Uganda

the Bradt Travel Guide

Philip Briggs

updated by
Andrew Roberts

edition
5

www.bradtguides.com

Bradt Travel Guides Ltd, UK
The Globe Pequot Press Inc, USA

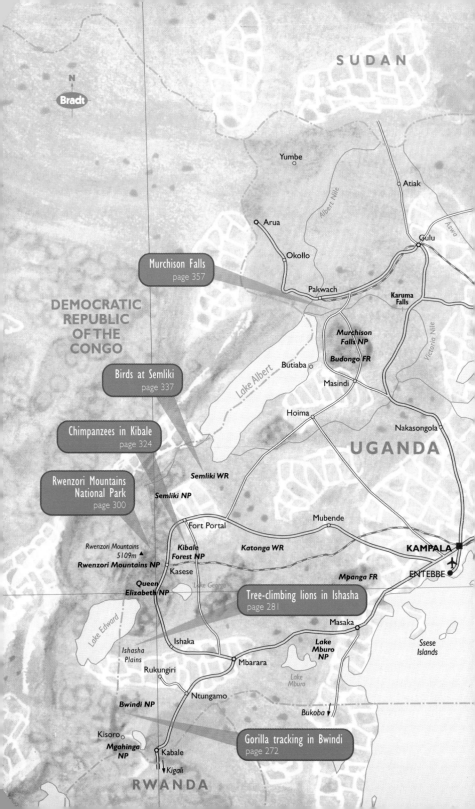

SUDAN

N

Bradt

Yumbe

Atiak

Arua

Okollo

Gulu

Murchison Falls
page 357

Pakwach

Karuma
Falls

DEMOCRATIC
REPUBLIC
OF THE
CONGO

*Murchison
Falls NP*

Budongo FR

Butiaba

Lake Albert

Masindi

Birds at Semliki
page 337

Hoima

Nakasongola

UGANDA

Chimpanzees in Kibale
page 324

Semliki WR

**Rwenzori Mountains
National Park**
page 300

Semliki NP

Fort Portal

Mubende

KAMPALA

Rwenzori Mountains
5109m ▲
Rwenzori Mountains NP

*Kibale
Forest NP*

Katonga WR

ENTEBBE

Kasese

Lake George

Mpanga FR

**Queen
Elizabeth NP**

Tree-climbing lions in Ishasha
page 281

Masaka

Lake Edward

Ishaka

Masaka

*Lake
Mburo
NP*

*Ssese
Islands*

*Ishasha
Plains*

Rukungiri

Mbarara

*Lake
Mburo*

Ntungamo

Bukoba

Bwindi NP

Kisoro

Gorilla tracking in Bwindi
page 272

*Mgahinga
NP*

Kabale

↓ *Kigali*

RWANDA

Kidepo
Valley NP

Kaabong

Loyoro

Kitgum

Kotido

Patonga

Mount Moroto
3084m

Moroto

Lira

Orungo

KENYA

Lake Turkana

Amudat

Soroti

Lake Kyoga

Kumi

Kapchorwa

Mount
Elgon NP ▲ Mount Elgon
4321m

Kamuli

Mbale

Iganga

Tororo

→ Nairobi,
Eldoret

Bujagali

Busia

→ Nairobi,
Kisumu

Mabira
FR

JINJA

Nile rafting at Bujagali
page 161

Lake

Victoria

TANZANIA

0 ————— 50km
0 ————— 50 miles

KEY
Capital city ■
Main town ●
Other town ○
Airport ✈
Main road
Other road
Railway
International boundary

Uganda
Don't
miss...

Murchison Falls
— 43 metres high
page 357

Tree-climbing lion
Ishasha Plains
page 281

White-water rafting
Bujagali Falls
page 161

Mountain-gorilla tracking
Bwindi
page 272

Mwamba Crater lake
near Fort Portal
page 337

above **People drink local beer through straws from a communal pot, Sipi** page 448

centre **Natural hot springs, Sempaya, Semliki National Park** page 455

left **Nyero rock paintings: 400–1,000 years old** page 344

Author/Updater

Philip Briggs is a travel writer and tour leader specialising in east and southern Africa. Born in Britain and raised in South Africa, he started travelling in East Africa in 1986, and his first book *Guide to South Africa* was published by Bradt in 1991. Since then, Philip has divided his time between exploring and writing about the highways and byways of Africa. In addition to authoring or co-authoring ten Bradt Travel Guides covering countries such as Tanzania, Rwanda, Uganda, Ghana, Ethiopia, Malawi and Mozambique, he has contributed to numerous other books and contributes regularly to various travel and wildlife magazines.

Ariadne Van Zandbergen, who took most of the photographs for this book and contributed to the research, is a freelance photographer and tour guide. Born and raised in Belgium, she travelled through Africa from Morocco to South Africa in 1994/5 and is now resident in Johannesburg. She has visited 25 African countries and her photographs have appeared in several books, magazines, newspapers, maps, periodicals and pamphlets. She has recently established her own photo library (*www.africaimagelibrary.com*).

Andrew Roberts, who updated this book for the fifth edition, is a landscape architect who has lived in Uganda since 1994. Born in Britain, he first visited Uganda with a backpack in 1990 and returned three years later to help the Forest Department set up ecotourism projects. Fourteen years later he's still in Uganda with his wife and two daughters. Andrew considers himself lucky to have worked in every national park in Uganda, settings which he greatly prefers to his office in Kampala. In August 2006 he published his first book, *Uganda's Great Rift Valley* and he is currently working on a history of the Rwenzori Mountains.

EMAIL US FOR A FREE UGANDA UPDATE NEWSLETTER!

As of March 2007, Bradt Travel Guides will hold on file an update newsletter for Uganda, regularly updated by Philip Briggs based on feedback from readers and from other local sources. To obtain the free newsletter, email Bradt at info@bradtguides.com and it will normally be forwarded to your email address by return. For those UK readers who aren't on email, please send a SAE to Bradt Travel Guides, 23 High Street, Chalfont St Peter, Bucks SL9 9QE and we will post it to you.

The newsletter is provided as a free service and without obligation. But if you have benefited from it, we would be grateful if you could return the favour by writing to us on your return with any information that may be of use to future travellers. Volunteers, hotel owners and other tourist-related persons working in Uganda are also invited to contact us with their news. Please also have a look at Philip Briggs's blog at http://philipbriggs.wordpress.com for interactive, regularly updated travel information for Uganda.

> Uganda is a fairy tale. You climb up a railway instead of a bean-stalk and at the top
> there is a wonderful new world. The scenery is different, and most of all the people
> are different from anywhere else in Africa.
>
> Winston Churchill, 1908

On our trip north from Cape Town to Cairo in 1976, George and I liked Uganda more
than any other country – and that despite being arrested during the aftermath of the
Entebbe Raid. It wasn't necessarily the most interesting, but the people, landscape and
wildlife were superb. For overlanders backpacking through Africa, the welcome (or
otherwise) you get at the border post can colour your impressions for the rest of your
stay. It took us three days to walk and hitch to the Ugandan border post from what was
then Zaire, and, in the politically turbulent Amin era, we were afraid that we would be
refused entry. George wrote: 'A Ugandan border guard walked towards us, starched
khaki shorts, crisply ironed shirt, bright boots, and said, "Welcome to Uganda!" We
were completely overwhelmed… After he'd finished stamping us in he said, "But there
is one problem…" Our hearts sank. "…about transport. But some men are driving into
Kasese tonight if you'd care to wait for them."'

I have not had the opportunity to return to Uganda since that memorable trip,
but reading Andy's excellent update to Philip's ground-breaking Uganda guide
convinces me that I must not leave it much longer.

Reprinted June 2007, February 2008, December 2008
Fifth edition published January 2007
First published in 1994

Bradt Travel Guides Ltd, 23 High Street, Chalfont St Peter, Bucks SL9 9QE, England.
www.bradtguides.com
Published in the USA by The Globe Pequot Press Inc, 246 Goose Lane,
PO Box 480, Guilford, Connecticut 06475-0480

Text copyright © 2007 Philip Briggs
Maps copyright © 2007 Bradt Travel Guides Ltd
Photographs © 2007 Individual photographers

ISBN-10: 1 84162 072 182 X   ISBN-13: 978 1 84162 072 182 1
British Library Cataloguing in Publication Data
A catalogue record for this book is available from the British Library

Photographs Ariadne Van Zandbergen, FLPA
Front cover Infant chimpanzee (Jan Vermeer/Foto Natura/FLPA)
Back cover Sipi Falls (AZ), Bambuti Pygmy (AZ)
Title page Karimojong girl portrait (AZ), Shoebill (AZ), Fishing canoes on source of the Nile, Jinja
(AZ)
Illustrations Annabel Milne, Mike Unwin   **Maps** Steve Munns

Typeset from the author's disc by Wakewing
Printed and bound in India by Nutech Photolithographers, New Delhi

Acknowledgements

FROM PHILIP BRIGGS This fifth edition was updated almost single-handedly by Andrew Roberts, which leaves me little to say other than echoing the acknowledgements below, and to thank Andrew for his abundant dedication to the task – may the travellers who use this edition come to appreciate the thoroughness of his efforts as much as I do!

FROM ANDREW ROBERTS Thanks are due to many people for providing up-to-date information both in person in Uganda and by email. These include Dr Dick Stockley, Arjan van den Bos, Pearl Horeau, Paul Holdsworth, Paul Rippey, The Eye magazine, John Hunwick, David and Joanna Evans, Keith Mills, Kevin O' Connor, Phil Woodcock, Marc Hempling, Brian and Irene McWeeney, Britta Adema, Pia Jeppesen, Michael Keizer, Rick Simpson, Andy Creeden, David Parrish, Richard Curley, Carol Berman, Simon Eyre, Jessica Mjelde, Margaret Noblin, Virgo Ssempebwa, Paul and Jane Goldring, Renzo Blasa, Jason Gerber, Fred Hodgson, John Osman, Robert Hall, Tony Wilder, Tara Anderson, Robert Springett, Fried Hauchecorne, Paola Ricceri, Susie Jones, Pernille Boerendtsen, Chris Kidd and Andy Gratt. Thanks to Dr Richard Lamprey for updating us on some wildlife issues. Thanks also to the staff at Uganda Wildlife Authority for responding to my reams of questions, notably Tom Okello, Patrick Tushabe, Moses Mapesa, Sam Mwandha, Damian Akankwasa and John Makombo. For their assistance and hospitality while we were on the road I'm indebted to Aubrey Price (Ndali Lodge), Ivan Mbabazi (Lake Bunyonyi Resort), Roni Madvhani (Marasa), Steve and Catherine in Kidepo (Uganda Safari Company), Norrie and Traxier Searle, Landmark Inn (Mbale), Bruce Martin (Lake Albert Safari Lodge), Eagle Air, Kampala Aeroclub, Nile River Explorers, the Haven and the Woods family in Entebbe (The Boma). On a personal note, thanks to my wife Sarah and my daughters Eleanor and Caitlin for their company along some of the roads travelled. I'm also obliged to Philip Briggs for having handed over his guidebook, nurtured by him over the course of 12 years and four previous editions, for me to update. Thanks also to Phil for updating the history section in *Chapter 1*.

Contents

LIST OF MAPS

Introduction

Almost 15 years ago, in the introduction to the first edition of this guide, I wrote that Uganda's attractions 'tend towards the low-key'. Four editions later, when I re-read this assertion for the first time in years, my initial reaction was – well – bemusement, unease, even embarrassment.

Meeting the eyes of a mountain gorilla on the bamboo-clumped slopes of the Virungas? Rafting grade-five rapids on the Nile? Following a narrow rainforest trail awhirl with the heart-stopping pant-hoot chorusing of chimpanzees? Cruising the Kazinga Channel in the shadow of the Ruwenzoris while elephants drink from the nearby shore? Watching a prehistoric shoebill swoop down on a lungfish in the brooding reed-beds of Mabamba Swamp? The roaring, spraying sensory overload that is standing on the tall rocks above Murchison Falls... Low-key? Goodness me – short of landing on the moon, what exactly would I have classified as a must-do or must-see attraction when I wrote that line?

But as I flicked through that yellowing first edition, all 150 pages of it, my unease slowly dissipated. It had not, I realised, been a reflection of any significant change in my own perceptions during the intervening decade, but rather of the remarkable strides made by Uganda in general, and its tourist industry specifically.

Uganda has changed. And how! When I first visited in 1988, Uganda's economy, infrastructure and human spirit – every aspect of the country, really – were still tangibly shattered in the aftermath of a 15-year cycle of dictatorship and civil conflict that had claimed an estimated one million human lives. Come 1992, when I researched the first edition of this guide, Uganda was visibly on the mend, but, a steady trickle of backpackers aside, its tourist industry remained in the doldrums. Incredible as it seems today, there was no facility to track gorillas within Uganda in 1992, no white-water rafting, no realistic opportunity to get close to chimpanzees, and the likes of Queen Elizabeth and Murchison Falls national parks were practically void of game. And many other tourist sites that today seem well established either didn't exist in their present form, were off-limits or unknown to travellers, or were far less accessible than they are now.

Uganda today does not lack for accessible travel highlights. There is the opportunity to trek within metres of one of the world's last few hundred mountain gorillas, arguably the most exciting wildlife encounter Africa has to offer – though observing chimps in the Kibale or Budongo runs it a damn close second. There is the staggering recovery made by Uganda's premier savanna reserves, where these days one can be almost certain of encountering lions, elephants and buffaloes, etc. There are the Ruwenzoris and Mount Elgon, where one can explore East Africa's bizarre montane vegetation without the goal-oriented approach associated with ascents of mounts Kilimanjaro or Kenya. And there is Bujagali Falls, which – with its white-water rafting, kayaking and recently introduced bungee jump – is rapidly emerging as East Africa's answer to that more southerly 'adrenalin capital' Victoria Falls.

Nor does Uganda lack for tourist facilities. As recently as ten years ago, international-class hotels and restaurants were all but non-existent outside of the capital. Today, by contrast, practically every major attraction along the main tourist circuits is serviced by one – or two, or three – luxury lodges and/or tented camps. Trunk roads have improved beyond recognition, as has the overall standard of local tour operators, public transport, budget accommodation, restaurants and service in general.

It should be noted, too, that the country's natural attractions far exceed the opportunity to see gorillas and lions and so on. Somebody once said that if you planted a walking stick overnight in the soil of Uganda, it would take root before the morning dawned. And it is certainly true that of all Africa's reasonably established safari destinations, Uganda is the most green, the most fertile – the most overwhelmingly tropical!

Uganda, in an ecological nutshell, is where the eastern savanna meets the west African jungle – and it really does offer visitors the best of both these fantastic worlds. In no other African destination can one see a comparable variety of primates with so little effort – not just the great apes, but also more than ten monkey species, as well as the tiny wide-eyed bushbaby and peculiar potto. And if Uganda will have primate enthusiasts wandering around with imbecile grins, it will have birdwatchers doing cartwheels. Uganda is by far the smallest of the four African counties in which more than 1,000 bird species have been recorded, and it is particularly rich in western rainforest specialists – in practical terms, undoubtedly the finest birdwatching destination in Africa.

And yet for all that, Uganda does feel like a more intimate, unspoilt and – dare I say it? – low-key destination than its obvious peers. For starters, it has no semblance of a package tourist industry: group tours seldom exceed eight in number, and even the most popular game-viewing circuits retain a relatively untrammelled atmosphere. The country's plethora of forested national parks and reserves remain highly accessible to independent travellers and relatively affordable to those on a limited budget, as do such off-the-beaten-track gems as the Ssese Islands, Katonga Wildlife Reserve, Sipi Falls and Kasenda Crater Lakes.

Uganda has changed. More than 25 years after Idi Amin was booted into exile, and two decades after President Museveni took power, the country bears few obvious scars of what came before. True, there are corners of Uganda that couldn't by any stretch of the imagination be described as safe or stable – these are highlighted elsewhere in this book – but then the same might be said of specific quarters in many Western cities not otherwise regarded to be dangerous. Uganda enjoys one of the healthiest reputations of any African country when it comes to crime directed at tourists. The level of day-to-day hassle faced by independent travellers is negligible. And Ugandans as a whole – both those working within the tourist industry and the ordinary man or woman on the street – genuinely do come across as the most warm, friendly and relaxed hosts imaginable.

It's been with growing pleasure that I've documented Uganda's progress, as a country and as a tourist destination, over the course of five editions of this guidebook. And this progress is, I hope, reflected in the evolution of the book – from its backpacker-oriented earliest incarnation into this totally reworked and vastly expanded fifth edition, which provides thorough coverage of all aspects of the country for all tastes and budgets. But progress begets progress, and doubtless the next few years will see a host of new and exciting tourist developments in Uganda.

Part One

GENERAL INFORMATION

Area 235,796km² (91,041 square miles), similar to Great Britain or the state of Oregon

Location Equatorial Africa between latitudes 4°12' N and 1°29' S and longitudes 29°35' W and 25° E. Bordered by Rwanda (169km) and Tanzania (396km) to the south, Kenya (933km) to the east, Sudan (435km) to the north and the Democratic Republic of Congo (DRC) for 765km to the west.

Altitude 85% of the country lies between 900m and 1,500m above sea level. The lowest region is the Lake Albert basin (612m) and the Albert Nile. The highest point is Mount Stanley (Ruwenzoris) at 5,110m.

Population 28.2 million (July 2006), 13% urban. Previous results were 16.7 million (1991), 12.6 million (1980), 9.5 million (1969), 6.5 million (1959), 5 million (1940), 3.5 million (1931), 2.9 million (1921) and 2.5 million (1911).

Capital Kampala (population 1.2 million in 2002)

Other major towns Gulu, Lira, Jinja. Other towns with more than 50,000 are Mbale, Mbarara, Masaka, Entebbe, Kasese and Njeru in descending order.

Language English, the official language, is spoken by most reasonably educated Ugandans. Among the country's 33 indigenous languages, Luganda is the closest to being a lingua franca.

Religion Christian (85%), Islam (11%), also some Hindu and Jewish, while tribes such as the Karimojong adhere to a traditional animist faith.

Currency Uganda shilling, Ush1,850 = US$1 in 2006

Head of State President Yoweri Museveni (since 1986)

Time zone GMT+3

International dial code +256 (Kampala: 414)

Electricity 240 volts at 50Hz

Mineral resources Copper, cobalt, limestone, salt, alluvial gold. In July 2006, significant oil reserves were discovered below the shores of Lake Albert at Kaiso-Tonya.

Major exports Coffee (55%), fish (7.5%), tea (5%), tobacco (4%)

Other crops Bananas, maize, millet, sorghum, cotton, rice, cassava, groundnuts, potatoes

GDP US$7 million per annum (US$1,800 per capita, annual growth rate 4% in 2005)

Human development Average life expectancy 39.5 years; under-five mortality rate 13.7%; rate of HIV infection 8–10% (estimate); primary school completion 38%; secondary school enrolment 13%; adult literacy 65%; access to safe water 45%; access to electricity 4%

Land use Arable land 25%; agriculture 9%; pasture 9%; forest & woodland 28%; open water 18%; marsh 4%; other 7%

National flag Two sets of black, yellow and red horizontal stripes, with a white central circle around the national bird, the grey crowned crane

National anthem
Oh! Uganda, May God uphold thee, We lay our future in thy hand,
United, free, for liberty, Together, We always stand.
Oh! Uganda the land of freedom, Our love and labour we give,
And with neighbours all at our country's call, In peace and friendship we'll live.
Oh! Uganda the land that feeds us, By sun and fertile soil grown,
For our own dear land we'll always stand, The Pearl of African's crown.

1

Background Information

GEOGRAPHY AND CLIMATE

Uganda lies on the elevated basin which rises between the eastern and western branches of the Great Rift Valley. Most of the country is over 1,000m in altitude, and the topography is generally quite flat. The most mountainous part of Uganda is the Kigezi region in the southwest. North of Kigezi, on the Congolese border, the 70km-long and 30km-wide Rwenzori Mountains form the highest mountain range in Africa; Margherita Peak (5,109m), the highest point in the Rwenzori, is exceeded in altitude on the African continent only by the free-standing Mount Kenya and Mount Kilimanjaro. Other large mountains in Uganda include the volcanic Virunga range on the border with Rwanda and DRC, and Mount Elgon, a vast extinct volcano straddling the Kenyan border. There are several smaller volcanic mountains in the north and east.

With the exception of the semi-desert in the extreme northeast, most of Uganda is well watered and fertile. Almost 25% of the country's surface area is covered by water. Lake Victoria, the largest lake in Africa and second-largest freshwater body in the world, is shared by Uganda with Tanzania and Kenya. Lakes Albert, Edward and George lie on or close to the Congolese border, while the marshy and ill-defined Lake Kyoga lies in the centre of Uganda. At Jinja, on the Lake Victoria shore, Owen Falls (now submerged by the Owen Falls Dam) is regarded as the official source of the Nile, the world's longest river. The Nile also passes through lakes Kyoga and Albert.

Uganda's equatorial climate is tempered by its elevated altitude. In most parts of the country, the daily maximum is between 20°C and 27°C and the minimum is between 12°C and 18°C. The highest temperatures in Uganda occur on the plains immediately east of Lake Albert, while the lowest have been recorded on the glacial peaks of the Rwenzori. Except in the dry north, where in some areas the average annual rainfall is as low as 100mm, most parts of Uganda receive an annual rainfall of between 1,000mm and 2,000mm. There is wide regional variation in rainfall patterns. In western Uganda and the Lake Victoria region it can rain at almost any time of year. As a rough guide, however, the wet seasons are from mid September to November and from March to May (see the *Climate chart* box overleaf).

HISTORY

Africa is popularly portrayed as a continent without history. Strictly speaking, this is true, as history by definition relies upon written records, and there are no written records of events in central Africa prior to the mid 19th century. All the same, it would be foolish to mistake an absence of documentation for an absence of incident, as do those historical accounts of African countries which leap in the space of a paragraph from the Stone Age to the advent of colonialism.

KAMPALA (1,155m)	Jan	Feb	Mar	Apr	May	Jun	Jul	Aug	Sep	Oct	Nov	Dec
Ave max (°C)	28	28	27	26	26	25	25	26	27	27	27	27
Ave min (°C)	18	18	18	18	17	17	17	16	17	17	17	17
Rainfall (mm)	45	60	125	170	135	75	50	85	90	100	125	105

ENTEBBE (1,145m)	Jan	Feb	Mar	Apr	May	Jun	Jul	Aug	Sep	Oct	Nov	Dec
Ave max (°C)	27	26	26	25	25	25	25	25	26	26	26	26
Ave min (°C)	17	18	18	18	17	16	16	16	16	17	17	17
Rainfall (mm)	75	95	155	250	240	115	75	75	75	80	130	115

FORT PORTAL (1,540m)	Jan	Feb	Mar	Apr	May	Jun	Jul	Aug	Sep	Oct	Nov	Dec
Ave max (°C)	27	27	26	26	25	25	25	25	25	25	25	26
Ave min (°C)	12	13	14	14	14	13	13	13	13	14	14	12
Rainfall (mm)	20	75	125	190	130	85	60	110	195	210	165	75

KABALE (1,950m)	Jan	Feb	Mar	Apr	May	Jun	Jul	Aug	Sep	Oct	Nov	Dec
Ave max (°C)	24	24	23	22	22	23	23	24	24	24	23	23
Ave min (°C)	10	10	11	12	11	10	9	10	11	11	11	10
Rainfall (mm)	50	100	125	120	95	25	20	45	95	100	115	90

GULU (1,110m)	Jan	Feb	Mar	Apr	May	Jun	Jul	Aug	Sep	Oct	Nov	Dec
Ave max (°C)	32	32	31	29	28	28	26	27	28	29	29	31
Ave min (°C)	17	18	18	18	18	17	17	17	17	17	17	16
Rainfall (mm)	10	35	85	160	200	140	155	215	165	140	95	30

MASINDI (1,145m)	Jan	Feb	Mar	Apr	May	Jun	Jul	Aug	Sep	Oct	Nov	Dec
Ave max (°C)	31	31	30	29	29	28	27	27	28	29	30	30
Ave min (°C)	12	12	13	13	13	12	12	12	12	12	13	12
Rainfall (mm)	20	50	10	140	135	95	100	45	120	125	110	45

MBALE (1,150m)	Jan	Feb	Mar	Apr	May	Jun	Jul	Aug	Sep	Oct	Nov	Dec
Ave max (°C)	32	32	31	29	28	28	27	28	28	29	30	31
Ave min (°C)	16	17	17	17	17	16	16	15	15	16	16	16
Rainfall (mm)	25	60	90	160	175	130	110	135	105	80	65	40

JINJA (1,145m)	Jan	Feb	Mar	Apr	May	Jun	Jul	Aug	Sep	Oct	Nov	Dec
Ave max (°C)	29	30	29	28	27	27	27	28	28	29	30	29
Ave min (°C)	15	15	15	15	15	14	14	15	15	15	15	14
Rainfall (mm)	50	70	120	170	130	65	50	105	80	95	100	85

Without written records to draw from, scholars of pre-colonial African history have to rely on two main resources, archaeological evidence and oral traditions. As a rule these resources are riddled with contradictions and open to a diversity of interpretations, making it impossible to say with any certainty what happened in any given region prior to the arrival of Europeans.

Events in Uganda between AD1100 and the present appear to be a happy exception to the above rule. As I read over various sources, I was struck by the remarkable degree of correlation between the oral traditions of the various kingdoms of Uganda and the more objective evidence unearthed by modern archaeologists. When stripped of the quasi-religious trappings and mythologising which are to be expected in any folk history, the oral traditions of Uganda seem to me to be a reasonably accurate and consistent account of actual events.

A NOTE ON TERMINOLOGY Most Bantu languages use a variety of prefixes to form words so that several similar words are made from a common root. When discussing the various peoples and kingdoms of Uganda, this can be somewhat confusing.

The most common prefixes are *mu-*, *ba-* and *bu-*, the first referring to an individual, the second to the people collectively, and the third to the land they occupy. In other words, a Muganda is a member of the Baganda, the people who live in Buganda. The language of the Baganda is Luganda and their religion and customs are Kiganda. To use another example, the Banyoro live in Bunyoro, where they speak Runyoro and follow Kinyoro customs.

There is not a great deal of consistency in the use of these terms in the English-language books. Some use the adjective *Ganda* to describe, for instance, the *Ganda kabaka* (King of Buganda). Others will call him the Muganda or Baganda kabaka. Standards are more flexible when dealing with ethnic groups other than the Baganda: the Ankole people are usually referred to as the Banyankole but I've never seen the kingdom referred to as Bunyankole; the people of Toro are often referred to as the Batoro but I've not come across the term Butoro. In this following historical account, I've generally stuck with what seems to be the most common usage: prefixes for -ganda, -nyoro and -soga; no prefixes for Ankole and Toro.

The name Uganda of course derives from the word Buganda. The most probable reason why the British protectorate came to be known by this abbreviated name is that most Europeans had their initial contact with Buganda through KiSwahili-speaking guides and translators. In KiSwahili, the prefix *u-* is the equivalent of the Luganda *bu-*, so that the Swahili speakers would almost certainly have referred to the Ganda kingdom as Uganda. Although many Baganda writers evidently find it annoying that their country has been misnamed in this way, it does simplify my task that there is a clear distinction between the name of Uganda the country and that of Buganda the kingdom.

When referring to the leaders of the various Ugandan groups, the title *kabaka* is bestowed on the Baganda king, the title *omakuma* on the Banyoro king, and *omugabe* on the Ankole king.

EARLY PREHISTORY It is widely agreed that the entire drama of human evolution was enacted in the Rift Valley and plains of East Africa. The details of this evolution are obscured by the patchy nature of the fossil record, but the combination of DNA evidence and two recent 'missing link' discoveries (the fossils of a 4.4-million-year-old hominid in the Ethiopian Rift Valley and a 5.6-million-year-old jawbone unearthed in the Turkana Basin in northern Kenya) suggests that the ancestors of modern humans and modern chimpanzees diverged roughly five to six million years ago.

Uganda has not thrown up hominid remains of comparable antiquity to those unearthed in Kenya, Tanzania and Ethiopia, largely because there are few places in the country where fossils of a suitable age might be sought. Nevertheless, it is reasonable to assume that Uganda has supported hominid life for as long as any other part of East Africa, an assumption supported by the discovery in Moroto district of fossils belonging to the semi-bipedal proto-hominid *Morotopithecus*, which is thought to have lived about 15 million years ago.

Stone-Age implements dating to over one million years ago have been discovered throughout East Africa, and it is highly probable that this earliest of human

Ggulu, the creator, sent his daughter Nambi and her siblings on a day trip to earth, where they chanced upon its only human inhabitant: poor lonely Kintu, who lived in the vicinity of Lake Wamala, west of present-day Kampala, his sole companion a beloved cow. Nambi was at once attracted to Kintu and upset at his enforced solitude, and she determined there and then to marry and keep him company on earth. Nambi's brothers were appalled at her reckless decision, and attempted to dissuade her, eventually reaching the compromise that she and Kintu would return to heaven to ask Ggulu's permission to marry. Ggulu reluctantly blessed the union, but he did advise the couple to descend to earth lightly packed and in secret, to avoid being noticed and followed by Nambi's brother Walumbe, the spirit of disease and death.

The next morning, before dawn, the delighted newlyweds set off for earth, carrying little other than Nambi's favourite chicken. When they arrived, however, Nambi realised that she had forgotten to bring millet to feed the chicken and decided to return to heaven to fetch it. Kintu implored Nambi to stay, fearing that she might encounter Walumbe, and suggesting that a substitute chicken feed would surely be available on earth. But Nambi ignored Kintu's pleadings and returned to heaven, where sure enough she bumped into Walumbe, who – curious as to where his sister might be headed so early in the morning – followed her all the way back to join Kintu.

A few years later, Kintu, by then the head of a happy family, received a visit from Walumbe, who insisted that he be given one of their children to help with his household chores. Heedful of his father-in-law's warning, Kintu refused Walumbe, who was deeply angered and avenged himself by killing Kintu's eldest son. When Kintu returned to heaven to ask for assistance, Ggulu chastised him for ignoring the warning, but he agreed nevertheless to send another son Kayikuzi to bring Walumbe back to heaven. Walumbe refused to leave earth, however, so that Kayikuzi was forced to try and evict him against his will. The brothers fought violently, but the moment Kayikuzi gained an upper hand, Walumbe vanished underground. Kayikuzi dug several large holes, found Walumbe's hiding place, and the two resumed their fight, but soon Walumbe fled into the ground once again, and so the pattern repeated itself.

technologies arose in the region. For a quarter of a million years prior to around 8000BC, Stone-Age technology was spread throughout Africa, Europe and Asia, and the design of common implements such as the stone axe was identical throughout this area. The oldest Stone-Age sites in Uganda, Nsongezi on the Kigezi River and Sango Bay on Lake Victoria, were occupied between 150,000 and 50,000 years ago.

The absence of written records means that the origin and classification of the modern peoples of east and southern Africa are a subject of some academic debate. Broadly speaking, it is probable that East Africa has incurred two major human influxes since 1000BC, on both occasions, by people from west Africa.

The first of these influxes probably originated somewhere in modern-day DRC about 3,000 years ago. The descendants of these invaders, known locally as the Bambuti or Batwa, were slightly built hunter-gatherers similar in culture and physique to the Khoisan of southern Africa and the pygmoid people who still live in certain rainforests near the Congolese border. The rock paintings on several shelters near Mbale in eastern Uganda show strong affinities with Khoisan rock art, suggesting that at one time these people occupied most of Uganda, as did they most of east and southern Africa at the beginning of the 1st millennium AD.

The second human influx, which reached the Lake Victoria hinterland in roughly 200BC, apparently coincided with the spread of Iron-Age technology in the region. There is good reason to suppose that the people who brought iron-working

After several days, Kayikuzi, now nearing exhaustion, told Kintu and Nambi he would try one last time to catch Walumbe, at the same time instructing them to ensure that their children stayed indoors and remained silent until his task was done. Kayikuzi chased Walumbe out of hiding, but some of Kintu's children, who had disobeyed the instruction, saw the sparring brothers emerge from underground and they started screaming, giving Walumbe the opportunity to duck back into his subterranean refuge. Kayikuzi, angry that his earthly charges had ignored his instructions, told them he was giving up the chase, and the embarrassed Kintu did not argue. He told Kayikuzi to return to heaven and said: 'If Walumbe wishes to kill my children, so be it. I will keep having more, and the more he kills, the more I will have. He will not be able remove them all from the face of the earth.'

And so ends the Kiganda creation myth, with its Old Testament association between human disobedience and the arrival of death and disease on earth. And one question raised by this story is the connection between Kintu the first man and Kintu the founding kabaka of Buganda. It is often assumed that these two seminal Kintus of Kiganda lore are one and the same figure, a mythical embodiment of the creation of both mankind and Buganda. But certain Muganda traditionalists assert otherwise. Kintu, the first person on earth, they concede, is clearly an allegorical figure whose story has no basis in historical fact. But Kintu the founder of Baganda is a wholly separate person, and quite possibly a genuine historical figure.

The 'two Kintus' claim is legitimised by the contrast between the unambiguous absence of other humans in the creation myth, and the presence of humanity explicit in any foundation legend in which one king defeats another king and rules over his former subjects. There is a popular Kiganda saying, derived from the mythical Kintu's last words, that translates as 'Kintu's children will never be removed from the face of the earth'. And if this saying does pre-date the foundation of Buganda, then it is plausible – even likely – that the founder of Buganda would have adopted Kintu as his throne name, with the deliberate intention of legitimising his rule by association with the mythical father of mankind.

techniques into the region were the ancestors of the Bantu speakers who probably occupied most of sub-equatorial Africa by AD500. Few conclusive facts are known about the political and social structures of the early Bantu-speaking peoples who inhabited Uganda, but it is reasonable to assume that they lived in loosely assembled chiefdoms similar to the pre-colonial *ntemi* structures which existed in the Tanzanian interior until colonial times.

It has been established beyond doubt that relatively centralised political systems made an early appearance in Uganda. The origin of the first of these kingdoms, Bunyoro-Kitara, is shrouded in legend, and the rough date of its foundation has yet to be determined by scholars. Nevertheless, a number of archaeological sites in the Mubende and Ntusi districts of central Uganda suggest that Bunyoro-Kitara was established long before AD1500.

THE BATEMBUZI AND BACWEZI (AD1100–1500) Kinyoro and several other local oral traditions assert that the first dynasty to rule over Bunyoro-Kitara was the Batembuzi. These traditions place the Batembuzi as having ruled between AD1100 and AD1350, and there is ample physical evidence at Ntusi to confirm that a highly centralised society existed in this area as early as the 11th century.

The origin of the Batembuzi is obscured by legend and myth, but they must have ruled for several generations, as various local traditions list between ten and

22 dynastic kings. Oral traditions name Ruhanga, the King of the Underworld, as the founder of the dynasty (the Kinyoro Underworld is evidently closer to the Christian notion of heaven than to that of hell) and they consider the Batembuzi to have been deities with supernatural powers. Descriptions of the Batembuzi's physical appearance suggest that they may have migrated to the area from modern-day Sudan or Ethiopia. Whatever their origins, they evidently became culturally and linguistically integrated into the established Bantu-speaking culture of Bunyoro-Kitara.

Most traditions identify Isuza as the last Batembuzi ruler. Isuza is said to have fallen in love with a princess of the Underworld, and to have followed her into her homeland, from where he couldn't find his way back to Bunyoro-Kitara. Years later, Isuza's son Isimbwa visited Bunyoro-Kitara, and he impregnated the only daughter of the unpopular stand-in king, Bukuku. Their child, Ndahura, was thrown into a river shortly after his birth at the order of Bukuku, who had been told by diviners that he should fear any child born by his daughter; but his umbilical cord stuck in a tree, keeping him afloat, and he was rescued by a royal porter. Ndahura was raised by the porter and, after he reached adulthood, he drove Bukuku's cattle from his home, stabbed the king in the back, and claimed the throne as his own. His claim was supported by the people of Bunyoro-Kitara, who accepted that the true royal lineage was being restored because of Ndahura's striking physical resemblance to his grandfather Isuza.

Ndahura – 'the uprooter' – is remembered as the founder of the Bacwezi dynasty. The Bacwezi were most probably migrants from Ethiopia or Sudan (hence the physical resemblance between Ndahura and Isuza?), who like the Batembuzi before them adopted the language and culture of the local Bantu speakers over whom they assumed rule. Ndahura was almost certainly a genuine historical figure, and he probably came to power in the second half of the 14th century. In addition to having supernatural powers, Ndahura is traditionally credited with introducing Ankole cattle and coffee cultivation to Uganda.

The Mubende and Ntusi areas are identified by all traditional accounts as lying at the heart of Bunyoro-Kitara during the Bacwezi era, an assertion which is supported by a mass of archaeological evidence, notably the extensive earthworks at Bigo bya Mugenyi and Munsa. This suggests that the Bacwezi Empire covered most of Uganda south and west of the Nile River. Traditional accounts claim that it covered a much larger area, and that Ndahura was a militant expansionist who led successful raids into parts of western Kenya, northern Tanzania and Rwanda.

Ndahura was captured during a raid into what is now northern Tanzania. He eventually escaped, but he refused to reclaim the throne, instead abdicating in favour of his son Wamala. Ndahura then disappeared, some claim to the Fort Portal region. He abandoned his capital at Mubende Hill to his senior wife, Nakayima, who founded a hereditary matriarchy that survived into the colonial era. Wamala moved his capital to an unidentified site before eventually relocating it to Bigo bya Mugenyi.

Considering the immense Bacwezi influence over modern Uganda – almost all the royal dynasties in the region claim to be of direct or indirect Bacwezi descent – it is remarkable that they ruled for only two generations. Tradition has it that Wamala simply disappeared, just like his father before him, thereby reinforcing the claim that the Bacwezi were immortal. It is more likely that the collapse of the dynasty was linked to the arrival of the Luo in Bunyoro-Kitara towards the end of the 15th century. Whatever their fate, the Bacwezi remain the focus of several religious cults, and places like the Nakayima Tree on Mubende Hill and the vast earthworks at Bigo bya Mugenyi near Ntusi are active sites of Bacwezi worship to this day.

BUNYORO, BUGANDA AND ANKOLE (1500–1650) In the second half of the 15th century, the Nilotic-speaking Luo left their homeland on the plains of southeastern Sudan, and migrated southwards along the course of the Nile River into what is now Uganda. After settling for a period on the northern verge of Bunyoro-Kitara at a place remembered as Pubungu (probably near modern-day Pakwach), they evidently splintered into three groups. The first of these groups remained at Pubungu, the second colonised the part of Uganda west of the Nile, and the third continued southwards into the heart of Bunyoro-Kitara.

It was probably the Luo invasion which ended Bacwezi rule over Bunyoro-Kitara. The Bacwezi were succeeded by the Babiito dynasty, whose founder Rukidi came to Bunyoro from Bukidi (a Runyoro name for anywhere north of Bunyoro). The tradition is that Rukidi was the son of Ndahura and a Mukidi woman, and that he was invited to rule Bunyoro by the Bacwezi nobles before they disappeared. Many modern scholars feel that the Luo captured Bunyoro by force, and that they integrated themselves into the local culture by claiming a genetic link with the Bacwezi, adopting several Bacwezi customs and rapidly learning the local Runyoro tongue.

The arrival of the Luo coincided with the emergence of several other kingdoms to the south and east of Bunyoro, notably Buganda and Ankole in modern-day Uganda, as well as Rwanda, Burundi and the Karagwe kingdom in what is now northwest Tanzania. All these kingdoms share a common Bacwezi heritage. Kinyoro and Kiganda traditions agree that Buganda was founded by an offshoot of the Babiito dynasty, while Ankole traditions claim that Ruhinda, the founder of their kingdom, was yet another son of Ndahura. Ankole retained the strongest Bacwezi traditions, and its most important symbol of national unity was a royal drum or Bagyendwaza said to have been owned by Wamala.

Bunyoro was the largest and most influential of these kingdoms until the end of the 17th century. It had a mixed economy, a loose political structure, and a central trade position on account of its exclusive control of the region's salt mines. Bunyoro was presided over by an *omakuma*, who was advised by a group of special counsellors. The omakuma was supported at a local level by several grades of semi-autonomous chiefs, most of whom were royally appointed loyalists of aristocratic descent.

Prior to 1650, Buganda was a small kingdom ruled over by a *kabaka*. Unlike those in Bunyoro, the local chiefs in Buganda were hereditary clan leaders and not normally of aristocratic descent. Buganda was the most fertile of the Ugandan kingdoms, for which reason its economy was primarily agricultural. Ankole, by contrast, placed great importance on cattle, and its citizens were stratified into two classes: the cattle-owning Bahima, who claimed to be descendants of Ruhinda, and the agriculturist Bairu. Ankole was ruled by an *omugabe*. As with the omakuma of Bunyoro and the kabaka of Buganda, this was a hereditary title normally reserved for the eldest son of the previous ruler. Positions of local importance were generally reserved for Bahima aristocrats.

Another identifiable polity to take shape at around this time was the Busoga, which lies to the east of Buganda and is bordered by Lake Kyoga to the north and Lake Victoria to the south. The Basoga show strong linguistic and cultural affiliations to the Baganda, but their oral traditions suggest that their founder, remembered by the name of Mukama, came from the Mount Elgon region and had no Bacwezi or Babiito links. Busoga has apparently assimilated a large number of cultural influences over the centuries, and it seems to have remained curiously detached from the mainstream of Ugandan history, probably by allying itself to the dominant power of the time.

An indication of Bunyoro's regional dominance in the 16th century comes from the traditional accounts of the wars fought by Olimi I, the fifth omakuma. Olimi is said to have attacked Buganda and killed the kabaka in battle, but he declined to occupy the conquered territory, opting instead to attack Ankole (of the several explanations put forward for this superficially peculiar course of action, the only one that rings true is that Olimi was after cattle, which were scarce in Buganda but plentiful in Ankole). Olimi occupied Ankole for some years, and according to Kinyoro traditions he withdrew only because of a full solar eclipse, an event which Banyoro traditionalists still consider to be portentous. If this tradition is true (and there is no reason to doubt it), Olimi must have been ruling Bunyoro at the time of the solar eclipse of 1520. Assuming that the four Babiito rulers who preceded Olimi would together have ruled for at least 30 or 40 years, this suggests that the Babiito dynasty and the Buganda and Ankole kingdoms were founded between 1450 and 1500.

BUNYORO, BUGANDA AND ANKOLE (1650–1850)

At its peak in the 17th century, Bunyoro covered an area of roughly 80,000km² south and west of the Nile and Lake Victoria. Buganda was at this time no more than 15,000km² in area, and Ankole covered a mere 2,500km² north of the Kagera River. Similar in size to Buganda, the relatively short-lived kingdom of Mpororo, founded in about 1650, covered much of the Kigezi region of Uganda, as well as parts of what is now northern Rwanda, until its dissolution in the mid 17th century.

The period between 1650 and 1850 saw Bunyoro shrink to a fraction of its former area and relinquish its regional dominance to Buganda. The start of this decline can be traced to the rule of Omakuma Cwa I (or Cwamali) in the late 17th or early 18th century. During Cwa's reign, Bunyoro suffered an epidemic of cattle disease. Cwa ordered all the cattle in the kingdom to be killed, and he then raided Ankole to seize replacements. Cwa occupied Ankole for three years, after which he attempted to extend his kingdom into Rwanda. He was killed in Rwanda and his returning troops were evicted from Ankole by Omugabe Ntare IV, who thereby earned himself the nickname Kitabunyoro – 'the scourge of Bunyoro'. After chasing out the Banyoro, Ntare IV extended Ankole's territory north to the Karonga River.

Bunyoro descended into temporary disarray as the aristocracy tried to cover up the omakuma's death, and the empty throne was seized by one of his sisters, stimulating a succession war that lasted for several years. Buganda took advantage of Bunyoro's weakness by taking control of several of its allied territories, so that in the years following Cwa's death it doubled in area. It is unclear whether Buganda acquired these territories by conquest or merely by exploiting the faltering loyalty of chiefs who were traditionally allied with Bunyoro.

Also linked to the upheavals following Cwa's death was the migration of the Palwo, the name given to the Luo speakers who had settled in the north of Bunyoro two centuries earlier. Some of the Palwo settled in Acholi, the part of northern Uganda east of the Albert Nile, where they founded several small Luo-speaking kingdoms modelled along the traditions of Bunyoro. Others migrated through Busoga in eastern Uganda to the Kisumu region of what is now western Kenya, where they are still the dominant group. A few groups settled in Busoga, south of modern-day Tororo, to found a group of small kingdoms known collectively as Jopadhola.

In 1731, Omakuma Duhaga took the Banyoro throne. Kinyoro traditions remember him as being small, light-skinned, hairy and difficult, and as having had the second-greatest number of children of any omakuma (the third omakuma, Oyo I, reputedly had 2,000 children, a record which will take some beating). During Duhaga's 50-year reign, Buganda annexed the area around Lake Wamala, as well as the land immediately west of the Victoria Nile, from where it plundered large parts of Busoga. Duhaga died in battle along with 70 of his sons, attempting to protect Bunyoro from Baganda expansionists.

By the reign of Omakuma Kyebambe III (1786–1835), Buganda was firmly entrenched as the major regional power. During the late 17th century, Kabaka Mutebi consolidated his power by dismissing some traditional clan leaders and replacing them with confirmed loyalists; by the end of the 18th century, practically every local chief in Buganda was one of the so-called 'king's men'. Buganda forged loose allegiances with Busoga and Karagwe (in northern Tanzania), and they maintained a peaceful equilibrium with Ankole, which had in the meantime further expanded its territory by absorbing several parts of the former Mpororo kingdom. Towards the end of Kyebambe III's rule, Bunyoro was dealt a further blow as several local princes decided to rebel against the ageing omakuma. The most significant rebellion was in Toro, where a prince called Kaboyo declared autonomous rule in 1830, depriving Bunyoro of its important salt resources at Katwe.

By the mid 19th century, Buganda stretched west from the Victoria Nile almost as far as Mubende and over the entire Lake Victoria hinterland as far south as the Kagera River. Ankole covered an area of roughly 10,000km² between the Karonga and Kagera rivers, and the newly founded Toro kingdom occupied a similar area north of the Karonga. Bunyoro had been reduced to a quarter of its former size; although it had retained the Nile as its northern boundary, there was now no point at which it stretched further than 50km south of the Kafu River.

BUNYORO AND EGYPT (1850–89) The death of Omakuma Kyebambe III was followed by a period of internal instability in Bunyoro, during which two weak omakumas ruled in succession. In 1852, the throne was seized by Kamurasi, who did much to stop the rot, notably by killing a number of rebellious princes at the Battle of Kokoitwa. Kamurasi's rule coincided with the arrival of Arab traders from the north, who were admitted into Bunyoro in the recognition that their support could only strengthen the ailing kingdom. The Arabs based themselves at Gondoroko, from where they led many brutal raids into the small and relatively defenceless Luo kingdoms of Acholi.

In 1862, Kamurasi's court welcomed Speke and Grant, the first Europeans to reach Bunyoro. Two years later, Bunyoro was entered from the north by Samuel Baker, a wealthy big-game hunter and incidental explorer who travelled everywhere with his wife. The Bakers spent a year in Bunyoro, during which time they became the first Europeans to see Lake Mwatanzige, which they renamed Lake Albert. Baker also developed an apparently irrational antipathy towards his royal host, which almost certainly clouded his judgement when he returned to the region eight years later.

The years following the Bakers' departure from Bunyoro saw radical changes in the kingdom. Omakuma Kamurasi died in 1869, prompting a six-month succession battle that resulted in the populist Kabalega ascending to the throne. Omakuma Kabalega is regarded by many as the greatest of all Banyoro rulers who, were it not for British intervention, would surely have achieved his goal of restoring the kingdom to its full former glory. Kabalega introduced a set of military and political reforms which have been compared to those of Shaka in Zululand: he divided the army into battalions of 1,500 men, each of which was led by a trained soldier chosen on merit as opposed to birth, and he minimised the influence of the eternally squabbling Banyoro aristocracy by deposing them as local chiefs in favour of capable commoners with a sound military background.

In 1871, the imperialist Khedive Ismail of Egypt appointed the recently knighted Sir Samuel Baker to the newly created post of Governor General of Equatoria, a

In 1862, Speke spent weeks kicking his heels in the royal capital of Buganda, awaiting permission to travel to the river he suspected might be the source of the Nile. His sojourn is described in four long and fascinating chapters in *The Journal of the Discovery of the Source of the Nile*, the earliest and most copious document of courtly life in the kingdom. The following extracts provide some idea of the everyday life of the subjects of Kabaka Mutesa – who is remembered as a more benevolent ruler than his predecessor Suuna or successor Mwanga. The quotes are edited to modernise spellings and cut extraneous detail.

> A more theatrical sight I never saw. The king, a good-looking, well-figured, tall young man of 25, was sitting on a red blanket spread upon a platform of royal grass, scrupulously well dressed in a new *mbugu*. His hair was cut short, excepting on the top, where it was combed up into a high ridge, running from stem to stern like a cockscomb. On his neck was a large ring of beautifully worked small beads, forming elegant patterns by their various colours. On one arm was another bead ornament, prettily devised; and on the other a wooden charm, tied by a string covered with snakeskin. On every finger and every toe, he had alternate brass and copper rings; and above the ankles, halfway up to the calf, a stocking of very pretty beads. Everything was light, neat, and elegant in its way; not a fault could be found with the taste of his 'getting up'.
>
> Both men, as is the custom in Uganda, thanked Mutesa in a very enthusiastic manner, kneeling on the ground – for no-one can stand in the presence of his majesty – in an attitude of prayer, and throwing out their hands as they repeated the words N'yanzig, N'yanzig, ai N'yanzig Mkahma wangi, etc, etc, for a considerable time; when, thinking they had done enough of this, and heated with the exertion, they threw themselves flat upon their stomachs, and, floundering about like fish on land, repeated the same words over again and again, and rose doing the same, with their faces covered with earth; for majesty in Uganda is never satisfied till subjects have grovelled before it like the most abject worms…
>
> The king loaded one of the carbines I had given him with his own hands, and giving it full-cock to a page, told him to go out and shoot a man in the outer court; which was no sooner accomplished than the little urchin returned to announce his success, with a look of glee such as one would see in the face of a boy who had robbed a bird's nest, caught a trout, or done any other boyish trick. I never heard, and there appeared no curiosity to know, what individual human being the urchin had deprived of life…
>
> The Namasole entered on a long explanation, to the following effect. There are no such things as marriages in Uganda; there are no ceremonies attached to it. If any man possessed of a pretty daughter committed an offence, he might give her to the king as a peace offering; if any neighbouring king had a pretty daughter, and the King of Uganda wanted her, she might be demanded as a fitting tribute. The men in Uganda are supplied with women by the king, according to their merits, from seizures in battle abroad, or seizures from

loosely defined province in the south of Egyptian-ruled Sudan. When Baker assumed his post in 1872, he almost immediately overstepped his instructions by declaring Bunyoro to be an annexe of Equatoria. Kabalega responded to Baker's pettiness by attacking the Egyptian garrison at Masindi. Baker was forced to retreat to Patiko in Acholi, and he defended his humiliating defeat by characterising Kabalega as a treacherous coward, thereby poisoning the omakuma's name in Europe in a way that was to have deep repercussions on future events in Uganda.

The second Governor General of Equatoria, General Gordon, knew of Kabalega only what his biased predecessor had told him. Gordon further antagonised the omakuma by erecting several forts in northern Bunyoro without first asking

refractory officers at home. The women are not regarded as property, though many exchange their daughters; and some women, for misdemeanours, are sold into slavery; whilst others are flogged, or are degraded to do all the menial services of the house...

Congow was much delighted with my coming, produced *pombe*, and asked me what I thought of his women, stripping them to the waist. I asked him what use he had for so many women? To which he replied, 'None whatever; the king gives them to us to keep up our rank, sometimes as many as one hundred together, and we either turn them into wives, or make servants of them, as we please...

The king was giving appointments, plantations, and women, according to merit, to his officers. As one officer, to whom only one woman was given, asked for more, the king called him an ingrate, and ordered him to be cut to pieces on the spot; and the sentence was carried into effect -- not with knives, for they are prohibited, but with strips of sharp-edged grass, after the executioners had first dislocated his neck by a blow delivered behind the head...

Nearly every day, I have seen one, two, or three of the wretched palace women led away to execution, tied by the hand, and dragged along by one of the body-guard, crying out, as she went to premature death, at the top of her voice, in the utmost despair and lamentation; and yet there was not a soul who dared lift hand to save any of them, though many might be heard privately commenting on their beauty... One day, one of the king's favourite women overtook us, walking, with her hands clasped at the back of her head, to execution, crying in the most pitiful manner. A man was preceding her, but did not touch her; for she loved to obey the orders of her king voluntarily, and in consequence of previous attachment, was permitted, as a mark of distinction, to walk free. Wondrous world!...

A large body of officers came in with an old man, with his two ears shorn off for having been too handsome in his youth, and a young woman who had been discovered in his house. Nothing was listened to but the plaintiff's statement, who said he had lost the woman for four days, and, after considerable search, had found her concealed by the old man. Voices in defence were never heard. The king instantly sentenced both to death; and, to make the example more severe, decreed that, being fed to preserve life as long as possible, they were to be dismembered bit by bit, as rations for the vultures, every day, until life was extinct. The dismayed criminals, struggling to be heard, in utter despair, were dragged away boisterously in the most barbarous manner, to the drowning music of drums...

A boy, finding the king alone, threatened to kill him, because he took the lives of men unjustly. The king showed us, holding the pistol to his cheek, how he had presented the muzzle to the boy, which so frightened him that he ran away... The culprit, a good-looking young fellow of 16 or 17, brought in a goat, made his n'yanzigs, stroked the goat and his own face with his hands, n'yanzigged again with prostrations, and retired... There must have been some special reason why, in a court where trifling breaches of etiquette were punished with a cruel death, so grave a crime should have been so leniently dealt with; but I could not get at the bottom of the affair.

permission. Kabalega refrained from attacking the forts, but relations between Bunyoro and the Egyptian representative became increasingly uneasy. Outright war was probably averted only by the appointment of Emin Pasha as governor general in 1878. Sensibly, Emin Pasha withdrew from Bunyoro; and, instead of using his position to enact a petty vendetta against Kabalega, he focused his energy on the altogether more significant task of wresting control of the west Nile and Acholi regions from Arab slave traders. In 1883, following the Mahdist rebellion in Sudan, Emin Pasha and his troops were stranded in Wadelai. In 1889, they withdrew to the East African coast, effectively ending foreign attempts to control Uganda from the north.

The combined efforts of Baker and Gordon did little to curb Kabalega's empire-building efforts. In 1875, the Banyoro army overthrew Nyaika, the King of Toro, and the breakaway kingdom was reunited with Bunyoro. Kabalega also reclaimed several former parts of Bunyoro which had been annexed to Buganda, so that Bunyoro doubled in area under the first 20 years of his rule. Even more remarkably, Kabalega's was the first lengthy reign in centuries during which Bunyoro was free of internal rebellions. Following the Emin Pasha's withdrawal from Equatoria in 1889, the continued expansion, stability and sovereignty of Bunyoro under Kabalega must have seemed assured.

EUROPEANS IN BUGANDA (1884–92) In the mid 19th century, when the first Swahili slave traders arrived in central Africa from the east coast, the dominant regional power was Buganda, ruled over by Kabaka Mutesa from his capital at Kampala. Mutesa allowed the slave traders to operate from his capital, and he collaborated in slave-raiding parties into neighbouring territories. The Swahili converted several Baganda clan chiefs to their Islamic faith, and later, when Kampala was descended upon by the rival French Catholics and British Protestants, even more chiefs were attracted away from traditional Kiganda beliefs. Mutesa's court rapidly descended into a hotbed of religious rivalry.

Mutesa died in 1884. His son and successor, Mwanga, was a volatile and headstrong teenager who took the throne as religious rivalries in Buganda were building to a climax. Mwanga attempted to play off the various factions; he succeeded in alienating them all. In 1885, under the influence of a Muslim adviser, Mwanga ordered the execution of Bishop Hannington and 50 Christian converts (many of whom were roasted to death on a spit). In 1887, Mwanga switched allegiance to the traditionalist Kiganda chiefs, who in return offered to help him expel converts of all persuasions from Buganda. Threatened with expulsion, Muslims and Christians combined forces to launch an attack on the throne. Mwanga was overthrown in 1888. His Muslim-backed replacement, Kiwewa, persecuted Christians with even greater fervour than Mwanga had in 1885–86, but when Kiwewa's Kiganda leanings became apparent the Muslims rebelled and installed yet another leader. Events came to a head in 1889, when a civil war erupted between the Christian and Muslim factions, the result of which was that all Muslims were driven from the capital, later to join forces with Kabalega in Bunyoro. Mwanga was re-installed as kabaka.

The rival European powers were all eager to get their hands on the well-watered and fertile kingdom of Buganda, where, with the Muslims safely out of the way, rivalry between Francophile Catholics and Anglophile Protestants was increasingly open. In February 1890, Carl Peters arrived at Mengo clutching a treaty with the German East Africa Company. Mwanga signed it readily, possibly in the hope that German involvement would put an end to the Anglo-French religious intrigues which had persistently undermined his throne. Unfortunately for Mwanga, German deliverance was not to be: a few months after Peters's arrival, Germany handed Buganda and several other African territories to Britain in exchange for Heligoland, a tiny but strategic North Sea island.

In December 1890, Captain Lugard, the representative of the British East Africa Company, arrived at Kampala hoping to sign a treaty with an unimpressed Mwanga. The ensuing religious and political tensions sparked a crisis in January 1892, when a Catholic accused of killing a Protestant was acquitted by Mwanga on a plea of self-defence. Lugard demanded that the freed man be handed to him for a retrial and possible execution. Mwanga refused, on the rightful grounds that he was still the kabaka. Lugard decided it was time for a show of strength, and with the support of the Protestants he drove Mwanga and his Catholic supporters to an island on Lake

Victoria. He then sent troops to rout Mwanga from the island; the kabaka fled to Bukoba in Karagwe (northern Tanzania) before returning in March to his kingdom, which was by then on the verge of civil war. Mwanga was left with no real option but to sign a treaty recognising the Company's authority in Buganda.

Lugard returned to Britain in October 1892, where he rallied public support for the colonisation of Buganda, and was instrumental in swaying a Liberal government which under Gladstone was opposed to the acquisition of further territories. In November, the British government appointed Sir Gerald Portal as the commissioner to advise on future policy towards Buganda. Portal arrived in Kampala in March 1893, to be greeted by a flood of petitions from all quarters. Swayed by the fact that missionaries of both persuasions felt colonisation would further their goals in the kingdom, Portal raised the Union Jack over Kampala in April; a month later he signed a formal treaty with the unwilling but resigned Mwanga, offering British protectorateship over Buganda in exchange for the right to collect and spend taxes.

THE CREATION OF UGANDA (1892–99) The protectorate of Uganda initially had rather vague boundaries, mimicking those of the indigenous kingdom to which it nominally offered protection. It is not at all clear to what extent the early British administrators conceived of their protectorate extending beyond the boundaries of the kingdom, but all accounts suggest that Uganda was as chaotic an assemblage as can be imagined.

Captain Lugard had done a fair bit of tentative territorial expansion even before he signed a treaty with Buganda. It was evidently his intention to quell Bunyoro's rampant Omakuma Kabalega, against whom he had been prejudiced by the combination of Baker's poisonous reports, the not entirely unpredictable antipathy held for the Banyoro in Buganda. In August 1891, Lugard signed a treaty with the omugabe of Ankole in a vain attempt to block arms reaching Bunyoro from the south. Lugard drove the Banyoro army out of Toro and installed Kasagama, an exiled prince of Toro, to the throne. He then built a line of forts along the southern boundary of Bunyoro, effectively preventing Kabalega from invading Toro. The grateful Kasagama was happy enough to reward Lugard's efforts by signing a treaty of friendship between Britain and Toro.

Britain's predisposition to regard Kabalega as a villain became something close to a legal obligation following the treaty of protectorateship over Buganda, and it was certainly paralleled by the residual suspicion of foreigners held by Kabalega after the Equatoria debacle. Elements opposing British rule over Buganda fled to Kabalega's court at Mparo (near Hoima), notably a group of Muslim Baganda and Sudanese soldiers whose leader Selim Bey was deported in 1893 following a skirmish with the imperial authorities in Entebbe. With the assistance of the Baganda exiles, Kabalega re-invaded Toro in late 1893, driving Kasagama into the Rwenzori Mountains and the only British officer present back to Buganda.

In December 1893, Colonel Colville led a party of eight British officers, 450 Sudanese troops and at least 20,000 Baganda infantrymen on to Mparo. Kabalega was too crafty to risk confrontation with this impressive force: he burnt his capital and fled with his troops to the Budongo Forest. During 1894, Kabalega led several successful attacks on British forts, but as he lost more men and his supplies ran low, his guerrilla tactics became increasingly ineffective. In August 1894, on the very same day that the formal protectorateship of Uganda was announced by Colville, Kabalega launched his biggest assault yet on the fort at Hoima. The fort was razed, but Kabalega lost thousands of men. He was forced to leave Bunyoro to go into hiding in Acholi and Lango, from where he continued a sporadic and increasingly unsuccessful series of attacks on British targets. Kabalega's kingdom was unilaterally appended to the British Protectorate on 30 June 1896; the first formal agreement between Britain and Bunyoro was signed only in 1933.

Meanwhile, back in Kampala, Kabaka Mwanga and his traditionalist chiefs were becoming frustrated at the power which the British had invested in Christian converts in general and Protestants in particular. In July 1897, Mwanga left Kampala and raised a few loyalist troops to launch a feeble attack on the British forces. Swiftly defeated, Mwanga fled to Bukoba where he was captured by the German authorities. The British administration officially deposed Mwanga and they installed his one-year-old son Chwa as kabaka under the regency of three Protestant chiefs led by Apollo Kaggwa. The administration adopted the same tactic in Bunyoro, where a blameless 12-year-old son of Kabalega was installed as omakuma in 1898 – only to be removed four years later for what the administration termed incompetence!

Mwanga escaped from his German captors in late 1897, after which he joined forces with his former rival Kabalega. After two years on the run, Mwanga and Kabalega were cornered in a swamp in Lango. Following a long battle, Kabalega was shot (a wound which later necessitated the amputation of his arm) and the two former kings were captured and exiled to the Seychelles, where Mwanga died in 1903 and Kabalega died 20 years later. Kabalega remained the spiritual leader of Bunyoro until his death: it is widely held that the unpopular Omakuma Duhaga II, installed by Britain in place of his 'incompetent' teenage brother, was tolerated by the Banyoro only because he was Kabalega's son.

Ankole succumbed more easily to British rule. Weakened by smallpox and rinderpest epidemics in the 1870s, the kingdom then suffered epidemics of tetanus and jiggers in the early 1890s, and it only just managed to repel a Rwandan invasion in 1895. Omugabe Ntare died later in the same year, by which time all the natural heirs to the throne had died in one or other epidemic. Following a brief succession war, a youthful nephew of the Ntare was installed on the throne. In 1898, Britain occupied the Ankole capital at Mbarara; the battered kingdom offered no resistance.

The southeast also fell under British rule without great fuss, due to the lack of cohesive political systems in the region. Much of the area was brought into the protectorate through the efforts of a Muganda collaborator called Semei Kakungulu who, incidentally, had assisted in the capture of Kabalega and Mwanga in Lango. Kakungulu set up a fiefdom in the Lake Kyoga region, where he installed a rudimentary administrative system over much of the area west of what is now the Kenyan border and south of Mount Elgon. Characteristically, the British administration eventually demoted Kakungulu to a subordinate role in the very system which he had implemented for them. Kakungulu's life-story, as recounted in Michael Twaddle's excellent biography (see *Appendix 3*, *Further Information*, page 478), is as illuminating an account as any of the formative days of the protectorate.

By the end of the 19th century, the Uganda protectorate formally included the kingdoms of Buganda, Bunyoro, Ankole and Toro. Three of them were ruled by juveniles, while Toro was under the rule of the British-installed Kasagama. Whether through incompetence or malicious intent, the British administration was in the process of creating a nation divided against itself: firstly by favouring Protestants over Baganda of Catholic, Muslim or traditionalist persuasion, and secondly by replacing traditional clan leaders in other kingdoms with Baganda officials.

It is often asked whether colonialism was a good or a bad thing for Africa. There is no straightforward answer to this question. When writing about Malawi in 1995, I was forced to the conclusion that British intervention was the best thing to happen to that country in the troubled 19th century. By contrast, the arrogant, myopic and partial British administrators who were imposed on Uganda in the late 19th century unwittingly but surely sowed the seeds of future tragedy.

BRITISH RULE (1900–52) Ironically, the first governor of Uganda was none other than Sir Harry Johnston, whose vigorous anti-slaving campaign in the 1890s was as much as anything responsible for Britain's largely positive influence over Malawi. Johnston's instructions were to place the administration of the haphazardly assembled Uganda protectorate under what the Marquis of Salisbury termed 'a permanently satisfactory footing'. In March 1900, the newly appointed Governor of Uganda signed the so-called Buganda Agreement with the four-year-old kabaka. This document formally made Buganda a federal province of the protectorate, and it recognised the kabaka and his federal government conditional upon their loyalty to Britain. It divided Buganda into 20 counties, each of which had to pass the hut and gun taxes collected in their region to the central administration, and it forbade further attempts to extend the kingdom, a clause inserted mostly to protect neighbouring Busoga.

The Buganda Agreement also formalised a deal which had been made in 1898, in recognition of Buganda's aid in quelling Kabalega. Six former counties of Bunyoro were transferred to Buganda and placed under the federal rule of the kabaka, a decision described by a later district commissioner of Bunyoro as 'one of the greatest blunders' ever made by the administration of the protectorate. For lying within the Lost Counties (as the six annexed territories came to be called) were the burial sites of several former omakumas, as well as Mubende, a town which is steeped in Kinyoro traditions and the normal coronation site of an incoming omakuma. In 1921, the Banyoro who lived in the Lost Counties formed the Mubende Bunyoro Committee to petition for their return to Bunyoro. This, and at least three subsequent petitions, as well as five petitions made by the omakuma between 1943 and 1955, were all refused by the British administration on the basis that 'the boundaries laid down in 1900 could not be changed in favour of Bunyoro'. The issue of the Lost Counties caused Banyoro resentment throughout the colonial era, and it is arguably the trigger which set in motion the tragic events which followed Uganda's independence.

When Johnston arrived in Kampala in 1900, Uganda's borders were ill-defined. The first 15 years of the 20th century saw the protectorate expand further to incorporate yet more disparate cultural and linguistic groups, a growth which was motivated as much as anything by the desire to prevent previously unclaimed territories from falling into the hands of other European powers. The Kigezi region, a mishmash of small kingdoms which bordered German and Belgian territories to the south and west, was formally appended to Uganda in 1911. Baganda chiefs were installed throughout Kigezi, causing several uprisings and riots until the traditional chiefs were restored in 1929.

In the first decade of protectorateship, Britain had an inconsistent and ambiguous policy towards the territories north of the Nile. In 1906, it was decided not to incorporate them into Uganda, since they were not considered to be appropriate for the Kiganda system of government which was being imposed on other appended territories. More probably the administration was daunted by the cost and effort that would be required to subdue the dispersed and decentralised northern societies on an individual basis. In any event, the policy on the north was reversed in 1911, when the acting governor extended the protectorate to include Lango, and again in 1913, when Acholi and Karamoja were placed under British administration. The final piece in the Ugandan jigsaw was west Nile province: leased to the Belgian Congo until 1910, after which it was placed under the administration of the Sudan, west Nile was found a permanent home as part of Uganda in 1914.

Obsessed with the idea of running the protectorate along what it termed a Kiganda system of indirect rule, the British administration insisted not only on

Alexander Calder and Dr Joseph Kivubiro

Since its foundation in 1937, the School of Fine Art at Kampala's Makerere University has been the nucleus for East Africa's most influential and widespread contemporary art movement. While indigenous arts have flourished and evolved for centuries throughout East Africa, Makerere provided the region's first formal instruction in modern fine-art techniques, including drawing, painting and modern sculpture. Over the years, many students and graduates of this school became recognised innovators of striking new techniques and original styles.

During the particularly active 1950s and 1960s, artists held solo and group exhibitions at numerous locations. Growing interest in exhibitions by local artists led to the establishment of sizeable art collections by public museums, corporations, and government institutions throughout the country. Further stimulating Uganda's environment for advancing local art during this time, Esso and Caltex held widely publicised annual art competitions, publishing work by awarded artists on calendars distributed locally and abroad.

Until 1961, Makerere generally emphasised representative art, using drawing, perspective and shading in compositions inspired from local imagery. Following independence, however, a cadre of leading artists embraced a new role as visual cultural historians, producing interpretative works that document the early post-independence era – often using representative forms and figures to symbolise uncertainties and ideals within a rapidly changing society.

In 1966, artist Norbert Kaggwa underscored the importance of representational art in Uganda's rapidly evolving culture: 'Wedged into a single generation, my own, is a double vision; we are the beginning of an industrialised, urban society and we are probably – to be realistic – the end of the nomadic and village ways of life. The two eras are usually separated by hundreds of years. Here they are separated by a few dozen miles. I am personally very moved by this phenomenon and feel some special responsibility towards it. This is at least one of the reasons why I am a realistic and not an abstract painter. In one way, I suppose, I consider myself as much a cultural historian as an artist... or rather, in my case, they are one and the same thing.'

Artists debated their perceived role and the purpose of their works against the backdrop of independence. Art of this period consequently benefited from rich cross-fertilisation: several artists embraced both idioms to find unique and expressive visual forms that drew from abstract as well as representational influences. The late Henry Lumu, Augustine Mugalula Mukiibi, Teresa Musoke and Elly Kyeyune were early leaders of Uganda's emerging modernist school, spawning the distinctive semi-abstract styles that characterised much art of this era.

In 1968, Makerere graduate Henry Lumu was hired as art director by Uganda National Television, initiating regular broadcasts of televised art instruction classes. Exposure through this new medium further stimulated Kampala's burgeoning art community, which by that time extended well beyond the campus. The Uganda Art Club organised exhibitions throughout Kampala in the early to mid 1970s, prompting prominent hotels, banks and commercial buildings to amass and display collections of outstanding original works. During this period, artists attained unprecedented standing within Kampala's thriving cosmopolitan circles and among the country's élite.

By the late 1970s, political unrest had taken a dreadful toll among Uganda's artistic

exporting its bastardised Kiganda system throughout the country, but also on placing its implementation in the hands of Baganda officials. In effect, Britain ruled Uganda by deploying the Baganda in a sub-imperialistic role; as a reward for their

community. Professionals and intellectuals were targeted by the Obote and Amin regimes, and museums and galleries were looted or reoccupied – destroying numerous significant art collections. Forced to choose between seclusion, alternative occupations or self-imposed exile, many Ugandan artists emigrated to Kenya, South Africa, Europe or North America. The expatriate artists incorporated visual elements from their new surroundings into mediums, styles and colour palettes that still remained faithful to their Ugandan experience.

A large number of artists, including Henry Lumu, Joseph Mungaya, Dan Sekanwagi, Emmy Lubega, David Kibuuka, Jak Kitarikawe, David Wasswa Katongole and James Kitamirike, left for neighbouring Kenya. The colourful, innovative and uniquely stylised works of the Ugandan painters transformed Nairobi's art scene. Kenyan artist Nuwa Nnyanzi reflected recently: 'The impact of Ugandan artists in Kenya in the seventies and eighties was so great that it is still felt and highly visible today.'

Restored political stability in the late 1980s encouraged the homecoming or resurfacing of many Ugandan artists. Expressing rediscovered peacetime ideals through their art, many artists also reminded their audience of struggles and horrors endured during the troubled years. Exhibitions by Ugandan artists were held regularly at London's Commonwealth Institute, while other shows opened in Paris and Vienna. In 1992, President Museveni marked the opening of a Vienna show featuring Geoffrey Mukasa and Fabian Mpagi with these remarks:

As those destructive years have regrettably shown, art cannot flourish in a situation plagued with terror and human indifference. Peace and security has returned to our country. We have gone a long way to encourage the revival of arts. The fine works exhibited are a vivid testimony that art has come to life again in Uganda. Certainly, both the public and the critics will recognise that Uganda has taken up her place in the world of modern art. It is an opportune moment for us to portray through these paintings a promising new picture of the 'New Uganda'.

Exhibitions by and for Ugandan artists have also been held in Stockholm, Amsterdam, Berlin, Frankfurt, Rome, Johannesburg and seven cities in the USA. In North America, expatriate artists such as James Kitamirike, David Kibuuka, Dan Sekanwagi and Fred Makubuya have united to spearhead renewed interest in their art through the Fine Arts Centre for East Africa, which opened in San Francisco in 1998. Organising group exhibitions in the USA and Canada, this active contingent of artists continues to garner recognition for their innovative styles, mediums and potent individual voices within Uganda's art movement.

In Kampala today, Uganda's renewed art scene embodies a vibrant and vital country redefining its past yet also reaching for a hopeful future. Sharing their unique visual arts legacy, Uganda's fine-art pioneers have become the country's cultural ambassadors, creating global awareness of their homeland's unique colours, cultures, peoples and art.

Locations to view art in Kampala include the Uganda Museum, Nommo Gallery, Tuli Fanya Gallery, Gallery Café, Okapi Gallery, Cassava Republic and Nnyanzi Art Studio. For relevant websites, see page 482.

Reprinted with minor edits from the website of the Fine Arts Centre for East Africa in San Francisco, with permission from Alexander Calder (☎ 415 333 9363; e gadart@aol.com; www.theartroom-sf.com).

doing the administration's dirty work, Buganda was run as a privileged state within a state, a status it enjoyed right through to independence, when it was the only former kingdom to be granted full federality.

This divisive arrangement worked only because the administration had the legal and military clout to enforce it – even then, following regular uprisings in Bunyoro and Kigezi, traditional chiefs were gradually reinstated in most parts of the country. The 1919 Native Authority Ordinance delineated the powers of local chiefs, which were wide-ranging but subject always to the intervention of British officials. The Kiganda system was inappropriate to anywhere but Buganda, and it was absolutely absurd in somewhere like Karamoja, where there were no traditional chiefs, and decisions were made on a consensual basis by committees of recognised elders.

For all its flaws, the administrative system which was imposed on Uganda probably gave indigenous Ugandans far greater autonomy than was found elsewhere in British-ruled Africa. The administration discouraged alien settlement and, with the introduction of cotton, it helped many regions attain a high degree of economic self-sufficiency. Remarkably, cotton growing was left almost entirely to indigenous farmers – in 1920, a mere 500km^2 of Uganda was covered in European-run plantations, most of which collapsed following the global economic slump of the 1920s and the resultant drop in cotton prices. Political decentralisation was increased by the Local Government Ordinance of 1949, which divided Uganda along largely ethnic lines into 18 districts, each of which had a district council with a high degree of federal autonomy. This ordinance gave even greater power to African administrators, but it also contributed to the climate of regional unity and national disunity which characterised the decades immediately preceding and following Uganda's independence.

The area that suffered most from this federalist policy was the 'backward' north. Neglected in terms of education, and never provided with reliable transport links whereby farmers could export their product to other parts of the country, the people of the north were forced to send their youngsters south to find work. There is some reason to suppose it was deliberate British policy to underdevelop an area which had become a reliable source of cheap labour and of recruits to the police and army. This impression is reinforced by the fact that when Africans were first admitted to the Central Legislative Council, only Buganda, the east and the west were allowed representation – the administrative systems which had been imposed on the north were 'not yet in all districts advanced to the stage requiring the creation of centralised native executives'. In other words, instead of trying to develop the north and bring it in line with other regions in Uganda, the British administration chose to neglect it.

Writing before Amin ascended to power, the Ugandan historian Samwiri Karugire commented that 'the full cost of this neglect has yet to be paid, not by the colonial officials, but by Ugandans themselves'. More recent writers have suggested that it is no coincidence that Milton Obote and Idi Amin both hailed from north of the Nile.

THE BUILD-UP TO INDEPENDENCE (1952–62) The cries for independence which prevailed in most African colonies following World War II were somewhat muted in Uganda. This can be attributed to several factors: the lack of widespread alien settlement, the high degree of African involvement in public affairs prior to independence, the strongly regional character of the protectorate's politics, and the strong probability that the status quo rather suited Uganda's Protestant Baganda élite. Remarkably, Uganda's first anti-colonial party, the Uganda National Congress (UNC), was founded as late as 1952, and it was some years before it gained any marked support, except, significantly, in parts of the underdeveloped north.

The first serious call for independence came from the most unlikely of sources. In 1953, the unpopular Kabaka Mutesa II defied the British administration by vociferously opposing the mooted federation of Uganda with Kenya and Tanzania.

When the Governor of Uganda refused to give Mutesa any guarantees regarding federation, Mutesa demanded that Buganda – alone – be granted independence. The governor declared Mutesa to be disloyal to Britain, deposed him from the throne, and exiled him to Britain. This won Mutesa immense support, and not only in Buganda, so that when he was returned to his palace in 1955 it was as something of a national hero. Sadly, Mutesa chose not to use his popularity to help unify Uganda, but concentrated instead on parochial Kiganda affairs. A new Buganda Agreement was signed on 18 October 1955, giving the kabaka and his government even greater federal powers – and generating mild alarm among the non-Baganda.

Uganda's first indigenous party of consequence, the Democratic Party (DP), was founded in 1956 by Matayo Mugwanya after Mutesa had rejected him as a candidate for the Prime Minister of Buganda on the grounds of his Catholicism. The party formed a platform for the legitimate grievances of Catholics, who had always been treated as second-class citizens in Uganda, and it rose to some prominence after party leadership was handed to the lawyer Benedicto Kiwanuka in 1958. However, the DP was rightly or wrongly perceived by most Ugandans as an essentially Catholic party, which meant it was unlikely ever to win mass support.

The formation of the Uganda People's Union (UPU) came in the wake of the 1958 election, when for the first time a quota of Africans was elected to national government. The UPU was the first public alliance of non-Buganda leaders, and as such it represented an important step in the polarisation of Ugandan politics: in essence, the Baganda versus everybody else. In 1959, the UNC split along ethnic lines, with the non-Baganda faction combining with the UPU to form the Uganda People's Congress (UPC), led by Milton Obote. In 1961, the Baganda element of the UNC combined with members of the federal government of Buganda to form the overtly pro-Protestant and pro-Baganda Kabaka Yekka (KY) – which literally means 'The Kabaka Forever' (and was nicknamed 'Kill Yourselves' by opponents).

As the election of October 1961 approached, the DP, UPC and KY were clearly the main contenders. The DP won, largely through a Baganda boycott which gave them 19 of the seats within the kingdom – in East Kyaggwe, for instance, only 188 voters registered out of an estimated constituency of 90,000. The DP's Benedicto Kiwanuka thus became the first Prime Minister of Uganda when self-government was granted on 1 March 1962 – the first time ever that Catholics had any real say in public matters. Another general election was held in April of that year, in the build-up to the granting of full independence. As a result of the DP's success the year before, the UPC and KY formed an unlikely coalition, based on nothing but their mutual non-Catholicism. The UPC won 43 seats, the DP 24 seats, and the KY 24 (of which all but three were in Buganda), giving the UPC–KY alliance a clear majority and allowing Milton Obote to lead Uganda to independence on 9 October 1962.

THE FIRST OBOTE GOVERNMENT (1962–71) Obote, perhaps more than any other Commonwealth leader, inherited a nation fragmented along religious and ethnic lines to the point of ungovernability. He was also handed an Independence Constitution of singular peculiarity: Buganda was recognised as having full federal status, the other kingdoms were granted semi-federal status, and the remainder of the country was linked directly to central government. His parliamentary majority was dependent on a marriage of convenience based solely on religious grounds, and he was compelled to recognise Kabaka Mutesa II as head of state. Something, inevitably, was going to have to give.

The Lost Counties of Bunyoro became the pivotal issue almost immediately after independence. In April 1964, Obote decided to settle the question by holding a referendum in the relevant counties, thereby allowing their inhabitants to decide whether they wanted to remain part of Buganda or be reincorporated into Bunyoro. The result of the referendum, almost 80% in favour of the counties being reincorporated into Bunyoro, caused a serious rift between Obote and Mutesa. It also caused the fragile UPC–KY alliance to split; no great loss to Obote since enough DP and KY parliamentarians had already defected to the UPC for him to retain a clear majority.

Tensions between Obote and Mutesa culminated in the so-called Constitutional Crisis of 1966. On 22 February, Obote scrapped the Independence Constitution, thereby stripping Mutesa of his presidency. Mutesa appealed to the UN to intervene. Obote sent the army to the royal palace. Mutesa was forced to jump over the palace walls and into exile in London, where he died, impecunious, three years later. Ominously, an estimated 2,000 of the Baganda who had rallied around their king's palace were loaded on to trucks and driven away. Some were thrown over Murchison Falls. Others were buried in mass graves. Most of them had been alive when they were taken from the palace.

In April 1966, Obote unveiled a new constitution in which he abolished the role of prime minister and made himself 'Life President of Uganda'. In September 1967, he introduced another new constitution wherein he made Uganda a republic, abolished the kingdoms, divided Buganda into four new districts, and gave the army unlimited powers of detention without trial. In sole control of the country, but faced with smouldering Baganda resentment, Obote became increasingly reliant on force to maintain a semblance of stability. In September 1969, he banned the DP and other political parties. A spate of detentions followed: the DP leader Benedicto Kiwanuka, perceived dissidents within the UPC, the Baganda royal family, Muslim leaders, and any number of lawyers, students, journalists and doctors.

On 11 January 1971, Obote flew out of Entebbe for the Commonwealth Conference in Singapore. He left behind a memorandum to the commander of the Ugandan army, demanding an explanation not only for the disappearance of four million US dollars out of the military coffers, but also for the commander's alleged role in the murder of a brigadier and his wife in Gulu a year earlier, a dual murder for which he was due to be brought to trial. The commander decided his only option was to strike in Obote's absence. On 25 January 1971, Kampala was rocked by the news of a military coup, and Uganda had a new president – a killer with the demeanour of a buffoon, and charisma enough to ensure that he would become one of the handful of African presidents who have achieved household-name status in the West.

THE AMIN YEARS (1971–79) Idi Amin was born in January 1928 of a Muslim father and Christian mother at Koboko near the border with DRC and Sudan. As a child, he moved with his mother to Lugazi in Buganda. Poorly educated and barely literate, Amin joined the King's African Rifles in 1946. He fought for Britain against the Mau-Mau in Kenya, after which he attended a training school in Nakuru. In 1958, he became one of the first two Africans in Uganda to be promoted to the rank of lieutenant. In 1962, he showed something of his true colours when he destroyed a village near Lake Turkana in Kenya, killing three people without provocation; a misdeed for which he only narrowly escaped trial, largely through the intervention of Obote.

By 1966, Amin was second in command of the Ugandan army, and, following the 1966 Constitution Crisis, Obote promoted him to the top spot. It was Amin who led the raid that forced Mutesa into exile, Amin who gave the orders when 2,000 of the kabaka's Baganda supporters were loaded into trucks and killed, and Amin who co-ordinated the mass detentions that followed the banning of the DP in 1969. For years, Amin was the instrument with which Obote kept a grip on power, yet, for reasons that are unclear, by 1970 the two most powerful men in Uganda were barely talking to each other. It is a measure of Obote's arrogance that when he wrote that fateful memorandum before flying to Singapore, he failed to grasp not only that its recipient would be better equipped than anybody else to see the real message, but also that Amin was one of the few men in Uganda with the power to react.

Given the role that Amin had played under Obote, it is a little surprising that the reaction to his military takeover was incautious jubilation. Amin's praises were sung by everybody from the man in the street to the foreign press and the Baganda royals whose leader Amin had helped drive into exile. This, quite simply, was a reflection less of Amin's popularity than of Obote's singular unpopularity. Nevertheless, Amin certainly played out the role of a 'man of peace', promising a rapid return to civilian rule, and he sealed his popularity in Buganda by allowing the preserved body of Mutesa to be returned for burial.

On the face of it, the first 18 months of Amin's rule were innocuous enough. Arguably the first public omen of things to come occurred in mid 1972, when Amin expelled all Asians from the country, 'Africanised' their businesses, and commandeered their money and possessions for 'state' use. In the long term, this action proved to be an economic disaster, but the sad truth is that it won Amin further support from the majority of Ugandans, who had long resented Asian dominance in business circles.

Even as Amin consolidated his public popularity, behind the scenes he was reverting to type; this was, after all, a man who had escaped being tried for murder not once but twice. Amin quietly purged the army of its Acholi and Lango majority: by the end of 1973, 13 of the 23 officers who had held a rank of lieutenant-colonel or higher at the time of Amin's coup had been murdered. By the end of 1972, eight of the 20 members of Obote's 1971 cabinet were dead, and four more were in exile. Public attention was drawn to Amin's actions in 1973, when the former prime minister, Benedicto Kiwanuka, was detained and murdered by Amin, as was the vice-chancellor of Makerere University.

By 1974, Amin was fully engaged in a reign of terror. During the eight years he was in power, an estimated 300,000 Ugandans were killed by him or his agents (under the guise of the State Research Bureau), many of them tortured to death in horrific ways. His main targets were the northern tribes, intellectuals and rival politicians, but any person or group that he perceived as a threat was dealt with mercilessly. Despite this, African leaders united behind Uganda's despotic ruler: incredibly, Amin was made President of the Organisation of African Unity (OAU) in 1975. Practically the sole voice of dissent within Africa came from Tanzania's Julius Nyerere, who asserted that it was hypocritical for African leaders to criticise the white racist regimes of southern Africa while ignoring similarly cruel regimes in 'black' Africa. Nyerere granted exile to several of Amin's opponents, notably Milton Obote and Yoweri Museveni, and he refused to attend the 1975 OAU summit in Kampala.

As Amin's unpopularity with his own countrymen grew, he attempted to forge national unity by declaring war on Tanzania in 1978. Amin had finally overreached himself; after his troops entered northwest Tanzania, where they bombed the towns of Bukoba and Musoma, Tanzania and a number of Ugandan exiles retaliated by invading Uganda. In April 1979, Amin was driven out of Kampala into an exile from which he would never return prior to his death of multiple organ failure in a Saudi Arabian hospital in August 2003.

UGANDA AFTER AMIN (1979–86)
When Amin departed from Ugandan politics in 1979, it was seen as a fresh start by a brutalised nation. As it transpired, it was Uganda's

third false dawn in 17 years – most Ugandans now regard the seven years which followed Amin's exile to have been worse even than the years which preceded it.

In the climate of high political intrigue which followed Amin's exile, Uganda's affairs were stage managed by exiled UPC leaders in Arusha (Tanzania), most probably because the UPC's leader Milton Obote was understandably cautious about announcing his return to Ugandan politics. The semi-exiled UPC installed Professor Lule as a stand-in president, a position which he retained for 68 days. His successor, Godfrey Binaisa, fared little better, lasting about eight months before he was bundled out of office in May 1980. The stand-in presidency was then assumed by two UPC loyalists, Paulo Muwanga and David Oyite-Ojik, who set an election date in December 1980.

The main rivals for the election were the DP, led by Paul Ssemogerere, and the UPC, still led by Milton Obote. A new party, the Uganda Patriotic Movement (UPM), led by Yoweri Museveni, was formed a few months prior to the election. Uganda's first election since 1962 took place in an atmosphere of corruption and intimidation. Muwanga and Oyite-Ojik used trumped-up charges to prevent several DP candidates from standing, so that the UPC went into the polling with 17 uncontested seats. On the morning of 11 December, it was announced that the DP were on the brink of victory with 63 seats certain, a surprising result that probably reflected a strong anti-Obote vote from the Baganda. In response, Muwanga and Oyite-Ojik quickly drafted a decree ensuring that all results had to be passed to them before they could be announced. The edited result of the election saw the DP take 51 seats, the UPM one seat, and the UPC a triumphant 74. After some debate, the DP decided to claim their seats, despite the overwhelming evidence that the election had been rigged.

Yoweri Museveni felt that people had been cheated by the election, and that under Obote's UPC the past was doomed to repeat itself. In 1982, Museveni formed the National Resistance Movement (NRM), an army largely made up of orphans left behind by the excesses of Amin and Obote. The NRM operated from the Luwero Triangle in Buganda north of Kampala, where they waged a guerrilla war against Obote's government. Obote's response was characteristically brutal: his troops waded into the Luwero Triangle killing civilians by their thousands, an ongoing massacre which exceeded even Amin's. The world turned a blind eye to the atrocities in Luwero, and so it was left to 'dissident' members of the UPC and the commander of the army, Tito Okello, to suggest that Obote might negotiate with the NRM in order to stop the slaughter. Obote refused. On 27 July 1985, he was deposed in a bloodless military coup led by Tito Okello. For the second time in his career, Obote was forced into exile by the commander of his own army.

Okello assumed the role of head of state and he appointed as his prime minister Paulo Muwanga, whose role in the 1980 election gave him little credibility. With some misgivings, the DP allied itself with Okello, largely because Ssemogerere hoped he might use his influence to stop the killing in Luwero. In a statement made in Nairobi in August 1985, Museveni announced that the NRM was prepared to co-operate with Okello, provided that the army and the other instruments of oppression used by previous regimes were brought under check. The NRM entered into negotiations with Okello, but after these broke down in December 1985, Museveni returned to the bush. On 26 January 1986, the NRM entered Kampala, Okello surrendered tamely, and Museveni was sworn in as president – Uganda's seventh head of state in as many years.

THE NRM GOVERNMENT (1986–2003)
In 1986, Museveni took charge of a country that had been beaten and brutalised as have few others. There must have been

many Ugandans who felt this was yet another false dawn, as they waited for the cycle of killings and detentions to start all over again. Certainly, to the outside world, Uganda's politics had become so confusing in all but their consistent brutality that the NRM takeover appeared to be merely another instalment in an apparently endless succession of coups and civil wars.

But Museveni was far from being another Amin or Obote. He shied away from the retributive actions which had destroyed the credibility of previous takeovers; he appointed a broad-based government which swept across party and ethnic lines, re-established the rule of law, appointed a much-needed Human Rights Commission, increased the freedom of the press, and encouraged the return of Asians and other exiles. On the economic front, he adopted pragmatic policies and encouraged foreign investment and tourism, the result of which was an average growth rate of 10% in his first decade of rule. Museveni has also tried to tackle corruption, albeit with limited success, by gradually cutting the civil service. Most significantly, Uganda under Museveni has visibly moved away from being a society obsessed with its ethnic and religious divisions. From the most unpromising material, Museveni has, miraculously, forged a real nation.

In 1993, Museveni greatly boosted his popularity (especially with the influential Baganda) by his decision to grant legal recognition to the old kingdoms of Uganda. In July 1993, the Cambridge-educated son of Mutesa II, Ronald Mutebi, returned to Uganda after having spent over 20 years in Britain; in a much-publicised coronation near Kampala, he was made the 36th kabaka of Buganda. The traditional monarchies of Bunyoro and Toro have also been restored, but not that of Ankole.

In the 1990s, the most widespread criticism of Museveni and the NRM was its tardiness in moving towards a genuine multi-party democracy. At the time, Museveni argued rather convincingly that Uganda needed stability offered by a 'no party' system more than it needed a potentially divisive multi-party system that risked igniting the ethnic passions that had caused the country so much misery in its first two decades of independence. As a result, the NRM remained the only legal political party until as recently as 2005, though the country's first open presidential elections were held in 1996, slightly more than ten years after Museveni had first assumed power. Museveni won with an overwhelming 74% of the vote, as compared with the 23% polled by his main rival, Paul Ssemogerere, a former DP leader who once served as prime minister under Museveni. A similar pattern was registered in the 2001 presidential elections, which returned Museveni to power with 70% of the vote, as compared to the 20% registered by his main rival Kizza Besigye. At the time, and for several years afterwards, Museveni reiterated his commitment to stand down from the presidency in 2006, in accordance with the maximum of two presidential terms specified by a national constitution drawn up years earlier by the NRM constitution.

During the course of 2004, Museveni made two crucial political about faces. In July, during the build up to holding a national referendum on the question of a return to multi-partyism, he actively travelled the country rallying support for a vote in favour of change. The results of this poll were somewhat ambiguous. On the one hand, an impressive majority of 92.5% of votes cast were in favour of Museveni's proposed reversion to multi-party politics. On the other, a polling turnout of only 47% suggested that many agreed with the opposition, which claimed that the referendum was a waste of time and money and called upon voters to boycott it. Just weeks after this political landmark, Museveni pushed a constitutional amendment to scrap presidential term limits through parliament, clearing the way for him to seek a third term in the looming elections. In November, barely three months before the election was due, the main opposition leader Kizza Besigye, having recently returned from exile, was imprisoned and charged with terrorism, only to be released on bail in January 2006. A month later, Uganda's first multi-party election in 25 years was largely held to be free and fair by international observers, though this verdict was loudly disputed by Besigye, who polled 37% of the vote as compared to Museveni's 59%. Once again, this result can be viewed as ambiguous – the gap between the two primary candidates, though by no means insubstantial, had halved since the 2001 presidential election, and it is difficult to say to what extent the vote for Museveni represented overt support for his presidency and to what extent it simply reflected a fear of change.

On 26 August 2006, the Ugandan government announced what is potentially the most important landmark in the country's recent history, ie: the mutual agreement to a three-week ceasefire with the LRA aimed at ending the civil war that has caused so much death and suffering in northern Uganda over the past 20 years (see box *Joseph Kony and the Lord's Resistance Army* page 396–7). At the time of writing, the major stumbling block to the ongoing peace talks would appear to be a warrant for the arrest of Kony and five other LRA leaders issued by the International Criminal Court in Hague in October 2005. However, Museveni has offered the LRA leaders full immunity if peace talks in southern Sudan lead to a firm agreement, and – following a two-week extension of the ceasefire into early October – most observers regard this to be best chance yet of ending the protracted conflict in the north.

ECONOMY

Uganda has, by and large, a free market economy. This suffered greatly under the presidencies of Amin and Obote, but since Museveni took power in 1986 Uganda's economy has maintained a growth rate of 5–6% per annum. Agriculture accounts for about 60% of the GDP, with major export crops including coffee, tea and tobacco. Over 90% of Ugandans are either subsistence farmers or work in agriculture-related fields.

PEOPLE

The 2002 census showed Uganda to have a population of 24.6 million, of which 87% live rurally. This represents an almost 50% increase on the 1991 figure of 16.7 million, an annual growth rate of more than 4% as compared with 2.5% per annum between 1980 and 1991. The majority of Uganda's people are concentrated in the south and west. The most populous ethnic group are the Bantu-speaking Baganda, who account for about 20% of the population and are centred around Kampala. Other significant Bantu-speaking groups are the Ankole, Toro, Banyoro and Basoga. The east and north of the country are populated by several groups of Nilotic or Cushitic origin, including the Teso, Karimojong, Acholi and Lango.

The most populous city in Uganda is Kampala at 1.2 million in 2002. Jinja is generally cited as the country's second-largest city, but the 2002 census would suggest that the ongoing instability in the north and associated flood from rural areas into the towns has seen it overtaken by Gulu (population 113,000) and Lira (90,000). Having said that, add the 50,000-plus residents of Njeru, which lies on the opposite bank of the Nile, to Jinja's 86,500, and it remains comfortably the largest urban centre in Uganda after the capital. The table above, showing the ten largest urban centres in Uganda in 2002 and in earlier censuses, is a good indicator of the dramatic post-independence shifts in urban growth around the country.

Note that exact figures are not yet published for Mbarara and lower-ranked towns in 2002, except that the population of each exceeds 50,000. Aside from Gulu

	1959		1991		2002	
1	Kampala	46,000	Kampala	775,000	Kampala	1.2 million
2	Gulu	30,000	Jinja	65,000	Jinja	113,000
3	Lira	14,000	Mbale	54,000	Mbale	90,000
4	Jinja	11,500	Masaka	49,500	Entebbe	86,500
5	Mbale	11,000	Entebbe	42,700	Kabale	76,000
6	Mbarara	8,500	Mbarara	41,000		
7	Masaka	8,000	Soroti	40,900		
8	Entebbe	7,000	Gulu	38,300		
9	Kasese	6,000	Njeru	37,000		
10	Njeru	5,000	Fort Portal	32,800		

and Lira, the most rapid growth centre in Uganda in the past decade would appear, somewhat improbably, to be Kasese, which ranked 18th in 1991 with a population of only 18,000. As with Gulu and Lira, this rapid expansion might well be linked to the instability in the Rwenzori area in the late 1990s. If this author's impressions count for anything, the most visibly expanded town since I first visited Uganda in 1988 is without question Mbarara.

LANGUAGE

The official language, English, is spoken as a second language by most educated Ugandans. More than 33 local languages are spoken in different parts of the country. Most of these belong to the Bantu language group: for instance, Luganda, Lusoga and Lutoro. Several Nilotic and Cushitic languages are spoken in the north and east, some of them by only a few thousand people. An unusual language of the extreme northeast is Karimojong, which has a vocabulary of only 180 words. Many Ugandans speak a limited amount of KiSwahili, a coastal language which spread into the East African interior via the 19th-century Arab slave traders. Few Ugandans speak any indigenous language other than their home language, so KiSwahili and English are the most useful languages for tourists, and they are widely used between Ugandans of different linguistic backgrounds.

RELIGION

Some 85% of Ugandans are Christian, divided roughly equally between the Protestant Church of Uganda (an offshoot of the Church of England) and the Roman Catholic Church. In most rural areas, these exotic religions have not entirely replaced traditional beliefs, so that many people practise both concurrently. Roughly 11% of Uganda is Islamic, a legacy of the Arab trade with Buganda in the late 19th century. There is little or no friction between Christian and Muslim in modern Uganda, though post-independence political conflict did follow Catholic–Protestant lines. Although the country's Asian population was forced into exile by Amin in 1972, many individuals, both Islamic and Hindu, have been repatriated since 1986. The main centre of animism is the northeast, where the Karimojong – like the affiliated Maasai and other Rift Valley pastoralists – largely shun any exotic faith in favour of their own traditional beliefs.

2

Natural History

What most distinguishes Uganda from any other recognised African safari destination is quite simply its relatively high proportion of closed canopy forest. This embraces Afro-montane forest such as that found on Mount Elgon, which has strong affinities to similar habitats on mounts Kilimanjaro and Kenya, as well as the likes of Semliki National Park, effectively an easterly extension of the lowland rainforest that blankets the Congolese Basin and west Africa. Uganda thus harbours a wide variety of vertebrate and other species absent elsewhere in east and southern Africa, and the accessibility of its major forests by comparison to those in west Africa makes it an unbeatable destination for viewing African forest creatures – from gorillas and chimps to a colourful array of butterflies and birds – in their natural habitat.

When it comes to more conventional game viewing, Uganda is not a safari destination to bear comparison with Tanzania or Kenya, or for that matter the majority of countries in southern Africa. It is too small to have any reserves on the grand scale of Tanzania's Selous or Serengeti, or the Luangwa, Chobe, Hwange and Kruger national parks further south. Nevertheless, its savanna reserves are gradually recovering from the heavy poaching that took place during the years of civil war and political unrest. Today, Queen Elizabeth and Murchison Falls national parks offer as good a chance of encountering perennial safari favourites such as lion, elephant, buffalo, giraffe and even leopard as many more celebrated game reserves – with the added bonus of lying on a circuit that also offers some of the best forest primate viewing in Africa. For independent travellers on a limited budget, these two parks are also among the most accessible and affordable, comparably worthwhile savanna reserves anywhere in Africa.

A striking feature of the Ugandan landscape, with the exception of the semi-desert and dry acacia woodland of the far north, is its relatively moist climate. A high precipitation level makes the countryside far greener and more fertile than elsewhere in East Africa, while lakes, rivers and other wetland habitats account for almost 25% of the country's surface area. The most extensive freshwater bodies that lie within Uganda or along its borders are, in descending order, lakes Victoria, Albert, Kyoga, Edward, Kwania and George. Lesser expanses include Lake Wamala near Mityana, lakes Bunyonyi and Mutanda in Kigezi, lakes Bisina and Opeta in the east, and almost 100 small crater lakes dotted around the Rwenzori foothills. Of particular interest to birdwatchers are the half-dozen species associated exclusively with papyrus swamps – most notably the exquisite papyrus gonolek and eagerly sought-after shoebill, the latter seen more easily in Uganda than anywhere else.

Although most of Uganda is topographically relatively undramatic – essentially an undulating plateau perched at altitudes of 1,000–1,200m between the eastern and western arms of the Rift Valley – it is bordered by some of the continent's most impressive mountains. Foremost among these are the

The Uganda Wildlife Authority or (as it's more commonly referred to) UWA (pronounced ooh-er!) is the body responsible for all national parks and wildlife reserves in Uganda. Details of its headquarters and booking office in Kampala, as well as its excellent website, are listed in Chapter 6, page 158. These prices are based on a draft for a revised UWA tariff applicable from August 2006 to July 2008.

The visitation fee for most protected areas under its supervision falls into one of two categories. Murchison Falls, Queen Elizabeth, Bwindi Impenetrable, Mgahinga Gorilla, Lake Mburo, Kibale, Kidepo Valley and Rwenzori Mountains national parks are classed as Category A. Entrance for foreign non-residents costs US$25 for one night, US$35 for two nights and US$50 for three or more nights. East African residents who are able to show proof of residency pay US$15/20/25, respectively. Semuliki Mount Elgon national parks and Katonga, Semliki and Pian Upe wildlife reserves are classed as Category B. Non-residents pay US$20/25/30 and East African residents US$15/20/25 for one/two/three or more nights, respectively. Children of five–15 years pay rather less than half the adult rate and under fives enter for free. Ugandan citizens pay Ush5,000/7,500/10,000 (Ush – Uganda shilling) for Category A parks and Ush3,000 per night for other protected areas. Note that although UWA publishes most of its entrance and activity fees in US$ they can be paid in local currency.

If after a night in a park you decide to stay another, it's possible to top up your permit at a gate or information office. In other words, if you pay US$25 to enter Queen Elizabeth National Park (QENP) you can stay a second night on payment of US$10 and a third on payment of US$15 to total US$50. This highlights an anomaly in the system. As several travellers have pointed out the three-day plus permit is only good value if you spend four or more days in the park. Entrance permits do not apply to special activities such as mountaineering on the Rwenzori and Mount Elgon, gorilla tracking in Bwindi and the Kibale chimp habituation experience which are subject to all-inclusive fees.

In Mount Elgon National Park daily mountaineering fees of US$30 for both foreign residents and non-residents and Ush20,000 for Ugandan citizens includes the entrance fee, camping fee (this is not included) and ranger/escort fee: a flat rate of US$40/Ush20,000 per day applies to the same visitor categories for volcano climbing in Mgahinga Gorilla National Park. For the Rwenzoris, the mountaineering fee for a seven-day, six-night hike costs US$500 for non-residents, US$460 for East African residents or US$254 for Ugandan citizens. This fee is paid to Rwenzori Mountaineering Services and covers hut fees rescue, fuel and guide fees, as well as the services of four porters per hiker. It excludes park entrance of US$25/day (totaling US$175) which is paid to UWA.

Rwenzori, which follows the Congolese border and is topped by the third-highest point in Africa, the 5,109m Margherita Peak on Mount Stanley. Other major mountains include Elgon (4,321m) on the Kenyan border, the Virungas on the Rwandan border (of which Muhabura is at 4,127m the highest of the Ugandan peaks), and Moroto (3,084m), Kadam (3,068m) and Morungole (2,750m) on the Kenyan border north of Elgon. Rising in solitude from the surrounding plains, these high mountains all support isolated microhabitats of forest and high grassland. The higher reaches of the Rwenzori, Elgon and to a lesser extent the Virungas are covered in Afro-alpine moorland, a fascinating and somewhat other-worldly habitat noted for gigantism among plants such as lobelias, heather and groundsel, as well as habitat-specific creatures such as the dazzling scarlet-tufted malachite sunbird.

Accommodation charges for units operated by UWA vary widely from US$6–20 per person depending on the standard of accommodation and whether they are sharing. Camping at all UWA public campsites costs US$6 per person. The services of a ranger/guide for game drives costs US$20 per vehicle for day game drives and US$25 for night drives. Half day rates no longer apply. Guided walks cost US$10 per person. The most glaring exception is of course the popular gorilla-tracking excursions in Bwindi, which must normally be booked well in advance through the UWA headquarters in Kampala, at a charge of US$375 for non-residents, US$355 for East African residents and Ush100,000 for Ugandan citizens. As of July 2007, this will increase to US$500 for foreigners, US$475 for residents and Ush150,000 for citizens. Primate/chimp walks in Kibale National Park have recently been hiked substantially, costing US$70 for non-residents, US$50 for East African residents, and Ush50,000 for Ugandan citizens (excludes park entrance fee). The same visitor categories pay US$30/US$20/Ush20,000 respectively for chimp tracking in Kyambura Gorge (QENP). Chimp tracking is considerably cheaper in Budongo and Kalinzu forests which are managed by the National Forest Authority; US$30 for non-residents and US$20 for East African residents. These exclude entrance fees (see below). Further details on charges for activities and accommodation in the national parks and wildlife reserves are included under the relevant headings in the main body of this guidebook.

A discount of 50% on all visitation fees is offered to children aged 15 or younger and 25% to foreign students with valid international student cards. Residents of East Africa can buy a special pass allowing them free entrance to all national parks for a year at US$100 for one person, US$150 for a couple or US$200 for a family with up to four children aged 15 or younger. It has always been possible to pay visitation and other UWA fees (including gorilla tracking) in local currency and in recent years this has been the best way to pay aside from the hassle of carrying large numbers of small-denomination US dollar bills. Note that while UWA only accepts US$100 bills issued during or since 1997, UWA uses a conversion rate lower than you'll get in Kampala, so the double conversion generally works in your favour. Expect UWA fees to be revised in mid 2008. Several UWA accommodation facilities are currently being privatised so prices are likely to change. In addition to personal entrance fees, private 4x4 vehicles pay an entrance fee of US$16 for Ugandan registrations and US$40 for foreign vehicles. Ugandan saloon cars pay US$11 (Ush20,000) and foreign ones US$30. Note that though parking is provided, vehicle entrance fees are not levied for forested national parks such as Kibale and Mgahinga. A proposed revision of fees for forest reserves suggests that entrance for Budongo and Kalinzu will rise to US$20 daily for foreign visitors, US$15 for foreign residents and Ush5,000 for Ugandan citizens. Entrance to other forest reserves will cost US$15/US$10/Ush3,000 respectively.

CONSERVATION AREAS

Uganda's list of gazetted conservation areas embraces ten national parks and several other wildlife reserves and forest reserves. National parks are accorded a higher status and conservation priority than other reserves, and from the visitor's point of view they are generally better developed for tourism.

Bureaucratic considerations aside, the most meaningful way to categorise Uganda's various national parks and reserves is on the basis of the type of habitat they protect. I will occasionally refer to some national parks as game or savanna reserves, forest reserves and montane reserves. In this sense, the term 'game reserve' applies to any reserve or national park that protects a savanna habitat and supports typical plains animals, whereas the term 'forest reserve' refers to any reserve or

	Area	Habitat	Special attractions
BWINDI IMPENETRABLE	310km²	forest	mountain gorillas, forest birds
KIDEPO VALLEY	1,344km²	savanna	dry-country antelopes, predators and birds
KIBALE FOREST	766km²	forest	chimpanzees, monkeys, forest birds
LAKE MBURO	256km²	savanna	wide variety of antelope and waterbirds
MGAHINGA GORILLA	33km²	montane	mountain gorillas, hiking, volcanic peaks
MOUNT ELGON	1,145km²	montane	hiking, forest birds
MURCHISON FALLS	3,900km²	savanna	Murchison Falls, big game, waterbirds
RWENZORI	996km²	montane	hiking, forest birds, Afro-montane plants
QUEEN ELIZABETH	1,978km²	savanna	big game, chimps, 612 bird species
SEMLIKI	220km²	forest	hot springs, Rift Valley setting, 45 birds found nowhere else

national park that protects a forest environment and associated animals. The three montane national parks can in some circumstances be bracketed with forest reserves, since they all support montane and bamboo forests up to around 3,000m above sea level, though this habitat gives way to Afro-montane moorland at higher altitudes. For Uganda's ten national parks see the box *National parks* above.

Although several other wildlife reserves are gazetted in Uganda, most are merely adjuncts to one of the savanna national parks. The only ones that have any tourist facilities at present are Semliki, Katonga, Bugungu, Pian Upe, Kabwoya and Kyambura wildlife reserves. Also of interest to tourists are Uganda's forest reserves, of which the Budongo and Kanyiyo Pabidi forest reserves south of Murchison Falls National Park have well-established tourist sites offering camping facilities, *bandas* and guided forest walks. The Lake Victoria region supports large tracts of forest, the most accessible of which are protected in Mpanga Forest Reserve near Mpigi and the Mabira Forest Reserve near Jinja, both of which also now offer accommodation, camping and guided walks. Kalinzu Forest Reserve between Mbarara and Queen Elizabeth National Park is also developed for tourism. Chimp tracking in Budongo and Kalinzu forests is significantly cheaper than in the national parks.

Several other sites are also of interest for their natural history. These include Lake Nkuruba, Amabere Caves and Bigodi Wetland near Fort Portal, Lake Bunyonyi and the Echuya Forest in Kigezi, and the Sipi Falls near Mbale. For birders in particular, it is easy to view Uganda, with its lush natural vegetation and dense tropical cultivation, as nothing less than one giant nature sanctuary. There are extensive forests on Buggala and other islands in Lake Victoria's Ssese archipelago, while the small relict forest protected in the Entebbe Botanical Garden offers an excellent introduction to Uganda's forest birds and is a good place to get a close look at black-and-white colobus monkeys. Even the Backpackers' Hostel 2km from the heart of Kampala offers the opportunity to see such colourful species as Ross's turaco, woodland kingfisher, white-throated bee-eater and a variety of robin-chats and weavers.

MAMMALS

The official checklist of mammals found in Uganda numbers 342 species, with both west and East African mammals being well represented. Using the same distinction between small and large mammals as that of the checklist, 132 of the species recorded in Uganda can be classified as large mammals and the remainder are small mammals, the latter group comprising 94 bat species, 70 rats and mice, 33 shrews and otter shrews, eight gerbils, four elephant shrews and a solitary golden mole.

What follows is an overview of the large mammal species known to occur in Uganda. Several useful field guides to African mammals are available for the purpose of identification (see *Appendix 3, Further Information*, pages 478–9), but they all lack specific distribution details for individual countries. The following notes thus place emphasis on distribution and habitat within Uganda: they are not intended to replace a regional or continental field guide, but to be a Uganda-specific supplement to such a book.

PRIMATES Primates are exceptionally well represented in Uganda. There is widespread disagreement about the taxonomic status of many primate species and subspecies, but the present checklist includes 13 diurnal and six nocturnal species. Six of the diurnal primates found in Uganda are guenon monkeys, members of the taxonomically controversial genus *Cercopithecus*. The vervet and blue guenon monkeys, for instance, are both widespread African species known by at least five different common names, and both have over 20 recognised races, some of which are considered by some authorities to be separate species. Having been forced to try to make sense of this taxonomic maze in order to work out what is what, I might as well save you the effort and provide details of local races where they are known to me.

Apes The great apes of the family Pongidae are so closely related to humans that a less partial observer might well place them in the same family as us (it is thought that the chimpanzee is more closely related to humans than it is to any other ape). There are four ape species, of which two are found in Uganda (for further details see the boxes on gorillas and chimpanzees on pages 264–5 and pages 324–5).

Gorilla (*Gorilla gorilla*) This is the bulkiest member of the primate family: an adult gorilla may grow up to 1.8m high (although they seldom stand fully upright) and weigh up to 210kg. Three subspecies of gorilla are recognised. The most common race, the western lowland gorilla (*G. g. gorilla*), is not present in Uganda, but an estimated 40,000 live in the rainforests of west and central Africa. The endangered eastern lowland gorilla (*G. g. graueri*) is restricted to patches of forest in eastern DRC, where there are estimated to be 4,000 animals. The most threatened race of gorilla is the mountain gorilla (*G. g. beringei*). The total number is now estimated at around 700 (a significant increase over the past few years): at least 380 in the Virunga Mountains (shared between Uganda, DRC and Rwanda) and 320 in Uganda, where mountain gorillas are resident in Bwindi Impenetrable National Park and Mgahinga Gorilla National Park. These reserves, along with the mountain gorilla reserves in Rwanda and DRC, are both covered in *Chapter 10*, and so I have included more detailed information on gorilla behaviour in that chapter.

Mountain gorilla

Common chimpanzee (*Pan troglodytes*) This distinctive black-coated ape, more closely related to man than to any other living creature, lives in large, loosely bonded communities based around a core of related males with an internal

In this chapter, I've made widespread use of taxonomic terms such as genus, species and race. Some readers may not be familiar with these terms, so a brief explanation follows.

Taxonomy is the branch of biology concerned with classifying living organisms. It uses a hierarchical system to represent the relationships between different animals. At the top of the hierarchy are kingdoms, phyla, subphyla and classes. All vertebrates belong to the animal kingdom, phylum Chordata, subphylum Vertebrata. There are five vertebrate classes: Mammalia (mammals), Aves (birds), Reptilia (reptiles), Amphibia (amphibians) and Pisces (fish). Within any class, several orders might be divided in turn into families and, depending on the complexity of the order and family, various suborders and subfamilies. All baboons, for instance, belong to the Primate order, suborder Catarrhini (monkeys and apes), family Cercopithecoidea (Old World monkeys) and subfamily Cercopithecidae (cheek-pouch monkeys, ie: guenons, baboons and mangabeys).

Taxonomists accord to every living organism a Latin binomial (two-part name) indicating its genus (plural genera) and species. Thus the savanna baboon *Papio cyenephalus* and hamadrayas baboon *Papio hamadrayas* are different species of the genus *Papio*. Some species are further divided into races or subspecies. For instance, taxonomists recognise four races of savanna baboon: yellow baboon, olive baboon, chacma baboon and Guinea baboon. A race is indicated by a trinomial (three-part name), for instance *Papio cyenephalus cyenephalus* for the yellow baboon and *Papio cyenephalus anubis* for the olive baboon. The identical specific and racial designation of *cyenephalus* for the yellow baboon make it the nominate race – a label that has no significance other than that it would most probably have been the first race of that species to be described by taxonomists.

Taxonomic constructs are designed to approximate the real genetic and evolutionary relationships between various living creatures, and on the whole they succeed. But equally the science exists to help humans understand a reality that is likely to be more complex and less absolute than any conceptual structure used to contain it. This is particularly the case with speciation – the evolution of two or more distinct species from a common ancestor – which might occur over many thousands of generations, and like many gradual processes may lack for any absolute landmarks.

Simplistically, the process of speciation begins when a single population splits into two mutually exclusive breeding units. This can happen as a result of geographic isolation (for instance mountain and lowland gorillas), habitat differences (forest and savanna elephants) or varied migratory patterns (the six races of yellow wagtail intermingle as non-breeding migrants to Africa during the northern winter, but they all have a discrete Palaearctic breeding ground). Whatever the reason, the two breeding communities will share an

hierarchy topped by an alpha male. Females are generally less strongly bonded to their core group than are males; emigration between communities is not unusual. Mother–child bonds are strong. Daughters normally leave their mother only after they reach maturity, at which point relations between them may be severed. Mother–son relations have been known to survive for over 40 years. A troop has a well-defined core territory which is fiercely defended by regular boundary patrols.

Chimpanzee

Chimpanzees are primarily frugivorous (fruit eating), but they do eat meat and even hunt on occasion – red colobus monkeys are regularly hunted in Tanzania's Gombe Stream and Mahale Mountains national parks, while researchers in

identical gene pool when first they split, but as generations pass they will accumulate a number of small genetic differences and eventually marked racial characteristics. Given long enough, the two populations might even deviate to the point where they wouldn't or couldn't interbreed, even if the barrier that originally divided them was removed.

The taxonomic distinction between a full species and a subspecies or race of that species rests not on how similar the two taxa are in appearance or habit, but on the final point above. Should it be known that two distinct taxa freely interbreed and produce fertile hybrids where their ranges overlap, or it is believed that they would in the event that their ranges did overlap, then they are classified as races of the same species. If not, they are regarded as full species. The six races of yellow wagtail referred to above are all very different in appearance, far more so, for instance, than the several dozen warbler species of the genus *Cisticola*, but clearly they are able to interbreed, and they must thus be regarded as belonging to the same species. And while this may seem a strange distinction on the face of things, it does make sense when you recall that humans rely mostly on visual recognition, whereas many other creatures are more dependent on other senses. Those pesky *cisticolas* all look much the same to human observers, but each species has a highly distinctive call and in some cases a display flight that would preclude crossbreeding whether or not it is genetically possible.

The gradual nature of speciation creates grey areas that no arbitrary distinction can cover – at any given moment in time there might exist separate breeding populations of a certain species that have not yet evolved distinct racial characters, or distinct races that are on their way to becoming full species. Furthermore, where no conclusive evidence exists, some taxonomists tend be habitual 'lumpers' and others eager 'splitters' – respectively inclined to designate any controversial taxa racial or full specific status. For this reason, various field guides often differ in their designation of controversial taxa.

Among African mammals, this is particularly the case with primates, where in some cases up to 20 described taxa are sometimes lumped together as one species and sometimes split into several specific clusters of similar races. The savanna baboon is a case in point. The four races are known to interbreed where their ranges overlap. But they are also all very distinctive in appearance, and several field guides now classify them as different species, so that the olive baboon, for instance, is designated *Papio anubis* as opposed to *Papio cyenephalus anubis*. Such ambiguities can be a source of genuine frustration, particularly for birdwatchers obsessed with ticking 'new' species, but they also serve as a valid reminder that the natural world is and will always be a more complex, mysterious and dynamic entity than any taxonomic construct designed to label it.

Kalinzu Forest in Uganda have observed blue and red-tailed monkeys being eaten by chimps, as well as unsuccessful attempts to hunt black-and-white colobus. The first recorded instance of chimps using tools was at Gombe Stream in Tanzania, where they regularly use modified sticks to 'fish' in termite mounds. In west Africa, they have been observed cracking nuts open using a stone and anvil. Chimpanzees are amongst the most intelligent of animals: in language studies in the USA they have been taught to communicate in American sign language and have demonstrated their understanding, in some instances by even creating compound words for new objects (such as rock-berry to describe a nut).

Chimpanzees are typical animals of the rainforest and woodlands from Guinea to western Uganda. Their behaviour has been studied since 1960 by Jane Goodall and others at Gombe Stream and other sites across Africa, including the Budongo and Kibale forests in Uganda. Chimpanzees live in most of the forests of western Uganda, and they have been habituated for tourists in Kibale Forest

National Park, the Chambura Gorge in Queen Elizabeth National Park, Semliki Wildlife Reserve and the Budongo and Kanyiyo Pabidi forests near Murchison Falls National Park.

Monkeys All the monkeys found in Uganda are members of the family Cercopithecidae (Old World Monkeys). They fall into five genera: *Colobus* (closely related to the leaf-eating monkeys of Asia), *Cercopithecus* (guenons), *Papio* (baboons), *Erythrocebus* (patas) and *Cercocebus* (mangabeys).

Baboons (*Papio spp*) Heavily built and mainly terrestrial, baboons can be distinguished from any other monkey found in Uganda by their larger size and

DANGEROUS ANIMALS

The dangers associated with African wild animals are frequently overstated by hunters and others trying to glamorise their way of life. In reality, most wild animals fear us far more than we fear them, and their normal response to seeing a person is to leg it off as quickly as possible. But while the risk posed to tourists by wild animals is very low, accidents do happen, and common sense should be exercised wherever they are around.

The need for caution is greatest near water, particularly around dusk and dawn, when hippos are out grazing. Responsible for more human fatalities than any other large mammal, hippos are not actively aggressive to humans, but they do panic easily and tend to mow down any person that comes between them and the safety of the water, usually with fatal consequences. Never cross deliberately between a hippo and water, and avoid well-vegetated riverbanks and lakeshores in overcast weather or low light unless you are certain no hippos are present. Be aware, too, that any path leading through thick vegetation to an aquatic hippo habitat was most probably created by grazing hippos, so there's a real risk of a heads-on confrontation in a confined channel at times of day when hippos might be on land.

Crocodiles are more dangerous to locals but represent less of a threat to travellers, since they are unlikely to attack outside of their aquatic hunting environment. That means you need to swim in crocodile-infested waters to be at appreciable risk, though it's wise to keep a berth of a metre or so from the shore, since a large and hungry individual might occasionally drag in an animal or person from the water's edge. In the vicinity of a human settlement, any crocodile large enough to attack an adult will most likely have been consigned to its maker by its potential prey. The risk is greater away from habitation, but the rule of thumb is simple: don't bathe in any potential crocodile habitat unless you have reliable local information that it is safe.

There are parts of Malawi where hikers might stumble across an elephant or a buffalo, the most dangerous of Africa's terrestrial herbivores. Elephants almost invariably mock charge and indulge in some hair-raising trumpeting before they attack in earnest. Provided that you back off at the first sign of unease, they seldom take further notice of you. If you see them before they see you, give them a wide berth, bearing in mind they are most likely to attack if surprised at close proximity. If an animal charges you, the safest course of action is to head for the nearest tree and climb it. And should an elephant or buffalo stray close to your campsite or lodge, do suppress any urge to wander closer on foot – it may well react aggressively if surprised!

An elephant is large enough to hurt the occupants of a vehicle, so if it doesn't want your vehicle to pass, back off and wait until it has crossed the road or moved off. Never switch off the engine around elephants until you're certain they are relaxed, and avoid allowing your car to be boxed in between an elephant and another vehicle (or boxing in another

Common baboon

distinctive dog-like head. They live in large troops with a complex and rigid social structure held together by matriarchal lineages. Males frequently move between troops in their search for social dominance. Baboons are omnivorous and highly adaptable, for which reason they are the most widespread primate in Africa. Four types of baboon live in sub-Saharan Africa. The olive baboon, the only type found in Uganda, is accorded full species status (*P. anubis*) by some authorities and designated as a race of the yellow/savanna baboon (*P. cyanocephalus*) by others. Baboons are widespread and common in Uganda: they occur in all but the three

vehicle yourself). If an elephant does threaten a vehicle in earnest and backing off isn't an option, them revving the engine hard will generally dissuade it from pursuing the contest.

Monkeys, especially vervets and baboons, can become aggressive where they associate people with food. For this reason, feeding monkeys is highly irresponsible, especially as it may ultimately lead to their being shot as vermin. If you join a guided tour where the driver or guide feeds any primate, tell him not to. Although most monkeys are too small to be more than a nuisance, baboons have killed children and maimed adults with their vicious teeth. Unless trapped, however, their interest will be food, not people, so in the event of a genuine confrontation, throw down the food before the baboon gets too close. If you leave food (especially fruit) in your tent, monkeys might well tear the tent down. Present only in a handful of African countries, chimps and gorillas are potentially dangerous, but only likely to be encountered on a guided forest walk, where you should obey your guide's instructions at all times.

Despite their fierce reputation, large predators generally avoid humans and are only likely to kill accidentally or in self-defence. Lions are arguably the exception, though they seldom attack unprovoked. Of the rest, cheetahs represent no threat to adults, leopards seldom attack unless cornered, and hyenas – though often associated with human settlements and potentially dangerous – are most likely to slink off into the shadows when disturbed. Should you encounter any other large predator on foot, the most important thing you need to know is that running away will almost certainly trigger its 'chase' instinct and it *will* win the race. Better to stand still and/or back off very slowly, preferably without making eye contact. If (and only if) the animal looks really menacing, then noisy confrontation is probably a better tactic than fleeing. In areas where large predators are still reasonably common, sleeping in a sealed tent practically guarantees your safety – but don't sleep with your head sticking out or you risk being decapitated through predatorial curiosity, and *never* store meat in the tent.

As for the smaller stuff, venomous snakes and scorpions are present but unobtrusive, though you should be wary when picking up the wood or stones under which they often hide. Snakes generally slither away when they sense the seismic vibrations made by footfall, though be aware that rocky slopes and cliffs are a favoured habitat of the slothful puff adder, which may not move off in such circumstances. Good walking boots protect against the 50% of snakebites that occur below the ankle, and long trousers help deflect bites higher on the leg. But lethal bites are a rarity – in South Africa, which boasts its fair share of venomous snakes, more people are killed by lightning! Some discussion of treatment is included on page 126.

When all's said and done, Africa's most dangerous non-bipedal creature, and exponentially so, is the malaria-carrying mosquito. Humans, particularly when behind a steering wheel, come in a close second!

montane national parks and are frequently seen on the fringes of forest reserves and even along the roadside elsewhere in the country.

Patas monkey (*Erythrocebus patas*) Another terrestrial primate, restricted to the dry savanna of north-central Africa, the patas could be confused with the vervet monkey, but it has a lankier build, a light reddish-brown coat, and a black stripe above the eyes (the vervet is greyer and has a black face mask). In Uganda, the patas monkey is restricted to the extreme north, where it can be seen in Kidepo and Murchison Falls national parks, as well as the Pian Upe Wildlife Reserve. It is also known as the hussar monkey. The race found in Uganda is the Nile patas or nisras (*E. p. pyrrhonotus*).

Patas monkey

Vervet monkey (*Cercopithecus aethiops*) This light-grey guenon is readily identified by its black face and the male's distinctive blue genitals. Associated with a wide variety of habitats, it's the only guenon you're likely to see outside of forests and it is thought to be the most numerous monkey species in the world. The vervet monkey is also known as the green, tantalus, savanna and grivet monkey. More than 20 races are recognised, and some authorities group these races into four distinct species. At least four races are found in Uganda: the black-faced vervet (*C. a. centralis*), Naivasha vervet (*C. a. callidus*), Jebel Mara tantalus (*C. a. marrensis*) and Stuhlmann's green monkey (*C. a. stuhlmanni*). Vervet monkeys are widespread and common in Uganda, even outside of national parks, but they are absent from forest interiors and Afro-alpine habitats.

Vervet monkey

Blue monkey (*Cercopithecus mitis*) The blue monkey is the most widespread forest guenon in East Africa – uniform dark blue-grey in colour except for its white throat and chest patch, with thick fur and backward-projecting hair on its forehead. The blue monkey is common in most Ugandan forests, where it lives in troops of between four and 12 animals and frequently associates with other primates. It is also known as the diademed guenon, samango monkey, Sykes's monkey, gentle monkey and white-throated guenon (the last regarded as a separate species by some authorities). Over 20 races are identified, of which three are found in Uganda, including the striking and very localised golden monkey, which is more-or-less restricted to bamboo forest in the Virunga Mountains. Blue monkeys occur in all but two of Uganda's national parks (Murchison Falls and Lake Mburo being the exceptions) and in practically every other forest in the country.

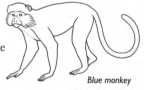

Blue monkey

Red-tailed monkey (*Cercopithecus ascinius*) Another widespread forest guenon, the red-tailed monkey is brownish in appearance with white cheek whiskers, a coppery tail and a distinctive white, heart-shaped patch on its nose, giving rise to its more descriptive alternative name of black-cheeked white-nosed monkey. It is normally seen singly, in pairs or in small family groups, but it also associates with other monkeys and has been known to accumulate in groups of up to 200. The race found in Uganda is *C. a. schmidti*. Red-tailed and blue monkeys regularly interbreed in the Kibale Forest. Red-tailed monkeys occur in Kibale Forest, Bwindi, Semliki and Queen Elizabeth national parks, as well as in Budongo, Mpanga and several other forest reserves.

De Brazza's monkey (*Cercopithecus neglectus*) This spectacular thickset guenon has a relatively short tail, a hairy face with a reddish-brown patch around its eyes, a white band across its brow and a distinctive white moustache and beard. Primarily a west African species, De Brazza's monkey is very localised in East Africa, most likely to be seen in the vicinity of Mount Elgon and Semliki national parks.

L'Hoest's monkey (*Cercopithecus lhoesti*) This handsome guenon is less well known and more difficult to see than most of its relatives, largely because of its preference for dense secondary forest and its terrestrial habits. It has a black face and backward-projecting white whiskers that partially cover its ears, and is the only guenon which habitually carries its tail in an upright position. In Uganda, L'Hoest's monkey is most likely to be seen in Kibale Forest, Bwindi or Maramagambo Forest in Queen Elizabeth National Park.

Grey-cheeked mangabey (*Cercocebus algigena*) This greyish-black monkey has few distinguishing features. It has baboon-like mannerisms, a shaggier appearance than any guenon, light-grey cheeks and a slight mane. Grey-cheeked mangabeys live in lowland and mid-altitude forests. In Uganda, they are most likely to be seen in the Kibale Forest, where they are common, as well as in Semliki National Park. The race found in Uganda is also known as Johnston's mangabey (*C. a. johnstoni*).

Black-and-white colobus (*Colobus guereza*) This beautifully marked and distinctive monkey has a black body, white facial markings, long white tail and, in some races, a white side-stripe. It lives in small groups and is almost exclusively arboreal. An adult is capable of jumping up to 30m, a spectacular sight with its white tail streaming

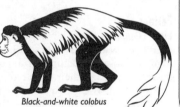
Black-and-white colobus

behind. This is probably the most common and widespread forest monkey in Uganda, occurring in most sizeable forest patches and even in well-developed riparian woodland. The Rwenzori race of the closely related **Angola colobus** (*Colobus angolensis*) occurs alongside the black-and-white colobus in forested parts of the Rwenzori National Park.

Red colobus (*Piliocolobus badius*) This relatively large red-grey monkey has few distinguishing features other than its slightly tufted crown. It is highly sociable and normally lives in scattered troops of 50 or more animals. About 15 races of red colobus are recognised, many of which are considered by some authorities to be distinct species. In Uganda, red colobus monkeys are largely restricted to Kibale Forest National Park and environs, where they are especially common in the Bigodi Wetland sanctuary, though they do also occur in small numbers in Semliki National Park.

Nocturnal primates Seldom observed on account of their nocturnal habits, the prosimians are a relict group of primitive primates more closely related to the lemurs of Madagascar than to the diurnal monkeys and apes of the African mainland.

Bushbabies Also called galagoes, these small, nocturnal primates are widespread in wooded habitats in sub-Saharan Africa. The bushbaby's piercing cry is one of the distinctive sounds of the African night. If you want to see a bushbaby, trace the cry to a tree, then shine a torch into it and you should easily pick out its large round eyes. Five galago species are found in Uganda, of which the lesser bushbaby (*Galago senegalensis*) is the most common. An insectivorous creature, only 17cm long excluding its tail, the lesser bushbaby is a creature of woodland as opposed to true forest, and it has been recorded in all of Uganda's savanna reserves. The eastern needle-clawed bushbaby (*G. inustus*), Thomas's bushbaby (*G. thomasi*) and dwarf bushbaby (*G. demidovii*) all occur in the Kibale and Bwindi forests, and the dwarf bushbaby has also been recorded in Lake Mburo and Queen Elizabeth national parks. I have no distribution information for Matschie's bushbaby (*G. matschiei*).

Lesser bushbaby

Potto (*Perodicticus potto*) This medium-sized sloth-like creature inhabits forest interiors, where it spends the nights foraging upside down from tree branches. It can sometimes be located at night by shining a spotlight into the canopy. The potto occurs in Kibale, Bwindi and Queen Elizabeth national parks, as well as most other major rainforests, and it is most likely to be seen in guided night walks in Kibale Forest.

CARNIVORES A total of 38 carnivores have been recorded in Uganda: five canid species, seven felines, three hyenas, ten mongooses, six mustelids (otters, badgers and weasels) and seven viverrids (civets and genets).

Felines

Lion (*Panthera leo*) The largest African carnivore, and the one animal that everybody wants to see on safari, the lion is the most sociable of the large cats, living in loosely structured prides of typically five to 15 animals. They normally hunt at night, and their favoured prey consists of buffalo and medium-to-large antelope such as Uganda kob. Females, working in teams of up to eight animals, are responsible for most hunts. Rivalry between male lions is intense: prides may have more than one dominant male working in collaboration to prevent a takeover and young males are forced out of their home pride at about three years of age. Pride takeovers are often fought to the death; after a successful one, it is not unusual for all the male cubs to be killed. Lions are not very active by day: they are most often seen lying in the shade looking the picture of regal indolence. They occur naturally in most woodland and grassland habitats, and are now fairly common in certain parts of Murchison Falls and Queen Elizabeth national parks. A healthy lion population survives in Kidepo National Park, but they are no longer present in Lake Mburo.

Leopard

Leopard (*Panthera pardus*) The most common of Africa's large felines, the leopard often lives in close proximity to humans, but it is rarely seen because of its secretive, solitary nature. Leopards hunt using stealth and power, often getting to within 5m of their intended prey before pouncing, and they habitually store their kill in a tree to keep it from being poached by other large predators. They can be distinguished from cheetahs by their rosette-shaped spots and more powerful build, as well as by their preference for wooded or rocky habitats. Leopards are found in virtually all habitats which offer adequate cover, and are present in most Ugandan national parks and forest reserves. The only place in Uganda where they are seen with regularity is along the Channel Track in Queen Elizabeth National Park.

Cheetah

Cheetah (*Acinonyx jubatus*) Superficially similar to the leopard, the cheetah is the most diurnal of Africa's cat species, and it hunts using speed as opposed to stealth. Cheetahs are the fastest land mammals, capable of running at up to 70km/h in short bursts. Male cheetahs are strongly territorial and in some areas they commonly defend their territory in pairs or trios. Cheetahs are the least powerful of the large predators: they are chased from a high percentage of their kills and 50% of cheetah cubs are killed by other predators before they reach three months of age. Like leopards, cheetahs are heavily spotted and solitary in their habits, but their greyhound-like build, distinctive black tear-marks and preference for grassland and savanna habitats precludes confusion. In Uganda, cheetahs are traditionally present only in the vicinity of Kidepo National Park, though several sightings in the north of Murchison Falls in 2002 suggest that they might yet recolonise this park.

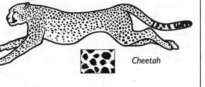
Cheetah

Smaller cats (*Felis spp*) The **caracal** (*F. caracal*) is a medium-sized cat found in open habitats, and easily identified by its uniform reddish-brown coat and tufted ears. In Uganda, it occurs only in Kidepo National Park. The slightly larger **serval** (*F. serval*) has a pale spotted coat, making it possible to confuse it with some genet species. It favours moister habitats than the caracal, ranging from woodland to forest, and it is widespread in Uganda. The **African golden cat** (*F. aurata*) is a rarely seen creature of the west African forest: it is widespread in western Uganda, where it has been recorded in every forested national park except Semliki. The **African wild cat** (*F. silvestris*) is reminiscent of the domestic tabby, with which it has been known to interbreed successfully, and it is found in most savanna habitats in Uganda.

Caracal

Canids The Canidae is a family of medium-sized carnivores of which the most familiar is the domestic dog. Five species – all recognisably dog-like in appearance and habits – are present in Uganda, though none is very common.

Jackals (*Canis spp*) Jackals are small to medium-sized dogs associated with most savanna habitats. Although often portrayed as carrion-eaters, they are in fact opportunistic omnivores, hunting a variety of small mammals and birds with some regularity and also eating a substantial amount of fruit and bulbs. The most widespread canid in Uganda is the **side-striped jackal** (*C. adustus*), which occurs

Black-backed jackal

in all four savanna national parks as well as in Bwindi and Mgahinga, and is most likely to be seen in the north of Murchison Falls. Within Uganda, the similar **black-backed jackal** (*C. mesomelas*) is restricted to Kidepo National Park, Pian Upe and environs, while the **golden jackal** (*C. aureus*), though it appears on the national checklist, has been recorded in no national park and is presumably a vagrant.

Bat-eared fox

Bat-eared fox (*Otocyon megalotis*) This small but striking silver-grey insectivore, rendered unmistakable by its huge ears and black eye-mask, is most often seen in pairs or small family groups during the cooler hours of the day. Associated with dry open country, the bat-eared fox is quite common in the Kidepo and Pian Upe, but absent elsewhere in Uganda.

African hunting dog (*Lycaon pictus*) The largest African canid, and the most endangered after the rare Ethiopian wolf, the African hunting dog (also known as the wild or painted dog) lives in packs of five–50 animals and is distinguished by its cryptic black, brown and cream coat. Hunting dogs are highly effective pack hunters and were once widely distributed and common throughout sub-Saharan Africa. Hunted as vermin and highly susceptible to epidemics spread by domestic dogs, hunting dogs today have a very localised and scattered distribution pattern, with perhaps 25% of the estimated wild population of 5,000 confined to the Selous ecosystem in southern Tanzania. The African hunting dog is locally extinct in roughly half the countries it once inhabited, Uganda included. Recolonisation, though unlikely, is not impossible, since hunting dogs are great wanderers and small populations do still survive in parts of western Tanzania and Kenya.

African hunting dog

Other carnivores

Spotted hyena (*Crocuta crocuta*) In Uganda, as elsewhere in Africa, the spotted hyena is by far the most common member of a family of large, hunchbacked carnivores whose somewhat canid appearance belies a closer evolutionary relationship to mongooses and cats. Often portrayed as an exclusive scavenger, the spotted hyena is an adept hunter capable of killing an animal as large as a wildebeest. In ancient times, the spotted hyena was thought to be hermaphroditic: the female's vagina is blocked by a false but remarkably realistic-looking scrotum and penis. Most hyena species live in loosely structured clans of around ten animals, and their social interaction is fascinating to observe. Clans are led by females, which are stronger and larger than males. The spotted hyena is bulky with a sloping back, a light-brown coat marked with dark-brown spots and an exceptionally powerful jaw which enables it to crack open bones and slice through the thickest hide. The spotted hyena is found in all of Uganda's savanna national parks, as well as in Mgahinga, but is only seen with great regularity in Queen Elizabeth. Note that the secretive **striped hyena** (*Hyaena hyaena*) and the insectivorous **aardwolf** (*Proteles cristatus*) are present but uncommon in Kidepo National Park and environs.

Spotted hyena

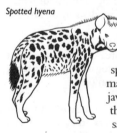

African civet (*Civetticus civetta*) This bulky, long-haired, cat-like viverrid has been kept in captivity for thousands of years (its anal secretions were used in making perfumes until a synthetic replacement was found). Surprisingly, little is known about their habits in the wild. Civets are widespread and common in most wooded habitats, and

African civet

they have been recorded in most of Uganda's national parks, but they are seen very rarely on account of their secretive, nocturnal habits.

Genets (*Genetta spp*) Closely related to civets, but often referred to mistakenly as cats because of various superficial similarities in appearance, the genets are slender, low-slung viverrids characterised by beautiful spotted coats and extraordinarily long tails. Secretive except when habituated, and subject to some taxonomic debate, genets are attracted to human waste and are occasionally seen slinking around campsites and lodges after dark. The servaline genet (*G. tigrina*), large-spotted genet (*G. tigrina*) and small-spotted genet (*G. genetta*) are all widespread in Uganda, with the latter two generally occurring in more lightly wooded areas than the former, and sometimes observed on night drives in the Semliki Wildlife Reserve. A west African species, the giant forest genet (*G. victiriae*), has been recorded in Maramagambo Forest in Queen Elizabeth National Park.

Otters Three species of these familiar aquatic predators occur in sub-Saharan Africa, and their ranges overlap in western Uganda, where all three have been recorded in certain areas such as Lake Mburo National Park. The Cape clawless otter (*Aonyx capensis*) and DRC clawless otter (*A. congica*), regarded to be conspecific by some authorities, are the largest African otters, growing up to 1.6m long, with a rich brown coat and pale chin and belly. Associated with most wetland habitats, the clawless otters are most active between dusk and dawn, and are hence less likely to be observed than the smaller and darker spotted-necked otter (*Lutra maculicollisi*), a diurnal species that is unusually common and visible on Lake Bunyonyi in Kigezi.

Ratel (honey badger) (*Mellivora capensis*) The ratel is a medium-sized mustelid with a puppy-like head, black sides and underparts and a grey-white back. It is an adaptable creature, eating whatever comes its way – it's said that they've been known to kill buffaloes by running underneath them and biting off their testicles which, if true, is certainly taking opportunism to a wasteful extreme. When not Bobbiting bovines, the ratel occasionally indulges in a symbiotic relationship with a bird called the greater honeyguide: the honeyguide takes the ratel to a beehive, which the ratel then tears open, allowing the honeyguide to feed on the scraps. Ratels are widespread in Uganda, but uncommon and rarely seen. Other mustelids found in Uganda include the **zorilla** (or striped polecat) and the **striped weasel**.

Mongooses Ten mongoose species have been recorded in Uganda, none of which – as is commonly assumed – feeds predominantly on snakes. Five species are widespread and common enough to have been recorded in at least half the national parks. They are the marsh mongoose (*Atilax paludinosus*), Egyptian mongoose (*Herpestes ichneumon*), slender mongoose (*Herpestes sanguineus*), white-tailed mongoose (*Ichneumia albicauda*) and banded mongoose (*Mungos mungo*). Of these the banded

Banded mongoose

mongoose is the most regularly observed, particularly on the Mweya Peninsula in Queen Elizabeth National Park.

ANTELOPE Some 29 antelope species – about one-third of the African total – are included on the checklist for Uganda, a figure that fails to acknowledge a recent rash of near or complete local extinctions. There are probably no more than ten roan antelope remaining in Uganda, for example, while no oryx are left at all. Of the species that do still occur, five fall into the category of large antelope, having a shoulder height of above 120cm (roughly the height of a zebra); eight are in the category of medium-sized antelope, having a shoulder height of between 75cm and 90cm; and the remainder are small antelope, with a shoulder height of between 30cm and 60cm.

Large antelope

Common eland (*Taurotragus oryx*) The world's largest antelope is the common or Cape eland (*T. oryx*) which measures over 1.8m in height, and which can be bulkier than a buffalo. The eland has a rather bovine appearance: fawn-brown in colour, with a large dewlap and short, spiralled horns, and in some cases light white stripes on its sides. The common eland occurs in open habitats throughout eastern and southern Africa. In Uganda, it is most likely to be seen in Lake Mburo National Park, but also occurs in Kidepo Valley and Pian Upe Wildlife Reserve.

Common eland

Greater kudu (*Tragelaphus strepsiceros*) This is another very large antelope, measuring up to 1.5m high, and it is also strikingly handsome, with a grey-brown coat marked by thin white side-stripes. The male has a small dewlap and large spiralling horns. The greater kudu live in small groups in woodland habitats. In Uganda, it occurs only in small numbers in Kidepo.

Greater kudu

Hartebeest (*Alcelaphus buselaphus*) This large and ungainly looking, tan-coloured antelope – a relative of the wildebeest, which is absent from Uganda – has large shoulders, a sloping back and relatively small horns. It lives in small herds in lightly wooded and open savanna habitats. The typical hartebeest of Uganda is Jackson's hartebeest (*A. b. jacksoni*), though it is replaced by the Lelwel hartebeest (*A. b. lelweli*) west of the Nile. The closely related and similarly built topi (*Damaliscus lunatus*) has a much darker coat than the hartebeest, and distinctive blue-black markings above its knees. Jackson's hartebeest is most frequently seen in Murchison Falls, though it also occurs in Kidepo Valley.

Hartebeest

Defassa waterbuck (*Kobus ellipsyprymnus defassa*) Shaggy-looking, with a grey-brown coat, white rump and large curved horns, the Defassa waterbuck is considered by some authorities to be a distinct species, *K. defassa* (the common waterbuck found east of the Rift Valley has a white ring on its rump), but the two races interbreed where they overlap. Defassa waterbuck live in small herds and are most often seen grazing near water. They are found in suitable habitats in all four of Uganda's savanna national parks.

Defassa waterbuck

Roan antelope

Roan antelope (*Hippotragus equinus*) This handsome animal has a light red-brown coat, short backward-curving horns and a small mane on the back of the neck. It is present only in small numbers in Pian Upe having become locally extinct in Kidepo Valley and Lake Mburo national parks.

Medium-sized antelope

Kobus kob

Uganda kob (*Kobus kob thomasi*) Uganda's national antelope is a race of the west African kob confined to grassy floodplains and open vegetation near water in Uganda and the southern Sudan. Although closely related to waterbuck and reedbuck, the kob is reddish-brown in colour and similar to the impala, but bulkier in appearance and lacking the impala's black side-stripe. Uganda Kob live in herds of up to 100 animals in Queen Elizabeth and Murchison Falls and neighbouring conservation areas, as well as in Semliki and Katonga wildlife reserves.

Bushbuck (*Tragelaphus scriptus*) Probably the most widespread antelope in Uganda is the bushbuck, which lives in forest, riverine woodland and other thicketed habitats. The male bushbuck has a dark chestnut coat marked with white spots and stripes. The female is lighter in colour and vaguely resembles a large duiker. Although secretive and elusive, the bushbuck is very common in suitable habitats in most forests and national parks in Uganda.

Bushbuck

Sitatunga (*Tragelaphus spekei*) This semi-aquatic antelope is similar in appearance to the closely related bushbuck, but the male is larger with a shaggier coat, both sexes are striped, and it has uniquely splayed hooves adapted to its favoured habitat of papyrus and other swamps. It is found in suitable habitats throughout Uganda, including six national parks, but is likely to be seen only in the Katonga Wildlife Reserve.

Lesser kudu (*Tragelaphus imberbis*) This pretty, dry-country antelope is similar in appearance to the greater kudu, but much smaller and more heavily striped (greater kudu have between six and ten stripes; lesser kudu have 11 or more). Lesser kudu are present in Pian Upe and environs.

Grant's gazelle (*Gazella granti*) Yet another dry-country antelope which in Uganda has been reduced to 100 animals roaming the contiguous Pian Upe, Matheniko and Bokora wildlife reserves in Karamoja. This typical gazelle is lightly built, tan in colour, and lives in herds.

Reedbuck *Reedbuck (Redunca spp)* Also restricted to Kidepo is the mountain reedbuck (*R. fulvorufula*), a grey-brown antelope with small crescent-shaped horns. The very similar Bohor reedbuck (*R. redunca*) is more widespread, occurring in all four savanna national parks. Both reedbuck species are usually seen in pairs in open country near water, with the mountain reedbuck occurring at higher altitudes.

Impala (*Aepyceros melampus*) This slender, handsome antelope, though superficially similar to the gazelles, belongs to a separate subfamily that is more closely related to hartebeest and oryx. The impala can be distinguished from any gazelle by its chestnut colouring, sleek appearance and the male's distinctive lyre-shaped horns. An adult impala can jump up to 3m high and has been known to broad-jump for over 10m. Impala live in herds of between 20 and a few hundred animals. They favour well-wooded savanna and woodland fringes, and are often abundant in such habitats. In Uganda, impalas are found only in Lake Mburo National Park and Katonga Wildlife Reserve.

Impala

Small antelope Nine of the small antelope species present in Uganda are **duikers**, a family of closely related antelopes which are generally characterised by their small size, sloping back, and preference for thickly forested habitats. Between 16 and 19 duiker species are recognised, many of them extremely localised in their distribution.

Grey duiker (*Sylvicapra grimmia*) Also known as the common or bush duiker, this is an atypical member of its family in that it generally occurs in woodland and savanna habitats. It has a grey-brown coat with a vaguely speckled appearance. The grey duiker is widespread in east and southern Africa, and it occurs in all four of Uganda's savanna national parks as well as in Mount Elgon.

Forest duiker (*Cephalophus spp*) The striking yellow-backed duiker (*C. sylviculter*) is also atypical of the family, due to its relatively large size – heavier than a bushbuck – rather than any habitat preference. It is a west African species, but has been recorded in several forests in western Uganda, including those in Bwindi, Mgahinga, Rwenzori and Queen Elizabeth national parks; it's sometimes encountered fleetingly along the forest track leading uphill from the Buhoma headquarters at Bwindi. Of the more typical duiker species, Harvey's red duiker (*C. harveyi*) is a tiny chestnut-brown antelope found in forested parts of Queen Elizabeth National Park and in the Kibale Forest. The blue duiker (*C. monticola*), even smaller and with a grey-blue coat, is known to occur in Queen Elizabeth, Murchison Falls, Kibale and Bwindi national parks. Peter's duiker (*C. callipygus*) has been recorded in Bwindi, Kibale and Queen Elizabeth; the black-fronted duiker (*C. nigrifrons*) in Mgahinga and Bwindi; and there have been unconfirmed sightings of the white-bellied duiker (*C. leucogaster*) for Bwindi and Semliki. The red-flanked duiker (*C. rufilatus*) and Weyn's duiker (*C. weynsi*)

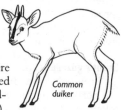

Common
duiker

have not been recorded in any national park, but they most probably occur in the Budongo Forest.

Bates's pygmy antelope (*Neofragus batesi*) Not a duiker, but similar both in size and its favoured habitat, this diminutive antelope – the second-smallest African ungulate – is a Congolese rainforest species that has been recorded in Semliki National Park and in forests within and bordering the southern half of Queen Elizabeth National Park.

Klipspringer (*Oreotragus oreotragus*) This distinctive antelope has a dark-grey bristly coat and an almost speckled appearance. It has goat-like habits and is invariably found in the vicinity of koppies or cliffs (the name *klipspringer* means rock-jumper in Afrikaans). It lives in pairs in suitable habitats in Kidepo Valley and Lake Mburo national parks.

Oribi (*Ourebia ourebi*) This endearing gazelle-like antelope has a light red-brown back, white underparts, and a diagnostic black scent gland under its ears. It is one of the largest 'small' antelopes in Africa, not much smaller than a Thomson's gazelle. When disturbed, the oribi emits a high-pitched sneezing sound, then bounds off in a manner mildly reminiscent of a pronking springbok. The oribi favours tall grassland, and it occurs in all of the savanna national parks except for Queen Elizabeth. It is remarkably common in the Borassus grassland in the northern part of Murchison Falls National Park, most often seen in pairs or groups of up to five animals, consisting of one male and his 'harem', but also sometimes in larger groups.

Guenther's dik-dik (*Modoqua guentheri*) This pretty, small antelope has a dark red-brown coat and distinctive white eye markings. It is found in the dry savanna in and around Kidepo Valley.

Other herbivores
African elephant (*Loxodonta africana*) The world's largest land animal is also one of the most intelligent and entertaining to watch. A fully grown elephant is about 3.5m high and weighs around 6,000kg. Female elephants live in closely knit clans in which the eldest female takes a matriarchal role over her sisters, daughters and granddaughters. Mother–daughter bonds are strong and may exist for up to 50 years. Males generally leave the family group at around 12 years, after which they either roam around on their own or form bachelor herds. Under normal circumstances, elephants range widely in search of food and water but, when concentrated populations are forced to live in conservation areas, their habit of uprooting trees can cause serious environmental damage. Two races of elephant are recognised: the savanna elephant of east and southern Africa (*L. a. africana*) and the smaller and slightly hairier forest elephant of the west African rainforest (*L. a. cyclotis*). The two races are thought to interbreed in parts of western Uganda. Despite severe poaching in the past, elephants occur in all national parks except for Lake Mburo. They are most likely to be seen in Murchison Falls, Queen Elizabeth and Kidepo national parks.

Rhinoceros The black rhinoceros (*Diceros bicornis*) and northern white rhinoceros (*Ceratotherium simum cottoni*) both occur naturally in Uganda, but they have been poached to local extinction. The northern white rhino is a geographically isolated race of the white rhino of southern Africa: formerly common in

Black rhino

Uganda west of the Albert Nile, and at one time introduced into Murchison Falls National Park, its long-term future rests on the survival of one remaining breeding herd in eastern DRC.

Hippopotamus (*Hippopotamus amphibus*) This large, lumbering aquatic animal occurs naturally on most African lakes and waterways, where it spends most of the day submerged, but emerges from the water to graze at night. Hippos are strongly territorial, with herds of ten or more animals being presided over by a dominant male. The best places to see them are in Murchison Falls, Queen Elizabeth and Lake Mburo national parks, where they are abundant in suitable habitats. Hippos are still quite common outside of reserves, and they are responsible for killing more people than any other African mammal.

African buffalo

African buffalo (*Syncerus caffer*) Africa's only wild ox species is an adaptable and widespread creature that lives in large herds on the savanna and smaller herds in forested areas. Herds are mixed-sex and normally comprise several loosely related family clans and bachelor groups. Buffaloes can be seen in just about all of Uganda's national parks and large forests. In Queen Elizabeth and Murchison Falls national parks, you may see hybrids of the savanna buffalo (*S. c. caffer*) of East Africa and the red buffalo (*S. c. nanus*) of the west African forest.

Giraffe (*Giraffa camelopardus*) The world's tallest animal (up to 5.5m) lives in loosely structured mixed-sex herds, typically numbering between five and 15 animals. As herd members may be dispersed over an area of up to 1km, they are frequently seen singly or in smaller groups, though unusually large aggregations are often seen in Uganda. The long neck of the giraffe gives it a slightly ungainly appearance when it ambles; giraffes look decidedly absurd when they adopt a semi-crouching position in order to drink. The race found in Uganda is Rothschild's giraffe, rare elsewhere in its former range but very common in the northern part of Murchison Falls National Park. A small herd is present in Kidepo Valley.

Burchell's zebra (*Equus burchelli*) This unmistakable striped horse is common and widespread throughout east and southern Africa. Zebras are often seen in large herds but their basic social unit is the small, relatively stable family group, which typically consists of a stallion, up to five mares, and their collective offspring. In Uganda, zebras are present only in Lake Mburo and Kidepo Valley national parks.

Swine The most visible pig species in Uganda is the **warthog** (*Phacochoerus aethiopicus*), a common resident of the savanna national parks. Warthogs are uniform grey in colour and both sexes have impressive tusks. They are normally seen in family groups, trotting away briskly in the opposite direction with their tails raised stiffly and a determinedly nonchalant air. The bulkier and hairier **bushpig** (*Potamochoerus porcus*) is found mainly in thickets and dense woodland. Although bushpigs occur in all national parks except for Rwenzori, they are not often seen due to their nocturnal habits and the cover afforded by their favoured habitat. The **giant forest hog** (*Hylochoerus meinertzhageni*) is the largest African pig species. It is a nocturnal creature of the forest interior, and so very rarely seen, but it

Warthog

probably occurs in all national parks in western Uganda, and is often seen by day along Channel Drive in Queen Elizabeth National Park.

Hyraxes and other oddities Uganda's five hyrax species are guinea-pig-like animals, often associated with rocky habitats, and related more closely to elephants than to any other living creatures – difficult to credit until you've heard a tree hyrax shrieking with pachydermal abandon through the night. Four types of **pangolin** (similar in appearance to the South American scaly anteaters) occur in Uganda, as does the **aardvark**, a bizarre, long-snouted insectivore which is widespread in savanna habitats but very seldom seen due to its nocturnal habits. Also regarded as large mammals by the official checklist are 12 squirrel species, three flying squirrels (anomalures), three porcupines, three hares, two cane-rats, a hedgehog and the peculiar chevrotain.

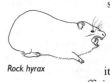
Rock hyrax

BIRDS

Uganda is arguably the most attractive country in Africa to birdwatchers, not only because of the unusually high number of species recorded within its borders, but also because it offers easy access to several bird-rich habitats that are difficult to reach elsewhere. Uganda's remarkable avian diversity – 1,008 species recorded in an area similar to that of Great Britain – can be attributed to its location at a transitional point between the East African savanna, the west African rainforest and the semi-desert of the north.

Indicative of Uganda's transitional location is the fact that only one bird is endemic to the country, the somewhat nondescript Fox's weaver. However, if you take only East Africa into consideration, then roughly 150 bird species (more than 10% of the regional checklist) are found only in Uganda. This list includes seven of the 20 hornbill species recorded in the region, five out of 14 honeyguides, seven out of 21 woodpeckers, 11 out of 36 bulbuls and greenbuls, five out of 20 bush shrikes, as well as 13 members of the thrush family, 11 warblers, ten flycatchers, eight sunbirds, eight weavers, eight finches, four tinkerbirds, four pigeons or doves, three kingfishers, three sparrowhawks, three cuckoos and three nightjars.

Most of these 'Uganda specials' are west African and Congolese forest birds that would be very difficult to see elsewhere, for the simple reason that the other countries in which they occur are poorly developed for tourism. The rainforests of western Uganda must be seen as the country's most important bird habitat, and the one that is of greatest interest to birdwatchers, particularly if they are already reasonably familiar with typical East African birds. The most alluring forest in terms of localised species is probably Semliki, closely rivalled by Budongo, Kibale and Bwindi. However, in practical terms, Kibale Forest is probably Uganda's best single stop for forest birds, because of the proficiency of the guides who take tourists into the forest and the nearby Magombe Swamp. That said, just about any forest in Uganda will be rewarding; even the relatively tame botanical garden in Entebbe will throw up several interesting species.

Unfortunately, most forest birds are very secretive, and it can be difficult to get even a glimpse of them in the dense undergrowth, let alone a clear enough look to make a positive identification. You would probably identify more bird species in ten minutes at the Backpackers' Hostel in Kampala than you would in an afternoon walking through the Semliki Forest. For this reason, first-time visitors to Africa might do better concentrating on locations other than forests – if you want to see a wide range of Ugandan birds, try to visit Entebbe (water and forest birds), Lake

Most of Uganda's forest inhabitants have a wide distribution in the Democratic Republic of Congo (DRC) and/or west Africa, while a smaller proportion comprises eastern species that might as easily be observed in forested habitats in Kenya, Tanzania and in some instances Ethiopia. A significant number, however, are endemic to the Albertine Rift: in other words their range is more-or-less confined to montane habitats associated with the Rift Valley Escarpment running between Lake Albert and the north of Lake Tanganyika. The most celebrated of these regional endemics is of course the mountain gorilla, confined to the Virungas and Bwindi mountains near the eastern Rift Valley Escarpment. Other primates endemic to the Albertine Rift include several taxa of smaller primates, for instance the golden monkey and Rwenzori colobus, while eight endemic butterflies are regarded as flagship species for the many hundreds of invertebrate taxa that occur nowhere else.

Of the remarkable tally of 37 range-restricted bird species listed as Albertine Rift endemics, roughly half are regarded to be of global conservation concern. All 37 of these species have been recorded in the DRC, and nine are endemic to that country, since their range is confined to the western escarpment forests. More than 20 Albertine Rift endemics are resident in each of Uganda, Rwanda and Burundi, while two extend their range southward into western Tanzania. All 24 of the Albertine Rift endemics recorded in Uganda occur in Bwindi National Park, including the highly sought African green broadbill, which is elsewhere known only from the Itombwe Mountains and Kahuzi-Biega National Park in the DRC. Other important sites in Uganda are the Rwenzori Mountains with 17 Albertine Rift endemics, the Virungas with 14 and the Echuya Forest with 12.

Outside of Uganda, all but one of the 29 endemics that occur on the eastern escarpment have been recorded in Rwanda's Nyungwe Forest, a readily accessible site that is highly recommended for the opportunity to observe several species absent from, or not as easily located in, Uganda. Inaccessible to tourists at the time of writing, the Itombwe Mountains, which rise from the Congolese shore of northern Lake Tanganyika, support the largest contiguous block of montane forest in East Africa. This range is also regarded to be the most important site for montane forest birds in the region, with a checklist of 565 species including 31 Albertine Rift endemics, three of which are known from nowhere else in the world. The most elusive of these birds is the enigmatic Congo bay owl, first collected in 1952, and yet to be seen again, though its presence is suspected in Rwanda's Nyungwe Forest.

Several Albertine Rift forest endemics share stronger affinities with extant or extinct Asian genera than they do with any other living African species, affirming the great age of these forests, which are thought to have flourished during prehistoric climatic changes that caused temporary deforestation in lower-lying areas such as the Congo Basin. The Congo bay owl, African green broadbill and Grauer's cuckoo-shrike, for instance, might all be classed as living fossils – isolated relics of a migrant Asian stock that has been

Mburo (water- and acacia-associated birds), Queen Elizabeth (a wide variety of habitats; over 600 species recorded), Murchison Falls (a wide variety of habitats; the best place in East Africa to see the papyrus-associated shoebill) and Kidepo (northern semi-desert specials; over 50 raptors recorded).

Several noteworthy developments have occurred in Uganda since the last edition of this guide went to print, all of which have assisted in making the country an even more alluring destination for birdwatchers. The first has been a blanket increase in the avian knowledge of ranger/guides working in national parks and other conservation areas – this is now to a standard that compares favourably with any part

superseded elsewhere on the continent by indigenous genera evolved from a common ancestor.

Among the mammals endemic to the Albertine Rift, the dwarf otter-shrew of the Rwenzoris is one of three highly localised African mainland species belonging to a family of aquatic insectivores that flourished some 50 million years ago and is elsewhere survived only by the related tenrecs of Madagascar. A relict horseshoe bat species restricted to the Rwenzoris and Lake Kivu is anatomically closer to extant Asian forms of horseshoe bat and to ancient migrant stock than it is to any of the 20-odd more modern and widespread African horseshoe bat species, while a shrew specimen collected only once in the Itombwe Mountains is probably the most primitive and ancient of all 150 described African species.

A full list of the Albertine Rift endemic birds that occur in Uganda follows, with species regarded to be of global conservation concern marked with an asterisk. All are present in Bwindi National Park; those present elsewhere are indicated as M (Mgahinga), E (Echuya), R (Rwenzori) and/or K (Kibale Forest).

Handsome francolin	*Francolinus nobilis*	M E R
Rwenzori Turaco	*Tauraco johnstoni*	M E R
Rwenzori nightjar	*Caprimulgus rwenzori*	R
Dwarf honeyguide	*Indicator pumilio* *	
African green broadbill	*Pseudocalyptomena grauri* *	
Kivu ground thrush	*Zoothera tanganjicae* *	
Red-throated alethe	*Alethe poliophrys*	E R
Archer's robin-chat	*Cossypha archeri*	M E R
Collared apalis	*Apalis rwenzori*	M E R K
Mountain masked apalis	*Apalis personata*	M R
Grauer's scrub warbler	*Bradypterus grauri* *	M R
Grauer's warbler	*Graueria vittata*	
Neumann's warbler	*Hemetisia neumanni*	
Red-faced woodland warbler	*Phylloscopus laetus*	M E R K
Yellow-eyed black flycatcher	*Melaeornis ardesiascus*	
Chapin's flycatcher	*Musicapa lendu* *	
Rwenzori batis	*Batis diops*	M E R
Stripe-breasted tit	*Parus fasciiventer*	M R
Blue-headed sunbird	*Nectarinia alinae*	R K
Regal sunbird	*Nectarinia regia*	M E R
Purple-breasted sunbird	*Nectarinia purpureiventris*	R K
Dusky crimsonwing	*Cryptospiza jacksoni*	M E R K
Shelley's crimsonwing	*Cryptospiza shelleyi* *	M R
Strange weaver	*Ploceus alienus*	M E R

of Africa. The best local guides are capable of identifying most species by call, and even calling up more responsive species. Levels of knowledge do vary from one guide to the next, however, so specify your interest when you ask for a guide. A not unrelated development has been the formation of the prestigious Uganda Bird Guides Club (❭ 077 518290; e ugandabirdguides@hotmail.com), an organisation whose membership includes most of the country's best bird guides. Ibrahim Senfuma from Mabira Forest (see *Chapter 12*, pages 425–8) is one of Uganda's best bird guides and he's happy to take a break to conduct nationwide safaris (❭ 0712 920515). Finally, the publication of Stevenson and Fanshawe's superb *Field Guide to the Birds of East Africa* in 2002 means that for the first time birdwatchers have access to accurate depictions, descriptions and distribution details for every species recorded in the country, complemented by the equally useful site descriptions in Russouw and Sacchi's exemplary *Where to Watch Birds in Uganda*.

Few visitors to Uganda will depart totally unmoved by its avian wealth, but they will tend to arrive in the country with a wide variety of expectations. Those European visitors for whom birdwatching ranks as a pursuit on a perversity level with stamp collecting might well revise that opinion when first confronted by a majestic fish eagle calling high from a riverine perch, or a flock of Abyssinian ground hornbills marching with comic intent through the savanna. First-time African visitors with a stated interest in birds are more likely to be blown away by their first sighting of a lilac-breasted roller or Goliath heron than by most of the country's long list of western forest specials. Birdwatchers based in Africa's savanna belt will generally want to focus more on forest birds, but mostly on such common and iconic species as great blue turaco or black-and-white casqued hornbill rather than on glimpsing a selection of more localised but duller forest greenbuls. The more experienced the individual birdwatcher in African conditions, the greater the priority they will place on the pursuit of Albertine Rift endemics and Semliki 'specials'. And at the extreme end of the scale there are those whose life's mission is to tick every bird species in the world, in which case dedicating several days to seeking out the endemic Fox's weaver might rank above all other considerations in planning a Ugandan itinerary.

At almost every level, the sheer variety of bird species in Uganda can be daunting, not only for first-timers to Africa, but also for bird enthusiasts familiar with other parts of the continent. Experienced South African birdwatchers, for instance, are likely to struggle with identification of the plethora of small warblers, forest greenbuls, Ploceus weavers, sunbirds and raptors that occur in Uganda (and one might argue that entering into serious battle with these difficult groups is best left for a repeat visit). Bearing the above in mind, two annotated lists follow, each containing concise details of 50 key birds resident in various parts of Uganda. The *Beginner's list* details some common and/or highly singular birds that are likely to make an impact on first-time visitors to Africa (or in some cases visitors from elsewhere in Africa), whether or not they have any great prior interest in ornithology. The *Twitcher's list* highlights a selection of species that are reasonably likely to be seen in the course of a normal birdwatching trip, and which for one reason or another (often relating to a specialised habitat or distribution) will feature high on the wish list of many experienced African birdwatchers visiting Uganda for the first time. Excluded from both of these lists in order to keep things manageable are the 30–40 species whose Ugandan range is restricted to Semliki National Park (discussed under the park itself on pages 342–3), the country's 24 Albertine Rift endemics (already listed in the box on pages 50–1), and the true weavers (see separate box, pages 58–9). Even allowing for these omissions, the *Twitcher's list* might easily run to more than 100 species, so preference is given to more common, striking and/or individualistic birds over the likes of greenbuls and cisticolas. For ease of reference, the plate number in Stevenson and Fanshawe is provided at the end of each entry.

BEGINNER'S LIST

Common ostrich (*Struthio camelus*) World's largest bird, a flightless savanna resident, in Uganda restricted to Kidepo and the far northeast. Plate 1

Pelicans (*Pelecanus spp*) Large, charismatic water-birds often seen swimming in tight flotillas on open lakes and the Kazinga Channel, Queen Elizabeth National Park (QENP). Two species are present in Uganda. 7

African darter (*Anhinga rufa*) Also referred to as the snake-bird after its habit of swimming low with elongated rufous neck (longer than any cormorant) extended in serpentine fashion, fairly common in most freshwater habitats with fringing vegetation, perches openly, often with wings spread open to dry. 8

Goliath heron (*Ardea goliath*) As the name suggests, an immense heron – 1.5m tall – with lovely cryptic purple-grey and orange markings, commonly seen from launch trips in Murchison Falls. 12

Hamerkop (*Scopus umbretta*) Peculiar, medium-sized, brown waterbird with no close allies, a backward-pointing crest and long bill that combine to create the hammerhead effect for which it is named. Builds a vast scruffy nest, a good example of which can be seen on the Mweya Peninsula, QENP. 13

Saddle-billed stork (*Ephippiorhynchus senegalensis*) The largest and most handsome of several storks common in Uganda, up to 1.4m high, with black-and-white feathering and gaudy red, yellow and black bill, usually seen in pairs, regular on game drives north of Murchison Falls. 15

Marabou stork (*Leptoptilos crumeniferus*) Macabre carrion-eating stork, 1.5m tall, with large expandable air-sac below neck, and black-and-white feather pattern reminiscent of an undertaker's suit. Common in rural and urban environments – nowhere more so than in downtown Kampala. 15

Shoebill (*Balaeniceps rex*) Unmistakable large grey swamp-dweller, distantly related to pelicans, and the main motivating factor behind many an ornithological tour to Uganda. Most easily seen in Mabamba Swamp near Kampala, on the Nile below Murchison Falls, and Lake Albert in Semliki Wildlife Reserve. 15

Flamingos (*Phoenicopterus spp*) Stunning and gregarious pink-white algae-eaters, most likely to be seen in large concentrations in Katwe and Flamingo crater lakes in QENP and adjacent Chambura Wildlife Reserve. Two species in Uganda. 17

Secretary bird (*Sagittarius serpentarius*) Unique grey snake-eating raptor, with stork-like build, up to 1.5m tall, red face markings, black head quills, rare and localised in northern Uganda. 24

African fish eagle (*Haliaeetus vocifer*) Stunning fish-eating raptor, resident on most lakes and waterways, as notable for its high, eerie duetting as its bold black, white and chestnut feather pattern. 25

Palmnut vulture (*Gypohierax angolensis*) Superficially similar to the fish eagle, and also associated with palm-fringed waterways and lakes, but with more white than black, no chestnut, and a red rather than yellow cere. 25

Lappet-faced vulture (*Torgos tracheliotus*) Africa's largest vulture, dark black with a bare red head, often seen singly or in pairs alongside smaller vultures at kills in Uganda's savanna reserves. 27

Bateleur (*Terathopius ecaudatus*) Arguably the most striking of Uganda's large raptors, a predominantly black short-tailed eagle with unique red collar and face and bold white underwings seen clearly in flight. Common in savanna reserves, often seen soaring with a tilting motion reminiscent of the tightrope walkers from which its name derives. 39

Long-crested eagle (*Lophaetus occipitalis*) Handsome, medium-sized eagle, with diagnostic foppish long crest. Unlike many other large raptors it's common outside of game reserves, often, though by no means exclusively, seen close to water. 39

With its distinctive tall green stem topped by a luxuriant clump of thick, wide leaves, the banana (or plantain) is such an integral feature of the Ugandan landscape that it may come as a surprise to learn that it is not indigenous to the country. Kiganda folklore claims that the first banana plant was brought to the kingdom by Kintu, whose shrine lies on a hill called Magonga (almost certainly a derivative of a local name for the banana) alongside a tree said to have grown from the root of the plant he originally imported. If this legend is true, it would place the banana's arrival in Uganda in perhaps the 13th–15th century, probably from the Ethiopian highlands. Most botanists argue, however, that the immense number of distinct varieties grown in modern Uganda could not have been cultivated within so short a period – a time span of at least 1,000 years would be required.

Only one species of banana (*Musa ensete*) is indigenous to Africa, and it doesn't bear edible fruit. The more familiar cultivated varieties have all been propagated from two wild Asian species (*M. acuminata* and *M. balbisiana*), and hybrids thereof. Wild bananas are almost inedible and riddled with hard pits, and it is thought that the first edible variety was cultivated from a rare mutant of one of the above species about 10,000 years ago – making the banana one of the oldest cultivated plants in existence. Edible bananas were most likely cultivated in Egypt before the time of Christ, presumably having arrived there via Arabia or the Indian Ocean. The Greek sailor and explorer Cosmas Indicopleustes recorded that edible bananas grew around the port of Adulis, in present-day Eritrea, cAD525 – describing them as 'moza, the wild-date of India'.

The route via which the banana reached modern-day Uganda is open to conjecture. The most obvious point of origin is Ethiopia, the source of several southward migrations in the past two millennia. But it is intriguing that while the banana is known by a name approximating to the generic Latin *Musa* throughout Asia, Arabia and northEast Africa – *moz* in Arabic and Persian, for instance, or *mus* or *musa* in various Ethiopian languages and Somali – no such linguistic resemblance occurs in East Africa, where it is known variously as *ndizi*, *gonja*, *matoke*, etc. This peculiarity has been cited to support a hypothesis that the banana first travelled between Asia and the East African coast either as a result of direct trade or else via Madagascar, and that it was entrenched there before regular trade was established with Arabia. A third possibility is that the banana reached Uganda via the Congolese Basin, possibly in association with the arrival of Bantu speakers from west Africa.

However it arrived in Uganda, the banana has certainly flourished there, forming the main subsistence crop for an estimated 40% of the population. Some 50 varieties are grown in the country, divided into four broad categories based on their primary use – *matoke* for boiling, *gonja* for roasting, *mbide* for distillation into banana beer (*mwenge*) or wine (*mubisi*), and the more familiar sweet *menvu* eaten raw for a snack or dessert. Within these broad categories, many subtleties of nomenclature and cultivation are applied to different varieties. And first-time visitors to Uganda might take note of the above names when they shop for bananas in the market – or sooner or later you'll bite into what looks to be a large, juicy sweet banana, but is in fact a foul and floury uncooked *matoke* or *gonja*!

Helmeted guineafowl (*Numida meleagris*) Gregarious and largely terrestrial wildfowl with striking white-speckled grey feathering and blue head with ivory casque. Panic-prone flocks common in savanna. The similar crested guineafowl is a forest resident with an unruly set of black head feathers. 46

African jacana (*Actophilornis africanus*) Unusual chestnut, white and black wader, also known as lily-trotter for its habit of walking across floating vegetation on its splayed feet, common in most wetlands in Uganda. 55

The banana's uses are not restricted to feeding bellies. The juice from the stem is traditionally regarded to have several medicinal applications, for instance as a cure for snakebite and for childish behaviour. Pulped or scraped sections from the stem also form very effective cloths for cleaning. The outer stem can be plaited to make a strong rope known as Byai in Luganda, while the cleaned central rib of the leaf is used to weave fish traps and other items of basketry. The leaf itself forms a useful makeshift umbrella, and was traditionally worn by young Buganda girls as an apron. The dried leaf is a popular bedding and roofing material, and also used to manufacture the head pads on which Ugandan women generally carry their loads.

The banana as we know it is a cultigen – modified by humans to their own ends and totally dependent on them for its propagation. The domestic fruit is the result of a freak mutation that gives the cells an extra copy of each chromosome, preventing the normal development of seeds, thereby rendering the plant edible, but also sterile. Every cultivated banana tree on the planet is effectively a clone, propagated by the planting of suckers or corms cut from 'parent' plants. This means that, unlike sexually reproductive crops, which experience new genetic configurations in every generation, the banana is unable to evolve mechanisms to fight off new diseases.

In early 2003, a report in the *New Scientist* warned that cultivated bananas are threatened with extinction within the next decade, because of their lack of defence against a pair of fungal diseases rampant in most of the world's banana-producing countries. These are black sigatoka, an airborne disease first identified in Fiji in 1963, and the soil-borne Panama disease, also known as fusarium wilt. Black sigatoka can be kept at bay by regular spraying – every ten days or so – but it is swiftly developing resistance to all known fungicides, which in any case are not affordable to the average subsistence farmers. There is no known cure for Panama disease.

So far as can be ascertained, Panama disease does not affect any banana variety indigenous to Uganda, but it has already resulted in the disappearance of several introduced varieties. Black sigatoka, by contrast, poses a threat to every banana variety in the world, and is present throughout Uganda. Buganda has been especially hard hit – a progressive reduction exceeding 50% has been experienced in the annual yield of the most seriously affected areas. In addition to reducing the yield of a single plant by up to 75%, black sigatoka can also cut its fruit-bearing life from more than 30 years to less than five.

International attempts to clone a banana tree resistant to both diseases have met with one limited success – agricultural researchers in Honduras have managed to produce one such variety, but it reputedly doesn't taste much like a banana. Another area of solution is genetic engineering – introducing a gene from a wild species to create a disease-resistant edible banana. Although ecologists are generally opposed to the genetic modification of crops, the domestic banana should perhaps be considered an exception, given its inability to spread its genes to related species – not to mention its pivotal importance to the subsistence economies of some of world's poorest countries, Uganda among them.

Grey crowned crane (*Balearica regulorum*) Uganda's national bird, 1.1m tall, grey and white feathering and a unique golden crest, common in swamp and associated moist grassland. North of the Nile, check carefully, since the northern black crowned crane has been recorded. 56

African green pigeon (*Treron calva*) Large, dove-like inhabitant of riparian woodland with cryptic green-grey feathering, often seen in fruiting fig trees. In north, check against Bruce's green pigeon, distinguished by yellow chest. 83

African grey parrot (*Psittacus erithacus*) Familiar caged bird – large, grey, with red tail feathers. Flocks are liable to be seen in any forested habitat, listen out for the loud squawking call emitted in flight. 89

Great blue turaco (*Corythaeola cristata*) Like a psychedelic turkey, this awesome blue-green forest dweller measures up to 75cm from the tip of its red-and-yellow bill to the end of its blue black-barred tail. Small flocks widespread in forested habitats countrywide, including Entebbe Botanical Gardens. 91

Ross's turaco (*Musophaga rossae*) Another stunner – deep purple with a bold yellow facemask and red crest and underwings. Widespread – but nowhere abundant – resident of forested habitats bordering wetlands or rivers. 91

Eastern grey plantain-eater (*Crinifer zonurus*) Large grey turaco-like bird with bold yellow bill and off-white crest, common in woodland and savanna countrywide, its loud chuckling call a characteristic sound of suburban Kampala and Entebbe. Check against black-faced go-away bird in acacia woodland of Lake Mburo. 93

African emerald cuckoo (*Chrysococcyx cupreus*) Brilliant green-and-yellow cuckoo associated with forest, where its deliberate, clear four-note call is as ubiquitous seasonally as the bird itself is impossible to locate in the high canopy. In breeding season, the three-note call of the red-chested cuckoo, variously rendered as 'it-will-rain' or 'Piet-my-vrou', also forms an unforgettable element in the Ugandan soundscape, but the bird itself is slightly less elusive. 97

Coucals (*Centropus spp*) Large, clumsy-looking relatives of the cuckoos, associated with rank grassland and swamp, with four species in Uganda of which the blue-headed and swamp-dwelling black coucal are the most enticing. 98

Verreaux's eagle-owl (*Bobo lacteus*) Largest of 13 owl species in Uganda, most of which might be seen by chance on night drives or roosting in large trees by day. 101

Pennant/Standard-winged nightjars (*Macrodipteryx spp*) Most spectacular of 11 nocturnal nightjars recorded in Uganda, the males of both species acquire wing streamers twice the length of their body during the breeding season. It might be seen in display flight in any savanna habitat, especially close to water, but there's no better place to seek them out than on the road to the top of Murchison Falls after dusk. 106

Pied kingfisher (*Ceryle rudis*) Boldly marked black-and-white kingfisher that hovers still above water for long periods and is ubiquitous in practically any wetland habitat. 111

Giant kingfisher (*Mageceryle maxima*) Like an overgrown pied kingfisher but with distinctive chestnut chest; widespread near water with tall fringing vegetation, but nowhere common. 111

Malachite kingfisher (*Alcedo cristata*) Exquisite African counterpart to European kingfisher, with blue back and wings and orange chest. Perches still on low reeds or twigs next to rivers and lakes; away from water, check against pink-cheeked but otherwise similar pygmy kingfisher. 113

Red-throated bee-eater (*Merops bulocki*) Stunning green, red and turquoise bee-eater, essentially west African though range extends into northwest Uganda. Breeds in tall sandbanks on Lake Albert and the Nile below Murchison Falls. 116

Northern carmine bee-eater (*Merops nubicus*) Bold red and blue bee-eater, not uncommon and perches openly north of the Nile in Murchison Falls. 117

Broad-billed roller (*Eurostymos glaucurus*) Dark chestnut and blue bird with bright-yellow bill, usually seen in pairs perched high but openly in woodland. Common countrywide including around Entebbe golf course. 117

Lilac-breasted roller (*Coracias caudata*) Dazzling pigeon-sized bird with chestnut back, lilac breast, blue chest and long tail streamers. Common in savanna habitats throughout East Africa, where it perches openly. A popular safari favourite, check it against the Abyssinian roller (no lilac) in Murchison Falls, where both species are present. 118

Hoopoe (*Upupa epops*) Distinctive orange, white and black bird with prominent crest, mainly terrestrial though it flies into trees when disturbed. Not uncommon in most wooded savanna habitats. 120

Black-and-white casqued hornbill (*Bycanistes brevis*) Characteristic Ugandan forest resident, a turkey-sized black-and-white bird with gross ivory bill, often first detected through its raucous braying and heavy wing flaps. 124

Abyssinian ground hornbill (*Bucorvus abyssinicus*) Predominantly terrestrial hornbill, over 1m tall, very heavily built with black feathering with white underwings, blue and red face patches, and effete long eyelashes. A common savanna resident in Murchison Falls and Semliki Wildlife Reserve. 125

Double-toothed barbet (*Lybius bidentatus*) Colourful thrush-sized bird, black with bold red breast, chest and face, yellow eye-patch and heavy pale bill. Might be seen in any wooded habitat, especially near fruiting fig trees. In north of Murchison Falls, check against rather similar but more localised black-breasted barbet. 130

White-browed robin-chat (*Cossypha heuglini*) The most common of seven similar thrush-sized species, most of which have orange-red chest, dark blue-black back and bold white eye-stripe. Associated with forest edge, well-developed gardens and other lush vegetation but not forest interiors. 166

Grey-capped warbler (*Eminia lepida*) Distinctive sparrow-sized resident of rank undergrowth, has green back, grey cap, black eye-stripe and red bib. Seldom comes out into the open, but very vocal and widespread, and especially common close to water. 198

Brown-throated wattle-eye (*Platysteira cyanea*) Delightful, highly vocal, common and widespread resident of woodland and forest edge, with neat black-and-white markings, bold red eye-wattle and (female only) chestnut-brown throat. 211

African paradise flycatcher (*Terpsiphone viridis*) Stunning and ubiquitous woodland and forest resident, usually blue-black on head and chest, rufous on back, male with extended tail up to twice the body length. A black-and-white morph is common in some parts of Uganda, and intermediate forms exist. In forested habitats, especially Kibale Forest, check against similar red-bellied paradise flycatcher. 212

Silverbird (*Empidornis semipartitus*) Striking silver-backed, orange-chested dry-country flycatcher, often seen perching openly in Murchison Falls. 212

Scarlet-chested sunbird (*Chalcomitra senegalensis*) Represented by more than 30 species in Uganda alone, sunbirds are small, colourful and often iridescent nectar-eaters, with long curved bills reminiscent of the unrelated hummingbirds which fill a similar niche in the New World. This is one of the more common species in Uganda, jet-black with a bold scarlet chest patch and green head markings. 228

Black-headed gonolek (*Laniarius erythrogaster*) Brilliant black-and-red thrush-sized bird, common in most savanna habitats, especially riverine thickets. Secretive but

Placed by some authorities in the same family as the closely related sparrows, the weavers of the family Ploceidae are a quintessential part of Africa's natural landscape, common and highly visible in virtually every habitat from rainforest to desert. The name of the family derives from the intricate and elaborate nests – typically but not always a roughly oval ball of dried grass, reeds and twigs – that are built by the dextrous males of most species.

It can be fascinating to watch a male weaver at work. First, a nest site is chosen, usually at the end of a thin hanging branch or frond, which is immediately stripped of leaves to protect against snakes. The weaver then flies back and forth to the site, carrying the building material blade by blade in its heavy beak, first using a few thick strands to hang a skeletal nest from the end of a branch, then gradually completing the structure by interweaving numerous thinner blades of grass into the main frame. Once completed, the nest is subjected to the attention of his chosen partner, who will tear it apart if the result is less than satisfactory, and so the process starts all over again.

All but 12 of the 113 described weaver species are resident on the African mainland or associated islands, with some 40 represented within Uganda alone. A full 25 of the Ugandan species are placed in the genus *Ploceus* (true weavers), which is surely the most characteristic of all African bird genera. Most of the *Ploceus* weavers are slightly larger than a sparrow, and display a strong sexual dimorphism. Females are with few exceptions drab buff or olive-brown birds, with some streaking on the back, and perhaps a hint of yellow on the belly.

Most male *Ploceus* weavers conform to the basic colour pattern of the 'masked weaver' – predominantly yellow, with streaky back and wings, and a distinct black facial mask, often bordered orange. Eight Ugandan weaver species fit this masked weaver prototype more-or-less absolutely, and a similar number approximate it rather less exactly, for instance by having a chestnut-brown mask, or a full black head, or a black back, or being more chestnut than yellow on the belly. Identification of the masked weavers can be tricky without experience – useful clues are the exact shape of the mask, the presence and extent of the fringing orange, and the colour of the eye and the back.

The golden weavers, of which only two species are present in Uganda, are also brilliant yellow and/or light orange with some light streaking on the back, but they lack a mask or any other strong distinguishing features. The handful of forest-associated *Ploceus* weavers, by contrast, tend to have quite different and very striking colour patterns, and although sexually dimorphic, the female is often as boldly marked as the male. The most aberrant among these are Vieillot's and Maxwell's black weavers, the males of which are totally black except for their eyes, while the black-billed weaver reverses the prototype by being all black with a yellow facemask.

Among the more conspicuous *Ploceus* species in Uganda are the black-headed, yellow-backed, slender-billed, northern brown-throated, orange and Vieillot's black weavers – for

not especially shy, its presence is often revealed by loud duetting, alternating loud liquid notes with a softer churring response. 234

Fork-tailed drongo (*Dicrurus absimilis*) Pugnacious all-black bird with deep forked tail, common in wooded savanna where it perches openly and often emits a series of harsh, nasal notes. Could be confused with similar but more lightly built northern black flycatcher. 241

Piacpiac (*Ptilostomus afer*) Smaller and more lightly built than other African crows, glossy black with a red eye, often seen in the vicinity of riverine palms and frequently associates with livestock or wild bovines, eating disturbed insects. Common in Jinja and Murchison Falls. 241

the most part gregarious breeders forming single or mixed species colonies of hundreds, sometimes thousands, of pairs. The most extensive weaver colonies are often found in reed-beds and waterside vegetation – the mixed species colonies in Entebbe Botanical Garden or Ngamba Island are as impressive as any in Uganda. Most weavers don't have a distinctive song, but they compensate with a rowdy jumble of harsh swizzles, rattles and nasal notes that can reach deafening proportions near large colonies. One of the more cohesive songs you will often hear seasonally around weaver colonies is a cyclic 'dee-dee-dee-Diederik', often accelerating to a hysterical crescendo when several birds call at once. This is the call of the Diederik cuckoo, a handsome green-and-white cuckoo that lays its eggs in weaver nests.

Oddly, while most East African *Ploceus* weavers are common, even abundant, in suitable habitats, seven highly localised species are listed as range-restricted, and three of these – one Kenyan endemic and two Tanzanian endemics – are regarded to be of global conservation concern. Of the other four, Fox's weaver (*Ploceus spekeoides*) is the only bird species endemic to Uganda: a larger-than-average yellow-masked weaver with an olive back, yellow eyes and orange-fringed black facemask, confined to acacia woodland near swamps and lakes east of Lake Kyoga. The strange weaver (*Ploceus alienus*) – black head, plain olive back, yellow belly with chestnut bib – is an Albertine Rift endemic restricted to four sites in Uganda.

Most of the colonial weavers, perhaps relying on safety in numbers, build relatively plain nests with a roughly oval shape and an unadorned entrance hole. The nests of certain more solitary weavers, by contrast, are far more elaborate. Several weavers, for instance, protect their nests from egg-eating invaders by attaching tubular entrance tunnels to the base – in the case of the spectacled weaver, sometimes twice as long as the nest itself. The Grosbeak weaver (a peculiar, larger-than-average brown-and-white weaver of reed-beds, distinguished by its outsized bill and placed in the monospecific genus *Amblyospiza*) constructs a large and distinctive domed nest, which is supported by a pair of reeds, and woven as precisely as the finest basketwork, with a neat raised entrance hole at the front. By contrast, the scruffiest nests are built by the various species of sparrow- and buffalo-weaver, relatively drab but highly gregarious dry-country birds, poorly represented in Uganda except for in the vicinity of Kidepo.

Black-winged red bishop (*Euplectes hordaecrus*) The most widespread of three red bishop species found in Uganda, all of which are small, bright, black-and-red birds, associated with reeds and rank grassland. 268

Red-cheeked cordon-bleu (*Uraeginthus bengalus*) Diminutive finch with blue underparts and (male only) bold red cheek-patch. Restless flocks regularly encountered in savanna habitats throughout Uganda. 274

Pin-tailed wydah (*Vidua macroura*) Black-and-white male is small, but with a bright-red bill and tail streamers twice the length of the body. Often accompanied by harem of nondescript females, common in grassland and open savanna. 280

TWITCHER'S LIST

African finfoot (*Podica senegalensis*) Widespread but elusive red-billed resident of quiet lakes and rivers with overhanging vegetation. Ranks high on many African birdwatchers' wish list and seen very regularly from boat trips on Lake Mburo, and also on the crater lake at Jacana Lodge, QENP. 8

Nahan's francolin (*Francolinus nahan*) Small dark forest wildfowl with white-barred chest, and a red facemask and bill. In Uganda restricted to Bwindi and Mabira Forest, where it's most likely to be seen hurriedly crossing forest paths. 47

Jackson's francolin (*Francolinus jacksoni*) Large pale-headed wildfowl, localised on East African mountains, and in Uganda restricted to forest edge and open country on Mount Elgon, where it's common. 47

Denham's bustard (*Neotis denhami*) Localised ground bird, up to 1.2m tall and very heavily built. Open country north of the Nile in Murchison Falls is perhaps the most reliable site for it anywhere in Africa. 57

Black-headed lapwing (*Vanellus tectus*) Long black crest makes it arguably the most striking of seven Ugandan lapwing species; uncommon in East Africa generally, but seen very regularly on game drives in the north of Murchison Falls. 64

African skimmer (*Rynchops flavirostris*) Handsome tern-like build and black-and-white feathering complemented by long, bold red bill; often seen flocked on sandbanks or skimming above the water in Murchison Falls. 80

White-headed turaco (*Tauraco leocolophus*) Striking purple-green turaco with distinctive white crest/head. Widespread but secretive in woodland and riparian forest, and often seen along Nile in Murchison Falls. 91

Black-billed turaco (*Tauraco schuetti*) Bright-green turaco with white markings above and below eye, white-tipped crest and small black bill. Resident and vocal in most forest interiors, but often difficult to see clearly. 92

Long-tailed nightjar (*Caprimulgus climacurus*) Unusually large nightjar, easily identified by long tail with narrow white outer feathers. Seasonally common in north, it's likely to be seen diving from the top of Murchison Falls after dark. 103

Bar-tailed trogon (*Apaloderma vittatum*) Stunning forest bird, similar to more widespread Narina trogon but with blue breast band and barred (as opposed to white) tail. Secretive and often sits motionless for long periods, it's generally quite easy to locate along the road leading uphill from Buhoma (Bwindi) especially if you have a local guide who knows the call. 110

Blue-breasted kingfisher (*Halcyon malimbica*) Similar to the more widespread woodland kingfisher but with unique blue breast band. Common in several forests, especially Budongo and Chambura Gorge, where it often sits motionless, revealing its presence by a high scolding trill. 112

Chocolate-backed kingfisher (*Halcyon badia*) Localised forest kingfisher with unique chocolate-brown back and bold red bill; nowhere common, but fairly likely to be seen in Budongo Forest. 112

African dwarf kingfisher (*Ispidina lecontei*) Small forest kingfisher, differs from other blue-backed, rufous-fronted kingfishers in having red crown with a black frontal mark. Resident in most forests in Uganda, most common perhaps in Budongo. 113

Shining blue kingfisher (*Alcedo quadribrachys*) Considerably larger than other kingfishers, a blue-backed, rufous-fronted, localised denizen of rivers and pools within forest interiors. Sometimes seen at roadside pools and river crossings in Budongo and Kibale forests. 113

Black bee-eater (*Merops gularis*) The most eagerly sought of the 12 brightly coloured bee-eater species recorded in Uganda, with a distinctive blue-black colour and scarlet throat. Often found perched high on bare branches in forests such as Bwindi, or riparian woodland along Chambura and Ishasha rivers. 115

Blue-throated roller (*Eurystomus gularis*) Similar to broad-billed roller but with clear blue throat patch, generally associated with forest interiors and regularly seen on the trail through Bigodi Wetland. 117

Forest/white-headed wood-hoopoe (*Phoeniculus castaneiceps/bolloi*) A pair of patchily distributed and generally scarce forest birds, similar in appearance (and noisy behaviour) to familiar green wood-hoopoe though *castaneiceps* has black bill and variable head colour (white, black or brown) and *bolloi* has white head and bright red bill. The former is common only in Mabira Forest, while the latter is most likely to be seen in Bwindi or Kibale. 119

Black scimitarbill (*Rhinopomastus aterrimus*) In East Africa, confined to northwest of Uganda, the only scimitarbill present in Murchison Falls, where it's quite common in acacia woodland north of the Nile. 120

African pied hornbill (*Tockus fasciatus*) Medium-sized black-and-white hornbill with black-tipped ivory bill. The most common forest hornbill in Uganda after black-and-white casqued, it's resident in Entebbe Botanical Garden and also common in Kibale, Budongo and Mabira forests. 122

Piping hornbill (*Bycanistes fistulator*) Similar to but significantly larger than above, with heavier bill and more white in flight pattern. Common only in Semliki National Park but also regular in Budongo Forest. 123

White-thighed hornbill (*Bycanistes cylinddricus*) Large forest hornbill, distinguished from rather similar black-and-white casqued by diagnostic white tail with solitary black bar; present in several Ugandan forests, common in Budongo and forest patches along the Masindi–Hoima road to the south. 124

Grey-throated barbet (*Gymnobucco bonapartei*) Dull grey-brown forest barbet with diagnostic pale tufts standing erect on either side of the bill. Unique silhouette emphasised by habit of perching openly on dead trees, common in most Ugandan forests. 127

Hairy-breasted barbet (*Tricholaema hirsute*) Black, yellow and white forest barbet, not uncommon in most Ugandan forests, often seen in Bigodi Wetland Sanctuary. 129

Yellow-spotted barbet (*Buccanodon duchaillui*) Black barbet with yellow streaking on breast and red forehead; common in most Ugandan forests, especially Kibale and Mabira. 129

Yellow-billed barbet (*Trachylaemus purpuratus*) Unique large barbet, glossy purple-black with yellow bill, face and chest. Widespread in forested and wooded habitats, regular in Bigodi Wetland Sanctuary. 131

Green-breasted pitta (*Pitta riechenowi*) Terrestrial forest bird with brilliant green breast, red vent, black-and-white face. Nowhere common, and unlikely to be seen unless accompanied by a knowledgeable guide, the best sites are Budongo and Kibale forests. 139

Uganda's wealth of invertebrate life – more than 100,000 species have been identified countrywide – is largely overlooked by visitors, but is perhaps most easily appreciated in the form of butterflies and moths of the order Lepidoptera. An astonishing 1,200 butterfly species, including almost 50 endemics, have been recorded in Uganda, as compared with fewer than 1,000 in Kenya, roughly 650 in the whole of North America, and a mere 56 in the British Isles. Several forests in Uganda harbour 300 or more butterfly species, and one might easily see a greater selection in the course of a day than one could in a lifetime of exploring the English countryside. Indeed, I've often sat at one roadside pool in the like of Kibale or Budongo forests and watched ten–20 clearly different species converge there over the space of 20 minutes.

The Lepidoptera are placed in the class Insecta, which includes ants, beetles and locusts among others. All insects are distinguished from other invertebrates, such as arachnids (spiders) and crustaceans, by their combination of six legs, a pair of frontal antennae, and a body divided into a distinct head, thorax and abdomen. Insects are the only winged invertebrates, though some primitive orders have never evolved them, and other more recently evolved orders have discarded them. Most flying insects have two pairs of wings, one of which, as in the case of flies, might have been modified beyond immediate recognition. The butterflies and moths of the order Lepidoptera have two sets of wings and are distinguished from all other insect orders by the tiny ridged wing scales that create their characteristic bright colours.

The most spectacular of all butterflies are the swallowtails of the family Papilionidae, of which roughly 100 species have been identified in Africa, and 32 in Uganda. Named for the streamers that trail from the base of their wings, swallowtails are typically large and colourful, and relatively easy to observe when they feed on mammal dung deposited on forest trails and roads. Sadly, this last generalisation doesn't apply to the African giant swallowtail (*Papilio antimachus*), a powerful flier that tends to stick at canopy levels and seldom alights on the ground, but the first two generalisations certainly do. With a wingspan known to exceed 20cm, this black, orange and green gem, an endangered west African species whose range extends into Bwindi, Kibale, Semliki, Budongo and Kalinzu forests, is certainly the largest butterfly on the continent, and possibly the largest in the world. One of the most common large swallowtails in Uganda is *Papilio nobilis*, which has golden or orange wings, and occurs in suburban gardens in Kampala, Entebbe, Jinja and elsewhere.

The Pieridae is a family of medium-sized butterflies, generally smaller than the swallowtails and with wider wings, of which almost 100 species are present in Uganda, several as seasonal intra-African migrants. Most species are predominantly white in colour, with some yellow, orange, black or even red and blue markings on the wings. One widespread member of this family is the oddly named angled grass yellow (*Eurema desjardini*), which has yellow wings marked by a broad black band, and is likely to be seen in any savanna or forest-fringe habitat in southern Uganda. The orange-and-lemon *Eronia leda* also has yellow wings, but with an orange upper tip, and it occurs in open grassland and savanna countrywide.

The most diverse family of butterflies within Uganda is the Lycaenidae, with almost 500 of the 1,500 African species recorded. Known also as gossamer wings, this varied

Petit's cuckoo-shrike (*Campephaga petiti*) Male all black with yellow gapes, female yellow with vertical bars on side of breast, fairly regular on walk uphill from Buhoma in Bwindi. 154

Red-tailed bristlebill (*Bleda syndactyla*) Large yellow-breasted greenbul with diagnostic blue eye-wattle, fairly common in most Ugandan forests. 161

family consists mostly of small to medium-sized butterflies, with a wingspan of 1–5cm, dull underwings, and brilliant violet blue, copper or rufous-orange upper wings. The larvae of many Lycaenidae species have a symbiotic relationship with ants – they secrete a fluid that is milked by the ants and are thus permitted to shelter in their nests. A striking member of this family is *Hypolycaena hatita*, a small bluish butterfly with long tail streamers, often seen on forest paths throughout Uganda.

Another well-represented family in Uganda, with 370 species present, is the Nymphalidae, a diversely coloured group of small to large butterflies, generally associated with forest edges or interiors. The Nymphalidae are also known as brush-footed butterflies, because their forelegs have evolved into non-functional brush-like structures. One of the more common and distinctive species is the African blue tiger (*Tirumala petiverana*), a large black butterfly with about two-dozen blue-white wing spots, often observed in forest paths near puddles or feeding from animal droppings. Another large member of this family is the African queen (*Danaus chrysippus*), which has a slow, deliberate flight pattern, orange or brown wings, and is as common in forest-edge habitats as it is in cultivated fields or suburbia. Also often recorded in Kampala gardens is the African Mother of Pearl (*Salamis parhassus*), a lovely light-green butterfly with black wing dots and tips.

The family Charaxidae, regarded by some authorities to be a subfamily of the Nymphalidae, is represented in Uganda by 70 of the roughly 200 African species. Typically large, robust, strong fliers with one or two short tails on each wing, the butterflies in this family vary greatly in colouration, and several species appear to be scarce and localised since they inhabit forest canopies and are seldom observed. Bwindi is a particularly good site for this family, with almost 40 species recorded, ranging from the regal dark-blue charaxes (*Charaxes tiridates*) (black wings with deep blue spots) to the rather leaf-like green-veined charaxes (*Charaxes candiope*).

Rather less spectacular are the 200 grass-skipper species of the family Hersperiidae recorded in Uganda, most of which are small and rather drably coloured, though some are more attractively marked in black, white and/or yellow. The grass-skippers are regarded as the evolutionary link between butterflies and the generally more nocturnal moths, represented in Uganda by several families of which the most impressive are the boldly patterned giant silk-moths of the family Saturniidae.

An obstacle to developing a serious interest in Uganda's butterflies has been the absence of useful literature and field guides to aid identification. The recent publication of Nanny Carter and Laura Tindimubona's *Butterflies of Uganda* (Uganda Society, 2002) goes a long way to rectifying this situation, illustrating and describing roughly 200 of the more common and striking species, with basic information about distribution and habitat. It's not quite the same as a comprehensive field guide, since many allied butterfly species are very similar to each other in appearance, while other species are highly localised or endemic to one specific forest. But certainly this book does pave the way for a greater appreciation of Uganda's most colourful invertebrate order, and as such it is highly recommended to anybody with even a passing interest in butterflies. If you can't find it in a bookshop, it can be bought at the Uganda Society shop at the National Museum in Kampala (e *ugsociety@bushnet.com*).

Blue-shouldered robin-chat (*Cossypha cyanocampter*) Similar in appearance to more common white-browed robin-chat, but significantly smaller and with distinctive light-blue shoulder patch, widespread but never common in forest interiors throughout southern Uganda. 166

Snowy-headed robin-chat (*Cossypha niveicapella*) Similar in appearance to more common white-browed robin-chat, but larger, white stripe through top of head replaces white eye-stripe. Widespread and generally fairly common in forest interiors throughout southern Uganda. 166

African thrush (*Turdus pelios*) Western counterpart to the ubiquitous olive thrush found elsewhere in eastern and southern Africa, very common and often quite tame in lodge gardens. 168

Spotted morning thrush (*Cichladusa guttata*) Lively streaky-breasted small thrush, attractively vociferous and common in lodges at Murchison Falls. 177

Papyrus yellow warbler (*Chloropeta gracilrostris*) Large yellow warbler restricted exclusively to papyrus swamps; very scarce in southwest of Uganda. 178

White-winged warbler (*Bradypterus carpalis*) Another papyrus endemic, large streaky warbler, widespread but secretive; resident in suitable habitats throughout Uganda. 180

Black-faced rufous warbler (*Bathmocercus rufus*) Striking, secretive resident of forest undergrowth, most common at higher altitudes such as Bwindi and Mount Elgon. 189

Red-winged grey warbler (*Drymocichla incana*) Attractive, restless northern warbler whose range extends into Murchison Falls, where quite common in riverine scrub. 197

Black-throated apalis (*Apalis jacksoni*) Neat apalis with bright yellow belly and black, grey and white head markings, resident in most Ugandan forests, also riverine woodland; commonest at higher altitudes. 203

Black-and-white shrike-flycatcher (*Bias musicus*) Patchily distributed and heavily built small flycatcher with long black crest, yellow eye, white belly, black back in male, chestnut back in female. Amazing circular display flights undertaken from treetops. Not uncommon garden bird in Entebbe and Kampala. 210

Chestnut-bellied wattle-eye (*Dyaphorophyia castanea*) The most likely to be seen of three blue- or yellow-wattled small forest birds in this genus, all reasonably common in suitable habitats in the southwest, but rather unobtrusive. 211

African blue flycatcher (*Elminia longicauda*) Pretty grey-blue flycatcher with distinct crest and long tail, common throughout Uganda, even in gardens in Entebbe and Kampala. 214

Chestnut-capped flycatcher (*Erythrocercus mccallii*) Diminutive and gregarious olive-grey flycatcher with streaked chestnut cap. In East Africa known only from Budongo Forest, where it's quite common. 214

Tit hylia (*Pholidornis rushae*) Tiny yellow-bellied, streaky-headed bird, moves around in small highly vocal parties, in East Africa known only from Budongo, Semliki and Mabira forests, most common in the last. 219

Green-headed sunbird (*Cyanomitra verticalis*) The wealth of sunbird diversity in Uganda is amazing, and several forest and highland species are likely to be seen in the course of a visit. This olive-bodied, green-headed resident of forest edge and wooded habitats is one of the more singular and common species. 222

Mackinnon's fiscal (*Lanius mackinnoni*) Boldly patterned grey, black and white shrike of forest edge and open woodland, most common at higher altitudes, especially around Buhoma in Bwindi. 232

Papyrus gonolek (*Laniarius mufumbiri*) Similar to black-headed gonolek but with bright-yellow cap complementing crimson breast, and white bar on the black wing. Endemic to papyrus habitats, where locally common and often heard but difficult to see. 234

Luhder's bush-shrike (*Laniarius luehderi*) Distinctive black-and-white gonolek-like shrike with unique orange crown and belly. Widespread but secretive forest resident most likely to be traced by call, and often observed around Buhoma in Bwindi. 234

Lagden's bush-shrike (*Malaconotus lagdeni*) Handsome yellow, green, grey and orange bird, similar in size and appearance to widespread grey-headed bush-shrike, within East Africa confined to forests of the Albertine Rift, where common and vocal but difficult to locate. 238

Red-billed helmetshrike (*Prionops caniceps*) Remarkably colourful helmetshrike, grey above, orange below, white on face, uncommon in western forests, but gregarious, noisy and highly active when present. 240

Grey-headed negro-finch (*Nigrita canicapilla*) Endearing finch with grey head separated from black body by thin white stripe. One of Uganda's more widespread and visible small forest birds. 269

Red-headed bluebill (*Spermophaga ruficapella*) Gobsmackingly pretty finch, with black back and chest (the latter spotted white in the female), red head and breast, and bright blue-and-red bill. Often seen in lodge grounds in Buhoma (Bwindi) and in Bigodi Wetland Sanctuary. 273

REPTILES

NILE CROCODILE The order Crocodilia dates back at least 150 million years, and fossil forms that lived contemporaneously with dinosaurs are remarkably unchanged from their modern ancestors, of which the Nile crocodile is the largest living reptile, regularly growing to lengths of up to 6m. Widespread throughout Africa, the Nile crocodile was once common in most large rivers and lakes, but it has been exterminated in many areas in the past century – hunted professionally for its skin as well as by vengeful local villagers. Contrary to popular legend, Nile crocodiles generally feed mostly on fish, at least where densities are sufficient. They will also prey on drinking or swimming mammals where the opportunity presents itself, dragging their victim underwater until it drowns, then storing it under a submerged log or tree until it has decomposed sufficiently for them to eat. A large crocodile is capable of killing a lion or wildebeest, or an adult human for that matter, and in certain areas such as the Mara or Grumeti rivers in the Serengeti, large mammals do form their main prey. Today, large crocodiles are mostly confined to protected areas. The gargantuan specimens that lurk on the sandbanks along the Nile below Murchison Falls National Park are a truly primeval sight, silent and sinister, vanishing under the water when the launch approaches too closely. Other reliable sites for crocs are Lake Mburo and increasingly the Kazinga Channel in QENP.

SNAKES A wide variety of snakes is found in Uganda, though – fortunately, most would agree – they are typically very shy and unlikely to be seen unless actively sought. One of the snakes most likely to be seen on safari is Africa's largest, the **rock python**, which has a gold-on-black mottled skin and regularly grows to lengths exceeding 5m. Non-venomous, pythons kill their prey by strangulation,

Common and widespread in Uganda, but not easily seen unless they are actively searched for, chameleons are arguably the most intriguing of African reptiles. True chameleons of the family Chamaeleontidae are confined to the Old World, with the most important centre of speciation being the island of Madagascar, to which about half of the world's 120 recognised species are endemic. Aside from two species of chameleon apiece in Asia and Europe, the remainder is distributed across mainland Africa.

Chameleons are best known for their capacity to change colour, a trait that has often been exaggerated in popular literature, and which is generally influenced by mood more than the colour of the background. Some chameleons are more adept at changing colour than others, with the most variable being the **common chameleon** (*Chamaeleo chamaeleon*) of the Mediterranean region, with more than 100 colour and pattern variations recorded. Many African chameleons are typically green in colour but will gradually take on a browner hue when they descend from the foliage in more exposed terrain, for instance while crossing a road. Several change colour and pattern far more dramatically when they feel threatened or are confronted by a rival of the same species. Different chameleon species also vary greatly in size, with the largest being Oustalet's chameleon of Madagascar, known to reach a length of almost 80cm.

A remarkable physiological feature common to all true chameleons are their protuberant round eyes, which offer a potential 180° degree vision on both sides and are able to swivel around independently of each other. Only when one of them isolates a suitably juicy-looking insect will the two eyes focus in the same direction as the chameleon stalks slowly forward until it is close enough to use the other unique weapon in its armoury. This is its sticky-tipped tongue, which is typically about the same length as its body and remains coiled up within its mouth most of the time, to be unleashed in a sudden, blink-and-you'll-miss-it lunge to zap a selected item of prey. In addition to their unique eyes and tongues, many chameleons are adorned with an array of facial casques,

wrapping their muscular bodies around it until it cannot breathe, then swallowing it whole and dozing off for a couple of months while it is digested. Pythons feed mainly on small antelopes, large rodents and similar. They are harmless to adult humans, but could conceivably kill a small child. A slumbering python might be encountered almost anywhere in East Africa, and one reasonably relaxed individual is often present at the bat cave near the visitors' centre in Maramagambo Forest, Queen Elizabeth National Park (QENP).

Of the venomous snakes, one of the most commonly encountered is the **puff adder**, a large, thick resident of savanna and rocky habitats. Although it feeds mainly on rodents, the puff adder will strike when threatened, and it is rightly considered the most dangerous of African snakes, not because it is especially venomous or aggressive, but because its notoriously sluggish disposition means it is more often disturbed than other snakes. The related **Gabon viper** is possibly the largest African viper, growing up to 2m long, very heavily built, and with a beautiful cryptic geometric gold, black-and-brown skin pattern that blends perfectly into the rainforest litter it inhabits. Although highly venomous, it is more placid and less likely to be encountered than the puff adder.

Several **cobra** species, including the spitting cobra, are present in Uganda, most with characteristic hoods that they raise when about to strike, though they are all very seldom seen. Another widespread family is the **mambas**, of which the black mamba – which will only attack when cornered, despite an unfounded reputation for unprovoked aggression – is the largest venomous snake in Africa, measuring up to 3.5m long. Theoretically, the most toxic of Africa's snakes is said to be the

flaps, horns and crests that enhance their already somewhat fearsome prehistoric appearance.

In Uganda, you're most likely to come across a chameleon by chance when it is crossing a road, in which case it should be easy to take a closer look at it, since most chameleons move painfully slowly and deliberately. Chameleons are also often seen on night game drives, when their ghostly nocturnal colouring shows up clearly under a spotlight – as well as making it pretty clear why these strange creatures are regarded with both fear and awe in many local African cultures. More actively, you could ask your guide if they know where to find a chameleon – a few individuals will be resident in most lodge grounds.

The **flap-necked chameleon** (*Chamaeleo delepis*) is probably the most regularly observed species of savanna and woodland habitats in East Africa. Often observed crossing roads, the flap-necked chameleon is generally around 15cm long and bright green in colour with few distinctive markings, but individuals might be up to 30cm in length and will turn tan or brown under the right conditions. Another closely related and widespread savanna and woodland species is the similarly sized **graceful chameleon** (*Chamaeleo gracilis*), which is generally yellow-green in colour and often has a white horizontal stripe along its flanks.

Characteristic of East African montane forests, three-horned chameleons form a closely allied species cluster of some taxonomic uncertainty. Typically darker than the savanna chameleons and around 20cm in length, the males of all taxa within this cluster are distinguished by a trio of long nasal horns that project forward from their face. Perhaps the most alluring of East Africa's chameleons is the **giant chameleon** (*Chamaeleo melleri*), a bulky dark-green creature with yellow stripes and a small solitary horn, mainly associated with the Eastern Arc forests, where it feeds on small reptiles (including snakes) as well as insects.

boomslang, a variably coloured and, as its name – literally tree snake – suggests, largely arboreal snake that is reputed to have accounted for not a single known human fatality, as it is back-fanged and very non-aggressive.

Most snakes are in fact non-venomous and not even potentially harmful to any other living creature much bigger than a rat. One of the more non-venomous snakes in the region is the **green tree snake** (sometimes mistaken for a boomslang, though the latter is never as green and more often than not brown), which feeds mostly on amphibians. The **mole snake** is a common and widespread grey-brown savanna resident that grows up to 2m long, and feeds on moles and other rodents. The remarkable **egg-eating snakes** live exclusively on birds' eggs, dislocating their jaws to swallow the egg whole, then eventually regurgitating the crushed shell in a neat little package. Many snakes will take eggs opportunistically, for which reason large-scale agitation among birds in a tree is often a good indication that a snake (or small bird of prey) is around.

LIZARDS All African lizards are harmless to humans, with the arguable exception of the **giant monitor lizards**, which could in theory inflict a nasty bite if cornered. Two species of monitor occur in East Africa, the water and savanna monitor, the latter growing up to 2.2m long and occasionally seen in the vicinity of termite mounds, the former slightly smaller but far more regularly observed by tourists, particularly along the Kazinga Channel in QENP. Their size alone might make it possible to fleetingly mistake a monitor for a small crocodile, but their more colourful yellow-dappled skin precludes sustained confusion. Both species are predatorial, feeding on anything from birds' eggs to smaller reptiles and mammals, but will also eat carrion opportunistically.

Visitors to East Africa will soon become familiar with the **common house gecko**, an endearing bug-eyed, translucent white lizard, which as its name suggests reliably inhabits most houses as well as lodge rooms, scampering up walls and upside-down on the ceiling in pursuit of pesky insects attracted to the lights. Also very common in some lodge grounds are various **agama** species, distinguished from other common lizards by their relatively large size of around 20–25cm, basking habits, and almost plastic-looking scaling – depending on the species, a combination of blue, purple, orange or red, with the flattened head generally a different colour from the torso. Another common family are the **skinks**: small, long-tailed lizards, most of which are quite dark and have a few thin black stripes running from head to tail.

TORTOISES AND TERRAPINS These peculiar reptiles are unique in being protected by a prototypal suit of armour formed by their heavy exoskeleton. The most common of the terrestrial tortoises in the region is the **leopard tortoise**, which is named after its gold-and-black mottled shell, can weigh up to 30kg, and has been known to live for more than 50 years in captivity. It is often seen motoring along in the slow lane of game reserve roads in Uganda. Four species of terrapin – essentially the freshwater equivalent of turtles – are resident in East Africa, all somewhat flatter in shape than the tortoises, and generally with a plainer brown shell. They might be seen sunning on rocks close to water or peering out from roadside puddles. The largest is the **Nile soft-shelled terrapin**, which has a wide, flat shell and in rare instances might reach a length of almost 1m.

3

Planning Your Trip

This chapter covers most practical aspects of planning a trip to Uganda, including overland crossings between Uganda and neighbouring countries. Practical advice relating to day-to-day travel in Uganda is covered separately in *Chapter 4, Travelling in Uganda,* but in some instances it might bear on planning, so do at least skim through it before you travel. Aspects of trip planning relating to health – for instance organising vaccinations and putting together a medical kit – are covered separately in *Chapter 5, Health.*

WHEN TO VISIT

Uganda has a warm climate all year round and, because it lies on the Equator, seasonal temperature variations are insignificant. The main factor you should consider when planning a trip to Uganda is the rainfall pattern, especially if you plan on hiking in the Rwenzori Mountains. The wettest months are April, May, October and November. During these months camping isn't very practical (you'll be packing up your tent in the rain as often as not), hiking can be an endurance test and some unsurfaced roads may be impassable.

TOURIST INFORMATION

Ugandan embassies or high commissions can give limited advice. There is no longer a Ugandan Tourist Centre in London. A good source of current information is the website of Tourism Uganda (*www.visituganda.com*), previously the Uganda Tourist Board, along with various other sites listed under *Uganda online* in *Appendix 3*, page 481. Don't leave without emailing info@bradtguides.com for a free copy of our regularly revised update newsletter.

TOUR OPERATORS

An ever-growing number of local and international tour operators offer a range of standard and customised private safaris to Uganda. Two-week itineraries typically cover the full western circuit from Murchison Falls to Lake Mburo via Kibale Forest, Queen Elizabeth and Bwindi or Mgahinga national parks, sometimes nipping across the border to Rwanda to go gorilla tracking when no permits are available within Uganda. Shorter itineraries generally omit the long drive to and from Murchison Falls, and one-stop gorilla tours of three days' duration are also available out of Kampala. Several other variations are available, depending on the individual's interests and how much time they have available. The high cost of vehicle maintenance, fuel and upmarket accommodation in Uganda is reflected in the price of private safaris, but this can be reduced by opting to use cheaper accommodation, such as the rest camp at Paraa and hostel at Mweya in QENP, or by camping.

Uganda, mercifully, shows no signs of trying to establish itself as a package destination, nor is it likely to for as long as its premier attraction remains the relatively exclusive experience of tracking mountain gorillas in Bwindi or the Virungas. The country is, however, well suited to small group tours that offer the same standard of accommodation and service as private safaris, but generally at a reduced individual price because transport and related costs are divided between several passengers. In addition to general group tours, packages are also available for special-interest groups such as birdwatchers, primate enthusiasts and photographers. The South African company Wild Frontiers runs regular general- and special-interest small group tours led by the highly regarded ornithologists Malcolm Wilson and Ian Davidson as well as – unabashed plug, I admit it! – the author of this guidebook.

The following locally based and international operators can all be recommended as experienced and reliable:

Great Lakes Safaris Ltd m 0772 426 368; e info@safari-uganda.com; www.safari-uganda.com. This relatively new tour company has been recommended by travellers as being helpful and efficient.

Kimbla-Mantana African Safaris ↘ 0414 321552; f 0414 320152; e mantana@africaonline.co.ug; www.kimbla-mantana.co.ug. Entebbe-based company with over 20 years' experience of conducting safaris in Uganda. Operates permanent tented camps at Kibale, Bwindi and Lake Mburo.

Ku Tunza Travel m 0772 456303; e info@ kutunza.com or admin@kutunza.com; www.kutunza.com. This new Jinja-based tour company provides the usual national range of tours with an emphasis on 'responsible tourism'.

Pearl of Africa Tours and Travel (Kampala) ↘ 0414 340533; m 0772 403614; f 0414 236255; e info@pearlofafricatours.com; www.pearlofafricatours.com. Solid local operation offering tours countrywide, car hire and travel agent services. Office in Impala Hse on Kimathi Av.

Uganda Safari Company (Kampala) ↘ 0414 251182; m 0772 489497; f 0414 344653; e tusc@ africaonline.co.ug; www.safariuganda.com. Guided safaris and tracking tours countrywide. The USC operates a long-standing luxury tented camp in the Semliki Valley and has recently opened a new lodge in Kidepo Valley National Park. They are set to develop an additional facility to serve Bwindi Impenetrable National Park's new gorilla-tracking site at Nkuringo.

Volcanoes Safaris (London and Kampala) PO Box 16345, London SW1X 0ZD; ↘ +44 0870 870 8480 (UK) or 0414 346464/5 (Uganda); f +44 0870 870 8481 (UK) or 0414 341718 (Uganda); e ukinfo@ volcanoessafaris.com (UK) or salesug@ volcanoessafaris.com (Uganda); www.volcanoessafaris.com. Highly regarded joint UK–Uganda company, specialising in gorilla tracking out of its tented camps at Bwindi, Mgahinga, Sipi Falls and near Ruhengeri in Rwanda, as well as tours to other parts of Uganda and Rwanda. The local office is at 27 Lumumba Av.

Wild Frontiers (Johannesburg and Entebbe) ↘ +27 11 702 2035 (South Africa) or 0414 321479 (Uganda); m 0772 502155 (Uganda); f +27 11 315 4850 (South Africa) or 0414 321479 (Uganda); e wildfront@icon.co.za (South Africa) or info@wildfrontiers.co.ug or gctours@imul.com (Uganda); www.wildfrontiers.com or www.wildfrontiers.co.ug. Excellent, competitively priced Johannesburg-based tour operator with more than a decade of experience arranging safaris to all corners of East Africa. It operates in Uganda through its own well-equipped ground operation in Entebbe, **G&C Tours**. In addition to creating customised private safaris, it offers a good range of fixed-departure photographic, birdwatching, primate and other interest tours led by experts in their fields. G&C is expanding its operations to include accommodation at Bwindi and in the beautiful Ishasha sector of Queen Elizabeth National Park.

The above companies will provide you with tailor-made itineraries. Both Backpackers and Red Chilli hostels (see *Chapter 6, Where to Stay*, pages 147–8) offer low-budget, fixed-itinerary tours to specific destinations, eg: Murchison Falls and Queen Elizabeth national parks. All of the above are (I believe) members of AUTO (Association of Ugandan Tour Operators), an accreditation intended to imply a certain standard of operation, experience and integrity. There are also a few smaller and cheaper operators, often Ugandan safari guides setting up on their own with a vehicle. These are invariably not AUTO members and may not offer the same 'fully comprehensive' service as the operators listed above. Nevertheless, they may well provide you with an affordable compromise between a fully fledged safari and the bus.

African Connection m 0782 016655; www.ac-safaris.com. A single-vehicle, Kampala-based outfit.
Trekkers Budget Travel m 0752 296197 or 0772 552819; e trekkers@susnow.org;

www.lakebunyonyi.net. This is an offshoot of the American-run Byoona Amagara resort at Lake Bunyonyi.

Other Ugandan tour operators include:

Adrift Adventure Company ✆ 0312 237 438; m 0772 237 438; e adrift@surfthesource.com; www.surfthesource.com
East African Safaris ✆ 0414 344332; e info@eastafricansafaris.net; www.eastafricansafaris.net
Magic Safaris ✆ 0414 342 926; e info@magic-safaris.com; www.magic-safaris.com

Mihingo Lodge ✆ 0752 410 509; e safari@mihingolodge.com; www.mihingolodge.com
Nalubale Rafting ✆ 0782 638 939; e bookings@nalubalerafting.com; www.nalubalerafting.com
Paraa and Mweya Lodges ✆ 0414 259 390/4/5; e marasa@starcom.co.ug
Volvo Safaris and Travel ✆ 0782 404330; e vst@travel-safaris.com; www.travel-safaris.com

Overseas-based tour operators include:

UK

Aardvark Safaris RBL Hse, Ordnance Rd, Tidworth, Hants SP9 7QD; ✆ John Spence or Richard Smith on 01980 849160; f 01980 849161; e mail@aardvarksafaris.com; www.aardvarksafaris.com. Private and small-group tailored itineraries.
Abercrombie and Kent Sloane Sq Hse, Holbein Pl, London SW1W 8NS; ✆ 0845 070 0611 (for UK reservations); www.abercrombiekent.co.uk. A specialist in luxury and adventure travel with over 40 years of experience.
Absolute Africa 41 Swanscombe Rd, Chiswick, London W4 2HR; ✆ 020 8742 0226; f 020 8995 6155; e absaf@actual.co.uk; www.absoluteafrica.com
Acacia Adventure Holidays 23a Craven Terrace, Lancaster Gate, London W2 3QH; ✆ 020 7706 4700; f 020 7706 4686; e info@acacia-africa.com; www.acacia-africa.com
Africa Travel Centre Leigh St, London WC1H 9EW; ✆ 020 7387 1211; f 020 7383 7512; e sales@africatravel.co.uk; www.africatravel.co.uk
African & Indian Explorations Afex House, Holwell, Burford, Oxon OX18 4JS; ✆ 01993 822443; e info@africanexplorations.com; www.explorationcompany.com
Cazenove and Loyd Safaris 9 Imperial Studios, 3–11 Imperial Rd, London SW6 2AG; ✆ 020 7384 2332; f 020 7384 2399; www.caz-loyd.com. Specialists in tailor-made private travel in Africa and the Indian Ocean.
Cox and Kings Travel Gordon Hse, 10 Greencoat Pl, London SW1P 1PH; ✆ (brochure requests) 01235

824404, (reservations) 020 7873 5000; f 020 7630 6038; e cox.kings@coxandkings.co.uk. Group and individual tours.
Nile Safaris 5 St Albans Mansions, Kensington Court Pl, London W8 5QH; ✆/f 020 7938 4066; e Suthjans@aol.com; www.nilesafaris.8m.com
Okavango Tours Marlborough Hse, 298 Regents Park Rd, London N3 2TJ; ✆ 020 8343 3283; f 020 8343 3287; e info@okavango.com; www.okavango.com
Oksana Travel 98b Water Lane, Wilmslow, Cheshire SK9 5BB; ✆ 01625 530035; f 0870 442 3303; e steve@oksana.co.uk; www.oksana.co.uk
Rainbow Tours 305 Upper St, London N1 2TU; ✆ 020 7226 1004; f 020 7226 2621; e info@rainbowtours.co.uk; www.rainbowtours.co.uk. Dynamic Africa specialists offering tailor-made safaris and other tours to Uganda, Rwanda and elsewhere.
Roxton Bailey Robinson Worldwide 25 High St, Hungerford, Berks RG17 0NF; ✆ 01488 689700; f 01488 681973; e safaris@rbrww.com; www.rbrww.com. Specialises in top-end safaris to east and southern Africa.
Safari Consultants Orchard Hse, Upper Rd, Little Cornard, Suffolk CO10 0NZ; ✆ 01787 228494; f 01787 228096; e bill@safariconsultantuk.com; www.safari-consultants.co.uk or www.safariconsultantuk.com. Tailor-made and small-group departures.
Scott Dunn World Fovant Mews, 12 Noyna Rd, London SW17 7PH; ✆ 020 8682 5010; f 020

3

8682 5090; e world@scottdunn.com;
www.scottdunn.com

Steppes Africa 51 Castle St, Cirencester, Glos GL7
1QD; ☏ 01285 650011; f 01285 885888;
e safari@steppesafrica.co.uk;
www.steppesafrica.co.uk

Uganda Experience Ridgeway Farm, Powick, Worcester
WR2 4SN; ☏ 01905 830745; f 01905 831745;
e ugexp@aol.com. Personally arranged upmarket
Uganda safaris.

Wildlife Worldwide Chameleon Hse, 162 Selsdon Rd,
South Croydon, Surrey CR2 6PJ; ☏ 020 8667 9158;
f 020 8667 1960; e sales@wildlifeworldwide.com;
www.wildlifeworldwide.com. Tailor-made and small-
group wildlife holidays.

World Odyssey 32 Sansome Walk, Worcester WR1
1NA; ☏ 01905 731 373; e info@world-
odyssey.com; www.world-odyssey.com

Zambezi Safari and Travel Co Ltd *UK head office:*
Ermington Mill, Ivybridge, Devon PL21 9NT;
☏ 01548 830059; f 01548 831352; e info@
zambezi.co.uk; www.zambezi.com. *Zimbabwe office:*
1 School Rd, Kariba; ☏ +263 61 3351; f +263 61
2291

US

Classic Africa Safaris 354 Meadowland Way,
Kearneysville, WV 25430; ☏ +1 304 724 8235;
f +1 304 724 8341; e phil.ward3@juno.com.
Fully escorted safaris. In Uganda; ☏ 0414 320121;
e classic@africaonline.co.ug

The African Adventure Company 5353 North Federal
Highway, Ste 300, Fort Lauderdale, Florida 33308;
☏ +954 491 8877; e safari@africa-
adventure.com; www.africanadventure.com

Volcanoes Safaris 4850 Manget Court, Dunwoody, GA
30338; ☏ +1 770 730 0960; f +1 305 946
0593; e salesusa@volcanoessafaris.com;
www.volcanoessafaris.com

ELSEWHERE

Hauser Exkursionen International GmbH Spiegelstr 9,
81241 München, Germany; ☏ +49 89 235 0060;
f +49 89 235 00699; e info@hauser-
exkursionen.de; www.hauser-exkursionen.de

KK United Travel Service International KK Uti Hse, 4-
5-5, Nakakasai, Edogawa-ku, Tokyo 134 0083;
☏ +81 3 3675 6636; f +81 3 3877 4779;
e waliangulu@aol.com

Pulse Africa PO Box 2417, Parklands 2121,
Johannesburg, South Africa; ☏ +27 11 325 2290 or
+44 020 8995 5909 (UK); f +27 11 325 2226;
e info@africansafari.co.za or
pulseafricauk@easynet.co.uk; www.africansafari.co.za
or www.pulseafrica.com

Sanctuary Lodges East Africa Njiro Hill, PO Box 427,
Arusha, Tanzania; ☏ +255 27 250 8346/7/8 or
+255 27 250 9816; f +255 27 250 8273/4112;
e malpers@sanctuarylodges.com;
www.sanctuarylodges.com

RED TAPE

Check well in advance that you have a valid **passport** and that it won't expire
within six months of the date on which you intend to *leave* Uganda. Should your
passport be lost or stolen, it will generally be easier to get a replacement if you have
a photocopy of the important pages.

If there is any possibility you'll want to drive or hire a vehicle while you're in
the country, do organise an **international driving licence**, which you may be
asked to produce together with your original licence. Any AA office in a country in
which you're licensed to drive will do this for a nominal fee. You may sometimes
be asked at the border or international airport for an **international health
certificate** showing you've had a yellow fever shot.

For security reasons, it's advisable to detail all your important information on
one sheet of paper, photocopy it, and distribute a few copies in your luggage, your
moneybelt, and amongst relatives or friends at home. The sort of things you want
to include are your travellers' cheque numbers and refund information, travel
insurance policy details and 24–hour emergency contact number, passport number,
details of relatives or friends to be contacted in an emergency, bank and credit card
details, camera and lens serial numbers, etc.

VISAS Nationals of most countries require a visa in order to enter Uganda. This can be bought in advance at any Ugandan embassy or high commission abroad, but usually it's simpler to buy the visa upon arrival, a straightforward procedure that takes a few minutes at Entebbe International Airport or any overland border. Though inevitably some queuing is involved most people will still find it more convenient, not to mention cheaper, than travelling twice into the middle of London (for example) to submit and later collect their visa. Visa rulings are prone to change, so all visitors are advised to check the current situation with their travel agent or a Ugandan diplomatic mission before they travel. A standard single-entry visa, valid for three months, costs US$30. Student visas cost US$20 while multiple-entry visas cost US$80 for up to six months or US$160 for one year. An inland transit visa costs US$15. Travellers with a single-entry visa intending to leave and return to Uganda (eg: to track gorillas in Uganda or DRC) must purchase another US$30 visa on re-entry. If however you intend to spend less than seven days in Uganda before leaving again, you can purchase a transit visa for only US$15. Otherwise you have to get another visa for US$30 and most nationals also require a visa to enter Rwanda, which costs US$50 and can be bought on arrival at any border.

Important note It seems that immigration authorities will now generally only stamp your passport for a maximum of one month upon arrival. This can be extended to three months at any immigration office. In Kampala, you will almost certainly be asked to provide an official letter from a sponsor or the hotel where you are staying. In Jinja, recent reports suggest you are more likely to have your stay extended to three months without producing any paperwork.

E UGANDAN DIPLOMATIC MISSIONS ABROAD

Belgium Av de Tervurn 317, 1150 Brussels; ☎ +32 11 762 58 25 (3 lines); f +32 11 763 04 38

Canada 231 Cobourg St, Ottawa KIN 8J2; ☎ +1 613 613 7797; f +1 613 232 6689

China 5 San Lt Tun Dong Jie, Beijing; ☎ +86 10 532 1708; f +86 10 532 2242

Denmark Sofievej 15, DK-2900, Heller up, Copenhagen; ☎ +45 31 62066; f +45 39 610148

Egypt 9 Midan El Messaha, Dokki, Cairo; ☎ +593 248 5975; f +593 348 5980

Ethiopia Africa Av H-18, K-36, Addis Ababa; ☎ +251 513531; f +251 514355

France 13 Av Raymond Poincaré, 75116, Paris; ☎ +33 53 70 62 70; f +33 53 70 85 15

Germany Dorenstrasse 14, 531 Bonn; ☎ +37 0228 355 02738; f +37 0228 351 692

India C-6/11 Vasant Vihar, New Delhi 110-05; ☎ +91 1 11 687 7687; f +91 1 11 687 4445

Italy Via Ennio Quirino Viscount S, 00193, Rome; ☎/f +39 322 52 20

Japan 39-15 Oyama-cho Shibuya-Ku, Tokyo 151; ☎ +81 3465 4552; f +81 3465 4970

Kenya Uganda Hse, 5th Fl, Kenyatta Av, Nairobi; ☎ +254 2 330801/34; f +254 2 330970

Nigeria Ladi Kwali Way, Maitama, PMB 143, Abuja FCT; ☎ +234 9 804384; f + 234 9 5234826

Russian Federation Per Sadovskikh 5, Moscow; ☎ +7 251 0060/2; f +7 200 1200

Rwanda Av de la Paix, BP, 656, Kigali; ☎ +250 72115; f +250 73551

South Africa 35B Trafalgar Court, 634 Park St, Pretoria; ☎ +27 12 344 4100; f +27 12 343 2809

Tanzania 25 Msasani Rd, Dar es Salaam; ☎ +253 22 266 7391; f +253 22 266 7224

UK Uganda Hse, 58/5 Trafalgar Sq, London WC2; ☎ +44 20 7839 5783; f +44 20 7839 8925. *Open 09.30–17.30. Ask for the information desk.*

UN (New York) Uganda Hse, 336 E 45th St, New York, NY 10017; ☎ +1 212 949 0110; f +1 212 687 4517. Permanent representative ☎ +1 212 697 2918.

US 5911 16th St, NW, Washington, DC 20011; ☎ +1 202 726 7100; f +1 202 726 1727

CUSTOMS The following items may be imported into Uganda without incurring customs duty: 400 cigarettes or 500g of tobacco; one bottle of spirits and wine and 2.5 litres of beer; 1oz bottle of perfume. Souvenirs may be exported without restriction but game trophies such as tooth, bone, horn, shell, claw, skin, hair, feather or other durable items are subject to export permits.

GETTING THERE AND AWAY

Uganda's international airport is at Entebbe, 40km from Kampala. A full list of international airlines that fly to Uganda is included under the *Kampala* listings in *Chapter 6*, page 154. People flying from Europe or North America to Uganda might find it easier to get a cheap ticket to Nairobi, the capital of Kenya and East Africa's major entry point. You can normally get between Nairobi and Kampala overland in a day (see *To/from Kenya* below).

In Europe, the best place to find cheap tickets to Africa is London. Two London travel agents specialise in Africa: **African Travel Specialists** (*Glen Hse, Stag Pl, London SW1E 5AG;* ↘ *020 7630 5434*) and **Africa Travel Centre** (*4 Medway Court, Leigh St, London WC1H 9QX;* ↘ *020 7387 1211;* f *020 7383 7512*). The website www.cheapflights.co.uk has been recommended by a traveller who got 30% off the standard British Airways fare to Entebbe.

Trailfinders (*42–48 Earls Court Rd, London W8 6EJ;* ↘ *020 7938 3366*) and STA (*117 Euston Rd, London WC1;* ↘ *020 7465 0486;* f *020 7388 0944*) are both respected agents who do cheap flights worldwide, and particularly worth speaking to for round-the-world-type tickets. There are STA branches in Bristol, Cambridge, Oxford, Leeds, Brighton, Glasgow, Newcastle, Aberdeen, Cardiff and Manchester.

Provided that you have a valid passport and a return ticket, you should whizz through the entrance formalities at Entebbe with no hassle. Visitors who arrive by air are often asked to produce a yellow fever vaccination certificate. If you arrive without this, you'll probably just be asked to bring it next time you fly in.

The only reason why a fly-in visitor would be likely to arrive in Uganda without a return ticket is because they intend to travel more widely in Africa. Not many people start their African travels in Uganda, because from most parts of the world it's far cheaper to fly to Nairobi; but if for some reason you will be arriving with a one-way ticket, there is a small but real possibility that you will be given a rough time by immigration officials concerned that you won't have enough funds to buy a flight out of the country. Obviously, the more money you have, the less likely they are to query your finances. And a credit card will almost certainly convince them to let you in. Assuming that you do intend to travel to neighbouring countries, you can underline this intention by arranging a visa or visitor's pass for the next country you plan to visit before you land in Uganda. Finally, an onward ticket technically is an entry requirement for Uganda, so there is little point in arguing the toss or becoming needlessly aggressive with immigration officials who are only doing the job they are paid to do – patient diplomacy is a far better approach.

The very worst that will happen if you arrive without a return ticket is that you will have to buy a ticket back to your home country before being allowed entry. Assuming you intend to leave Uganda overland, it is important you check with the relevant airline that this ticket will be refundable once you have left Uganda, and also that you select a departure date that will give you time to get to a country where you can organise the refund.

Once through customs and immigration, the first thing you will want to do is get some local currency. There are 24-hour foreign-exchange facilities at the airport, though the rates are lower than at private forex bureaux in town, so I wouldn't exchange any more money than I had to. A private taxi from the airport to Entebbe costs around US$2 and one to Kampala should cost no more than US$30. The alternative is to take a shared taxi between the airport and Entebbe, where you can pick up a minibus to the old taxi park in Kampala for roughly US$1 per person.

The airport departure tax of US$20 is now included in the final price of a return ticket to Uganda.

ARRIVING (AND LEAVING)

✈ By air With backing from South Africa and Switzerland, Uganda has launched its own airline. Victorian International Airlines (VB) will fly twice daily from Entebbe to Nairobi; from Entebbe to Johannesburg three times a week on Tuesday, Thursday and Sunday and to the Sudan capital, Juba, four times a week on Monday, Wednesday, Friday and Saturday. There are also plans to operate flights from Entebbe to Mombasa and Lusaka.

🚗 Overland Uganda borders five countries: Kenya, Tanzania, Rwanda, DRC and Sudan. A high proportion of visitors to Uganda enters and leaves the country overland at the borders with Kenya or Tanzania. Few people enter or leave Uganda from DRC or Rwanda, though a fair number cross briefly into these countries from Uganda to see mountain gorillas. I've not heard of any traveller crossing between Sudan and Uganda in years. Although international NGOs and other organisations are now active in southern Sudan following an apparent end to that country's interminable civil war it must still be considered, if no longer a no-go area, one that still entails extreme caution. Uganda's land borders are generally very relaxed. Provided that your papers are in order, you should have no problem, nor is there a serious likelihood of being asked about onward tickets, funds or vaccination certificates. About the worst you can expect at Ugandan customs is a cursory search of your luggage. It may be necessary to exchange money at any overland border in or out of Uganda; take a look at the box *Changing money at borders*, pages 90–1 for advice.

To/from Kenya Crossing between Kenya and Uganda couldn't be more straightforward, and there are several ways you can go about it. There is no longer a direct rail service between Nairobi and Kampala, but several bus services run directly between these cities. These take 12–15 hours including a couple of rest stops along the way. Your best bet seems to be the **Scandinavian Express** (✆ *0414 348895;* m *0312 260409 or 0772 377174; international contact numbers are as follows: Arusha;* ✆ *027 250 0153; Dar es Salaam;* ✆ *022 218 4833/4 or 0741 325474;* e *scandinavia@raha.com).* This company operates an exceptionally comfortable daily coach service departing at 13.00 (check-in 45 minutes earlier) from new premises on Lumumba Avenue near the French embassy on the leafy and affluent Nakasero Hill. It's an unexpectedly pleasant place that includes a good café and comfortable waiting room. One-way tickets cost Ush45,000. Connecting services to Tanzania are available from Nairobi. Through tickets from Kampala cost Ush65,000 to Arusha and Ush90,000 to Dar es Salaam.

Also recommended is the long-serving **Akamba Bus Company** (✆ *0414 250412;* m *0772 505539;* f *0414 250411; the Nairobi numbers are 02 340430 or 221779),* whose Kampala depot is on De Winton Street near the national theatre. Executive coaches leave twice daily in either direction at 07.00 and 15.00 and take between 12 and 15 hours. Tickets cost Ush30,000 to Nairobi with intermediate fares charged for stops in-between such as Kisumu, Nakuru and Naivasha. A more comfortable and faster Royal Coach costing Ush44,000 departs daily at 07.00, stopping only at Kisumu and Nairobi. A through ticket to Mombasa using a connecting service costs Ush50,000. Additional connecting coaches link to destinations in Tanzania. Through-ticket rates from Kampala cost Ush49,000 to Moshi; Ush47,000 to Arusha and Ush74,000 to Dar es Salaam.

The cheapest tickets to Nairobi cost Ush22,000 by Busscar at 8 Burton Street, and Ush23,000 at Gateway. It must be said that in terms of comfort and safety you generally get what you pay for; I'd certainly be reluctant to travel all the way to Nairobi with Gateway.

It is also possible to do the trip between Nairobi and Kampala in stages, which will take two days by road now that the passenger train service between Nairobi and Malaba, the border town, has been suspended. Plenty of transport connects Kisumu, Eldoret and other major centres in western Kenya to either the Malaba or Busia border post. Another option, currently little used, is the Suam border to the north of Mount Elgon (see *Sipi Falls*, pages 448–9, and *Suam*, page 453).

If you are crossing from Kenya in your own vehicle, bear in mind that fuel prices in Uganda are double those in Kenya, so stock up accordingly.

To/from Tanzania Following the suspension of the ferry service between Mwanza and Port Bell, the best way to cross between Uganda and Tanzania depends on which part of Tanzania you want to visit. The only direct road between the two countries connects Masaka to the port of Bukoba, crossing at the Mutukula border post. From Bukoba, overnight ferries continue to Mwanza thrice weekly. It is possible to travel between Kampala and Bukoba in hops, but far easier to use the new direct bus services run by Falcon and Tawfiq buses. These leave from the central bus park in Kampala on Tuesday, Thursday and Sunday at 10.30, in time to connect with the overnight ferry to Mwanza, and return on the following day. Tickets cost Ush20,000.

Most road routes heading south from Mwanza are pretty awful. Far better to use the thrice-weekly passenger-train service via Tabora to Dar es Salaam on the coast or Kigoma on Lake Tanganyika. It is also possible to travel by road from Mwanza to Arusha in northeastern Tanzania. A couple of buses or Land Rovers daily do the 12–18-hour trip from Mwanza to Arusha via the Serengeti and Ngorongoro, a good way of seeing something of the Serengeti if you're not planning on doing an organised safari – but you will have to pay at least US$80 in national park entrance fees, so it isn't a cheap option. There is also a bus service from Mwanza to Arusha via Singada, but this is very uncomfortable and often takes as long as three days!

Frankly, if you are in Uganda and want to get to Arusha or Moshi (or even to a lesser extent to Dar es Salaam), it will be quicker, cheaper and more comfortable to travel via Nairobi. Scandinavian Coaches have a link service straight from Kampala through Nairobi to Arusha. There are also regular shuttle buses between Nairobi and Arusha, taking around five hours and costing in the region of US$15, assuming that you're permitted to pay residents' rates (which you normally will be).

You can do the same trip in about seven hours and at considerably less cost by using local transport and changing vehicles at the Namanga border post. But one word of warning: Nairobi is East Africa's crime capital: if you are merely passing through *en route* to Arusha, wandering around with all your luggage on your back is practically asking to be mugged. However and wherever you arrive in Nairobi, you are urged to get a private taxi directly to a hotel, or if you're heading on straight to Tanzania, to Ronald Ngala Street, where you'll find plenty of minibuses heading to Namanga. A taxi shouldn't cost much more than US$3, and the driver will be able to put you on the next minibus heading in the direction you want. Once on the minibus, ignore the slimeballs who've been setting up travellers for the past few years by inventing problems relating to changing money at Namanga – whatever anybody tells you (driver, fellow passenger, doesn't matter) there is a bank at Namanga and it's no problem to change money privately when it's closed, ideally on the more chilled Tanzanian side of the border.

To/from Sudan The 'Nile Route' via Juba was once very popular with travellers but the ongoing civil war in Sudan has meant that the south of that country has been completely closed to tourists for longer than a decade. This may change following a 2005 peace agreement that has attracted a flood of NGOs and commercial opportunists into southern Sudan. Almost without exception, such people report a beautiful country with friendly people, but they also emphasise that a lot of work – not to mention marketing – will be necessary before any level of tourism activity is possible or advisable. Ongoing problems include widespread gun ownership amongst a population for whom war has been the norm for decades, landmines, and the fact that southern Sudan is the favoured retreat for the murderous rebel army that has plagued northern Uganda for 20 years. For further information, you might want to get hold of Paul Clammer's pioneering Bradt guide to Sudan (*www.bradtguides.com*).

To/from Rwanda/DRC See the boxes on pages 252–3 (Rwanda) and pages 256–7 (DRC) for further information.

$ FINANCES

From the security point of view, it's generally advisable to bring the bulk of your money to Africa in the form of **travellers' cheques**, which will be refunded if they are lost or stolen. Bear in mind however that outside the capital, options for changing TCs are frequently limited to the local branch of Stanbic Bank in major regional towns. For more details, see the section on foreign exchange on pages 89–92. The most widely recognised currencies are the US dollar, pound sterling and euro. The **euro** is now as widely accepted as the US dollar and is increasingly favoured by European travellers as a hard currency cash source (no need to change euro to dollars to Uganda shillings) with the added advantage that (besides its current strength) there are no problems with older notes being rejected. Other internationally recognised currencies will be fine in major cities, but they may cause some confusion at banks in smaller centres.

Assuming that you do bring travellers' cheques, you should choose American Express, this being the only brand presently widely accepted, with Thomas Cook as a second option. Bring your proof of purchase with you, as you'll need it to exchange the travellers' cheques in Uganda, but carry it separately. Buy your travellers' cheques in a healthy mix of denominations, since you may sometimes need to change a small sum only, for instance when you're about to cross into another country. On the other hand, you don't want an impossibly thick wad of cheques. For a trip to one country, I'd take five US$20 cheques and the remainder in denominations of US$100. Whatever your bank at home might say, currency regulations and other complications make it practically impossible to break down a large denomination travellers' cheque into smaller ones in most African countries, so don't bring travellers' cheques in denominations larger than US$100.

Visitors who opt to carry most of their funds in the form of travellers' cheques should still bring some **hard currency** cash, ideally US dollars. Large denomination bills (US$50/100) attract a better exchange than travellers' cheques. Smaller denominations (US$20 and less) attract a lousy rate, but they can be useful in some situations, for instance direct hard-currency payments or when you want to exchange a small sum shortly before departure. I would advise bringing all the cash you intend to exchange directly in US$100 bills, but also carrying a few smaller denomination notes just in case, and taking them back home should you ever need them. Note that US dollar bills issued before 2000 are not accepted.

3

No matter how long you are travelling in Uganda (or elsewhere in Africa except South Africa) make sure that you bring enough money so that you won't need to have any more transferred or drafted across. This is a notoriously tedious process and there is a real risk the money will never arrive. Even if it does arrive safely, you will battle to have it given to you in hard currency. Credit cards are accepted in most upmarket hotels and in some shops and restaurants in the capital, Visa being far more widely accepted than MasterCard or any other option. Some nationwide banks allow you to draw a limited amount of cash in local currency against an internationally recognised credit or debit card at their ATMs (automated teller machines) in Kampala and upcountry. If you do intend to use credit cards, and you'll be away for a while, it's worth arranging some mode of payment at home, whether direct debit from your bank or a few signed cheques left with your folks. As far as purchasing power is concerned, outside Kampala, credit cards are close to useless except at a few safari lodges where a 5% surcharge applies. In my view, credit cards are best carried to Uganda as a contingent rather than primary source of funds.

CARRYING MONEY AND VALUABLES It is advisable to carry all your hard currency as well as your passport and other important documentation in a moneybelt. The ideal moneybelt for Africa is one that can be hidden beneath your clothing. External moneybelts may be fashionable, but wearing one in Africa is as good as telling thieves that all your valuables are there for the taking. Use a belt made of cotton or another natural fabric, bearing in mind that such fabrics tend to soak up a lot of sweat, so you will need to wrap plastic around everything inside.

The best insurance against complete disaster should you be robbed is to keep things well documented. If you carry a photocopy of the main page of your passport, you will be issued with a new one more promptly. In addition, note down details of your bank, credit card (if you have one), travel insurance policy and camera equipment (including serial numbers), as well as your travellers' cheque numbers and *a record of which ones you have cashed*, and the international refund-assistance telephone number and local agent. If all this information fits on one piece of paper, you can keep photocopies on you and with a friend at home.

BUDGETING Independent travel in Uganda is inexpensive by most standards, but your budget will depend greatly on how and where you travel. The following guidelines may be useful to people trying to keep costs to a minimum.

In most parts of the country, it will be difficult to keep your basic travel expenses (food, transport and accommodation) to much below US$20 per day. You could spend considerably less – say around US$10 per day – by camping everywhere and by staying put for a few days at somewhere cheap like the Ssese Islands or Lake Nkuruba. Typically a room in the most basic sort of local hotel will cost US$3–5, camping around US$2 per person, and a meal US$2–5 depending on whether you're content to stick to the predictable local fare or want to eat a more varied menu. A treat in one of Kampala's best restaurants won't cost more than US$8 for a main course. Transport costs will probably work out at around US$4–5 daily, assuming that you're on the move every other day or thereabouts. If you don't want *always* to stay in the most basic room and *always* to go for the cheapest item on the menu, I would bank on spending around US$20–25 per day on basic travel costs. You could travel a lot more comfortably for around US$50 per day.

Unless you go on an organised safari, the only expenses over and above your basic travel costs will be national park fees. You can probably expect to spend around an extra US$25–35 per day for every 24-hour period you spend in a national park though this is difficult to quantify, since after the first day (US$25 for foreign

From a letter by Steve Lenartowicz

Ugandans are very interested in children and make them most welcome. On buses and *matatus*, the rule seems to be that you pay full fare for the seats you occupy, and so children sitting on a lap go free. Similarly, hotels are usually happy for children (and adults!) to share beds, and we usually negotiated to pay per bed rather than per person. Often, hotels were able to provide an extra bed or mattress on the floor. We travelled light, taking no camping gear or bedding, but we carried mosquito nets and often used them (although mosquitoes were never bad). Don't take white clothing, as the ubiquitous red dust and mud get everywhere. It was easier to order adult portions of meals and to share them rather than to try to negotiate children's portions. National park fees are significantly reduced for children.

If you are taking children to Uganda, you might like to get hold of the book *Your Child's Health Abroad: A Manual for Travelling Parents*, by Dr Jane Wilson-Howarth and Dr Matthew Ellis (Bradt, 2005).

tourists), fees for subsequent days reduce while food/accommodation may be slightly more expensive than elsewhere and activities such as launch trips and nature walks will incur additional expense. Gorilla tracking, whether you do it in Uganda, Rwanda or DRC, will cost between US$300 and US$400 in fees and visas.

If funds are tight, it is often a useful idea to separate your daily budget from one-off expenses. At current prices, a daily budget of around US$20–25 with US$300–500 set aside for expensive one-off activities (excluding gorilla tracking) would be comfortable for most travellers.

WHAT TO TAKE

Two simple rules to bear in mind when you decide what to take with you to Uganda – particularly if you expect to use public transport – are to bring with you *everything* that might not be readily available when you need it, and to carry as little as possible. Somewhat contradictory rules, you might think, and you'd be right – so the key is finding the right balance, something that probably depends on personal experience as much as anything. Worth stressing is that most genuine necessities are surprisingly easy to get hold of in the main centres in Uganda, and that most of the ingenious gadgets you can buy in camping shops are unlikely to amount to much more than dead weight on the road. If it came to it, you could easily travel in Uganda with little more than a change of clothes, a few basic toiletries and a medical kit.

CARRYING YOUR LUGGAGE Visitors who are unlikely to be carrying their luggage for any significant distance will probably want to pack most of it in a conventional suitcase. Make sure the case is tough and durable, and that it seals well, so that the contents will survive bumpy drives to the game reserves. A lock is a good idea, not only for flights, but for when you leave your case in a hotel room – theft from upmarket hotels is unusual in Uganda, but it can happen anywhere in the world, and even a flimsy lock will act as a serious deterrent to casual finger-dipping. A daypack will be useful on safari, and you should be able to pack your luggage in such a manner that any breakable goods can be carried in the body of the vehicle, and on your lap when necessary – anything like an mp3 player or camera will suffer heavily from vibrations on rutted roads.

If you are likely to use public transport, then an internal frame backpack is the most practical way to carry your luggage. Once again, ensure your pack is durable, that the seams and zips are properly sewn, and that it has several pockets. If you intend doing a lot of hiking, you definitely want a backpack designed for this purpose. On the other hand, if you'll be staying at places where it might be a good idea to shake off the sometimes negative image attached to backpackers, then there would be obvious advantages in using a suitcase that converts into a backpack.

Before I started travelling with my wife Ariadne and her heavy camera equipment, my preference over either of the above was for a robust 35l daypack. The advantages of keeping luggage as light and compact as possible are manifold. For starters, you can rest it on your lap on bus trips, avoiding complications such as extra charges for luggage, arguments about where your bag should be stored, and the slight but real risk of theft if your luggage ends up on the roof. A compact bag also makes for greater mobility, whether you're hiking or looking for a hotel in town. The sacrifice? Leave behind camping equipment and a sleeping bag. Do this, and it's quite possible to fit everything you truly need into a 35l daypack, and possibly even a few luxuries – I refuse to travel without binoculars, a bird field guide and at least five novels, and am still able to keep my weight down to around 8kg. Frankly, it puzzles me what the many backpackers who wander around with an enormous pack and absolutely no camping equipment actually carry around with them!

If your luggage won't squeeze into a daypack, a sensible compromise is to carry a large daypack in your rucksack. That way, you can carry a tent and other camping equipment when you need it, but at other times reduce your luggage to fit into a daypack and leave what you're not using in storage. Travellers carrying a lot of valuable items should look for a pack that can easily be padlocked.

CAMPING EQUIPMENT There is a strong case for carrying a tent to Uganda, particularly if you are on a tight budget. Campsites exist in most Ugandan national parks, forest reserves and towns. Travellers who intend doing a fair bit of off-the-beaten-track hiking will find a tent a useful fallback where no other accommodation exists.

If you decide to carry camping equipment, the key is to look for the lightest available gear. It is now possible to buy a lightweight tent weighing little more than 2kg, but make sure that the one you buy is reasonably mosquito-proof. Usable sleeping bags weighing even less than 2kg can be bought, but, especially as many lightweight sleeping bags are not particularly warm, my own preference is for a sheet sleeping bag, supplemented by wearing heavy clothes in cold weather. Also essential is a roll-mat, which will serve as both insulation and padding. In Uganda, there is no real need to carry a stove, as firewood is available at most campsites where meals cannot be bought. If you do carry a stove, it's worth knowing that Camping Gaz cylinders are not readily available. Try the Game store in Kampala's Lugogo Mall. If you are camping in the rainy season, bring a box of firelighter blocks: they will get a fire going in the most unpromising conditions. It would also be advisable to carry a pot, plate, cup and cutlery – lightweight cooking utensils are available at most camping shops in Western countries.

CLOTHES Assuming that you have the space, you ought to carry at least one change of shirt and underwear for every day you will spend on safari. Organising laundry along the way is a pain in the neck, and the dusty conditions will practically enforce a daily change of clothes. It's a good idea to keep separate one or two shirts for evening use only.

Otherwise, and especially if you are travelling with everything on your back, try to keep your clothes to a minimum, bearing in mind that you can easily and cheaply replace worn items in markets. In my opinion, the minimum you need is one or possibly two pairs of trousers and/or skirts, one pair of shorts, three shirts or T-shirts, one light sweater, maybe a light waterproof windbreaker during the rainy season, enough socks and underwear to last five to seven days, one solid pair of shoes or boots for walking, and one pair of sandals, thongs or other light shoes.

Trousers It's widely held that jeans are not ideal for African travel, since they are bulky to carry, hot to wear and take ages to dry. I've repeated this advice in earlier editions of this guide, and seldom used to travel in jeans myself, but these days I almost always do, since they have the advantages of durability and comfort, and of hiding the dust and dirt that tends to accumulate on public transport A good alternative is light cotton trousers, which dry more quickly and weigh less. Try to avoid light colours, as they show dirt more easily. If you intend spending a while in montane regions, instead of bringing a second pair of trousers, you might prefer to carry tracksuit bottoms. These can serve as thermal underwear and as extra cover on chilly nights, and they can also be worn over shorts on chilly mornings. Shorts on men are acceptable for travel and informal situations, though many Ugandans consider them inappropriate on grown men whose schooldays are clearly long past. Before travelling in shorts, it's worth considering whether you'll be able to don longer trousers before mosquitoes start snapping at your ankles.

Skirts Like trousers, these are best made of a light natural fabric such as cotton. For reasons of protocol, it is advisable to wear skirts that go below the knee: short skirts will cause needless offence to many Ugandans (especially Muslims) and, whether you like it or not, they may be perceived as provocative in some quarters. There are parts of Africa where it's still considered slightly off for women to wear trousers or jeans rather than a skirt, but this isn't a real issue in Uganda. In rural areas, women are probably best off not wearing shorts.

Shirts T-shirts are arguably better than button-up shirts, because they are lighter and less bulky. That said, I've found that the top pocket of a shirt (particularly if the pocket buttons up) is a good place to carry my spending money in markets and bus stations, as it's easier to keep an eye on than trouser pockets.

Sweaters Uganda is generally warm at night, though at higher altitudes (for instance in Fort Portal) it can cool down in the evening. For general purposes, one warm sweater, fleece jacket or sweatshirt should be adequate. If you intend hiking on Mount Elgon or the Rwenzoris, you will need very warm clothing. Western Uganda has a wet climate, and showers are normal even during the supposed dry seasons. A light waterproof jacket is close to essential. Alternatively, a lightweight umbrella can be useful against rain and sun (local ones are flimsy so bring this with you).

Socks and underwear These must be made from natural fabrics, and bear in mind that re-using them when sweaty will encourage fungal infections such as athlete's foot, as well as prickly heat in the groin region. Socks and underpants are light and compact enough for it to be worth bringing a week's supply.

Shoes Unless you're serious about off-road hiking, bulky hiking boots are probably over the top in Uganda. They're also very heavy, whether they are on your feet or in your pack. A good pair of walking shoes, preferably made of leather and with some ankle support, is a good compromise. It's also useful to carry sandals, thongs or other light shoes.

Ariadne Van Zandbergen

EQUIPMENT Although with some thought and an eye for composition you can take reasonable photos with a 'point-and-shoot' camera, you need an SLR camera if you are at all serious about photography. Modern SLRs tend to be very clever, with automatic programmes for almost every possible situation, but remember that these programmes are limited in the sense that the camera cannot think, but only makes calculations. Every starting amateur photographer should read a photographic manual for beginners and get to grips with such basics as the relationship between aperture and shutter speed.

Always buy the best lens you can afford. The lens determines the quality of your photo more than the camera body. Fixed fast lenses are ideal, but very costly. Zoom lenses allow you to change the composition without having to change lenses the whole time. If you carry only one lens, a 28–70mm (digital 17–55mm) or similar zoom should be ideal. For a second lens, a lightweight 80–200mm or 70–300mm (digital 55–200mm) or similar will be excellent for candid shots and varying your composition. Wildlife photography will be very frustrating if you don't have at least a 300mm lens. For a small loss of quality, tele-converters are a cheap and compact way to increase magnification: a 300mm lens with a 1.4x converter becomes 420mm, and with a 2x it becomes 600mm. Note, however, that 1.4x and 2x tele-converters reduce the speed of your lens by 1.4 and 2 stops respectively.

For wildlife photography from a safari vehicle, a solid beanbag, which you can make yourself very cheaply, will be necessary to avoid blurred images, and is more useful than a tripod. A clamp with a tripod head screwed on to it can be attached to the vehicle as well. Modern dedicated flash units are easy to use; aside from the obvious need to flash when you photograph at night, you can improve a lot of photos in difficult 'high contrast' or very dull light with some fill-in flash. It pays to have a proper flash unit as opposed to a built-in camera flash.

DIGITAL/FILM Digital photography is now the preference of most amateur and professional photographers, with the resolution of digital cameras improving the whole time. For ordinary prints a 6 megapixel camera is fine. For better results and the possibility to enlarge images and for professional reproduction, higher resolution is available up to 16 megapixels.

Memory space is important. The number of pictures you can fit on a memory card depends on the quality you choose. Calculate in advance how many pictures you can fit on a card and either take enough cards to last for your trip, or take a storage drive onto which you can download the content. A laptop gives the advantage that you can see your pictures properly at the end of each day and edit and delete rejects, but a storage device is lighter and less bulky. These drives come in different capacities up to 80GB.

Rather than spending a fortune outfitting yourself for Africa before leaving home, you might follow the lead of informed travellers and volunteers who pack a minimum of clothes and buy the remainder in Kampala's superb Owino Market. This sells secondhand clothes from Europe and the US which have been bought by exporters in bulk from charity shops for export to the Third World where they are sorted, graded and priced accordingly for sale in markets and by hawkers. An American journalist recently trailed a T-shirt from a US charity shop to eventual purchase in a remote village on Mount Elgon. You'll benefit a Ugandan when you purchase a nearly new pair of cotton chinos for around US$4–5, and you'll also have saved yourself US$30 on a new pair as well as saving luggage space and weight. Bargains include cotton clothing, lightweight fleece jackets, hiking boots

Bear in mind that digital camera batteries, computers and other storage devices need charging, so make sure you have all the chargers, cables and converters with you. Most hotels have charging points, but do enquire about this in advance. When camping you might have to rely on charging from the car battery; a spare battery is invaluable.

If you are shooting film, 100 to 200 ISO print film and 50 to 100 ISO slide film are ideal. Low ISO film is slow but fine grained and gives the best colour saturation, but will need more light, so support in the form of a tripod or monopod is important. You can also bring a few 'fast' 400 ISO films for low-light situations where a tripod or flash is not an option.

DUST AND HEAT Dust and heat are often a problem. Keep your equipment in a sealed bag, stow films in an airtight container (eg: a small cooler bag) and avoid exposing equipment and film to the sun. Digital cameras are prone to collecting dust particles on the sensor which results in spots on the image. The dirt mostly enters the camera when changing lenses, so be careful when doing this. To some extent photos can be 'cleaned' up afterwards in Photoshop, but this is time-consuming. You can have your camera sensor professionally cleaned, or you can do this yourself with special brushes and swabs made for the purpose, but note that touching the sensor might cause damage and should only be done with the greatest care.

LIGHT The most striking outdoor photographs are often taken during the hour or two of 'golden light', after dawn and before sunset. Shooting in low light may enforce the use of very low shutter speeds, in which case a tripod will be required to avoid camera shake.

With careful handling, side lighting and back lighting can produce stunning effects, especially in soft light and at sunrise or sunset. Generally, however, it is best to shoot with the sun behind you. When photographing animals or people in the harsh midday sun, images taken in light but even shade are likely to be more effective than those taken in direct sunlight or patchy shade, since the latter conditions create too much contrast.

PROTOCOL In some countries, it is unacceptable to photograph local people without permission, and many people will refuse to pose or will ask for a donation. In such circumstances, don't try to sneak photographs as you might get yourself into trouble. Even the most willing subject will often pose stiffly when a camera is pointed at them; relax them by making a joke, and take a few shots in quick succession to improve the odds of capturing a natural pose.

Ariadne Van Zandbergen is a professional travel and wildlife photographer specialising in Africa. She runs The Africa Image Library. For photo requests, visit www.africaimagelibrary.com or contact her by email at ariadne@hixnet.co.za.

and brand-name frocks. Owino Market (officially renamed St Balikudembe Market in 2004) is conveniently located near the bus and taxi parks. Jinja and Fort Portal markets are also pretty good for secondhand clothes.

OTHER USEFUL ITEMS Most backpackers, even those with no intention of camping, carry a **sleeping bag**. A lightweight sleeping bag will be more than adequate in most parts of Uganda; better still in this climate would be to carry a sheet sleeping bag, something you can easily make yourself. The one time when you will definitely need an all-weather sleeping bag is on high mountains. You might meet travellers who, when they stay in local lodgings, habitually place their own sleeping bag on top of the bedding provided. Nutters, in my opinion, and I'd imagine that a sleeping bag placed on a flea-ridden bed would be unlikely to provide significant protection, rather more likely to become flea-infested itself.

I wouldn't leave home without **binoculars**, which some might say makes *me* the nutter. Seriously though, if you're interested in natural history, it's difficult to imagine anything that will give you such value-for-weight entertainment as a pair of light compact binoculars, which these days needn't be much heavier or bulkier than a pack of cards. Binoculars are essential if you want to get a good look at birds (Africa boasts a remarkably colourful avifauna, even if you've no desire to put a name to everything that flaps) or to watch distant mammals in game reserves. For most purposes, 7x21 compact binoculars will be fine, though some might prefer 7x35 traditional binoculars for their larger field of vision. Serious birdwatchers will find a 10x magnification more useful.

Some travellers like to carry their own **padlock**. This would be useful if you have a pack that is lockable, and in remote parts of the country it might be necessary for rooms where no lock is provided. If you are uneasy about security in a particular guesthouse, you may like to use your own lock instead of or in addition to the one provided. Although combination locks are reputedly easier to pick than conventional padlocks, I think you'd be safer with a combination lock in Uganda, because potential thieves will have far more experience of breaking locks with keys.

Your **toilet bag** should at the very minimum include soap (secured in a plastic bag or soap holder unless you enjoy a soapy toothbrush!), shampoo, toothbrush and toothpaste. This sort of stuff is easy to replace as you go along, so there's no need to bring family-sized packs. Men will probably want a **razor**. Women should carry at least enough **tampons** and/or **sanitary pads** to see them through at least one heavy period, since these items may not always be immediately available. Nobody should forget to bring a **towel**, or to keep handy a roll of **loo paper** which, although widely available at shops and kiosks, cannot always be relied upon to be present where it's most urgently needed.

Other essentials include a **torch**, a **penknife** (or arguably more useful, a **Leatherman**-style tool) and a compact **alarm clock** for those early morning starts. As load shedding (a euphemism for scheduled power cuts) becomes an increasingly important factor of day-to-day life, so does a powerful **torch** rank as an increasingly important item of luggage. If you're interested in what's happening in the world, you might also think about carrying a **short-wave radio**. Some travellers carry **games** – most commonly a pack of cards, less often chess or draughts or Travel Scrabble. Many older hotels have baths but no bath plugs, so you might want to consider carrying your own **universal bath plug**.

You should carry a small **medical kit**, the contents of which are discussed in *Chapter 5, Health*, as are **mosquito nets**. If you wear **contact lenses**, bring all the fluids you need, since they are not available in Uganda. You might also want to bring a pair of glasses to wear on long bus rides, and on safari – many lens wearers suffer badly in dusty conditions. In general, since many people find the intense sun and dry climate irritate their eyes, you might consider reverting to glasses. For those who wear **glasses**, it's worth bringing a spare pair, though a new pair can be made up cheaply and quickly in most towns, provided that you have your prescription available.

Novels are difficult to get hold of outside of Kampala. Either bring a supply with you or visit the excellent Aristoc bookshops on Kampala Road and in Garden City which stock an excellent range of literature, present bestsellers, Africana, and local-interest material (including this guidebook). Books are competitively priced and sometimes cheaper than UK prices.

4

Travelling in Uganda

TOURIST INFORMATION AND SERVICES

Tourism Uganda has a tourist information office in Impala House on Kimathi Avenue in Kampala (see *Chapter 6*, page 161) while the Uganda Wildlife Authority (UWA) has an information and booking office in Kampala as well as local information offices in Masindi (for Murchison Falls) and Kabale and Kisoro (for Bwindi and Mgahinga) and Mbale (Mount Elgon). See listings for individual towns in the regional chapters for further details.

Otherwise, there are few official sources of travel information in Uganda. The best source of reliable up-to-date information is other travellers and popular travel hubs such as the Backpackers and Red Chilli in Kampala, Explorers Backpackers at Jinja and nearby Bujagali Falls, and the Bunyonyi Overland Resort at Lake Bunyonyi near Kabale.

$ MONEY

The local currency is the Uganda shilling, which trades at around Ush1,850 to the US dollar at the time of writing (2006), representing a devaluation of around 60% since the late 1990s after having held fairly steady for most of that decade. Notes are printed in denominations of Ush50,000, 20,000, 10,000, 5,000 and 1,000. Ush500, 200, 100, 50 notes have been replaced by coins and are no longer legal tender.

FOREIGN EXCHANGE Assuming that you're carrying all your money in US dollars cash (denominations of US$50 or higher printed after the year 2000) or in pounds sterling and euro, that you never stray outside of Kampala, and that you hibernate over weekends and public holidays, the process of converting these funds into local currency in Uganda could scarcely be more straightforward. Banks and bureaux de change (known locally as forex bureaux) all around the capital will convert US dollars cash to local currency at a moment's notice. At a private 'forex,' this transaction seldom takes more than a minute or two, and no passport or other documentation is required. A bit more paperwork is involved at banks. The exchange rate against US dollars is generally more favourable at a forex than at any bank, and the previous day's rate offered by a selection of the capital's more prominent bureaux is listed daily in the *Monitor* and *New Vision* newspapers.

Banks are open from 09.00 to 15.00 on weekdays (though some banks on Kampala Road do stay open later) and from 09.00 to 12.00 on Saturdays. Forex offices may open up earlier, they typically close at 17.00, and are also open on Saturday mornings. All banks and practically all forexes close on Sundays and public holidays. Most upmarket hotels in the capital and some elsewhere in the country will exchange money outside of normal banking hours, but generally at less favourable rates, and most offer this service only to hotel residents. In

CHANGING MONEY AT BORDERS

The black market that previously thrived in Uganda was killed off by private forex bureaux some years ago, and the only circumstance where it is still normal to change money on the street is at overland borders. There is generally nowhere else to change money both legally and conveniently at borders. (Some crossings do have a branch of Stanbic Bank. However even if you do arrive during opening hours, if you're crossing the border by bus your driver will have sped onwards towards Kampala long before you get to the front of the queue.) Nevertheless, you'll almost certainly need some local currency, perhaps to pay for an onward bus ride to the next town and a room when you get there. Moreover, if you expect to arrive in that town after banks have closed or over the weekend, you will need sufficient local currency to see you through until the next banking day. One way around this, assuming that the opportunity presents itself, is to ask travellers coming from the country you plan to enter whether they have any leftover cash to swap.

Failing that, most border crossings are spiced up with the added adventure of trying to locate some local cash – technically illegal on some borders, but usually handled openly and with no risk of running into trouble with the authorities. As a rule you won't get the greatest rate of exchange, which is fair enough, considering that moneychangers, like banks, need to make a cut on the deal by offering different rates of conversion in either direction. Nevertheless, there's no sense in exchanging more money than you'll require before you reach a bank or forex bureau. The only exception is when you have a surfeit of cash from the country you're leaving and no intention of returning there – the border may be the last place you can offload it.

Many of the private moneychangers at borders are also part-time con artists. It will help you in dealing with these guys if you've checked the approximate exchange rate in advance with a fellow passenger and calculated roughly what sum of local currency you should expect. I prefer to carry a small surplus of the currency of the country I am leaving (the equivalent of about US$10) to change into the currency of the country I am entering. Whether I exchange local or hard currency, I routinely stash whatever bill(s) I intend to change in a pocket discrete from my main stash of foreign currency before I arrive at the border. Personally, I'm not too worried about being offered a slightly lower rate than might be expected, since pushing too hard carries the risk of weeding out the honest guys and leaving only the con artists (and if I'm offered an exceptionally good rate, I know I'm being set up). I am wary of allowing a quick-talking moneychanger in a chaotic environment to exploit the decimal shifts involved in many African currency transactions.

Should you be surrounded by a mob of yelling moneychangers, pick any one of them and tell him that you will only discuss rates when his pals back off. Having agreed a rate, insist on taking the money and counting it before you hand over, or expose the location of, your own money. Should the amount that the moneychanger hands you be incorrect, it is almost certainly not a mistake, but phase one of an elaborate con trick, so it's safest to hand the wad of cash back and refuse to have anything further to do with him. Alternatively, if you do decide to continue, then recount the money after he hands it back to you and keep doing so until you have the correct amount counted in your hand. The reason for this is that some crooked moneychangers have such sleight of hand that they can seemingly add notes to a wad while actually removing a far greater number, all right in front of your eyes. Only when you are sure you have the right amount should you hand over your money.

Kampala, your best bet on Sunday is the private forex office within the Speke Hotel which is open seven days a week, as are forex bureaux and banks at Entebbe International Airport which normally stay open late enough to serve passengers on all incoming and outgoing flights. If later you do find you exchanged more than you actually required in Uganda, it's straightforward to convert it back to foreign currency in a matter of minutes at any forex bureau in Kampala or at Entebbe International Airport, albeit at a slight loss.

So far, so good! But there are a few complications. In Uganda, as elsewhere in East Africa, US dollar banknotes printed before 2000 are not accepted, owing to a prevalence of forgeries dating from this period. Nor will banks or forex bureaux accept any torn or blemished notes, no matter how insignificant the damage. Also, significantly poorer rates – up to 20% lower – are offered for denominations of US$20 or less. Furthermore, many financial institutions will look upon with suspicion – or reject altogether – your travellers' cheques. The story is that a few years back some Ugandan banks were defrauded by a series of forgeries that left the banks substantially out of pocket and understandably reluctant to accept travellers' cheques at all, let alone without backup documentation. The prime exceptions are a few major international banks, notably Stanbic, Barclays (a maximum of US$500) and Standard Chartered which will accept American Express travellers' cheques. They may also accept Thomas Cook cheques but this seems to be at the discretion of the branch. As is normally the case, you'll need to show the bank your passport, but it is also likely they'll demand to see the proof of purchase.

This situation presents something of a quandary to anybody carrying travellers' cheques. The sole advantage of travellers' cheques over cash (and the reason that they effectively cost more) is the guarantee of a refund should they be lost or stolen, which will be nullified should the proof of purchase be lost or stolen at the same time. In other words, while the issuing companies decree that one should never carry travellers' cheques and the related proof of purchase in the same place, the banking rules in Uganda enforce one to do precisely this, and in the circumstance where arguably they are most exposed to theft – walking the streets of the capital. Fortunately, unlike Nairobi, Kampala is not a city that carries a significant risk of daylight theft, but clearly it does make sense to carry the travellers' cheques and proof of purchase separately on your person, or for couples to divide the two between them, reducing the risk of both being stolen at the same time. Should you not have your proof of purchase to hand, the Standard Chartered Bank on Kampala Road may exchange travellers' cheques after a grilling by the bank manager, but this is a lengthy process, with an uncertain outcome. It's worth double-checking before you sign any travellers' cheques that you have presented all the necessary paperwork and have an acceptable brand, *and* that the cashier is ready to accept them. Should you do so and the bank decides for whatever reason to decline them, you won't, of course, be able to use them elsewhere

Out of Kampala, forex complications have become things of the past with the expansion of private banks, notably Stanbic, into most regional towns. It's a pleasure to find that you can change cash or travellers' cheques for US dollars, pounds sterling and euro at fair rates established by the banks' head offices in Kampala. While these rates are slightly inferior to those offered by private forex bureaux in the capital, they are an improvement on the rotten rates usually offered by their upcountry counterparts. In fact, in the face of corporate competition, most regional forex bureaux outside hotels and other umbrella institutions have disappeared. The most extensive banking network is operated by Stanbic which occupies the upcountry branches of the former Uganda Commercial Bank in Jinja, Mbale, Fort Portal, Kisoro, Mbarara, Hoima and Masindi. Nile Bank operates in Jinja, Entebbe and Mbale; Crane Bank operates in Jinja and Mbale. Standard

Chartered has branches in Mbarara, Jinja and Mbale. All of these banks accept American Express travellers' cheques at rates scarcely inferior to cash. If this seems all too convenient to be true; it's refreshing to note that the usual prejudices concerning small denomination and older dollar bills still apply.

If you are in Uganda for an extended tour, visit or volunteer stint, you might consider opening a bank account to access your shillings through ATMs. If you'll be doing a lot of travelling, choose Stanbic. If you expect to be based in Kampala, Mbale or Jinja, then Nile, Crane, or Standard Chartered banks will do just as well. In addition to the usual photos and ID, you'll need proof of local address and a form of recommendation signed by an existing account holder.

It's worth planning ahead with regard to changing money upcountry. Do check the list of public holidays on pages 103–4 to avoid being inconvenienced or left short of funds over long weekends. Stanbic branches are often very busy and since all transactions, including forex, are handled by the same counters you'll probably find yourself in a long queue. Either get there early or leave yourself plenty of time. Nile Bank branches, though fewer in number, have a specific forex counter and provide swifter service with better rates. If your itinerary is tight, perhaps with one-night stopovers outside banking hours, plan accordingly.

CREDIT CARDS AND MONEY TRANSFERS Major credit cards are accepted by most upmarket hotels and quality restaurants in Kampala, and by a high proportion of upmarket lodges and hotels elsewhere in the country, though a levy of up to 5% will often be added to the bill. There are very few other circumstances in which credit cards will be much use for direct payments. However they can be used to obtain cash. Barclays on Kampala Road will provide you with pounds sterling or dollars (up to a limit of US$700 per day) but expect to pay about Ush30,000 in local charges. It's cheaper to obtain local currency (up to US$200 equivalent per day) from the 24-hour Visa- and MasterCard-enabled ATMs outside the Standard Chartered and Barclays banks (Stanbic is likely to follow suit). The rates are inferior to those offered by the forex bureaux and a nominal fee of about Ush5,000 (US$3) is automatically debited. If you intend to use these facilities, it's worth checking before you leave home what additional fees will appear on your credit card bill at home. While this a reasonably reliable service, it's not unknown for ATMs in Uganda – as is the case anywhere – to be out of order, or out of funds, or otherwise out of sorts. So, to give an example, depending on being able to draw funds from an ATM on the morning you're meant to leave on a ten-day safari might be reasonably regarded as practically asking for Mr Sod to lay down his law and delay your departure.

It's worth knowing that in an emergency, a friend or relative can send you money quickly and safely using Western Union or Money Gram. These allow you to collect Ugandan shillings converted from a sum paid to an agent in your home country as little as ten minutes earlier. It will take you this long to receive – by phone, email or text message – a codeword registered by your Good Samaritan which you must quote to obtain your money. The service is not cheap but it has the advantage that you receive all the money that is sent; if you are sent US$500 then you'll receive US$500 in Ugandan shillings while your transferer will pay about US$30 in commission separately. Branches are found in Kampala, Entebbe and several towns upcountry. Western Union operates out of Nile Bank branches. Check the websites (*www.westernunion.com or www.moneygram.com*) with a friend or relative before you travel to identify your local agent in case the need arises.

PRICES QUOTED IN THIS BOOK Practically everything in Uganda can be paid for in the local currency, and in most instances hard currency will not be accepted except in upmarket hotels and lodges. Within the country, prices are most often quoted in Uganda shillings, but some hotels and backpacker hostels do have set US dollar rates, which can be paid in local currency at the current rate of exchange. This duality is epitomised in the official UWA rate sheet. Visitation fees, for instance, are quoted in US dollars, though they can be paid either in US dollars or in Uganda shillings. Gorilla-tracking permits are also quoted in US dollars, but cannot be paid for in local currency, while fees for accommodation, guided walks and launch trips are quoted in local currency, and are normally paid for in Uganda shillings.

Such inconsistencies present a slight dilemma in the context of presenting prices in a travel guide. There is a case for quoting all rates in US dollars, which are likely to mean more to readers at the planning stage of the trip, and which, given the instability of African currencies in general, is likely to be more accurate than local currency rates in the long term. There is, too, a case for following the normal custom among local establishments and quoting all prices in Uganda shillings, especially as these have changed little in the past five years, while over the same period a 60% devaluation in the local currency has deflated many prices in hard-currency terms. And there is a case for quoting prices in the currency used by the relevant establishment, since it most accurately reflects the actual situation, though it does also have the real disadvantage of complicating the process of comparing the rates of different hotels etc.

There is no perfect solution, but in general I have opted to follow the local practice. If the visitation fee for a national park is US$10, and a guided walk in the same park costs Ush10,000, then these prices will respectively be quoted in US dollars and Uganda shillings in this book. The most significant exceptions are those instances where comparative rates will often be of greater significance to readers than actual rates, ie: accommodation and restaurants. All accommodation rates are quoted in US dollar terms, converted where appropriate at an approximate rate of Ush1,850. Restaurant prices, by contrast, are uniformly given in Uganda shillings, since very few establishments, even the most upmarket hotels, express the prices on their menus in any other currency. Conversions throughout are rounded off to the nearest dollar.

Finally, please note that prices quoted in this book were collected during the middle of 2006. They will almost certainly increase noticeably during the lifetime of this edition due to increased costs resulting from the present electricity crisis and exacerbated by international increases in oil prices.

GETTING AROUND

✈ **BY AIR** That there are no scheduled domestic flights within Uganda is presumably linked to the fact that the driving distance between the capital and most major urban centres is no more than five hours. The exception is Eagle Air which provides a regular service to towns in the insecure northern part of the country. Airstrips do serve most of the major national parks, however, and charter flights can be arranged through any tour operator, albeit it at a serious price. The only destination in Uganda which is reached by air more often than it is by road is Kidepo Valley National Park, partly because the drive up from Kampala takes two days, and partly because of the risk of banditry *en route* (see *Chapter 13, Kidepo*, pages 462–3).

Eagle Air 11 Portal Av; ☎ 0414 344292   **Kampala Aeroclub** Kajjansi Airstrip; ☏ 0772 706105

🚗 **SELF-DRIVE** By East African standards, Uganda's major roads are generally in good condition. Surfaced roads run east, connecting Kampala to Jinja, Busia, Malaba,

Tororo, Mbale and Soroti, southwest to Masaka, Mbarara and Kabale and west to Fort Portal. Note that the Jinja–Tororo highway is presently 'surfaced' in name only and won't justify this categorisation until a continually delayed roadworks programme is completed. The other major surfaced road in Uganda runs north from Kampala to Gulu while the Kampala–Hoima road is in the process of being sealed. Other surfaced roads connect Mbale to Sipi Falls, Masaka to the Tanzanian border, Mbarara to Ibanda, and Ntungamo to Rukungiri.

SELF-DRIVE IN UGANDA

Edited from notes sent by Dr Fritz Esch

Most readers of Bradt guides live in countries where heavy traffic, congestion and ice and snow are almost the only problems encountered by drivers. They are therefore unaware of the hassles they are likely to meet once on the road in Uganda. Based on personal experience of over ten years of daily driving in the outback of Uganda, Kenya and Malawi I have compiled the following dos and don'ts readers should be advised to keep in mind in order to make their self-drive trip an enjoyable one:

1 Never travel without the following:
   • First-aid kit
   • Spare petrol to last for not less than 300km allowing for low-gear driving on rough roads (use jerry cans as the caps of plastic spare tanks often leak)
   • Oil enough to refill the sump
   • Water of drinkable quality and for refilling the engine's cooling system if it bursts
   • Plastic bonding goo to fix sump, distributor cap, etc.

2 On corrugated roads, the most comfortable driving speed is about 60km/h. Always drive with anticipation and foresight and abstain from sudden steering movements, or steering and braking at the same time, both of which can result in skidding. For slowing down early, gentle breaking alternating with cautiously dosed accelerator application prevents the car from going out of control.

3 Before negotiating flooded stretches of road, or rivers that aren't too deep for the car (wade through to find out!) remove the fan belt to stop water from spraying around, which could upset the electrical systems of the engine. Traverse the flooding in first gear with high revs to blow water from the exhaust. To remove water from electrical parts, use the hollow stem of tall-growing roadside grass as a pipette to drain less accessible areas of the engine compartment.

4 Stop well ahead of bush fires. The fire's front could well be 500m in length, and it doesn't always travel in a straight line as one might assume, making it difficult to judge the course and progress from a moving vehicle with bends, slopes, trees, anthills and other obstacles obscuring the view ahead. Traversing the fire in the belief that it can be negotiated without first checking the situation carefully is simply foolish: many a daring driver misjudging this type of scenario has found himself surrounded by choking smoke and intense heat in the middle of an inferno with no chance to retreat or get away. When in doubt, fire has the right of way!

5 When you have to change a right-hand wheel, park on the left side of the road, and vice versa. African roads are seldom level and are most likely to slope down towards the shoulders, leaving insufficient clearance for the jack if the punctured tyre is on the road edge. Do beware of passing traffic!

Kampala lies at the centre of a number of surfaced radial roads entering from Entebbe, Mbarara, Fort Portal, Hoima, Masindi, Gayaza and Jinja. Getting to the edge of Kampala is not difficult, though increased traffic volume including trucks inevitably slows speeds as the metropolis is approached. However getting from one side of the city to the other is becoming increasingly time consuming. Hopefully this will be eased by the completion of a Northern bypass in 2007/8. This long-awaited development will make life considerably easier for guests at, say, Blue

6 If the petrol tank leaks due to small holes caused by flying stones, try a cake of ordinary household soap to be rubbed on and around the holes in the same way an eraser is applied for removing pencil marks from paper.

7 During the dry season, patches of grass or savanna should be avoided when looking for a place to park, as there is a risk that the exhaust pipe or other hot engine parts will ignite the parched vegetation and spark off a fire, possibly damaging or destroying the car. If possible, leave the car in a field of young cotton, maize, groundnuts or other green vegetation. Provided the crops are small and the car is parked close to the perimeter of the field, with the wheels resting on empty furrows, the damage caused to the crops will be negligible. The owner of the field should, however, be informed. A dry riverbed would be an ideal alternative, but be aware that out of the blue it could become a raging stream – a slight risk during the dry season.

8 It's a good idea to have a fire extinguisher on board, of the professional type large enough to last for several minutes and also good for electrical fires. Drivers should be familiar with the technicalities of their extinguisher! Forget about fire-fighting sprays marketed like deodorants in little push-button spray-cans of a size fitting in the car's glove compartment – they run dry within seconds.

9 Petrol from remote filling stations or dubious pumps, drums or jerry cans might be dirty. To protect the engine, it may be prudent to use nylon stockings or some similar material to filter the petrol while filling up.

10 For elementary on-the-road maintenance and repair jobs, having a workshop manual in the car would be an excellent idea.

11 Beware of any snake crossing the road ahead, since it may rear up and (if not killed first) could strike at any arm, elbow or hand sticking out of a window. Should you accidentally run over the snake, look in your rear-view mirror or reverse to check it is dead. If it has vanished altogether, it could have lodged in your chassis or undercarriage, ready to attack when you alight, open the bonnet or boot, or change a wheel. A snake trapped in this manner will be very scared and aggressive, and I've witnessed several snakebites, some fatal, inflicted under such circumstances.

12 In the unfortunate event that you collide with a person or livestock, it's not advisable to stop. Assuming that the car still drives, it's safer to continue on to the next police station. This might sound harsh, but the reality is that an accident of this sort will often attract an angry *panga*- and stick-wielding crowd, possibly containing a drunken element, which will not hesitate to threaten and possibly attack the car's occupants.

Mango Club in eastern Kampala, to head out towards the national parks in the west of the country. Similarly, the bypass will make it far easier for rafters staying at Kampala Backpackers in the west of the city to and from the Nile at Jinja, 80km to the east.

Most other roads in Uganda – for instance from Fort Portal or Masindi to Hoima, from Masindi to Murchison Falls, and from Kabale to Kisoro – are unsurfaced. The condition of these and other more minor unsurfaced roads is discussed under the relevant section in the regional part of the guide. As a rule, however, unsurfaced roads tend to be very variable from one season to the next, with conditions likely to be most tricky during the rains and least so towards the end of the dry season. Even within this generalisation, an isolated downpour can do major damage to a road that was in perfectly good nick a day earlier, while the arrival of a grader can transform a pot-holed 4x4 track into a road navigable by any saloon car. The type of soil is also a big factor in how prone any given road is to deterioration, and in wet conditions one should always be conscious that firm soil or gravel can give way abruptly to a mushy depression or a black cotton-soil quagmire. Put simply, advice in this guide regarding road conditions is of necessity a snapshot of conditions in mid 2006 and should not be taken as gospel. When in doubt, ask local advice – if minibus-taxis are getting through, then so should any 4x4, so the taxi station is always a good place to seek current information.

The main hazard on Ugandan roads, aside from unexpected pot-holes, is other drivers. Minibus-taxi drivers in particular have long been given to overtaking on blind corners, and speed limits are universally ignored except when enforced by road conditions. As big a threat as minibus-taxis these days are the spanking new coaches that bully their way along trunk routes at up to 120km/h – keep an eye in your rear-view mirror and if necessary pull off the road in advance to let the closing loony past. The coaches are in reality just a heavyweight manifestation of a more widespread road-hog mentality that characterises Ugandan drivers. Larger vehicles show little compunction when it comes to overtaking smaller ones so tightly that they are practically forced off the road, and vehicles passing in the opposite direction will often stray across the central white line forcing oncoming traffic to cut onto the verge. Bearing the above in mind, a coasting speed of 80km/h in the open road would be comfortable without being over cautious, and it's not a bad idea to slow down and cover the brake in the face of oncoming traffic. In urban situations, particularly downtown Kampala, right of way essentially belongs to he who is prepared to force the issue – a considered blend of defensive driving tempered by outright assertiveness is required to get through safely without becoming too bogged down in the traffic.

A peculiarly African road hazard – one frequently taken to unnecessary extremes in Uganda – is the giant sleeping policeman, or 'speed bump' as it's known locally. A lethal bump might be signposted in advance, it might be painted in black-and-white stripes, or it might simply rear like a macadamised wave a full 30cm or so above the road without warning. It's to be assumed that the odd stray bump will exist on any stretch of a major road that passes through a town or village, so slow down at any looming hint of urbanisation. Other regular obstacles include bicycles laden with banana clusters, which can often force traffic to leave its lane, as well as livestock and pedestrians wandering around blithely in the middle of the road. Be aware that piles of foliage placed in the road at a few metres interval warn of a broken-down vehicle. Red warning triangles are not used for the purpose as these would quickly be stolen; however these items are useful to have to show at Rwandan police checks.

Indicator lights, according to local custom, are not there to signal an intent to turn. Instead, they are switched on only in the face of oncoming traffic with the intention of warning following drivers not to attempt to overtake. Ugandans, like many Africans, display a strong and inexplicable aversion to switching on their headlights except in genuine darkness – switch them on at any other time and every passing vehicle will blink its lights back at you in bemusement. In rainy, misty or twilight conditions, it would be optimistic to think that you'll be alerted to oncoming traffic by headlights, or for that matter to expect the more demented element among Ugandan drivers to avoid overtaking or speeding simply because they cannot see more than 10m ahead. It's strongly recommended that you avoid driving at night on main highways outside towns since a significant proportion of vehicles either lack a full complement of functional headlights (never assume a single glow indicates a motorcycle) or keep their lights permanently on blinding full beam! Another very real danger is unlit trucks that, invariably overloaded, have broken down in the middle of the road.

If you decide to rent a self-drive vehicle, check it over carefully and ask to take it for a test drive. Even if you're not knowledgeable about the working of engines, a few minutes on the road should be sufficient to establish whether it has any seriously disturbing creaks, rattles or other noises. Check the condition of the tyres (bald is beautiful might be the national motto in this regard) and that there is at least one spare, better two, both in a condition to be used should the need present itself. If the tyres are tubeless, an inner tube of the correct size can be useful in the event of a repair being required upcountry. Ask to be shown the wheel spanner, jack and the thing for raising the jack. If the vehicle is a high-clearance 4x4 make sure (and I write from experience here) that the jack is capable of raising the wheel high enough to change the wheel. Do also ensure that the licence is valid for the duration of your trip. Ask also to be shown filling points for oil, water and petrol and check that all the keys do what they are supposed to do – we've left Kampala before with a car we later discovered could not be locked! Once on the road, check oil and water regularly in the early stages of the trip to ensure that there are no existing leaks. See also the box *Self-drive in Uganda*, pages 94–5, for further survival tips.

Fuel is expensive in Uganda – the equivalent of around US$1.30 per litre for petrol and slightly less for diesel – and this price is likely to rise further. If you are arriving overland it is worth stocking up before you enter the country. While driving in Uganda the following documentation is required at all times: the vehicle registration book (a photocopy is acceptable; ensure it is a recent one with the most recent vehicle licence entry recorded on the back page); the vehicle certificate of insurance (heavy fines are imposed for driving an uninsured vehicle); and an international or domestic driver's licence. Ugandans follow, albeit somewhat loosely on occasions, the British custom of driving on the left side of the road. The general speed limit on the open road is 100km/h and 65km/h in built-up areas unless otherwise indicated. For details of recommended car-rental agencies, see the appropriate heading under in *Chapter 6*, page 155.

MOUNTAIN BIKING Uganda is relatively compact and flat, making it ideal for travel by mountain bike. New quality bikes are not available in Uganda so you should try to bring one with you (some airlines are more flexible than others about carrying bicycles; you should discuss this with your airline in advance). However if you are prepared to look around Kampala, some excellent bikes can be bought from a few private importers for as little as US$200; the adventure/rafting company Adrift recommends a chap called Joe (m 0772 490311). Adrift also organises regular weekend social mountain biking/cycling activities around Kampala (m 0772 223438). Main roads in Uganda are generally in good condition and buses will allow you to take your bike on the roof, though you should expect to be charged extra for this. Minor roads are variable in condition, but in the dry season you're unlikely to encounter any problems. Several of the more far-flung destinations mentioned in this book would be within easy reach of cyclists.

Before you pack that bicycle, do consider that cyclists – far more than motorists – are exposed to an estimable set of hazards on African roads. The 'might-is-right' mentality referred to in the section about self-drive above is doubly concerning to cyclists, who must expect to be treated as second-class road users, and to display constant vigilance against speeding buses etc. It is routine for motorised vehicles to bear down on a bicycle as if it simply didn't exist, hooting at the very last minute, and enforcing the panicked cyclist to veer off the road abruptly, sometimes resulting in a nasty fall. Should this not put you off, do at least ensure that your bicycle is fitted with good rear-view mirrors, a loud horn and luminous strips, and that you bring a helmet and whatever protective gear might lessen the risks. Cycling at night is emphatically not recommended.

The **International Bicycle Fund** (IBF) (*4887 Columbia Drive South, Seattle, WA 98108-1919, USA;* e *intlbike@scn.org*) is an organisation promoting bicycle travel internationally. It produces a useful publication called *Bicycling in Africa* at a cost of US$14.95 plus US$5 post and packing, as well as several regional supplements including one about Malawi, Tanzania and Uganda.

ROAD TRANSPORT Following the permanent suspension of all passenger rail and ferry services over the past few years, public transport in Uganda essentially boils down to buses and other forms of motorised road transport. The only exceptions are the new passenger/vehicle ferry between Entebbe and the Ssese Islands and local boat services connecting fishing villages on lakes Victoria, Albert and Kyoga. Details of these services are given under the appropriate sections in the regional part of the guide, but it's worth noting here that overloading small passenger boats is customary in Uganda, and fatal accidents are commonplace, often linked to the violent storms that can sweep in from nowhere during the rainy season.

Buses Coach and bus services cover all major routes and, all things being relative, they are probably the safest form of public road transport in Uganda. On all trunk routes, the battered old buses of a few years back have been replaced or supplemented by large modern coaches that typically maintain a speed of 100km/h or faster, allowing them to travel between the capital and any of the main urban centres in western Uganda in less than five hours. The Horizon bus service is by far the best. The better services mostly have fixed departure times, with one or other coach leaving in either direction between Kampala and the likes of Mbale, Mbarara, Kabale, Kasese, Fort Portal and Masindi every hour or so from around 07.00 to mid afternoon. The Post Buses, which depart from the yard behind the post office on Kampala Road at 08.00 daily, are recommended on account of being relatively soberly driven. Coach and bus fares countrywide typically work out at around Ush1,500 per 50km.

Minibus-taxis In addition to buses, most major routes are covered by a regular stream of white minibuses, which have no set departures times, but simply leave when they are full – every ten to 30 minutes on busier routes. It is no longer the case that minibuses are significantly faster than buses, but the drivers tend to be more reckless. Fares are generally slightly higher than for buses, and it's customary on most routes to pay shortly before arriving rather than on departure, so there is little risk of being overcharged provided that you look and see what other passengers are paying. Minibuses are referred to as taxis in Uganda (though in this book I've called them minibus-taxis to preclude confusion with special hire taxis) and as *matatus* in Kenya, a term that is generally understood but not used by Ugandans. They are also sometimes called *kigatis*, in reference to their resemblance to a bread loaf. A law enforcing a maximum of three passengers per row is stringently enforced in most parts of Uganda, meaning that minibus travel is far more comfortable than in the majority of African countries where four bums per row is customary. Seat belts are now mandatory. All minibus-taxis by law now have to have a distinctive blue-and-white band round the middle, and special hire cars have to have a black-and-white band.

Shared taxis Shared taxis, generally light saloon cars that carry four to six passengers, come into their own on routes that attract insufficient human traffic for minibuses, for instance between Katunguru and Mweya in Queen Elizabeth National Park. They tend to be crowded and slow in comparison with minibuses, and on routes where no other public transport exists, fares are often highly inflated. The drivers habitually overcharge tourists, so establish the price in advance.

Special hire You won't spend long in Uganda before you come across the term *special hire* – which means hiring a vehicle privately to take you somewhere. There are situations where it is useful to go for a special hire, but beware of people at *matatu* stations who tell you there are no vehicles going to where you want, but that they can fix you up a special hire. Nine times out of ten they are trying their luck. If you organise a special hire vehicle, bargain hard. Urban taxis are also known locally as special hires.

Boda-boda One of the most popular ways of getting around in Uganda is the bicycle-taxi or *boda-boda*, so-called because they originated as bicycles with large panniers, used for smuggling goods across borders by rural footpaths. Now fitted with pillions and powered by foot or by 50 to 100cc engines, they are a convenient form of suburban transport and also great for short side trips where no public transport exists. Fares are negotiable and not at all daunting. If you're reliant on public transport it's inevitable that you'll use a *boda-boda* at some stage. Before hopping aboard however, you should be aware of a pretty poor urban safety record. *Boda-boda* riders are invariably lacking in formal training, road safety awareness and, it is frequently suggested, much between the ears. In December 2005, 1,383 vehicles were involved in accidents sufficiently serious to be reported. Of these, 22% (predictably enough) involved *matatu*-taxis and 15% *boda-bodas*. *Boda-bodas* and their passengers are of course far more vulnerable than the occupants of larger vehicles and in the same month 15 *boda-boda* drivers were killed. By all means use *boda-bodas* but do try to identify a relatively sensible-looking operator, tell him to drive slowly and carefully, and don't be afraid to tell him to slow down (or even stop for you to get off) if you don't feel safe. Officially, helmets for *boda-boda* drivers and their passengers have been mandatory since 2005; however the Regional Traffic Officer informs me that her officers are choosing to 'sensitise' *boda-boda* users before enforcing the law.

Hitching Although some guides to East Africa carry severe warnings against hitching, this strikes me as a knee-jerk reaction based on the type of risk associated with hitching in Western countries. Being picked up by a psychopath should be the least of your concerns when travelling around Uganda – there is a far greater risk of being injured or killed in a car accident, and since drivers of private vehicles are generally (but not always) less reckless than their professional counterparts, this is arguably reduced by hitching. An even greater risk attached to trying to hitch a lift is that you won't succeed. It is customary to pay for lifts in Uganda, so a free ride is likely only in the instance that you're picked up by a foreigner or a wealthy Ugandan with some exposure to Western ways. While waiting for a lift, you can expect to attract a stream of opportunists offering you a special hire. Hitching may be the only way to reach some reserves. Manic arm-flapping, as opposed to a gently raised thumb, is the standard way of signalling to passing traffic for a lift.

ACCOMMODATION

Wherever you travel in Uganda, and whatever your budget, you'll seldom have a problem finding suitable accommodation. Most towns have a good variety of moderately priced and budget hotels, and even the smallest villages will usually have somewhere you can stay for a dollar or so. Upmarket accommodation, by contrast, is generally available only in major towns and other tourist centres such as national parks. Budget accommodation in Uganda used to be rather expensive by comparison with most of its neighbours, but this is no longer the case. The main reason for this is that the local currency has devalued by 60% against the US dollar since 1998, but many hotels have not (as yet) changed their prices to reflect this, so that in hard-currency terms they cost considerably less than they did eight years ago. The present electricity crisis means that prices are set to rise however (see the box, *Dark days in Uganda*, on pages 110–11). All accommodation entries in this travel guide are placed in one of five categories: upmarket, moderate, budget, shoestring and camping. The purpose of this categorisation is twofold: to break up long hotel listings that span a wide price range, and to help readers isolate the range of hotels that will best suit their budget and taste. Any given hotel is thus categorised on its overall feel as much as its actual prices (rack-rates are quoted anyway) and in the context of general accommodation standards in the town or reserve where it is situated. Comments relating to the value for money represented by any given hotel should also be read in the context of the individual town and of the stated category. In other words, a hotel that seems to be good value in one town might not be such a bargain were it situated in a place where rates are generally cheaper. Likewise, a hotel that I regard to be good value in the upmarket category will almost certainly seem to be madly expensive to a traveller using budget hotels.

Before going into further detail about the different accommodation categories, it's worth noting a few potentially misleading quirks in local hotel-speak. In Swahili, the word *hoteli* refers to a restaurant while what we call a hotel is generally called a lodging, guesthouse or *gesti* – so if you ask a Ugandan to show you to a hotel you might well be taken to an eatery (see *Appendix 1, Language*, page 465). Another local quirk is that most East African hotels in all price ranges refer to a room that has en-suite shower and toilet facilities as self-contained, a term that is also used widely in this guide. Several hotels offer accommodation in *bandas*, a term used widely in Africa to designate rooms or cottages that are detached from any other building.

Be aware, too, that Ugandan usage of the terms single, double and twin is somewhat inconsistent and not always in accord with Western conventions. Rather than automatically asking for a double room, couples might also check the size of a bed in a single room. Several hotels now provide ³/₄-size beds in which two people may sleep at the single tariff. However, if the rate is for bed and breakfast, usually only one guest will be provided with breakfast. Some double rooms offer similar scope for triple occupancy, being furnished with a double and single bed.

UPMARKET This category embraces all hotels, lodges and resorts that cater primarily to the international leisure or business traveller and would probably be accorded a two- to four-star ranking internationally. Most hotels in this category offer smart, modern accommodation with en-suite facilities, mosquito netting, air conditioning or fans (depending on the local climate) and in cities DSTV in all rooms. A smaller subset within this category consists of smaller game lodges and tented camps that typically consist of no more than ten double accommodation units, built and decorated in a style that complements the surrounding environment, and catering to the exclusive end of the market. Hotels in this upmarket bracket will generally charge more than US$100 for a double room, rising in some instances to US$300 or higher. Room rates for upmarket city hotels invariably include breakfast but exclude all other meals, while at game lodges they normally also include lunch and dinner. This is the category to look at if cost is not a major consideration and you require hotel accommodation of a standard you'd expect at home.

MODERATE In Uganda, as in many African countries, there is often a huge gap between the price and quality of the very cheapest hotels that meet international standards, and that of the most expensive hotels that are geared primarily towards locals and budget travellers. For this reason, the moderate bracket is rather more nebulous than other accommodation categories. Essentially, it embraces those hotels which, for one or other reason, could not truly be classified as upmarket but are also too expensive or of a sufficiently high standard that they cannot be considered budget lodgings. Many places listed in this range are superior local hotels that suffice in lieu of any genuinely upmarket accommodation in a town that sees relatively few tourists. The category also embraces decent lodges or hotels in recognised tourist areas that charge considerably lower rates than their upmarket competitors, but are clearly a notch or two above the budget category. Hotels in this range normally offer comfortable accommodation in self-contained rooms with hot water, fan and possibly DSTV, and they will have a decent restaurant and employ a high ration of English-speaking staff. Most moderate hotels charge around US$40–80 for a double room inclusive of breakfast, but some are slightly more expensive or cheaper. This is the category to look at if you are travelling on a limited but not a low budget and expect a reasonably high but not luxurious standard of accommodation.

BUDGET The hotels in this category are generally aimed largely at the local market and they definitely don't approach international standards, but they will usually be reasonably clean and comfortable, and a definite cut above the basic guesthouses that proliferate in most towns. Hotels in this bracket will more often than not have a decent restaurant attached, English-speaking staff, and comfortable rooms with en-suite facilities, running cold or possibly hot water, fans (but not air conditioning) and good mosquito netting. Room rates are typically around US$10–40 for a double, including breakfast, which may or may not be very substantial. This is the category to look at if you are on a limited budget, but want to avoid total squalor!

SHOESTRING This category includes a small number of establishments aimed very specifically at backpackers, most of which are run by Westerners and very affordable but also fairly comfortable. The greater part of the accommodation in this category, however, consists of the small local guesthouses that proliferate in most towns, catering almost exclusively to locals. The typical guesthouse consists of around ten cell-like rooms forming three walls around a central courtyard, with a reception area or restaurant at the front. Guesthouse standards tend to vary widely both within towns and between them, far more so than do their prices.

The places listed in this guide are the pick of what may be a much larger selection of basic guesthouses clustered together in the vicinity of the bus station or market, and often there is little to choose between them. If you're looking around, my experience is that guesthouses run by women or with a strong female presence are generally cleaner and more hospitable than those run by men, and that – standards of maintenance being low – the newest guesthouse will be the cleanest and the brightest. Shoestring accommodation typically costs around US$4–8 for a double, with some establishments nudging the US$10 mark. Almost without exception, toilets and showers are common as opposed to en suite and breakfast will not be included in the room rate, or will be very insubstantial if it is. This category is the one to look at for travellers who want the cheapest possible accommodation irrespective of quality, though it does often include perfectly pleasant hotels that just happen to be cheap.

CAMPING There has been a great increase in the number of organised campsites in recent years, and there are now very few established tourist centres where you can't pitch a tent in a guarded site with good facilities. Camping typically costs around US$2–3 per person per night.

EATING AND DRINKING

EATING OUT If you are not too fussy and don't mind a lack of variety, you can eat cheaply almost anywhere in Uganda. In most towns numerous local restaurants (often called *hotelis*) serve unimaginative but filling meals for under US$2. Typically, local food is based around a meat or chicken stew eaten with one of four staples: rice, chapati, *ugali* or *matoke*. *Ugali* is a stiff maize porridge eaten throughout sub-Saharan Africa. *Matoke* is a cooked plantain dish, served boiled or in a mushy heap, and the staple diet in many parts of Uganda. Another Ugandan special is groundnut sauce. *Mandazi*, the local equivalent of doughnuts, are tasty when they are freshly cooked, but rather less appetising when they are a day old. *Mandazi* are served at *hotelis* and sold at markets. You can often eat very cheaply at stalls around markets and bus stations.

Cheap it may be, but for most travellers the appeal of this sort of fare soon palls. In larger towns, you'll usually find a couple of better restaurants (sometimes attached to upmarket or moderate hotels) serving Western or Indian food for around US$3–5. There is considerably more variety in Kampala, where for around US$5–10 per head you can eat very well indeed. Upmarket lodges and hotels generally serve high-quality food. Vegetarians are often poorly catered for in Uganda (the exception being Indian restaurants) and people on organised tours should ensure that the operator is informed in advance about this or any other dietary preference.

Note that Swahili names for various foods are widely used in Uganda (see *Appendix 1, Language*, page 465).

COOKING FOR YOURSELF The alternative to eating at restaurants is to put together your own meals at markets and supermarkets. The variety of foodstuffs you can buy varies from season to season and from town to town, but in most major centres, with the exception of Kisoro, you can rely on finding a supermarket that stocks frozen meat, a few tinned goods, biscuits, pasta, rice and chocolate bars.

Fruit and vegetables are best bought at markets, where they are very cheap. Potatoes, sweet potatoes, onions, tomatoes, bananas, sugarcane, avocados, paw-paws, mangoes, coconuts, oranges and pineapples are available in most towns.

For hikers, packet soups are about the only dehydrated meals that are available throughout Uganda. If you have specialised requirements, you're best off doing your shopping in Kampala, where a wider selection of goods is available in the supermarkets.

⚲ DRINKS Brand-name soft drinks such as Pepsi, Coca-Cola and Fanta are widely available in Uganda and cheap by international standards. If the fizzy stuff doesn't appeal, you can buy imported South African fruit juices at supermarkets in Kampala and other large towns. Tap water is reasonably safe to drink in larger towns, but bottled mineral water is widely available if you prefer not to take the risk.

Locally, the most widely drunk hot beverage is *chai*, a sweet tea where all ingredients are boiled together in a pot. In some parts of the country *chai* is often flavoured with spices such as ginger (an acquired taste, in my opinion). Coffee is one of Uganda's major cash crops, but you'll be lucky if you ever meet a Ugandan who knows how to brew a decent cup – coffee in Uganda almost invariably tastes insipid and watery except at upmarket hotels and quality restaurants.

The main alcoholic drink is lager beer. Jinja's Nile Breweries (a subsidiary of South African Breweries) brews Nile Special, Club, ESB and Castle, whilst Uganda Breweries at Port Bell near Kampala brews Bell, Pilsner, Tusker Export and Guinness. All local beers come in 500ml bottles, which cost less than US$1 in local bars and up to US$2.50 in some upmarket hotels. Nile Special is probably the most popular tipple with locals and travellers alike, though I must admit a preference for the milder Bell. If you're serious about getting drunk, try Extra Special Brew (ESB), which has an alcohol level of 7.5%. Two of Africa's most pleasant lagers, Kenya Tusker and Congo Primus, are sometimes sold in towns near the respective borders. If you've never been to Africa before, you might want to try the local millet beer. It's not bad, though for most people once is enough.

A selection of superior plonk-quality South African wines is available in most tourist-class hotels and bars, as well as in some supermarkets, generally at around US$10–20 per bottle – outrageous to South Africans who know that exactly the same wine would cost 20% of that in a supermarket at home, but not unreasonable in international terms. Based on our experience, all wines – white or red – of more than two or three years' vintage are best avoided in preference for younger bottles, presumably because they are poorly stored. Bond 7 Whisky and a local gin called Waragi can be bought very cheaply in a variety of bottle sizes or in 60ml sachets – very convenient for hiking in remote areas or taking with you to upmarket hotels for an inexpensive nightcap in your room. A box of 20 sachets costs around US$5, and local bars increasingly sell whisky and gin by the sachet. These are known by the rather endearing term 'tot pack' though the African fondness for tacking an additional vowel to the end of a noun has actually resulted in 'totter pack'; you may appreciate this inadvertent irony if you overindulge.

PUBLIC HOLIDAYS

In addition to the following fixed public holidays, Uganda recognises as holidays the Christian Good Friday and Easter Monday and the Muslim Eid-el-Fitr and Eid-el-Adha, all of which generally fall in March or April. Expect any institutions that would be closed on a Sunday – banks and forex bureaux, for instance, or government and other offices – to also be closed on any public holiday, but most shops and other local services will function as normal. Public transport is typically more intermittent than normal on public holidays, but it still operates.

1 January	New Year's Day
26 January	NRM Anniversary Day
8 March	International Women's Day
1 May	Labour Day
3 June	Martyrs' Day
9 June	Heroes' Day
9 October	Independence Day
25 December	Christmas Day
26 December	Boxing Day

SHOPPING

Until a few years ago it was difficult to buy anything much in Uganda, but things have improved greatly of late. A fair range of imported goods is available in Kampala, though prices are often inflated. If you have specific needs (unusual medications or slide film, for instance), then you'd be safest bringing what you need with you. Toilet rolls, soap, toothpaste, pens, batteries and locally produced foodstuffs are widely available. Shopping hours are normally between 08.30 and 17.00, with a lunch break between 13.00 and 14.00.

CURIOS Items aimed specifically at tourists are available, but there is nothing like the variety you'll find in Kenya or Tanzania. Typical curios include carvings, batiks, musical instruments, wooden spoons and various soapstone and malachite knick-knacks. There are several curio shops in Kampala, and there's a good craft market next to the National Theatre.

*MEDIA AND COMMUNICATIONS

NEWSPAPERS Uganda has a good English-language press, with the daily *New Vision* and *Monitor* offering the best international coverage as well as local news. The *East African*, a Kenyan weekly, has excellent regional coverage and comment. *Time* and *Newsweek* can be bought at street stalls in Kampala.

RADIO AND TELEVISION An increasingly varied selection of local and national radio stations service Uganda, most of them privately run, and offering listeners a lively mix of talk, hard and soft news, local and other current music – not to mention a litany of dodgy 1970s' disco anthems you'd probably forgotten about! The national television channels aren't up to much, but most international hotels and many smaller ones subscribe to DSTV, a South African multi-channel satellite service featuring the likes of CNN or Sky News as well as good movie and sports channels. Bars and restaurants with DSTV tend to be packed solid on Saturday afternoons during the English football season, and for all other major football events.

TELEPHONE Uganda's land telephone system is reasonably efficient – from overseas, it's definitely one of the easiest African countries to get through to first time. The international code is +256, and area codes are as follows:

Entebbe	0414	Kampala	0414	Mbarara	04854
Fort Portal	04834	Kasese	04834	Mityana	0464
Jinja	0434	Masaka	04814	Mubende	046444
Kabale	04864	Mbale	04544	Tororo	04544

A major recent development in Uganda has been the upsurge of mobile satellite telephones, most notably the South African company MTN. It's unusual nowadays to meet an employed Ugandan who doesn't own a mobile phone (rather more unusual, admittedly, to meet one who actually has any remaining airtime!). Peak-rate domestic calls between all phone networks cost Ush380–520/min depending on which tariff option you select. Calls to East Africa cost Ush900/min and international calls Ush1,000 per minute. Mobile phones can use various tariff options. In larger towns, MTN shops, stalls and booths on every block offer calls at slightly higher rates. MTN numbers are prefixed 0772 or 0782. Numbers prefixed 0712 belong to Mango, the mobile network of the indigenous Uganda Telecom. Just occasionally, you might come across a number beginning 0752. This is a real collector's item, the telephonic equivalent of a shoebill sighting, and identifies a loyal customer of the increasingly sidelined CelTel service. The MTN satellite network grid is remarkably widespread, extending into significant chunks of Queen Elizabeth and Murchison Falls national parks. All safari drivers and guides now carry them on safaris and game drives. Self-drive visitors should give serious thought to buying or renting a new or secondhand phone in case of emergency, making hotel bookings and even calling home given the now reasonable rates. Better still, if you bring a compatible phone with you, a local SIM card costs next to nothing and can be inserted in place of your normal SIM card, giving you your own phone number in Uganda at cheap local rates – pay-as-you-go airtime cards are available everywhere. There's nothing whatsoever wrong with Mango or CelTel in Kampala and the main urban centres but to enjoy the reassurance of maximum possible network coverage of mind out in the sticks, MTN is the best bet. Mobile numbers are included in this guidebook alongside conventional phone numbers, and generally you're more likely to get through to them more quickly than to land lines, though they also tend to change with greater frequency. If you're calling from outside the country, dial +256 then the full mobile number minus the leading zero. Note that many of the mobile numbers given here are actually the manager's personal line, so don't be surprised if a high proportion of those listed in this book become obsolete a couple of years down the line.

INTERNET AND EMAIL Email is by far the easiest way to keep in contact with people at home, much cheaper than the telephone, but almost as instantaneous. Assuming that you already have an email address, do check in advance whether your server offers the facility to browse email online through the internet (it will be both costly and complicated to dial your own server internationally to download messages). If not, it's probably worth setting up a temporary address with hotmail, yahoo or any other similar free facility for the duration of your trip, and giving out that address to anybody that might want to contact you.

The number of internet cafés in Kampala seems to increase with every passing week, while browsing rates keep dropping. At the time of writing, there must be a dozen cafés on Kampala Road alone offering cheap internet facilities. Communication by email used to be extremely limited outside Kampala but this has changed. Jinja, Mbale, Masaka, Mbarara, Fort Portal, Kasese and Kabale all offer a choice of internet cafés (expect to pay double Kampala prices – Ush50 per minute) while internet facilities are even available by satellite link at such out-of-the-way locations as Lake Bunyonyi and Buhoma (Bwindi).

INTERACTING WITH UGANDANS

Ugandans are generally relaxed, friendly and tolerant in their dealings with tourists, and you would have to do something pretty outrageous to commit a serious faux pas there. But, like any country, it does have its rules of etiquette, and while allowances will always be made for tourists, there is some value in ensuring that they are not made too frequently!

GENERAL CONDUCT Perhaps the single most important point of etiquette to be grasped by visitors to Africa is the social importance of formal greetings. Rural Africans tend to greet each other elaborately, and if you want to make a good impression on somebody who speaks English, whether they be a waiter or a shop assistant (and especially if they work in a government department), you would do well to follow suit. When you need to ask directions, it is rude to blunder straight into interrogative mode without first exchanging greetings. Most Ugandans speak some English, but for those who don't the Swahili greeting 'jambo' delivered with a smile and a nod of the head will be adequate.

Among Ugandans, it is considered to be in poor taste to display certain emotions publicly. Affection is one such emotion: it is frowned upon for members of the opposite sex to hold hands publicly, and kissing or embracing would be seriously offensive. Oddly, it is quite normal for friends of the same sex to walk around hand-in-hand. Male travellers who get into a long discussion with a male Ugandan shouldn't be surprised if that person clasps them by the hand and retains a firm grip on their hand for several minutes. This is a warm gesture, one particularly appropriate when the person wants to make a point with which you might disagree. On the subject of intra-gender relations, homosexuality is as good as taboo in Uganda, to the extent that it would require some pretty overt behaviour for it to occur to anybody to take offence.

It is also considered bad form to show anger publicly. It is difficult to know where to draw the line here, because some minibus-taxi conductors in particular act in a manner that positively invites an aggressive response, and I doubt that many people who travel independently in Uganda will get by without the occasional display of impatience. Frankly, I doubt that many bystanders would take umbrage if you responded to a pushy tout with a display of anger, if only because the tout's behaviour itself goes against the grain. By contrast, losing your temper will almost certainly be counter-productive when dealing with obtuse officials, dopey waiters and hotel employees, or unco-operative safari drivers.

Visitors should be aware of the Islamic element in Ugandan society, particularly in Kampala. In Muslim society, it is insulting to use your left hand to pass or receive something or when shaking hands (a custom adhered to in many parts of Africa that aren't Muslim). If you eat with your fingers, it is also customary to use the right hand only. Even those of us who are naturally right-handed will occasionally need to remind ourselves of this (it may happen, for instance, that you are carrying something in your right hand and so hand money to a shopkeeper with your left). For left-handed travellers, it will require a constant effort.

TIPPING AND GUIDES The question of when and when not to tip can be difficult in a foreign country. In Uganda, it is customary to tip your driver/guide at the end of a safari or hike, as well as any cook or porter that accompanies you. A figure of roughly US$5 per day would be a fair benchmark, though do check this with your safari company in advance. I see no reason why you shouldn't give a bigger or smaller tip based on the quality of service. It is not essential to tip the guides who take you around in national parks and other reserves, but it is recommended, and the money will be greatly appreciated by the recipient; assuming the service has been good, anything from Ush2,000–5,000 is fine.

In some African countries, it is difficult to travel anywhere without being latched on to by a self-appointed guide, who will often expect a tip over and above any agreed fee. This sort of thing is comparatively unusual in Uganda, but if you do take on a freelance guide, then it is advisable to clarify in advance that whatever price you agree is final and inclusive of a tip.

It is not customary to tip for service in local bars and *hotelis*, though you may sometimes *want* to leave a tip (in fact, given the difficulty of finding change in Uganda, you may practically be forced into doing this in some circumstances). A tip of 5% would be very acceptable and 10% generous. Generally any restaurant that caters primarily to tourists and to wealthy Ugandan residents will automatically add a service charge to the bill, but since there's no telling where that service charge ends up, it would still be reasonable to reward good service with a cash tip.

BARGAINING AND OVERCHARGING Tourists to Uganda will sometimes need to bargain over prices, but generally this need exists only in reasonably predictable circumstances, for instance when chartering a private taxi, organising a guide, or buying curios and to a lesser extent other market produce. Prices in hotels, restaurants and shops are generally fixed, and overcharging in such places is too unusual for it to be worth challenging a price unless it is blatantly ridiculous.

You may well be overcharged at some point in Uganda, but it is important to keep this in perspective. After a couple of bad experiences, some travellers start to haggle with everybody from hotel owners to old women selling fruit by the side of the road, often accompanying their negotiations with aggressive accusations of dishonesty. Unfortunately, it is sometimes necessary to fall back on aggressive posturing in order to determine a fair price, but such behaviour is also very unfair on those people who are forthright and honest in their dealings with tourists. It's a question of finding the right balance, or better still looking for other ways of dealing with the problem.

The main instance where bargaining is essential is when buying curios. What should be understood, however, is that the fact a curio seller is open to negotiation does not mean that you were initially being overcharged or ripped off. Curio sellers will generally quote a price knowing full well that you are going to bargain it down (they'd probably be startled if you didn't) and it is not necessary to respond aggressively or in an accusatory manner. It is impossible to say by how much you should bargain the initial price down. Some people say that you should offer half the asking price and be prepared to settle at around two-thirds, but my experience is that curio sellers are far more whimsical than such advice allows for. The sensible approach, if you want to get a feel for prices, is to ask the price of similar items at a few different stalls before you actually contemplate buying anything.

At markets and stalls, bargaining is the norm, even between locals, and the healthiest approach to this sort of haggling is to view it as an enjoyable part of the African experience. There will normally be an accepted price band for any particular commodity. To find out what it is, listen to what other people pay and try a few stalls. A ludicrously inflated price will always drop the moment you walk away. It's simpler when buying fruit and vegetables which are generally piled in heaps of Ush500 or Ush1,000. You'll elicit a smile and a few extra items thrown in if you ask '*Yongela ko*' meaning 'addition'. Above all, bear in mind that when somebody is reluctant to bargain, it may be because they asked a fair price in the first place.

Minibus-taxi conductors often try to overcharge tourists. The best way to counter this is to check the correct ticket price in advance with an impartial party, and to book your ticket the day before you travel. Failing that, you will have to judge for yourself whether the price is right, and if you have reason to think it isn't, then question the conductor. In such circumstances, it can be difficult to find the right balance between standing up for your rights and becoming overtly obnoxious.

Uganda has been an acceptably safe travel destination ever since Museveni took power in 1986, and the most significant threat to life and limb comes not from banditry or political instability, but rather from the malaria parasite and car or boat accidents. Nevertheless, as the fatal attack by Rwandan rebels on tourists staying at Bwindi in 1999 so brutally demonstrated, Uganda's location at the heart of a perennially unstable part of Africa does mean that its border areas in particular are bound to suffer intermittent security problems.

The only part of Uganda that suffers from genuine internal instability lies northwest of Murchison Falls, an area that traditionally sees few tourists and has few compelling attractions in the first place. The northwest has been plagued in recent years by the Lord's Resistance Army (LRA – see box, pages 396–7). In addition to the direct political and social consequences attached to this ongoing upheaval, banditry is rife, and several attacks on buses and other vehicles have taken place at the Karuma Bridge and points further north towards Gulu. Travel in the vicinity of Gulu, Lira and other areas north of the Nile is highly risky, if not downright suicidal, and cannot be recommended. Murchison Falls, as far as we can ascertain, is safe enough, though it would be prudent to seek current advice before heading there (see the box in *Chapter 11*, pages 380–1). The northeast is also rather dodgy, due to banditry related to Karamojong cattle rustlers. Encouragingly, as I write in September 2006, ongoing negotiations between the government and the LRA appear closer to reaching a lasting peace than any previous efforts, in which case northern Uganda may become safe for travel during the life of this edition.

The problems afflicting the DRC and Rwanda have also frequently spilt over into neighbouring parts of Uganda. The most sustained instance of this overflow was the emergence of the Allied Democratic Forces (ADF) in the mid 1990s. This small and somewhat mysterious 'rebel' army – thought to consist solely of Congolese thugs – has been responsible for several brutal attacks in the Rwenzori border area, including the massacre of 60 students at the Kichwamba Technical School near Fort Portal in June 1998. The activities of the ADF forced the closure of the Rwenzori and Semliki national parks in 1997. Since then, Ugandan government troops have managed to drive the ADF back into the DRC, and there have been no subsequent incidents of concern. Semliki National Park reopened in 1999, as did the Rwenzoris in July 2002, and it can be assumed that they would close again at the first hint of trouble.

In August 1998, four travellers were abducted in the DRC after crossing there from Uganda – one elderly women was released but the other three are missing, presumed dead – an incident that at the time seemed to have little bearing on security in Uganda. Six months later, tragedy struck closer to home, when the park headquarters at Bwindi

A final point to consider on the subject of overcharging and bargaining is that it is the fact of being overcharged that annoys; the amount itself is generally of little consequence in the wider context of a trip to Uganda. Without for a moment wanting to suggest that travellers should routinely allow themselves to be overcharged, I do feel there are occasions when we should pause to look at the bigger picture. Backpackers in particular tend to forget that, no matter how tight for cash they are, it was their choice to travel on a minimal budget, and most Ugandans are much poorer than they will ever be. If you find yourself quibbling over a pittance with an old lady selling a few piles of fruit by the roadside, you might perhaps bear in mind that the notion of a fixed price is a very Western one. When somebody is desperate enough for money, or afraid that their perishable goods might not last another day, it may well be possible to push them down to a price lower than they would normally accept. In such circumstances, I see nothing wrong with erring on the side of generosity.

was attacked by an army of exiled Rwandan rebels, killing two rangers and eight tourists. If, as seems probable, the aim of the attack was to destabilise Uganda's tourist industry, then it could not have been better calculated, given that the mountain gorillas at Bwindi had done more than anything to help Uganda overcome a negative international image generated by the barbarities of the Amin and Obote regimes.

Prior to March 1999, Bwindi was considered to be safe by almost everybody involved in Uganda. The attack on the unprotected park headquarters came as a complete shock, but in hindsight it could so easily have been averted by a greater military presence. Since Bwindi reopened in May 1999, security levels have been very high, with soldiers accompanying visitors on all walks. Uganda's battered tourist industry took longer to recover, but things started to return to normal in 2000, and tour operators based in the country for the best part of a decade have reported 2002 to be their busiest year ever – a figure made doubly remarkable when contrasted against the global downswing in tourism post-9/11. Still, any reader who is thinking of visiting Uganda might reasonably ask of the Bwindi incident whether something similar might happen again. The honest answer is that nobody knows. The official line, and one followed by all local tour operators, is that it was an isolated tragedy, and certainly Bwindi itself is now so well protected that it would make an unlikely target for any further attacks. The country was recently visited by military attachés from three Western countries, and proclaimed safe for travel (with the obvious exception of the little-visited north). Overall, then, there seems little cause for serious concern with regard to security along Uganda's established tourist circuits.

It might also be worth touching briefly on the implications of broader global events on travel to Uganda, especially as two of its neighbours have suffered terrorist attacks attributed to Al Qaeda. My feeling is that Uganda forms no more likely a target for this particular threat than do most other countries – and less, perhaps, than the US or UK – because its Islamic population is small by comparison with that of Tanzania or Kenya, and it lacks the centuries-old trade links that bind the East African coast to the Middle East.

To place things in some perspective, I would regard Uganda to be safer overall than Kenya or South Africa, both of which suffer from very high rates of armed crime. Equally, I'm a travel writer, not a political sage, and as such I'd regard it to be irresponsible to state categorically that the Bwindi massacre was a one-off event, or that nothing of the sort could ever happen again. The decision to visit Uganda, and the responsibility, rests on the individual traveller. Assuming that you do, I would recommend you keep your ear to the ground, read the local newspaper, and avoid visiting known trouble spots – fortunately, the authorities are unlikely to allow tourists to visit reserves and national parks where there is a security problem.

WOMEN TRAVELLERS Women generally regard sub-equatorial Africa as one of the safest places in the world to travel alone. Uganda in particular poses few if any risks specific to female travellers. It is reasonable to expect a fair bit of flirting and the odd direct proposition, especially if you mingle with Ugandans in bars, but a firm 'no' should be enough to defuse any potential situation. And, to be fair to Ugandan men, you can expect the same sort of thing in any country, and for that matter from many male travellers. Ugandan women tend to dress conservatively. It will not increase the amount of hassle you receive if you avoid wearing clothes that, however unfairly, may be perceived to be provocative, and it may even go some way to decreasing it.

More mundanely, tampons are not readily available in smaller towns, though you can easily locate them in Kampala, Entebbe and Jinja, and in game lodge and hotel gift shops. When travelling in out-of-the-way places, carry enough tampons to see you through to the next time you'll be in a large city, bearing in mind that

Uganda's electricity is supplied primarily by two hydro-power dams built along the Nile close to its overflow from Lake Victoria near Jinja. Generation began with the opening of the Nalubaale Power Station at the Owen Falls Dam by Queen Elizabeth in 1954. Capacity was increased in 1998 with a second dam at nearby Kiira, which brought the total capacity to 300MW. The national capacity was set to increase further with the planned construction of an additional dam 8km downriver near Bujagali (see pages 418–19). When this project collapsed in 2003, an energy crisis was inevitable, given that the existing output, though sufficient to cater for the daytime consumption of 260MW, could not meet a peak evening load of 380MW. Greater problems were envisaged ahead, with growing urban demands and the extension of the national grid ever further upcountry under the government's Rural Electrification Scheme. Moreover, with all eggs packed into the ill-fated Bujagali basket, no similar backup scheme existed as an immediate substitute.

The power crisis transpired sooner rather than later when the Lake Victoria basin endured two years of extended drought during 2004/5 causing the lake to drop by over 1m to its lowest level since 1961. This fall is popularly blamed by Kenyan and Tanzanian lakeshore communities on technicians at the dams who, despite reduced flow *into* Lake Victoria, reportedly continued to let the same volume out through their turbines and down the Nile. Ugandan officials point out that constant loss by evaporation from the lake surface is nine times the amount released down the river. Whatever the truth, the volume of water available for power generation has dropped from 73.5 million m^2 per day to 64.8 million m^2 per day, with disastrous effects on the combined output of the dams, which has dropped from 300MW to 135MW. As a result, UMEME (the power distribution body) has been forced to reinstate 'load shedding,' the loathed system of phased power cuts that dogged Uganda before the commissioning of the Kira II Dam at Jinja.

Even at its previous nadir in 1997, load shedding involved a system of power cuts on alternate evenings (19.00–22.00) followed by an 08.00–14.00 outage (or 'outrage' as Ugandans like to say) on alternate days. By contrast, the current system, imposed in May 2006, involves alternating 24-hour periods. That's 24 hours with power followed by 24 without. This system is further complicated by an additional schedule of 'supplementary load shedding' from 19.00–22.00 every few nights, plus additional outages when a fault occurs. All of which made Uganda a difficult place to watch the FIFA 2006 World Cup! Shortly after an unscheduled power failure, guests at Kampala Backpackers were amused to learn that residents of a city suburb in Australia were treated to restaurant vouchers to go eat out rather than staying home to endure a *two-hour* power cut while a new transformer was commissioned. UMEME is not so quite considerate.

In August 2006, the Minister of Energy and Mineral Development announced a further reduction in hydro-power capacity to 120MW per day, increasing the energy deficit during peak hours to 180MW. The authorities are however making efforts to close the gap. A 50MW thermal (diesel) generation plant has increased output to 170MW. Another 50MW plant will be installed, which combined with energy-saving measures is expected to eliminate daytime power cuts by mid 2007. Distribution of 800,000 subsidised low-energy light bulbs, for example, is expected to save up to 50MW during

travelling in the tropics can sometimes cause heavier or more regular periods than normal. Sanitary pads are available in most towns of any size.

BRIBERY AND BUREAUCRACY For all you read about the subject, bribery is not the problem to travellers in Africa it is often made out to be. The travellers who are most often asked for bribes are those with private transport; and even they only

evening hours. Up to 30MW may also be imported from Kenya subject to availability.

Plans for a long-term solution still remain at the paperwork stage. Following the collapse of the controversial Bujagali dam project (see box, pages 418–9), attention shifted to Karuma Falls, which lies along the Nile at the eastern boundary of Murchison Falls National Park. Frustratingly, however, construction of this eagerly awaited project by a Norwegian company, Norpak Power, was set back many months by irregularities in the tender process in 2006. The deal was scrapped and it was back to square one! In the meantime, the Bujagali dam project has been resuscitated and is once again to the fore. Construction is expected to start in 2007.

The extent to which the crisis will affect visiting tourists varies. Hotels have adapted by installing backup systems, so in all probability, other than the dull vibration of a hotel generator out in the back courtyard, the average tourist won't be inconvenienced too much. Rooms will be lit (most of the time), DSTV will function and the drinks will be cold. But electrical self-sufficiency is costly, so these services will come at a price. In order to be spared darkness in their rooms, visitors will inevitably experience an additional lightness in their wallets and moneybelts as costs are passed on to the consumer. This means more expensive hotel rooms, beer, food and bus fares.

Rising costs are a function not only of installing operating backup systems but also of all-round inflation caused by rising transport and manufacturing costs. The situation has been further complicated by a sharp rise in oil prices. It takes a lot of oil to run a 50MW thermal generator and in June 2006, UMEME added insult to injury for its long-suffering customers by hiking electricity tariffs by almost 40% and prices may rise by an additional 25% in September 2006. This is rather a nuisance for residential consumers but the financial implications for the business and industrial sector are of course huge. Factory workers presently mill around idle or work through the night. Businesses adapt or close down. As firms in all sectors invest in alternative sources of power, prices across the board must rise. Generator systems of adequate capacity are expensive and fuel to run them is a recurrent drain. Solar systems might harness free energy but the panels, inverters and battery banks require significant capital investment upfront. You'll find that it's increasingly common for internet cafés and photocopy shops to double their prices on days when they are forced to run generators. It's fair enough paying Ush100 rather than Ush50 per photocopy but it'll hurt rather more if the same principle is applied across the board to food, transport and hotels. I'm not suggesting that the price of everything will double like internet access and photocopying but it would be reasonable to expect the prices that I've compiled during June and July of 2006 to date rather more quickly than is usual even over the duration of a guidebook edition.

Most rural Ugandans remain untroubled by electricity or the lack of it for the simple reason that it has not reached them yet. Similarly, bush lodges and camps either manage without it or took steps long ago to generate their own requirements. If urban Uganda seems destined to suffer electricity shortages for some years to come, the solution for tourists is of course to get out of the towns to rural locations – such as the Ssese Islands, Kasenda craters, Sipi Falls and Lake Bunyonyi – where electric light is simply a nuisance that interferes with the appreciation of Africa's vast starry skies.

have a major problem at some borders and from traffic police in some countries (notably Mozambique and Kenya). If you are travelling on public transport or as part of a tour, or even if you are driving within Uganda, I don't think that you need to give the question of bribery serious thought.

There is a tendency to portray African bureaucrats as difficult and inefficient in their dealings with tourists. As a rule, this reputation says more about Western prejudices than it does about Uganda. Sure, you come across the odd unhelpful official, but then such is the nature of the beast everywhere in the world. The vast majority of officials in the African countries I've visited have been courteous and helpful in their dealings with tourists, often to a degree that is almost embarrassing. In Uganda, I encountered nothing but friendliness from almost every government official I had dealings with, whether they were border officials, policemen or game reserve staff. This, I can assure you, is far more than most African visitors to Europe will experience from officialdom.

A factor in determining the response you receive from African officials will be your own attitude. If you walk into every official encounter with an aggressive, paranoid approach, you are quite likely to kindle the feeling held by many Africans that Europeans are arrogant and off-hand in their dealings with other races. Instead, try to be friendly and patient, and accept that the person to whom you are talking does not speak English as a first language and may thus have difficulty following everything you say. Treat people with respect rather than disdain, and they'll tend to treat you in the same way.

THEFT Uganda is widely and rightly regarded as one of the most crime-free countries in Africa, certainly as far as visitors need be concerned. Muggings are comparatively rare, even in Kampala, and I've never heard of the sort of con tricks that abound in places like Nairobi. Even petty theft such as pick-pocketing and bag snatching is relatively unusual, though it does happen from time to time. Walking around large towns at night is also reputedly safe, though it would be tempting fate to wander alone along unlit streets. On the basis that it is preferable to err on the side of caution, I've decided to repeat a few tips that apply to travelling anywhere in east and southern Africa:

- Most casual thieves operate in busy markets and bus stations. Keep a close watch on your possessions in such places, and avoid having valuables or large amounts of money loose in your daypack or pocket.
- Keep all your valuables and the bulk of your money in a hidden moneybelt. Never show this moneybelt in public. Keep any spare cash you need elsewhere on your person; I feel that a button-up pocket on the front of the shirt is the most secure place as money cannot be snatched from it without the thief coming into your view. It is also advisable to keep a small amount of hard currency (ideally cash) hidden away in your luggage so that, should you lose your moneybelt, you have something to fall back on.
- Where the choice exists between carrying valuables on your person or leaving them in a locked room I would tend to favour the latter option (only one of the hundreds of thefts I've heard about in Africa happened from a locked hotel room, and that was in Nairobi where just about anything is possible). Obviously you should use your judgement on this and be sure the room is absolutely secure. A factor to be considered is that some travellers' cheque companies will not refund cheques which were stolen from a room.
- Leave any jewellery of financial or sentimental value at home.

People new to exotic travel often worry about tropical diseases, but it is accidents that are most likely to carry you off. Road accidents are very common in many parts of Uganda so be aware and do what you can to reduce risks: try to travel during daylight hours, always wear a seatbelt and refuse to be driven by anyone who has been drinking. Listen to local advice about areas where violent crime is rife too.

5

Health and Safety

with Dr Jane Wilson-Howarth, Dr Felicity Nicholson, and Dr Dick Stockley

People new to exotic travel often worry about tropical diseases, but it is accidents that are most likely to carry you off. Road accidents are very common in many parts of Uganda so be aware and do what you can to reduce risks: try to travel during daylight hours, always wear a seatbelt and refuse to be driven by anyone who has been drinking. Listen to local advice about areas where violent crime is rife too.

PREPARATIONS

Preparations to ensure a healthy trip to Uganda require checks on your immunisation status: it is wise to be up to date on **tetanus**, **polio**, **diphtheria** (now given as an all-in-one vaccine, Revaxis, that lasts for ten years), and hepatitis A. Immunisations against meningococcus and rabies may also be recommended. Proof of vaccination against **yellow fever** is needed for entry into Uganda if you are coming from another yellow fever endemic area. The World Health Organisation (WHO) recommends that this vaccine should be taken for Uganda by those over nine months of age, although proof of entry is only officially required for those over one year of age. If the vaccine is not suitable for you then obtain an exemption certificate from your GP or a travel clinic. Immunisation against cholera is no longer required for Uganda.

Hepatitis A vaccine (Havrix Monodose or Avaxim) comprises two injections given about a year apart. The course costs about £100, but may be available on the NHS; protects for 25 years and can be administered even close to the time of departure. **Hepatitis B** vaccination should be considered for longer trips (two months or more) or for those working with children or in situations where contact with blood is likely. Three injections are needed for the best protection and can be given over a three-week period if time is short. Longer schedules give more sustained protection and are therefore preferred if time allows. Hepatitis A vaccine can also be given as a combination with hepatitis B as 'Twinrix', though two doses are needed at least seven days apart to be effective for the hepatitis A component, and three doses are needed for the hepatitis B.

The newer injectable typhoid vaccines (eg: Typhim Vi) last for three years and are about 85% effective. Oral capsules (Vivotif) are currently available in the US (and soon in the UK); if four capsules are taken over seven days it will last for five years. They should be encouraged unless the traveller is leaving within a few days for a trip of a week or less, when the vaccine would not be effective in time. **Meningitis** vaccine (ideally containing strains A, C, W and Y, but if this is not available then A+C vaccine is better than nothing), especially for trips of more than four weeks (see *Meningitis*, page 123). Vaccinations for **rabies** are ideally advised for everyone, but are especially important for travellers visiting more remote areas, especially if you are more than 24 hours from medical help and definitely if you will be working with animals (see *Rabies* pages 123–4).

Experts differ over whether a BCG vaccination against **tuberculosis** (TB) is useful in adults: discuss with your travel clinic.

Ideally you should visit your own doctor or a specialist travel clinic (see pages 116–17) to discuss your requirements if possible at least eight weeks before you plan to travel. Several travellers report that anti-malarial drugs (and other medicines) in Kampala are far cheaper than in the UK, but you will still need to start the course of anti-malarial tablets before you leave home.

PROTECTION FROM THE SUN Give some thought to packing suncream. The incidence of skin cancer is rocketing as Caucasians are travelling more and spending more time exposing themselves to the sun. Keep out of the sun during the middle of the day and, if you must expose yourself to the sun, build up gradually from 20 minutes per day. Be especially careful of exposure in the middle of the day and of sun reflected off water, and wear a T-shirt and lots of waterproof suncream (at least SPF15) when swimming. Sun exposure ages the skin, makes people prematurely wrinkly; and increases the risk of skin cancer .Cover up with long, loose clothes and wear a hat when you can. The glare and the dust can be hard on the eyes, too, so bring UV-protecting sunglasses and, perhaps, a soothing eyebath.

MALARIA Along with road accidents, malaria poses the single biggest serious threat to the health of travellers in most parts of tropical Africa, Uganda included. It is unwise to travel in malarial parts of Africa whilst pregnant or with children: the risk of malaria in many parts is considerable and these travellers are likely to succumb rapidly to the disease. The risk of malaria above 1,800m above sea level is low.

Malaria in Uganda The *Anopheles* mosquito that transmits the parasite is most commonly found near marshes and still water, where it breeds, and the parasite is most abundant at low altitudes. Parts of Uganda lying at an altitude of 2,000m or higher (a category that includes only high mountains such as the Rwenzoris and Elgon) are regarded to be free of malaria. In mid-altitude locations, malaria is largely but not entirely seasonal, with the highest risk of transmission occurring during the rainy season (March to May and October to December). Moist and low-lying areas such as the Nile at Murchison Falls are high risk throughout the year, but the danger is greatest during the rainy season. This localised breakdown might influence what foreigners working in Uganda do about malaria prevention, but all travellers to Uganda must assume that they will be exposed to malaria and should take precautions throughout their trip (see below).

Malaria prevention There is not yet a vaccine against malaria that gives enough protection to be useful for travellers, but there are other ways to avoid it; since most of Africa is very high risk for malaria, travellers must plan their malaria protection properly. Seek current advice on the best antimalarials to take: usually mefloquine, Malarone or doxycycline. If mefloquine (Lariam) is suggested, start this two-and-a-half weeks (three doses) before departure to check that it suits you; stop it immediately if it seems to cause depression or anxiety, visual or hearing disturbances, severe headaches, fits or changes in heart rhythm. Side effects such as nightmares or dizziness are not medical reasons for stopping unless they are sufficiently debilitating or annoying. Anyone who has been treated for depression or psychiatric problems, has diabetes controlled by oral therapy or who is epileptic (or who has suffered fits in the past) or has a close blood relative who is epileptic, should probably avoid mefloquine.

In the past doctors were nervous about prescribing mefloquine to pregnant women, however, experience has shown that it is relatively safe and certainly safer than the risk of malaria. It is now an option at some stages, however, there are other issues and if you are travelling to Uganda whilst pregnant, seek expert advice before departure.

Malarone (proguanil and atovaquone) is as effective as mefloquine. It has the advantage of having few side effects and need only be continued for one week after returning. However, it is expensive and because of this tends to be reserved for shorter trips. Malarone may not be suitable for everybody, so advice should be taken from a doctor. The licence in the UK has been extended for up to three months' use and a paediatric form of tablet is also available, prescribed on a weight basis.

Another alternative is the antibiotic doxycycline (100mg daily). Like Malarone it can be started one day before arrival. Unlike mefloquine, it may also be used in travellers with epilepsy, although certain anti-epileptic medication may make it less effective. In perhaps 1–3% of people there is the possibility of allergic skin reactions developing in sunlight; the drug should be stopped if this happens. Women using the oral contraceptive should use an additional method of protection for the first four weeks when using doxycycline. It is also unsuitable in pregnancy or for children under 12 years.

Chloroquine and proguanil are no longer considered to be effective enough for Uganda but may be considered as a last resort if nothing else is deemed suitable

All tablets should be taken with or after the evening meal, washed down with plenty of fluid and, with the exception of Malarone (see above), continued for four weeks after leaving.

Despite all these precautions, it is important to be aware that no anti-malarial drug is 100% protective, although those on prophylactics who are unlucky enough to catch malaria are less likely to get rapidly into serious trouble. In addition to taking anti-malarials, it is therefore important to avoid mosquito bites between dusk and dawn (see *Avoiding insect bites*, page 122).

There is unfortunately the occasional traveller who prefers to 'acquire resistance' to malaria rather than take preventive tablets, or who takes homeopathic prophylactics thinking these are effective against killer disease. Homeopathy theory dictates treating like with like so there is no place for prophylaxis or immunisation in a well person; bone fide homoeopathists do not advocate it. Travellers to Africa cannot acquire any effective resistance to malaria, and those who don't make use of prophylactic drugs risk their life in a manner that is both foolish and unnecessary.

Malaria diagnosis and treatment Even those who take their malaria tablets meticulously and do everything possible to avoid mosquito bites may contract a strain of malaria that is resistant to prophylactic drugs. Untreated malaria is likely to be fatal, but even strains resistant to prophylaxis respond well to prompt treatment. Because of this, your immediate priority upon displaying possible malaria symptoms – including a rapid rise in temperature (over 38°C), and any combination of a headache, flu-like aches and pains, a general sense of disorientation, and possibly even nausea and diarrhoea – is to establish whether you have malaria, ideally by visiting a clinic.

Diagnosing malaria is not easy, which is why consulting a doctor is sensible: there are other dangerous causes of fever in Africa, which require different treatments. Even if you test negative, it would be wise to stay within reach of a laboratory until the symptoms clear up, and to test again after a day or two if they don't. It's worth noting that if you have a fever and the malaria test is negative, you may have typhoid or paratyphoid, which should also receive immediate treatment.

5

Travellers to remote parts of Uganda – for instance in the game reserves and most of the popular hiking areas - would be wise to carry a course of treatment to cure malaria, and a rapid test kit. With malaria, it is normal enough to go from feeling healthy to having a high fever in the space of a few hours (and it is possible to die from falciparum malaria within 24 hours of the first symptoms). In such circumstances, assume that you have malaria and act accordingly – whatever risks are attached to taking an unnecessary cure are outweighed by the dangers of untreated malaria. Experts differ on the costs and benefits of self-treatment, but agree that it leads to over-treatment and to many people taking drugs they do not need; yet treatment may save your life. There is also some division about the best treatment for malaria, but either Malarone or Coarthemeter are the current treatments of choice. Discuss your trip with a specialist either at home or in Uganda.

TRAVEL CLINICS AND HEALTH INFORMATION A full list of current travel clinic websites worldwide is available from the International Society of Travel Medicine on www.istm.org. For other journey preparation information, consult www.tripprep.com. Information about various medications may be found on www.emedicine.com. For information on malaria prevention, see www.preventingmalaria.info.

UK

Berkeley Travel Clinic 32 Berkeley St, London W1J 8EL (near Green Park tube station); ✆ 020 7629 6233

Cambridge Travel Clinic 48a Mill Rd, Cambridge CB1 2AS; ✆ 01223 367362; e enquiries@travelcliniccambridge.co.uk; www.travelcliniccambridge.co.uk. Open Tue–Fri 12.00–19.00, Sat 10.00–16.00.

Edinburgh Travel Clinic Regional Infectious Diseases Unit, Ward 41 OPD, Western General Hospital, Crewe Rd South, Edinburgh EH4 2UX; ✆ 0131 537 2822; www.link.med.ed.ac.uk/ridu. Travel helpline (0906 589 0380) open weekdays 09.00–12.00. Provides inoculations and antimalarial prophylaxis and advises on travel-related health risks.

Fleet Street Travel Clinic 29 Fleet St, London EC4Y 1AA; ✆ 020 7353 5678; www.fleetstreetclinic.com. Vaccinations, travel products and latest advice.

Hospital for Tropical Diseases Travel Clinic Mortimer Market Bldg, Capper St (off Tottenham Ct Rd), London WC1E 6AU; ✆ 020 7388 9600; www.thehtd.org. Offers consultations and advice, and is able to provide all necessary drugs and vaccines for travellers. Runs a healthline (0906 133 7733) for country-specific information and health hazards. Also stocks nets, water purification equipment and personal protection measures.

Interhealth Worldwide Partnership House, 157 Waterloo Rd, London SE1 8US; ✆ 020 7902 9000; www.interhealth.org.uk. Competitively priced, one-stop travel health service. All profits go to their affiliated company, InterHealth, which provides health care for overseas workers on Christian projects.

MASTA (Medical Advisory Service for Travellers Abroad) MASTA Ltd, Moorfield Rd, Yeadon LS19 7BN; ✆ 0870 606 2782; www.masta-travel-health.com. Provides travel health advice, anti-malarials and vaccinations. There are over 25 MASTA pre-travel clinics in Britain; call or check online for the nearest. Clinics also sell mosquito nets, medical kits, insect protection and travel hygiene products.

NHS travel website www.fitfortravel.scot.nhs.uk. Provides country-by-country advice on immunisation and malaria, plus details of recent developments, and a list of relevant health organisations.

Nomad Travel Store/Clinic 3–4 Wellington Terrace, Turnpike Lane, London N8 0PX; ✆ 020 8889 7014; travel-health line (office hours only) 0906 863 3414; e sales@nomadtravel.co.uk; www.nomadtravel.co.uk. Also at 40 Bernard St, London WC1N 1LJ; ✆ 020 7833 4114; 52 Grosvenor Gardens, London SW1W 0AG; ✆ 020 7823 5823; and 43 Queens Rd, Bristol BS8 1QH; ✆ 0117 922 6567. For health advice, equipment such as mosquito nets and other anti-bug devices, and an excellent range of adventure travel gear.

Trailfinders Travel Clinic 194 Kensington High St, London W8 7RG; ✆ 020 7938 3999; www.trailfinders.com/clinic.htm

Travelpharm The Travelpharm website, www.travelpharm.com, offers up-to-date guidance on travel-related health and has a range of medications available through their online mini-pharmacy.

Irish Republic

Tropical Medical Bureau Grafton Street Medical Centre, Grafton Bldgs, 34 Grafton St, Dublin 2; ℡ 1 671 9200; www.tmb.ie. A useful website specific to tropical destinations. Also check website for other bureaux locations throughout Ireland.

US

Centers for Disease Control 1600 Clifton Rd, Atlanta, GA 30333; ℡ 800 311 3435; travellers' health hotline 888 232 3299; www.cdc.gov/travel. The central source of travel information in the USA. The invaluable *Health Information for International Travel*, published annually, is available from the Division of Quarantine at this address.
Connaught Laboratories PO Box 187, Swiftwater, PA 18370; ℡ 800 822 2463. They will send a free list of specialist tropical-medicine physicians in your state.

IAMAT (International Association for Medical Assistance to Travelers) 1623 Military Rd, 279, Niagara Falls, NY14304-1745; ℡ 716 754 4883; e info@iamat.org; www.iamat.org. A non-profit organisation that provides lists of English-speaking doctors abroad.
International Medicine Center 920 Frostwood Drive, Suite 670, Houston, TX 77024; ℡ 713 550 2000; www.traveldoc.com

Canada

IAMAT Suite 1, 1287 St Clair Av W, Toronto, Ontario M6E 1B8; ℡ 416 652 0137; www.iamat.org

TMVC Suite 314, 1030 W Georgia St, Vancouver BC V6E 2Y3; ℡ 1 888 288 8682; www.tmvc.com. Private clinic with several outlets in Canada.

Australia, New Zealand, Singapore

TMVC ℡ 1300 65 88 44; www.tmvc.com.au. Clinics in Australia, New Zealand and Singapore, including: *Auckland* Canterbury Arcade, 170 Queen St, Auckland; ℡ 9 373 3531
Brisbane 6th floor, 247 Adelaide St, Brisbane, QLD 4000; ℡ 7 3221 9066

Melbourne 393 Little Bourke St, 2nd floor, Melbourne, VIC 3000; ℡ 3 9602 5788
Sydney Dymocks Bldg, 7th floor, 428 George St, Sydney, NSW 2000; ℡ 2 9221 7133
IAMAT PO Box 5049, Christchurch 5, New Zealand; www.iamat.org

South Africa and Namibia

SAA-Netcare Travel Clinics P Bag X34, Benmore 2010; www.travelclinic.co.za. Clinics throughout South Africa.

TMVC 113 D F Malan Drive, Roosevelt Park, Johannesburg; ℡ 011 888 7488; www.tmvc.com.au. Consult website for details of other clinics in South Africa and Namibia.

Switzerland

IAMAT 57 Chemin des Voirets, 1212 Grand Lancy, Geneva; www.iamat.org

For further information see page 480.

PERSONAL FIRST-AID KIT A minimal kit contains:

- A good drying antiseptic, eg: iodine or potassium permanganate (don't take antiseptic cream)
- A few small dressings (Band-Aids)
- Suncream
- Insect repellent; anti-malarial tablets; impregnated bed-net or permethrin spray
- Aspirin or paracetamol
- Antifungal cream (eg: Canesten)
- Ciprofloxacin or norfloxacin, for severe diarrhoea
- Tinidazole for giardia or amoebic dysentery (see below for regime)

Dr Jane Wilson-Howarth

Long-haul air travel increases the risk of deep vein thrombosis. Although recent research has suggested that many of us develop clots when immobilised, most resolve without us ever having been aware of them. In certain susceptible individuals, though, clots form on clots and when large ones break away and lodge in the lungs this is dangerous. Fortunately this happens in a tiny minority of passengers.

Studies have shown that flights of over five-and-a-half-hours are significant, and that people who take lots of shorter flights over a short space of time can also form clots. People at highest risk are:

- Those who have had a clot before – unless they are now taking warfarin
- People over 80 years of age
- Anyone who has recently undergone a major operation or surgery for varicose veins
- Someone who has had a hip or knee replacement in the last three months
- Cancer sufferers
- Those who have ever had a stroke
- People with heart disease
- Those with a close blood relative who has had a clot

Those with a slightly increased risk:

- People over 40
- Women who are pregnant or have had a baby in the last couple of weeks
- People taking female hormones, the combined contraceptive pill or other oestrogen therapy
- Heavy smokers
- Those who have very severe varicose veins
- The very obese
- People who are very tall (over 6ft/1.8m) or short (under 5ft/1.5m)

- Antibiotic eye drops, for sore, 'gritty', stuck-together eyes (conjunctivitis)
- A pair of fine pointed tweezers (to remove hairy caterpillar hairs, thorns, splinters, coral, etc)
- Alcohol-based hand rub or a bar of soap in a plastic box
- Condoms or femidoms
- Malaria diagnostic kits (5) and a digital thermometer (for those going to remote areas)

IN UGANDA

MEDICAL FACILITIES Private clinics, hospitals and pharmacies can be found in most large towns, and doctors generally speak fair to fluent English. The main hospital is the International Hospital Kampala (*Namuwongo;* ✆ *0312 200400*). Private clinics include The Surgery in Kampala (✆ *0414 256003, 0752 756003; www.thesurgeryuganda.org*).

Consultation fees and laboratory tests are remarkably inexpensive when compared to most Western countries, so if you do fall sick it would be absurd to let financial considerations dissuade you from seeking medical help. Commonly required medicines such as broad-spectrum antibiotics are widely available and cheap throughout the region, as are malaria cures and prophylactics, but wherever possible, take medicines with you. If you are on any medication prior

A deep vein thrombosis (DVT) is a blood clot that forms in the deep leg veins. This is very different from irritating but harmless superficial phlebitis. DVT causes swelling and redness of one leg, usually with heat and pain in one calf and sometimes the thigh. A DVT is only dangerous if a clot breaks away and travels to the lungs (pulmonary embolus). Symptoms of a pulmonary embolus (PE) include chest pain that is worse on breathing in deeply, shortness of breath, and sometimes coughing up small amounts of blood. The symptoms commonly start three to ten days after a long flight. Anyone who thinks that they might have a DVT needs to see a doctor immediately who will arrange a scan. Warfarin tablets (to thin the blood) are then taken for at least six months.

PREVENTION OF DVT Several conditions make the problem more likely. Immobility is the key, and factors like reduced oxygen in cabin air and dehydration may also contribute. To reduce the risk of thrombosis on a long journey:

* Exercise before and after the flight
* Keep mobile before and during the flight; move around every couple of hours
* Drink plenty of water or juices during the flight
* Avoid taking sleeping pills and excessive tea, coffee and alcohol
* Perform exercises that mimic walking and tense the calf muscles
* Consider wearing flight socks or support stockings (see www.legshealth.com)
* Ideally take a meal each week of oily fish (mackerel, trout, salmon, sardines, etc) ahead of your departure. This reduces the blood's ability to clot and thus DVT risk. It may be even worth just taking a meal of oily fish 24 hours before departure is this is more practical.

If you think you are at increased risk of a clot, ask your doctor if it is safe to travel.

to departure, or you have specific needs relating to a known medical condition (for instance if you are allergic to bee stings or you are prone to attacks of asthma), then you are strongly advised to bring any related drugs and devices with you.

WATER STERILISATION You can fall ill from drinking contaminated water so try to drink from safe sources eg: bottled water where available. If you are away from shops such as half way up the Rwenzori and your bottled water runs out, make tea, pour the remaining boiled water into a clean container and use it for drinking. Alternatively, water should be passed through a good bacteriological filter or purified with iodine or the less-effective chlorine tablets (eg: Puritabs).

COMMON MEDICAL PROBLEMS
Travellers' diarrhoea Travelling in Uganda carries a fairly high risk of getting a dose of travellers' diarrhoea; perhaps half of all visitors will suffer and the newer you are to exotic travel, the more likely you will be to suffer. By taking precautions against travellers' diarrhoea you will also avoid typhoid, paratyphoid, cholera, hepatitis, dysentery, worms, etc. Travellers' diarrhoea and the other faecal-oral diseases come from getting other peoples' faeces in your mouth. This most often happens from cooks not washing their hands after a trip to the toilet, but even if the restaurant cook does not understand basic hygiene you will be safe if your food

has been properly cooked and arrives piping hot. The most important prevention strategy is to wash your hands before eating anything. You can pick up salmonella and shigella from toilet door handles and possibly bank notes. The maxim to remind you what you can safely eat is:

PEEL IT, BOIL IT, COOK IT OR FORGET IT.

This means that fruit you have washed and peeled yourself, and hot foods, should be safe but raw foods, cold cooked foods, salads, fruit salads which have been prepared by others, ice cream and ice are all risky, and foods kept lukewarm in hotel buffets are often dangerous. That said, plenty of travellers and expatriates enjoy fruit and vegetables, so do keep a sense of perspective: food served in a fairly decent hotel in a large town or a place regularly frequented by expatriates is likely to be safe. If you are struck, see box above for treatment.

Eye problems Bacterial conjunctivitis (pink eye) is a common infection in Africa; people who wear contact lenses are most open to this irritating problem. The eyes feel sore and gritty and they will often be stuck together in the mornings. They will need treatment with antibiotic drops or ointment. Lesser eye irritation should settle with bathing in salt water and keeping the eyes shaded. If an insect flies into your eye, extract it with great care, ensuring you do not crush or damage it otherwise you may get a nastily inflamed eye from toxins secreted by the creature. Small elongated red and black blister beetles carry warning colouration to tell you not to crush them anywhere against your skin.

Prickly heat A fine pimply rash on the trunk is likely to be heat rash; cool showers, dabbing dry, and talc will help. Treat the problem by slowing down to a relaxed schedule, wearing only loose, baggy, 100%-cotton clothes and sleeping naked under a fan; if it's bad you may need to check into an air-conditioned hotel room for a while.

Skin infections Any mosquito bite or small nick in the skin gives an opportunity for bacteria to foil the body's usually excellent defences; it will surprise many travellers how quickly skin infections start in warm humid climates and it is essential to clean and cover even the slightest wound. Creams are not as effective as a good drying antiseptic such as dilute iodine, potassium permanganate (a few crystals in half a cup of water), or crystal (or gentian) violet. One of these should be available in most towns. If the wound starts to throb, or becomes red and the redness starts to spread, or the wound oozes, and especially if you develop a fever, antibiotics will probably be needed: flucloxacillin (250mg four times a day) or cloxacillin (500mg four times a day). For those allergic to penicillin, erythromycin (500mg twice a day) for five days should help. See a doctor if the symptoms do not start to improve within 48 hours.

Fungal infections also get a hold easily in hot, moist climates so wear 100%-cotton socks and underwear and shower frequently. An itchy rash in the groin or flaking between the toes is likely to be a fungal infection. This needs treatment with an antifungal cream such as Canesten (clotrimazole); if this is not available try Whitfield's ointment (compound benzoic acid ointment) or crystal violet (although this will turn you purple!).

Insect-borne diseases Malaria (see pages 114–16) is by no means the only insect-borne disease to which the traveller may succumb. Others include sleeping sickness and river blindness (see box, *Avoiding insect bites* page 122). Dengue fever is rare in Uganda but there are many other similar arboviruses. These mosquito-borne diseases may mimic malaria but there is no prophylactic medication against them. The mosquitoes that carry dengue fever viruses bite during the daytime, so it is worth applying repellent if you see any mosquitoes around. Symptoms include strong headaches, rashes and excruciating joint and muscle pains and high fever. Viral fevers usually last about a week or so and are not usually fatal. Complete rest and paracetamol are the usual treatment; plenty of fluids also help. Some patients are given an intravenous drip to keep them from dehydrating. It is especially important to protect yourself if you have had dengue fever before, since a second infection with a different strain can result in the potentially fatal dengue haemorrhagic fever.

Bilharzia or schistosomiasis
with thanks to Dr Vaughan Southgate of the Natural History Museum, London, and Dr Dick Stockley, The Surgery, Kampala

Bilharzia or schistosomiasis is a disease that commonly afflicts the rural poor of the tropics. Two types exist in sub-Saharan Africa – *Schistosoma mansoni* and *Schistosoma haematobium*. It is an unpleasant problem that is worth avoiding, though can be treated if you do get it. This parasite is common in almost all water sources in Uganda, even places advertised as 'bilharzia free'. Lake Bunyoni is genuinely free of bilharzia. The most risky shores will be close to places where infected people use water, wash clothes, etc.

It is easier to understand how to diagnose it, treat it and prevent it if you know a little about the life cycle. Contaminated faeces are washed into the lake, the eggs hatch and the larva infects certain species of snail. The snails then produce about

As the sun is going down, don long clothes and apply repellent on any exposed flesh. Pack a DEET-based insect repellent (roll-ons or stick are the least messy preparations for travelling). You also need either a permethrin-impregnated bednet or a permethrin spray so that you can 'treat' bednets in hotels. Permethrin treatment makes even very tatty nets protective and prevents mosquitoes from biting through the impregnated net when you roll against it; it also deters other biters. Otherwise retire to an air-conditioned room or burn mosquito coils (which are widely available and cheap in Uganda) or sleep under a fan. Coils and fans reduce rather than eliminate bites. Travel clinics usually sell a good range of nets, treatment kits and repellents.

Aside from avoiding mosquito bites between dusk and dawn, which will protect you from elephantiasis and a range of nasty insect-borne viruses, as well as malaria (see pages 114–15), it is important to take precautions against other insect bites. During the day it is wise to wear long, loose (preferably 100% cotton) clothes if you are pushing through scrubby country; this will keep off ticks and also tsetse and day-biting *Aedes* mosquitoes which may spread viral fevers, including yellow fever.

Tsetse flies hurt when they bite and it is said that they are attracted to the colour blue; locals will advise on where they are a problem and where they transmit sleeping sickness.

Minute pestilential biting **blackflies** spread river blindness in some parts of Africa between 190°N and 170°S; the disease is caught close to fast-flowing rivers since flies breed there and the larvae live in rapids. The flies bite during the day but long trousers tucked into socks will help keep them off. Citronella-based natural repellents (eg: Mosi-guard) do not work against them.

Mosquitoes and many other insects are attracted to light. If you are camping, never put a lamp near the opening of your tent, or you will have a swarm of biters waiting to join you when you retire. In hotel rooms, be aware that the longer your light is on, the greater the number of insects will be sharing your accommodation.

Tumbu flies or *putsi*, often called mango flies in Uganda, are a problem where the climate is hot and humid. The adult fly lays her eggs on the soil or on drying laundry and when the eggs come into contact with human flesh (when you put on clothes or lie on a bed) they hatch and bury themselves under the skin. Here they form a crop of 'boils' each with a maggot inside. Smear a little Vaseline over the hole, and they will push their noses out to breathe. It may be possibly to squeeze them out but it depends if they are ready to do so as the lavae have spines that help them to hold on.

In putsi areas either dry your clothes and sheets within a screened house, or dry them in direct sunshine until they are crisp, or iron them.

Jiggers or **sandfleas** are another flesh-feaster, which can be best avoided by wearing shoes. They latch on if you walk barefoot in contaminated places, and set up home under the skin of the foot, usually at the side of a toenail where they cause a painful, boil-like swelling. They need picking out by a local expert.

10,000 cercariae a day for the rest of their lives. The parasites can digest their way through your skin when you wade, or bathe in infested fresh water.

Winds disperse the snails and cercariae. The snails in particular can drift a long way, especially on windblown weed, so nowhere is really safe. However, deep water and running water are safer, while shallow water presents the greatest risk. The cercariae penetrate intact skin, and find their way to the liver. There male and female meet and spend the rest of their lives in permanent copulation. No wonder you feel tired! Most finish up in the wall of the lower bowel, but others can get lost and can cause damage to many different organs. *Schistosoma haematobium* goes mostly to the bladder.

Although the adults do not cause any harm in themselves, after about 4–6 weeks they start to lay eggs, which cause an intense but usually ineffective immune reaction, including fever, cough, abdominal pain, and a fleeting, itching rash called 'safari itch'. The absence of early symptoms does not necessarily mean there is no infection. Later symptoms can be more localised and more severe, but the general symptoms settle down fairly quickly and eventually you are just tired. 'Tired all the time' is one of the most common symptoms among expats in Africa, and bilharzia, giardia, amoeba and intestinal yeast are the most common culprits.

Although bilharzia is difficult to diagnose, it can be tested at specialist travel clinics. Ideally tests need to be done at least six weeks after likely exposure and will determine whether you need treatment. Fortunately it is easy to treat at present.

Avoiding bilharzia If you are bathing, swimming, paddling or wading in fresh water which you think may carry a bilharzia risk, try to get out of the water within ten minutes.

- Avoid bathing or paddling on shores within 200m of villages or places where people use the water a great deal, especially reedy shores or where there is lots of water weed.
- Dry off thoroughly with a towel; rub vigorously.
- If your bathing water comes from a risky source try to ensure that the water is taken from the lake in the early morning and stored snail-free, otherwise it should be filtered or Dettol or Cresol added.
- Bathing early in the morning is safer than bathing in the last half of the day.
- Cover yourself with DEET insect repellent before swimming: it may offer some protection.

HIV/AIDS The risks of sexually transmitted infection are extremely high in Uganda, whether you sleep with fellow travellers or locals. About 80% of HIV infections in British heterosexuals are acquired abroad. If you must indulge, use condoms or femidoms, which help reduce the risk of transmission. If you notice any genital ulcers or discharge, get treatment promptly since these increase the risk of acquiring HIV. If you do have unprotected sex, visit a clinic as soon as possible; this should be within 24 hours, or no later than 72 hours, for post-exposure prophylaxis. It costs US$15.

Meningitis This is a particularly nasty disease as it can kill within hours of the first symptoms appearing. The telltale symptoms are a combination of a blinding headache (light sensitivity), a blotchy rash and a high fever. Immunisation protects against the most serious bacterial form of meningitis and the tetravalent vaccine ACWY is recommended for Uganda by British travel clinics, but if this is not available then A+C vaccine is better than nothing.

Although other forms of meningitis exist (usually viral), there are no vaccines for these. Local papers normally report localised outbreaks. A severe headache and fever should make you run to a doctor immediately. There are also other causes of headache and fever; one of which is typhoid, which occurs in travellers to Uganda. Seek medical help if you are ill for more than a few days.

Rabies Rabies is carried by all mammals (beware the village dogs and small monkeys that are used to being fed in the parks) and is passed on to man through

Gordon Rattray www.able-travel.com

Uganda's highlights often involve trekking in rough terrain, and as a result do not lend themselves to people with mobility problems. On top of that, the country as a whole has a tourist industry that is relatively young by east African standards, meaning access for disabled people is rarely a consideration and never a priority. However, depending on your determination and ability, and aided by African resourcefulness, a rewarding trip is possible for most travellers.

ACCOMMODATION In general, it is not easy to find disabled-friendly accommodation in Uganda. Only top of the range hotels and lodges have 'accessible' rooms. Occasionally (more by accident than through design), bathrooms are wheelchair accessible, but where this is not the case, you should be prepared to be lifted, or do your ablutions in the bedroom. Budget disabled travellers will definitely need to compromise, as cheap guesthouses and lodgings are often small and campsites are basic and not ideal for wheelchairs.

The best advice is to research your options in advance. Tour operators will normally take time to listen to your needs, or if you prefer, many hotels can be found and contacted directly via the internet.

TRANSPORT

By air Entebbe International Airport has wheelchairs but there is no guarantee that a narrow aisle chair will be present. This means that unless you can walk to some degree, entering and exiting the aircraft will be a manhandling affair. Staff will be prepared to help but this service is not as slick as you may be used to.

By bus Buses and matatus are cramped, with no facilities for wheelchairs, and getting off and on is often a hectic affair. You may need fellow passengers to help you to your seat, it will often be crowded and there will not be an accessible toilet. Therefore, unless you can walk at least to some degree then taxi is going to be your only easy way of getting around. If you can cope with these difficulties, then travelling by bus is feasible and is the most affordable method of transport.

By car Most tour companies use 4x4s and minibuses, which are higher than normal cars, making transfers more difficult. Drivers and guides are normally happy to help, but they

a bite, scratch or a lick of an open wound. You must always assume any animal is rabid, and seek medical help as soon as possible. Meanwhile scrub the wound with soap under a running tap or while pouring water from a jug. Find a reasonably clear-looking source of water (but at this stage the quality of the water is not important), then pour on a strong iodine or alcohol solution of gin, whisky or rum. This helps stop the rabies virus entering the body and will guard against wound infections, including tetanus.

Pre-exposure vaccinations for rabies is ideally advised for everyone, but is particularly important if you intend to have contact with animals and/or are likely to be more than 24 hours away from medical help. Ideally three doses should be taken over a minimum of 21 days, though even taking one or two doses of vaccine is better than none at all. Contrary to popular belief these vaccinations are relatively painless.

If you are bitten, scratched or licked over an open wound by a sick animal, then post-exposure prophylaxis should be given as soon as possible, though it is never too late to seek help, as the incubation period for rabies can be very long. Those

are not trained in this skill so you must thoroughly explain your needs and stay in control of the situation during any transfers.

Distances are great and roads are often bumpy, so if you are prone to skin damage you need to take extra care. If you use one, place your own pressure-relieving cushion on top of (or instead of) the original car seat and if necessary, pad around knees and elbows.

ACTIVITIES Gorilla tracking is literally a stumble in the jungle, even for able-bodied people. The guides follow the gorillas from their previous nest and it can mean several hours of hacking through vegetation. You don't need to be super-fit, but check with your tour operator if you think your disability may exclude you. Kibale Forest trails and other primate walks are generally less arduous, but are not designed with wheelchair users in mind. It is also worth remembering that Uganda has a fairly high rainfall and because most of these paths are not purpose built and rather hewn from continued use, they quickly become muddy in wet conditions. On the plus side, although you may need to be helped over obstacles and up steps, there will always be plenty of willing hands to do this. I would offer money for this kind of help but this is often refused.

HEALTH Ugandan hospitals and pharmacies are often basic, so if possible, take all essential medication and equipment with you. It is advisable to pack this in your hand luggage during flights in case your main luggage gets lost. Doctors will know about 'everyday' illnesses, but you must understand and be able to explain your own particular medical requirements.

SECURITY It is also worthwhile remembering that as a disabled person, you are more vulnerable. Stay aware of where your bags are and who is around you, especially during car transfers and similar. These activities often draw a crowd, and the confusion creates easy pickings for an opportunist thief.

SPECIALIST OPERATORS I know of no operators in Uganda who specialise in disability. Having said that, most travel companies will listen to your needs and try to create an itinerary suitable for you. For the independent traveller, it is possible to limit potential surprises by contacting local operators and establishments by email in advance.

who have not been immunised will need a full course of injections. The vast majority of travel health advisors including WHO recommend rabies immunoglobulin (RIG), but this product is expensive (around US$800) and may be hard to come by – another reason why pre-exposure vaccination should be encouraged.

Tell the doctor if you have had pre-exposure vaccine, as this should change the treatment you receive. And remember that, if you do contract rabies, mortality is 100% and death from rabies is probably one of the worst ways to go.

Tickbite fever African ticks are not the rampant disease transmitters they are in the Americas, but they may spread tick-bite fever and a few dangerous rarities in Uganda. Tick-bite fever is a flu-like illness that can easily be treated with doxycycline, but as there can be some serious complications it is important to visit a doctor.

Ticks should ideally be removed as soon as possible as leaving ticks on the body increases the chance of infection. They should be removed with special tick tweezers that can be bought in good travel shops. Failing that you can use your finger nails by grasping the tick as close to your body as possible and pull steadily and firmly away at right angles to your skin. The tick will then come away complete as long as you do not jerk or twist. If possible douse the wound with alcohol (any spirit will do) or iodine. Irritants (eg: Olbas oil) or lit cigarettes are to be discouraged since they can cause the ticks to regurgitate and therefore increase the risk of disease. It is best to get a travelling companion to check you for ticks and if you are travelling with small children remember to check their heads, and particularly behind the ears.

Spreading redness around the bite and/or fever and/or aching joints after a tick bite imply that you have an infection that requires antibiotic treatment, so seek advice.

Snakebite Snakes rarely attack unless provoked, and bites in travellers are unusual. You are less likely to get bitten if you wear stout shoes and long trousers when in the bush. Most snakes are harmless and even venomous species will dispense venom in only about half of their bites. If bitten, then, you are unlikely to have received venom; keeping this fact in mind may help you to stay calm. Many so-called first-aid techniques do more harm than good: cutting into the wound is harmful; tourniquets are dangerous; suction and electrical inactivation devices do not work. The only treatment is antivenom. In case of a bite that you fear may have been from a venomous snake:

- Try to keep calm – it is likely that no venom has been dispensed.
- Prevent movement of the bitten limb by applying a splint.
- Keep the bitten limb BELOW heart height to slow the spread of any venom.
- If you have a crêpe bandage, wrap it around the whole limb (eg: all the way from the toes to the thigh), as tight as you would for a sprained ankle or a muscle pull.
- Evacuate to a hospital that has antivenom. At the time of writing this is only known to be available in Kampala. Many centres have an Indian antivenom that does not include the most common biting snakes in Uganda. The Surgery has South African antivenom that includes all the common biters. The best option is to phone for advice.

And remember:

- NEVER give aspirin; you may take paracetamol, which is safe.
- NEVER cut or suck the wound.
- DO NOT apply ice packs.
- DO NOT apply potassium permanganate.

If the offending snake can be captured without risk of someone else being bitten, take this to show the doctor – but beware since even a decapitated head is able to bite.

Travel from and to the heart of Africa..

...For the safari of a life time

From one of the last natural habitats of the famous mountain gorilla to the last montane rainforest in East and Central Africa. Rwanda is a destination that will surprise and enthral.

Rwandair Express , the national carrier, connects to all the main centres in the region with onward links to the rest of the world

For a safari of a lifetime, you need to visit the Heart of Africa.

Centenary Building Ground & 2nd floor
P.O Box 7275 Kigali, Rwanda Tel: +250 503687, 575757/
+250 08306050 Fax: + 250 503686/9
Website: www.rwandair. com   Email: info@rwandair.com

Rwandair Express
From the heart of Africa

Part Two

THE GUIDE

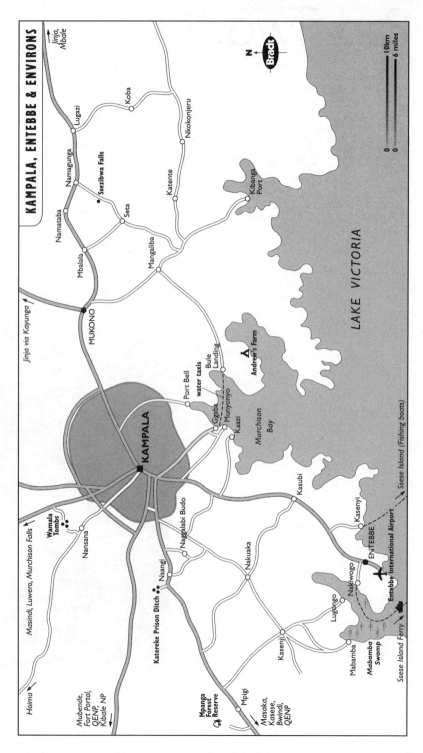

KAMPALA, ENTEBBE & ENVIRONS

N

Bradt

0 ___ 10km
0 ___ 6 miles

Jinja,
Mbale

Lugazi

Koba

Namagunga

Nkokonjeru

Ssezibwa Falls

Katente

Namataba

Seta

Mbalala

Mangaliba

Kibanga
Port

MUKONO

LAKE VICTORIA

Jinja via Kayunga

Port Bell

water taxis

Bule
Landing

Andrew's Farm

Ggaba

Munyonyo

Kaazi

Murchison
Bay

Masindi, Luwero, Murchison Falls

KAMPALA

Kasubi

**Wamala
Tombs**

Nansana

Naggalabi Budo

Kasenyi

Kateleke Prison Ditch

Nsangi

Nakuaka

ENTEBBE

Nakiwogo

Entebbe International Airport

Ssese Island (Fishing boats)

Hoima

Mubende,
Fort Portal,
QENP,
Kibale NP

**Mpanga
Forest
Reserve**

Mpigi

Kasenji

Lugongo

Mabamba

Mabamba
Swamp

Ssese Island Ferry

Masaka,
Kasese, Bwindi,
QENP

130

6

Kampala, Entebbe and Environs

Although they lie only 35km apart on the northern Lake Victoria hinterland, the twin cities of Kampala and Entebbe – present and former capital of Uganda respectively – could scarcely be more different in character. Situated on rolling hills some 10km inland of the lake, Kampala is the archetypal African capital – more verdant than many of its counterparts, not quite so populous or chaotic as others – but essentially the familiar juxtaposition of a bustling compact high-rise city centre rising from a leafy suburban sprawl, increasingly organic in appearance as one reaches its rustic periphery.

Entebbe, by contrast, scarcely feels like a town at all. Straddling the Equator some 30 minutes' drive south of Kampala, it is a remarkably unfocused urban centre, carved haphazardly into the tropical lakeshore jungle in such a manner that one might reasonably wonder whether most of its 50,000-plus residents haven't packed up their tents and gone on holiday. Indeed, Entebbe is quite possibly the only African capital past or present to enter the new millennium with a golf course more expansive than its nominal city centre, or whose tallest buildings are dwarfed by the antiquated trees of the botanical garden.

With their contrasting atmospheres of modern urban bustle and time-warped equatorial languor, Kampala and Entebbe – linked by a smooth surfaced road passing through a lush cover of broad-leaved plantains and other tropical cultivation – make for a fascinating introduction to Uganda. Coming by air, you'll land at Entebbe International Airport, 3km from the town centre, and if your main interest is natural history then you'd be well advised to stay over in Entebbe rather than heading on to the capital. Kampala, on the other hand, is the pulsating heart of Uganda's cultural and intellectual life – not to mention its nightlife – and it also lies at the hub of the international and domestic long-haul bus network, making it the more attractive base to independent travellers seeking a taste of urban Africa.

KAMPALA

The capital city and economic and social hub of Uganda, Kampala is also the country's largest urban centre by a factor of ten, with a population of 1.2 million according to the 2002 census. Kampala, like Rome, was originally built across seven hills – today, that figure is more like two dozen – and although its founder is generally cited as Captain Lugard, who set up camp on Kampala Hill in 1890, the surrounding hills had in fact lain at the political centre of Buganda for several decades before that. Kasubi Hill, only 2.5km northwest of the modern city centre, served briefly as the capital of Kabaka Suuna II in the 1850s, and it also housed the palace of Kabaka Mutesa I from 1882–84, while Mengo Hill formed the capital of Mutesa's successor Mwanga, as it has every subsequent kabaka. The name Kampala derives from the Luganda expression Kosozi Kampala – Hill of Antelope – a reference to the domestic impala that cropped the lawns of Mengo during Mutesa's reign.

Kampala lies at the political and geographical heart of the Kingdom of Buganda, home to the Baganda (singular Muganda), who form the largest single ethnic group in Uganda, comprising more than 20% of the national population. The kingdom originally consisted of four counties: Kyadondo, Busiro, Busujju and Mawokota. It expanded greatly during the early to mid 18th century, mainly at the expense of Bunyoro, to extend over 20 counties, as well as the semi-autonomous Ssese Islands. During the colonial era, Buganda remained a kingdom with unique privileges, but it was relegated to provincial status after Obote abolished the monarchy in 1966. Today, Buganda is divided across nine administrative districts: Kampala, Mpigi, Mukono, Masaka, Kalangala, Kiboga, Rakai, Sembabule and Mubende.

Buganda is ruled by a *kabaka*, an autocratic monarch whose position, though hereditary, is confined to no single clan. Traditionally, the kabaka would marry into as many clans as possible – Stanley estimated Mutesa's female entourage to number 5,000, of which at least one-tenth were members of the royal harem – and his heir would take the clan of his mother, a custom that encouraged loyalty to the throne insofar as each of the 52 clans could hope that it would one day produce a king. Mutesa, who held the throne when Speke arrived in Buganda in 1862, is listed by tradition as the 30th kabaka. Although the dates of Mutesa's predecessors' reigns are a matter for conjecture, an average duration of a decade would place the foundation of Buganda in the mid 16th century, while 20 years would push it back into the 13th century.

The founding kabaka of Buganda was Kintu, who, it is widely agreed, came to power after defeating a despotic local ruler called Bemba. Kintu is otherwise the subject of several conflicting traditions. Some say that he descended from the heavens via Bunyoro, others that he originated from the Ssese Islands, or was indigenous to the area, or – most credible perhaps – that he arrived in Buganda from beyond Mount Elgon, suggesting an origin in Sudan or Ethiopia. The identity of Kintu is further confused by the Kiganda creation legend asserting that Kintu was the name of the first man on earth (see the box in *Chapter 1, In the beginning…*, pages 184–5). A common tradition holds that Kintu, having defeated the unpopular Bemba, took over his house at Nagalabi Buddo, about 20km west of present-day Kampala, as a spoil of victory. The house was called Buganda, a name that was later transferred to all the territory ruled by Kintu. Nagalabi Buddo remains the coronation site of the kabaka to this day.

Traditional Buganda society allowed for some upward and downward mobility – any talented person could rise to social prominence – but it was nevertheless strongly stratified, with three distinct classes recognised. The highest class was the hereditary Balangira (aristocracy), which based its right to rule on royal blood. In addition to the kabaka, several aristocratic figureheads were recognised, including the *namasole* (queen mother), *lubuga* (king's sister) and *katikiro* (prime minister). Other persons who occupied positions of political and social importance were the *gabunga* and *mujasi*, the respective commanders of the royal navy and army.

In the first decade of the post-independence era, Kampala was widely regarded to be the showpiece of the East African community: a spacious garden city with a cosmopolitan atmosphere and bustling trade. It was also a cultural and educational centre of note, with Makerere University regarded as the academic heart of East Africa. Under Amin, however, Kampala's status started to deteriorate, especially after the Asian community was forced to leave Uganda. By 1986, when the civil war ended, Kampala was in complete chaos: skeletal buildings scarred with bullet holes dotted the town centre, shops and hotels were boarded up after widespread

The middle class in Baganda society consisted of chiefs or *baami*. Initially, the status of the baami was hereditary, enjoyed solely by the *bataka* (clan heads). After 1750, however, bakopi men could be promoted by royal appointment to baami status, on the basis of distinguished service and/or ability. A hierarchic system of chieftaincy existed, corresponding with the importance of the political unit over which any given chief held sway. The most important administrative division was the Saza (county), each of which was ruled by a Saza chief. These were further sub-divided into Gombolola (sub-counties), then into parishes and sub-parishes, and finally Bukungu, which were more-or-less village units. The kabaka had the power to appoint or dismiss any chief at will, and all levels of baami were directly responsible to him.

At the bottom of the social stratum was a serf class known as the *bakopi*: literally, the people who don't matter. The bakopi were subsistence farmers, whose labour (as tends to be the case with those who matter not to their more socially elevated masters) formed the base of Buganda's agricultural economy. Many bakopi kept chickens and larger livestock, but they were primarily occupied with agriculture – the local staple of bananas, supplemented by sweet potatoes, cassava, beans and green vegetables. The bakopi were dependent on land to farm, but they had no right to it. All land in Buganda was the property of the kabaka, who could allocate (or rescind) the right of usage to any subsidiary chief at whim. The chiefs, in turn, allocated their designated quota of land as they deemed fit – a scenario that encouraged the bakopi to obedience. Peasant men and women were regularly sacrificed by the aristocracy – Kabaka Suuna, during one bout of illness, is said to have ordered 100 bakopi to be slaughtered daily until he was fully recovered.

Kiganda, the traditional religion of Buganda (discussed more fully in the box on pages 184–5) is essentially animist, in thrall not to a supreme being but rather a variety of ancestral and other spirits. Temples dedicated to the most powerful spirits were each served by a medium and a hereditary priest, who would liase between the spirit and the people. The priests occupied a place of high religious and political importance – even the most powerful kabaka would consult with appropriate spirit mediums before making an important decision or going into battle. The kabaka appointed at least one female slave or relative to tend each shrine and provide food and drink to its priest and medium.

The traditions of Buganda are enormously complex, and the kingdom's history is packed with incident and anecdote. The above is intended as a basic overview, to be supplemented by more specific information on various places, events, characters and crafts elsewhere in this book. Readers whose interest is whetted rather than sated by this coverage are pointed to the informative website (www.buganda.com) and to Richard Reid's excellent *Political Power in Pre-Colonial Buganda* (James Currey, 2002), a comprehensive source of information about most aspects of traditional Baganda society. Many old and out-of-print editions of the *Uganda Journal* also contain useful essays on pre-colonial Buganda – they can be viewed at the Uganda Society library in the National Museum of Uganda in Kampala.

looting, and public services had ground to a halt, swamped by the huge influx of migrants from war-torn parts of the country.

Kampala today is practically unrecognisable from its pot-holed, war-scarred incarnation of the mid 1980s. The main shopping area along Kampala Road could be that of any African capital, and has recently been supplemented by a clutch of bright, modern supermarkets and shopping malls. The area immediately north of Kampala Road, where foreign embassies and government departments rub shoulders with renovated tourist hotels, is smarter than any part of Nairobi or Dar

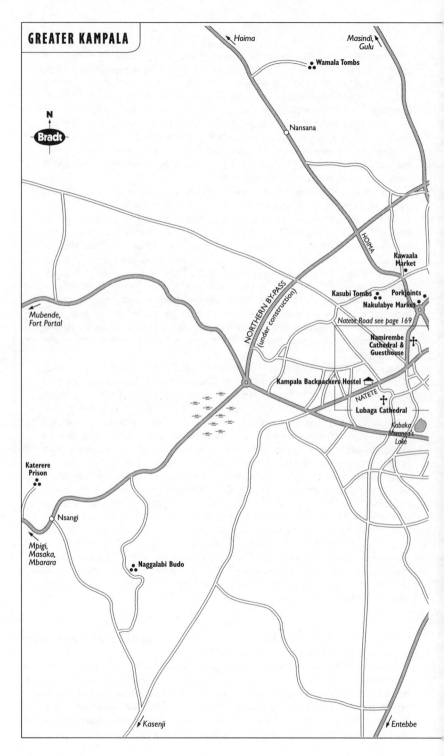

GREATER KAMPALA

Hoima

Masindi,
Gulu

Wamala Tombs

N
Bradt

Nansana

HOIMA

Kawaala
Market

Kasubi Tombs   Porkjoints
Nakulabye Market

Mubende,
Fort Portal

NORTHERN BY-PASS
(under construction)

Natete Road see page 169

Namirembe
Cathedral &
Guesthouse

Kampala Backpackers Hostel

NATETE

Lubaga Cathedral

Kabaka
Mwanga's
Lake

Katerere
Prison

Nsangi

Mpigi,
Masaka,
Mbarara

Naggalabi Budo

Kasenji

Entebbe

134

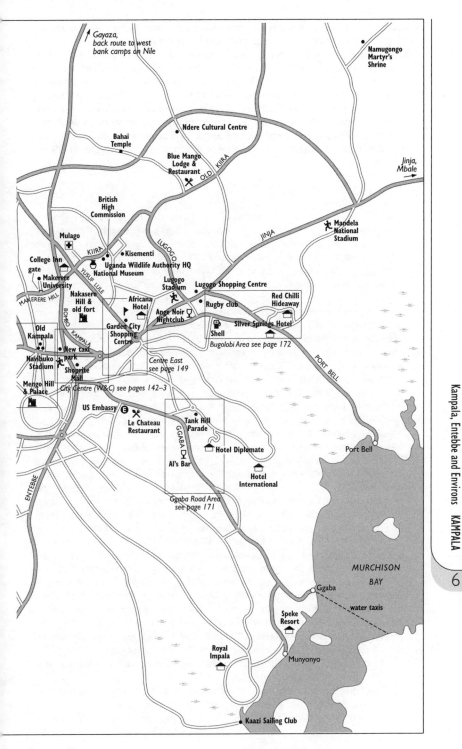

Gayaza,
back route to west
bank camps on Nile

Namugongo
Martyr's
Shrine

Ndere Cultural Centre

Bahai
Temple

Blue Mango
Lodge &
Restaurant

OLD KIIRA

Jinja,
Mbale

British
High
Commission

JINJA

Mandela
National
Stadium

Mulago

KIIRA

Kisementi

College Inn
gate

Uganda Wildlife Authority HQ
National Museum

LUGOGO

YUSUF LULE

Makerere
University

Lugogo
Stadium

Lugogo Shopping Centre

MAKERERE HILL

Nakasero
Hill &
old fort

Africana
Hotel

Red Chilli
Hideaway

BOMBO

Ange Noir
Nightclub

Rugby club

Silver Springs Hotel

KAMPALA

Garden City
Shopping
Centre

Shell

Old
Kampala

New taxi
park

Bugolobi Area see page 172

Navibuko
Stadium

Shoprite
Mall

Centre East
see page 149

PORT BELL

Mengo Hill
& Palace

City Centre (W&C) see pages 142–3

ENTEBBE

US Embassy

Le Chateau
Restaurant

GGABA

Tank Hill
Parade

Hotel Diplomate

Port Bell

Al's Bar

Hotel
International

Ggaba Road Area
see page 171

MURCHISON
BAY

Ggaba

water taxis

Speke
Resort

Munyonyo

Royal
Impala

Kaazi Sailing Club

es Salaam – an image compromised somewhat by the scavenging marabou storks that flop gracelessly between their treetop and lamppost nests.

Walk through the city's various other quarters for a fascinating and rather depressing cross-section of the extremes of wealth and poverty that characterise so much of Africa. The overcrowded back streets running downhill from Kampala Road, congested with hooting minibus-taxis and swerving *boda-boda* drivers, reveal a more representative facet of Kampala – the city as most of its residents see it – yet even so the rundown streets sparkle with an economic dynamism that was absent as recently as 1995. Further from the city centre, and again very different, are the green and hilly outer suburbs, which come across more like an overgrown village than a capital city.

EARLY DAYS IN KAMPALA

The original city centre – little more than a fort and a few mud houses – stood on the hill known today as Old Kampala. Its early expansion and urbanisation from 1897 onwards is best catalogued in the memoirs of two early settlers, the medical pioneer Sir Albert Cook (arrived 1897) and W E Hoyle (arrived 1903), both of which were published in early (and long out of print) editions of the *Uganda Journal*, the main sources of what follows. Unattributed quotes relating to before 1903 are from Cook.

Conditions for the few settlers in Kampala in 1897 were rudimentary. Imported provisions were scarce, and when available at the town's two English stores they were very expensive. Most settlers suffered ongoing health problems, often related to malaria, which had not yet been connected to mosquito bites. The settlers lived in simple abodes made of reeds, elephant grass and thatch, with a stamped mud floor 'cow-dunged once a week to keep out jiggers'. Cook, a doctor, performed his first operations 'on a camp bedstead, the instruments sterilised in our cooking saucepans, and laid out in vegetable dishes filled with antiseptics'. A 12-bed hospital, built in the local style, opened in May 1897, and a larger one was constructed three years later, only to be destroyed in a lightning strike in 1902. Still, Cook 'introduced the natives to the advantages of anaesthetics and antiseptics' and also started a programme of vaccinations after a chief warned him that a smallpox epidemic was approaching the capital.

The arrival of the telegraph line in April 1900 was a major boon to the remote community, allowing it regular contact with the coast and to keep abreast of world affairs. Cook notes that 'this happy condition of affairs did not last long, however, for where the line passed through the Nandi country it was constantly being cut down. On one occasion no less than sixty miles [100km] of wire were removed and coiled into bracelets or cut into pieces and used as slugs for their muzzle-loading guns'. More significant still was the arrival of the Mombasa Railway at Kisumu, in December 1901, connected by a steamer service to Entebbe. Not only did this facilitate personal travel between Kampala and the coast, but it also allowed for the freight of imported goods on an unprecedented scale.

Prior to the arrival of the railway, most buildings in Kampala had been thatched firetraps, routinely destroyed by lightning strikes – not only Cook's hospital, but also the first cathedral at Namirembe, the telegraph office, a trading store and several private homesteads. Now, permanent brick buildings could be erected, with corrugated iron roofing, proper guttering and cement floors, all of which made for more hygienic living, as well as reducing the risk of destruction by fire. The railway also improved the quality of life for the small European community by attracting 'a flood of Indian shopkeepers' and associated 'influx of European trade goods'.

The original European settlement, as already mentioned, stood atop Old Kampala Hill. To its east, an ever-growing local township sprawled downhill to where Navibuko Stadium and Owino Market stand today. The present-day city centre took shape as an

Kampala is a pleasant enough city, remarkably safe by comparison with the likes of Nairobi or Dar es Salaam, and its glut of restaurants, nightclubs, bars, cinemas and other modern facilities has made it a popular place for overlanders and backpackers to hang out for a few days. Its attractions are perhaps less compelling to fly-in tourists with greater time restrictions. Conventional sightseeing within the city limits is restricted to the Kasubi Tombs and National Museum, but several other worthwhile sites of interest lie within day-tripping distance. These include organised excursions to raft the Nile near Jinja or visit the chimpanzees of Ngamba Island, as well as more low-key goals such as the Entebbe Botanical Garden, Mabira and Mpanga forest reserves, and Mbamba Swamp.

indirect result of the improved transportation to the coast via Kisumu. It was, Hoyle writes: 'realised by the government that the space below Kampala Fort was inadequate to meet growing trade, and they decided to start a new township on the more expansive hill named Nakasero, half a mile [1km] to the east. Already by 1903 a new fort had been built there [and] by 1905 practically all government offices and staff and traders' shops had been moved to Nakasero.' Over the next few years, writes Cook, the government had 'good roads cut and well laid out in the new town... bordered with trees' – essentially the nascent modern city centre, which slopes across the valley dividing Old Kampala from Nakasero Hill.

The Mombasa Railway also facilitated the export trade out of Uganda, which until 1906 consisted primarily of wild animal produce such as hide, skins and ivory, controlled by an Italian and an American firm, as well as the Indian storekeeper Allidina Visram. Hoyle writes: 'It was a memorable sight to see frequent safaris laden with ivory tusks filing towards Kampala from the strip of country between the Congo Free State and Uganda Protectorate, which at that point was in dispute, a kind of no-man's-land and therefore the elephant-hunters' paradise.' Hoyle writes elsewhere of Allidina Visram's store that in 1903 it was 'to Europeans, the most important... existence almost entirely depended on [it], for his firm not only supplied the necessities of life, but in the absence of any bank it provided ready money in exchange for a cheque'.

Oddly, perhaps, English money held no currency in Kampala's early days. The Indian rupee was effectively the official currency, equivalent to one English shilling and four pence. But Hoyle writes that: 'the most generally used currency among the Baganda was cowrie shells... one thousand to the rupee... through which a hole had been made for threading... using banana fibre. The Baganda were very adept at counting shells, usually strung in hundreds... It was amusing, having paid a porter... five thousand shells, to see him sit down and count them... report that he was one, two, or maybe up to five short, and it was easier to throw these to him from a quantity of loose shells kept in a bag for that purpose.' Cowries continued in general use until about 1905, and were still employed in petty trade until 1922, when the shilling was introduced.

Last word to Hoyle, and an improbable anecdote relating to Sir Hesketh Bell, Governor of Uganda from 1905–09: 'Bell conceived the idea that elephants might be trained to do the many useful jobs they do in India. The experiment was made of bringing a trained elephant from India. It was a great business getting the elephant aboard the [ferry] at Kisumu and landing it in Entebbe. [Bell] came to Kampala to make a triumphant entry riding the elephant, mounting it two miles outside the township. He was greeted by a large crowd of Europeans and Baganda. Some young elephants were caught, but the experiment of training them was not successful, and eventually the Indian elephant was sold to a menagerie in Europe.'

GETTING THERE AND AWAY

✈ **By air** Fly-in visitors will arrive in Uganda at Entebbe International Airport, which lies on the Lake Victoria shore about 3km from Entebbe Town. If you arrive outside of banking hours, there are 24-hour foreign-exchange facilities at the airport. Historically, these used to offer dreadful rates compared with private forex bureaux in Kampala, and while their rates have improved of late, it's still worth waiting until you get into town for larger sums. Special hire taxis from the airport cost around US$3 to Entebbe and US$20 to Kampala. Airport collection can also be arranged in advance through most tour operators and upmarket hotels in Kampala and Entebbe. Several of the latter send their buses along to pick pre-booked clients and hopefully some additional trade. If you're stuck for a lift into town, you might have a quiet word with one of these and see if it's not possible to come to some arrangement. The cheapest option however is to take a shared taxi from the airport to Entebbe (around US$3 divided between four passengers) where you can pick up a minibus to Kampala for no more than US$1 per person. This is safe enough during daylight hours, but probably not too sensible after dark, and if you do arrive in central Kampala with all your luggage at any time of day, you're strongly advised to catch a special hire taxi to a hotel rather than walking the streets looking for a room. (In such circumstances, as with any major African city, its better to find a reasonable bed quickly and wait for the morning to locate more comfortable/affordable/quieter lodgings if this proves necessary.) If you're heading out to the airport from Kampala, minibuses to Entebbe leave from both the old and the new taxi park.

🚊 **By rail** There used to be two internal rail services in Uganda, one connecting Kampala to Kasese in the west, and the other connecting Kampala to Pakwach via Tororo and Gulu. Neither service was much used by travellers, because the trains were very slow and unreliable, and both were suspended in 1997 with little likelihood of resuming in the foreseeable future. The weekly overnight train service between Kampala and Nairobi, at one time the most attractive means of transport between these cities, has also been suspended on an indefinite basis.

🚢 **By boat** Uganda's main ferry port in Kampala is Port Bell, which is about 30 minutes from Kampala and reached by regular minibuses from the old taxi park. At the time of writing, however, no passenger boats operate out of Port Bell. The ferry service between Port Bell and Mwanza (Tanzania) was aborted following the sinking of the MV *Bukoba* in 1996 (in which as many as 1,000 people are thought to have drowned) and although it resumed briefly at one point, it is unlikely it will again in the near future. Cargo boats between Port Bell and Mwanza will sometimes take passengers, however, and many travellers crossing between Tanzania and Uganda use the thrice-weekly overnight ferry from Mwanza to Bukoba, which connects with a direct bus service to Kampala via Masaka. For further information, try ringing the Port Bell ferry office (✆ 0414 221336) though ominously it was out of order when we tried it.

🚌 **By bus** Kampala's minibus-taxi station was once the most chaotic in East Africa: several hundred minibuses, identical in appearance bar the odd bit of panel-beating and with no indication as to their destination, all sardine-packed into a couple of acres of seething madness. To counter this, the city council built a second taxi station about 100m from the first – which means that Kampala now boasts the two most chaotic taxi parks in East Africa. Minibuses to most destinations west of Kampala leave from the new taxi park, while minibuses to Port Bell and destinations east of Kampala leave from the old taxi park. Local minibuses leave for

Entebbe from both taxi parks every few minutes. Prices are generally slightly higher than the bus fares quoted below, but departures are far more regular – before noon, you're unlikely to wait for more than 30 minutes for a minibus to leave for Jinja, Tororo, Mbale, Kabale, Kasese, Mityana, Mubende, Fort Portal, Masindi, Gulu or Hoima.

Most bus services operate out of the central bus station, which lies between the two taxi parks, enhancing the general aura of chaos in this congested part of town. There are regular departures – every one to two hours from around 07.00 until noon – for most of the destinations listed above, though it's worth checking out departure times and booking a day ahead to save waiting around on the day. However, by the time you read this, buses serving western Uganda from the Central Bus Park will probably have been relocated from the Central Bus Park at Nakasero to Natete on the western edge of the city. Buses for Fort Portal, Masaka, Kabale, Kisoro, etc will leave and arrive from a site close to the Masaka Road at Natete (behind the Total fuel station). This will obviously have significant implications for travellers, not least since the city's main concentration of budget hotels around the central bus and taxi parks will no longer be convenient for stumbling out of bed and onto an early morning bus (or vice versa later in the day). To catch your early morning bus out west you'll need to find a hotel in the vicinity or find a special hire or taxi for the 4km journey from the city centre to Natete. Kampala's Masaka Road is an unlovely locale which constitutes the city's western industrial suburb. Hotels will quickly mushroom up to cater for travellers: in the meantime the hotels and hostel listed along the Natete Road around Mengo are the best bet.

Do check that the new bus park is operational before heading down to Natete. Initial attempts by the City Council to relocate westbound buses in October 2006 met strong resistance from transport operators. It is quite possible that opponents may delay or even stall the development.

Sample fares are as follows: Butogota Ush17,000, Fort Portal Ush10,000–11,000, Hoima Ush6,000, Kabale Ush12,000, Kasese Ush10,000, Kisoro Ush18,000, Masaka Ush2,500, Masindi Ush8,000 and Mbale Ush10,000.

The excellent **Horizon Bus** coach to Kisoro via Mbarara and Kabale leaves every hour or so between 06.30 and 16.00 daily from its office on Luwum Street (m 0752 690549 or 0772 504555; e horizon@swiftuganda.com). It also connects Fort Portal to Kabale. The most extensive network is operated by the **Gateway** bus company, whose drivers are not renowned as the most considerate or careful of road users. Far better to take the popular and relatively safe **Post Bus** (↘ 0414 236436/256539) which operates from the main post office on Kampala Road. Services leave from the parking yard at the back here at 08.00 daily Monday to Saturday. The most useful services for tourists are Masaka Ush3,000, Mbarara Ush8,000 and Kabale Ush12,000; Masindi Ush8,000 and Hoima Ush10,000; Jinja Ush2,000, Tororo Ush8,000 and Mbale Ush9,000; and Mubende Ush5,000 and Fort Portal Ush10,000. Note that public transport fares are hiked immediately before holiday periods such as Easter and Christmas when Kampala's multi-tribal society moves out *en masse* to their home areas. These increases are not so much to maximise profits but to compensate for buses etc returning almost empty to Kampala at these times. For details of international bus services to and from Kampala, see *Chapter 3, Getting there and away*, pages 76–9.

WHERE TO STAY Uganda is to host the British Commonwealth Heads of Government Meeting (CHOGM) in November 2007 when Queen Elizabeth II is expected to travel to Uganda for her first visit since 1954. Kampala anticipates this week-long event with a mixture of national pride and economic expectation, one

The life of a *mumbeja* – a Muganda princess – wasn't quite so romantic as it might sound. The sisters of the kabaka generally lived a life close to bondage, as ladies-in-waiting to the king, at risk of being put to death for any perceived breach of conduct. Marriage was forbidden to the king's sisters and daughters, as was casual sex or becoming pregnant – and the punishment for transgressing any of these taboos was death by cremation.

The first princess to break the mould was Clara Nalumansi, a daughter of Mutesa I. Nalumansi angered Mwanga by converting to Islam during the first year of his reign, and further aggravated him by publicly reconverting to Catholicism in May 1886. Then, in early 1887, Princess Clara capitalised on her rights as a Christian – in the process scandalising the whole of Buganda – by tying the marital knot with another convert, a former page of Mwanga named Yosef Kadu.

The admirable princess didn't stop there. Shortly after her marriage, Clara was appointed to succeed the recently deceased *namasole* of Kabaka Junju, a charge that, traditionally, would have entailed her moving permanently to a house alongside Junju's tomb and tending the royal shrine in solitude for the rest of her days. Instead, Clara and Yosef arrived at the tomb, chased away the attendant spirit medium, then cleared the previous namasole's house of every last fetish and charm, and dumped the lot on a bonfire.

Clara's next move? Well, it's customary for the umbilical cord of a Muganda princess – and all other royals for that matter – to be removed with care and preserved until they die, when it is buried with the rest of the body. So Clara dug out her umbilical cord from wherever it was stored, cut it into little pieces, and chucked it out – leading to further public outcry and a call for both her and her husband to be executed.

The general mood of unrest in Buganda in late 1887 diverted attention from the Christian couple and gave them temporary respite. But not for long. In December, Clara placed herself back in the spotlight when she arranged for an immense elephant tusk, placed by her grandfather Kabaka Suuna at a shrine dedicated to the water god Mukasa, to be removed from its sacred resting place.

The errant princess's luck ran out in August 1888, a month before Mwanga was forced into exile, when she was killed by a gunshot fired by a person or persons unknown. Not entirely incredibly, her relatives claimed that the assassination was arranged by Mwanga, who – characteristically paranoid – feared that the English Christians might follow the British example and name the princess as the new ruler of Buganda.

More than a century after her death, it's impossible to know what to make of Princess Clara Nalumansi's singular story. Quite possibly she was just a religious crank, recently converted to Christianity and set on a self-destructive collision course with martyrdom. But it's more tempting, and I think credible, to remember her as a true rebel: a proto-feminist whose adoption of Christianity was not a matter of blind faith, but rather a deliberately chosen escape route from the frigid birthright of a mumbeja.

consequence of which has been a rash of hotel construction and renovation. Most prominent are some luxurious new developments in the upmarket sector which is competing to attract heads of state and their immediate entourages. Visitors will of course include numerous lower budget categories and by mid 2007 every hotelier who can afford a tin of paint will surely have daubed it over the peeling patches on his walls.

City centre
Upmarket

⌂ **Emin Pasha Hotel** (20 rooms) 27 Akii Bua Rd, Nakasero; ✆ 0414 236977/8/9; e info@eminpasha.com; www.eminpasha.com. Located on leafy Nakasero Hill, the Emin Pasha proclaims itself to be 'Kampala's first boutique hotel', a marketing term that is for once justifiable, as this really is the most attractive and atmospheric hotel in the city. Set in an effectively converted and expanded two-storey 1930s' townhouse, the hotel bristles with taste and character. Terraces, balconies and courtyards abound beside a landscaped garden and swimming pool. A creation of the Uganda Safari Company, the hotel was inspired by their clients' evident disappointment when their African safari began at one of the ubiquitous 'international' hotels that dominate the remainder of this section. The brasserie is gaining a reputation for good food. Rooms contain large and comfortable beds, gorgeous antique hardwood furniture and framed artwork. *US$220–300 inc b/fast.*

⌂ **Kampala Serena** (150 rooms) Nile Av; ✆ 0414 309000; f 0414 259130; e kampala@serena.co.ug. The former Nile Hotel, a facility remembered primarily for its gruesome associations with Idi Amin's secret service, has just enjoyed a spectacular US$12 million facelift courtesy of the Serena Hotel chain, and opened its doors as The Kampala Serena in August 2006 to mark yet another quantum leap in Ugandan hotel standards. Set in newly landscaped grounds, the Nile's sterile 1960s' 4-storey block is now unrecognisable inside and out, following a somewhat eclectic – but wholly effective – rebirth that comes across as something along the lines of Indiana Jones and his Temple of Doom transplanted to a Moroccan palace. Be warned, however, that a journey of discovery through the Serena's revolting glass portal is only for adventurers of comfortable means. The rewards for those who wind their way between the stone pillars and traverse the indoor ponds (a bridge is provided) range from a beer (Ush5,000) in the Explorers Bar/Italian Restaurant to lunch buffet (Ush37,000) in the Lakes Restaurant or dinner (main courses Ush20,000–35,000) in the plush 1st-floor restaurant. The north African theme is picked up in the rooms which are spacious, inviting and (in Kampala) comparable to the Emin Pasha Hotel for ambience. Rooms at the front of the hotel overlook the spectacular water garden. Kampala Serena enjoys a convenient central location which is considerably quieter than other upmarket options nearby. *Sgl/dbl rooms cost US$350/450 B&B standard/executive (excluding 18% VAT).*

⌂ **Kampala Sheraton** (200 rooms) Between Nile and Ternan avs; ✆ 0414 420000/7; f 0414 356696; e reservation.kampala@sheraton.com. A 15-storey skyscraper, the Sheraton stands in beautiful landscaped grounds verging the city centre. Long billed as Kampala's only 5-star hotel, this was for many years a dubious classification, but one which is rather more deserved following the completion of a much-needed facelift in 2005. Now fitted with marbled tiles and fountains, the ground floor is now a plush environment enjoying an extensive lounge, coffee shop, business centre and a shopping arcade, plus the Rhino Bar, a perennial favourite with Kampala's late-night crowd. Sports facilities include a gym, swimming pool, squash and tennis courts. For all this, the objective remains firmly on providing an AC refuge for the international business traveller rather than any sort of vernacular experience for the discerning visitor to Africa. The rooms, though smart and with super city views, are small. *US$265/290 sgl/dbl.*

⌂ **Hotel Africana** (115 rooms) Wampeko Av; ✆ 0414 348080/6; m 0772 748080 or 0752 748081; f 0414 348090/1; e africana@hotelafricana.com; www.hotelafricana.com. Situated opposite the golf course, immediately west of the city centre, this new and modern-looking hotel offers similar facilities and standard of accommodation to its competitors, but in prettier surrounds and at a more realistic price. Facilities include a vast swimming pool, health club, free golf club membership, a forex bureau, a bar with live music at weekends, shops and hair salons, 2 restaurants, business and internet services and 24hr room service. It can be noisy with parties at weekends. Neat s/c (self-contained) rooms, all with AC and DSTV. *US$90/110 sgl/dbl B&B.*

⌂ **Fairway Hotel** ✆ 0414 259571/257171; f 0414 234160; e fairway@starcom.co.ug; www.fairwayhotel.com. This veteran Kampala hotel faces the golf course valley and is only a short walk from the new Garden City Shopping Centre. Facilities include free hotel pick-up, swimming pool, gym, business and conference centres, 2 restaurants and a garden bar. The comfortable AC rooms with DSTV are good value. *US$76/96/106 sgl/dbl/apts.*

⌂ **Grand Imperial Hotel** (100 rooms) Nile Av; ✆ 0414 250681-5; f 0414 250606; e imperialhotels@utlonline.co.ug; www.imperialhotels.co.ug. This long-serving and recently renovated hotel has a useful central location and all the facilities you'd expect of a popular

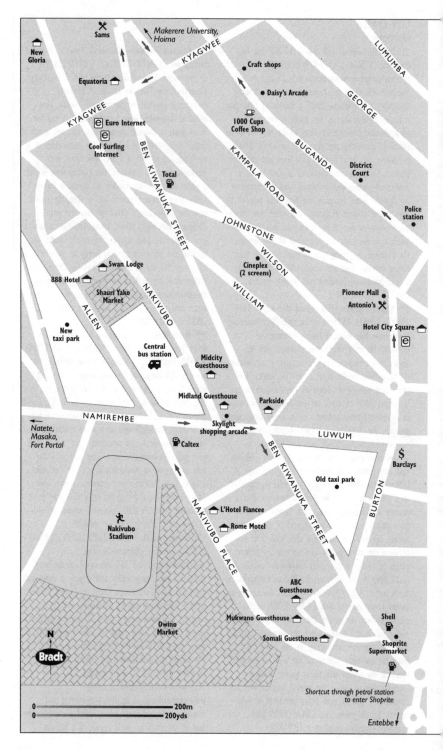

Sams

New Gloria

Makerere University, Hoima

KYAGWEE

Equatoria

KYAGWEE

Craft shops

Daisy's Arcade

LUMUMBA

GEORGE

BUGANDA

Euro Internet

Cool Surfing Internet

1000 Cups Coffee Shop

BEN KIWANUKA STREET

Total

KAMPALA ROAD

District Court

Police station

JOHNSTONE

WILSON

Swan Lodge

888 Hotel

Shauri Yako Market

NAKIVUBO

Cineplex (2 screens)

WILLIAM

Pioneer Mall

Antonio's

New taxi park

ALLEN

Central bus station

Midcity Guesthouse

Hotel City Square

Midland Guesthouse

Parkside

NAMIREMBE

Natete, Masaka, Fort Portal

Caltex

Skylight shopping arcade

LUWUM

BEN KIWANUKA STREET

BURTON

$ Barclays

Old taxi park

Nakivubo Stadium

NAKIVUBO PLACE

L'Hotel Fiancee

Rome Motel

ABC Guesthouse

N

Bradt

Owino Market

Mukwano Guesthouse

Somali Guesthouse

Shell

Shoprite Supermarket

Shortcut through petrol station to enter Shoprite

Entebbe

0   200m
0   200yds

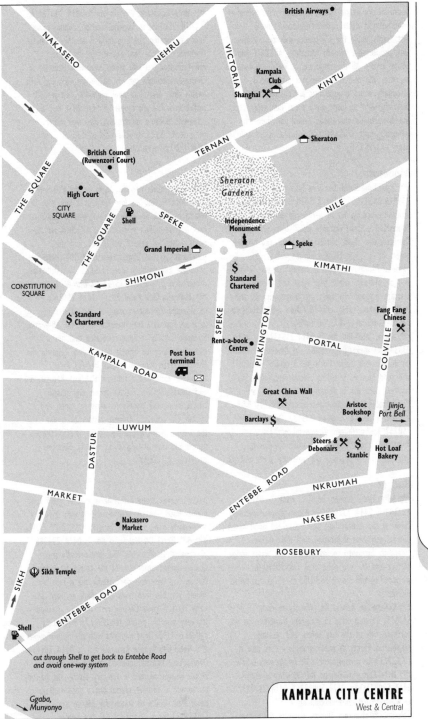

KAMPALA CITY CENTRE
West & Central

businessmen's haunt. There's a health club, swimming pool, business centre, conference room and 3 restaurants, while the s/c rooms and stes all come with comfortable modern furnishing, AC, DSTV and in-house movies. All the same, unless you're on business expenses, the cost is a steep ask for what is essentially bland transatlantic functionalism. You'd certainly want to insist on a room well away from the distressingly loud 'Good Fellas' Bar above the swimming pool. *US$140/160 for a standard sgl/dbl, rising to US$250.,*

Moderate

🏠 **Fang Fang Hotel** Ssezibwa Rd; ☎ 0414 235828/233115; f 0414 233620; e fangfang@africaonline.co.ug. Set in a restored colonial homestead a short distance uphill from the Sheraton, this clean, comfortable, family-run hotel is noted for its good Chinese cuisine and large gardens. Facilities include an airport shuttle service and an in-house clinic, hair salon and Chinese massage parlour. The large s/c rooms with AC and DSTV are good value. *US$38/60/64 sgl/twin/dbl; stes are available at US$75/90 sgl/dbl.*

🏠 **Speke Hotel** Nile Av; ☎ 0414 235332/5; f 0414 235345; e speke@spekehotel.com. Recently renovated, the long-serving Speke Hotel has a central location and good facilities including several restaurants. The adjacent Rock Bar is disturbingly noisy until late. *Comfortable s/c sgl/dbl rooms all cost US$110 B&B.*

🏠 **Hotel Havana** ☎ 0414 343532; ☎/f 0414 250762; e hotelhavana@hotmail.com. This reasonably smart hotel seems oddly misplaced, situated directly opposite the new taxi park, and it's

🏠 **Hotel Equatoria** William St; ☎ 0414 250781/8; f 0414 250146; e imperialhotel@utlonline.co.ug. Centrally located, the Equatoria is another business-oriented high rise that's undergone extensive refurbishment but still seems somewhat deficient in character. Facilities include an on-site shopping mall, health club, swimming pool, nightclub and several restaurants. The s/c rooms all have DTSV but are otherwise nothing special, and they feel rather overpriced.*US$125/140 sgl/dbl with AC or US$100/120 without.*

potentially rather noisy at night – but also very convenient if you bus into town at a late hour or intend to catch an early morning bus or minibus-taxi. A good Indian restaurant is attached, serving main dishes for around Ush10,000, and the pavement bar has large-screen DSTV. The rooms are adequate but nothing special.*US$25/30 sgl/dbl using a common shower, US$35/41 s/c with AC.*

🏠 **Kampala Club** Kintu Rd; ☎ 0414 250366; e shanghai@infocom.co.ug or hotel@shangri-la.co.ug. Formerly the Shanghai Hotel, the 10-year-old Kampala Club is recently renovated and has a convenient location almost immediately opposite the Sheraton. Free services include laundry, local telephone calls, and a substantial b/fast. Recreational and sports facilities include tennis and squash courts, swimming pool, gym, massage, sauna and squash. The attached Chinese restaurant is one of the best in town. *Executive s/c rooms US$70/86 sgl/dbl with fan or US$70/85 with AC. Stes are available at US$95.*

Budget

🏠 **Jeliza Hotel** Bombo Rd (City end); ☎ 0414 232249; f 0414 232460; e jelkam@utlonline.co.ug. Formerly the Antlers Inn, this creaky old hotel has a conveniently central location, and the spacious, pleasantly furnished rooms with TV, hot water, fridge, netting and AC is a good deal. *US$30/40 for standard sgl/dbl rooms and US$35/45 for executive rooms.*

🏠 **College Inn** Bombo Rd (Wandegere end); ☎ 0414 533835. Situated close to Makerere University on the northern side of the city centre and recently refurbished. Plenty of public transport runs past it. *US$22/33 for a comfortable s/c sgl/dbl with DSTV.*

🏠 **Hotel Catherine** Bombo Rd (Wandegere end) ☎ 0414 530871; m 0772 509902; f 0414 257473; e walusumo@walusumo.com or walusimbi@afsat.com. Directly opposite the College

Inn, the newer Hotel Catherine is another good budget hotel. The s/c accommodation with DSTV is particularly good value for couples. *US$22/25 sgl/dbl.*

🏠 **888 Hotel** Off Nakivuko Rd. ☎ 0414 234888; e chpalace@afsat.com. This unexpectedly smart Chinese-owned hotel around the corner from the bus station and new taxi park seems like a safe bet should you bus into town after dark or want an early start. A good Chinese restaurant is attached. It's very sensibly priced, too.*US$12/19 for a s/c sgl/dbl or US$10/14 for ones with common showers.*

🏠 **Hotel City Square** Kampala Rd; ☎ 0414 251451. Overlooking Constitutional Sq, this is one of the better budget options in the city centre. The balcony restaurant is nothing special but a good vantage point from which to watch city life go by. *US$19/25 for a s/c sgl/dbl with hot water.*

🏠 **Hotel New Gloria** William St; ✆ 0414 257790. This long-serving hotel is centrally located, and one of the best budget hotels in the city centre. *US$25 for a clean s/c dbl.*

Shoestring

🏠 **Lusam Inn Resthouse** Namirembe Rd; ✆ 0414 348355. This pleasant no-frills lodge is conveniently located a few hundred metres from the bus and taxi parks, and it seems good value.*US$8/9 for a sgl/dbl using common showers or US$14 for a s/c dbl.*

🏠 **Motel Rome** Navibuko Pl. Centrally located between the old taxi park and the market.*US$11 for clean s/c dbls with tiled floors and hot water.*

🏠 **Hotel Fiancée** Navibuko Pl; ✆ 0414 236144; 📱 0772 408870. Above-average budget hotel.*US$10/12 for a clean s/c sgl/dbl with nets and hot water.*

🏠 **Midland Guesthouse** ✆ 0414 340264. Set directly opposite the bus station, this adequate no-frills guesthouse has a top-floor bar with great views and DSTV. *US$7/9 for a clean s/c sgl/dbl.*

🏠 **Samalien Hotel** Off Navibuko Pl; ✆ 0772 575811. Easily the best of some grubby places in Nakivubo Pl (conveniently located between the new Taxi Park and Owino Market), this friendly place is currently under renovation and s/c rooms are being introduced. *US$7/8 for sgl/dbl rooms using shared facilities.*

🏠 **Parkside Hotel** This atmospheric establishment is located within the architecturally notable Corner House at the junction of Luwum St and Ben Kiwanuka St. Realistically, you'd only stay here if you were a travel writer (as opposed to a guidebook writer) hungry for warts 'n' all book material, or possibly an entomologist. The upstairs bar is worth a visit for the lively street views. *US$5/8 for 's/c' (tap, basin and hole-in-floor) sgl/dbl rooms, the use of a low-wattage light bulb and a considerate plywood partition to enable you and your neighbours to enjoy a degree of visual if not acoustic privacy.*

🏠 **YMCA** Buganda Rd (Wandegere end). This once-popular backpackers' standby is seldom used by travellers now that other, better hostels exist, but it remains about the cheapest place to stay in Kampala.*US$1.50 pp to camp or US$2.50 pp for a mattress on a classroom floor, which you'll have to vacate by 07.00 on weekdays.*

Suburbs
Upmarket

🏠 **Speke Resort & Country Lodge** ✆ 078 227111; 📠 0414 227110; 📧 spekeresort@spekeresort.com; www.spekeresort.com. Opened in August 2001, this superb all-suite resort is on the Lake Victoria shore at Munyonyo, about 10km from central Kampala along the Ggaba Road. An 80% price hike since the last edition of this book means that the resort no longer offers quite the same value for money but it is still difficult to beat for quality. The s/c stes are airy and spacious, with tiled floor, modern wrought-iron furnishings, a private balcony, lounge with DSTV, fan and self-catering kitchen with fridge. There's a large swimming pool in the grounds, along with a marina facing a lushly forested island, while horseriding, fishing and other boat excursions are all available. The restaurant serves good meals in the Ush10–15,000 range. *US$120/130 sgl/dbl ste and US$150–200 for 1–2-bedroom apts. Superb 2-storey round cottages which sleep 4 cost US$250. W/end packages are better value at US$95/125 sgl/dbl (FB) per night (+ VAT).*

🏠 **Hotel Bougainvillier** Off Port Bell Rd, Bugolobi; ✆ 0414 220966; 📧 bougainvillier@utl.co.ug; www.bougainvillier.com. A new establishment, this truly delightful French-owned hotel is located opposite Shell Bugolobi on the east side of town. Inspired by classic Mediterranean villa architecture, the accommodation surrounds a terraced and landscaped courtyard with a small swimming pool. The rooms are airy and spacious with stone tiled floors, a safe, AC and wireless internet connection. They extend out through glass doors to the patio and central garden. A restaurant is attached for residents. *US$85/90 sgl room/dbl ste. The excellent dbl studio apts, with fitted kitchen and gas stove each have a large dbl bed raised on a small mezzanine floor (US$110).*

🏠 **Royal Impala Hotel** ✆ 0414 577413. This smart new multi-storeyed hotel is tucked away on a back road behind Speke Resort at Munyonyo in somewhat eccentric but attractively landscaped grounds. There's no lake view but the hotel overlooks an expansive papyrus swamp which must be worth scanning for wildlife. Main courses on a varied menu cost around Ush7,000. The tiled and s/c rooms are effectively furnished with metal furniture, though some are more generously sized than others. Just outside the hotel is a shrine to St Andrew Kaggwa, a Baganda Christian who fell victim to the murderous 19th-century Kabaka Mwanga. *US$41/53 sgl/dbl.*

Moderate

Blue Mango ☎ 0414 543481/2/3; **m** 0772 398880; **f** 0414 541154; **e** bluemango@infocom.ug. The popular Blue Mango, situated a few kilometres north of the city centre, is a favourite expatriate hangout. Excellent food and the selection of small, simple but brightly painted s/c rooms have long made the Blue Mango popular with upcountry expats visiting the big city. The premises include a coffee shop, swimming pool and a booking office for the Nalubale Rafting Company. *Rooms with shared facilities cost US$25–35 and a choice of s/c rooms US$35–55/45–70 sgl/dbl. Dormitory accommodation costs US$8 pp.*

Kampala Regency Hotel Namirembe Rd; ☎ 0414 270186; **e** kasigwa@excite.com/ munialo@excite.com. A smart and very reasonably priced new hotel about 1km from the city centre. If you arrive at Entebbe with no pre-arrangements, you could do worse than hop onto this hotel's free shuttle bus. *Large s/c rooms US$51/68 sgl/dblwith a fan and DSTV, stes US$71/81 sgl/dbl. Smaller rooms in an annexe are also very good value at US$27/41 sgl/dbl.*

Hotel Diplomate ☎ 0414 267655/572828; **e** diplomatekampala@hotmail.com. Perched on the top of Tank Hill, this pleasantly low-key hotel is most notable for panoramic views north to the city centre. The restaurant serves grills, pizzas and other dishes at around Ush8,000. The s/c carpeted rooms with DSTV are pretty good value too. *US$35/45 standard sgl/dbl, US$55 ste.*

Hotel International ☎ 0414 510200/4; **e** musa@hotel-international.biz. Situated at the southern end of Tank Hill Rd, this recently opened hotel is perhaps a bit bland, but it's also very comfortable and peaceful, with a large swimming pool area offering views across to Lake Victoria. Some rooms are better than others, and not all have a balcony, so ask to see a room before you check in. *Large, attractively furnished dbl rooms with DSTV US$60/76 standard/executive.*

Budget

Namirembe Guesthouse ☎ 0414 237981/273778; **f** 041 273904; **e** ngh@utlonline.co.ug; www.namirembe-guesthouse.com. The Church of Uganda's sprawling guesthouse near the Namirembe Cathedral has long been popular with travellers for its clean accommodation, friendly atmosphere, decent canteen and attractive views over the city centre. A variety of rooms is available, most s/c with hot water and DSTV. The New Taxi Park–Natete minibus route passes within 100m of the guesthouse. *US$19–32/32–38 sgl/dbl. Family rooms cost US$41/43/56/88 3/4/5/9 bed.*

Hotel Yovani Situated along Namirembe Rd less than 1km from the city centre, close to a minibus-taxi route, this unremarkable hotel offers a good compromise between price and comfort., *US$13 dbl B&B (common showers) or US$17 s/c dbl.*

Hotel Olympia ☎ 0414 266743; **m** 0772 686300. Set along a quiet side road close to the popular cluster of pubs and restaurants on Ggaba Rd, the Olympia is a smart new reasonably priced 3-storey hotel. *US$17/22 for a comfortable carpeted s/c sgl/dbl or US$28 for a semi-ste with DSTV.*

Shine Hotel Off Ggaba Rd; ☎ 0414 510241; **m** 0712 885792. This smart new hotel offers clean s/c accommodation with carpets, fans and nets. A bar-restaurant with DSTV is attached though the Le Petit Bistro out on the main road is more tempting. *US$14/20/28 with a sgl/3/4 /dbl bed.*

Sam Sam Hotel Natete Rd; ☎ 0414 274211. This smart new hotel stands on the side of Namirembe Hill close to shops and bars in Mengo. *Rather small sgls US$16, more spacious dbls US$32.*

Pearl Guesthouse (8 rooms) Muyenga Rd; ☎ 0414 510346. Set in a quiet garden off Ggaba Rd, this small guesthouse consists of 8 bright and airy *s/c rooms* with fan and tiled floor.*US$11/17 sgl/dbl.*

Silver Springs Hotel Port Bell Rd. ☎ 0414 505976. Centred on a large swimming pool and the Woodcutter Restaurant, this rather odd hotel consists of a couple of dozen double-storey *bandas. The cheapest bandas cost US$17 and although the décor is slightly tacky, they are very spacious, with a large bedroom, lounge and bathroom. Other dbl bandas for US$33 have DSTV though they are not otherwise significantly better, while family bandas with 2 dbl rooms and DSTV cost US$56.*

Bugolobi Guesthouse **m** 0772 800247. This clean double-storey guesthouse lies alongside the Port Bell Rd near Bugolobi Market. *US$10/14 sgl/dbl using common showers or US$20 s/c dbl.*

Ndere Centre (3 rooms) ☎ 0414 288123. A new purpose-built cultural entertainment centre set in expansive green grounds 2km north of Ntinda. It's a beautiful setting, obviously convenient for almost nightly theatre and musical events and also close to the northern bypass (under construction). *There are 2 comfortable s/c dbl rooms for US$32. A non-s/c room with 4 beds costs US$14 pp.*

Andy Roberts

The choice of accommodation options along Natete Road around Mengo/Namirembe has made this area Kampala's main focus for independent and budget travellers. It's therefore appropriate to note a few useful locations which I'll describe in relation to the Backpackers' Hostel. Firstly, an excellent 20m swimming pool has just opened 200m from the hostel opposite Lyna Day Care kindergarten on the steep road leading to Rubaga Cathedral. At the time of writing, the pool is open but the adjacent club buildings remain incomplete. The caretaker, Patricia, is a tricky customer who will try to overcharge you so check the going rate (probably Ush5,000 by 2007) with the hostel. It's well worth wandering up to the Catholic cathedral 500m beyond the pool for the superb view across the city. A less precipitous route to the cathedral turns right out of the Backpackers' gate and then left at the nearby crossroads, then head uphill at successive junctions. On the tarmac Lungujja road behind the hostel, Mama Winnie's shop sells basic provisions and drinks. Heading up the main road from the hostel towards Kampala, market produce and cheap local food is available in Mengo Market. Some small supermarkets and eateries (of the liver/sausage/deep-fried object with chips ilk) can be found further up the hill in Mengo trading centre. Most pedestrian travellers pop into the long-serving Maggie's Bar at some stage for a drink. The veranda is a good place to watch the world pass by and to enjoy a plate of roast pork. Having patronised the place over 12 years I feel qualified to say that the service can approach astonishing levels of incompetence but this is all part of the great Maggie's tradition so relax and enjoy it. From Mengo it's a pleasant stroll up to the Anglican Cathedral on Namirembe hill which enjoys good city views.

Shoestring

Ⓧ Andrew's Farm ⓜ 0772 or 0712 462646; **ⓔ** andrewslakefarm@gmail.com; www.andrewslakefarm.com. Or check at Kampala Backpackers for details. While the Lake Victoria shoreline near Kampala is blighted by unmitigated suburban tat, the eastern side of Murchison Bay remains almost totally undeveloped. Andrew's Farm, scheduled to open in the first months of 2007, is a low-key campsite arranged around a croquet lawn on the quiet side of the bay, sharing a delightful lakeside site with fish eagles, kingfishers and monitor lizards. It'll be a self-catering site (in the short term anyway) and while beers, sodas, tea, fresh lake fish and BBQ equipment will be available you should (unless you hear otherwise), bring other provisions with you; there's an excellent market at Ggaba port. To get to the campsite, head south of Kampala to Ggaba where you can either hire a fishing boat for a scenic 40 minute voyage (boats carry up to 12 people and cost Ush.20,000 each way) or take a 'water taxi' (Ush1000 each) across the bay to Bule landing (15 minutes) then continue by boda boda (10 minutes: Ush.1500). Self contained self catering cottages are planned but in the meantime, *camping*

with your own tent will cost US$4pp; tent hire an additional US$3, and US$16 s/dbl for a permanent tent with a bed and net.

🏠 Kampala Backpackers' Hostel and Campsite
◟ 0414 274767; **ⓜ** 0772 430587/502758; **ⓔ** backpackers@infocom.co.ug; www.backpackers.co.ug. Entering its 14th year of service in 2007, this excellent and popular Australian-owned travellers' hangout is situated on the main Kampala–Natete Rd in Lungujja, about 3km out of town, directly on the Natete Rd minibus-taxi route. A good range of facilities including internet, gorilla-tracking information and permit bookings, white-water rafting bookings and pick-up, an international MTN payphone, a DSTV and video lounge, free luggage storage, clean ablution blocks with hot water, a good bar, craft shop and a restaurant serving filling pizzas, burgers and daily 'specials'. Valuables, laptops, etc, can be left in secure lockers provided with individual keys and padlock fittings for additional security for Ush1,000 per day. The large, green grounds are teeming with birds, and also host a resident troop of vervet monkeys and a ground squirrel colony. To get to the hostel, go to the new taxi park and ask for a

minibus-taxi to 'Backpackers' — all the drivers know it and you'll never wait more than 5mins for something to leave. If you're headed west in your own vehicle, Backpackers is ideally placed for a traffic-free escape from the city. A range of accommodation is available. *From the bottom upwards, camping in the lovely garden costs US$4 pp while dormitory beds are US$5.50 or US$6.50 pp with nets and bedding. A popular option in the latter category is the open fronted 4-bed 'Nature's dorm' on a 1st-floor balcony above the gardens. Twin-bed bandas in the garden cost US$16 sharing a smart new communal bathroom. 2 s/c rooms with verandas facing the garden cost US$23 and US$26. A new 1st-floor flat with 4 twin/dbl rooms at US$27 each sharing a bathroom, lounge with TV and veranda is ideal for small groups.*

🏠 **Uganda Protestant Medical Bureau** This clean and quiet hostel is located on Balintuma Rd between Mengo and Natete. It's an institutional establishment decidedly lacking in atmosphere but the staff are friendly and helpful and the rooms are excellent value. Meals are available but no beer is served on the premises. Still, Maggie's Bar in Mengo is just 10mins' walk up the road (Take a torch for the way home down unlit Balintuma Rd!). *Rooms with shared facilities US9/13 sgl/dbl, s/c rooms US14/16 sgl/dbl.*

🏠 **Red Chilli Hideaway** Sunderland Rd; ☎ 0414 223 903 (office); m 0772 509150 *(bar open 07.00–midnight)*; e chilli@infocom.co.ug; www.redchillihideaway.com. Another excellent backpackers' hostel, Red Chilli lies in a 2.5-acre garden in the leafy suburb of Bugolobi, some 4km east of the city centre. A good range of facilities including white-water rafting bookings and pick-up, DSTV, laundry service, clean ablution blocks with hot water, a very lively bar, and a restaurant serving a good range of reasonably priced Western and local snacks and meals from Ush1,500–7,500. Free internet is available from 09.00–21.00. Red Chilli lies about 500m from the Port Bell Rd. To get there, catch any minibus-taxi to Bugolobi, Luzira, Nakawa or Port Bell, disembark at Colgate Factory Junction (200m past the Silver Springs Hotel), take Kireka Rd to the left, then follow the second left for about 200m. If you're headed east in your own vehicle, Red Chilli is conveniently located to dodge the traffic and get out of town. *Accommodation*

options using shared facilities are: camping US$3.50 pp; dormitory beds US$5; rooms US$12/14 twin/dbl. S/c cottages are also available. 1-bedroom unit (>3 people) US$35 and 2-bedroom units (>4) US$46.

🏠 **Vellavue Hotel** Ggaba Rd; ☎ 0414 510640; m 0772 868669. This hotel has a great location close to numerous bars and restaurants. The rooms at the back overlook Kansanga's slum roofscapes across the green swamp valley towards the affluent leafy suburb of Makynde Ridge. This and the slightly smarter Embassy Hotel (below) have to be the best non-backpackers' budget deals in Kampala. It's also very good value. *US$8 for a clean sgl/dbl using common showers or US$14 s/c.*

🏠 **Embassy Hotel** ☎ 0414 267672. This excellent new hotel stands above the Western Union office in the middle of the popular Kabalagala nightspot close to numerous bars and restaurants. With smart and spacious s/c rooms, it's unbeatable value! *US$14 s/c, larger (ste) rooms US$16 (b/fast is Ush5,000 extra).*

🏠 **Tal Cottages** ☎ 0414 273330. This curiously suburban development is found off Kabusu Rd on the side of Rubaga hill between the Catholic Cathedral and Kabaka Lake, 5 storied cottages line a narrow private lane leading to a 3-floor conference centre and swimming pool, a row of drab bungalows faces 5 round, storied cottages, The latter are altogether more inspired as are their room names which include Marie Antoinette, Princess Diana, Lewinsky, Venus de Milo and Black Eyed Susan. Rather ordinary meals are available while the popular Wallet Time bar on Kabusu road serves some excellent roasted pork. *Cottages are divided into 4 smallish s/c rooms which each cost a (negotiable) US$27 B&B.*

🏠 **Kenrock Hotel** Situated just off Tank Hill Rd, opposite the better known but presently closed Grand Pearl Hotel. *US$7/11 for a rather scruffy but adequate s/c sgl/dbl.*

🏠 **Deep Guesthouse** Located right opposite Al's Bar and Half London, this cheapie is perfectly placed to crash after partying the night away at the Ggaba Rd hotspots. It's bound to be dreadfully noisy but the chances are that if you're staying there, you won't be crawling into bed until late anyway. No food is served but with some of Kampala's best eateries within a short stroll, who cares! *Clean s/c rooms US$8/11 sgl/dbl.*

✕ **WHERE TO EAT AND DRINK** This section has been updated with the help of Adrift Adventure Company, an energetic crew that manages to juggle busy workdays (rafting the Nile and tossing punters off their bungee tower) with nights spent ensuring that they keep constantly abreast of new opportunities to eat, drink and dance their way around Kampala. It's an exhausting and never-ending task and I

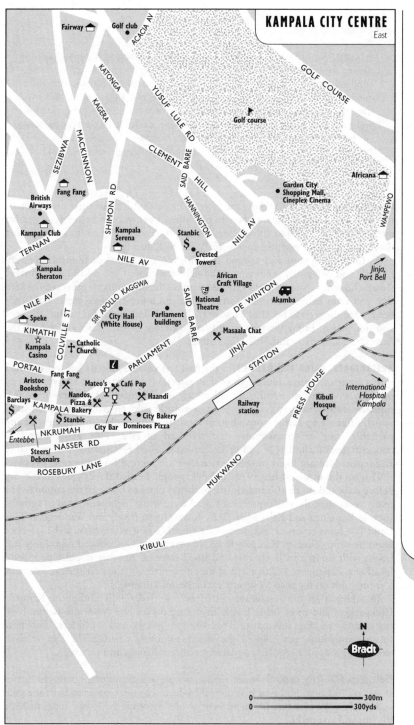

KAMPALA CITY CENTRE
East

Fairway
Golf club
ACACIA AV
KATONGA
KAGERA
SEZIBWA
MACKINNON
YUSUF LULE RD
CLEMENT BARRE HILL
SAID BARRE HILL
GOLF COURSE
Golf course
WANPEWO
Africana
Garden City
Shopping Mall,
Cineplex Cinema
British
Airways
Fang Fang
SHIMON RD
Kampala
Serena
Stanbic
Crested
Towers
NILE AV
Jinja,
Port Bell
Kampala Club
TERNAN
Kampala
Sheraton
NILE AV
NILE AV
SIR APOLLO KAGGWA
African
Craft Village
National
Theatre
DE WINTON
Akamba
Speke
KIMATHI
Kampala
Casino
City Hall
(White House)
Parliament
buildings
SAID BARRE
Masaala Chat
JINJA
PORTAL
Catholic
Church
PARLIAMENT
COLVILLE ST
STATION
International
Hospital
Kampala
Aristoc
Bookshop
Fang Fang
Mateo's
Café Pap
Barclays
Nandos,
Pizza &
Bakery
Haandi
PRESS HOUSE
KAMPALA RD
Stanbic
City Bakery
Railway
station
Kibuli
Mosque
Entebbe
City Bar
Dominoes Pizza
NKRUMAH
Steers/
Debonairs
NASSER RD
MUKWANO
ROSEBURY LANE
KIBULI

N

Bradt

0 ——————— 300m
0 ——————— 300yds

hope you'll join me in thanking the boys and girls of Adrift for their dedication to this important cause. The numbers in parentheses below refer to highly subjective ratings (on a scale of 0 to 10) allocated by Adrift. A star ★ is given to locations that they consider to be essential to any 'real' visit to Kampala.

As for finding your way around at night, most residents of Kampala are very friendly and will gladly point you in the right direction if you ask. The cab drivers (locally known as 'special hires') are also very on the ball, and can get you anywhere that you want to go. Just don't forget to bargain a pre-arranged price. *Boda-boda* drivers are also a good bet after a few beers (provided it's you who has had the beer and not them). Enjoy yourselves and have one for us, the guides of Adrift, the Adventure Company and Nile High Bungee.

Restaurants, cafés and bars Over the past ten years, Kampala has transformed into a diner's paradise. Hundreds of new eateries have sprung up all over the city offering a variety of cuisine for all tastes and budgets. There are of course numerous small take-aways, pork joints, roadside chicken grills and market stalls which offer cheap and reasonable local food. It is impossible to recommend any particular one or to guarantee the standard of fare. This guide therefore concentrates on the larger and/or longer-established restaurants, whose quality and reputations are likely to ensure that they are around for some time to come.

During the troubled late 1970s and 80s, people headed directly out of the city before dark and drank (Ugandans like to drink) close to home in the suburbs. For many years after, the city centre was a dead zone while nightlife shifted to suburbs such as Kansanga and Kabalagala (3km down Ggaba Road) and Wandegeya. This trend has been reversed and many of Kampala's best restaurants and bars once again lie on or close to Kampala Road. However the Ggaba Road nightspots still boom with numerous lively bars and good eateries. Another popular peripheral location is Kisementi, 1.5km north of the city centre, and the nearby Acacia Avenue (recently put on the map by several exclusive restaurants).

In addition to the restaurants listed below, Red Chilli Hideaway, Kampala Backpackers and most other hotels in the upmarket and moderate ranges have restaurants serving international cuisine to guests and outsiders. For new recommendations, get hold of the free bi-monthly ad-mag *The Eye* (*or check www.theeye.co.ug*) for regularly updated restaurant listings and reviews.

Nakasero Hill (city centre) Smart restaurants are mushrooming across the upper slopes of Nakasero Hill which is capped by State House. Opportunities for eating and drinking become steadily more basic as one descends the lower slopes towards the bus and taxi parks.

✕ **1,000 Cups** Buganda Rd; ✆ 0772 505619; 📱 0782 544313. Drink in or take-away – a wide selection of packaged Uganda coffees make novel presents to take home. (6)

✕ **Alleygators** Karaoke bar and bowling alley on the 3rd floor of the Garden City Complex. The place to be on Thu or Sat evenings.

✕ **Nawab Restaurant** ✆ 0414 263333. This new Indian restaurant in the Garden City Shopping Centre has 2 sister branches in Dubai! Very good food (especially the tandoori), provided that you can ignore the naff astro-turf grass outside and the pictures on the menu – the actual food looks nothing like them! The atmosphere is slightly lacking, which shouldn't really be surprising in a shopping centre. *Prices around Ush10,000 for a main course with rice/naan.* (7)

✕ **The Venue** Top fl, new Garden City Shopping Centre, Yusuf Lule Rd directly beside Nawab. A popular retreat with Ugandans visiting Kampala's latest and smartest shopping centre. A good place for a drink after a trip to the cinema downstairs. (7)

✕ **Bancafé** ✆ 0414 346834; 📱 0312 263003. Located in the Grand Imperial Hotel complex, this is a good spot for a cup of Java and a muffin. (6)

✕ **Baldwins Café** 2nd Floor, Crested Towers Bldg. Very good cocktails (according to our seasoned tasters), coffee and teas. (7)

✕ **Blue Africa Bar and Restaurant** ✆ 0414 233506. Set in the shadow of Crested Towers (the big blue ones) this is a popular place for continental food. (7)

✕ **Café Pap** 13 Parliament Av; ✆ 0414 254647; 📱 0772 652443. *The place for coffee connoisseurs.* Excellent coffee, good food and fast internet access make it a popular stop for laptop owners. (9)

✕ **City Bar and Restaurant** 11 Kampala Rd; ✆ 0414 346460. Old-fashioned décor with a snooker table, so a popular afternoon spot during the rains. Also good outdoor set-up. (6)

✕ **Dominoes Pizza** Kampala Rd; ✆ 0414 251513. Almost fast food, Dominoes near City Bar offers excellent pizzas and burgers to eat in or take-away/deliver. (6)

✕ **Ekitoobero** 21 Kitante Rd; ✆ 0414 346834. *The place to sample traditional Ugandan food in a restaurant rather than a market stall.* Ekitoobero is a very informal restaurant with a massage parlour/beautician's out the back! *Meals cost between Ush4,000 and Ush8,000.* (8)

✕ **Fang Fang Restaurant and Hotel** ✆ 0414 344806. Excellent Chinese food. There are 2 locations, the Roof Terrace in Communications Hse on Colville St. and the (less atmospheric) hotel on Ssezibwa Rd (8)

✕ **Garden City Food Court** The excellent food court in the Garden City Shopping Centre, adjacent to the golf course, has 5 different outlets: Haandi (Indian – see below), Iranian, Magic Wok (Chinese), Chick'n Express and Sub 'n' Bun Sandwiches. Eat in/take-away. *Most meals in Ush4,000–10,000 range.*

✕ **Haandi Restaurant** Commercial Plaza, Kampala Rd; ✆ 0414 346283. Odd setting for Uganda's best Indian food. (8)

✕ **Kampala Casino** Pan Africa Hse, Kimathi Av; ✆ 0414 343628/343630. This plush casino is worth visiting for the food even if you don't fancy a flutter – they have a range of good continental dishes for around Ush10,000. Thu is particularly popular as there's live music and a very reasonable Ugandan buffet *Ush7,500 pp.* (6)

✕ **Kyoto Japanese Restaurant** 1 Shimoni Rd, Nakasero; ✆ 0414 237078. One of the latest additions to the Kampala restaurant scene. Excellent sushi and sashimi for lovers of authentic Japanese food. Don't miss the *miso* soup either. (9)

✕ **Mamba Point** Akii Bua Rd; ✆ 0772 243225. Excellent Italian food at corporate prices. (9)

✕ **Mamma Mia** Speke Hotel; ✆ 0414 346340; 📱 0772 630211. The corner plot of Nile/Kimathi avs has served Italian food since the mid 1960s (albeit with a few interruptions in service). The present management provides some of the best pizzas in town, and they are to be recommended over anything else on the menu. Handily located within the Speke Hotel complex and with an attractive garden setting, the restaurant is popular for lunch and dinner alike. *Main meals are in the Ush7,000–12,000 range.* (8)

✕ **Masala Chaat House** De Winton Rd; ✆ 0414 236487. Popular with travellers as an informal, good-value Indian restaurant, this place is located just opposite the National Theatre (and craft market). The food is reasonable – not as good as the more upmarket Indian restaurants, but significantly cheaper. Boozers note – no alcohol on the premises! *Expect to pay around Ush8,000 for a main course.* (9)

✕ **Music Club** Located in the National Theatre.. ✆ 0414 254567. Every Mon night around 19.00, local musicians gather for excellent impromptu jam sessions. Free admission and if you play an instrument, you'll be welcome to join in. (10)*

✕ **Mateo's** Kampala Rd; ✆ 0414 340840. The best cocktail bar in Kampala. Great place to kick off your Friday evening. (6)

✕ **Nando's** Kampala Rd; ✆ 0414 340840/3. Downstairs from Mateo's, this fast-food complex offers ice creams, pizzas, barbecue chicken, etc.

✕ **Vasilis Bakery** Good bread, pies and pastries. (10)

✕ **Steers Food Court** ✆ 0414 231623/4. South African franchises Steers (steaks and burgers) and Debonairs (pizza) have outlets on the corner of Kampala and Entebbe Rd but their operation is not a patch on nearby Nandos. Eat in/take-away/deliver. *Most meals in Ush4,000–8,000 range.*

✕ **Sam's Restaurant** 78 Kampala Rd (Bombo Rd end); ✆ 0414 251694. This popular restaurant caters for absolutely everyone: there's a whole range of Indian dishes, homemade burgers, pies and salads and the carnivore's favourites – ranging from the conventional fillet steak to the more adventurous ostrich and crocodile. Particularly busy at lunchtimes, Sam's has a buzzing atmosphere and efficient service. *Prices for main courses range from Ush7,000–15,000.* (9)

Bugolobi

✕ **Katch the Sun** Bandali Rise; m 0774 0331253. Bright and interesting décor and good food. (8)

✕ **Shanghai Hotel** 8/10 Ternan Av, near Sheraton Hotel; ✆ 0414 250372. Nice Chinese food, open 7 days. (7)

✕ **T and J's** Buganda Rd, near the YMCA; ✆ 0414 348417. This sports bar has recently been remodelled with a snappy new look. (6)

✕ **Uganda Crafts Bat Valley** 28–30 Bombo Rd; ✆ 0414 250077. Really good, authentic African food: *posho* (aka *ugali*), *matoke*, *kalo*. Try this one for lunch. (6)

✕ **Parkside Inn** Found on the corner of Ben Kiwanuka and Luwum sts next to the old taxi park this is a great place to watch the craziness of Kampala go by while relaxing over a cold beer on the balcony. (7 for the view)

✕ **Afrique Hotel** Allen Rd, across from New Taxi Park. Same idea as the Parkside Inn but this overlooks the new taxi park. You can watch soccer games in Nakivubo Stadium for free from up here. (6)

✕ **Italia** Behind Shell Bugolobi; m 0772 956882. Genuine Italian food in relaxed garden atmosphere. (8)

Rubaga and Mengo

✕ **MM Pub** Good little pub close to the main Masaka Rd and a lively place to watch a premier league game. (5)

✕ **Wallet Time Pub** Enjoy excellent roast pork in shady thatch shelters. On Kabusu Rd below Rubaga Cathedral.

✕ **Maggie's Bar, Natete Rd.** Perennial stop-off in Mengo at the top of the long walk up the hill from the Backpackers' Hostel.

Wandegeya/Makerere and Nakulabye

✕ **The Bermuda Triangle** Just off Makerere Hill Rd. Near Makerere University, so a very popular student hangout. Not so much a bar as a collection of tables and stores selling the coldest beer in Uganda.

✕ **Tipsy's Takeaway** (10 for the grease), just down the road, is a mandatory pilgrimage after a night's drinking for a late-night snack. The rolexes are great (see box, page 150); try the 'double bugger' if you dare (and do let us know afterwards). (7)

✕ **Deep Blue and 2 stars** Two in one located next to Shell Wandegeya. Another pork festival awaits. (7)

✕ **Joys Joint** Next to Wandegeya Post Office. For the best pork in Kampala. (7)*

✕ **Teachers Grill** Next to the basement of College Inn. Trendy, classy and full of university students. (7).

✕ **Club 5** This affordable café at Club 5 is located just inside the Makerere University gate and is worth a visit if you have cause to be on campus. It occupies a pleasant semi-outdoor setting and serves affordable local and international staples plus some good Indian specials. The complex includes a bar with DSTV, a well-equipped gym with a sauna, and an internet café. To get there take the first left inside the main gate and follow the road downhill.

✕ **Nakulabye Pork Joints** 1km west of the University, Makerere Hill Rd is lined with pork joints/bars where roast pork is served with 'accompaniments' (tomato, avocado, onion, cassava). It's strictly a dining-with-fingers place. What you do is drip chilli sauce onto a sliced tomato then mash it into a pulp with your thumb to make a delicious dip. Very popular with Ugandans on evenings and weekend afternoons before the (English Premier League) football on TV.

Kisementi and Acacia Avenue (Kololo)

✕ **Bubbles O' Leary** 30 Windsor Cres. Authentic Irish pub (fittings imported from a bankrupt bar in Eire) unfortunately without the Guinness. Popular expat pub particularly on Fri.

✕ **The Crocodile** ☎ 0414 254593; m 0772 486630. The Crocodile has a real continental feel about it and serves consistently good food, though sometimes a little slowly. Particularly popular with expatriates, there are good sandwiches, steaks, pasta and other main dishes. *Sandwiches at around Ush8,000 and other main meals around Ush12,000.* (9)

✕ **Just Kicking** Cooper Rd, Kisementi; ☎ 0414 235134. Uganda's most popular expat bar. Fri and Sat nights are particularly lively as are showings of soccer and rugby internationals. (9)*

✕ **Khana Khazana** Acacia Av; ☎ 0414 233049/ 347346. The best setting of all of Uganda's restaurants with creamy rich Indian food. Splash out! (8)

✕ **Krua Thai** Windsor Cres. Best Thai food in Uganda in a wonderful setting. (9)

✕ **Rocks and Roses** 2 Acacia Av (part of The Surgery complex). Great homemade scones and teas in traditional UK style. (7)

Kabalagala

✕ **7th Happiness** Tucked away in Tank Hill Road between all the nightclubs, this is excellent, authentic Chinese food. (8)

✕ **Café Roma** m 0772 501847. Situated on Muyenga Hill close to the Hotel International, this cheerful Italian café serves good coffee and a selection of sandwiches, snacks and pasta dishes. (9)

✕ **Fasika** ☎ 0414 510441; m 0772 303716.. This good-value Ethiopian restaurant next to Payless supermarket offers tasty and authentic Ethiopian dishes — pancake-like *injera* with spicy *wat* sauces — for around Ush5,000–7,000 in a pretty garden setting. A good option for combining eating with a night out, since the notorious Al's Bar and Capital Pub lie just up the road. (8)

✕ **Punchline** Popular local pub and pork joint frequented by students from nearby Kampala International University (8)*

✕ **Le Chateau** Ggaba Rd; ☎ 0414 510404; e sales@qualitycuts.net. Excellent Belgian restaurant with African décor at the Quality Hill Shopping Mall. There is a cheaper, rather uninspiring lunchtime snack menu, but the formal main menu is much more imaginative. They serve a wide variety of food — from steaks to snails and guinea fowl and not forgetting the essential Belgian *frites*. They even occasionally import mussels from Belgium at Ush45,000 per head. A venue worthy of a special occasion. *Main meals are between Ush15,000 and Ush20,000. Open 7 days.*

Kansanga

✕ **Half London 2000** 70 Ggaba Rd, next to Al's; ☎ 0414 268910. Reopened under new management, this one is proving to be a popular spot for both dinner and drinks. Live music on Wed and Sat. (6)

✕ **Hunters' Bar** Ggaba Rd. Good place to relax with lively crowd and live bands. (6)

✕ **Le Petit Bistro** ☎ 0772 403080. A local roadside café with no visible signs to distinguish it from any of the hundreds in Kampala. Be not deterred, however, as although the rest of the menu is not anything in particular to write home about, the steaks are by far and away the best in Kampala. Huge, wonderfully tender fillet steaks with a choice of sauces, they are the carnivore's dream-come-true. And the prices are great too. *Ush8,000 for the steaks and less for the other dishes.* (7)

Nightclubs
It's perfectly possible to visit all of the places mentioned above for a meal and a couple of drinks and retire happily before midnight. If that doesn't appeal, try the locations listed below which exist to keep you entertained until very late.

City centre

☆ **Sabrinas** ☎ 0414 250174. The original karaoke pub in Kampala with tasty buffet lunches and a good atmosphere. (7)

☆ **TLC** Buganda Rd; m 0772 404456. Really good party music with plenty of food, swimming pool and a slide! (8)

☆ **Faze 2** Buganda Rd, above YMCA; ☎ 0392 700815; m 0772 345808. Great bar/club with good music. (7)

☆ **The Basement** William St, below the Hotel Equatoria; m 0772 501345. Popular for Afro-Caribbean music. (6)

Kabalagala/Kansanga

☆ **Al's Bar** Ggaba Rd. The wildest bar in town. Cool music, cheap snacks, great service. Anything goes. Open until b/fast time and very quiet before 02.00 when it fills up with partygoers from around town. (8)*

☆ **Capital Pub** 119 Tank Hill Rd, across from Fasika; ✆ 0414 269676. For alternative entertainment. Pay a visit and test your fear threshold. (7 for shock value)

Industrial area (off Jinja Road)

☆ **Club Silk** 15–17 First St; ✆ 0414 250907. Go on the first Fri of the month (TFI Friday). Otherwise, cheap drinks and expensive admission. (6)

☆ **Ange Noir** Off Jinja Rd, between First and Third sts; ✆ 0414 230190. Another popular student hangout; features good DJs, cheap drinks, and a guaranteed lively crowd. Check out Ange Mystique upstairs for a more sophisticated crowd. (9)*

☆ **Club Obbligatto** Old Port Bell Rd, next to Meatpackers; m 0772 923988. Afrigo band, one of Uganda's best known, play there at weekends. (7)

LISTINGS
Airlines

✈ **Uganda Travel Bureau (UTB-2004 Ltd)** ✆ 0312 223255/5 /0414 335335; emergency 24hr line, m 0772 232555; e info@utb.co.ug or ruth@utb.co.ug; www.utb.co.ug. A useful first contact for good deals on flights out of Uganda. They also often offer special fares to London, Johannesburg and other major European and African cities.

The following international airlines fly into/out of Entebbe:

✈ **Air Tanzania** Ground Fl, Workers Hse, Pilkington Rd; ✆ 0414 255501; f 0414 345774; www.airtanzania.com. Flights to and from Dar es Salaam on Tue, Thu, Fri and Sun.

✈ **British Airways** Centre Crt, 4 Ternan Av; ✆ 0414 257414/5/6; f 0414 259181; e contactba.1.uganda@britishairways.com; www.britishairways.com. Overnight flights from London Heathrow on Tue, Thu and Sun, returning daytime Mon, Wed and Fri.

✈ **Dairo Air** 8 Colville St, ✆ 0414 256135/256213; f 0414 256137; e dairoair@dasair.com. 3 flights to Sudan on Wed, Fri and Sun.

✈ **EgyptAir** Grand Imperial Arcade, Speke Rd; ✆ 0414 233960; m 0772 200119; e egyptairuganda @africaonline.com; www.egyptair.com. Flights to and from Cairo on Sun only, with good connections to Europe.

✈ **Emirates** FNC Bldg, Kimathi Av; ✆ 0414 349941/2/3/4; f 0414 340076; www.emirates.com. Daily flights to Dubai with connections to Europe, the Far East and the US.

✈ **Ethiopian Airways** United Assurance Bldg, Kimathi Av; ✆ 0414 345577/8 and 0414 254796/7; f 0414 231455; www.flyethiopian.com. 5 flights weekly to/from Addis Ababa, with connections to two dozen other African cities, several European capitals, as well as the US.

✈ **Kenya Airways** Jubilee Centre, 11 Parliament Av; ✆ 0312 236000041 233068; f 0414 259472; www.kenya-airways.com. Several flights daily between Entebbe and Nairobi, with connecting flights most days to London Heathrow, Dar es Salaam and Johannesburg.

✈ **KLM Royal Dutch Airlines** 14 Parliament Av, Jubilee Insurance Bldg, 3rd Fl, ✆ 0414 338000/1.Direct night flights to Amsterdam 3 times a week on Tue, Fri and Sat with connections to Europe, the US and Canada.

✈ **Rwandair Express** 1st Fl, Garden City Mall; ✆ 0414 346666/7; f 0414 346666. Flights to Kigali (Rwanda) daily except Sat and daily to Nairobi.

✈ **South Africa Airways** Workers Hse, Pilkington Rd; ✆ 0414 255501/2; f 0414 255825; www.saa.co.za. Flights to/from Johannesburg on Wed, Fri and Sun.

✈ **SN Brussels** Rwenzori Hse, Lumumba Dr; ✆ 0414 234200/1/2; f 0414 342790. Overnight flights from Entebbe to Brussels on Mon, Wed and Fri; daytime flights Brussels to Entebbe on the same days.

✈ **Precision Air** c/o Kenya Airways, Jubilee Centre, 11 Parliament Av; ✆ 0312 236000041 233068; f 0414 259472. Flights to Kilimanjaro and Mwanza on Mon and Sat.

Art galleries Several good art galleries are scattered around Kampala. Highly recommended, the **Nommo National Art Gallery** (e *culture@africaonline.co.ug; gallery and attached shop open Mon–Fri 09.00–17.00, Sat and Sun 09.00–15.00; admission free*) is housed in a converted colonial residence on Victoria Street in Nakasero, and displays a wide variety of work by Ugandan and other East African artists. The gallery at the **Faculty of Fine Art** in Makerere University displays work by several of the country's leading or most promising talents. Also worth a visit are the private **Okapi Gallery** on Ggaba Road (✆ *0414 343532;* m *0772 480015*), **Cassava Republic** on Bukoto Street in Kisementi (m *0772 407318;* e *cassava@hotmail.com*) and **Tulifanya Art Gallery** on Hannington Road (✆ *0414 254183*).

Bakeries The **Hot Loaf Bakery** on Kampala Road, opposite the intersection with Parliament Road, bakes good fresh bread and serves various take-away snacks. Other good bakeries include the **Shoprite** supermarkets, and **Nando's** and **Baker's World** on Kampala Road.

Bookshops There are several bookshops in Kampala, though most focus exclusively on religious tracts. The main exception is the superb **Aristoc Book Shop** on Kampala Road, which stocks an impressive selection of current novels, travel guides, field guides and publications about Ugandan history. A second branch of Aristoc opened recently in the new Garden City Shopping Mall. To buy or exchange secondhand novels, the best selections are available at the centrally located **Rent-A-Book Centre** in Colline House on Pilkington Road, **Seconds R' Us** on Bombo Road and in the little arcade in Kabalagala (Ggaba Rd) opposite the Shell station.

Car hire The major international car-hire companies **Avis** (✆ *0414 320516;* m *0752 694843*) and **Hertz** (✆ *0414 347191;* e *hertz-u@africaonline.co.ug*) are both represented in Kampala. Hertz charges US$51 per day for a saloon car inside Kampala and US$86 outside (exclusive of fuel). A 4x4 costs US$85 per day (Kampala) and US$155 (outside). It is advisable to make arrangements before you travel using their freephone central reservations services or websites. For Avis dial 0870 606 0100 (UK) or +1 800 230 4898 (US) or log on at www.avis.com. For Hertz contact 0870 848 4848 (UK), +1 800 654 3131 (US) or log on at www.hertz.com.

Better rates for vehicle rental are generally available through locally based operators, of which the following can be recommended:

🚗 **City Cars & 4x4s** Tank Hill Parade, Muyenga; m 0772 412001; e citycars@bushnet.com; www.driveuganda.com

🚗 **Phoenix Car Rental** UWA Head Office, Kintu Rd; ✆ 0414 236096; m 0772 200605; f 0414 236097; e phoenix@starcom.co.ug

🚗 **Walter Egger** ✆/f 0434 121314; m 0772 221113; e wemtec@source.co.ug. Jinja-based private rental offers reasonable rates on 4 Land Rovers, an AC van with fridge, a 4x4 Pajero and a 29-seater bus. Rates US$70–135 per day inc a driver (self drive not available).

Cinema The **Cineplex Cinema** at 10 Wilson Road shows a good selection of current American and European films while you'll find brand new international releases opening at the 3-screen Cineplex in the Garden City Shopping Centre within a day or so of their premieres in London and New York and (at a fraction of the cost). Pick up a copy of the *New Vision* or *Monitor* to find out what's showing when you're in town.

Clubs and societies The following clubs and societies may be worth contacting by travellers with special interests. A fuller list is contained in Kampala's free bimonthly ad-mag, *The Eye*.

International Women's Organisation m 0712 700007 or 0752 742646. Regular meetings on the first Thu of the month at the National Museum on Kiira Rd. Special events.

Mountain Club of Uganda m 0772 200745; e hostetter@spacenet.com. Meets at 17.30 on the second Thu of each month at the Athina Club, Windsor Cres (next to Bubbles Irish pub).

Nature Uganda ↘ 0414 540719; **f** 0414 533528. Ring for details of free monthly nature walks around Kampala.
Uganda Bird Guides Club m 0772 518290; **e** ugandabirdguides@hotmail.com. The country's top bird guides all belong to this club, which is well worth contacting if you're looking for a reliable freelance guide with local knowledge.

Courier services Although post into and out of Kampala is fairly reliable, it is rather slow and best avoided for any valuable or urgent dispatches. More expensive but safer to use a major international courier service such as **DHL** on Clement Hill Road (↘ *0414 251608–12*) or **TNT** in the Nile Hotel's conference centre (↘ *0414 230005/ 342923*).

Credit cards Most upmarket hotels in Kampala accept major international credit and debit cards, as do some of the smarter restaurants, but you will normally need to pay cash for other services and purchases. The equivalent of up to around US$200 in local currency can be drawn against all major credit cards at ATMs outside the Standard Chartered and Barclays banks on Kampala Road.

Dental services Recommended dentists include the **Sterling Dental Clinic** in Bhatia House, Kampala Road (m *0772 488592*), **Doctors A & G Madan** (m *0772 433058/9*) and **Dr Paul Aliker** (↘ *0414 531259*).

Diplomatic missions Embassies and high commissions likely to be of interest to visitors to Uganda are as follows:

ⓔ Algeria 14 Acacia Av, Kololo; ↘ 0414 232918/232689; **f** 0414 341015
ⓔ Austria 3 Portal Av; ↘ 031 235104/5; **f** 0312 235160; **e** franzbreitwieser@ada.or.at
ⓔ Belgium 1 Lumumba Av, Rwenzori Hse, 3rd Fl; ↘ 0414 349559/349569/70; **f** 0414 347212; **e** ambelkam@infocom.co.ug
ⓔ Canada IPS Bldg, 14 Parliament Av; ↘ 0414 258141/348141 and 0312 260511; **f** 0414 349484; **e** canada.consulate@utlonline.co.ug
ⓔ China 37 Malcolm X Av, Kololo; ↘ 0414 236895/259881; **f** 0414 235087; **e** chinaemb_ug@mfa.gov.cn
ⓔ Cyprus Athina Club Hse, 30 Windsor Close; ↘ 0414 341428/236053; **f** 0414 236089; **e** athina@infocom.co.ug
ⓔ Denmark 3 Lumumba Av; ↘ 0312 263211/2; **f** 0312 264624; **e** kmtamb@um.dk
ⓔ Egypt 33 Kololo Hill Drive; ↘ 0414 254525/345152; **f** 0414 232103; **e** egyembug@utlonline.co.ug
ⓔ Ethiopia Kiira Rd; ↘ 0414 348340; **f** 0414 341885; **e** ethiokam@starcom.co.ug
ⓔ European Union 15th Fl, Crested Towers, Hannington Rd; ↘ 0414 233303/4 and 0414 231226; **f** 0414 233708; **e** delegation-uganda@cec.eu.int
ⓔ France 16 Lumumba Av, Nakasero; ↘ 0414 342120/342176; **f** 0414 349812; **e** mbasrance.kampala@diplomatie.jouv.fr
ⓔ Germany 15 Philip Rd; ↘ 0414 501111; **f** 0414 501115; **e** germemb@africaonline.co.ug
ⓔ India 11 Kyadondo Rd; ↘ 0414 342994/344631; **f** 0414 254943; **e** hc@hicomindkampala.org
ⓔ Ireland 25 Kitante Rd; ↘ 0414 344344/344348; **f** 0414 344353; **e** hom@ireland.co.ug
ⓔ Italy 11 Lourdel Rd; ↘ 0414 250450/250442; **f** 0414 250448; **e** ambkamp@imul.com
ⓔ Japan EADB Bldg, 4 Nile Av; ↘ 0414 349542/3/4/5; **f** 0414 349547; **e** jambassy@jembassy.or.ug
ⓔ Kenya 41 Nakasero Rd; ↘ 0414 258235/6 and 0414 268232; **f** 0414 258239; **e** kenhicom@africaonline.co.ug
ⓔ Netherlands 4th Fl, Rwenzori Hse, Lumumba Av; ↘ 0414 346000; **f** 0414 231861; **e** kam@minbuza.nl
ⓔ Nigeria 33 Nakasero Rd; ↘ 0414 233691/2; **f** 0414 232543; **e** nighcom-sgu@africaonline.co.ug

Some other diplomatic missions accredited to Uganda are in Nairobi; for instance Australia, Canada, Japan, Greece, Zimbabwe and Zambia. Australians and Canadians can contact the UK high commission in an emergency. Quite a number of backpackers pick up their Ethiopian visas in Kampala because the Ethiopian high commission in Nairobi often refuses to issue visas to travellers who don't have an air ticket to Addis Ababa.

Foreign exchange (cash) Private forex bureaux are dotted all over the city, with the main concentration along Kampala Road, and will readily exchange US dollars and other hard currencies into Uganda shillings. Most bureaux are open from 09.00 to 17.00 on weekdays and a few are also open on Saturday mornings – exchange rates at the major forex bureaux are pretty uniform, and better than at the banks, though you might want to shop around before you change large sums of money. The only place where you can be certain of being able to exchange money over weekends and in the evenings is the forex in Speke Hotel or those at Entebbe International Airport. You could also try other upmarket hotels, but generally they change money only for hotel residents.

Foreign exchange (travellers' cheques) Most private forex bureaux will not exchange travellers' cheques under any circumstances, and nor will many of the banks. Also be aware that opportunities for changing euro travellers' cheques in Kampala are presently few and far between. The best places to change travellers' cheques are Barclays, Stanbic and Standard Chartered banks on Kampala Road, all of which offer rates only slightly less favourable than for cash. A commission equivalent to about US$3 is charged per transaction (not per cheque), which works out to be negligible if you're changing several hundred dollars, but will eat heavily into smaller sums. It is not possible to exchange travellers' cheques without a passport and proof of purchase (the receipt you obtained when you bought them). Standard Chartered may waive the latter requirement on production of as much paperwork as you can find to back up your identity, but this is a lengthy and less-than-certain procedure.

Gorilla-tracking permits Permits for reserves in Uganda can be bought directly from the new UWA headquarters on Kiira Road between the Uganda Museum and the British High Commission (see *National Parks and reserves* below) or through any major tour operator. The Kampala Backpackers' Hostel can usually arrange permits for reserves in Uganda, Rwanda and DRC (if in Jinja contact Nile River Explorers).

Hair and beauty salons Recommended salons include the **Pearl Royale Beauty Parlour** on the ground floor of Rwenzori House on Lumumba Avenue (✆ 0414 254534/342037), **AVOA** on Buganda Avenue near Daisy Mall (✆ 0414 341607; m 0772 493902) and the **Maryland Parlour** in Colline House on Pilkington Road (✆ 0414 255620; m 0772 430475). Several of the upmarket hotels in the city centre have in-house salons. Gents looking for a haircut can either get a Ush2, 000 crew-cut from any local barber (it's worth making sure your trip doesn't coincide with a scheduled power cut!) or try **Tas Salon** at Kisementi (✆ 0414 252380) at Ush15,000.

Handicrafts and curios A number of good craft shops and stalls are clustered on Buganda Road close to the Daisy Mall, as well as in the central market. The atmospheric and long-established **Uganda Crafts** on Bombo Road (✆ 0414 250077) is recommended. It's also worth a wander around the African Craft Village which consists of more than 30 stalls on De Winton Road near the National Theatre, and the craft shop attached to Kampala Backpackers. Though home-produced crafts are increasing and improving, there is still too much of the ubiquitous Kenyan wood and soapstone carvings of animals and Maasai warriors on offer. The best place to head for quality crafts is **'Banana Boat'** (✆ *0414 232885;* e *bananaboat@infocom.co.ug*) which has branches at Kisementi (by Crocodile Restaurant), Garden City and Lugogo Mall. It displays an excellent variety of locally made crafts produced by over 90 small Ugandan artisans and workshops. Banana Boat includes many bespoke items, notably jewellery, tribal art handmade paper products produced by a group of Ugandan women on the shores of Lake Victoria (*Paper Craft;* m *0782 224026*) and the idiosyncratic wrought-iron figurines produced by internationally exhibited sculptor John Odoch. Highly recommended. Also worth a look is **A&K '97** in the Crested Towers Building.

Samaki Fashions, found in Quality Hill Mall on Ggaba Road (✆ *0414 510566;* m *0772 375001;* e *acha@imul.com; http://uga.edu/internationalpso/ugandatextiles/ samaki.html*), designs and prints its own patterned fabrics to make African outfits with a contemporary feel.

Internet and email It's scarcely possible to walk more than 100m in the city centre without tripping over an internet café. Standards are generally high, and a fairly uniform rate of Ush25 per minute (around US$0.80 per hour) is charged, though as access keeps improving this is likely to drop further. It would be pointless attempting to compile a full list of cafés, but Lotus, Cyberworld and Globenet on Kampala Road are all recommended as fast and efficient.

Libraries The **Uganda Society** (✆ *0414 234964;* e *ugsociety@bushnet.net; www.africa.upenn.edu/ugandasoc/ugandasociety.htm; open Mon–Fri 08.00–12.30, closed public holidays; a nominal daily membership fee is charged to casual visitors*) in the National Museum Building on Kiira Road houses what is probably the most comprehensive collection of current and out-of-print books about Uganda in existence.

Medical services Hospitals and medical services are not generally up to Western standards, and it's worth seeking current recommendations from your hotel before contacting any of the following private clinics.

✚ **The Surgery** 2 Acacia Av; ✆ 0414 256003, 24hr emergency and ambulance service; m 0752 756003. Previously the clinic in the British high commission, this is the choice of many expatriates. Several travellers have found the website useful (*www.thesurgeryuganda.org*). If you're not too sick, there's a coffee shop and hairdressers' in the complex.

✚ **International Medical Centre** (IMC) KPC Bldg, Bombo Rd; ✆ 0312 200400 or Kitgum Hse, Jinja Rd; ✆ 0312 341291; 24hr emergency line; m 0772 741291; 24hr ambulance service; m 0772 200400/1. IMC also has several branches upcountry.

✚ **International Hospital Kampala (IHK)** ✆ 0312 200400; e ihk@africaonline.co.ug. This smart new hospital (allied to the IMC clinic) is located in Namuwongo/Kisugu. It can be approached either from Kabalagala (off Ggaba Rd), heading behind the Reste Corner Hotel (see Ggaba Rd map, page 171) or from the junction just west of the 'Mukwano' roundabout railway crossing junction on Mukwano Road (see Kampala city centre: east map, page 149).

✚ **Case Medical Centre** 69–71 Buganda Rd; ✆ 0414 250362, 24hr emergency line; ✆ 0312 250362

✚ **Kim's Medical Centre** 4 Entebbe Rd; ✆ 0414 341777, 24hr emergency and ambulance; m 0752 722000

National parks and reserves The **Uganda Wildlife Authority (UWA)** (✆ *0414 355000/346290;* f *0414 346291;* e *uwa@uwa.or.ug; www.uwa.co.ug; information office open Mon–Fri 08.00–13.00 and 14.00–17.00, Sat 09.00–13.00*) is in charge of all of Uganda's national parks and game reserves. The main office is on Kiira Road between the Uganda Museum and the British High Commission. All gorilla-viewing permits for Bwindi and Mgahinga must be booked and paid for here, as can *banda* accommodation in the various national parks and game reserves, and you can also pick up some informative brochures. This office is the best place to check on current developments in game reserves such as Bugungu and Katonga, which are being developed for low-key tourism with the assistance of Peace Corps volunteers. For information about Budongo, Mpanga, Mabira, Kalinzu and other forest reserves, contact the **National Forest Authority** (☏ *0414 230365*).

Newspapers The main local English-language newspapers are *New Vision* and *Monitor*, both of which include reasonable coverage of African and international affairs and are widely available in Kampala, as is the excellent Nairobi-published weekly *East African*. Current and old issues of the American *Time* and *Newsweek* magazines can be bought from street vendors. The best place to pick up recent UK and US newspapers is **Uchumi** in Garden City or the **Sheraton Bookshop**. The **Rhino Bar** in the same hotel usually has a selection for customers' use.

Photography Although film stock and developing services are widely available in Kampala, the range of film available is not what it is in most Western cities, and there is a risk of buying expired or badly stored stock, while development standards are not always of the highest quality. Ideally, bring all the film you need with you, and take it home to be processed. If that isn't possible, among the more reliable photographic services are the **Camera Centre** on Wilson Road (☏ *0414 236991*) and **Colour Chrome** on Kampala Road (☏ *0414 230556*). The latter also offers digital photographic and slide-processing services.

Post The main post office on the corner of Kampala and Speke roads has a *poste restante* service as well as selling stamps etc.

Shopping malls By far the best mall in Kampala is the **Garden City Shopping Centre** on Yusuf Lule Road overlooking the golf course, which opened in October 2002. In addition to a cinema complex and Kampala's first bowling alley, it contains a good supermarket, half-a-dozen restaurants, a branch of the excellent Aristoc Bookshop, several banks and a forex bureau and some trendy clothes shops. The newer **Lugogo Mall** on the east side of the city contains two South African 'megastores,' a large Shoprite supermarket and an equally expansive 'Game' store with a wide-ranging stock including camping accessories. If you're using public transport, the **Shoprite Mall** by the old taxi park will be more convenient. **The Pioneer Mall** on Kampala Road contains the economical **Antonio's Restaurant** but an otherwise unremarkable selection of shops.

Supermarkets The best supermarkets in Kampala are the two branches of the South African **Shoprite** (see *Shopping malls* above). Almost as good is the branch of the Kenyan '**Uchumi**' in Garden City. There are also several smaller supermarkets along Kampala/Bombo Road around or northwest of the Pioneer Mall. The **Luisin Delicatessen** next to the Jeliza Hotel is an Italian-owned place selling as good a variety of cold meats and cheeses as you'll find in East Africa, as well as fresh bread and sensibly priced take-away dishes such as pizza and lasagne. There are some excellent little supermarkets in the suburbs. Guests at the Backpackers' Hostel will find pretty much what they need at the **Top Shop/Kenjoy Supermarket** up the hill in nearby Mengo. There's a sister branch **Kenjoy** just outside the Blue Mango in Bukoto.

Taxis (shared) A steady stream of minibus-taxis plies along most trunk roads through Kampala, picking up and dropping off passengers more-or-less at whim, and charging around Ush200–500 per person depending in the routing. Unlike in many other African capitals, the minibuses are seldom overcrowded – police and passengers alike actively ensure that conductors adhere to the maximum of three passengers per row – and I've neither experienced nor heard of anything to suggest that pickpockets are a cause for concern. It can be confusing coming to terms with minibus-taxi routes in Kampala, particularly as the routes are unnumbered and the minibuses seldom have their destination marked. Heading from the suburbs into central Kampala is pretty straightforward, since you can safely assume that any minibus pointed towards the city centre along a trunk route is going your way. Heading out from the city centre can be more daunting. In essence, if you're heading to anywhere along the Natete and Hoima roads (for instance Kampala Backpackers, Namirembe Guesthouse, Kasubi Tombs) you're best off heading straight to the new taxi park to pick up a vehicle. Minibuses to most other parts of the city leave from the old taxi park, but in several instances it's easier to intercept them along Kampala Road – east of the junction with Entebbe Road for Red Chilli Hideaway and other places along Port Bell Road, northwest of the junction with Burton Street for Bombo Road, Makerere University, the National Museum, etc. When in doubt, the conductors are normally pretty helpful, assuming that they can speak English, or you can ask one of your fellow passengers.

Taxis (special hire) Conventional taxis – generally referred to as special hires – are usually easy to locate within the city centre and usually charge a negotiable Ush3,000–5,000 for short trips and up to Ush15,000 for longer rides. Taxi stands can be found outside most of the upmarket hotels, on Dastur Street close to the intersection with Kampala Road, on Ben Kiwanuka Street opposite the old taxi park, near the junction of Navibuko and Kyagwe Streets behind the new taxi park, and at the roundabout at the junction of Bombo and Makerere Hill roads. To book a taxi, contact **Belex Taxis** (↘ *0414 344105;* m *0772 443491*), **New Lines** (↘ *0414 251752;* m *0752 721111*) or **Phone-A-Taxi** (↘ *0414 221978*).

Boda-boda The easiest way to get around Kampala's increasingly congested traffic system is by *boda-boda* (moped taxi). However, you shouldn't hop aboard without reading about their poor road safety record in *Chapter 4*, page 99. The City Council announced in August 2006 that *boda-bodas* are to be banned from the city centre. You'll find out for yourself whether this is enforced.

Telephone Mobile phones, in particular the South African MTN network (numbers mostly beginning 0772 or 0782), have rendered the parastatal land line services all but obsolete when it comes to international calls. All over the city centre you'll see shops and kiosks offering domestic and international calls. Calls to Uganda's MTN and Mango mobile networks cost Ush250 per minute, it's Ush1,000 per minute to other East African countries and Ush2,000 (just over US$1) per minute to the rest of the world. An international payphone is available at the Kampala Backpackers, and most upmarket hotels can book international calls at inflated rates. The MTN office in the city centre is at 22 Hannington Road (m *0782 212333/212013*).

Useful telephone numbers

Directory enquiries (domestic)	↘ 901
Directory enquiries (international)	↘ 0901
Operator services	↘ 0900
Emergencies (ambulance, fire or police assistance)	↘ 999 or 0414 342222/3
Central police station	↘ 0414 254561/2

See also *Medical services* above for clinics with 24-hour emergency and ambulance services.

Theatres Kampala has an active English-language theatre community, which mainly stages locally written plays in English. The impressive **National Theatre** (✆ *0414 344490*), which opened in 1959 on the corner of Siad Barre Avenue and De Winton Road, puts on productions most weekends. Tickets cost around US$8 and forthcoming events are pinned up on the noticeboard. There is an art gallery in the theatre complex and a restaurant in the gardens. English-language productions are also put on at the **Pride Theatre** near the old fort. Tickets cost US$3.

Tour operators Full details of international and local tour operators servicing Uganda are listed in *Chapter 3, Tour operators*, page 72.

Tourist information The **Tourism Uganda** information office is on the ground floor of Impala House on Kimathi Avenue (✆ *+256 0414 342196/7;* e *utb@starcom.co.ug; www.visituganda.com*). A 2006 rebranding of the once rather ineffectual Uganda Tourist Board, the Tourism Uganda staff are friendly and genuinely interested. The lady I met had made it her business to be informed on everything from the best bus company waiting room to details of new developments in the national parks. For budget travellers, a better source of current practical information is the staff of the Kampala Backpackers Hostel and Campsite or Red Chilli Hideaway (see *Where to stay*, pages 147–8). The owners of these places keep their ears to the ground, particularly regarding the southwest of Uganda and Rwanda, and you're bound to meet plenty of travellers who've been in Uganda a while at either hostel.

A bi-monthly 100-page booklet called **The Eye** (✆ *0312 251117;* e *theeye@ theprinthouse.co.ug; www.theeye.co.ug*) is available for free at most upmarket hotels, selected booksellers, tour agents and the information office at Entebbe International Airport. It contains useful and regularly updated listings covering the whole of Uganda, as well as a few short travel pieces and plenty of ads, but is focused mainly on Kampala.

White-water rafting The daily rafting excursions on the Nile below Bujagali Falls run by **Adrift** (m *0772ADRIFT/ 237438 or 0782BUNGEE/ 286433*), **Equator** (✆ *0434 123712 or 0712 720906*), **Nile River Explorers** (✆ *0434 120236;* m *0772 422373*) and **Nalubale** (m *0782 638938*) can be undertaken as a day trip out of Kampala inclusive of a free road transfer. Ring the various companies for details, or book through Kampala Backpackers, Red Chilli Hideaway, or any other upmarket hotel or tour operator. See also *Bujagali Falls*, pages 421–2.

WHAT TO SEE AND DO The National Museum, Kasubi Tombs and other sites of interest situated more-or-less within the city limits of Kampala are covered below. As with any city, however, just strolling around can be illuminating; the contrast between the posh part of town north of Kampala Road and the sleazier area near the bus and taxi parks is striking. Sites of interest in Entebbe are covered later in the chapter, while those further afield are covered under *Day Trips out of Kampala/Entebbe*, pages 183–9.

City centre Kampala's modern city centre – which sprawls across a valley about 2.5km east of Kabaka Mwanga's former capital on Kasubi Hill, immediately east of Lugard's original fort on Old Kampala Hill – boasts little in the way of compelling sightseeing. The most important cluster of architecturally noteworthy buildings is centred on the acacia-lined **Parliament Avenue** on the east side of the city centre. On Parliament Avenue itself, the imposing though not exactly inspiring **Parliament Building**, built during the colonial era and still the seat of national government today, is a vast white monolith entered via an angular and some might say rather ugly concrete arch, built to commemorate independence in 1962. On the same block lies the so-called **White House**, occupied by the Kampala City Council, while immediately to its east, on De Winton Road, stand the **National Theatre** and attached **African Crafts Village**. Arguably more attractive than any of the above is the **Railway Station**, which lies on Jinja Road about 200m further south, and was built in the 1920s but has fallen into virtual disuse since passenger services out of Kampala were suspended a few years ago.

For those seeking leafy respite from the city centre, the attractive **Sheraton Gardens**, entered via a gate near the junction of Speke Road and Nile Avenue, was originally set aside to commemorate the jubilee of King George VI but is now effectively managed as an extension of the Kampala Sheraton. The **Independence Monument** on Nile Avenue, just outside the fenced gardens, is well worth a minor diversion – a tall, attractively proportioned neo-traditional statue of a mother and child.

Old Kampala Kampala Hill, which rises gently to the immediate west of city centre, less than five minutes' walk from the new taxi park, was the site of the original fort and capital founded by Captain Lugard in 1890. Enclosed within the oval Old Kampala Road, the hill is dotted with a few fine colonial-era buildings of Asian design, now generally rather rundown though some have been strikingly renovated. Old Kampala is most notable today as the focal point for Kampala's Islamic community and the sight of an imposing new **mosque**. This was initiated by Idi Amin in the 1970s but the project stalled after the dictator's overthrow and has only recently been completed using money provided by the Libyan leader, Colonel Ghadaffi. The structure lay dormant as an ugly concrete monolith with a lofty minaret with a decided list. In its shadow stood the old museum (see below), one of Kampala's oldest surviving buildings, sadly being slowly dismantled by the grip of a strangler fig tree. When work on the mosque restarted after a 25-year delay, the building was demolished and a replica with the same vaguely Arcadian frontage erected at a more prominent location beside Old Kampala Road. Lip service having been paid to the conservation lobby, the gate appears to have been locked and the new structure left to fall down once again.

Makerere University The main campus of Uganda's respected Makerere University, which was founded in 1922, lies about 1km north of the city centre and can be entered via the main gate on Makerere Hill Road, some 200m west of Wandegeyre traffic lights on Bombo Road. The university library has an extensive Africana section, while the campus bookshop stocks a wide selection of local-interest academic works. The gallery in the Faculty of Fine Arts is highly regarded. The spacious green grounds possess an aura of academic gentility at odds with the hustle and bustle of downtown Kampala, while the older buildings – in particular the whitewashed Main Hall with its handsome bell tower – will be of interest to students of colonial architecture.

National Museum of Uganda (*Kiira Rd, about 2km from the city centre; open daily 08.00–17.00; a small admission fee is charged*) The National Museum of Uganda is the oldest in East Africa, and perhaps the best, rooted in an ethnographic collection first exhibited in 1905 in a small Greek temple near Lugard's fort on Old Kampala Hill. Formally established in 1908, the museum was initially known by the local

Baganda as Enyumba ya Mayembe (House of Fetishes) and its exhibits were believed to bestow supernatural powers on the colonial administration. In 1954, the museum relocated to its present site on Kiira Road. For those with an interest in pre-colonial African history, there are stimulating displays on the Nakayima Tree, Ntusi and Bigo bya Mugenyi, as well as other aspects of Ugandan history. Of more general interest is a fantastic collection of traditional musical instruments from all over the continent, and the ethnographic gallery, which houses a variety of exhibits relating to traditional Ugandan lifestyles. On foot or in a private vehicle, follow Kampala/Bombo Road north out of the city centre, turning right at the traffic lights at Wandegeyre into Haji Kasule Road, crossing straight across another roundabout after 400m into Kiira Road. The museum is clearly signposted to the right, 600m past this roundabout. Minibuses between the new taxi park and Kamwokya will drop passengers roughly opposite the museum entrance, and can be picked up at taxi ranks along Kampala/Bombo Road north of the junction with Burton Road. The **Uganda Society Library** in the main museum building (*open Mon–Fri 08.00 to 12.00*) has a comprehensive collection of published works relating to Uganda.

Hoima Road Two important sets of royal tombs, collectively housing the bodies of the four *kabakas* of Buganda to have died since the 1850s, lie within walking distance of the road running northwest from central Kampala towards Hoima. The

JAWBONE SHRINES

The Baganda traditionally believe that the spirit of a dead man resides in his jawbone, for which reason it is customary for the jawbone of a deceased king to be removed and preserved in a separate shrine before the rest of the body is buried. The jawbone shrine is normally located at the last capital site used by the dead ruler, and is housed within a miniature reproduction of his palace. Jawbone shrines associated with almost all of the kabakas that preceded Mutesa I lie scattered across an area of less than 500km² northwest of present-day Kampala. Most are now untended, and have suffered from serious neglect over the past century, but their location remains well known to locals.

According to the historian Roland Oliver: 'after the dislocation of the jawbone, the body of the king was handed over to the chief executioner, Senkaba, who took it away... to the royal cemetery. There, the body was placed on a bed and certain friends and officials of the dead kabaka were killed and their bodies were thrown upon the heap. These sites did not, like the jawbone shrines, become places of pilgrimage. Nevertheless they were guarded by Senkaba and his representatives.' While jawbone shrines are associated with one specific king, the royal burial grounds are more centralised entities. At least ten tombs of the earlier kings are situated within a 1km² area at Gombe, 20km north of Kampala, while a similar number of more recent kings are buried at Merera along the Hoima Road.

The last ruler of Buganda to receive a traditional royal burial was Kabaka Suuna II, whose jawbone shrine is preserved in a large traditional structure at the site of his last kibuga at Wamala. Suuna's successors – influenced by Islam and Christianity – were buried at Kasubi with their jawbones intact. There is some ambiguity about where the rest of Suuna's remains are located: one tradition asserts that he was the last king to be buried at Merera, while others claim that he was buried at Wamala. The most likely explanation is that Suuna was originally buried at Merera, but his body was later exhumed by his son Mutesa I to be buried alongside the jawbone at Wamala.

THE FUNERAL OF KABAKA MWANGA

Edited from the 'Uganda Notes' of September 1910

Mwanga was deported in the year 1899 [and] moved to the Seychelles, where he died in May 1903… Nothing can be more distressing to the Baganda mind than that a near relative should not be buried in his own Butaka [home]… So the leading chiefs and the descendants of Mwanga have been agitating to exhume the body and have it transferred to Uganda, and at last permission was obtained.

2 August [1910] was a day of great excitement, and business, as far as natives was [sic] concerned, was suspended. A large crowd proceeded to meet the steamer at Kampala Port to bring up the large packing case in which was enclosed the leaden coffin containing the body of the deceased king [Mwanga], and at 15.00 an enormous concourse followed the body to Namirembe Cathedral… The funeral cortège entered the church, filling it from end to end, and part of the Burial Service was read… The body was then removed to Kasubi, the burial place of King Mutesa… [where] a vault had been carefully prepared of brick and cement, and a double coffee was in readiness.

On the morning of Wednesday [3 August], everyone of any importance in or near Mengo was present at the tomb and the gruesome process of opening the leaden shell in order to examine the remains was gone through. Repugnant though it seems to open a coffin so many years after a death has taken place, it was insisted that as King Daudi had never seen his father in the flesh he must on no account miss seeing his corpse, and to the surprise of everyone concerned the features were quite recognisable… Daudi took hold of a barkcloth together with Mugemo and Kago and covered up the corpse, this being the custom of a father whose son is dead, and then the body was buried… In the afternoon the concluding part of the Burial Service was read; Bishop Tucker and a very large number of Europeans were present, together with a crowd of natives, to perform the last rites.

To follow old custom, Mwanga should really have been buried inside his own court [on Mengo Hill], and many of the natives were inclined to follow precedent; but it was finally decided that if he were to be buried in Mengo, the Kabaka Daudi would have to turn out [of his] comfortable and permanent residence, [which] seemed inadvisable, especially when there is the difficulty of securing a suitable site for the new court in the Capital. On the morning of Thursday 4 August, a very interesting ceremony took place,

---

Kasubi Tombs are the more publicised of the two sites, but the Wamala Tombs are no less worthwhile, and its caretakers are less accustomed to tourist visits.

Kasubi Tombs (m *0752 960446;* e *kasubiheritage@yahoo.com; open daily 08.00–18.00; admission Ush3,000, including the services of a knowledgeable guide*) In 1882, Kabaka Mutesa relocated his *kibuga* (palace) to Nabulagala Hill, briefly the capital of his father Suuna II some 30 years earlier, and renamed it Kasubi Hill after his birthplace some 50km further east. Mutesa constructed a large hilltop palace called Muziba Azala Mpanga (roughly translating as 'a king is born of a king'), where he died in 1884 following a prolonged illness. As was the custom, Kasubi Hill was abandoned after the king's death – his successor Mwanga established a new capital at Mengo Hill – but rather less conventionally Mutesa was the first kabaka to be buried with his jawbone intact, in a casket built by the Anglican missionary Alexander Mackay. In a further break with tradition, Kasubi rather than Mengo was chosen as the burial place of Kabaka Mwanga in 1910, seven years after his death in exile (see box *The funeral of Kabaka Mwanga*, above). It also houses the tombs of his successor Daudi Chwa II, who ruled from 1897 to 1939, and of Edward Mutesa

which had been deemed impossible until such time as Mwanga should be buried in his own country…

The following is a translation of an account of the ceremony written by the Rev Henry Wright Duta:

[King Daudi] came and stood outside his court [on] the coronation chair… Mugema opened proceedings by bringing a barkcloth and hanging it about the king from his shoulders… He then put on a calfskin to remind [Daudi] that his first forefather was thus dressed… Then came Kasuju, who brought a second barkcloth and also a leopard skin, with which he also proceeded to dress the king… the meaning of the leopard skin is that it separates him from all other princes and makes him into the king… The reason why he is dressed in two barkcloths is because he is called the 'father of twins', that is to say he gives birth to many people and he rules over many people…

[Kasuju] brought the king a sword… saying 'take this sword and with it cut judgement in truth (distribute justice equally and fairly), anyone who rebels against you, you shall kill with this sword'. Then they brought before him the drum which is called Mujagazo which is very old indeed and which has carved on it a python (once sacred to the Baganda)… this is supposed to be the drum which Kimera had with him when he came from Bunyoro… A shield was then presented to the king and… two spears… [and] a bow and arrows… the weapons with which Kimera first came to Uganda… Then came a long string of people bringing offerings too numerous to mention.

After that the king was placed on the shoulders of Namutwe so that the crowd might all have a good look at him, saying 'This is your king' and the crowd set up a loud yell beating their hands with their mouths to produce a tremulant effect. Then the king together with the Lubuga (queen sister) and an old woman to represent the head of the king's wives were all carried on the shoulders of their attendants back into the [royal] Court… Then came the whole of the visitors to the king to congratulate him on his accession, he sitting down on the seat called Mubanga, which resembles a drum, and old Prince Mbogo, the brother of [the late king] Mutesa, came and wrapped some cents around his wrist in place of the cowrie shells which used to obtain here… Every member of the king's tribe – princes, princesses and everyone else who could be present – brought him presents of money… and for days afterwards all his relatives came in batches and went through the same ceremony.

II, whose body was returned to Uganda in 1971, two years after his death in exile.

The tombs are housed within the original palace built by Mutesa, a fantastic domed structure of poles, reeds and thatch, which – aside from the addition of a concrete base and sliding glass doors in 1938 – has changed little in appearance over the intervening 130 years. The former palace contains a fascinating collection of royal artefacts, ranging from traditional musical instruments, weapons, shields and fetishes to exotic gifts donated by Queen Victoria – as well as a stuffed leopard once kept as a pet by Mutesa I. The giant rings in the roof of the hut each represent one of the 52 clans of Buganda. The four royal tombs, obscured behind a red barkcloth veil, are off-limits to the public, and visitors must remove their shoes before entering the palace.

The tombs are maintained by the wives of the various kings – or more accurately by female descendants of their long-deceased wives – some of whom live on the property, while others do a one-month shift there twice every year. Many of the kings' wives, sisters and other female relations are also buried at Kasubi, not in the main palace but in the series of smaller buildings that flank the driveway. The complex is entered via a large traditional reception hut known as

The centre of political power in Buganda for several centuries prior to the colonial era was the *kibuga* (capital) of the *kabaka* (king), generally situated on a hilltop for ease of defence. Based on the knowledge that at least ten different kibuga sites were used by three kabakas between 1854 and 1894, it would appear that the capital was regularly relocated, possibly for security reasons. It was also customary for a kibuga to be abandoned upon the death of its founder, at least until 1894, when Kabaka Mwanga founded a new capital on Mengo Hill, one that remained in use until the Baganda monarchy was abolished in 1966. Mengo Palace, damaged by the military during the Amin era, remains in poor shape, but following the reinstitution of the monarchy in 1993, a new kibuga has been established 10km east of Kampala at Banda.

Banda was also the site of the first capital of Kabaka Mutesa, visited in 1862 by Speke, who wrote: 'the palace or entrance quite surprised me by its extraordinary dimensions, and the neatness with which it was kept. The whole brow and sides of the hill on which we stood were covered with gigantic grass huts, thatched as neatly as so many heads dressed by a London barber, and fenced all round with the tall yellow reeds of the common Uganda tiger-grass; whilst within the enclosure, the lines of huts were joined together, or partitioned off into courts, with walls of the same grass.' The next European visitor to Mutesa's capital – by then relocated to Rubaga – was Stanley, in 1875, who was equally impressed: 'Broad avenues [of] reddish clay, strongly mixed with the detritus of hematite… led by a gradual ascent to the circular road which made the circuit of the hill outside the palace enclosure… his house is an African palace, spacious and lofty'. Visitors to Kabaka Mwanga's kibuga some ten years later were less complimentary – Gedge, for instance, described it as a 'miserable collection of huts [where] dirt and filth reign supreme' – but this was probably a temporary decline linked to the instability that characterised Mwanga's early rule.

The most detailed description of a kibuga was published by the Rev John Roscoe in 1911:

> The king lived upon a hill situated in the neighbourhood of the lake. The summit of the hill was levelled, and the most commanding site overlooking the country was chosen for the king's dwelling houses, court houses, and shrine for fetishes, and for the special reception room… The whole of the royal enclosure was divided up into small courtyards with groups of huts in them; each group was enclosed by a high fence and was under the supervision of a responsible wife. Wide paths between high fences connected each group of houses with the king's royal enclosure. In the reign of the famous King Mutesa, there were several thousand residents in the royal enclosure; he had five hundred wives, each of whom had her maids and female slaves; and in addition to the wives there were fully two hundred pages and hundreds of retainers and slaves. A high fence of elephant grass surrounded the royal residence, so that it was impossible for an enemy with the ordinary primitive weapons to enter… There was one plan followed, which has been used by the kings for years without variation. The [royal] enclosure was oval shaped, a mile in length and half a mile wide, and the capital extended five or six miles in front and two miles on either side.

a *bujjabukula*. This is tended by the chief gateman, known as Mulamba (a hereditary title), who customarily dresses in a brilliant yellow barkcloth robe, as do his assistants.

An excellent booklet on the tombs is sometimes on sale at the site, and well worth buying for its background information on Baganda culture. To get there from the city centre, follow Namirembe/Natete Road east for about 1km until you reach the pinkish Kampala Regency Hotel, immediately before which you need to turn right into Hoima Road. After nearly 2km you'll cross over Nakulabye roundabout and 2km further on you'll reach Kasubi Market at the junction with Kimera Road, from where the tombs – signposted to the left – lie about 500m uphill along Masiro Road. Plenty of minibus-taxis run from the city centre to Kasubi Market. Alternatively head out of town past Makerere University to Nakulabye roundabout and turn right.

Wamala Tomb Situated on the crest of a low hill some 12km northwest of central Kampala, Wamala Tomb is housed in an attractive, traditional, thatched domed building, slightly smaller and older than its counterpart at Kasubi. The hill is the former palace and sacred resting place of Kabaka Mutesa I's father and predecessor Kabaka Suuna, who ascended the throne circa 1830 and died in 1856. Suuna is remembered as a despotic ruler and keen hunter. The menagerie he maintained at Wamala – said to have included lions, leopards, elephants and various smaller creatures – sufficiently impressed the first Arab traders to reach Buganda that word of it reached Sir Richard Burton at the Swahili Coast.

Wamala is neither as well known as Kasubi, nor as carefully tended, but it is just as interesting in its comparatively low-key way. A diverse array of royal artefacts – spears, shields, drums and other musical instruments – is displayed in front of the barkcloth drape that veils the tomb itself. Opposite the main building stands the former palace and tomb of Suuna's mother, Namasole Kanyange, according to tradition a very beautiful woman and also highly influential – it's said that Suuna insisted the Namasole live alongside him so that he could keep an eye on her doings. In keeping with Kiganda royal custom, Kanyange appointed a successor as Namasole before her death. The lineage survives to this day: the fourth Namasole to Suuna is resident at Wamala and still performs traditional duties such as tending the royal tomb.

To reach Wamala, follow the Hoima Road out of Kampala, passing the junction for Kisubi, then after another 6km the trading centre of Nansana. Only 2km past Nansana, a small faded purple signpost on the right side of the road indicates the turn-off to Wamala. From this junction, a rough dirt 1.5km track marked with wooden signs leads to the hilltop tomb, which is visible from some distance away.

Natete Road A number of minor historical sites lie within 1km of the Natete Road, which runs east out of central Kampala, past the popular Namirembe Guesthouse and Kampala Backpackers, in the direction of Masaka.

Namirembe Cathedral The Anglican (now Church of Uganda) cathedral perched atop Namirembe Hill, roughly 1.5km west of the city centre off Natete Road, is one of the most impressive colonial-era constructions in Kampala, and it also offers superb views over the city centre and suburbs. The original cathedral, completed in 1903 and consecrated a year later (see box, overleaf), was built entirely by Baganda artisans, albeit under the supervision of a British missionary, and could hold a congregation of 3,000 people. It was described contemporaneously by W E Hoyle as 'a remarkable building with walls of sun-dried bricks, and brick columns supporting the thatch roof, containing 120 tons of thatch [and a] ceiling covered with washed reeds of elephant grass'. This building was destroyed by lightning in 1910 and the present cathedral, a more conventional red-brick structure, built to vast dimensions and graced by some attractive stained-glass windows, was completed in 1919. The cemetery contains

6

the grave of Bishop Hannington, murdered near Jinja in 1885, as well as that of Sir Albert Cook, a pioneering medical doctor who arrived in Kampala in 1896 and whose extensive writings about the early colonial era are quoted elsewhere in this guide. Brass memorial plaques on the wall testify to the often short lives of Europeans in those early days.

Bulange Building Less than 500m past the turn-off to Namirembe, the Bulange Building – traditional seat of the Buganda Parliament – stands on the south side of Natete Road, directly opposite the junction with Sentema Road. It is one of the most impressive colonial-era buildings in Uganda, and though much of it is obscured by a tall enclosing wall, the roof and its trio of spires is clearly visible from the main road. Entrance to the enclosure is allowed unless the building is in official use. Mr Kalanzi, a venerable and well-informed old gentleman with the title of Sergeant of Arms to the Kabaka, will be more than pleased to show you around. There's no charge but he'll appreciate a tip (it's worth doing this just before he invites you to buy a Buganda kingdom lapel pin for Ush20,000). About 200m downhill from the Bulange, on Kabakanjagala Road, two exotic giant tortoises dawdle around the gardens of the impressive blue (if dilapidated) building, once the home of Stanley Kisingire, one of the regents of the infant king, Daudi Chwa. Local wisdom is that they are all around 500 years old, but they apparently came to Mengo as recently as 1945. Stanley's rather annoying grandson Kizito will charge you what he can to see the reptiles.

Kabaka Mwanga's Lake, Lubaga Cathedral and Mengo Palace In 1885, Mwanga settled on the ultimately over-ambitious scheme of digging a large lake near his capital and linking it with Lake Victoria. The lake was completed in 1888, but the intended link was abandoned when Muslim dissenters drove the *kabaka* from his capital. The lake was once more of a health hazard than it was a tourist attraction, but the surrounding area has recently been cleared and there are some interesting birds to be seen on its fringes – notably large colonies of cattle egrets and weavers. Follow the Natete Road out of the city centre for about 2km then turn left just beyond the spired Bulange Building. As you descend the hill, you'll see the lake. The shore can be reached about 1km further on, by taking a steep dirt road on your left towards the Miracle Church where the deep pockets of born-again Christians – or *savedees* as they are known – have funded a massive new auditorium and a fleet of British double-decker buses to bring the faithful to worship.

The lake can easily be visited in conjunction with the Catholic cathedral on Lubaga (or Rubaga) Hill, which lies about 500m south of Natete Road along Mutesa Road, but is neither as old nor as impressive as its Church of Uganda equivalent at Namirembe. Also close to the lake is the Kabaka's Twekobe Palace on the low Lubiri Hill, the site chosen by Mwanga after his coronation in 1884. The ill-fated Kabaka Edward Mutesa was driven from this palace in 1966 by Idi Amin on Obote's orders. The army subsequently occupied the site until 1993, gaining a reputation for terror. Hundreds were taken through its gates by the agents of Amin and Obote, never to be seen again while ill-paid and ill-disciplined troops terrorised the leafy suburbs of Rubaga and Mengo. Tourist visits are not officially sanctioned but for a small consideration the caretaker will show you around the hill on which the 'attractions' include Idi Amin's specially constructed underground cells and execution chambers, where there's some movingly defiant graffiti scrawled in charcoal by the doomed inmates if you have a translator. It's quite a relief to get out again under open skies into Mengo's picturesque environs and be thankful that those days are past.

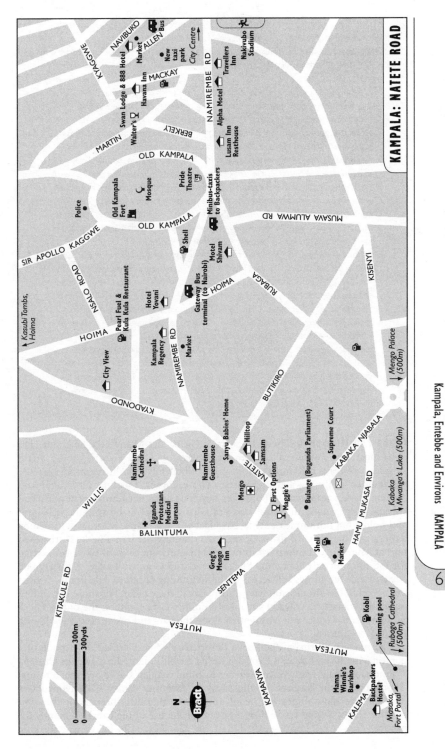

KAMPALA: NATETE ROAD

Kampala, Entebbe and Environs **KAMPALA**

6

169

The consecration of Namirembe Cathedral on 21 July 1904 was described vividly in the *Mengo Notes* a month after the event:

> A great crowd began to assemble at 6am, and… the crush at the doors so great that they had to be opened to prevent people being crushed to death. There was a considerable amount of struggling and good-natured fighting among the Baganda desirous of gaining admission, for not more than 3,000 could get in, and the crowd must have numbered nearly 10,000… Numbers climbed through the windows and jumped down on to those seated inside… Mr Savile had a bone in the hand broken in trying to repress a rush. To while away the time of waiting Mr Hattersley gave half an hour's organ recital… The European and native clergy, over 40 in number, assembled at the west door, and all in procession marched up to the Church, repeating the opening sentences of the Consecration Service… in English and Luganda… Then came morning prayer… and the wonderful way in which the congregation responded, and joined in the hymns and chants, will long be remembered.
>
> Instead of dispersing, the vast crowd unable to gain admission to the service had filled all the school rooms around the church, and still enough remained to nearly fill the yard. [They] contributed to the collection just as though they had taken part in the service. This considerably delayed matters, and it seemed as though the bringing in of offerings would never cease… The collection consisted of rupees, pice, and cowrie shells… in bundles more than enough to fill a whole collecting bag. Then came goats led up by ropes to the communion rails… fowls in a coop and singly; one, trussed feet and wings, was solemnly handed by the sideman to the Bishop along with his bag of shells… More than 30 head of cattle had been sent in by chiefs, but it was wisely decided that it would not be well to admit these to the church. The proceeds of the collection thus totalled up to over £80, the exact amount we cannot give, as the cattle have not all been sold at the time of writing.

Ggaba and Munyonyo The twin ports of Ggaba and Munyonyo lie about 1km apart near the southwest of Murchison Bay on Lake Victoria, some 10km southeast of central Kampala. Both ports, albeit for very different reasons, are worthwhile goals for a day's outing. The compact, bustling settlement and chaotic market at Ggaba spill onto the beach in a manner reminiscent of certain fishing villages along the Gold Coast of Ghana, as well as hosting the half-built and mildly but not unpleasantly seedy Ggaba Beach Hotel, where you can enjoy a quiet and inexpensive drink or meal overlooking the bay. The less-urbanised port at Munyonyo, by contrast, provides a magnificent tropical lakeshore setting for the sumptuously sprawling Speke Resort and Country Lodge. A Ush10,000 day entrance fee allows full access to the swimming pool and restaurant – a great place to chill out should you have a spare day in the capital. For those dependent on public transport, a steady stream of minibus-taxis connects the old taxi park in Kampala to Ggaba and Munyonyo along the bar- and restaurant-lined Ggaba Road.

The modern marina at the Speke Resort recalls Speke's 1862 description of a port on Murchison Bay as 'the royal yachting establishment, the Cowes of Uganda' – almost certainly Munyonyo, bearing in mind Stanley's 1875 reference to one 'Monyono' as the location of the kabaka's 'favourite canoes'. Munyonyo was probably the most important mainland port in Buganda throughout the 19th century, site of a large canoe fleet reserved for the use of the kabaka – mainly for pleasure cruises and hunting expeditions, but also on standby to evacuate the king

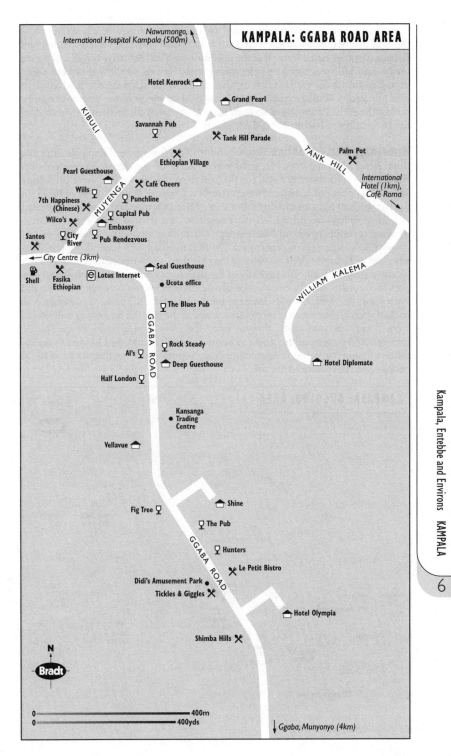

KAMPALA: GGABA ROAD AREA

Nawumongo,
International Hospital Kampala (500m)

KIBULI

Hotel Kenrock

Grand Pearl

Savannah Pub

Tank Hill Parade

TANK HILL

Palm Pot

Ethiopian Village

International
Hotel (1km),
Café Roma

Pearl Guesthouse

MUYENGA

Café Cheers

Wills

Punchline

7th Happiness
(Chinese)

Capital Pub

Wilco's

Embassy

Santos

City
River

Pub Rendezvous

City Centre (3km)

Shell

Fasika
Ethiopian

Lotus Internet

Seal Guesthouse

WILLIAM KALEMA

Ucota office

The Blues Pub

GGABA ROAD

Rock Steady

Al's

Deep Guesthouse

Hotel Diplomate

Half London

Kansanga
Trading
Centre

Vellavue

Shine

Fig Tree

The Pub

Hunters

GGABA ROAD

Le Petit Bistro

Didi's Amusement Park

Tickles & Giggles

Hotel Olympia

Shimba Hills

N

Bradt

0 ————————— 400m
0 ————————— 400yds

Ggaba, Munyonyo (4km)

from a succession of regularly shifted palace sites in times of emergency. It is thought that Munyonyo itself served as a royal palace site on several occasions, and Kabaka Mwanga based himself at the port for much of 1886 after his official palace on Mengo Hill was razed by a lightning strike. It was possibly then, but more probably during the earlier reign of Mutesa I, that the royal regatta at Munyonyo was initiated – similar regattas have been held at the port on several occasions during the 20th century, most recently in 1993 as part of the festivities surrounding the coronation of Kabaka Ronald Mutebi II.

Namugongo Martyrs' Shrine Situated about 12km from central Kampala along the Jinja Road, Namugongo, an established place of execution in pre-colonial Buganda, is remembered today for the massacre that took place there on 3 June 1886 at the order of Kabaka Mwanga (see box *Chaos in Buganda*, pages 176–7). In the last week of May, an unknown number of Baganda men and women, suspected or known to have been baptised, were detained near Mengo and forced to march, by some accounts naked, to Namugongo, where they were imprisoned for several days while a large pyre was prepared. On the morning of 3 June, those prisoners who had not already done so were given one final opportunity to renounce their recently adopted faith. Whether any of the neophyte Christians accepted this offer goes unrecorded, but 26 known individuals, divided evenly between Catholic and Protestant, declined. Charles Lwanga, the leader of the Catholic contingent, was hacked apart and burnt alive on the spot. Later in the day, the remaining individuals were bound in reed mats, thrown onto the pyre, and roasted alive. The 26 remembered victims of the massacre were all baptised, and thus known to one or other mission by name, but contemporary reports indicate that more than 30 people were thrown onto the fire.

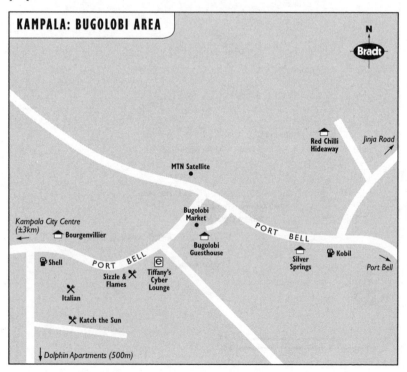

In 1920, Pope Benedict XV paved the way for future canonisation by declaring blessed the 13 known Catholic martyrs at Namugongo, together with another nine Catholic victims of separate killings in May 1886. The 22 Catholic martyrs were finally canonised by Pope Paul VI on 18 October 1964 during the Vatican II conference. In July 1969, Pope Paul VI visited Uganda – the first reigning pope to set foot in sub-Saharan Africa – to make a pilgrimage to Namugongo, where he instructed that a shrine and church be built on the spot where Lwanga had been killed. The Church of the Namugongo Martyrs, dedicated in 1975 and subsequently named a basilica church, is an unusual and imposing structure, modernistic and metallic in appearance, but based on the traditional Kasiisira style (epitomised, ironically, by the tombs of Mwanga and two other kabakas at Kasubi). The site of the massacre was visited by Archbishop Robert Runcie of Canterbury in 1984, and by Pope John Paul II in 1993. The 3 June massacre remains a public holiday in Uganda and is marked worldwide on the Church calendar in honour of the Uganda Martyrs.

Bahá'í Temple Opened on 15 January 1962, the Bahá'í Temple on Kikaya Hill, 6km from Kampala on the Gayaza Road, is the only place of worship of its kind in Africa. It is the spiritual home to the continent's Bahá'í, adherents to a rather obscure faith founded by the Persian mystic Bahá'u'lláh in the 1850s. Born in Tehran in 1812, Bahá'u'lláh was the privileged son of a wealthy government minister, but he declined to follow his father into the ministerial service, instead devoting his life to philanthropy.

In 1844, Bahá'u'lláh abandoned his Islamic roots to join the Bábí cult, whose short-lived popularity led to the execution of its founder and several other leading figures by the religious establishment – a fate escaped by Bahá'u'lláh only because of the high social status of his family. Bahá'u'lláh was nevertheless imprisoned, with his feet in stocks and a 50kg metal chain around his neck in Tehran's notoriously unsanitary and gloomy Black Pit. It was whilst imprisoned that Bahá'u'lláh received the Godly vision that led to the foundation of Bahá'í. Upon his release, Bahá'u'lláh dedicated the remaining 40 years of his life to writing the books, tracts and letters that collectively outlined the Bahá'í framework for the spiritual, moral, economic, political and philosophical reconstruction of human society.

Bahá'í teaches that heaven and hell are not places, but states of being defined by the presence or absence of spirituality. It is an inclusive faith, informed by all other religions – Hindu, Christian, Jewish, Zoroastrian, Buddhist and Islamic holy texts are displayed in the temple – which it regards to be stepping stones to a broader, less doctrinal spiritual and meditative awareness. It is also admirably egalitarian: it regards all humankind to be of equal worth, and any member of the congregation is free to lead prayers and meditations. Although not a didactic religion, Bahá'í does evidently equate spiritual well-being with asceticism: the consumption of alcohol and intoxicating drugs is discouraged in Bahá'í writings, and forbidden in the temple grounds, along with loud music, picking flowers and 'immoral behaviour'.

The Bahá'í Temple in Kampala, visible for miles around and open to all, is set in neatly manicured gardens extending over some 30ha atop Kikaya Hill. The lower part of the building consists of a white nontagon roughly 15m in diameter, with one door on each of its nine shaded faces. This is topped by an immense green dome, made with glazed mosaic Italian tiles, and a turret that towers 40m above the ground. The interior, which can seat up to 800 people, is illuminated by ambient light filtered through coloured glass windows, and decorated with lush Persian carpets. Otherwise, it is plainly decorated, in keeping with the Bahá'í belief that it would belittle the glory of God to place pictures or statues inside his temple. A solitary line of Arabic text repeated on the wall at regular intervals approximately translates to the familiar Christian text Glory of Glories.

Traditional dancing and music Ndere Centre (↘ *0414 288123*) This new purpose-built venue set in large lawns on the outskirts of the city at Ntinda is home to the well-known Ndere Troupe who perform every Sunday between 18.00 and 21.00 (Ush5,000). Additional performances include an excellent Afro-jazz night each Thursday (Ush5,000) and a talent show on Fridays for up-and-coming artists (free entrance). Contact the centre for other 'one-off plays and performances. Ndere Centre includes an outdoor auditorium, an indoor theatre, a restaurant and limited accommodation (see *Listings*, page 146). To get there, head past the Blue Mango to Ntinda trading centre. Turn left at the crossroads (north) for about 2km.

For people interested in traditional music, an old palace musician called Ssempeke (e *Sbakka99@yahoo.co.uk*) is the person to see for information or lessons on the *amadinda* xylophone/harp/flutes. He is based around the National Theatre – he did have an office there but it recently closed, though he may soon have a new one. His brother Serwanya is based by the instruments at the National Museum, and is also very knowledgeable. They can be contacted through another musician, Samuel Bakka, who is a fantastic drummer and can teach drum and dance, guide trips to villages or arrange to experience a traditional wedding.

ENTEBBE

In 1913, Sir Frederick Treves – coming fresh to Entebbe from the ports of Mwanza and Kisumu – described it as 'the prettiest and most charming town of the lake... a summer lake resort where no more business is undertaken than is absolutely necessary. The town spreads in a languid careless way to the lake... the golf links are more conspicuous than the capital.' Almost a century later, it is difficult to take issue with Treves's assessment – indeed, it could almost have been written yesterday!

Sprawling along the Lake Victoria shore some 35km south of Kampala, Entebbe exudes an atmosphere of tropical languor, and – particularly for those with a strong interest in natural history (and who aren't looking for budget accommodation) – it makes for an altogether more appealing introduction to Uganda than the capital. And even if you stay in Kampala, this pretty lakeshore town is worth a visit if only for its excellent botanical garden, which is teeming with birds and practically guarantees close-up views of black-and-white colobus monkeys.

Entebbe, the site of Uganda's only international airport, achieved instant immortality in June 1976 when an Air France airbus flying from Israel was hijacked by Palestinian terrorists and forced to land there. Non-Jewish passengers were released and the remainder held hostage against the demand that certain terrorists be freed from Israeli jails. In response, on 4 July 1976, a group of Israeli paratroopers stormed the airport in a daring surprise raid which resulted in all the hostages being freed. During the hijack, Amin pretended to play a mediating role between the Israeli government and the hijackers, but his complicity soon became apparent. A 75-year-old Israeli woman called Dora Bloch, rushed into a Ugandan hospital after choking on her food, was never seen again, presumably killed by Amin's soldiers. The raid also signalled the end of the already tenuous East African community when Amin broke off relations with Kenya (the Israeli raid was launched from Nairobi). The disused building where the hostages were held can be visited with permission from airport staff.

GETTING THERE AND AWAY Minibuses from Kampala to Entebbe leave from the old taxi park every ten minutes or so, and they take up to an hour. Entebbe is a sprawling place and the main taxi park is in Kitoro suburb 1km beyond the town centre. For details of flights, and getting between Kampala and the airport, see

The name Entebbe derives from the Luganda phrase Entebe za Mugala ('Headquarters of Mugala', head of the lungfish clan) and thus literally means 'Headquarters' – somewhat prescient, given that it would later serve as the British administrative capital of Uganda. Entebbe's prominence as a harbour is essentially a modern phenomenon: even into the 1890s, it was too remote from the centre of Baganda political activity to be of comparable significance to Munyonyo and Kaazi on Murchison Bay. But Entebbe's potential was hinted at as early as 1879 by the French missionaries Lourdel and Amans, who noted that 'the port… is large and very well sheltered; on the shore there are no more than three or four houses for travellers'.

Entebbe's potential was first realised in 1896, with the arrival of a European steamship on Lake Victoria – shipped from Scotland to Mombasa, from where it was transported to Port Florence (Kisumu) in pieces by a caravan of porters! And it was sealed in 1901, when the railway line from Mombasa finally reached Port Florence, allowing travellers to and from the coast to reach Entebbe directly by the combination of train and ferry. Within two years, Entebbe had replaced Kampala as the colonial administrative capital – though Kampala would remain capital of the Buganda kingdom throughout the colonial era.

W E Hoyle, who arrived in Uganda in 1903, would later recall that Entebbe, not Kampala, 'was then regarded as the "metropolis" of Uganda'. This switch evidently occurred in 1901, judging by a lamentation published in the *Mengo Notes* late that year: 'The traders in Uganda are not very numerous… we know of… only two Germans [who] have both left Kampala and now appear to be doing chiefly wholesale business in Entebbe.' By 1903, certainly, Entebbe had a greater population of European residents than Kampala, most prominently the commissioner of Uganda and his administrative officers, who were 'mostly living in houses with thatched roofs'. By 1904, Entebbe even boasted a hotel, the Equatorial, evidently the precursor of the present-day Lake Victoria Windsor, owned by an Italian couple whose 'charming daughter,' according to Hoyle, 'became engaged to the first English postmaster… neither knew the other's language, but both knew Swahili, so that little problem was solved'.

Entebbe served as administrative capital of Uganda into the 1960s, and still houses a few government departments to this day, but its claims to outrank Kampala in the metropolitan stakes were rather more short lived. Sir Frederick Treves wrote in 1913 that Entebbe 'is as unlike a capital as any place can well be, while as for administration it must be of that kind which is associated with a deck-chair, a shady veranda, the chink of ice on glass, and the curling smoke of a cigar'. Norma Lorimer, who visited 'gay little' Entebbe in the same year, paints a more pastoral picture: 'very tidy and clean and civilised… its gardens by the lake, full of gorgeous flowering trees and ferns, its red roads with no dust, and its enchanting views of the islands… Baganda moving about in their white kanzus on the red roads, silhouetted against a background of deep blue sky and tropical vegetation.'

Kampala, Getting there and away, pages 138–9. You can also reach Entebbe from Masaka via the Ssese Islands via the routes described in *Getting there and away* for these islands in *Chapter 7*.

WHERE TO STAY
Upmarket

Bulago Island m 0772 709970; e lodge@ islandinthesun.biz; www.islandinthesun.biz This

beautiful 500-acre island lies in Lake Victoria 10 miles east of Entebbe and a mile south of the

The succession of Kabaka Mwanga in October 1884 was an unusually smooth affair, accepted by his brothers and kin without serious infighting, and supported by the majority of Saza chiefs as well as the foreign factions that had by then settled around the royal capital. The five years that followed Mwanga's coronation were, by contrast, the most tumultuous in Buganda's 400-plus years of existence, culminating in three changes of kabaka within 12 months, and paving the way for the kingdom to relinquish its autonomy to a colonial power in 1890.

Mwanga's career comes across as the antithesis of the epithet 'come the moment, come the man'. In 1884, the missionary Alexander Mackay, who had witnessed Mwanga develop from 'a little boy… into manhood' described Mwanga as an 'amiable… young fellow' but 'fitful and fickle, and, I fear, revengeful', noting that 'under the influence of [marijuana] he is capable of the wildest unpremeditated actions'. These misgivings were echoed by other contemporary commentators: Robert Walker, for instance, dismissed Mwanga as 'frivolous… weak and easily led; passionate and if provoked petulant… possessed of very little courage or self-control'.

Whatever his personal failings, Mwanga was also forced to contend with a daunting miscellany of natural disasters, religious tensions and real or imagined political threats. Three months into his reign, he lost several wives and trusted chiefs to an epidemic that swept through his first capital at Nubulagala, while his second capital on Mengo Hill was destroyed by fire in February 1886 and again in 1887. Politically, Mwanga was threatened to the west by a resurgent Bunyoro, whose charismatic leader Kabalega inflicted several defeats on the Kiganda army in the 1880s. From the east, meanwhile, Buganda faced a more nebulous and less quantifiable threat, as news filtered through of the growing number and influence of European colonial agents on the coast.

Buganda c1884 was riddled with religious factionalism. Kiganda traditionalists had for some time co-existed uneasily with a growing volume of Islamic converts influenced by Arab traders. And both of these relatively established factions faced further rivalry from the late 1870s onwards, following the establishment of Catholic and Anglican missions near the capital. The divisions between these religious factions were not limited to matters purely ecclesiastical. Many established Kiganda and Islamic customs, notably polygamy, were anathema to the Christian missionaries, who also spoke out against participation in the slave trade – the lifeblood of the Arab settlers, and profitable to several prominent Kiganda traditionalists.

Mwanga's personal religious persuasions were evidently dictated by pragmatic concerns. During the early years of his rule, his views were strongly shaped by his *katikiro*, an influential Kiganda traditionalist who distrusted all exotic religions, but was relatively sympathetic to Islam as the lesser – or more tolerant towards Kiganda customs – of the two evils. It also seems likely that the traditionalist faction, not unreasonably, perceived a connection between the European missionaries and threat of European imperialism, and thus reckoned it had less to fear from the Arabs.

Three months after he took the throne, Mwanga signalled his hostility to Christianity by executing three young Anglican converts. Then, in October 1885, the king received news of Bishop Hannington's attempt to become the first European through the 'back door' of Busoga. In Kiganda tradition, the back door is used only by close friends or plotting enemies, and Hannington – a stranger to Mwanga – was clearly not the former. Motivated by fear more perhaps than any religious factor, Mwanga ordered the execution

Equator. The lake, sandy beaches, cliffs, grassy hills and forest are the setting for a wide range of activities ranging from pottering along nature trails (ticking off what you can from a 300+ bird list) to water sports and lake fishing (for Nile Perch up to 100kg!). Despite the location, Bulago manages some

of Hannington (see box, page 406). Weeks after the bishop's death, Joseph Mukasa, a Catholic advisor to the king, criticised Mwanga for having Hannington killed without first giving him an opportunity to defend himself, and was also executed for his efforts. These two deaths led to an increasing estrangement between the kabaka and the missionaries – Mackay included – who resided around his court, fuelled partially by Mwanga's fear of a European reprisal for the attack on Hannington.

Mwanga's distrust of Christianity exploded into blind rage on 25 May 1886. The catalyst for this was most probably the subversive actions of his sister Princess Clara Nalumansi (see box, *Buganda's first feminist?*, page 140), though it has been suggested by some writers that Mwanga was a homosexual paedophile whose temporary hatred of Christians stemmed from his rejection by a favoured page, recently baptised. Exactly how many Baganda Christians were speared, beheaded, cremated, castrated and/or bludgeoned to death over the next ten days is an open question – 45 deaths are recorded by name, but the actual tally was probably several hundred. The persecution culminated at Namugongo on 3 June 1886, when at least 26 Catholic and Anglican converts, having rejected the opportunity to renounce their new faith, were roasted alive.

His rage evidently spent, Mwanga set about repairing his relationship with the European missionaries, who had been not been directly victimised by the persecution, and who depended on the kabaka's tolerance to continue their work in the kingdom. Tensions resurfaced in June 1887, when, according to Mackay, Stanley's non-military expedition to Equatoria was described to Mwanga by an Arab trader as 'a Mazungu coming here with a thousand guns' – a ploy designed to reawaken the king's concern that Hannington's death would be avenged by his countrymen. In December 1887, Hannington's successor wrote Mwanga a letter, delivered by Rev E C Gordon, stating that 'we do not desire to take vengeance for this action of yours, we are teachers of the religion of Christ, not soldiers… We believe that you must see now that you were deceived as to the object for which [Hannington] had come.' The increasingly paranoid Mwanga interpreted this as a declaration of war, and Gordon was imprisoned for two months.

Over 1888, Mwanga's concerns about a foreign invasion were diverted by the domestic chaos induced by years of vacillation between the religious factions. On 10 September, Mwanga was forced to flee into exile. His successor, an Islamic convert called Kiwewa, enjoyed a six-week reign, marked by significant violence between the opposing converts, before he was ousted by another Islamic convert called Kalema. Under Kalema, Buganda descended into full-blown civil war, with an unexpected reversal of alliances in which the Christian and traditionalist Baganda lent their support to Mwanga, who was restored to power in February 1890. Three months later, Captain Lugard arrived in Kampala waving a treaty of protectorateship with England.

E B Fletcher, who knew Mwanga in his later years, regarded him to be 'nervous, suspicious, fickle, passionate… with no idea whatever of self-discipline, without regard for life or property, as long as he achieved his own end'. Yet in 1936 Fletcher also wrote an essay exonerating many of the king's excesses and flaws as symptomatic of the troubled times through which he'd lived. 'To steer a straight course through a time when such radical changes were taking place,' Fletcher concluded, 'needed a man of a strong character, a firm will and wide vision. Those characteristics Mwanga did not possess.'

delicious meals. The convenient fish-based menu (common to resorts throughout the Lake Victoria islands) enjoys welcome variations with Thai, Indian and Chinese recipes but if tilapia or Nile Perch really isn't your cup of tea (or kettle of fish), island-grown duck, lamb and salads are available.

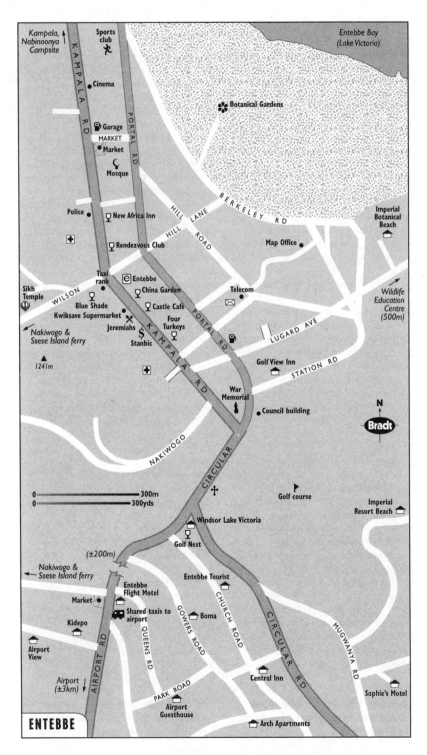

Kampala,
Nabinoonya
Campsite

Sports
club

Entebbe Bay
(Lake Victoria)

Cinema

Garage

MARKET

Market

Mosque

Botanical Gardens

Police

New Africa Inn

Imperial
Botanical
Beach

Rendezvous Club

Map Office

Sikh
Temple

Taxi
rank

Entebbe

China Garden

Telecom

Wildlife
Education
Centre
(500m)

Blue Shade

Kwiksave Supermarket

Castle Café

Nakiwogo &
Ssese Island ferry

Jeremiahs

Four
Turkeys

1241m

Stanbic

LUGARD AVE

Golf View Inn

STATION RD

War
Memorial

Council building

N

Bradt

0 _____ 300m

0 _____ 300yds

Golf course

Imperial
Resort Beach

Windsor Lake Victoria

(±200m)

Golf Nest

Nakiwogo &
Ssese Island ferry

Entebbe Tourist

Entebbe
Flight Motel

Market

Shared taxis to
airport

Boma

Kidepo

Airport
View

Central Inn

Airport
(±3km)

PARK ROAD

Sophie's Motel

Airport
Guesthouse

Arch Apartments

ENTEBBE

KAMPALA RD

PORTAL RD

HILL LANE

HILL ROAD

BERKELEY RD

PORTAL RD

WILSON

KAMPALA RD

NAKIWOGO

CIRCULAR

CIRCULAR RD

AIRPORT RD

QUEENS RD

GOWERS ROAD

CHURCH ROAD

MUGWANYA RD

The voyage to Bulago costs US$50pp return by speedboat from Garuga between Kampala and Entebbe or US$40 by Bulago's own Ssese canoe (fishing boat). Flights from Entebbe can also be arranged. Accommodation including dinner and breakfast is provided in luxury cottages sited along the lakeshore and in the resort gardens and costs US$89pp (US$10 supplement Fri–Sat nights). Ugandan residents enjoy a US$10 discount. Children cost about half price.

⌂ **Windsor Lake Victoria Hotel** ✆ 0414 351600/0312 310100; f 0312 310404; e windsor@imul.com. Despite the expanding list of large upmarket hotels in Entebbe, this refurbished, former government hotel remains the favourite choice for travellers starting or ending a safari. The 'Lake Vic' exudes an atmosphere of tropical grandeur within smallish but immaculate grounds overlooking the golf course and the lake. Facilities include AC and DSTV in all rooms, a swimming pool and health club, and secretarial and business services. The only drawback is that the hotel is some distance from the lake, though if you put practical considerations before aesthetics, this does mean that you are largely spared the harmless but annoying swarms of lake-flies which congregate along the shore in the evenings. *US$130/170 sgl/dbl.*

⌂ **Imperial Botanical Beach Hotel** ✆ 0414 320800; f 0414 320832; e ibbhotel@afsat.com. The Windsor's upmarket rival can boast the distinction of having accommodated Bill Clinton on his 1998 visit to Uganda. It is situated in large, green lakeshore grounds, adjacent to the botanical garden and a few hundred metres from the animal orphanage, and has a new swimming pool and gym complex. Other facilities include a grill restaurant with a lakeshore

Moderate

⌂ **Palm Resort Beach** ✆ 0414 321480/320840; m 0772 508939; f 0414 320840; e palmresort@utlonline.co.ug. The former Entebbe Resort has come a long way from its humble early 1990s incarnation as a likeably dopey and little-used lakeshore campsite. Today it is one of the more popular drinking and picnicking spots in the Greater Kampala area, with a swimming pool, health club, four bars, and several restaurants generating something of a carnival atmosphere at weekends. It's now overshadowed by the massive 'Blue Hotel' as the new Imperial Resort Beach Hotel is known locally. There's plenty of birdlife around, however, most notably an abundance of pied kingfishers hovering and darting above the lake, and the beach is said

annex, and canoe hire. AC rooms with DSTV *US$90/100 sgl/dbl inc a buffet b/fast.*

⌂ **The Boma** Plot 20a, Julia Sebutinde Rd (aka Gower Rd); m 0772 467929; e thebomaentebbe@infocom.co.ug. This new and welcoming guesthouse is the only establishment to rival the larger Lake Vic hotel in Entebbe's expanding upmarket category. Popular with inbound/outbound tourists and expatriates alike, it's a welcoming set-up in a tastefully restored colonial homestead in the leafy suburb behind the Lake Victoria Hotel. The homely lounge has DSTV and the comfortable s/c rooms are fitted with an attractive combination of English-colonial furnishings and African fabrics. From town, Gower Rd turns off Airport Rd, 400m beyond the Lake Victoria Hotel plot. A 'Boma II', apparently to be called 'The Peninsula', will open in early 2007. Overlooking the lake by the Entebbe Sailing Club, it will occupy a new storeyed structure of Zanzibari style. *US$75/100 sgl/dbl inc b/fast on a lovely veranda and airport transfers.*

⌂ **Imperial Resort Beach Hotel** ✆ 0414 303000; e information@irb.com; www.imperialhotels.com. This sumptuous new hotel takes your breath away. A 6-floor edifice, sinuous in plan and blue glass in façade encloses an astonishing central atrium that extends upwards all 6 storeys to a glass roof. Glass-sided lifts rise up its walls to 4.5m-wide carpeted corridors and internal balconies which lead to the truly sumptuous rooms. The building has been designed to suggest a wave which is unfortunate since waves don't have balconies and neither does this hotel. Actually after the initial awe it's really an AC prison. Worth a visit for a gawp and a drink though.

to be free of bilharzia (the close proximity of reed-beds gives cause to raise an eyebrow). To get to the Entebbe Resort, follow Circular Road southeast from the Windsor Lake Victoria Hotel around the golf course and past the Blue Hotel to the lake – about 15mins' walk. *An attached guesthouse, set some distance from the action, offers acceptable s/c accommodation with DSTV for US$46/55 sgl/dbl. There is also an attractive and reasonably secluded campsite, at a rather steep US$5 pp.*

⌂ **Sophie's Motel** ✆ 0414 320885/321370; f 0414 320897; e sophies@ieasy.com. This quiet and deservedly popular family-run hotel lies in the leafy residential suburbs between the town centre and the Palm Resort Beach. Facilities include a free airport shuttle and a good restaurant serving international and local cuisine. There's an attractive raised terrace, though the rear of the new Blue Hotel hasn't done anything to improve the view. *US$35/45 s/c sgl/dbl B&B, deluxe dbl rooms or cottages with DSTV and a fridge cost US$60.*

🏠 **Entebbe Flight Motel** ✆ 0414 320812; f 0414 320241. Conveniently situated and comfortable, the Entebbe Flight Motel lies close to the Windsor Lake Victoria right in front of the taxi ranks for Kampala and the airport. Facilities include an affordable garden restaurant and bar and satellite television. It's a pleasant old hotel presently being swallowed by a monolithic concrete extension which might account for a US$10 reduction in room rates since the last edition of this book. Don't bother negotiating discounted group rates because, as disgruntled delegates of the 2006 Entebbe Primatology Conference inform us, the motel won't honour them. *US$25/30/45 s/c sgl/dbl/triple inc b/fast.*

Budget

🏠 **Arch Apartments** ✆ 0414 323700. This small complex of small s/c apts on Coombe Rd at the Gower Rd junction is excellent value for money. *A terrace of flatlets (inc bathroom, kitchen, TV and fridge) around a central bar/dining shelter cost US$27/32 B&B.*

🏠 **Central Inn** ✆ 0414 322386; e centralinn@ yahooonline.co.ug. Enjoying a pleasant suburb location on Church Rd the Central Inn is also *good value at US$27/32 B&B.*

🏠 **Golf View Inn** ✆ 0414 321640. The management presumably thought it appropriate to highlight the fairway foreground rather than the lake backdrop. Small but clean s/c rooms with a hot bath are rather overpriced but not bad value for Entebbe.

Shoestring

🏠 **Entebbe Tourists Hotel and Campsite** Church Rd; ✆ 0414 320432; m 0712 849973; e frankstouristshostel@hotmail.com; www.traveluganda.co.ug/frankstouristshostel. This excellent and friendly family-run hostel fills a much-needed niche for decent shoestring accommodation in Entebbe. It's attractively located on Church Rd, one of the pleasant suburban avenues south of the town centre. Food is available and the lounge has DSTV. Church Road is the first turning off Airport Road immediately after the Lake Victoria Hotel. A special hire from the Kitoro taxi park costs about Ush3,000. *Camping costs less than US$3. A*

🏠 **Airport View Hotel** ✆ 0312 261754; e byagaba@airportviewhotel.com; www.airportviewhotel.com. Despite an unpromising location in the insalubrious suburb of Kitoro, this new hotel is smart and comfortable with spacious tiled rooms. It does indeed have an airport view. Birdwatchers should ask for Room 32 from which the balcony has a clear view across wetland to the runway and a good place to look for waterbirds. A pleasant in-house restaurant serves good dinners in the Ush5,000–15,000 range. *US$50/70–90/100 sgl/dbls/ste inc b/fast and airport transfers.* Turn off the Airport Road into Kitoro at Nile Bank and turn left at the signposted turning after 200m.

🏠 **Airport Guest House** (8 rooms) Mugula Rd; ✆ 0414 370932; m 0772 445805; e postmaster@ gorillatours.com. This new guesthouse off Park Rd offers smart and comfortable-looking good-value s/c rooms in an outside block facing a manicured lawn. It's a quiet suburban setting convenient for the airport. *US$30/40 inc b/fast and airport transfer.*

There's an acceptable restaurant with television attached, and a shady garden bar. *US$35/45 sgl/dbl.*

🏠 **Wildlife Education Centre** ✆ 0414 256041/320520 (there's never an answer, better to email); e uweced@infocom.co.ug. The WEC has recently introduced 3 roomy s/c bandas inside the compound with twin beds and an elevated platform for additional mattresses. There's a lake view and you should hear some interesting noises at night. There's a café in the zoo where you can wander for meals. It's a few hundred metres from the entrance to the bandas but you can hire a boda-boda if you've got luggage. *Dbl occupancy costs US$20 and additional mattress US$10, inc the zoo entrance fee.*

dormitory sleeping 5 people costs US$4.50 pp. Rooms with shared facilities US$7/8 sgl/dbl. Two s/c rooms are available; the larger costing US$16 and the smaller is US$11.

🏠 **Kidepo Hotel** A jumped-up local guesthouse on the edge of the less salubrious Kitoro suburb. An airport taxi costs Ush600 during the day and Ush10,000 at night. If you look, you're bound to find other basic but cheaper lodges in Kitoro though I suspect the emphasis may well be on 'short time' visits rather than full night stays. The Kidepo is cheap for Entebbe but not exactly a bargain! *US$8/13 for a small sgl/dbl using common showers.*

Nabinoonya Resort Beach m 0772 685264. Situated about 10km north of Entebbe, about 30mins' walk from the Kampala Rd, this quiet and secluded lakeshore resort is far cheaper and more attractive than any budget accommodation in Entebbe itself. Red-tailed monkeys inhabit the surrounding trees, and there's plenty of birdlife on the lake. To get there turn off at the large signpost on the Kampala–Entebbe road a few kilometres north of Entebbe. Weekdays are probably a better bet than weekends when it can be noisy. *S/c dbls US$12, twins using common showers US$9, a bed in a 4-berth dormitory US$3. Fish and chips Ush4,500.*

Camping

Bussi Island Kampala Backpackers (see contacts on pages 147–8) has developed an attractive lakeshore site, with beaches, cliffs and forest remnants, on the shores of Lake Victoria directly (and I mean *exactly*) on the Equator across the bay from Entebbe. To get there head either to Nakiwogo Port on the west side of Entebbe Peninsula or Kasenyi fishing village beyond the airport (follow the signs towards Merryland High School) and find a boat. You must book with Kampala Backpackers before you travel. There are birds and monkeys along the shore, hippos offshore while Mabamba Swamp across the bay is presently the best place in Uganda to find shoebills in the wild. To get there, catch an afternoon boat from Nakiwogo (Ssese ferry port) to Gulwe landing site on Bussi Island (Ush2,500 pp). Then it's a 2km walk. You could also charter a charter a boat from Nakiwogo to the camp for Ush35,000. Alternatively find your way to Mabamba Swamp (page 188) and cross to Bussi in a dugout canoe for Ush1,000 then take a *boda-boda* across the island to the campsite. *Camping with your own tent costs US$3.20 pp. Dormitory beds are US$6.50. Camping in permanent tents with a mattress is US$11 and bandas US$22 (Ush20,000/40,000). Fishing rods available, forest and birding walks organised. Entrance for day visitors Ush2,000 pp.*

Kisubi Beach Resort Camping is possible at this small site roughly 10km north of town along a 2km turn-off signposted from the Entebbe Road. *Camping costs US$2 pp, and a 'take-away' serves greasy chicken and chips etc.*

WHERE TO EAT AND DRINK

China Garden Restaurant The most interesting place to eat in Entebbe is this well-established Chinese restaurant in the old town centre – large portions of excellent food for around *Ush10,000 inc condiments.*

Four Turkeys This centrally located bar on Kampala Rd, very popular with the local expatriate crowd, serves filling and inexpensive snacks such as burgers and toasted sandwiches.

Jeremiah's Located on Kampala Rd near Four Turkeys, this new restaurant/bar is owned by the expat who does the food for the aeroplanes. Don't let that put you off; Jeremiah's serves a good range of local and international meals including some decent daily specials. *Meals Ush6,000–8,000.*

Golf Nest This commendable restaurant offers the alluring combination of a pleasant outdoor setting fringing the golf course and good grills, stews and burgers.Whole grilled tilapia is a house speciality. *Meals around Ush5,000.*

New Africa Inn No food to speak of, but plenty of cold beer flowing at this secluded garden bar tucked away on Kampala Rd, next to the Rendezvous Club.

Rendezvous Club One of a cluster of open-air bars on Kampala Rd where you can drink inexpensive beer and nibble on grilled meat, freshly cooked on the side of the street.

Windsor Lake Victoria Hotel The first-floor Indian restaurant at this plush hotel serves great food, and the Sat night buffet barbecue is great value if you're seriously hungry. *Meals around Ush10,000, Sat barbecue – all you can eat for Ush15,000. The buffet b/fast (Ush18,000) has long been a favourite with hungry in/outbound travellers.*

Café Victoria This basic set-up is located just north of Entebbe where the road passes within metres of the lake close to Ssese Gateway Beach. It's been recommended as a lovely spot to enjoy a grilled tilapia; you choose your fish. *Ush5,000 upwards depending on size, chips extra.*

LISTINGS

Foreign exchange Stanbic will change money and travellers' cheques on Kampala Road but expect a long queue. You'll get a better rate at Nile Bank at Kitoro junction on Airport Road. Out of banking hours, hop on a minibus-taxi to the airport, where a number of private forex bureaux offer rates that are reasonable, though somewhat lower than you'd get in Kampala.

Internet The only internet café is the Entebbe Cyber Link, which is situated on Kampala Road next to the China Garden Restaurant and charges Ush500 per 15 minutes.

Swimming pool The pool at the Windsor Lake Victoria Hotel is open to non-residents on payment of Ush5,000 The Imperial Botanical Beach Hotel has a huge covered pool which you can use for Ush5,000.

Luggage storage Not a standard topic for these listings, but included here since many outbound travellers head down early to Entebbe to enjoy a pleasant afternoon rather than risking getting stuck in the Kampala traffic. Both the Windsor Lake Victoria and Botanical Beach hotels seem happy to store luggage for day visitors who are paying to use the swimming pool or taking lunch. The Lake Vic is perhaps a more pleasant setting but the Botanical is convenient to wander down to the Botanical Garden or Wildlife Education Centre.

Map sales office Entebbe was the administrative capital of Uganda in the colonial era and many government departments are still dotted around the residential area between the town centre and Botanical Beach Hotel in Entebbe. Most likely to be of interest to tourists is the Department of Lands and Surveys, where a well-stocked map sales office sells 1:50,000 sheets covering most of the country for Ush10,000 apiece. Do set aside a couple of hours for the adventure, which entails choosing the maps you want to buy, then walking up to the Stanbic Bank to pay (I queued for an hour on my most recent visit), before returning with the receipt to collect the booty.

Shopping The Kwiksave Supermarket on Kampala Road, opposite the China Garden Restaurant, is one of the best in town. For handicrafts, try the Banana Boat Arts and Crafts Shop at the entrance to the Entebbe Wildlife Centre.

WHAT TO SEE
Entebbe Botanical Garden (*Admission Ush1,000*) Established in 1902, Entebbe's botanical garden is an attractively laid-out mix of indigenous forest, cultivation and horticulture, and a highly attractive destination to birdwatchers. The botanical garden offers an excellent introduction to Uganda's birds, ranging from Lake Victoria specials such as grey kestrel, yellow-throated leaflove, slender-billed weaver and Jackson's golden-backed weaver to the more widespread but nonetheless striking black-headed gonolek, red-chested sunbird, grey-capped warbler and common wattle-eye. In addition to various shorebirds, the impressive palmnut vulture and fish eagle are both common, and a pair of giant eagle owls is resident. Forest birds include the splendid Ross's and great blue turaco, as well as the noisy black-and-white casqued hornbill.

It is said that some of the early *Tarzan* films were shot on location in Entebbe – a thus-far unverifiable legend that gains some plausibility when you compare the giggling of the plantain-eaters that frequent the botanical garden with the chimp noises that punctuate the old movies. There are some mammals around – no chimps, of course, nor even the sitatunga and hippos that frequented the lakeshore swamps into the 1960s – but you can be confident of seeing vervet and black-and-white colobus monkeys, as well as tree squirrels.

Uganda Wildlife Education Centre (*Admission Ush3,000/5,000/10,000 Ugandans/foreign residents/non-residents*) Often and rather misleadingly referred to as

a zoo, the animal orphanage near the former Game Department headquarters was established as a sanctuary for animals which would be unable to fend for themselves in the wild, and it has played an important role in the protection of rare and threatened animals. Residents include a few lions (whose nocturnal vocalisations add a distinct sense of place to a night in any nearby hotel), a pair of recently reintroduced black rhinos, and a variety of smaller predators that are seldom seen in the wild. The aviary provides the most reliable opportunity in Uganda of getting a close-up shot of the renowned shoebill.

DAY TRIPS OUT OF KAMPALA/ENTEBBE

Further afield, the Mpanga Forest (see *Chapter 7*, pages 191–3) and Mabira Forest (see *Chapter 12*, pages 425–8) would make good day trips, particularly if you are interested in birds and monkeys. You should take along a picnic lunch to these places. In a similar vein, the botanical garden in Entebbe is well worth an excursion (see above). A popular day excursion from Kampala is one of the white-water rafting trips conducted by Adrift (see page 161 for details).

NGAMBA ISLAND CHIMPANZEE SANCTUARY Situated 23km southeast of Entebbe, the 50ha Ngamba Island forms part of the Kome archipelago, a group of about 15 islands and islets separated from the northern shore of Lake Victoria by the 10km-wide Damba Channel. Ngamba was established as a chimpanzee sanctuary in 1998, when 19 orphaned chimps were relocated there from the Uganda Wildlife Education Centre (UWEC) in Entebbe and the smaller Isinga Island in Queen Elizabeth National Park. These chimpanzees had all been saved from a life in captivity or a laboratory when they were confiscated by the Ugandan authorities and brought to UWEC for care and rehabilitation, with some being released onto Isinga in the mid 1990s.

The island is divided into two unequal parts, separated by an electric fence. On one side of the fence, the visitors and staff centre extends over an area of about 1ha on a partially cleared stretch of northwestern shore notable for the immense weaver colonies it supports. The rest of the island is reserved more-or-less exclusively for the chimps and their attendants, the exception being tourists who opt to do the chimpanzee walk described below. In late 2002, an upmarket tented camp sleeping up to eight was established on the island by G&C Tours/Wild Frontiers.

Ngamba was chosen as a sanctuary because it was formerly uninhabited and its rainforest environment is almost identical to that of wild chimpanzees, with more than 50 plant species known to be utilised by free-ranging chimps in Uganda represented. There is plenty of room for the chimps to roam, but the forest isn't large enough to sustain the entire community – indeed its area corresponds roughly to the natural range of one chimpanzee – so the chimps are fed a porridge-like mixture for breakfast, and then fruits and vegetables twice during the day. The fruits are fed to the chimps from a viewing platform, which provides an opportunity for visitors to observe and photograph the chimps through a fence. The chimps have the choice of staying in the forest overnight or returning to a holding facility built to enhance social integration and veterinary management, with sleeping platforms and hammocks as well as grass for nest building.

The sanctuary exists to provide the best facilities and care to captive chimpanzees, for which reason the management has elected not to allow the chimps to breed. All sexually mature females in the island are given a contraceptive implant, which doesn't disrupt the community's normal sexual behaviour, but does prevent pregnancy in the same way as the human contraceptive pill. The

The spirit of Kiganda, the traditional religion of Buganda, 'is not so much adoration of a being supreme and beneficent', wrote Speke, 'as a tax to certain malignant furies... to prevent them bringing evil on the land, and to insure a fruitful harvest.' Certainly, like many traditional African religions, Kiganda does revolve largely around the appeasing and petitioning of ancestral and animist spirits both benign and malevolent. But Kiganda is unusual in that it combines these elements with a core of monotheism. The supreme being of the Baganda is Katonda – literally, Creator – who is not of human form, and has neither parents nor children, but who brought into being the heavens, the earth, and all they contain. Katonda is the most powerful denizen of the spiritual world, but also the most detached from human affairs, and so requires little attention by comparison to more hands–on subordinate spirits.

Ranking below Katonda, the *balubaale* (singular *lubaale*) are semi-deities who play a central role in the day-to-day affairs affecting Buganda. At least 30 balubaale are recognised (some sources claim a total of 70), and many are strongly associated with specific aspects or attributes of life. The balubaale have no real equivalent in the Judaic branch of religions. Certainly not gods, they are more akin perhaps to a cross between a saint and a guardian angel – the spirits of real men (or more occasionally women) whose exceptional attributes in life have been carried over to death. Traditionally, the balubaale form the pivot of organised religion in Buganda: prior to the introduction of exotic religions they were universally venerated, even above the kabaka, who in all other respects was an absolute ruler.

The most popular lubaale is Mukasa, the spirit of Lake Victoria, honoured at many temples around Buganda, the most important of which is on Bubembe in the Ssese Islands, where the kabaka would send an annual offering of cows and a request for prosperity and good harvests. Mukasa is also associated with fertility: barren women would regularly visit an adjacent shrine on Bubembe, dedicated to his wife Nalwanga, to ask her to seek her husband's blessing. Another important lubaale is Wanga, guardian of the sun and moon, who also has no earthly shrine, and is the father of Muwanga, literally 'the most powerful'. Other prominent male balubaale with specific areas of interest include Musoke (rainbows), Kawumpuli (plagues), Ndahura (smallpox), Kitinda (prosperity), Musisi (earthquakes), Wamala (Lake Wamala) and Ddunga (hunting).

Female balubaale are fewer, and in most cases their elevated status is linked to kinship to a male lubaale, but they include Kiwanuka's wife Nakayage (fertility) and Kibuuka's mother Nagaddya (harvests). Nabuzaana, the female lubaale of obstetrics, is possibly unique in having no kin among the other balubaale, furthermore in that she is tended by priestesses of Banyoro rather than Baganda origin. The male lubaale Ggulu, guardian of the sky, is a confusing figure. Listed in some traditions as the creator, his existence, in common with that of Katonda, pre-dated that of humanity, and he has no earthly shrine, furthering the suggestion that unlike other balubaale he is not the spirit of a dead person. Ggulu's children include the lightning spirit Kiwanuka as well as Walumbe, the spirit of sickness and death.

The balubaale are expected to intercede favourably in national affairs related to their speciality when petitioned with sacrifices and praise. Sacrifices to the lake spirit Mukasa might be made during periods of drought, in case he has forgotten that the people need rain. The rainbow spirit Musoke, by contrast, might be placated with sacrifices after extended rains that prevent harvesting or ploughing, and he will signal his assent to stop the rain with a

sanctuary may change this policy if it proves necessary or beneficial to allow breeding in the future.

Since 1998, UWEC has received an influx of orphaned chimpanzees, most of which were captured illegally in the forests of the DRC and smuggled across

rainbow. In past times, all the major temples would be consulted and offerings made before any major national undertaking – a coronation, for instance, or a war – and any kabaka who ignored this custom was inviting disaster. One main shrine or *ekiggwa* is dedicated to each lubaale, though many are also venerated at a number of lesser shrines scattered around Buganda. Every shrine is tended by a *mandwa*: a priest or medium who is on occasion possessed by the shrine's spirit and acts as its oracle. The mandwa for any given temple might be male or female, but will usually come from a specific clan associated with that temple. The three main shrines dedicated to Katonda – all situated in Kyaggwe, near the Mabira Forest – are, for instance, tended by priests of the Njovu (elephant) clan. Sacred drums, ceremonial objects and sometimes body parts of the deceased are stored in the temple, the upkeep of which is governed by elaborate customs.

While a relatively small cast of balubaale is concerned with national affairs, the day-to-day affairs of local communities and of individual Muganda are governed by innumerable lesser spirits. These are divided into two main categories: *mizimu* (singular *omuzimu*) are the spirits of departed ancestors, while *misambwa* (singular *omusambwa*) are spirits associated with specific physical objects such as mountains, rivers, forests or caves. Dealings with the ancestral spirits are a family matter, undertaken at a household shrine where small items, such as cowries or beans, are offered on a regular basis, while a living sacrifice of a chicken or goat might be offered before an important event or ceremony. Appeasing the misambwa, by contrast, is a community affair, with communal offerings made on regular basis. Unlike balubaale or mizimu, misambwa are generally cantankerous spirits: one's main obligation to an omusambwa is to keep out of its way and uphold any taboos associated with it.

The place of Kiganda in modern Buganda is difficult to isolate. In the latter half of the 19th century, when the kingdom was first infiltrated by evangelical foreigners – initially just Arabs, later also Europeans – a significant number of Muganda, especially the elite, converted to an exotic religion. Thereafter, the converts tended to regard their indigenous spiritual traditions as backward and superstitious, a stance that caused considerable friction within the kingdom during the 1880s. The trend against traditionalism continued throughout the 20th century. Today, most if not all Baganda profess to be either Christian or Islamic, and certainly very few educated and urbanised Baganda take Kiganda traditions very seriously, if they consider them at all.

I'm not at all certain this is the case in rural Buganda. From Ashanti to Zululand, it is my experience that rural Africans frequently adhere partially or concurrently to two apparently contradictory religious doctrines. They might be dedicated Christians or Muslims, but in times of trouble they will as likely consult a traditional oracle or healer as they will a priest or imam or a Western doctor. This dualism in Buganda is perhaps less conspicuous to outsiders than it would be in many other parts of Africa. But that it exists, I have no doubt. Shrines such as those at Ssezibwa Falls are clearly still in active use, while – further afield – the likes of Bigo and the Nakayima Tree both remain a focal point for traditionalist cults. In the past 20 years, Christian cults centred on the Acholi and Bakiga mediums Alice Lakwena and Credonia Mwerinde, though very different, have both possessed undeniable traditionalist undertones. It is out of respect for Kiganda traditions, rather than any wish to offend the many Baganda who reject them, that this box has been written not in the past tense but in the present.

Uganda for trade. By July 2006, 39 orphaned chimpanzees were resident on Ngamba Island. Workers on the island are constantly involved in helping the newly arrived orphans to integrate into the original community, which spans an age range of two to 19 years old, with an almost equal balance of males and females. In order to house the ceaseless influx of new orphans, a new sanctuary is currently being constructed on the adjacent Nsadzi Island, which covers about ten times the area of Ngamba.

Ngamba Island is the flagship project of the Chimpanzee Sanctuary and Wildlife Conservation Trust, jointly established in 1997 by the Born Free Foundation, the International Fund for Animal Welfare, the Jane Goodall Institute, UWEC and the Zoological Board of New South Wales (Australia). It is part of an integrated chimpanzee conservation programme that also includes an ongoing census study of wild chimpanzee populations in Uganda, two snare removal programmes, chimpanzee habituation for ecotourism, and education and outreach initiatives in local communities. Proceeds from tourist visits go directly back into the maintenance of the sanctuary and the organisation's other chimpanzee-related projects.

Day trips to the island are timed to coincide with the pre-arranged supplementary feeding times of 11.00 and 14.30, when the chimpanzees come to within metres of a raised walkway, offering an excellent opportunity to observe and photograph one of our closest animal relatives. Half-day trips by motorboat leave Entebbe at 09.30 and 13.00 daily by prior arrangement, and costs US$260 per party for up to four people, and an additional US$65 per person for additional passengers, inclusive of all fees. Full day trips using traditional Ssese canoes can also be arranged.

Overnight excursions were introduced in 2002, sleeping in smart self-contained tented accommodation with solar lighting. These allow for access to two daytime chimpanzee feedings from the visitors' platform, plus the early morning feeding in the holding facility. Kayaks are available to explore the island bays searching for monitor lizards, otters and some of the 154 recorded bird species, while other optional activities for overnight visitors include a visit to a local fishing village, a sunset cruise, and fishing. These excursions work out at around US$250–350 per person depending on group size and single or double occupancy, inclusive of boat transfers from Entebbe, all meals and most activities.

Also introduced in 2002 were one-hour chimpanzee walks with a group of infant chimpanzees through their forest habitat, either in the late afternoon or very early morning. A maximum of three visitors are allowed in the forest for each walk, always accompanied by trained staff. Even so, the chimpanzees are used to human contact and they will often play-bite visitors, climb on them, grab their glasses or pull their hair – or even just walk along holding their hand. This activity costs US$100 and is limited to people of between 18 and 65 years of age. Visitors are also required to be free of any flu-like disease or herpes (cold sores) outbreak at the time of the visit.

Visits to Ngamba can be arranged through most tour operators in Kampala, but they are run exclusively by G&C Tours, the Entebbe-based ground operator for Wild Frontiers, and can be booked through them directly (❨ *0414 321479;* m *0772 502155;* e *gctours@gctours.co.ug; www.gctours.co.ug*). Anybody thinking of booking on the chimpanzee walk should make advance contact with G&C Tours or check out their website for current medical requirements, which at the time of writing includes valid proof of a current vaccination against hepatitis A and B, measles, meningococcal meningitis, polio, tetanus, yellow fever, as well as a negative TB test within the past six months.

SSEZIBWA FALLS The Ssezibwa Falls, which lies 35km east of Kampala, is reputed to have been a favourite spot of kabakas Mwanga and Mutesa II, both of whom planted trees there that still flourish today. The waterfall, and the Ssezibwa River on which it lies, are also steeped in Kiganda folklore. Many hundreds of years ago, the legend goes, a woman called Nakangu, of the Achibe (fox) clan, gave birth not to twin children, as expected, but to a twin river, split into two distinct streams by an island immediately below the waterfall. It is believed locally that the spirits of Nakangu's unborn children – Ssezibwa and Mobeya – still inhabit the river, and it was once customary for any Muganda passing its source at Namukono, some 20km further east, to throw a handful of grass or stones into it for good luck. Even today, a thanksgiving sacrifice of barkcloth, beer and a cock is made at the river's source every year, usually led by a Ssalongo (father of twins).

It is not surprising, given the supernatural significance attached to the birth of twins in many Ugandan societies, that a number of shrines are maintained among the colourful quartzite rocks over which the river tumbles perhaps 15m before it divides into two. Specific gaps in the rock are dedicated to specific *lubaale*: including the river spirit Mukasa, the hunting spirit Ddungu and the rainbow spirit Musoke. There is also a fertility shrine in the rocks adjacent to the falls, associated with the thunder spirit Kiwanuka if I understand correctly, and generally used for individual rather than communal sacrifices. Women who have been blessed with twins, one of which is human, the other a benevolent spirit manifested in a python or leopard, often visit this shrine to leave eggs for their python spirit or a cock for its feline counterpart.

Communal sacrificial ceremonies, in which nine pieces of the meat most favoured by the individual spirit will be placed at the appropriate shrine, are still held at the waterfall, and sometimes even attended by the kabaka himself. Tourists are welcome to visit on such occasions, but unfortunately their timing is difficult to predict – ceremonies are not held every year, and the date is usually announced at short notice when a medium is consulted by a hungry spirit. Certain spirits, after having accepted a sacrifice and taken the requested action, appreciate having a live sheep or cock – white for Mukasa, brown for Kiwanuka – thrown over the waterfall itself, and they always ensure that the animal survives.

Ssezibwa is run as an ecotourism project, and although it is firstly a cultural attraction, the waterfall itself is very pretty, particularly during the rains, and the fringing trees harbour an interesting selection of birds. The falls can be reached by following the Jinja Road out of Kampala to Kayanja trading centre, then following a clearly signposted dirt road running southward for about 2km. Entrance costs Ush3,000 per person for non-residents and Ush1,000 for residents. There's no charge for being shown around by one of the knowledgeable guides, but it would be appropriate to tip them. No accommodation is available, but camping is permitted. Officially the rate is Ush25,000 per party, irrespective of whether that party constitutes one person or 20 but I've also been told Ush5,000 per person is acceptable.

KATEREKE PRISON The extensive prison ditch at Katereke is a relic of the instability that characterised Buganda in the late 1880s (see box *Chaos in Buganda*, pages 176–7). It was constructed by Kabaka Kalema, an Islamic sympathiser who was controversially placed on the throne in October 1888, less than two months after Kabaka Mwanga had been forced into exile. Kalema ordered that every potential or imagined rival to his throne be rounded up and sent to Katereke – which, given the fragility of his position in the divided kingdom, added up to an estimated 40 personages.

One of the first to be imprisoned at Katereke was Kiwewa, who had ruled Buganda for the brief period between Mwanga's exile and Kalema's ascent to the throne. Kiwewa was soon joined by a bevy of his wives, as well as the two infant sons of the exiled Mwanga, and the last two surviving sons of the late Kabaka Suuna. Kalema also feared a secession bid from his own brothers, and even his sisters – like Mwanga before him, Kalema was unsettled by the fact that the queen sat on the English throne – and most of them were imprisoned too.

Six months into his reign, sensing a growing threat from the budding alliance between the Christian faction in Buganda and its former persecutor Mwanga – the latter by this time openly resident on an island in Murchison Bay, only 10km from the capital – Kalema decided to wipe out the potential opposition once and for all. Most of the occupants of the prison were slaughtered without mercy. Other less significant figures, for instance some of the princesses and one elderly son of Kabaka Suuna, were spared when they agreed to embrace Islam. The massacre wasn't confined to the prison's occupants either: Mukasa, the traditionalist Katikiro who had served under Mwanga, was shot outside his house, which was then set on fire with the body inside. The wives of the former Kabaka Kiwewa, according to Sir John Milner Gray, were 'put to death in circumstances of disgusting brutality'.

Ultimately, this massacre probably hastened Kalema's downfall by strengthening the alliance between Buganda's Christians, who suffered several casualties, and the island-bound Mwanga, left mourning several bothers and sisters as well as his two sons. And the lingering death that Kalema had reserved for his predecessor set many formerly neutral chiefs and other dignitaries against him. Kiwewa was starved of food and water for seven days, then a bullet was put through his weakened body, and finally his remains were burnt unceremoniously in his prison cell – not, in the words of Sir Apollo Kaggwa, 'a fit manner in which to kill a king'.

Katereke Prison lies to the west of Kampala, and can be reached by following the Masaka Road out of town for about 15km, passing through Nsangi trading centre, then about 2km later turning right into a clearly signposted dirt road on a obvious bend in the road after a series of speed bumps (ignore another Katereke sign 1km back down the road towards Nsangi) that leads to the prison after another 2km. It's a surprisingly peaceful and leafy spot, considering its bloody historical associations, and guides are available to show you around what remains of the prison trench. A nominal entrance fee is charged. A visit to Katereke could be combined with a side trip to Nagalabi Buddo, which lies about 5km south of Nsangi trading centre and has reputedly served as the coronation site for the kabaka since Buganda was founded.

MABAMBA SWAMP No more than 15km west of Entebbe as the crow flies, the Mabamba Swamp extends across more than 100km² from a shallow, marshy bay on the northern shore of Lake Victoria. Listed as an Important Bird Area, Mabamba harbours an excellent selection of water-associated species, and is possibly now the most reliable place anywhere in the country for shoebill sightings. The villagers at the small lakeshore village of Mabamba offer dugout trips into the swamp for Ush20,000 per head (negotiable), and are usually capable of locating shoebills within a few minutes. Even if you're out of luck on that score, it's a lovely, mellow boat trip, and other localised birds likely to be seen include pygmy goose, lesser jacana, gull-billed tern, blue-breasted bee-eater and the papyrus-specific Carruthers's cisticola and white-winged warbler.

Despite their close geographical proximity, Entebbe and Mabamba lie at least 40km apart by road, and the trip there takes about one hour The most direct route out of Entebbe involves following the surfaced Kampala Road roughly 12km north as far as Kisubi, then turning left along a dirt side road to Nakauka, where another left turn leads to the small town of Kasanje, dominated by an outsized roundabout. Turn left again at the roundabout until after about 10km you reach the jetty from where the dugouts leave. Coming from Kampala, a better route is to follow the

Masaka Road out of town for 30km, then to turn left along a side road signposted for Buyege, shortly before Mpigi Town. After 12km this road leads to Kasanje, where you need to cross the roundabout and continue straight ahead for Mabamba. The route from Entebbe is a good place to look out for flocks of great blue turaco, while the route from Kampala passes through a large swamp where papyrus gonolek is resident about 6km before Kasanje, and could easily be combined with a visit to the Mpanga Forest Reserve near Mpigi (see *Chapter 7*, pages 191–3). Travellers dependent on public transport should have no problem getting to Kasanje, from where they will probably have to charter a *boda-boda* or taxi to get to the swamp. You can also get there from Bussi Island camp (see *Listings*, page 181).

6

Lake Mburo National Park

ROOM WITH A VIEW

Mihingo Lodge is a peaceful luxury retreat found just 3 and a 1/2 hours drive from Kampala. Stunningly situated amidst giant granite boulders it offers spectacular views across Lake Mburo National Park.

Entirely Solar powered, each of the 10 uniquely positioned, platform-mounted tents have the comfort and charm of wooden floors, four poster beds and en suite bathrooms. The spacious private verandas provide each guest with an individual and unforgettable African vista.

Unwind beside the lagoon style infinity pool, enjoy delicious home cooking in the thatched dining room and experience the rich wildlife through organised bird walks, game drives and walking safaris. Mihingo Lodge treats you to Africa at its most magical!

safari@mihingolodge.com
www.mihingolodge.com
+ 256 – 752 – 410509

7

The Mbarara Road

This chapter follows the 283km road running southwest from Kampala via Masaka to Mbarara, the bustling modern town located at the junction of the main roads southwest to Kisoro and north to Kasese and Fort Portal, as well as various sites of interest along the way. Many travellers, and organised tours in particular, rush along this smoothly surfaced road in their haste to reach the more lauded attractions of the Congolese border area, and certainly there is no reason to dally should you be pressed for time.

Equally, if there is no urgency to your travels, there are several places of interest between Kampala and Masaka, including the underrated Mpanga Forest and Lake Nabugabo. A more popular tourist draw in the region is the Ssese Islands, which – with its jungle-fringed tropical beaches, affordable lodgings and wonderfully relaxed atmosphere – has achieved something close to legendary status as a budget chill-out venue to rival Lamu in Kenya or Cape Maclear in Malawi.

Between Masaka and Mbarara, Lake Mburo National Park offers the best game viewing in the area – crocodiles and hippos in the lake, a surprising diversity of antelopes and other terrestrial herbivores, as well as a wealth of water- and acacia-associated birds. More esoteric, perhaps, but well suited to those who enjoy viewing game on foot, the remote but accessible Katonga Wildlife Reserve to the north of Mbarara is thinly populated by some 40 mammal species, and one of the best places in East Africa to see the shy aquatic sitatunga antelope.

MPANGA FOREST RESERVE

The 45km² Mpanga Forest Reserve, which lies near the small town of Mpigi, roughly 36km from Kampala along the Masaka road, makes for a fabulous rustic alternative to staying in the capital. The reserve protects an extensive patch of medium-altitude rainforest, characteristic of the vegetation that once extended over much of the northern Lake Victoria hinterland, but has largely been cleared over the past century due to human activity. The forest reserve was gazetted in the 1950s and is criss-crossed by an extensive network of wide footpaths, initially made by researchers, but now open to the public.

Mpanga harbours a less diverse fauna than the larger forests in the far west of Uganda, but there is still plenty to see, and its accessibility and proximity to Kampala provide more than enough justification for a visit. The most readily observed mammal is the red-tailed monkey, though bushpig, bushbuck and flying squirrels are also present. Blue-breasted kingfisher, black-and-white casqued hornbill, African pied hornbill, African grey parrot and great blue turaco are among the more striking and conspicuous of the 180-plus bird species recorded. Resident birds with a rather localised distribution elsewhere in Uganda include shining blue kingfisher, spotted greenbul, Uganda woodland warbler, green crombec, Frazer's ant-thrush, grey-green bush shrike, pink-footed puffback and

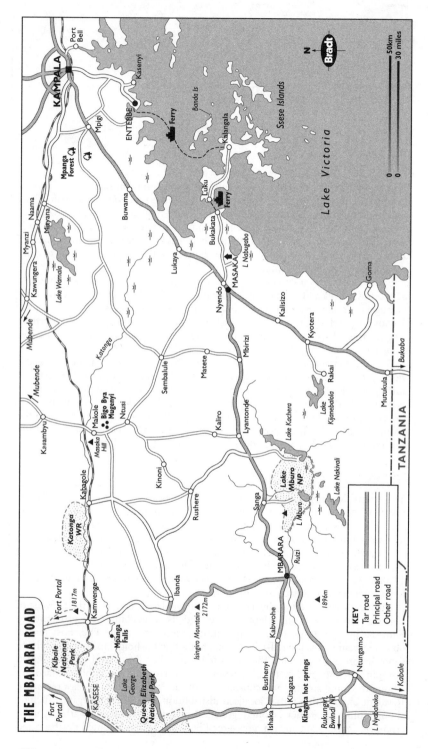

THE MBARARA ROAD

KEY

	Tar road
	Principal road
	Other road

Weyn's weaver. Mpanga Forest is also noted for its butterflies, which are abundant wherever you walk.

An ecotourism centre established in 1999 offers accommodation and forest walks. The NFA is in the process of revising its entrance fees upwards – considerably higher than the visitor-friendly Ush3,000/5,000 previously charged. According to the NFA tariff, residents will pay US$5 and non-residents US$15 for entrance. Both categories will pay an additional US$10 for a guided walk. It remains to be seen whether these prices will be justified by a similarly radical improvement in the presently woeful standard of services on the site.

The excellent and undemanding 3km Base Line Trail follows the main footpath west through the forest, crossing two streams before it emerges at Nakyetema Swamp, where sitatunga and shoebill are resident, though seldom seen. The 5km Hornbill Loop covers more undulating terrain, and involves fording several streams along minor footpaths, passing a striking tree-root arch along the way. For those with limited time, the 1km Butterfly Loop offers a good chance of seeing monkeys and common forest birds as well as a myriad colourful butterflies, and can be completed in less than an hour as can the short and easy Family Trail. Interpretive panels along the latter explore the surprisingly diverse theme of 'Movement in the Forest,' ants, seed dispersal, growth responses and the like.

ALONG THE MASAKA ROAD

Mpanga Forest is the only site along the Kampala–Masaka road that is likely to detain travellers for longer than half an hour. But there are several other points of interest to enliven the roughly two-hour drive. First up, about 2km after passing the turn-off to Mpanga, the road fords an extensive papyrus swamp – stretching all the way to Lake Victoria – in which the shoebill is resident and reportedly sometimes observed from the road. Just before the swamp, the small village of Mpambire, traditional home of the Buganda royal drum-makers, is lined with stalls selling drums (Ush10,000–50,000 apiece, depending on size) and other musical instruments. Even if you're not interested in buying drums, it's interesting to watch the craftsmen at work, and there's no hassle attached to wandering around. Another 5km further towards Masaka, a row of stalls sells colourful baskets and stools of a style not found elsewhere in Uganda.

Roughly 75km out of Kampala, the road crosses the Equator at the trading centre of Nabusanke (literally 'Small Parts'!), marked by a pair of unsightly but much-photographed white circles, and a cluster of good craft stalls and bars. A local entrepreneur has set up buckets and jugs to demonstrate – for a small fee – how water swirls in opposite directions in the northern and southern hemispheres. And if that isn't sufficiently exciting, you could always phone friends or family at home on the MTN payphone (international phonecards accepted) placed strategically along the Equator.

Some 30km before it reaches Masaka, the road from Kampala cuts through Lukaya, a small town fringing a marshy stretch of Lake Victoria, where a tall, bare tree on the roadside supports a substantial colony of pelicans and occasionally herons or storks. Also of ornithological interest is the Nyabajuzzi Ecotourism Project on the western edge of Masaka. Developed with support from Nature Uganda and the UK's RSPB, a raised wooden viewing deck overlooks the Nyabajuzzi papyrus wetland at 'Sitatunga Corner', where the Masaka Bypass meets the feeder road into town. Despite the unprepossessing foreground – the Masaka Water Treatment Plant – the wetland immediately beyond is home to sitatunga, shoebill, rufous-bellied heron, papyrus yellow warbler and other rarities. A mounted telescope is provided and entrance costs Ush2,000 per person.

In addition to forest walks, guided visits can also be arranged to two important Kiganda shrines that lie within walking distance of the forest. Less than 1km from the ecotourism centre, Nakibinge Shrine, dedicated to the eponymous 16th-century king, is housed in a small thatched building in the style of the Kasubi Tombs. The Kibuuka Shrine near Mpigi, 3–4km back along the Kampala road, is dedicated to a god of war who hailed from the Ssese Islands (see box, *Ssese history*, pages 202–3). Beyond the forest, the flat-topped hill south of the main road is worth climbing for the attractive grassland environment and views over the forest and surrounding swamp valleys.

GETTING THERE AND AWAY Mpanga Forest can easily be visited as a day or overnight trip out of Kampala or as a stop-off *en route* to Masaka. Coming from Kampala, about 3km past the turn-off to Mpigi, the road passes through a dip flanked by the southernmost tip of the forest. Immediately past the dip, a signposted turn-off to the right leads to the ecotourism centre after about 500m. Minibus-taxis to Mpigi leave Kampala from the new taxi park and cost Ush2,000. From Mpigi, you can arrange a *boda-boda* to the forest. Alternatively, any minibus or bus heading between Kampala and Masaka can drop you at the turn-off 500m from the ecotourism centre.

WHERE TO STAY

Mpanga Forest Ecotourism Site Tel (NFA Kampala): 0414 230035. Set around a pretty grassy picnic area fringing the forest, this slightly rundown site was improved in 2004 with a new layout, landscaping, new thatched picnic shelters with barbecue units, renovation of the old forest station house and the addition of a lovely elevated, reed-walled, self-contained cottage just inside the forest. The last contains a veranda, double bed, flush toilet and hot shower. With a few hours' notice, simple meals can be arranged for around Ush3,000 and basic foodstuffs can be bought at nearby trading centres on the main road. It is possible that the site may be privatised so these details will change and service may improve. *The present cost of the cottage is US$22 but the revised NFA tariff suggests US$11/14, presumably bearing in mind the entrance fee will impose a surcharge on non-residents of US$15. Bedding, towels, mosquito nets and kerosene lamps are provided. Rooms in the house cost US$6 and camping on the picnic site is available at US$2 pp.*

Homelands Guesthouse Probably the best of a few local hotels in Mpigi. The nearby Continental Restaurant serves good chicken and chips, as well as snacks such as samosas. *US$6 for a clean dbl room.*

WHERE TO TAKE A BREAK

Andy Roberts

It's a long way down the Mbarara road, especially if you're headed further west to Kabale and locations beyond. Fortunately, there are a few decent places providing good refreshments and, just as importantly, decent toilets. First along the way is the AidChild café at the Equator, which is a popular stop with tour groups, and serves tasty coffee and muffins. The setting is a large, round building which displays a variety of high-quality local crafts and artwork. It's not cheap and rather too close to Kampala for a natural break, but the money raised by AidChild goes to a self-explanatory good cause. If you're travelling by bus, you'll have to make do with ambivalent grilled snacks thrust up to your window at Lukaya by vendors all too happy to short-change you. Two hours from the capital, on the Masaka Bypass, the long-established Nyendo Takeaway is close to being an obligatory pull-over by private drivers for a cuppa and a snack, while over the years, thousands of Bwindi-bound tourists have dashed gratefully into the spotless toilets at Mbarara's smart Agip Motel, two hours further down the road, before enjoying the decent and reasonably priced lunch.

In October 1978, Amin ordered his Masaka-based Suicide Battalion and Mbarara-based Simba Battalion to invade Tanzania, under the pretext of pursuing 200 mutineers from his army. In the event, the Ugandan battalions occupied Tanzania's northwestern province of Kagera, and ravaged the countryside in an orgy of rape, theft and destruction that forced about 40,000 peasants to flee from the area.

In retaliation, Tanzania's Julius Nyerere ordered 45,000 Tanzanian troops, supported by the UNLA (a 1,000-strong army of exiled Ugandans), to drive Amin's army out of Kagera, then to create a military buffer zone by capturing the largest Ugandan towns close to the Tanzanian border, Masaka and Mbarara. Masaka was taken with little resistance on 24 February 1979. The outnumbered Suicide Battalion fled to a nearby hilltop, from where they watched helplessly as first the governor's mansion and several other government buildings collapsed under missile fire, then shops and houses were ransacked as the Tanzanian soldiers poured into the town centre.

Two days later, Nyerere achieved his stated aims for the campaign with the capture of Mbarara. But in early March it was announced that Amin would be enlisting the help of 2,500 Libyan and PLO soldiers to recapture Masaka and Mbarara, and possibly launch a counterattack on Tanzanian territory. Nyerere decided to retain the offensive, ordering his troops to prepare to march northeast towards the capital. Meanwhile, Radio Tanzania broadcast details of the fall of Masaka and Mbarara across Uganda, demoralising the troops, and prompting several garrisons to mutiny or desert as it became clear their leader's rule was highly tenuous. On 10 April 1979, the combined Tanzanian and UNLA army marched into Kampala, meeting little resistance along the way. Amin, together with at least 8,000 of his soldiers, was forced into exile.

MASAKA

Masaka, the fourth-largest town in Uganda, is attractively situated among the undulating green hills of the Lake Victoria hinterland. Founded as an Indian trading post c1900, Masaka suffered more than any other town during the 1979 Tanzanian invasion (see box *The sacking of Masaka* above). Despite some rebuilding in recent years, the town centre still has a rather down-at-heel appearance and offers little to excite travellers. The roads remain extensively pot-holed and lined with incomplete construction work, while the scars of battle are visible in the form of several derelict shells of bombed-out buildings along the old Kampala road. Masaka is of interest as the springboard for the main overland route to Bukoba in Tanzania and for the rather closer Lake Nabugabo and Ssese Islands. The town centre is bypassed by the main Kampala–Mbarara road, and also by most traffic heading to locations further west. Perhaps as a lack of exposure to purposeful through traffic, you'll find Masaka's drivers bumbling around the streets at grandmotherly speeds, stopping and starting without warning and creating a traffic chaos out of all proportion to their numbers.

GETTING THERE AND AWAY Masaka lies roughly 140km from Kampala along a good surfaced road. The drive should take about two hours depending on how easily the traffic around Kampala is cleared. Regular minibus-taxis to Masaka leave Kampala from the new taxi park, costing Ush3,500. There is also plenty of road transport from Masaka west to Mbarara: tickets cost Ush4,000. The small town of Nyendo, which lies 2km from Masaka back along the Kampala road, is an

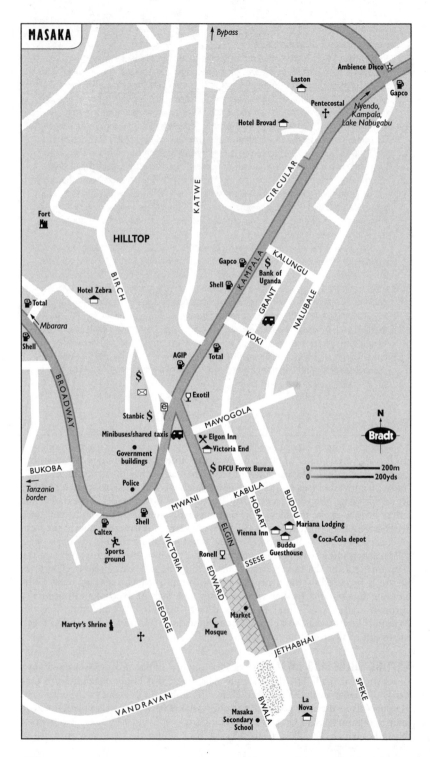

MASAKA

Bypass

Ambience Disco ☆

Laston

Gapco

Pentecostal

Hotel Brovad

Nyendo,
Kampala,
Lake Nabugabu

CIRCULAR

KATWE

Fort

HILLTOP

Gapco

KAMPALA

KALUNGU

Bank of
Uganda

Shell

GRANT

NALUBALE

Hotel Zebra

BIRCH

Total

Mbarara

KOKI

Shell

AGIP

Total

BROADWAY

$

Exotil

✉

Stanbic $

e

MAWOGOLA

N

Bradt

Minibuses/shared taxis

Elgon Inn

Victoria End

BUKOBA

Government
buildings

DFCU Forex Bureau

0   200m
0   200yds

Tanzania
border

Police

KABULA

BUDDU

MWANI

HOBART

Mariana Lodging

Caltex

Shell

Vienna Inn

Coca-Cola depot

Sports
ground

VICTORIA

ELGIN

Ronell

SSESE

Buddu
Guesthouse

GEORGE

EDWARD

Market

Martyr's Shrine

†

Mosque

JETHABHAI

SPEKE

VANDRAVAN

BWALA

La
Nova

Masaka
Secondary
School

important road junction and the place to pick up light vehicles heading towards Ntusi, Lake Nabugabo and the Ssese Islands.

WHERE TO STAY
Moderate

🏠 **Hotel Zebra** \ 04814 20936; e hotelzebra2005@yahoo.com. This new hotel occupies a quite delightful setting on the quieter side of the hill above Masaka town centre. The ground-floor terrace (and, even better, 1st-floor balcony) overlooks a small but pretty garden and green suburbs to the broad wetland of the Nyabajuzzi river valley and green hills. You won't spot a shoebill at this distance but it's by far the loveliest place in town for a drink or meal (items on the ubiquitous upcountry menu cost Ush4,500–6,000). The conifer-lined ridge top just above the hotel is a fine place for a stroll past

some beautifully restored colonial buildings. Unfortunately this aesthetic appreciation does not quite extend to the rather ordinary but fairly priced s/c rooms. *US$19/35 smallish single/dbl B&B.*

🏠 **Hotel Brovad** (75 rooms) \ 04814 21455; m 0772 425666; e hotelbrovad@utlonline.co.ug; www.hotelbrovad.com. The 4-storey Hotel Brovad is easily the smartest in Masaka, and although it lacks the character of the newer Hotel Zebra, its s/c rooms, all with DSTV, are superior and represent good value. Facilities include a restaurant and shopping arcade. *US$24/43/54 sgl/dbl/trpl B&B.*

Budget

🏠 **Laston Hotel** \ 04814 21883; m 0772 800757. Set in leafy suburbia, about 500m from the town centre, the clearly signposted Laston Hotel is a pleasant and friendly set-up, with clean s/c rooms with hot bath and television; there is also an attached restaurant. *US$13/16/22 sgl/dbl/larger dbls.*

🏠 **Hotel La Nova** \ 04814 21520. Also in the suburbs, and similar in standard to the above, the Hotel La Nova has long been the favourite of expatriates and other business travellers to Masaka. However its standing may well be affected by price increases since the 4th edition, though these are apparently 'negotiable.' *US$16/27 s/c sgl/dbl B&B.*

Shoestring

🏠 **Masaka Backpackers' Cottage and Campsite** \ 04814 21288; m 0752 619389; e masakabackpackers@yahoo.com; www.traveluganda/masakabackpackers. Situated 4km out of town, off the road towards Mutukula on the Tanzanian border, this excellent retreat is a great place to relax for a few days, especially if you've just slogged up overland from Tanzania. It boasts a homely atmosphere, enhanced by the large grounds, and the surrounding hills offer some good walking with great views back to Masaka. Tasty and inexpensive food is cooked to order, and there is a well-stocked drinks fridge and a platform bar. Other facilities include a book-swap service and cheap laundry. You could walk here from Masaka, but with a heavy pack you'd be better off picking up a shared taxi (Ush700 pp) or pick-up truck heading towards Kyotera and asking to be dropped at the signposted turn-off, from where it's a 5-min walk to the hostel. *Camping US$3 pp, dormitory bed US$3.50. Rooms with shared facilities US$6/8 sgl/dbl.*

🏠 **Mariana Bar and Lodging** Buddu Rd; m 0772 396544. A clean and friendly guesthouse. All the

rooms are reasonably spacious; those in the courtyard are superior. There's cold running water only, but a bucket of hot water can be supplied on request. *US$6/8 s/c sgl/dbl.*

🏠 **Buddu Guesthouse** m 0772 590989. Situated around the corner from the Mariana, the Buddu Guesthouse also seems friendly and comfortable, and is reasonably priced.*US$8/11 sgl/dbl with hot water.*

🏠 **Victoria End Rest House** Elgin Rd. This grotty guesthouse was the budget traveller's choice for many years before alternative options became available around Buddu Rd. *There's no longer any reason to pay US$6/8 for a rundown, s/c sgl/dbl with shared facilities.*

🏠 **Vienna Guesthouse** m 0782 457450. This smart new hotel stands just uphill from the Buddu Guesthouse. Clean and freshly painted s/c rooms are excellent value, though it's worth asking for a room with an external window rather than one facing into the corridor. Additional facilities include a restaurant/bar, sauna, steam room and massage. *US$8/11 sgl/dbl.*

✕ WHERE TO EAT AND DRINK In addition to the restaurants listed below, good (albeit rather predictable) international cuisine is available at the Hotels Brovad and Zebra, and to a lesser extent the Laston Hotel and Hotel La Nova.

✕ **Elgon Inn Bar and Restaurant** Situated next to the Victoria End Rest House, this serves a good variety of tasty local dishes at affordable prices.

✕ **Ambience Discothèque** The only nightclub in Masaka, this lies on Old Kampala Road about 500m downhill from the town centre.

LISTINGS

Foreign exchange Cash and American Express travellers' cheques can be exchanged at Stanbic bank next to the post office at the bank's national rates.

Shopping The supermarket opposite the Victoria End Rest House on Elgin Road sells a good range of imported foodstuffs, and there are a few other good supermarkets along the same road.

Internet The new building just above Old Kampala Road near the Elgin Road junction is where Masakans surf for news of the world beyond the Bypass. A choice of cafés charge Ush50 per minute.

LAKE NABUGABO

Lake Nabugabo, situated only 20km east of Masaka, formed some 4,000 years ago when a narrow bar of sand accumulated to impound what had formerly been a large, shallow bay on Lake Victoria. Silt accumulation has subsequently reduced the original extent of the open lake fourfold, so that today it covers about 25km^2, fringed on all but the western shore by the extensive Lwamunda Swamp. Despite its relatively recent formation, Nabugabo has a substantially different mineral composition from its larger neighbour: its calcium content, for instance, is insufficient for molluscs to form shells (hence the absence of the freshwater snails that transmit bilharzia). Five of the lake's nine cichlid fish species are endemics that evolved since it became separated from Lake Victoria, one of a handful of comparably recent incidents of speciation known from anywhere in the world.

More popular with Kampala weekenders than with foreign visitors, Nabugabo is nevertheless an excellent place to rest up for a day or two, with its bilharzia-free beaches serviced by two affordable and – on weekdays – tranquil resorts. The forest patches that line the lakeshore, interspersed with grassy clearings and cultivated smallholdings, are rustling with small animals such as tree squirrels, vervet monkeys and monitor lizards, and can easily be explored along several roads and footpaths. Birdlife is prolific, too – look out for broad-billed roller, Ross's turaco, black-and-white casqued hornbill, African fish eagle and a variety of sunbirds and weavers.

GETTING THERE AND AWAY Lake Nabugabo lies about 5km from the good dirt road that runs east from Nyendo (2km east of Masaka) to the Bukakata ferry jetty. The main turn-off out of Nyendo is clearly signposted, but after following it for about 300m, you need to take an unmarked left turn at a crossroads beside a Petro filling station. Roughly 14km out of Nyendo, a side road to the right, signposted for Sand Beach Camp, leads after 5km to the lake and its two resorts. The road is generally in good condition except for the last 5km, and the drive should take about 30–45 minutes in a private vehicle. Travellers driving themselves from Kampala can take a short cut to Lake Nabugabo (and to the Ssese Islands ferry at Bukakata) which leaves the Mbarara highway at a junction signposted for Lake Nabugabo Ramsar

Site. From Kampala, turn left about 7km past the old Road Toll at Lukaya Swamp (1km beyond Mukoko village). After about 12km, you'll reach the Nyendo–Bukakata road. Turn left for the ferry and right towards Masaka for the signposted turning to Sand Beach.

Using public transport, minibuses between Masaka and Nyendo run back and forth every few minutes throughout the day. Transport between Nyendo and Bukakata is rather erratic. You'll probably have to take a shared taxi, and can expect to wait around an hour for a lift. Another option is to catch a bus to Kalangala (on the Ssese Islands); these leave from the main bus station in Masaka at around 14.00 on Mondays, Wednesdays and Fridays, passing through Nyendo a few minutes later, then head on towards Bukakata. Either way, you will need to be dropped at the last junction and – unless you get lucky with a lift – walk the last 5km to the resorts. Another option would be to organise a special hire from Masaka directly to the resort, which should cost around Ush25,000. A *boda-boda* will be significantly cheaper.

⌂ WHERE TO STAY

⌂ **Church of Uganda Resort** m 0772 433332. This long-serving, if now slightly rundown, resort has a friendly atmosphere and a great location in a forested glade on the lakeshore. 2 double cottages are available and 2 family cottages with 4 beds apiece. All cottages have a private sitting room and shower, and are lit by generator from 19.00 until 22.00. If you want to cook for yourself, firewood is available but you must bring all the food you need. Alternatively, meals can be ordered from the restaurant: a heaped plate of fish and chips costs Ush4,000. Sodas and tea and coffee are sold, but no alcohol is available. Canoes can be hired at Ush3,500 per hr. It is advisable to enquire about room availability before you pitch up, either by phoning the number above or through the Masaka Safari Supermarket close to Nyendo taxi park. *US$12/17 for dbl cottages/family cottages (per unit). Camping US$3 per tent, dormitory beds US$4.*

⌂ **Sand Beach Resort** m 0772 802339/416047. More compact and conventionally resort-like than its Church-run neighbour, Sand Beach stands in attractive grassy grounds on a beach overlooking the lake. Accommodation is in a row of spacious good-value s/c rooms with cobbled floor, writing desk, large bed, hot water and a private veranda. There's a cheerful bar with a pool table and a restaurant serving decent meals for around Ush4,000. *US$11/14 sgl/dbl B&B. Camping is permitted at US$3 per private tent or US$6 in a hired double tent.*

THE SSESE ISLANDS

Situated in the northwest of Lake Victoria, the Ssese Islands form one of Uganda's prime destinations for casual rambling and off-the-beaten-track exploration, as well as for game fishing, in particular Nile perch. During the 1990s, the islands were Uganda's most popular backpackers' chill-out destination, at least until the ferry service from Port Bell (Kampala) was suspended in 1997. Inevitably, with access limited to less-than-comfortable 'lake-taxis' from Entebbe and a roundabout approach from Masaka to the Bukakata ferry, the islands lost their place in the hearts of independent travellers, the affection being grabbed by the more accessible Lake Bunyonyi, the site of burgeoning tourist development in recent years. However the Ssese Islands are experiencing a renaissance in tourism activity after nine years of relative isolation, following the inauguration of a superb new European-built passenger/vehicle ferry which cruises between Entebbe and Buggala Island in three easy hours. Drivers and backpackers alike will quickly spot that the new Entebbe ferry and the long-serving bucket ferry can be combined to enable a visit to the Ssese Islands *en route* to/from attractions further down the Masaka road.

The Ssese archipelago consists of 84 separate islands, some large and densely inhabited, others small and deserted, but all lushly forested thanks to an annual

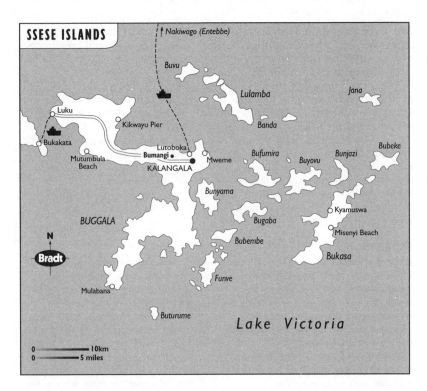

SSESE ISLANDS

Nakiwogo (Entebbe)

Buvu

Lulamba

Jana

Luku

Kikwayu Pier

Banda

Bukakata

Lutoboka

Bufumira

Bubeke

Mutumbula
Beach

Bumangi

Mweme

Buyovu

Bunjazi

KALANGALA

Bunyama

BUGGALA

Bugaba

Kyamuswa

Misenyi Beach

Bubembe

Bukasa

N

Funve

Mulabana

Buturume

Lake Victoria

0 — 10km
0 — 5 miles

Bradt

average rainfall in excess of 2,000mm. Only two islands regularly receive tourists. The more established of these is **Buggala**, the largest, most accessible and most developed of the islands. A significant number of travellers also head to tiny **Banda** Island, which is the site of a popular budget resort. Other islands that can be visited with varying degrees of ease are Bubeke, Bukasa and Bufumira.

Not least amongst the Ssese Islands' attractions are their rustic character and the sense of being well away from any established tourist circuit. But, as in other out-of-the-way places, it is suggested that you dress conservatively except in resort and campsite grounds, and to swim with a T-shirt on. It may also be worth mentioning that the Ssese Islands are reputed to have the highest proportion of HIV infection in Uganda.

BUGGALA ISLAND Extending over 200km² and measuring 43km from east to west, Buggala is the largest island set within the Ugandan waters of Lake Victoria, and the best developed for tourism, linked to the mainland by a regular motor ferry and dotted with accommodation to suit most tastes and budgets. **Kalangala**, the administrative centre for the islands, is an unremarkable small town situated on a ridge at the eastern end of Buggala, while the nearby **Lutoboka Bay** hosts the island's main cluster of beach resorts. Another important landmark on Buggala is **Luku**, the small village on the western extreme of the island where the motor ferry from the mainland docks. A good dirt road connects Luku to Kalangala, and several minor roads run to other villages lying further south on the island.

The most common large mammal on Buggala is the vervet monkey, often seen in the vicinity of Lutoboka and Kalangala. Bushbuck and black-and-white colobus are present but seldom observed. Over the 12,000 years that the island has been separate from the mainland, one endemic creek rat and three endemic butterfly species have evolved. Water and forest birds are prolific. Expect to see a variety of hornbills, barbets, turacos, robin-chats, flycatchers and weavers from the roads around Kalangala. Particularly common are the jewel-like pygmy kingfisher, the brown-throated wattle-eye and a stunning morph of the paradise flycatcher intermediate to the orange and white phases illustrated in most East African field guides. African fish eagles and palmnut vultures are often seen near the lake, while immense breeding colonies of little egret and great cormorant occur on Lutoboka and other bays.

Lutoboka Bay offers a variety of beach activities, building sandcastles, swimming (though bilharizia is certainly a risk; see *Chapter 5, Health*, pages 121–3 for more information) frisbee (bring your own), canoeing and volleyball at some resorts. The road behind the resorts terminating at Mirembe passes through grassland and a beautiful patch of forest which will interest birders. This may be enough for most visitors, but Buggala Island also offers some great possibilities for unstructured walking. Strike out in any direction from Kalangala and you'll be greeted with pleasing views over the forest and grassy clearings to the lakeshore and more distant islands. If you want to explore further afield you can either hike or try to hire a bicycle from Andronica Lodge. A popular cycling excursion is to **Mutumbula swimming beach** – reputedly free of bilharzia – off the road towards Luku. Travellers tend to concentrate on the Kalangala–Luku road, and justifiably so, since the road heading south from Kalangala is far more cultivated. One potentially interesting goal in this direction is the marshy southwestern shores, which harbour small numbers of hippo as well as a population of sitatunga antelope with larger horns than the mainland equivalent, regarded by some authorities to represent an endemic island race. Without a private vehicle, you would probably need to do an overnight walking or cycling trip to get to these swamps.

Getting there and away The brand new MV *Kalangala* ferry service to Lutoboka Port on Buggala Island operates out of Nakiwogo Port on the western side of Entebbe peninsula. To get there in a private vehicle turn off Kampala Road (ie: Entebbe High Street) at the Moneygram office and follow Wilson Road for 3km to the port. Parking is available either at the nearby police post or nearby the Delta fuel station for a small consideration. Those arriving by minibus taxi from Kampala should stay aboard until the trip terminates at the scruffy Kitoro suburb off Airport Road and then take a special hire or *boda-boda* along Nakiwogo Road to the port (again about 3km). The ferry leaves promptly at 14.00, arriving at Lutoboka equally promptly at 15.00. The supposed capacity is just 108 seated passengers (though I've heard reports of standing room only at busy times) and eight vehicles (less if a truck shows up) so foot passengers should turn up 30 minutes before departure and drivers at least an hour. Second-class passage on wooden benches costs Ush10,000 and first class (comfortable padded seats with tables) is Ush14,000. A car or 4x4 vehicle costs Ush50,000. Bottled drinks and snacks are available on board. The ferry overnights at Lutoboka, returning to Nakiwogo from 08.00–11.00. The return to Entebbe ferry can get busy at the end of holiday weekends, and returning drivers are advised to park on the jetty the night before and have a quiet word with the captain.

Other options, indeed the only options prior to the MV *Kalangala* are the (free) Bukakata–Buggala vehicle ferry near Masaka and lake-taxis (local fishing boats) operating from Kasenyi landing near Entebbe (See *Getting around* below). The former runs three times per day in either direction between Kabassese Jetty at Bukakata on the mainland and the island port of Luku. The trip should take around five hours coming from Kampala or two to three hours direct from

The Ssese Islands came into being about 12,000 years ago when a reduced Lake Victoria was refilled at the end of the last Ice Age, forming the lake as we know it today. Little is known about the earliest inhabitants of Ssese, but some oral traditions associated with the creation of Buganda claim that its founder Kintu hailed from the islands, or at least arrived in Buganda via them. The Baganda traditionally revere Ssese as the Islands of the Gods. In pre-colonial times it was customary for the kings of Buganda to visit the islands and pay tribute to the several *balubaale* whose main shrines are situated there. These include shrines to Musisi (spirit of earthquakes) and Wanema (physical handicaps) on Bukasa Island, as well as the shrine to Mukasa, spirit of the lake, on Bubembe. Some Baganda historical sources romanticise this relationship, claiming that in pre-colonial times Ssese, due to its exalted status, was never attacked by Buganda, nor was it formally incorporated into the mainland kingdom. In reality, while Ssese probably did enjoy a degree of autonomy, it was clearly a vassal of Buganda for at least a century prior to the colonial era. Furthermore, while the Baganda revered the islands' spirits, Stanley recorded that they looked down on their human inhabitants for their 'coal-black colour, timidity, superstition, and generally uncleanly life'.

The most popular legend associated with a deity from the Ssese Islands dates from the mid16th-century war, when Buganda, led by King Nakibinge, was being overwhelmed in a war against Bunyoro. Nakibinge visited the islands in search of support, and was offered the assistance of the local king's youngest son, Kibuuka, who leaped to the mainland in one mighty bound to join the war against Bunyoro. Tall and powerful though he was, Kibuuka – which means the flier – was also possessed of a somewhat more singular fighting skill. A deity in human form, he was able to fly high above the clouds and shower down spears on the enemy, who had no idea from where the deadly missiles emanated. Led by Kibuuka's aerial attacks, rout followed rout, and the tide of war reversed swiftly in Nakibinge's favour as the Baganda army proceeded deeper into Banyoro territory.

Although Buganda went on to win the war, Kibuuka didn't survive to enjoy the spoils of victory. After yet another successful battle, the Baganda soldiers captured several Banyoro maidens and gave one to Kibuuka as his mistress. Kibuuka told the Munyoro girl his secret, only to find that she had vanished overnight. The next day, Kibuuka sailed up into the sky as normal, and was greeted by a barrage of Banyoro spears and arrows projected up towards the clouds. Kibuuka fell wounded into a tall tree, where he was spotted the next morning by an elder, who attempted to rescue the wounded fighter, but instead accidentally let him drop to the ground, where he died on impact. The scrotum,

---

Masaka, assuming that your arrival at the jetty coincides with the departure of the ferry. Step one out of Masaka involves following the same directions as given above for Lake Nagubago, but instead of turning right at the junction 14km out of Nyendo, keep going straight for another 25km until you reach the jetty. The ferry, which takes 50 minutes to cross, theoretically leaves from Kabassese at 08.00, 11.00, 14.00 and 17.00 and from Luku at 09.00, 12.00, 15.00 and 18.00 daily except for Sundays when the earliest crossing in each direction is dropped. This timetable is somewhat loosely adhered to, however, making it advisable to be at the jetty a good hour before the scheduled crossing time. The road between Luku and Kalangala is generally in good condition, and can usually be covered in less than one hour, though some stretches might be slippery after heavy rain. Note that the Luku ferry occasionally stops running for a few days while repairs are undertaken, in which case you would have return on the Entebbe ferry.

A reliable **bus service** connects Kampala to Kalangala, leaving the new taxi park in Kampala at 08.00 daily except for Sunday and leaving from Kalangala at 11.00-ish daily except Sunday. Tickets cost Ush8,000.

testes, penis and certain other body parts of the great Ssese warrior – now regarded as the greatest lubaale of war – were preserved in a shrine, where his spirit could be called upon before important battles. The shrine, which lies close to the Mpanga Forest, can still be visited today, as can a nearby shrine to Nakibinge, also revered as a deity on account of his successful campaign against Bunyoro (see *Mpanga Forest Reserve*, pages 191–3). The shrine to Kibuuka was desecrated by the British during the colonial era, and the contents, including his jawbone, are on display in a museum in Cambridge.

The people of Ssese played a more verifiable – albeit less overtly aggressive – role in Baganda expansionism during the second half of the 19th century, when kabakas Suuna and Mutesa regularly dispatched fleets of 300-plus fighting canoes across Lake Victoria to present-day northwestern Tanzania. These military fleets comprised almost entirely canoes built on Ssese, which – by comparison with the simple dugouts used on the mainland – were highly sophisticated in design, constructed with several pieces of interlocking timber, and boasting an extended prow that could be used to batter other boats. Speke described one such fleet as follows: 'some fifty large [boats]... all painted with red clay, and averaged from ten to thirty paddles, with long prows standing out like the neck of a siphon or swan, decorated on the head with the horns of the Nsunnu [kob] antelope, between which was stuck upright a tuft of feathers exactly like a grenadier's plume.' The islanders were also more skilled oarsmen and navigators than their landlubber Baganda neighbours, and although they played no role in the fighting, it was they who generally powered and directed the war fleets.

The demands of the Buganda military became a heavy drain on the Ssese economy in the late 19th century. In 1898, the islanders petitioned the British governor, complaining that they were 'regarded in Uganda as being inferior and subordinate to that country' and that the 'severe strain upon the island labour resources [was] so serious as to endanger the canoe service, now so essential with the increasing demands on the Victoria Nyanza lake transport'. In 1900, an agreement between Buganda and Britain placed Ssese and nine other formerly autonomous counties under the full jurisdiction of Buganda. Over the next ten years, Ssese was hit by a sleeping sickness epidemic that claimed thousands of lives annually, forcing the government to relocate 25,000 islanders to the mainland. Resettlement of Ssese was gradual, and it is largely due to the sleeping sickness epidemic that the islands' total population is today estimated at fewer than 20,000, and so much of the land remains uncultivated.

Where to stay

Moderate The first four options described below are all found within a 15-min walk along the sandy Lutoboka Bay beach and are described in order of proximity to the new ferry landing. The final option, Palm Resort Beach, is comparatively isolated on a separate beach on the peninsula south of the port.

Pearl Gardens Beach m 0772 372164; e reservations@pearlgardensbeach.com; www.pearlgardensbeach.com. This new facility lies just metres from the ferry. Its beachfront cottages lack much character but compared with other options in this category on the same beach are affordably priced. A bar/reception at the top of the site provides DSTV and free internet for residents. On the downside, the peaceful atmosphere traditionally associated with the Ssese Islands can be shattered by private beach parties on long weekends. During a 2-night stay next door at Hornbill Campsite we were kept awake by a noisy and interminable corporate booze-up complete with a karaoke machine. When booking a weekend stay anywhere on Lutoboka Bay it's perhaps worth asking whether Pearl Gardens has anything planned! *US$22/32 sgl/dbl bed only, US$32/54 sgl/dbl FB.*

Ssese Islands Beach Hotel 0414 220065; m 0772 505098;

Known to the Baganda as Nalubaale – Home of the Spirit – Lake Victoria is the world's second-largest freshwater body, set in a shallow basin with a diameter of roughly 250km on an elevated plateau separating the eastern and western forks of the Great Rift Valley, and shared between Tanzania, Uganda and Kenya. The environmental degradation of the lake began in the early colonial era, when the indigenous lakeshore vegetation was cleared and swamps were drained to make way for plantations of tea, coffee and sugar. This increased the amount of topsoil washed into the lake, with the result that its water became progressively muddier and murkier. A more serious effect was the wash-off of toxic pesticides and other agricultural chemicals whose nutrients promote algae growth, and as a result a decrease in oxygenation. The foundation of several lakeshore cities and plantations also attracted migrant labourers from around the region, leading to a rapid increase in population and – exacerbated by more sophisticated trapping tools introduced by the colonials – heavy overfishing.

By the early 1950s, the above factors had conspired to create a noticeable drop in yields of popular indigenous fish, in particular the Lake Victoria tilapia (ngege), which had been fished close to extinction. The colonial authorities introduced the similar Nile tilapia, which restored the diminishing yield without seriously affecting the ecological balance of the lake. More disastrous, however, was the gradual infiltration of the Nile perch, a voracious predator that feeds almost exclusively on smaller fish, and frequently reaches a length of 2m and a weight exceeding 100kg. How the perch initially ended up in Lake Victoria is a matter of conjecture, but they regularly turned up in fishermen's nets from the late 1950s. The authorities, who favoured large eating fish over the smaller tilapia and cichlids, decided to ensure the survival of the alien predators with an active programme of introductions in the early 1960s.

It would be 20 years before the full impact of this misguided policy hit home. In a UN survey undertaken in 1971, the indigenous haplochromine cichlids still constituted their traditional 80% of the lake's fish biomass, while the introduced perch and tilapia had effectively displaced the indigenous tilapia without otherwise altering the ecology of the lake. A similar survey undertaken ten years later revealed that the perch population had exploded to constitute 80% of the lake's fish biomass, while the haplochromine cichlids – the favoured prey of the perch – now accounted for a mere 1%. Lake Victoria's estimated 150–300 endemic cichlid species, all of which have evolved from a mere five ancestral species since the lake dried out 10,000–15,000 years ago, are regarded to represent the most recent comparable explosion of vertebrate-adaptive radiation in the world. In simple terms, this is when a large number of species evolve from a limited ancestral stock in a short space of time, in this instance due to the lake having formed rapidly to create all sorts of new niches. Ironically, these fish also are currently undergoing what Boston University's Les Kauffman has described as 'the greatest vertebrate mass extinction in recorded history'.

For all this, the introduction of perch could be considered a superficial success within its own terms. The perch now form the basis of the lake's thriving fishing industry, with up to 500 metric tonnes of fish meat being exported from the lake annually, at a value of more than US$300 million, by commercial fishing concerns in the three lakeshore countries. The tanned perch hide is used as a substitute for leather to make shoes, belts, and purses, and the dried swim bladders, used to filter beer and make fish stock, are exported at a rate

e sibh @ sseseislandsbeachhotel.com; www.sseseislandsbeachhotel.com. This smart and under-utilised new hotel consists of a string of white cottages running along a sandy, forest-fringed beach on Lutoboka Bay, roughly 2km from Kalangala Town and 15 mins' walk up the beach from the ferry landing. Game fishing and other boat excursions can be arranged, along with guided forest walks and

of around US$10 per kg. The flip side of this is that as fish exports increase, local fishing communities are forced to compete against large commercial companies with better equipment and more economic clout. Furthermore, since the perch is too large to roast on a fire and too fatty to dry in the sun, it does not really meet local needs.

The introduction of perch is not the only damaging factor to have affected Lake Victoria's ecology. It is estimated that the amount of agricultural chemicals being washed into the lake has more than doubled since the 1950s. Tanzania alone is currently pumping two million litres of untreated sewage and industrial waste into the lake daily, and while legal controls on industrial dumping are tighter in Kenya and Uganda, they are not effectively enforced. The agricultural wash-off and industrial dumping has led to a further increase in the volume of chemical nutrients in the lake, promoting the growth of plankton and algae. At the same time, the cichlids that once fed on these microscopic organisms have been severely depleted in number by the predatorial perch.

The lake's algae levels have increased fivefold in the last four decades, with a corresponding decrease in oxygen levels. The lower level of the lake now consists of dead water – lacking any oxygenation or fish activity below about 30m – and the quality of the water closer to the surface has deteriorated markedly since the 1960s. Long-term residents of the Mwanza area say that the water was once so clear that you could see the lake floor; from the surface to depths of 6m or more. Today visibility near the surface is more like 1m.

A clear indicator of this deterioration has been the rapid spread of water hyacinth, which thrives in polluted conditions leading to high phosphate and nitrogen levels, and then tends to further deplete oxygen levels by forming an impenetrable mat over the water's surface. An exotic South American species, unknown on the lake prior to 1989, the water hyacinth has subsequently colonised vast tracts of the lake surface, and clogged up several harbours. To complete this grim vicious circle, Nile perch, arguably the main cause of the problem, are known to be vulnerable to the conditions created by hyacinth matting, high algae levels and decreased oxygenation in the water. On a positive note, hyacinth infestation on the Ugandan waters of Lake Victoria has decreased markedly since 1998. But a new threat to the lake's welfare has emerged with the recent opening of a major Tanzanian gold mine less than 20km from the lakeshore, a location that carries a genuine risk of sodium cyanide, used in the processing of gold, finding its way into Lake Victoria.

As is so often the case with ecological issues, what might at first be dismissed by some as an esoteric concern for bunny-huggers in fact has wider implications for the estimated 20–30 million people resident in the Lake Victoria basin. The infestation of hyacinth and rapid decrease in indigenous snail-eating fish has led to a rapid growth in the number of bilharzia-carrying snails. The deterioration in water quality, exacerbated by the pumping of sewage, has increased the risk of sanitary-related diseases such as cholera spreading around the lake. The change in the fish biomass has encouraged commercial fishing for export outside of the region, in the process depressing the local semi-subsistence fishing economy, leading to an increase in unemployment and protein deficiency. And there is an ever-growing risk that Africa's largest lake will eventually be reduced to a vast expanse of dead water, with no fish in it at all – and ecological, economic and humanitarian ramifications that scarcely bear thinking about.

birdwatching trips. Facilities include a swimming beach, pool table, beach volleyball, a bar with DSTV, and a restaurant serving reasonable meals for around Ush5,000. There is accommodation in s/c cottages with solar lighting and running hot water, and a rather bare dormitory, set on a hill some distance from the beach, a less alluring prospect. Camping is permitted. *US$38/65 sgl/dbl FB, dormitory US$3.50 pp.*

Ssese Island Club ✆ 0414 250757; m 0772 641376; e islandsclub@hotmail.com. About 300m along the beach from the Beach Hotel, the Ssese Island Club provides comfortable s/c wooden chalets or standing tents between the lake and enclosing forest. Full-day fishing excursions on motorised boats cost Ush200,000 for up to 4 people, while full-day bird walks cost the same for up to 6 people. *US$43/65 sgl/dbl FB.*

Mirembe Resort e miremberesortb@yahoo.com. Set in a quiet location at the northern end of the beach, this new resort provides attractive s/c rooms with a lake view. *US$27 pp FB.*

Ssese Palm Beach Resort ✆ 0414 254435; m 0772 503315; e ssese_2001@yahoo.com. Standing at the southern end of Lutoboka Bay, the round thatched cottages of Palm Beach with their forest backdrop are a picturesque sight as the ferry steams into port. Unfortunately, this visibility is enabled by extensive clearance within the resort grounds which detracts from their natural aesthetics when seen closer up, while the cottages and 'half cottages', identically sized structures divided into 2 rather cramped halves, are set rather too far back for a great lake view. It's better value opting for the bed only rate and purchasing your own meals – ideally elsewhere since the food by all accounts is poor (though being located on the southern tip of the beach, it's a bit of a hike to the culinary safety net offered by Hornbill Camp). *US$43/33 cottage/'half cottage' pp FB, US$16/11 respectively bed only.*

Budget

Panorama Lodge Situated in a forest clearing 500m inland from the ferry landing, this friendly lodge lacks a beachfront location, but has an attractive garden setting and a forest backdrop. Clean and spacious s/c chalets with solar lighting (hot water supplied on request) are good value. A bar and restaurant is provided. *US$16–21.*

Shoestring and camping

Hornbill Camping Site m 0772 729478; e loek.verburg@bigfoot.com; www.hornbillcamp.com. This admirably mellow Dutch-owned campsite lies in secluded lakeshore grounds, teeming with birds, most vociferously various colonial weavers and flocks of raucous black-and-white casqued hornbill. The lovely setting, relaxed atmosphere and good inexpensive food ensure that Hornbill is one of the best campsites anywhere in Uganda. Rather less attractive are the wooden dormitory and tiny bandas – far inferior to the accommodation at Panorama Lodge. The camp also rents out kayaks (Ush3,000 per hr), canoes (Ush2,000 per hour) and a motorboat carrying up to 25 (Ush40,000 per hour); lifejackets are available. Meals and snacks are available (see *Where to eat* below) favourites being the giant fish samosas (Ush3,000) and pancakes. *Camping US$2.70 pp; for tent hire, add US$3.20 per night. Dormitory US$4 pp, bandas US$11 dbl.*

PTA Andronica Lodge This long-established lodge in its ancient building is owned and presided over by a former schoolteacher and provides the only accommodation in Kalangala Town. It's the best place to overnight should you arrive after dark and not want to walk the 2km downhill to Lutoboka. PTA is certainly not lacking in character with its dominant green-and-white colour scheme and potted plants everywhere (even extending inside the latrine) but, despite recent improvements, remains a no-frills option. There's no food provided but simple meals are served in a separate *hoteli* at the front of the building. Bicycles are available for hire. *Rooms US$3 pp with shared facilities.*

Kalaya Guesthouse This Christian-oriented facility stands on an open hillside on the Mweena road about 1km out of Kalangala (take the left fork just beyond the town). It's notable for the elevated panorama looking east over the archipelago, perfect for the sunrise and full moon sky. Solar power is provided and meals are available but no alcohol is sold. However you can bring your own poison for your interpretation of a sunrise breakfast (as some have done). *A variety of rooms, some s/c, cost Ush10,000–25,000.*

Ssese Scorpion Lodge Situated at Luku, about 10 mins' walk from the ferry jetty pier along the Kalangala Roaad. Meals are served. *Rooms US$4, camping US$2 pp.*

✗ **Where to eat** It's fair to say that the Ssese Island resorts are not famed for their cooking. Nevertheless all of the resorts provide reasonably priced Ugandan and international meals (Ush5,000–8,000), albeit from limited menus on which fish, not surprisingly, features prominently. Fresh market produce in local markets is limited and expensive compared with the mainland. Meals must usually be ordered in advance; even so, service can be astonishingly slow and it is simply best to resign yourself to the pace of island life. The exception is the evening meal at **Hornbill Campsite** which is dished up at 20.00 sharpish. Though inevitably conforming to the fishy theme, a filling set meal (Ush6,000) is served to a communal table of pre-booked diners, invariably added to by 'refugees' from the other resorts.

OTHER ISLANDS The second-largest landmass in Ssese is **Bukasa Island**, which lies on the eastern end of the archipelago and is widely regarded by the few travellers who make it there to be even more attractive than Buggala. Extensively forested, the island supports a profusion of birds and monkeys, and can be explored on foot along a network of fair roads. Individual points of interest include an attractive beach at Misenyi Bay, 20 minutes' walk from Agnes's Guest House, and a plunge-pool ringed by forest and a waterfall, about one hour's walk from the guesthouse. For monkeys and views, the road to Rwanabatya Village has been recommended.

Also infrequently visited by travellers, **Bufumira Island** is readily accessible by fishing boat from Buggala, and there is a small guesthouse in its largest village Semawundu, though you are advised to bring all food with you. Far more popular is the small **Banda Island**, site of a backpacker resort that has become something of a legend among travellers in the last few years. Several other small, mostly uninhabited islands can be reached by fishing boat as day trips from Buggala.

Getting around The only public transport servicing islands other than Buggala are **motorised lake-taxis,** which link most of the larger inhabited islands daily, except on Sundays. These lake-taxis leave the mainland from Kasenyi, a fishing village which lies close to Entebbe and is connected to Kampala by a regular minibus-taxi service from the old taxi park, and sail to Banda, Bufumira and Bukasa islands as well as Buggala. Boats to Banda leave Kasenyi at around 15.00, arriving three hours later and cost Ush5,000 one way (see *Where to stay* below for additional options). The risk attached to using these lake-taxis should not be underestimated, particularly during the rainy season, when overloaded boats have a tendency to capsize during stormy weather, killing up to 100 people annually. Rather than relying on lifejackets being provided (though they increasingly are), I generally purchase a plastic jerrycan (top screwed on tight) and secure it to myself with a piece of rope. Kasenyi is a rather grotty place whose operatives are famous for overcharging and being generally annoying, and some time will usually elapse between booking your passage and your boat being considered full enough to leave, so it's best to wait it out at Kasenyi Takeaway where the formidable Mama Grace will protect you from sunburn and hassle.

Where to stay

Banda Island Resort m 0772 446669/222777; e banda_island@inorbit.com or bandaisland@2die4.com. In recent years, the laidback Banda Island Resort was the most popular budget hangout in the Ssese Islands, raved about by most who visit it, equally reviled by a few, depending almost entirely on whether they get on with the eccentric Kenyan *muzungu* owner-manager. Indeed Banda is somewhat similar to the Kenyan coast in that it's all too easy to stay 'just one more

day'. However the new Buggala Island ferry, being infinitely preferable to the lake-taxis, means that the budget traveller's most convenient island retreat is now Hornbill Camp and Banda is increasingly sidelined. Nevertheless, the legend lives on and a significant number of Hornbill clients form groups to charter the campsite's boat for the hour-long voyage to Banda at a shared cost of Ush80,000 return. Hornbill's Dutch owner (obligingly it must be said) will phone through to book lunch and pilot the boat himself. Banda's remote location and discreet forest setting attractively complements Lutoboka's expansive and relatively busy beaches and passengers moved to jump ship can stay in decidedly basic stone cottages inclusive of all (inevitably fish-based) meals (and other fresh produce). From Banda you can complete a loop through the islands by returning to Kasenyi by lake-taxi. It must be said that this itinerary, which limits your Kasenyi experience to landing and leaving is infinitely preferable to embarking from there. Prospective visitors are asked to ring or SMS the above numbers to give advance notice of their arrival. *Cottages US$16 pp daily.*

Bukasa Island

🏠 **Agnes's Guesthouse** Situated a short walk from the ferry pier in Bukasa Island, this basic but friendly and relaxed guesthouse has a veranda overlooking the lake, spectacular at sunset. You can camp for US$2 or take a room for US$4 per person. Meals are served, but it is a good idea to bring some food with you (wheat flour, margarine, garlic and sugar will be particularly appreciated).

🏠 **Father Christopher's Guesthouse** 30 mins' walk from the ferry jetty on Bukasa Island, this newer guesthouse also charges US$4 per person for a room and US$1.50 per person to camp. There is a kitchen, but you will need to bring food with you. Father Christopher is a good source of advice about walks on the island.

LAKE MBURO NATIONAL PARK

One of Uganda's smaller national parks, Lake Mburo extends over 260km^2 of undulating territory with an altitude range from 1,220m to 1,828m above sea level. The annual rainfall figure of around 800mm is relatively low, but roughly 20% of the park's surface area nevertheless consists of wetland habitats. The most important of these is Lake Mburo itself, the largest of five lakes that lie within the park boundaries, and part of a cluster of 14 lakes that are fed by the Rwizi River and connected by several permanent and seasonal swamps. The remainder of the park mainly consists of open savanna and acacia woodland, with some of the more common trees being *Acacia hockii, Acacia gerrardii, Acacia sieberiana* and *Acacia polycantha*. In the western part of the park, the savanna is interspersed with rocky ridges and forested gorges, while patches of papyrus swamp and narrow bands of lush riparian woodland line the verges of the various lakes.

Lake Mburo is an underrated gem of a park, dominated by the eponymous lake, which – with its forest-fringed shores hemmed in by rolling green hills – is scenically reminiscent of the more celebrated Lake Naivasha in the Kenyan Rift Valley. That the park is bypassed by the majority of safaris and independent travellers, despite its relative accessibility, is presumably down to the low 'big five' count, in particular the lack of elephant and lion, the latter not reliably observed in the area for several years now. Even in the absence of such heavyweights, however, Lake Mburo offers some excellent game viewing, and you're as likely to see as many different large mammal species over the course of a day as would be the case in any other Ugandan national park. More pragmatically, Lake Mburo is also ideally positioned to break up the long drive between Kampala and the national parks along the country's western border.

Lake Mburo harbours several species not easily observed elsewhere in Uganda. It is the only reserve in the country to support a population of impala, the handsome antelope for which Kampala is named, and one of only three protected areas countrywide where Burchell's zebra occurs, the other two being the far less accessible Kidepo and Pian-Upe. Other antelope species likely to be seen by casual visitors are topi, bushbuck, common duiker, oribi, Defassa waterbuck and Bohor reedbuck, while the lake and lush fringing vegetation support healthy populations of buffalo, warthog, bushpig and hippopotamus. Roan antelope, once common, are now locally extinct, but large herds of the majestic eland still move seasonally

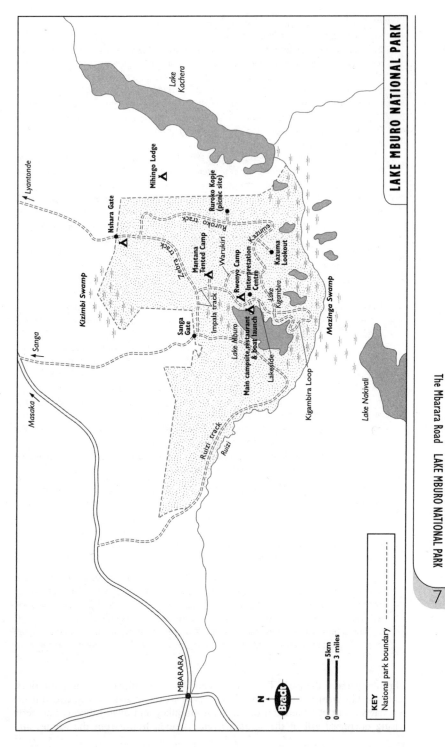

LAKE MBURO NATIONAL PARK

KEY
National park boundary

Many centuries ago, according to oral tradition, the valley in which Lake Mburo stands today was dry agricultural land, worked by a pair of brothers named Kigarama and Mburo. One night, Kigarama dreamed that he and his brother would be in danger unless they moved to higher land. The next morning, as Kigarama prepared to relocate to the surrounding hills, he shared the warning with Mburo, who shrugged it off and decided to stay put. Within days, the valley was submerged, and Kigarama watched on helplessly from the hills as his younger brother drowned. The lake was named for the unfortunate Mburo and the surrounding hills after Kigarama.

In pre-colonial times, the area around Lake Mburo, known as Nshara and referred to by Bahima pastoralists as Karo Karungyi (literally 'good grazing land'), was probably rather thinly populated. Pastoralist settlement would have been inhibited by the periodic prevalence of *Glossina morsitans*, a species of tsetse fly that transmits a strain of trypanosome harmless to wild animals and humans, but fatal to domestic cattle. Furthermore, the omugabe of Ankole favoured Nshara as a royal hunting ground, and forbade the Bahima from grazing and watering their cattle there except during times of drought.

In the early 1890s, Mburo – like the rest of Ankole – was hit severely by the rinderpest epidemic that swept through East Africa, and the resultant depletion of livestock precipitated a famine that claimed thousands of human lives. The decreased grazing pressure also led to widespread bush regeneration, paving the way for a devastating tsetse fly outbreak c1910. Those pastoralists who had resettled the Mburo area were forced to relocate their herds to the more arid savanna of Nyabushozi, north of the present-day Kampala–Mbarara road.

In 1935, the colonial government set aside the vast tract of largely depopulated land centred on Mburo as a Controlled Hunting Area in which both regulated hunting and traditional human activities were permitted. Ten years later, another tsetse outbreak – this time not only *G. morsitans*, but also *G. palpalis*, which spreads sleeping sickness to humans – forced the pastoralists out of the Mburo area. As a result, the colonial authorities instituted a radical programme to eradicate the tsetse from Ankole in the 1950s – its premise being that if every last wild animal in the area were killed, then the bloodsucking tsetse would surely be starved to extinction.

Brian Herne includes a scathing account of this first phase of the anti-tsetse campaign in his book *African Safaris* (see *Appendix 3, Further Information*, page 476):

> They employed vast teams of African hunters with shot-bolt rifles… with orders to shoot every single animal, irrespective of age or sex. Everything was to be exterminated. We watched in horror and anger. They did slaughter everything they could… anything and everything that crossed their gunsights. The wildlife was decimated almost out of existence… after the grass fires in July, the plains were richly scattered with bleached skeletons and gaunt sun-dried carcasses.

According to Herne, the 'wondrous final solution had proved a disastrous and expensive bloodbath… It is of course almost possible to kill off entire populations but some stock always survives, especially of more elusive animals like duiker and bushbuck. Of course, some did survive – enough to ensure the survival of the tsetse fly!'

The authorities reasoned that if it was not possible to starve the tsetse to death, then the only solution was to eradicate the shady bushes and trees around which it lived.

through parts of the park. The sitatunga antelope is confined to swamp interiors, and the klipspringer is occasionally observed in rocky areas. Only two diurnal primates occur at Lake Mburo: the vervet monkey and olive baboon. The eerie rising nocturnal call of the spotted hyena is often heard from the camps, and

Hundreds of square kilometres of bush around Mburo were stripped, cut and/or burned, until barely any trees were left. After the first rains fell, however, a dense cover of secondary undergrowth quickly established itself, offering adequate cover for tsetse flies to survive, Herne wrote, 'voracious and hungry and as indiscriminate in their hunger as ever'. Over the next season, the authorities implemented a new campaign, aimed directly at the tsetse, employing teams of locals to spray every inch of Ankole with insecticide. This final phase did result in the virtual elimination of the tsetse, but at considerable ecological cost, since it also took its toll on almost every other insect species, as well as insectivorous birds and small mammals.

In the early 1960s, with tsetse-borne diseases all but eradicated, Bahima pastoralists flocked back to the controlled hunting area. It soon became clear that, were any wildlife to survive, the resettlement of Mburo would need to be regulated. In 1964, the first Obote government de-gazetted a large portion of the controlled hunting area to make way for subsistence farmers and herders, while the remainder was upgraded to become the Lake Mburo Game Reserve. Pastoralists were granted transit and dry-season watering rights to the newly gazetted reserve, but were forbidden from residing within it.

This stasis was undermined in the 1970s, after some 650km² of gazetted land were excised to become a state cattle ranch. Conservation activities in what remained of the game reserve practically ceased, allowing for considerable human encroachment along the borders. The volume of wildlife, largely recovered from the anti-tsetse slaughter 20 years earlier, was again severely depleted, this time as a result of subsistence poaching. The park's lions – unpopular with local herders not only because they occasionally hunted cattle, but also for their long-standing reputation as man-eaters (one particularly voracious male reputedly accounted for more than 80 human lives in the 1960s) – were hunted to local extinction.

In 1983, the second Obote government gazetted Lake Mburo as a national park, following the boundaries of the original game reserve and forcibly evicting some 4,500 families without compensation. As a result, local communities tended to view the park somewhat negatively – a waste of an important traditional resource from which they had been wrongly excluded. As the civil war reached its peak in 1986, Lake Mburo was almost wholly resettled, its facilities and infrastructure were destroyed, and subsistence poaching once again reached critical levels. In 1987, the Museveni government agreed to reduce the area of the national park by 60%, and it allowed a limited number of people to live within the park and fish on the lake, but still tensions between the park and surrounding communities remained high.

The turning point in Mburo's fractious history came in 1991, with the creation of a pioneering Mburo Community Conservation Unit, established with the assistance of the Africa Wildlife Foundation. A community representative was appointed for each of the neighbouring parishes, to be consulted with regard to decisions affecting the future of the park, and to air any local grievances directly with the park management. Between 1991 and 1997, the remaining inhabitants of the park were relocated outside its borders and awarded a negotiated sum as compensation. Since 1995, 20% of the revenue raised by park entrance fees has been used to fund the construction of local clinics and schools, and for other community projects.

individuals are less frequently observed crossing the road shortly after dawn. Leopard, side-striped jackal and various smaller predators are also present, most visibly white-tailed mongoose (at dusk and dawn) and three otter species resident in the lakes. The lions for which Lake Mburo was famed in the 1960s were hunted to local extinction by the late 1970s and their present status is uncertain. One rather skittish pride, thought to have migrated from Akagera National Park in Rwanda, was observed sporadically over 1997–99, but I'm not aware of any more recent sightings.

Some 315 species of bird have been recorded in Lake Mburo National Park. It is probably the best place in Uganda to see acacia-associated birds, and Rwonyo Camp is as good a place as any to look for the likes of mosque swallow, black-bellied bustard, bare-faced go-away bird and Ruppell's long-tailed starling. A handful of birds recorded at Lake Mburo are essentially southern species at the very northern limit of their range, for instance the southern ground hornbill, black-collared and black-throated barbets, and green-capped eremomela. Of special interest to birders are the swamps, in which six papyrus endemics are resident, including the brilliantly coloured papyrus gonolek, the striking blue-headed coucal, and the highly localised white-winged and papyrus yellow warblers, the last recorded nowhere else in Uganda.

The superb 72-page *Lake Mburo National Park Guidebook*, published by the African Wildlife Foundation in 1994, contains complete bird and mammal checklists, as well as detailed ecological information and coverage of all roads within the park. When I last visited Lake Mburo, the booklet was unavailable at the gate and camp, so it's advisable to try to buy a copy in advance from the UWA headquarters in Kampala or the East African Wildlife Society office in the National Museum building. If you can't locate the booklet, a useful map is normally available at the entrance gate.

Non-residents pay a visitation fee of US$25/35/50 for one/two/three or more nights. East African residents pay discounted rates of US$15/20/25 on production of proof of residency. An entrance permit is valid for 24 hours from time of entrance. The standard vehicle entry fees are levied.

GETTING THERE AND AWAY Two different roads connect Lake Mburo National Park to the main surfaced road between Masaka and Mbarara. Coming from the west, the better approach road branches south at Sanga, 37km east of Mbarara. Coming from Kampala, it's easier to use the road branching south from the 50km marker for Mbarara, about 20km past Lyantonde. The drive from Kampala should take about four to five hours, not allowing for breaks. The approach roads are both quite rough, so a 4x4 vehicle is recommended, though not essential during the dry season, and either way you're looking at about an hour's drive between the main road and the rest camp.

There is no public transport along either of the approach roads, but it is possible to charter a special hire from Sanga (expect to pay something in excess of Ush30,000) or pick up a *boda-boda* (around Ush15,000). Another option is to ask the UWA headquarters in Kampala to radio through a day in advance to find out whether any park vehicle will be going to Mbarara, in which case you could wait for it at Sanga.

WHERE TO STAY
Upmarket
Kimbla-Mantana Tented Camp ✆ 0414 321552; m 0772 525736 or 401391; f 0414 320152; e mantana@africaonline.co.ug; www.kimbla-mantana.com. This is a classic luxury tented camp, offering a genuine bush experience in 8 secluded and fully furnished s/c tents on raised timber decks, all with solar lighting, eco-friendly toilet and private veranda. The camp runs along a thickly wooded ridge, which is rattling with birds, lizards and other small animals, and it offers great views across to the lake, as well as some fabulous nocturnal stargazing. The open-sided dining tent serves good full breakfasts, 3-course lunches and 5-course dinners. The tented camp lies off Impala Track along

From mountain gorillas to lions, from elephants to shoebills, Uganda is blessed with more than its fair share of impressive wild beasties. But it is also the major stronghold for what is unquestionably the most imposing of Africa's domestic creatures: the remarkable long-horned breed of cattle associated with various pastoralist peoples of the Ugandan–Tanzanian–Rwandan border area, but most specifically with the Bahima of Ankole.

Ankole cattle come in several colours, ranging from uniform rusty-yellow to blotched black-and-white, but they always have a long head, short neck, deep dewlap and narrow chest, and the male often sports a large thoracic hump. What most distinguish the Ankole cattle from any familiar breed, however, are their preposterous, monstrous horns, which grow out from either side of the head like inverted elephant tusks and, in exceptional instances, reach dimensions unseen on any Ugandan tusker since the commercial ivory poaching outbreak of the 1980s.

The ancestry of the Ankole cattle has been traced back to Eurasia as early as 15,000BC, but the precursors of the modern long-horned variety were introduced to northern Uganda only in late medieval times. Hardy, and capable of subsisting on limited water and poor grazing, these introduced cattle were ideally suited to harsh African conditions, except that they had no immunity to tsetse-borne diseases, which forced the pastoralists who tended them to kept drifting southward. The outsized horns of the modern Ankole cattle are probably a result of selective breeding subsequent to their ancestors' arrival in southern Uganda about 500 years ago. The Bahima value cows less for their individual productivity than as status symbols: the wealth of a man would be measured by the size and quality of his herd, and the worth of an individual cow by its horn size and, to a lesser extent, its coloration.

Traditionally, Bahima culture was as deeply bound up with its almost mystical relationship to cattle as the lifestyle of the Maasai is today. Like Eskimos and their physical landscape, the abiding mental preoccupation of the Bahima is reflected in the 30 variations in hide coloration that are recognised linguistically – the most valued being the uniform dark-brown *bihogo* – along with at least a dozen peculiarities of horn shape and size. The Bahima day is traditionally divided up into 20 periods, of which all but one of the daylight phases is named after an associated cattle-related activity. And, like the Maasai, the Bahima traditionally regarded any activity other than cattle herding as beneath contempt. They also declined to hunt game for meat, with the exception of buffalo and eland, which were sufficiently bovine in appearance for acceptable eating.

In times past, the Bahima diet did not, as might be expected, centre on meat, but rather on blood tapped from the vein of a living cow, combined with the relatively meagre yield of milk from the small udders that characterise the Ankole breed. The Bahima viewed their cattle as something close to family, so that slaughtering a fertile cow for meat was regarded as akin to cannibalism. It was customary, however, for infertile cows and surplus bullocks to be killed for meat on special occasions, while the flesh of any cow that died of natural causes would be eaten or bartered with the agriculturist Bairu for millet beer and other fresh produce. No part of the cow would go to waste: the hide would be used to make clothing, mats and drums, the dung to plaster huts and dried to light fires, while the horns could be customised as musical instruments.

Ankole is not as defiantly traditionalist as, say, Ethiopia's Omo Valley or Maasailand, and most rural Bahima today supplement their herds of livestock by practising mixed agriculture of subsistence and cash crops. But the Ankole cattle and their extraordinary horns, common in several parts of Uganda but most numerous in the vicinity of Mbarara and Lake Mburo, pay living tribute to the bovine preoccupations of Ankole past.

a 500m private road, clearly signposted about 7km from Sanga Entrance Gate and 4km from Rwonyo Rest Camp. *US$180/300 sgl/dbl FB, US$135/210 for East African residents.*

⌂ **Mihingo Lodge** m 0752 410509; e info@mihingolodge.com; www.mihingolodge.com. The lovely new Mihingo Lodge is spread across the side of a *koppie* in a privately owned wilderness of 238 acres, just outside Lake Mburo National Park. Accommodation is provided in luxurious and privately positioned tents on wooden platforms with attached shower and flush toilet. A thatched lounge/dining area, decidedly organic in feel, has been built using local rocks and gnarled olive wood branches to enjoy the sunsets over the park. A swimming pool with a view is also provided. Planned activities include mountain biking, walking safaris, horseriding, and visits to the national park. To get there, enter Lake Mburo national park at the Nshara gate and follow the Ruroko Track to the lodge. *US$280/350 for non-residents, less 30% for East African residents.*

Budget

⌂ **Rwonyo Rest Camp** Perched on a hillside no more than 1km from the lakeshore, the stalwart UWA rest camp has recently been expanded to offer two types of accommodation. At the centre of the camp is a cluster of individually named and idiosyncratically painted *bandas* using common showers. More recently, 5 comfortable standing dbl tents with private showers have been erected in secluded clearings in the thick bush uphill of the main camp, offering visitors a taste of tented camp atmosphere at a very reasonable price.

Firewood is available if you want to cook for yourself, but most people eat at the open-air restaurant at the main campsite 1km from Rwonyo (travellers without transport will need to be walked there by a ranger). At night, waterbuck, warthog and even the occasional bushpig wander through, and if you sit quietly they will often come very close. The camp often fills up over weekends and during the dry season, so do try to book accommodation in advance through the UWA headquarters in Kampala. *Bandas US$8/14 sgl/dbl, tents US$16/22 sgl/dbl.*

⋀ Camping

⋀ **Main Campsite** The main campsite, located on the lakeshore location only 1km from Rwonyo, is one of the most attractive in Uganda: spacious, grassy, shady, with a clean ablution block, and regularly visited by hippos, vervet monkeys, warthogs and various birds. The site doubles as the main jetty, so it is conveniently located for boat trips, especially for campers without private transport. An exceptionally pleasant and unexpectedly good stilted wooden restaurant serves decent meals in the Ush3,000–5,000 range as well as a selection of cold beers and sodas. Self-sufficient campers with transport might, however, prefer to pitch a tent at one of the quieter (but practically unfacilitated) campsites that lie further along the lakeshore. *US$6 pp.with or without your own tent.*

ACTIVITIES

Boat trips Probably the most popular activity in Lake Mburo is the motorboat trip on the lake, which leaves from the jetty at the main campsite 1km from Rwonyo Camp. In addition to the attractive scenery and simple pleasure attached to being out on the water, the boat trip reliably produces good sightings of hippo, crocodile, buffalo, waterbuck and bushbuck, and it's also worth looking out for the three species of resident otter. Among the more conspicuous waterbirds are African fish eagle, marabou stork, pied kingfisher and various egrets and herons, while Ross's turaco and Narina trogon are frequently seen in lakeside thickets. Lake Mburo is possibly the easiest place in Uganda to see the elusive African finfoot, which is generally associated with still water below overhanging branches. The boat carries up to eight people and costs US$5 per person with a minimum charge of Ush30,000.

Game drives The best way to explore the park fully is by road. The most frequently used roads are the Impala and Zebra tracks, which respectively connect Sanga Gate and Nshara Gate to Rwonyo Rest Camp. The quality of game viewing along these tracks is erratic but, particularly during the wet season, substantial concentrations of impala, zebra, waterbuck, topi and buffalo are often to be found only 2km from Rwonyo in the park-like savanna at the junction of Impala and Warukiri tracks.

In the dry season, when animals tend to congregate around the swamps and lakes, the most productive roads are likely to be the Lakeside Track and Kigambira Loop. At any time of year, these roads are the best places to see buffalo, hippopotamus, warthog, Defassa waterbuck, bushbuck and common duiker, as well as a variety of woodland- and water-associated birds. The Kigambira Loop gives access to lakes Mburo, Kigambira and Kibikwa. Branching to the east of the Lakeside Track, the Kazuma and Ruroko tracks pass through relatively open savanna interspersed with rocky hills where pairs of klipspringer are frequently observed. Visitors are permitted to walk to the top of Kazuma Hill, from where there is a view over four of the park's lakes.

To the west of Rwonyo, starting near Sanga Gate, the Rwizi Track leads through an area of light acacia savanna. Impala, eland and Burchell's zebra are common in this area, and the western shore of Lake Mburo is visible at times. After 12km, the track approaches the Rwizi River and fringing swamps. It then veers to the west, following the wooded watercourse for 33km before reaching Bisheshe Gate, a stretch that is particularly rewarding for birds. Note that the Rwizi Track deteriorates badly before reaching Bisheshe Gate, so unless you have a 4x4 vehicle you will probably have to turn back at some point.

Guided walks One of the major attractions of Lake Mburo is that you are permitted to walk anywhere in the park in the company of an armed ranger, at a cost of US$10 per person. Near to the camp, the road to the jetty remains a good place to walk: rich in birds and regularly visited by hippos. An even better target is the viewing platform that overlooks a salt lick about 2km from the camp – this is an excellent place to see a wide variety of animals. Of particular interest to walkers and birders is the **Rubanga Forest**, which lies off the Rwizi Track and can only be visited with the permission of the warden, who will provide you with an armed ranger. Visitors used to be allowed to walk unaccompanied along the 1km stretch of road between Rwonyo and the main campsite, but this practice was discontinued a few years ago after a tour leader was mauled by a buffalo.

MBARARA

In 1955, when Alan Forward arrived in Mbarara to serve as its new district officer, he found himself 'choking in the dust' of what 'seemed to have the atmosphere of a one-horse town'. Indeed, in the dying years of the colonial era, Mbarara was too small to be ranked among 12 towns countrywide whose population exceeded 4,000. By 1991, however, the one-horse town had grown to become the sixth-largest in Uganda, with a population exceeding 40,000. The past ten years have seen an even greater transformation. In the early 1990s, when I first visited Mbarara, it was a sleepy, nondescript junction town, still visibly scarred by the Tanzanian invasion during the Amin era. Subsequently, it has evolved into what is surely the only urban centre in western Uganda to which the adjectives 'modern' or 'vibrant' could be applied without a hint of facetiousness. Mbarara, in short, is the most rapidly expanding town in Uganda. Yet, paradoxically, while the town boasts perhaps the best selection of hotels and other tourist-related facilities anywhere in western Uganda – aimed mostly at local businessmen and the conference market – it lacks for any remotely scintillating sightseeing. Its bustling High Street almost qualifies, if only for the insight provided into the priorities of the modern Mbararan, for this contains what must be East Africa's highest

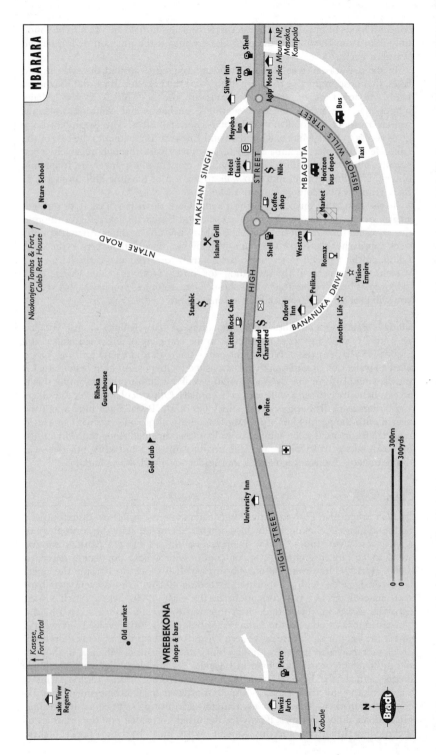

MBARARA

upcountry concentration of shops dealing exclusively in mobile phones and their accessories. Of potential interest is the royal drum house at Kamukazi, the last Ankole capital, situated 2km out of town along the Fort Portal road. Unfortunately, the royal drum, or *bagyendwaza*, an important symbol of Ankole national unity, said to have first belonged to the Bacwezi leader Wamala, was removed when the monarchy was banned in 1967, and Kamukuzi is now occupied by the military and off-limits to travellers. The Nkokonjeru Tombs, about 3km from the town centre, are the burial place of the last two kings of Ankole.

GETTING THERE AND AWAY Mbarara is a major route focus, situated at the junction of the surfaced roads east to Kampala via Masaka, southwest to Kabale and Kisoro, and northwest to Fort Portal via Kasese. Using public transport, the best way to get to or from Mbarara is with the Horizon Bus Company, whose modern and generally not overloaded vehicles run out of a private tout-free stand in the town centre. The staff at the stand use mobile phones to keep in touch with the buses, so they usually know when the next one is due to pass through *en route* to Kampala, Kabale or Kasese – you're unlikely to have to wait more than 30 minutes.

All other buses run out of the old bus park, where travellers are likely to be swamped by bus touts the moment they enter. Minibus taxis operate from the new taxi park: they are efficient for shorter journeys but in general they are not as comfortable or as safe as the big buses. Special-hire taxis are available all over town, especially around the central roundabout near the Shell station. A *boda-boda* trip within the town centre should cost around Ush500.

WHERE TO STAY
Moderate

🏠 **Lake View Regency Hotel** ☎ 04854 22112; e ivh@infocom.co.ug. The largest and smartest hotel in Mbarara, the 80-room Lake View lies in large grounds overlooking a manmade lake on the outskirts of the town centre along the Fort Portal road. It is popular as a conference centre and as a local leisure resort, since facilities include a large swimming pool, gym, sauna, aerobics classes and DSTV, as well as a poolside barbecue and disco every Fri night. Several restaurants serve a variety of good-quality international dishes for around Ush8,000–10,000. Credit cards are accepted for payments over US$50. *US$32/40 sgl/dbl for s/c rooms with DSTV.*

🏠 **Agip Motel** ☎ 04854 20060/21615; f 04854 20575. Although the name conjures up images of a dirty 1970s' motorway café, the Agip is a luxurious and modern small hotel, situated on the left as you enter town from the direction of Kampala. The roadside location can make it slightly noisy, but it has a friendly atmosphere and is close to all

amenities. The restaurant serves quality international dishes, specialising in Indian food and buffets, the latter costing Ush9,000. The fully carpeted, airy s/c rooms all have DSTV, and open out on to the gardens. *US$35/41/54 sgl/dbl/ste.*

🏠 **Rwizi Arch Hotel** ☎ 04854 20821; m 0712 648980 or 0772 622471; f 04854 20575. This only superficially attractive new hotel lies in attractive grounds in Wrebekona, the old market area of town along the Fort Portal road, and is named after the Rwizi River, which runs behind it. Be warned; the hotel is often used as a venue for musical and other events. The hotel is within safe and easy walking distance of a good market and cluster of shops during the day, and numerous local bars and restaurants by night. The restaurant serves a good selection of international dishes in the Ush6,000–9,000 range. We've had some dire reports of the food and service but in our experience the chicken Kiev is worth stopping for. *US$36/42/70 for s/c sgl/dbl/ste with DSTV.*

Budget

🏠 **Fort Coleb Rest House** (5 rooms) ☎/f 04854 20892; m 0772 502020. This small, friendly guesthouse, originally a family retreat for the daughter of the prime minister of Ankole region,

lies in a pleasant and leafy residential suburb 3km from the town centre. It is located on a hill, and the outside bar/restaurant, which serves international dishes for around Ush4,000, offers a

Mbarara lies at the heart of the former Ankole (or Nkore) kingdom, a centralised polity founded c1500 in the power vacuum created by the demise of the Bacwezi. Unlike the other pre-colonial kingdoms of Uganda, Ankole society was divided into two rigidly stratified but mutually inter-dependent castes, the pastoralist Bahima nobility and the agriculturist Bairu peasantry. Ankole was ruled by a king, called the *omugabe*, a hereditary title reserved for prominent members of the Bahinda clan of the Bahima, who was served under by an appointed *enganzi* (prime minister) and several local chiefs.

Ankole rose to regional prominence in roughly 1700, after the 11th omugabe, Ntare IV Kiitabanyoro, defeated the Banyoro army (Kiitabanyoro means 'Killer of the Banyoro'). By the mid 19th century, the kingdom, bounded by the Katonga River in the north and the Kagera River in the south, extended from east of Lake Mburo to the shores of Lake Albert in the west. After 1875, however, Ankole went into decline, attributable partly to a combination of disease and drought, but primarily to the rejuvenation of Bunyoro under Kabalega, who might well have co-opted Ankole into his realm were it not for outside intervention.

In 1898, Omugabe Kahaya decided that the only way to safeguard his kingdom against Bunyoro advances was to enter into an alliance with the British administration in Buganda, and John Macallister, a former railway engineer, was dispatched to Nkore to establish a British government station and fort – the future Mbarara. In January 1899, Macallister settled on a site called Muti, which was eminently defendable and boasted a perennial water supply in the form of the Rwizi River. There was also a strong historical basis for Macallister's choice of location. When Captain Lugard had visited Ankole a few years earlier, Muti was the capital of Omugabe Ntare, though it had been abandoned in the interim, after a smallpox epidemic claimed the lives of several of its prominent citizens and one of Ntare's sons. That the station built at Muti was called Mbarara evidently stemmed from some confusion on the part of Macallister. Mbarara (or more correctly Mburara, after a type of grass that grows locally) was actually the name of the site of another of Ntare's short-lived capitals, situated a few kilometres from the abandoned Muti.

Whatever other merits it might have possessed, the site selected by Macallister had one serious drawback. 'The more one journeys about,' wrote the missionary J J Willis, 'the more one is impressed with the fact that [Mbarara] is the one spot in all Ankole where you have to march a whole day or two days before you come on any cultivation worth the name'. The scarcity of food around Mbarara was rooted less in the area's geography than in local cultural attitudes – the Bahima, like so many other African pastoralists, had no tradition of cultivation. The British administration, supported by the enganzi (prime minister) Mbaguta, did much to encourage the growth of agriculture in Ankole during the early years of the 20th century. In 1905, Mbaguta remarked that, following the establishment of Mbarara, the annual famines were 'becoming yearly less severe'. Within a few years, the new capital of Ankole, accorded township status in 1906, would be practically self-sufficient in food, and its future role as the main centre of trade in Ankole was secure.

good view over the town. To get there, follow Ntare Rd out of the town centre, past the famous Ntare School, then take the next right turn and follow the signposts. A special hire or *boda-boda* from town costs around Ush3,000. *US$20/22 sgl/dbl (all rooms s/c).*

⌂ **Hotel Classic** ✆ 04854 21131; e hotclassic@ swiftuganda.com. This popular modern hotel is centrally located on High Street, and as a result it can be a bit noisy, though otherwise it's very good value. The lively balcony bar is a popular meeting place, and a good restaurant serves international dishes for around Ush7,000. *US$22/27 s/c sgl/dbl with DSTV.*

🏠 **Oxford Inn** Bananuka Drive, behind the post office; m 0772 546538. Another new and still-expanding hotel in the town centre. The comfortable outside latticed area and indoor restaurant make it a popular place to meet and to eat — most dishes cost around Ush6,000. Several bars and the Vision Empire Nightclub lie close by, making undisturbed Fri/Sat nights unlikely. *US$20/24 s/c sgl/dbl.*

🏠 **Pelikan Hotel** Bananuka Drive. An older hotel even closer to the Vision Empire. The restaurant serves international/local dishes for around Ush6,000. *US$11/21 for adequate s/c sgl/dbl inc b/fast.*

🏠 **Riheka Guest House** ☏ 04854 21314. This pleasant small hotel lies in a quiet residential area near to the golf course. It has an attractive garden and patio restaurant, serving international dishes for around Ush6,000, and the s/c rooms are very good value. Although it lies within walking distance of the town centre, it's better to have transport at night. *US$11/19 sgl/dbl.*

🏠 **University Inn** This long-serving hotel lies in leafy grounds along the main road through Mbarara, opposite the university teaching hospital, where it's set back sufficiently from the road to keep the traffic noise to a minimum. The large, s/c rooms have seen better times but are acceptable value. *US$16/19 sgl/dbl B&B.*

Shoestring

🏠 **Mayoba Inn** Centrally located on High St, close to all amenities, this multi-storey hotel is very good value. *US$7/8 for clean s/c sgl/dbl with hot water, and US$4/5 sgl/dbl with shared facilities.*

🏠 **Travellers Hotel and Lodgings** Situated in the old market area of Wrebekona along the Fort Portal road, this hotel is basic but clean and friendly, and located close to several local bars and restaurants. *Accommodation using common showers costs US$3 pp.*

🏕 Camping

🏕 **Agip Motel** This smart hotel has the only custom-built camping site in Mbarara. The well-kept grassy site is enclosed within a secure wall, and the ablution block offers hot showers and flush toilets. The site, though rather pricey, is close to all town amenities and the hotel has a pleasant outside bar and restaurant. Camping is also permitted in the grounds of the Fort Coleb Rest House and University Inn. *US$5 pp.*

✘ WHERE TO EAT AND DRINK

In addition to the restaurants listed below, several of the hotels recommended above have good restaurants attached. The **Lake View Regency Hotel** is good for a night out, especially on Fridays, and a special hire from the town centre should cost Ush3,000. The food at the **Motel Agip** is a few notches above the rest; the buffet is a quick and convenient lunch stop, while the steaks are a treat in the evening.

✘ **The Coffee Shop** High Street. Squeezed between the internet cafés and mobile phone shops, the Coffee Shop consists of a ground-floor restaurant and first-floor bar. It has DSTV and can be rather noisy at times. *A variety of spaghetti, steak and chicken dishes are available in the Ush4,000 range.*

✘ **Wrebekona** Numerous bars and *muchomo* (meat) joints come to life at night in this market area on the Fort Portal road near Rwizi Arch Hotel to serve cheap drinks and various affordable snacks including traditionally cooked tilapia, roast pork, chicken and goat served with *matoke*, cabbage and the like.

✘ **Little Rock Café** Kabale Rd, almost opposite the post office. Little Rock looks and feels much like a modern burger bar. It doesn't actually serve hamburgers, but sells very good chips with meat and eggs, as well as yoghurt and fruit salad. You can eat in or outdoors. *Meals cost around Ush3,000.*

✘ **Romax Bar** One of several bars on Bananuka Drive, the Romax has an outdoor seating area, as well as several pool tables and good music. *No food is served.*

✘ **Vision Empire** and **Another Life** Bananuka Drive is home to Mbarara's top two nightclubs. Vision Empire is dark and noisy but has a more exclusive upstairs area to which you can escape.

LISTINGS

Internet There are several internet cafés along High Street charging Ush50 per minute.

Foreign exchange Stanbic Bank, opposite the post office changes cash and American Express travellers' cheques at the bank's national rates. Out of banking hours, the Agip, Lake View and Rwizi Arch hotels will also exchange money, but at a poorer rate.

Swimming pool Day visitors can use the swimming pool at the Lake View Regency Hotel for a small fee.

Shopping Mbarara is well equipped with supermarkets, the best ones being clustered along High Street between the main Kampala roundabout and the post office.

WHAT TO SEE

Nkokonjeru Tombs The tombs of the last two kings of Ankole, Omugabe Edward Solomon Kahaya II, who died in 1944, and Omugabe Sir Charles Godfrey Rutahaba Gasyonga II, who ruled from 1944 until 1967 and died in 1982, can be visited at **Nkokonjeru**, 3km from central Mbarara. To anybody who has seen the impressive and lovingly tended traditional royal tombs at Kasubi and Mparo, however, an excursion to Nkokonjeru is bound to prove anti-climatic. Protected within an isolated, rundown – almost derelict – colonial-style house, the royal graves at Nkokonjeru consist of two bland concrete slabs, overgrown with vegetation and layered in sickly sweet-smelling bat shit, onto which the names of the late kings are unceremoniously hand-scrawled. Several other graves of minor royalty lie outside the main building.

To reach Nkokonjeru, follow Ntare Road out of the town centre, passing the Ntare School after about 1km. After another 500m, turn right into the road signposted for the Fort Coleb Rest House, ignoring a fork to the right after 200m. About 200m further, you reach a three-way junction, where the central fork leads after 500m to the tiled building housing the tombs.

Nsongezi Rock Shelter Overlooking the Kagera River near Kikagati, a former tin-mining centre set along the Tanzanian border 75km south of Mbarara, Nsongezi Rock Shelter is one of the most important Stone-Age sites in Uganda. A series of excavations in the shelter have yielded a large number of stratified pottery shards dating from around AD1000 into the 19th century, collectively representing the full range of styles characteristic of the period. Few people visit Nsongezi – the road through Gayaza and Nsongezi trading centres is poor, and pretty much a dead-end in terms of onward travel possibilities, and there's no site museum or anything else to see. Should you intend to be the exception, then do first check out the extensive display on the shelter in the National Museum in Kampala. The stretch of the Kagera around Nsongezi used to be known for its large pods of hippo, but it's unlikely that significant numbers survive today.

Ndija Anybody looking for a reason to break up the drive between Mbarara and Kabale could do far worse than stop over at the **Pan-Afric Motel** (m *0772 760146; US$11/13 sgl/dbl, camping US$3 pp; meals Ush2,000*) in Ndija, a small village straddling the main Kabale road roughly 35km past Mbarara. Ndija is surrounded by steep, volcanically formed hills, and the motel itself is set in an attractive garden ringed by *matoke* plantations and overlooking a papyrus-fringed river. There are clean self-contained rooms with running water or you can camp in the grounds. The restaurant serves meals and there is a bar. The Pan-Afric Motel can organise a variety of day excursions – monkey tracking, birdwatching, fishing, herbal medicine tours – from Ush5,000–10,000 per person. Equally, it's an area that keen

The untended state of the Nkokonjeru Tombs is symptomatic of a popular ambivalence to the Ankole royalty that stretches back to the early years of independence. In 1967, the constitutional abolition of the monarchies under Obote was hotly protested in Buganda, Bunyoro and Toro. In Ankole, by contrast, the reaction was closer to muted indifference. In 1971, Idi Amin opened a short-lived debate with regard to reinstating all the ancient monarchies, a notion that garnered strong support in Buganda and elsewhere. Not so in Ankole, where a committee of elders signed a memorandum stating that the matter 'should not be raised or even discussed', since it would 'revive political divisions and factionalism' and stand in the way of the 'march forward to our stated goal of freedom and progress'.

The widespread anti-royalist sentiment in Ankole is so fundamentally at odds with popular attitudes in the other kingdoms of Uganda that it requires explanation. Two main factors can be cited. The first is that the traditional social structure of Ankole, like that of pre-colonial Rwanda, but not of Buganda or Bunyoro, was informed by a rigid caste system. For the majority of Banyankole – who are of Bairu descent – reinstating the Bahima monarchy would smack of retrogression to that obsolete caste system. Secondly, Ankole as it was delineated from the early colonial era until post-independence was an artificial entity, one that encompassed several formerly independent kingdoms – Igara, Sheema, Bweju and parts of Mpororo – that had no prior historical affiliation or loyalty to the omugabe. Ankole is the only one of the ancient Ugandan kingdoms that was not officially restored by Museveni in 1993. And, despite ongoing lobbying from traditionalists (and the clandestine coronation of Prince Barigye, a ceremony that was immediately afterwards annulled by Museveni), it seems likely to remain that way for the foreseeable future.

hikers might want to explore on their own – the friendly, articulate Ugandan woman who runs the hotel will be able to give you advice.

Nshenyi Cultural Centre Shortly before going to print, we were sent information about this secluded new cultural centre in the village of Nshenyi, which lies about 90km (two–three hours) from Mbarara Town about 10km from the borders with Rwanda and Tanzania. Situated on a traditional Ankole farm, the centre offers basic accommodation in seven rooms using shared pit toilets and hot bucket showers, traditional meals, and a wide range of activities that encourage direct interaction with the local community. Activities include milking the long-horned Ankole cattle cows, joining the pastors as they graze the cattle, a market-day experience, nature walks and birdwatching on the undulating hills that overlook the village or along the Kagera River (the border with Tanzania), tribal encounters, visits to rock art and historical sites, traditional cooking, and cultural singing and dancing. For more details contact **Great Lakes Safaris** (\ *0414 267153 or 031 278757;* e *info@safari-uganda.com; www.safari-uganda.com*).

Ibanda Something of a minor route focus, the small town of Ibanda lies 67km north of Mbarara at the junction of the southern approach road to Katonga Wildlife Reserve and a little-used route north through Kamwenge to Kibale Forest National Park and Fort Portal. Unless you're heading between these places, however, it must be said that Ibanda is rather an out-of-the-way town, and – sprawling along one main road for about 1km – thoroughly unremarkable. But not so the newly surfaced road that connects Ibanda to Mbarara – possibly the smoothest drive in Uganda, and almost (but not quite) worth the diversion for that reason alone! This

The Mbarara Road **MBARARA**

7

road also bypasses **Isingiro Mountain**, at 2,172m the highest peak in Ankole, and reputedly climbable in a day from Lwesho trading centre. About 3km from Ibanda, a cairn-like memorial commemorates the murder of Harry St George Galt (see box *Murder in Ibanda*, below).

As for travel practicalities, Ibanda is connected to Mbarara by regular minibus-taxis, and there is also a fair amount of transport on to Kamwenge and to a lesser extent Kabagole (for Katonga Game Reserve). Should you need to overnight in Ibanda, there are several basic local guesthouses to choose from, with the **New Ibanda Lodge** probably the best bet.

KATONGA WILDLIFE RESERVE

This little-known wildlife reserve, the closest to Kampala as the crow flies, protects 207km² of mixed savanna, papyrus swamp and rainforest on the north bank of the Katonga River. The wildlife reserve was gazetted in 1964, at which time it

THE OLD KABALE ROAD AND KITAGATA SPRINGS

Readers travelling directly between Kasese and Kabale should, instead of following the 125km surfaced road through Mbarara, think about using the shortcut provided by the Old Kabale Road which links Ishaka to Ntungamo. This route is unsurfaced, though usually in pretty good shape, for 31km before emerging onto the brand new tarmac Rukungiri highway at Kagamaba. Turn left for Ntungamo (13km) or right for Rukungiri, Bwindi and Ishasha. If coming from Kabale, the Rukungiri road is clearly signposted off to the left from the Mbarara road 500m before Ntungamo but the next turn-off to the right after 13km is less obvious. The main site of interest along the Old Kibale Road is the **Kitagata Hot Springs**, which lie close to Kitagata trading centre, some 16km south of Ishaka. Kitagata is an oddly time-warped small town, dominated by a redundantly immense roundabout, and scattered with several colonial-era buildings including a rather pretty old church, all of which goes to suggest that urban development came to a standstill following the construction of the surfaced road via Mbarara. There are a few lodgings, should you be in the mood to linger – the **Fredon Tourists Bar and Lodging** looks the definite pick (*US$2 for a basic but clean sgl with nets*). The hot springs lie about 1.5km south of Kitagata, and you're unlikely to miss them – their vaguely sulphuric whiff should draw your attention even if the prominent signposts don't. The name Kitagata holds few mysteries for linguists – it translates somewhat unimaginatively as 'boiling water' – and it could be argued that the actual springs, too, are of no more than passing interest, bubbling as they do into a clear, shallow, steaming pool about 200m from the main road. Kitagata has long been believed to possess therapeutic qualities (and so probably it does, should you be suffering from creaky joints or aching muscles, though it's doubtful it would do much to cure malaria or several other ailments as it claims) and the surrounding rocks are generally draped in a couple of dozen half-naked bathers who, needless to say, will be less than enamoured of any passing tourist who pulls out a camera. The huge signpost announcing the presence of a rest camp at the springs flatters to deceive – you can pitch a tent, assuming you have one, for next to nothing, but facilities are limited to the communal hot bath created naturally by the springs. South of Kitagata, the road passes through some impressively scenic hills, a landscape characteristic of Kigezi, except that it is unusually grassy and lacking in cultivation. This stretch of road also follows a papyrus-fringed river for several kilometres, offering excellent views over patches of swamp that might potentially prove to be excellent for papyrus endemics.

supported large herds of resident zebra, elephant and buffalo, as well as serving as a corridor for game migration between western Uganda and Tanzania and the Sudan. Poaching and cattle encroachment took a heavy toll on the reserve's environment and wildlife in the 1970s and 1980s, but improved protection in recent years has ensured that the depleted populations are now on the increase. The current mammal checklist stands at 40 species, including black-and-white colobus, olive baboon, Uganda kob and small numbers of elephant and buffalo. Waterbuck, reedbuck and bushbuck are common and sufficiently habituated to approach on foot. Katonga is also one of perhaps three places in East Africa where the secretive sitatunga antelope is likely to be seen by a casual visitor. Katonga is also of great interest for its varied birdlife – over 150 species have been recorded to date and the checklist is likely to approach 300 species pending more detailed research. Among the more interesting species likely to be seen are green- and blue-headed coucal, Ross's and great blue turaco, crested malimbe and papyrus gonolek.

Totally undeveloped for tourism prior to 1998, Katonga is now the site of a worthwhile but sadly under-utilised ecotourism project – on average one party of tourists per month in 2002 – developed with Peace Corps assistance under the supervision of UWA. The main attraction is the unique canoe trail (US$5 per person with a minimum charge of Ush30,000) which follows a narrow channel through the heart of the swamp and offers a high chance of seeing sitatunga, river otter and various water- and papyrus-associated birds. Three guided half-day walking trails are available at US$10 per person. The Sitatunga Trail runs through a mixture of grassland and wetland habitats, offering a better than even chance of spotting the elusive antelope for which it is named. The Kisharara Trail passes through all the main habitats protected within the park – grassland, savanna and swamp fringes – and is also good for sitatunga, as well as monkeys and birds. The Kyeibale Trail loops away from the water into an area of drier scrub dotted with tall rock formations as well as forested valleys and caves. For details of further developments, ask at the UWA headquarters in Kampala. The guides are very knowledgeable about the local fauna and flora. Stays of one/two/three nights or more are charged at US$20/25/30 for foreign tourists and US$15/20/25 for East African residents.

GETTING THERE AND AWAY There are quite a number of ways of approaching the reserve, and the best route depends to some degree on the rest of your itinerary and whether or not you are dependent on public transport. Until recently, access from the south was complicated by the need to cross the Katonga by canoe, but this has changed with the recent construction of a motorable culvert between Kabagole and the reserve.

Coming by private vehicle from Kampala or Fort Portal, Katonga Wildlife Reserve is best approached from the north, branching south from the surfaced Kampala–Fort Portal road at a junction signposted in Kyegegwa, 50km west of Mubende. From this junction, a good 47km dirt road through Mparo and Kalwreni leads to the reserve entrance gate. This is the best route for those dependent on public transport. It's no hassle at all to get to Kyegegwa – any vehicle heading between Kampala and Fort Portal can drop you there – and you should also be able to find public transport on to Kalwreni, possibly changing vehicles at Mpora. Kalwreni lies 7km from the entrance gate, and if you can't find transport heading along this stretch it is possible to walk or to hire a *boda-boda*.

Coming directly from the southwest, the best route entails following the surfaced road north from Mbarara to Ibanda, from where a 75km dirt road leads northwest to Kabagole, on the south bank of the Katonga River, then crosses a culvert to the opposite bank, 500m from the reserve entrance gate. The dirt stretches of both routes are normally in reasonable shape, but a 4x4 may be required after heavy rain. At least two buses cover the Mbarara–Kabagole road daily, leaving Kabagole in the early morning to arrive at Mbarara shortly after midday, and starting the return trip out of Mbarara at around 14.00 to arrive back at Kabagole at dusk. From Kabagole, you can walk to the reserve, or hire canoes for a few hundred shillings to take you to the opposite bank.

It is also possible to approach Katonga from Kibale Forest National Park via Kamwenge, Ibanda and Kabagole. Plenty of public transport services all legs of this route.

✕ WHERE TO STAY AND EAT

🏠 **Katonga Visitors' Centre** The small campsite at the visitors' centre near the reserve entrance has a pleasant setting with a good covered dining area, locked kitchen and ablutions (key provided on payment of camping fee) – all looking very new and attractive. An education centre is located deeper in the bush. Meals are available from a canteen run by the local women's group. *Bandas* may be built at the site at some point in the future. *Camping US$6 pp.*

🏠 **Katonga View Tourist Lodge** This clean, comfortable and secure small lodge in Kabagole, on the south bank of the river about 1km from the reserve entrance gate, can be used as a base for day visits. The owner has trained as a cook, and can rustle together very enjoyable local meals. *Rooms around US$4.*

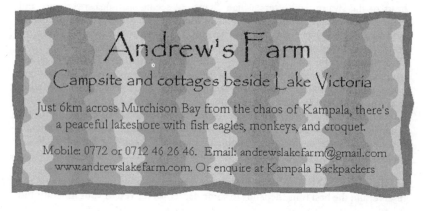

8

Kigezi

Kigezi is perhaps the most fertile and scenic region of Uganda: a landscape of expansive blue lakes and steep terraced slopes tumbling southwest towards the rainforest-swathed mountains of Bwindi National Park and the magnificent isolated peaks of the Virunga Volcanoes. But for most visitors, whatever scenic qualities are attached to this hilly southwestern corner of Uganda will be secondary to the region's outstanding attraction, which is the opportunity to track the endangered mountain gorilla in its natural habitat – arguably the most exciting wildlife encounter to be had anywhere in Africa.

The global population of at most 700 wild mountain gorillas is restricted to, and split more-or-less evenly between, the dense montane forest of Bwindi and the bamboo-clumped slopes of the Virungas. But, typical of the whimsical attitude to the carve-up of Africa in the 1880s, the Virungas were divided across three separate colonial territories, so that the mountain gorillas today are harboured within four independently managed national parks in three different countries. These are Bwindi and Mgahinga Gorilla national parks in Uganda, and – contiguous to the latter – the Parc National des Volcans in Rwanda and Parc National des Virungas in the DRC. However, while three habituated groups of gorillas can be seen in Bwindi, it's not clear when tracking will be possible in Mgahinga. The park's habituated group vanished over the volcanic watershed into Rwanda's Parc National des Volcans in late 2004 and, as I write in July 2006, has only been sighted on Ugandan soil within the last couple of days. Hopefully they will remain in Mgahinga and tracking will soon recommence. Since gorilla tracking in the adjoining parks in Rwanda and the DRC can easily be undertaken as an excursion out of Uganda, boxed text covering the relevant national parks in Rwanda and the DRC are also included in this chapter.

Mountain gorilla tracking is inevitably the most popular tourist activity in Kigezi, but the area does have much else to offer. The slopes of Mgahinga harbour a rich faunal diversity, and it is possible to organise guided forest walks as well as day hikes to the three volcanic peaks within the reserve. Bwindi, too, offers some excellent day-walking possibilities, and it has possibly the richest faunal diversity of any forest in East Africa, including two dozen bird species endemic to the Albertine Rift. National parks aside, the lovely, island-strewn Lake Bunyonyi has supplanted the Ssese Islands as Uganda's most popular beach chill-out venue, while a host of more obscure lakes and waterfalls form rewarding goals for more adventurous travellers.

The largest town in Kigezi, and main gateway to the region, is Kabale, which lies 430km from Kampala and 147km from Mbarara along one of the best roads in the country. The other important local urban centre is Kisoro, strategically situated at the base of the Virungas close to the borders with Rwanda and the DRC. The excellent 1:125,000 *Kigezi Tourist Map*, published in 1995, is no longer available for sale anywhere in the region, but copies are displayed at the national parks offices in Kabale and Kisoro and at Lake Bunyonyi's Overland Resort.

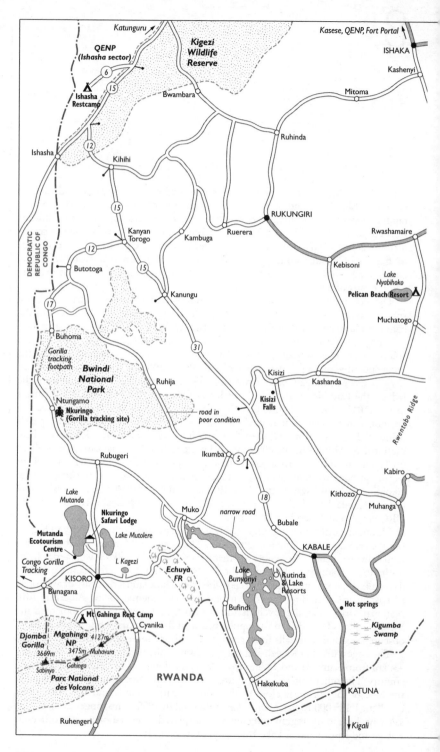

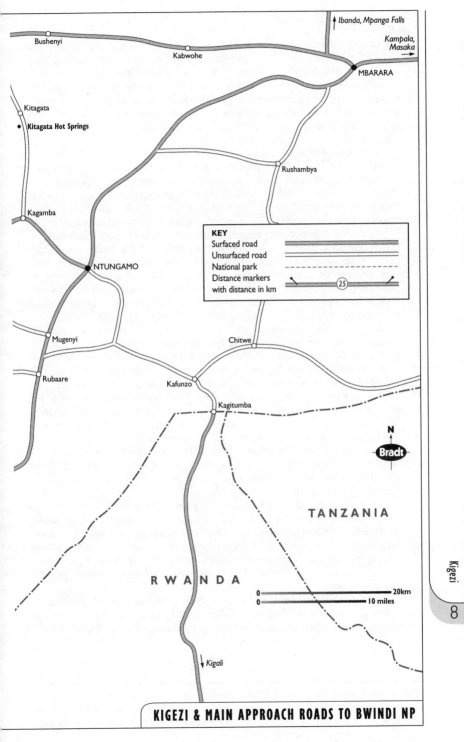

KIGEZI & MAIN APPROACH ROADS TO BWINDI NP

Tracking the mountain gorillas in the Virungas or Bwindi ranks among the absolute highlights of African travel. The exhilaration attached to first setting eyes on a wild mountain gorilla is difficult to describe. These are enormous animals: up to three times as bulky as the average man, their size exaggerated by a shaggily luxuriant coat. Yet despite their fearsome appearance, gorillas are remarkably peaceable creatures – tracking them would be a considerably more dangerous pursuit were they possessed of the aggressive temperament of, say, vervet monkeys or baboons, or for that matter human beings.

More impressive even than the gorillas' size and bearing is their unfathomable attitude to people, which differs greatly from that of any other wild animal I've encountered. Anthropomorphic as it might sound, almost everybody who visits the gorillas experiences an almost mystical sense of recognition. Often, one of the gentle giants will break off from the business of chomping on bamboo to study a human visitor, soft brown eyes staring deeply into theirs as if seeking a connection – a spine-tingling wildlife experience without peer.

That magical hour spent with the gorillas does not come cheaply – US$300–500 per person depending on which of the three reserves that offer gorilla tracking you elect to visit – but it's unusual to meet somebody who regretted the financial outlay. The experience offered at the three reserves is broadly similar, so the biggest factor in determining which you visit will probably be permit availability. The 32 daily permits available for Bwindi National Park are often booked up months ahead. On the Virunga volcanoes, up to 40 permits are available daily in Rwanda and 30 in DRC.

Travellers who track gorillas as part of an organised tour can safely assume that the operator will have booked permits in advance. Independent travellers, by contrast, will generally need to make their own booking, often at relatively short notice. Permits for the Ugandan reserves are generally best booked direct through the UWA headquarters in Kampala (for contact details see pages 158–9). The Backpackers' Hostel in Kampala can also book permits for Uganda, Rwanda and DRC as will Nile River Explorers in Jinja for pre-paid travellers. If it's possible to structure your travels around a set date, advance booking is strongly recommended. Should you be unwilling or unable to do this, then – depending on availability – permits for the Ugandan reserves can be bought more locally at the national parks offices in Kabale or Kisoro. The easiest place for which permits can be obtained at short notice is DRC, the most difficult is Bwindi, while Rwanda falls in between – permits are often booked solid during peak (ie: dry) seasons but there is usually some availability at other times of year.

Gorilla tracking should not present a serious physical challenge to any reasonably fit adult whatever their age, but the hike can be tough going. Exactly how tough varies greatly, and the main determining factor is basically down to luck, specifically how close the gorillas are to the trailhead on the day you trek (one to two hours is typical, anything from 15 minutes to six hours possible). Another variable is how recently it has rained, which affects conditions underfoot – June to August are the driest months and March to May are the wettest.

The effects of altitude should not be underestimated. Tracking in Bwindi takes place at around 1,500m above sea level, but in the Virungas the gorillas are often encountered at almost 3,000m – sufficient to knock the breath out of anybody who just flew in from low

KABALE

With a population of around 40,000, Kabale is one of the largest towns in western Uganda, as well as being an important travel hub and a useful base from which to visit mountain gorillas. It was founded in 1913, when the British

altitude. For this reason, visitors to the Virungas in particular might want to leave gorilla tracking until they've been in the region for a week and are reasonably acclimatised – most of Uganda lies above 1,000m.

Take advantage when the guides offer you a walking staff before the walk; this will be invaluable to help you keep your balance on steep hillsides. Once on the trail, don't be afraid to ask to stop for a few minutes whenever you feel tired, or to ask the guides to create a makeshift walking stick from a branch. Drink plenty of water, and do carry some quick calories such as biscuits or chocolate. The good news is that in 99% of cases, whatever exhaustion you might feel on the way up will vanish with the adrenalin charge that follows the first sighting of a silverback gorilla!

Put on your sturdiest walking shoes for the trek, and wear thick trousers and long sleeves as protection against vicious nettles. It's often cold at the outset, so bring a sweatshirt or jersey. The gorillas are used to people, and it makes no difference whether you wear bright or muted colours. Whatever clothes you wear are likely to get very dirty, so if you have pre-muddied clothes, use them! During the rainy season, a poncho or raincoat might be a worthy addition to your daypack, while sunscreen, sunglasses and a hat are a good idea at any time of year, as are gloves to protect against nettles.

In all reserves, tourists are permitted to spend no longer than one hour with the gorillas, and may not eat or smoke in their presence. It is forbidden to approach the gorillas within more than 5m, a rule that is difficult to enforce with those curious youngsters (and some adults) who enjoy approaching human visitors. Gorillas are susceptible to many human diseases, and it has long been feared by researchers that one ill tourist might infect a gorilla, resulting in the possible death of the whole troop should no immunity exist. For this reason, you should not track gorillas when you have a potentially airborne infection such as a flu or cold, and should turn away from the gorillas if you need to sneeze in their presence.

As for photography, my advice, unless you're a professional or serious amateur, is to run off a few quick snapshots, then put the camera away, enjoy the moment, and buy a postcard or coffee-table book later. Gorillas are tricky photographic subjects, on account of their sunken eyes, the gloomy habitat in which they are often found, and a jet-black skin that tends to distort light readings. Flash photography is forbidden, so you're unlikely to get sharp results without a tripod or monopod. It might be worth carrying an ISO 800 or 1600 film in case you need the speed, but where light conditions permit, low-speed ISO 50 or 100 film will generally produce far better results. Make sure, too, your camera gear is well protected – if your bag isn't waterproof, seal your camera and films in plastic bags.

Above all, do bear in mind that gorillas are still wild animals, despite the 'gentle giant' reputation that has superseded the old King Kong image. An adult is much stronger than a person and will act in accordance with its own social codes when provoked or surprised. The most serious incident to date occurred in Mgahinga in 1997 when a silverback took exception to a professional photographer who decided that he was the exception to the flash photography rule. The gorilla snatched the camera and charged, roughed up and sat upon an innocent party who did/didn't break a limb depending on which version of the story you hear. The point obviously, is to listen to your guide at all times regarding the correct protocol in the presence of gorillas.

government station at Ikumba was relocated to Makanga Hill – then known as Kabaare after a trough-like depression at its summit – above present-day Kabale town centre. The original hilltop site is dominated today by an expansive green golf course, a few old government buildings, and the venerable White Horse Hotel. Both the hill and the town centre below are studded with eucalyptus

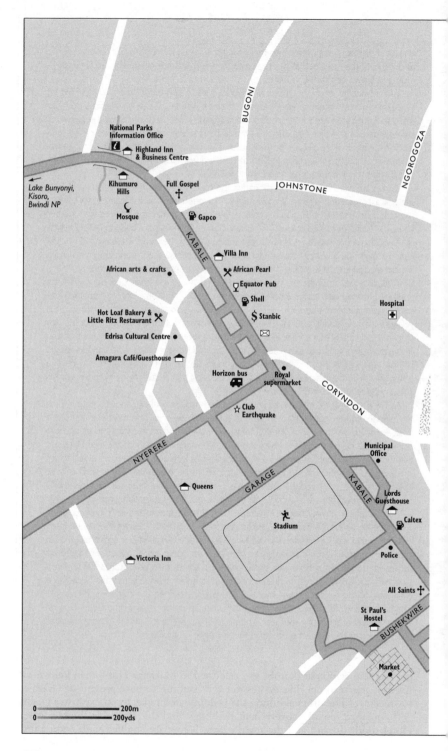

National Parks
Information Office

Highland Inn
& Business Centre

Kihumuro
Hills

Full Gospel

Gapco

Lake Bunyonyi,
Kisoro,
Bwindi NP

JOHNSTONE

BUGONI

NGOROGOZA

Mosque

KABALE

Villa Inn

African arts & crafts

African Pearl

Equator Pub

Shell

Hospital

Hot Loaf Bakery &
Little Ritz Restaurant

Stanbic

Edrisa Cultural Centre

Amagara Café/Guesthouse

Horizon bus

Royal
supermarket

CORYNDON

Club
Earthquake

NYERERE

Municipal
Office

Queens

GARAGE

KABALE

Lords
Guesthouse

Caltex

Stadium

Police

Victoria Inn

All Saints

St Paul's
Hostel

BUSHEKWIRE

Market

0 ━━━━━ 200m
0 ━━━━━ 200yds

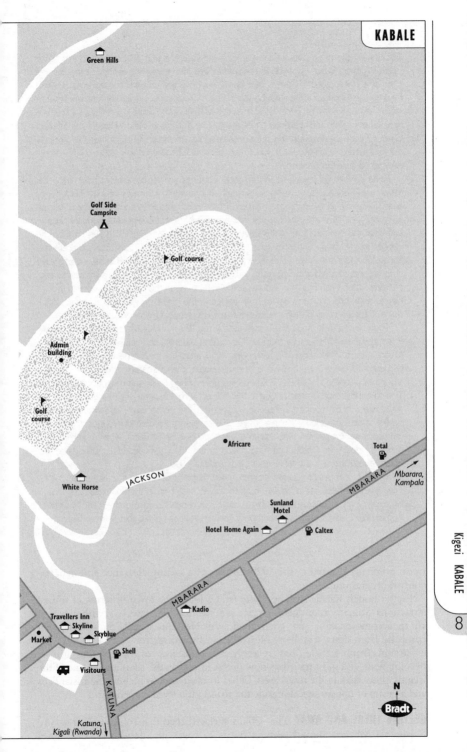

Green Hills

Golf Side
Campsite

Golf course

Admin
building

Golf
course

Africare

Total

White Horse

JACKSON

MBARARA

Mbarara,
Kampala

Sunland
Motel

Hotel Home Again

Caltex

MBARARA

Kadio

Travellers Inn
Skyline
Skyblue

Market

Shell

Visitours

KATUNA

Katuna,
Kigali (Rwanda)

N

Bradt

Traditionally the most popular spirit among the Bakiga is that of a respected rainmaker called Nyabingi, who – possibly in the mid to late 18th century – resided in the Bufundi Hills, at a place called Mukante, between Lake Bunyonyi and the modern border with Rwanda. Legend has it that after Nyabingi was murdered by a rival, her attendants were visited by a stream of ill or barren Bakiga villagers who made sacrifices to the late rainmaker's spirit, and were cured of their ailment if it approved of the items offered. Over subsequent decades, the spirit possessed a succession of Bakiga mediums, mostly but not always women, who would be blessed with Nyabinga's powers of healing, rainmaking and curing infertility.

Several Nyabingi mediums incited local uprisings against colonialism. The first such rebel was Muhumusa, of mysterious origin, but possibly a former wife of the recently dead Rwandan king, Rwabuguri Kigeri. Muhumusa was imprisoned by the German authorities in 1909 after threatening that her son Ndungutse would capture the throne and boot the colonists out of the kingdom. Upon her release in 1911, she crossed the border into Uganda and settled at Ihanga Hill near Bubale, 12km from present-day Kabale on the Kisoro road. She then announced that she had come in search of a cave wherein was secured a sacred drum which, she claimed, would call up a limitless stream of calves when beaten by her and her son. As the news of the magic drum spread though Kigezi, hundreds of young Bakiga men joined in the quest for its location, hoping for a share of the spoils, and Muhumusa received wide support from local chiefs.

The Christian Muganda chiefs installed by the British in Kigezi regarded the growing cult surrounding Muhumusa to be evil and insurrectionist, and refused to have anything to do with it. This angered Muhumusa, who attacked the home of one such chief, burning it to the ground and killing several people, then threatening to impale him and any other disrespectful chiefs on sharpened poles when finally she caught up with them. The colonial authorities responded to this indirect affront by attacking Muhumusa's Ihanga residence with 50 troops and a cannon. At least 40 of the medium's followers were killed on the spot and buried in a mass grave, and several more died of wounds after fleeing the battle site. Muhumusa was captured and imprisoned in Mbarara, where she remained until her death in 1945. The British authorities then proceeded to criminalise the Nyabingi cult through the Witchcraft Ordinance of 1912.

In 1917, a rebellion against an implanted Muganda chief was masterminded by the male medium Ntokibiri in the Nyabugoto Caves, which lie in the Rwanyabingi (Place of Nyabingi) Hills in Nyakishenyi sub-country. The rebels razed the chief's house on 17 August, killing some 60 family members and employees before they were chased away

trees, originally planted in the 1920s as part of a swamp clearance and malaria-control programme.

Pretty though Kabale may be, there isn't a lot to the town in terms of tourist attractions. Still, it's a comfortable place to settle into for a few days, with plenty of cheap accommodation and good food available, and usually no shortage of company from other travellers. Nearby Lake Bunyonyi, for years a popular day excursion from Kabale, has recently been subject to burgeoning tourist development, and most travellers now prefer to stay on the lakeshore or one of the islands rather than in the town itself. Other local attractions include the Kisizi Falls and a group of hot springs alongside the road to the Rwandan border.

GETTING THERE AND AWAY The 430km surfaced road that connects Kampala to Kabale via Mbarara should take six hours to cover in a private vehicle. Buses

by government troops. Two of the ringleaders were captured, to be executed by public hanging in Kabale six months later. Ntokibiri went into hiding, only to resurface almost two years later at Ikundu, where he attempted to plot another rebellion against an unpopular Muganda sub-country chief. His plans were leaked to the authorities, however, and he was shot dead in his bed by government troops on 21 June 1919.

The earliest missionaries to Kigezi, conscious of the significance of Nyabingi, attempted to convert the Bakiga by using local words associated with the cult in their sermons and descriptions of Christian rituals. The missionaries also portrayed the Mother of Jesus as a spiritual icon similar to but more powerful than Nyabingi, and many Bakiga came to perceive the Virgin Mary as a substitute for the traditional spirit associated with healing and fertility. By the 1930s, the Nyabingi cult, if not completely dead, had gone so far underground as to be undetectable. And in 1937, according to some Rastafarian cultists in Jamaica, the neglected Nyabingi spirit abandoned Uganda for good, and relocated to Ethiopia where it took possession of Haile Selassie during Mussolini's fascist invasion!

At least one shrine formerly associated with Nyabingi has more recently been used by a nominally Christian cult. The Nyabugoto Caves, where Ntokibiri fomented his 1817 rebellion, were in times past occupied by a Nyabingi medium visited by chronically barren Bakiga women, who would make sacrifices to the spirit and then wait, sometimes for weeks or months, for the oracle's blessing. In the late 1970s, it was reported that a local women called Blandina Buzigye witnessed a large rock formation in this cave transform into the Virgin Mary before her eyes. It was in the same cave, ten years later, that Credonia Mwerinde founded her own fertility cult, one that, before it mutated into the tragically fated Movement for the Restoration of the Ten Commandments of God, was essentially a variation on the old Nyabingi ritual but centred instead on the Virgin Mary.

Oddly enough, the term Nyabingi found its way across the Atlantic to Jamaica, where admirers of the rebellious Queen Muhumusa incorporated what are known as *nyabinghi* chants into their celebrations. Sometimes abbreviated to *bhingi*, the chants and dances were originally performed to invoke 'death to the black or white oppressors' but today they are purely ceremonial. Three differently pitched drums are used to create the nyabinghi beat, which – popularised in the late 1950s by the recording artist Count Ossie – has been a huge rhythmic influence on better-known secular Jamaican genres such as ska and reggae. Nyabinghi is also the name of a fundamentalist but strictly pacifist Rastafarian cult which regards the late Ethiopian Emperor Haile Selassie to have been an earthly incarnation of God.

between Kampala and Kabale leave throughout the morning, cost Ush15,000, and generally take six to seven hours, stopping at Mbarara *en route*. The Horizon Bus Company, which runs several buses daily, is recommended, as is the Post Bus that leaves Kampala from the rear of the main post office at 08.00 daily except for Sundays. There is also regular transport between Kabale and Kasese, Kisoro and the Rwandan border.

People driving between Kabale and Kasese might think about using a short cut avoiding Mbarara as described in the box in *Chapter 7, The Old Kabale Road and Kitagata Springs*, page 222. Another back route (far longer and slower but more rewarding) takes in Bwindi National Park and the Ishasha sector of Queen Elizabeth National Park. The Kabale–Bwindi leg of this route is covered in the *Getting there and away* section under *Bwindi National Park* later in this chapter, while the Bwindi–Katunguru leg is included under the corresponding section in *Chapter 9, Ishasha*, pages 282–3. Provided that you stick to the roads recommended in these sections (some other roads are in an appalling state), you could get between Kabale and Kasese in seven or eight hours, though you'd almost certainly want to stop at Bwindi and Ishasha along the way.

WHERE TO STAY
Moderate

White Horse Hotel ☎ 04864 26010; m 0772 459859; f 04864 23717. This former government hotel is perched in large green grounds adjacent to the golf course on Makanga Hill, overlooking the town centre, with carpeted rooms with DSTV and hot water. There is a cosy bar, lit by log fire on cooler nights, and the restaurant serves good international dishes in the Ush4,000–7,000 range. Facilities include 24hr room service, membership of the golf course, lawn and table tennis and a pool table. *US$37/46 sgl/dbl B&B.*

Green Hills Hotel ☎ 04864 24442. Situated on the opposite side of the golf course to the White Horse, the new Green Hills Hotel is smarter and more contemporary in feel than its only rival in this price bracket, but the rooms and grounds are far smaller and the whole is comparatively lacking in character. Still, the carpeted s/c rooms, all with DSTV and hot water, represent good value. *US$27/32 sgl/dbl B&B.*

Budget

Highland Hotel ☎ 04864 22175/23061; m 0772 462190; e highland@imul.com. This long-serving hotel is situated on the Kisoro side of the town centre. The s/c twin rooms all have hot baths which are welcome in the chilly Kabale climate, but are otherwise nothing special. Single rooms using common showers are also available. There's a cosy wood-panelled bar, complete with roaring log fire, and the restaurant serves adequate but unexciting fare in the Ush4,000–5,000 range. The attached business centre offers foreign exchange and serves as a booking agent for the Bunyonyi Overland Resort on nearby Lake Bunyonyi. *US$10/20 sgl/twin B&B.*

Victoria Inn ☎ 04864 22154. Another established favourite in this price range is the friendly Victoria Inn, which has a quiet back-road location only a couple of mins' walk from the town centre. The well maintained s/c rooms with hot running water are very good value. *US$9/13 sgl/dbl.*

Hotel Queens ☎ 04864 24054. This new hotel, conveniently located for the Main Street and

Amagara Café, has a plush appearance and clean tiled rooms with hot showers. The official rate for a room with a three-quarter sized bed is acceptable value for friendly couples while singles can negotiate a lower rate. The bar provides DSTV, the food is tasty in the Ush4,500–6,000 range and a generator backup is provided. *US$13/19 sgl/room with ³/₄-sized bed.*

Amagara Café and Guesthouse m 0772 959667; e amagara@susnow.org; lakebunyonyi.net. This excellent new guesthouse is a sister establishment to Byoona Amagara on lovely Lake Bunyonyi. The setting for the town guesthouse, 50m down a grubby back street behind the Edirisa Cultural Centre, is rather less attractive than that of the island resort but it's unbeatable value. Additional bonuses are the superb Amagara Café (see *Where to eat* below) and the cheapest internet outside Kampala (Ush25 per min). *US$6/8 sgl/dbl at the town guesthouse, US$32 family rooms.*

Shoestring

Skyblue and Skyline hotels These next-door neighbours occupy a convenient location directly opposite the bus park from which they have competed for the travel market for well over a decade. The pick of several-dozen cheap local guesthouses scattered around Kabale, there's little to choose between this pair. Both serve cheap and satisfying food in the Ush2,500–4,500 range. *Both charge US$4/6 sgl/dbl with common showers, and Skyblue (☎ 04864 22154) has introduced some s/c rooms for US$7/8 sgl/dbl.*

Edirisa Cultural Centre This new facility (see *Culture* below) is developing a small and

increasingly popular backpacker hostel with a limited number of rooms. Facilities include a lounge with book and DVD library and decent meals. Proceeds support community development activities beside Lake Bunyonyi. *Dormitory US$2, US$3 sgl, US$8 s/c dbl.*

Saint Paul's Hostel ☎ 04864 22267. Set in a green compound attached to the Catholic Church, this centrally located hostel is reasonable value and has rooms using common showers. A canteen serves basic meals and sodas but no alcohol. *US$3/5 sgl/dbl.*

Hotel Home Again The best of several shoestring lodges lining the Kampala road past the central bus station, with rooms with tiled floors using common showers. There's a sauna/aerobics club at the rear which is a popular spot in the evening for a beer and bib chicken. *US$5/6 sgl/dbl.*

Other options nearby, including the **Hotel Standard, London Image Inn** and **Silk Inn,** really don't warrant closer inspection despite smart exteriors.

Visitours Hotel Situated next to the bus station opposite the Skyline this hotel was for many years an established favourite with backpackers, with small but adequately clean rooms. However given the half-dozen or so reports of theft from locked rooms we've received and decline of the once-popular restaurant, it's difficult to recommend. *US$2 pp.*

✗ WHERE TO EAT AND DRINK

✗ **Amagara Café** m 0772 959667. Most hotels in Kabale serve affordable if predictable international (and local) food. However one location stands out, indeed deserves a stop in the town by itself. Following the much-lamented closure of Kabale's excellent Mbuzi Mbiri restaurant in 2004, one of the chefs, armed with photocopies of the original menu has surfaced at the new Amagara Café where the offerings are every bit as good as before. A steak (Ush6,500) ordered medium rare arrives as just that; deliciously tender, drenched with a honey and thyme sauce and accompanied by a side salad. If some criticism must be levelled, the backstreet setting is rather too grim to sit out in; though I'm assured the greater potential of the lawny back courtyard will be exploited before too long.

✗ **White Horse Hotel** This hilltop hotel serves smallish portions of rather ordinary grub but this is easily forgiven if you take lunch or an early dinner on the terrace to enjoy the expansive and immaculate gardens and surrounding hills.

✗ **Little Ritz Bar and Restaurant** Situated on the 1st floor of the same building as the Hot Loaf Bakery, this excellent restaurant serves a variety of Indian and continental dishes in the Ush4,000–5,000 range. A good bar with DSTV is attached. The breezy balcony is the most attractive spot in the town centre to eat outdoors or enjoy a drink while there's a warming log fire inside.

✗ **Hot Loaf Bakery** Located beneath the Little Ritz, the Kabale franchise of this national chain of bakeries stocks fresh bread (baked daily) and a variety of pies and pastries for take-away.

✗ **Golf Side Campsite** Overlooking the golf course on the hill above the town centre, this attractive spot doesn't actually permit camping, but the wood-and-bamboo double-storey bar is a great spot for a drink. A limited selection of food is available.

LISTINGS

Tourist information The Bwindi and Mgahinga national parks information office close to the Highland Hotel is open seven days a week and can provide current information about all aspects of visiting these two nearby national parks. It can also check the availability of gorilla-tracking permits and make bookings, though this is done in consultation with the UWA head office in Kampala, so it might take a few hours to sort out. Information about other local attractions is pinned on the walls, and the staff are generally willing to answer queries that are unrelated to the parks.

Foreign exchange As is the case throughout Uganda now, Stanbic Bank will change cash and American Express travellers' cheques at the rate set by the head office in Kampala. Outside banking hours, try Highland Business Centre (next to the Highland Inn) but expect poorer rates.

Internet Internet is available at Amagara Café for Ush25 per minute – the cheapest anywhere outside Kampala – and (6km out of town) at the Lake Bunyonyi Overland Resort for Ush100 per minute.

Shopping There are several good supermarkets in Kabale, the best being the one on the main road close to the post office. Handicrafts can be bought from the Edirisa Cultural Centre.

Culture The **Edirisa Cultural Centre** (*www.edirisa.org*) is located opposite the Hot Loaf/Little Ritz. This is a non-profit organisation striving to promote and preserve Bakiga culture. It was started several years ago by a Bakiga elder concerned at the erosion of his local culture and has developed with the help of young European volunteers into a community development project. Richard Curley writes that: 'The operation offers four high-value features: (1) a serviceable fast-food take-away (the giant vegetable samosas are a real triumph); (2) guided tours of an authentic fully furnished old Bakiga roundhouse; (3) honest, friendly advice about tourist activities and accommodation in the district, including field trips to Batwa villages; and most importantly (4), they now serve the best cup of coffee in Uganda outside of Kampala. In addition, there's a good gift shop, a library, and sitting room. It's a good place to park yourself for a few hours if you need to.' The Kabale operation supports community development activities beside Lake Bunyonyi.

Nightclubs Kabale's only nightclub is **Club Earthquake** on Nyerere Road. I vaguely remember some slightly disturbing entrance murals suggesting a fascination amongst local youth for outrageously busty females and hinting at activities that suggest that the traditional Bakiga taboo regarding pre-marital relations is a thing of the past.

WHAT TO SEE The most popular tourist attractions around Kabale are the nearby Lake Bunyonyi and more remote Bwindi and Mgahinga national parks, all covered under separate headings later in this chapter. The following more obscure sites might be of interest to those wanting to get away from the beaten track:

Hot springs There are some hot springs south of Kabale towards Katuna on the Rwandan border. Set in a eucalyptus stand, immediately to the left of the road from Kabale, the disappointing springs are no more than a muddy, lukewarm pool. To get there, either board a Katuna-bound pick-up truck and ask to be dropped at the springs, or else walk or cycle the 8km from Kabale. You can swim in the pool if you like – it's supposed to have therapeutic qualities, and you're bound to provide a few Ugandan bathers with some company and/or amusement.

Kisizi Waterfall This 30m-high waterfall lies on the Kyabamba River a few hundred metres from the Church of Uganda's Kisizi Hospital, some 65km from Kabale by road. It is a very pretty, peaceful spot, serviced by an excellent small guesthouse, and the surrounding forests and quiet roads offer pleasant rambling possibilities. The waterfall is used to provide hydro-electric power to the hospital – in Uganda's darker days, Kisizi was one of the few places countrywide that had a reliable 24-hour electricity supply and functional street lamps.

The tranquil atmosphere around the waterfall belies its macabre historical association with the local custom described somewhat euphemistically by one Ugandan source as 'damping'. In traditional Bakiga society, virginity was a highly prized asset and an unmarried girl who fell pregnant could, at best, hope to be a social outcast for the rest of her days. More often, however, the offender would be mortally punished: tied to a tree and left to the mercy of wild animals, or thrown from a cliff, or abandoned to starve on an island. And many disgraced girls were 'damped' at Kisizi: tossed over the waterfall, arms and legs tightly bound, to drown in the pool below.

Getting there and away To reach Kisizi, follow the surfaced Kampala road out of Kabale for 32km as far as Muhanga, from where a 33km dirt road leads north to the hospital and waterfall. The drive should take less than two hours in a private vehicle. Using public transport, regular minibus-taxis connect Kabale to Muhanga, from where a more erratic trickle of pick-up trucks bump their way to Kisizi. The Kisizi coach runs directly between Kampala and Kisizi daily, except for Sundays, leaving from Kisizi at 04.30 and from the main bus park in Kampala at 11.30. The trip takes up to eight hours and tickets cost Ush10,000.

Where to stay and eat

⌂ **Kisizi Hospital Cottages** ☎ +871 761 587164 (satellite phone); e kisiizi@bushnet.net. 2 clean, cosy and very reasonably priced cottages on the hospital grounds, primarily intended for expatriate hospital workers, will accommodate tourists when space is available. Although the accommodation is seldom full, room space cannot be guaranteed, so it's advisable to ring or email in advance. *Rose Cottage charges US$6 pp for a room using common hot showers, and serves home-cooked set meals at Ush1,500 for b/fast or Ush1,500 for lunch or dinner. The self-catering Round Cottage consists of 2 twin rooms and is rented out as a whole for US$24 (extra mattresses can be provided for larger groups).*

Lake Nyabihoko Perched at an altitude of roughly 1,500m above the western Rift Valley scarp, Lake Nyabihoko – like the better-known Lake Bunyonyi – is a long, narrow and relatively young body of water, created by the natural damming of what was formerly a river valley. Hemmed in by steep hills and studded with at least a dozen forested islands, Nyabihoko extends for about 7km from east to west, but it is nowhere much more than 1km wide. The 15m-high Nyakabare Falls on the Rwamunaba River lie about 2km north of the littoral, while a smaller set of rapids runs west out of the lake into the shallow Kakono Swamp. An extensive papyrus swamp at the eastern effluent is skirted by the main road past the lake. At

THE LEGEND OF MUTUMO

The relatively recent formation of Lake Nyabihoko is hinted at by a local legend relating to a farmer called Mutumo who once lived where the lake now lies. Mutumo had grown wealthy thanks to one of his cows, which produced a great many strong calves. One day, the fertile cow turned to Mutumo and surprised him by announcing that when she died, she should not be eaten, as was customary, but buried intact. Mutumo related this instruction to his wife and children, who understandably sceptical, but he insisted that the wishes of the cow should be respected. Some time later, Mutumo went away to Rwanda to look for a bull, and while he was away the cow died. Mutumo's wife pointed out to her sons that cows couldn't talk, so this burial business was nonsense – they would eat what meat they wanted and sell the rest.

The next morning, the valley started to flood. When Mutumo returned home a few days later, all his land was submerged by a lake in which all his cattle had drowned. Mutumo took refuge with his friend Mwamba, another cattle farmer, where he was offered the job of tending the calves. But Mutumo remained unhappy, seldom speaking to others, and muttering away to himself about his misfortune. Eventually, Mwamba asked Mutumo what the matter was, and when he heard the full story, he decided to share his friend's misery. The two men returned to Mutumo's land and prepared a feast for their families on the lakeshore. At the height of the festivities, Mwamba told the two families that when he died, they must share all his possessions between them. Then Mwamba and Mutumo walked off to a secluded part of the lakeshore, embraced each other, jumped into the lake, and drowned. The island closest to the northern lakeshore is still named in memory of Mutumo and is said to be all that is left of his farm.

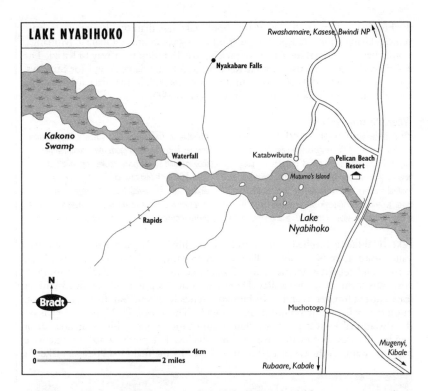

the fishing villages along the shore of Nyabihoko, it's possible to arrange to take a canoe to go looking for waterbirds and crocodiles, as well as the lake's solitary resident hippo. See box *The legend of Mutumo*, page 237.

Getting there and away The eastern shore of Lake Nyabihoko is skirted by the reasonable 27km dirt road that connects Omungeru trading centre, 60km from Kabale along the Kampala road, to Rwashamaire trading centre along the soon-to-be-surfaced main road between Ntungamo and Rukungiri. Coming from Kabale, the best route is via Omungeru, where the Pelican Beach Resort intends to erect a signpost at the turn-off in the near future. Coming from the north, the road to Nyabihoko branches south from Rwashamaire opposite the Petro filling station. The distance from Rwashamaire to the lakeshore is only about 12km, passing through Nkongoro trading centre, but there are a few ambiguous forks along the way, so keep asking directions. Coming from either direction, the road passes within about 200km of the Pelican Beach Resort. No public transport runs all the way to the lake, but it's straightforward and inexpensive to pick up a *boda-boda* either at Rwashamaire or at Omungeru. Should you get stuck along the way, there are a few basic guesthouses at Rwashamaire and the Skyblue Hotel in Ntungamo has good self-contained rooms.

Where to stay

⌂ **Pelican Beach Resort** m 0772 447764. This new resort has an attractive location on the eastern shore of the lake, not far from the swampy outlet, but as things stand that's about its only point of merit. The architecture epitomises an unfortunate Ugandan conception that stark concrete equates to aesthetic quality, and traveller feedback has been uniformly negative about the food ('the toughest old cock in all of Uganda', according to one reader), and the staff harassment and overcharging. *Camping around US$1.50 pp, bandas US$14 dbl B&B.*

LAKE BUNYONYI

Lake Bunyonyi, as its serpentine shape suggests, is essentially a flooded valley system, extending northwards from the Rwandan border over a distance of 25km through the contours of the steep hills that separate Kabale from Kisoro. It is thought to have formed about 8,000 years ago, as a result of a lava flow from local craters which blocked off the Ndego River at present-day Muko to create a natural dam. The lake has a total surface area of around 60km², but it forms the core of a 180km² wetland ecosystem, also incorporating the Ruvuma Swamp and several other permanent marshes. It lies at an altitude of 1,840m, but several of the enclosing hills rise up to 2,500m, and although reported estimates of its depth vary wildly, it is probably nowhere greater than 45m deep.

Dotted with at least 20 small islands and encircled by steep terraced hills, Bunyonyi is a magical spot, and it has been a popular day trip out of Kabale for decades. Over the past few years, the lake has further gained in popularity thanks to a proliferation of budget and other campsites and resorts around the small fishing village of Rutinda (also known as Kyabahinga) and nearby islands. Also in its favour is the high-altitude location, which ensures a moderate climate (often becoming quite chilly at night) and a relatively low incidence of malaria. Bilharzia is reliably reported to be absent from the lake, as are crocodiles and hippos, which means that swimming is very safe. Active travellers are catered for, with canoes, kayaks and mountain bikes available for hire, and enough potential excursions to keep one busy for days.

Bunyonyi translates as 'place of little birds', which is possibly a reference to the prolific weaver colonies along its shore, but larger birds are also represented by the likes of grey-crowned crane and a variety of herons and egrets. It is also probably the best place in Africa to see otters – the diurnal spotted-necked otter in particular – with several pairs resident around Rutinda and the nearby islands. It is difficult to say just why otters are so much more visible here than anywhere else I've visited in Africa, but it must be related to the absence of crocodiles, which would normally prey on and compete for prey with smaller aquatic carnivores.

GETTING THERE AND AWAY An all-weather dirt road connects Kabale to Rutinda, the focal point of tourist activity on Lake Bunyonyi. If you're driving yourself, follow the Kisoro road out of Kabale for 500m then, almost immediately after passing a Kobil filling station, turn left at a junction distinguished by several signposts to the various lakeshore resorts. After about 5km, the road reaches the summit of the hill above Bunyonyi, where there is a five-way junction – turn left for Acacia Cottages, but otherwise keep going straight ahead to reach Rutinda after another 2km or so. Note that the road branching right at this junction offers spectacular views over the lake, emerging at Muko on the main Kabale–Kisoro road after about 20km. Motorists who are heading out to Bushara Island can park their vehicle safely at the island's parking compound in Rutinda, and safe mainland parking is also offered for a small charge at Lake Bunyonyi Overland Camp.

For those without private transport, the Lake Bunyonyi Overland Camp runs a twice-daily shuttle to Rutinda, which leaves Kabale from in front of the Highland Inn at 09.30 and 16.30 daily, and costs Ush3,000 per person. This is subject to demand; it'll take a few people but won't make the trip for one individual. Regular minibus-taxis and pick-up trucks, costing Ush1,000, run between Kabale and Rutinda on market days (Monday and Friday) but the service is somewhat more erratic on other days. A special hire to Rutinda should cost Ush12,000, and a *boda-boda* about half that.

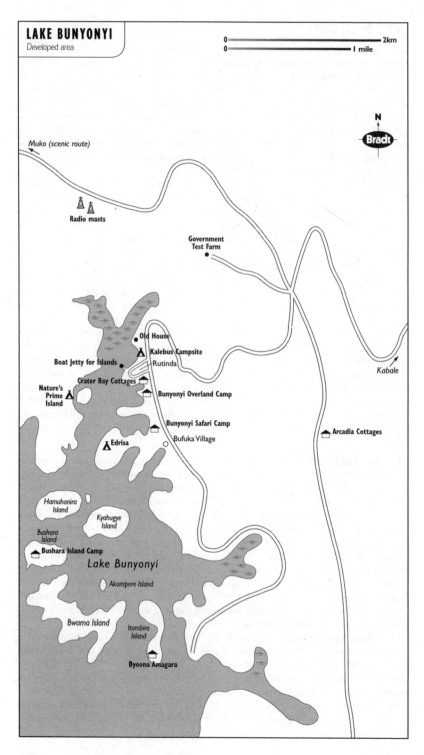

FISHY TALES

According to the late Paul Ngologoza, an eminent Kigezi politician and historian, Lake Bunyonyi harboured 'no fish at all, just *encere*, which are edible frogs' prior to 1919. While this claim seems rather unlikely, several other sources do imply that Bunyonyi naturally harbours very low fish densities. Presumably, this is because the lake slopes underwater too sharply and deeply from the shoreline to provide suitable habitat for shallow-water species such as tilapia and Nile perch, which would have lived in the river before Bunyonyi became a lake.

Whatever the situation before 1919, great efforts were made to stock Lake Bunyonyi during the colonial era. The most valiant of these was initiated in 1927 by District Commissioner Trewin, who arranged for a volume of fish to be relayed manually from Lake Edward to Lake Bunyonyi. 'This was a very involved task,' writes Ngologoza, 'because of the difficulty created by fish dying in transit. Many people [were] divided into groups... The first group brought fish from a place called Katwe... This group raced at great speed to hand over the fish to the second group, who raced to hand over to the third group, and so on, putting in fresh water, pouring out the old water, and finally bringing them to Lake Bunyonyi. It took a day and a night to cover the distance of about 80 miles [120km].'

Initially, the introduced fish flourished, as did commercial fishing, and the rapidly multiplying schools were used to restock several other lakes in the region. Then, in the early 1950s, for reasons that remain unclear, they died out *en masse*, so that 'one might see the whole lake full of floating bodies of dead fish'. Following this disaster, Ngologoza himself experimented with digging a shallow pool next to the lake and stocking it with 50 fish, which rapidly reproduced, allowing him to distribute 4,500 fish to local fishermen, to be bred in the same way.

The only fish to thrive in the lake today is *Claria mozambicus*, known locally as *evale*, which forms an important component of the local subsistence diet. Bunyonyi is also well known for its small but delicious freshwater crayfish, a staple at most of the tourist resorts along the shore, though in 2002 a temporary moratorium was placed on crayfish collection, to allow stocks to replenish after a period of overfishing.

Quotes extracted from the late Paul Ngologoza's excellent and often amusing introduction to the history and culture of Kigezi entitled 'Kigezi and its People', first published in 1967 and reprinted by Fountain Publishers in 1998.

It's also possible to walk to the lake along the road described above, with a slight chance of hitching a lift. A quieter, more scenic route involves following Butambuka Road west out of the town centre then following local footpaths – there are plenty of villagers around to point you in the right direction. Either way, the walk out is worthwhile in its own right, passing by traditional homesteads and patches of forest rustling with birdlife, and it should take the best part of two hours, involving a very stiff ascent as you approach the summit above the lake. One thing you don't want to do is hire a push bicycle to get to Bunyonyi – unless you are exceptionally fit, you'll probably spend as much time pushing the bike up steep hills as you will cycling.

If you want to go out on the lake, or to spend a night or two at one of the islands, you can hire a dugout or motorboat from Rutinda Jetty. Prices are negotiable, but expect to pay about Ush10,000 each way for the ten–15-minute motorboat trip to either Byoona Amagara or Bushara Island or Ush3,000 per person for a 30–45-minute ride in a dugout canoe. Bushara Island is closer than Byoona Amagara, but it's a more expensive place.

Derek Schuurman

Of all Uganda's peoples, the one group visitors most wish to visit is the Batwa, the Pygmies indigenous to the dense rainforests of the southwest. But, while meeting a Batwa community is easily achievable, visitors should be aware of the current situation of this tiny, ostracised minority, which has no land rights nor legal forest access, and remains subject to discrimination on local and institutional levels (see box *Batwa Pygmies*, pages 244–5).

Arguably the best place in which to meet Batwa is Bwindi National Park, where attendance at a Batwa music and dance performance is usually arranged as part of the Buhoma Community Forest Walk. Another possibility is Lake Bunyonyi, where an excursion to a local village is offered. But recent reports from both locations have mentioned distressing incidents in which the Batwa were exploited and/or subjected to rough treatment at the hands of other Ugandans. One organisation currently working hard to address the plight of the Batwa is the Forest Peoples Project (FPP) (↘ 01608 652893; e info@fppwrm.gn.apc.org; www.forestpeoples.org), a UK-based charity that supports forest peoples' rights to determine their own future, to control the use of their lands, and to carry out sustainable use of the forest resources.

The five main goals of the FPP aimed broadly at providing a voice for forest people, are as follows:

- To help establish an effective global movement of forest peoples.
- To promote the rights and interests of forest peoples in environmental and human rights circles.
- To co-ordinate support among environmental organisations for forest peoples' visions.
- To counter top-down projects which deprive local peoples of resources.
- To support community-based, sustainable forest management.

Presently, FPP is working with the Batwa in southwest Uganda to help them support and defend themselves against the problems and injustices they face. Should you happen to witness any incident where Batwa are exploited or victimised, please contact FPP and speak to your tour operator, who will follow up through the appropriate channels.

WHERE TO STAY AND EAT
Moderate

⌂ **Bushara Island Camp** ↘/f 04864 22447; m 0772 464585; e bushara@maf.co.ug; www.acts.ca/lbdc. The medium-sized island of Bushara, which lies about 10 mins from Rutinda by motorboat, has been developed as a community-run resort with the assistance of Canadian missionaries. It's come a long way since its first incarnation in 1993 when a few cramped standing tents were crammed with rickety beds to create a 'furnished tented camp'. From these humble origins Bushara Island has gone from strength to strength, today offering the winning combination of absolute tranquillity and isolation, tasteful rustic architecture, and as good value for money as you'll find anywhere in Uganda. Lake-view accommodation is available in spacious and secluded s/c standing tents, 2 three-quarter beds, and hot water supplied on request. An open-air hilltop restaurant serves pizzas, vegetarian dishes, meat, chicken and fish dishes in the Ush4,000–6,000 range. Several of the 100-plus bird species recorded on the island can be observed from a self-guided trail through the eucalyptus woodland, free to overnight guests. Guided day trips to the Muko and Nyombe swamps cost US$23 per boat plus US$4 pp, and local village and birding trips can be arranged at US$2–5 pp. Day visitors are welcome. The camp has its own motorboat for transfers and the captain is normally to be found at Rutinda Jetty. *S/c tents US$17–22 dbl, while a choice of equally pleasant and comfortable cottages are also available at US$22, US$30 and US$40 sgl/dbl. Rates given are for accommodation only. Camping US$3 pp per night.*

🏠 **Arcadia Cottages** ☎ 04864 26231; e arcadiacottages@yahoo.com. This new resort has 5 s/c brick cottages perched on the rim of a hill offering truly sensational views over Lake Bunyonyi and its myriad islands with the Virunga Volcanoes beyond. Meals are served in a spacious bar restaurant with a timber viewing deck outside. The menu (like that of Kabale's Amagara Café) is based on that of the excellent but now defunct Mbuzi Mbiri and has been related to me as being 'the best food in Uganda.' To get there, turn left at the five-way junction at the top of the hill as you approach Bunyonyi from Kabale (more or less as you get the first view of the lake) and follow the dirt track along the cusp of the hill for about 2km. *US$24/48 sgl/dbl inc full English b/fast.*

🏠 **Nature's Prime Island** m 0772 423215; e naturesprimeisland@yahoo.com. The acclaimed Far Out Camp, which was forced to close down in 2003, recently reopened under the management of the family that owns this now rather ambitiously named island. They tell us that: 'The beautiful island is offering quality services to the tourists in the form of new furnished log cabins and new luxury furnished tents with a fully operational bar and restaurant. The ambience at the island is still unique and it targets the upmarket tourists.' Initial reader feedback has been somewhat less elegiac, so updates to the Bradt Uganda email newsletter will be appreciated. The island is however conveniently close to the jetty at Rutinda. *Tents and cabins both US$25 pp B&B, US$3 to pitch your own tent.*

Budget

🏠 **Bunyonyi Overland Resort** ☎ 04864 23741/2/3; m 0772 409510; e highland@imul.com; www.edirisa.org/overland or www.traveluganda.co.ug/bunyonyi-overland. The justifiably popular Overland Resort, which lies adjacent to Rutinda village, sprawls down a terraced green slope to a lovely papyrus-fringed bay, frequented by at least one readily observed pair of otters and vast colonies of yellow-backed weavers. Excellent facilities include an open-sided restaurant/bar that serves affordable meals and has DSTV, a small curio and grocery shop, inexpensive kayak, canoe and mountain-bike hire, and emergency radio contact with the affiliated Highland Business Centre in Kabale. Set some distance from the main camping area are a row of comfortable s/c twin chalets with hot water, smaller twin rooms using common showers and furnished tents. A shuttle to the camp leaves from in front of the Highland Inn in Kabale at 09.30 and 16.30 daily, costing Ush4,000 pp. It's a truly excellent set-up for which the only criticism is a function of its high quality — up to 5 overland trucks might congregate on the campsite and bar on a busy night, a scenario that can be off-putting to independent travellers. *Chalets US$32/41 per unit, twin rooms US$16/22 sgl/dbl. Furnished tents US$19/24 sgl/dbl; tents can be rented for US$5 pp, US$4 pp with your own tent.*

🏠 **Crater Bay Cottages** ☎ 04864 26255; m 0772 643996/671458; e craterbay@yahoo.com. Situated within Rutinda on the opposite side of the same small bay as the Overland Camp, this new lodge consists of a row of clean and comfortably furnished round cottages set in compact flowering grounds that lead down to the lake. The restaurant/bar serves decent meals for around Ush5,000 and spills out onto a veranda overlooking the lake. On the whole, Crater Bay lacks the ambience of Overland Camp, but it's friendly, quiet and comfortable, and far less likely to become crowded. *US$16 for a s/c dbl with hot water or US$88 sgl/dbl using common shower. Camping slightly more than US$2 pp.*

🏠 **Bunyonyi Safari Camp** Standing silent sentinel over an otherwise pretty small bay situated between the fishing villages of Rutinda and Bufuka, this gaspingly inappropriate development was evidently conceived by somebody for whom the terms 'safari camp' and 'monolithic concrete eyesore' are more-or-less interchangeable. Construction of the main multi-storey tower block stalled several years ago, and although demolition would be the more certain bet aesthetically, its appearance might be slightly less confrontational if the finishing touches are ever applied. Until such time as that happens, 3 adjacent s/c cottages in the shadow of the edifice remain. *Around US$22 dbl.*

🏠 **Kalebas Campsite/Pizza Café** (4 rooms) m 0772 907892/0752 461913; e kalebas@yahoo.com. Previously the Karibuni Beach Campsite, the first backpackers' haunt on Lake Bunyonyi, Kalebas is located beside the lakeshore just as the road from Kabale enters Rutinda. Somewhat overtaken by subsequent developments on more expansive sites, this campground has been given a new lease of life

'We have always lived in the forest. Like my father and grandfathers, I lived from hunting and collecting in this mountain. Then the Bahutu came. They cut the forest to cultivate the land. They carried on cutting and planting until they had encircled our forest with their fields. Today, they come right up to our huts. Instead of forest, now we are surrounded by Irish potatoes!' – Gahut Gahuliro, a Mutwa born 100 years earlier on the slopes of the Virungas, talking in 1999.

The Batwa (singular Mutwa) Pygmies are the most ancient inhabitants of interlacustrine Africa, and easily distinguished from other Ugandans by their unusually short stature – an adult male seldom exceeds 1.5m in height – and paler, more bronzed complexion. Semi-nomadic by inclination, small egalitarian communities of Batwa kin traditionally live in impermanent encampments of flimsy leaf huts, set in a forest clearing, which they will up and leave when food becomes scarce locally, upon the death of a community member, or when the whim takes them. In times past, the Batwa wore only a drape of animal hide or barkcloth, and had little desire to accumulate possessions – a few cooking pots, some hunting gear, and that's about it.

The Batwa lifestyle is based around hunting, undertaken as a team effort by the male members of a community. In some areas, the favoured *modus operandi* involves part of the hunting party stringing a long net between a few trees, while the remainder advances noisily to herd small game into the net to be speared. In other areas, poisoned arrows are favoured: the hunting party will move silently along the forest floor looking for potential prey, which is shot from a distance, then they wait until it drops and if necessary deliver the final blow with a spear. Batwa men also gather wild honey, while the women gather edible plants to supplement the meat.

According to a survey undertaken in 1996, fewer than 2,000 Batwa reside permanently in Uganda, mostly concentrated in Kigezi. Only 2,000 years ago, however, east and southern Africa were populated almost solely by Batwa and related hunter-gatherers, whose lifestyle differed little from that of our earliest common human ancestors. Since then, agriculturist and pastoralist settlers, through persecution or assimilation, have marginalised the region's hunter-gatherers to a few small and today mostly degraded communities living in habitats unsuitable to agriculture or pasture, such as rainforest interiors and deserts.

The initial incursions into Batwa territory were made when the first Bantu-speaking farmers settled in Kigezi, some time before the 16th century, and set about clearing small tracts of forest for subsistence agriculture and pasture. This process of deforestation was greatly accelerated in the early 20th century: by 1930 the last three substantial tracts of forest remaining in Kigezi were gazetted as the Impenetrable and Echuya forest reserves and Gorilla Game Sanctuary by the colonial authorities. In one sense, this move to protect the forests was of direct benefit to the Batwa, since it ensured that what little remained of them would not be lost to agriculture. But the legal status of the Batwa was altered to their detriment – true, they were still permitted to hunt and forage within the reserves, but where formerly these forests had been recognised as Batwa communal land, they were now government property.

Only some three generations later would the Batwa be faced with the full ramifications of having lost all legal entitlement to their ancestral lands in the colonial era. In 1991, the Gorilla Game Sanctuary and Impenetrable Forest Reserve were re-gazetted to become Mgahinga

by a Dutch-Ugandan couple seeking to share their love of traditional art and pizzas. Small but adequate rooms with dbl beds have been recently extended to include bathrooms, Camping is available on the lovely lakeside lawn below a bar-dining shelter bedecked with traditional, carved artwork in which good pizzas (advance order preferred) are served. The range and standard of facilities is inferior to the rather slicker Overland Camp, but a growing number of independent travellers are coming

and Bwindi national parks, a move backed by international donors who stipulated that all persons resident within the newly proclaimed national parks were to be evicted, and that hunting and other forest harvesting should cease forthwith. Good news for gorillas, perhaps, but what about those Batwa communities that might have dwelt within the forest reserves for centuries? Overnight, they were reduced in status to illegal squatters whose traditional subsistence lifestyle had been criminalised. Adding insult to injury, while some compensation was awarded to non-Batwa farmers who had settled within the forest reserves since the 1930s and illegally cleared forest to make way for cultivation, the evicted Batwa received compensation only if they had destroyed part of the forest reserve in a similar manner.

Today, more than 80% of Uganda's Batwa are officially landless, and none has legal access to the forest on which their traditional livelihood depends. Locally, the Batwa are viewed not with sympathy, but rather as objects of ridicule, subject to regular unprovoked attacks that occasionally lead to fatalities. The extent of local prejudice against the Batwa can be garnered from a set of interviews posted on the website www.edrisa.org. The Batwa, report some of their Bakiga neighbours: 'smoke marijuana… like alcohol… drink too much… make noise all night long… eat too much food… cannot grow their own food and crops… depend on hunting and begging… don't care about their children… the man makes love to his wife while the children sleep on their side' – a collection of circumstantially induced half-truths and outright fallacies that make the Batwa come across as the debauched survivors of a dysfunctional hippie commune!

Prejudice against the Batwa is not confined to their immediate neighbours. The 1997 edition of Richard Nzita's otherwise commendable *Peoples and Cultures of Uganda* contrives, in the space of two pages, to characterise the pygmoid peoples of Uganda as beggars, crop raiders and pottery thieves – even cannibals! Conservationists and the Western media, meanwhile, persistently stigmatise the Batwa as gorilla hunters and poachers – this despite the strong taboo against killing or eating gorillas that informs every known Batwa community. Almost certainly, any gorilla hunting that might be undertaken by the Batwa today will have been instigated by outsiders.

This much is incontestable: the Batwa and their hunter-gatherer ancestors have in all probability inhabited the forests of Kigezi for some half a million years. Their traditional lifestyle, which places no rigorous demands on the forest, could be cited as a model of that professed holy grail of modern conservationists: the sustainable use of natural resources. The Batwa were not major participants in the deforestation of Kigezi, but they have certainly been the main human victims of this loss. And Batwa and gorillas cohabited in the same forests for many millennia prior to their futures both being imperilled by identical external causes in the 20th century. As Jerome Lewis writes: 'They and their way of life are entitled to as much consideration and respect as other ways of life. There was and is nothing to be condemned in forest nomadism… The Batwa… used the environment without destroying or seriously damaging it. It is only through their long-term custody of the area that later comers have good land to use.'

Quotes from Lewis and Gahuliro are sourced from Jerome Lewis's exemplary report 'Batwa Pygmies of the Great Lakes Region', downloadable at www.minorityrights. org/admin/Download/Pdf/Batwa%2520Report.pdf. See also the box Visiting the Batwa in Kigezi *on page 242.*

to appreciate the quiet and rustic setting. *Rooms US$11 pp (negotiable), camping US$3 pp.*
🏠 **Byoona Amagara Island Retreat** m 0752 652788; e amagara@susnow.org; www.lakebunyonyi.net. This new retreat is the most

southerly of the Lake Bunyonyi resorts. Quiet, scenic and distanced from the relative bustle of Rutindo it's fast becoming a popular getaway for budget travellers. A range of accommodation is available. The most popular option is the 'geodomes'; a fresh-air arrangement consisting of a round thatched roof and a rear wall over a dbl bed (net provided). An excellent library is provided with a solar-powered DVD-theatre. Byoona Amagara has a private compound for guests' parking at Rutindo. *Camping US$1.60 pp, dormitory beds US$4 pp using communal facilities, a trpl-bed log cabin US$9 pp and a guesthouse with dbl bed US$11 pp, each with their own ablutions. Geodomes US$7 pp.*

△ Camping The most popular place to pitch a tent is the Lake Bunyonyi Overland Camp, and in most respects this is also probably the best option, though nearby Kalebas and Crater Bay are might be quieter. Campers are also welcomed out on the lake at Bushara Island and Byoona Amagara.

EXCURSIONS AROUND BUNYONYI Lake Bunyonyi and surrounds offers numerous opportunities for organised excursions and casual exploration. Visits to most of the places of interest described below can be arranged through the lakeshore resorts and hotels, and it's also possible to reach some sites using public transport and/or dugout canoes chartered at a negotiable rate from the jetty at Rutinda.

The lakeshore near Rutinda Rutinda itself, though rather small and humdrum, is considerably enlivened on Mondays and Fridays, when dozens of canoes arrive in the early morning from all around the lake, carrying local farmers and their produce to a colourful market on the main jetty. A pleasant short stroll from Rutinda leads north along the lakeshore, following the Kabale road for roughly 1km before it begins the steep ascent to the summit above the lake.

A prominent local landmark, situated on a small peninsula alongside the Kabale road 700m north of Rutinda, is the semi-derelict colonial-style building that once housed the popular Bunyonyi Lake View Resort. The resort was established in 1965 by Frank Kalimuzo, a locally born politician who served as the permanent secretary to the prime minister in the first Obote government and was appointed Vice-chancellor of Makerere University in Kampala in 1969. It closed in 1972, after Amin's soldiers (or, as the official explanation had it at the time, 'men masquerading as security officers') abducted and permanently silenced Kalimuzo on suspicion of being a Rwandan spy. The building was partially restored as a short-lived backpacker hostel in 1998, but is once again uninhabited.

Having passed the abandoned resort, the road skirts a patch of papyrus swamp where various colourful bishop- and widow-birds breed and a few pairs of the peculiar thick-billed weaver construct their distinctive neat nests. From here, more energetic travellers could ascend to the top of the steep hills, via a series of switchbacks, to the five-way junction at the summit. Turn right here, and after about 2km you'll reach **Arcadia Cottages**, with its stunning view over the lake and islands. Using local footpaths, it's possible to descend directly from here to Bufuka, on the lakeshore about 1km south of Rutinda, but the paths are very steep and probably best avoided after rain.

The islands Several of the 20-plus islands on Bunyonyi are worth a visit, with the most accessible being the half-dozen or so situated in the central part of the lake close to Rutinda. Aside from Bushara Island, which uses its own motorboat for transfers, the best way to reach most of the islands is by dugout canoe, easily arranged with local fishermen at Rutinda Jetty.

Bwama Island is the largest on Lake Bunyonyi and the site of a well-known mission, school and handicraft centre for the disabled. Most of the buildings on Bwama date to 1929, when Leonard Sharp, a British doctor with several years' medical experience in southwest Uganda, established a leper colony on the island. Leprosy was a serious problem in Kigezi at that time, and for longer than three decades the island provided refuge to up to 100 victims of the disease. Leprosy was eradicated from Kigezi in the 1960s and the colony ceased operating in 1969. The island remains of interest for its scenery, architecture and handicraft shop, and it's possible to camp or rent a room at Byoona Amagara on neighbouring **Itambira Island**. The trip from Rutinda takes about 30 minutes in a local canoe.

Immediately north of Bwama, **Bushara Island** is well developed for tourism, and although the accommodation is highly recommended, day trips are also encouraged. The ideal would be to go to the island for a lingering lunch, then either arrange to take a dugout canoe around its circumference or else to walk the self-guided trail along the shore – both options cost US$2–3 to day visitors.

Shaded by one solitary tree, the tiny **Akampene Island**– Island of Punishment – is visible both from the north shore of Bwama and the east shore of Bushara. Like Kisizi Falls, this island is traditionally associated with the Bakiga taboo against pre-marital sex. In times gone by, unmarried girls who became pregnant would be exiled to Akampene, where they faced one of two possible fates. Any man who did not own sufficient cows to pay for an untainted bride was permitted to fetch the disgraced girl from the island and make her his wife. Failing that, the girl would usually starve to death.

A somewhat more fanciful legend is attached to the nearby island of **Akabucuranuka**, the name of which literally means 'upside down'. Many years ago, it is said, a group of male revellers on Akabucuranuka refused to share their abundant stock of beer with an old lady who had disembarked from her canoe to join them. Unfortunately for the drinking party, the woman was a sorceress. She returned to her canoe, paddled a safe distance away, and then used her magical powers to overturn the island – drowning everybody in the party – then flip it back the right way up as if nothing had happened.

Muko Forest Reserve and Ruvuma Swamp The small trading centre of Muko, on the northern tip of Bunyonyi, is the site of the vast papyrus expanses of Ruvuma Swamp, formed as the Ndego River flows out of the lake. Prior to the 1940s, the area around Muko was densely forested, and harboured a large population of elephants and other wildlife, but much of the indigenous vegetation was cleared in 1941 to make way for plantations of cypress and other conifers, and the large animals are long gone too. The neat plantations, which still dominate the scenery today, are of limited interest. Not so Ruvuma Swamp, which is one of the best places in Uganda to see a good variety of birds endemic to this habitat, including papyrus gonolek, papyrus canary and papyrus yellow warbler.

Muko lies along the main 80km road between Kabale and Kisoro, roughly equidistant from either town, and one elevated stretch of road affords good views over the swamps. A slightly rougher but shorter back road, roughly 20km long, runs north from the five-way junction on the hills above Rutinda to connect with the Kabale–Kisoro road at Muko, offering some fantastic views over the northern part of the lake. There is a fair amount of public transport along the main Kabale-Kisoro road, but little or none along the back route. It is also possible to visit Muko from Rutinda by boat. Bushara Island Camp charges US$25 for a motorboat plus US$4 per person for a six-hour guided excursion. The same trip can be done over a full day, more cheaply, by chartering a dugout canoe from Rutinda. There is no accommodation at Muko and the campsite that formerly operated within the forest reserve has closed.

Batwa Pygmies In the pre-colonial era, Kigezi – and in particular the present-day Echuya Forest Reserve and Bwindi National Park – supported a significant population of Batwa hunter-gatherers, an ancient pygmoid people who traditionally foraged mainly within the interior of forests (see box *Batwa Pygmies*, pages 244–5). The lifestyle of Kigezi's Batwa has subsequently been compromised by several factors, ranging from forest clearance to intermarriage with neighbouring tribes to misplaced missionary zeal. Most significant, perhaps, was the forced resettlement of Batwa living in forest reserves and national parks, coupled with tight restrictions on their utilisation of traditional resources within these protected areas, that occurred during the colonial and post-independence eras. Today, an estimated 1,700 Batwa eke out a peripheral existence in Kigezi, many of them living in artificial villages outside of their preferred forest home.

Visits to Batwa communities can be arranged through any of the lodges at Rutinda or the nearby islands. Although a few sites can be visited, most trips go to Ruhanga, which lies on the southwest lakeshore close to the Rwanda border. The excursion usually takes a full day, and it costs around Ush45,000 per group for boat hire plus a payment of Ush25,000 to the Batwa community, who will demonstrate their traditional dances. In theory, it is possible to visit the Batwa independently in a private vehicle, following a road that runs south from Muko on the Kabale–Kisoro road. We tried to do this but without any luck, so far as we could establish because no Batwa actually live in Ruhanga – they show up there by prior arrangement with the lodges. We were also told – reasonably reliably – that some Batwa communities are still resident or semi-resident in the southern part of the Echuya Forest Reserve.

KISORO

The amorphous and scruffy town of Kisoro, situated at the base of the Virunga Mountains, appears to have grown significantly in recent years, presumably as a result of its proximity to the borders with Rwanda and the DRC and sporadic influxes of refugees from both of these countries. As with so many towns in Uganda, Kisoro is a pleasant enough place with good facilities, but it is of little inherent interest to travellers. Should you be passing through at the right time of week, the enormous Monday and Thursday markets along the Kabale road are emphatically worth a look. Whenever you visit Kisoro, you're also bound to be approached about whether you want to visit a local Pygmy community, which has been evicted from the forest to be squatted in what amounts to a customised refugee camp. The answer to this query should be no, unless your motivations are charitable or journalistic – concrete suburbia is no place to gain an even faintly accurate impression of the rich culture of Uganda's oldest extant ethnic group.

What Kisoro lacks in intrinsic appeal is made up for by an utterly stupendous setting, with the tall volcanic peaks of the Virungas towering above the southern skyline and green hills rolling out of town in every direction. The town is also an important travel hub, passed through by all travellers who intend to visit Mgahinga National Park, and a popular springboard for cross-border gorilla-tracking excursions in Rwanda's Parc National des Volcans and the Congolese gorilla sanctuary at Djomba. And even if you have no intention of tracking gorillas, the undulating countryside around is studded with lakes, caves and craters that make ideal goals for off-the-beaten-track day walks.

Although plenty of accommodation is to be found in Kisoro, many travellers prefer to stay at the entrance gate to nearby Mgahinga National Park, which is a far more scenic and tranquil location. Since activities within the park depart from the entrance gate at 08.00, it also removes a lot of early-morning hassle to stay there overnight.

GETTING THERE AND AWAY Kisoro lies little more than 30km west of Kabale as the crow flies, but the distance by road is more than 80km, thanks to the obstacle presented by Lake Bunyonyi. The unsurfaced road between Kigezi's two principal towns – generally in good condition except after rain – is one of

left **Hippopotamus** *Hippopotamus amphibius*
page 48

above right **African elephant** *Loxodonta africana*
page 47

below left **Lion cub** *Panthera leo* page 40

below right **African buffalo** *Syncerus caffer* page 48

top	**Jackson's hartebeest** *Alcelaphus buselaphus* page 44
centre	**Oribi** *Ourebia ourebi* page 47
bottom left	**Uganda kob** *Kobus kob* page 45
bottom right	**Defassa waterbuck** *Kobus ellipsiprymnus defassa* page 44

above left	**African fish eagle** *Haliaeetus vocifer* page 53
top right	**Giant eagle owl** *Bubo lacteus* page 56
above right	**Senegal thick knee** *Buthinus senegalensis* page 391
left	**Red-chested sunbird** *Cinnyiris erythrocerca* page 57
below	**Spur-winged lapwing** *Vanellus spinosus* page 391

top **Slender-billed weaver**
Ploceus pelzelni
page 182

centre **Greater painted snipe**
Rostratula benghalensis

right **Male Abyssinian ground hornbill**
Bucorvus abyssinicus
page 57

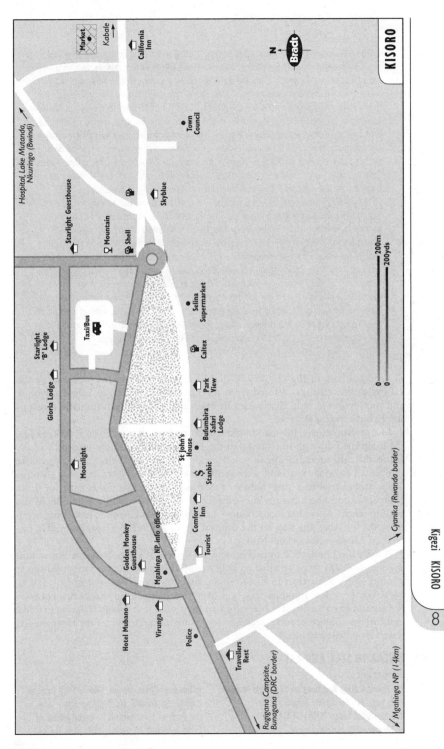

KISORO

Market

Kabale →

California
Inn

Town
Council

N

Bradt

Hospital, Lake Mutanda,
Nkuringo (Bwindi) ↗

Starlight Guesthouse

Mountain

Shell

Skyblue

200m

200yds

0

0

Starlight
'B' Lodge

Gloria Lodge

Taxi/Bus

Selina
Supermarket

Caltex

Park
View

Bufumbira
Safari
Lodge

Moonlight

St John's
House

Stanbic

Comfort
Inn

Tourist

Golden Monkey
Guesthouse

Mgahinga NP info office

Hotel Mubano

Virunga

Police

Travellers
Rest

Rugigana Campsite,
Bunagana (DRC border) ↙

Cyanika (Rwanda border) ↓

Mgahinga NP (14km) ↙

In 1910, Captain Coote was dispatched to the far southwest of Uganda to establish the first British government station in the region. He built the station next to a lake called Kagezi, a site that would be abandoned two years later in favour of Ikumba (near the present-day junction to Ruhija along the main Kabale–Kisoro road). But the name of Coote's short-lived station stuck and – bastardised to Kigezi – it would eventually be applied formally to the southwestern administrative district of Uganda. During the Amin era, the original Kigezi District was divided into two administrative components and in 1980 it was further subdivided and renamed to become the present-day districts of Kabale, Kisoro, Kanungu and Rukungiri. The name Kigezi thus has little historical validity, and it has also fallen into official disuse. Nevertheless, most locals still refer to the above four districts collectively as Kigezi.

On our most recent trip to Uganda, we couldn't resist the temptation to seek out the lake for which Kigezi is named. For those who're interested, it's easy enough to reach, situated only 800m from the Kisoro–Kabale road along a rough track leading north from alongside a conspicuous church. Whether the short diversion is worth the effort is another question. Lake Kagezi – or the lake we were shown, anyway – is little more than a grassy seasonal swamp, set in an approximately circular small depression, possibly an extinct crater, and no more than 200m in diameter. And no trace of any former government building remains either. Bizarrely, when we asked one passing local for confirmation that we were indeed looking at the legendary Kagezi, he nodded in proud agreement and expansively proclaimed the vegetated puddle to be the deepest lake in the whole of Uganda.

the most scenic in the country. Visual highlights include the view across the valleys to the Virungas offered from the Kanaba Gap north of Lake Bunyonyi, and the section of road that passes through the bamboo and montane forest of the Echuya Forest Reserve.

In a private vehicle, the trip should take around two hours. From Kabale, follow the main road through town out past the Highlands Inn and the turn-off to Lake Bunyonyi. After roughly 20km, you'll see the turn-off to Bwindi's Buhoma Gate signposted to your right, and after another 5km or so the turn-off to the Ruhija Gate. Roughly 40km past Kabale, the road skirts the northern tip of Lake Bunyonyi, and then crosses the Ndego River, shortly before reaching Muko trading centre. Note that an alternative – and more scenic – route, branching north from the five-way junction on the summit above Rutinda on Lake Bunyonyi, can be used between Kabale and Muko.

A daily bus connects Kampala directly to Kisoro. It leaves Kampala bus station at roughly 08.00, stops at Mbarara at between 11.00 and 12.00, stops at Kabale at around 14.00, and arrives in Kisoro in the late afternoon. Tickets cost Ush20,000. More locally, a few minibus-taxis and overcrowded pick-up trucks run between Kabale and Kisoro every day, leaving when they are full. It's worth bearing in mind that foreign volunteers and researchers in Kisoro always travel on the Horizon bus rather than Gateway bus.

⌂ WHERE TO STAY AND EAT
Upmarket

⌂ **Mount Gahinga Rest Camp** see *Mgahinga National Park*, page 260 for further details.
Nkuringo Safari Lodge ☏ 0414 543481;
e bluemango@infocom.co.ug or

go2nkuringo@hotmail.com; www.Fw02@gre.ac.uk.
Happily, the dreadful old Mgahinga Safari Lodge on the shore of Lake Mutanda is in the process of being renovated. It's nothing more than the site

deserves; you'll be hard put to find a lovelier backdrop than the Virunga volcano chain beyond this lovely lake. Accommodation is now provided in s/c tents on elevated decking and thatched cottages

Moderate

⌂ **Travellers Rest Inn** (8 rooms) ✆ 04864 30123; m 0772 533029; e postmaster@gorillatours.com; www.gorillatours.com. This pleasant old hotel, totally renovated in 2002, is centrally located in pretty gardens at the turn-off to Mgahinga National Park. It was built and managed in the 1950s by gorilla enthusiast Walter Baumgartel, and formed the first hub of gorilla-tracking activities in the Virungas — hosting such eminent personages as George Schaller and Dian Fossey — until it was taken over by the government during the Amin era. Recently reopened, it consists of 8 s/c twin rooms with hot water.There are also 2 dbl stes: Mutanda and Virunga. Meal prices range from Ush5,000 for a main course through to Ush15,000 pp for a buffet or barbecue. Cultural

Budget

⌂ **Hotel Virunga** ✆ 04864 30109; m 0782 776674. The cheery Hotel Virunga is evidently popular with local business, and it is undoubtedly the most inherently attractive budget option in Kisoro. Rooms using common showers are good value but the s/c dbls feel relatively overpriced. A decent restaurant serving Ugandan dishes (average Ush4000) is attached. US$6/8 sgl/dbl for rooms with common showers, US$16 s/c dbl. Camping US$3 pp.

⌂ **Mutanda Ecotourism Centre** m 0772 435148 or 0712 435148; e amajamcamp@yahoo.com. This development, a partnership between a charismatic

Shoestring

⌂ **Golden Monkey Hotel** m 0772 435148 or 0712 435148; e amajamcamp@yahoo.com. This small new hotel opposite the Virunga looks set to grab the backpacker market. Decorated with effective murals and including a tourist information point and curio shop, the Golden Monkey has a bit more atmosphere and warmth compared to the competition. Food, best ordered in advance if possible, costs about Ush3,000.

⌂ **Skyblue Hotel** ✆ 04864 30136. The restaurant here is one of the best in Kisoro, and most items

⚑ Camping

⚑ **Rugigana Campsite** m 0772 647660. Situated about 500m past the Travellers Rest along the road towards the Congolese border, this is a pretty

around a twin-deck stone and timber lodge. It's very reasonably priced. US$65/130 sgl/dbl for the tents and US$30/60 for the cottages (HB). Camping US$5.

village walks and gorilla tracking can be arranged, and mountain bikes are available for hire. US$35/45 sgl/dbl inc a good b/fast. Stes: Mutanda US$50; Virunga US$55.

⌂ **Kisoro Tourist Hotel** (c.15 rooms) ✆ 04864 30155. This smart and centrally located new multi-storey hotel, set in a grassy compound close to the national park office, lacks the individuality of the upmarket lodges listed above, but it seems competently managed, unpretentious and functional. Large, bright s/c rooms with tiled floor, DSTV, hot showers and a private balcony are decent value. Curries and grills cost Ush4,000—6,000 and cheaper snacks are also available. US$29/45 sgl/dbl.

local tourism entrepreneur and a Swede, occupies a stunning location on the southern shores of Lake Mutanda. Completed accommodation is limited to a single but lovely elevated log cottage but by the time you read this, there will be several, and also dormitory beds. Our man in Kisoro, Batwa researcher Chris Kidd reckons, 'It'll be very much like Bunyonyi Overland Camp but on a smaller friendlier scale'. Birdwatching, swimming, canoeing and snake-tracking safaris are available. Volunteers are welcomed for community development projects; they'll get free accommodation but pay for food. US$10/20 dormitory beds/cottage, both pp and FB.

on the varied menu — steaks, burgers, spaghetti, curries — are priced in the Ush3,000–5,000 range. This is just one of a regional chain of guesthouses known for value-for-money quality and service. From long experience however, the Kisoro Skyblue is where employees languishing at the bottom end of their professional learning curves are posted. US$5/7 for a clean sgl/dbl using common showers.

⌂ **Comfort Inn** Another above-par local guesthouse. US$2/6 basic sgls/a few s/c dbls.

campsite, popular with overland trucks. In addition to a bar, inexpensive meals are available by advance order. US$2 pp to pitch a tent.

In the 1980s, the Parc National des Volcans, which protects the Rwandan section of the Virungas and harbours approximately half of the range's gorillas, was the best-organised gorilla sanctuary in Africa and the country's leading earner of tourist revenue. The park was closed to tourism for much of the 1990s, both during and after the civil war, but it reopened in 1999 and has since become an increasingly popular goal for fly-in and cross-border tourist visits, which require an overnight stop in Rwanda, either at the gateway town of Musanze (known as Ruhengeri until early 2006 and still often referred to as such) or the near park headquarters at Kinigi, which lies about 20 minutes' drive north of Musanze.

The main attraction of the Parc National des Volcans, today as ever, is its five habituated gorilla troops, to which eight permits are issued daily, for a total of 40 permits on any given day, dependent on gorilla movements. The resident Susa Group, the second largest in the Virungas, consists of more than 30 individuals including two silverbacks, making for a delightfully chaotic and totally unforgettable encounter. Be warned, however, that this experience is only for the tolerably fit, since it involves a gaspingly steep hour-long ascent to the forest edge followed by anything from 20 minutes' to three hours' walking to locate the gorillas.

A far less strenuous prospect is the 11-strong Sabinyo Group, whose permanent territory is a lightly forested saddle between Mount Sabinyo and Mount Gahinga, and whose dominant silverback Guhondo is the heaviest gorilla (of any race) ever measured at 220kg. The walk to the forest boundary is gentle and typically takes 20–30 minutes. Once in the forest, the gorillas might take anything from ten minutes to an hour to reach, but the slopes aren't too daunting. Group Thirteen, which numbers 17 individuals, spends most of its time on the same saddle as the Sabinyo Group, and it is usually just as easy to reach. The other two groups are the Amahoro Group, numbering 14 and generally to be found on the slopes of Mount Visoke, and the more recently habituated Umubano Group, with eight individuals. Both of these groups have one silverback and the hikes to reach them are intermediate in difficulty between Susa and Sabinyo.

Gorilla-tracking permits in Rwanda cost US$375 apiece, but will soon increase in line with Ugandan permits, which will cost US$500 from July 2007. Advance booking is usually necessary, particularly during the peak season of June to September, and over the Christmas and New Year holiday period. Permits can be booked though any tour operator (saving a lot of hassle but attracting a small levy) or directly through the ORTPN (Rwanda's park authority) (e reservation@rwandatourism.com), which requires you to transfer a deposit of at least US$100 per permit a month prior to your tracking date. US dollars cash (but not travellers' cheques) or MasterCard (but not Visa) can be used to pay the balance at the ORTPN head office in Kigali, though a card attracts an additional charge of 4%. If you are prepared to take the risk, it does remain possible to pitch up at the ORTPN office in Kigali until 17.00 on the day before you want to track, and – assuming availability – to buy a permit on the spot. And if you are coming from across the Ugandan border and want to skip Kigali altogether, you can also buy a permit at the ORTPN office in Musanze or at the park headquarters at Kinigi at around 17.00–17.30 (when bookings are radioed through from Kigali) on the day before you want to track, or at Kinigi on the morning of departure. There is of course no guarantee that a permit will be available at such short notice, and you should be aware that the offices in Kinigi and Musanze take cash only.

✖ WHERE TO EAT

It's not wise to expect too much from Kisoro's eateries. By far the best food is served at the **Traveller's Rest** where evening buffets seem to be the order of the day. Three courses cost about Ush14,000 but they'll let you fill your plate with the main course for about Ush8,000. The **Tourist Hotel** continually promises

Gorilla-tracking excursions depart from the park headquarters at Kinigi at 07.00 (effectively 08.00 Uganda time, since Rwanda is an hour ahead) and you must now stay in Rwanda the night before you track, rather than nipping over from Kisoro in the morning, as many travellers used to do. Kinigi lies about 25 minutes' drive from the town of Musanze, which is situated 40km from Kisoro via the Cyanika border post. The road between Cyanika and Musanze is covered by plenty of public transport, though you may need to change vehicles at the border. Nationals of the US, the UK, Germany, Canada, Uganda, Sweden, South Africa and Hong Kong can enter Rwanda freely, but other visitors will need a visa, which can be obtained without fuss at Cyanika or any other port of entry, but costs a steep US$50. Independent travellers will also need to charter transport from Musanze to whichever trailhead they will be using – this comes to about US$60 per group for the round trip.

There are several good cheap lodges in Musanze. The relatively smart **Hotel Muhabura** (\f +250 546296; e muhabura12@yahoo.fr; US$25/35 dbl/ste with hot shower and bath) is set in compact green grounds on the outskirts of town. The pick of the cheapies is the **Home d'Accueil Moderne** (\ +250 546525; US$7.50 clean s/c dbl or twin with hot shower), diagonally opposite the market and only two minutes' walk from the minibus stand. Both of these places serve good food too. More commodious out-of-town options include Volcanoes Safaris' superb **Virunga Lodge** (\ +250 502452; e salesrw@volcanoessafaris.com; www.volcanoessafaris.com), which boasts one of the most stunning locations in Africa, on a hilltop overlooking lakes Burera and Ruhondo, and the somewhat more functional but very convenient **Mountain Gorilla's Nest** (\f +250 546331; e mgorillanest@yahoo.com) near Kinigi.

If you are heading to Kigali directly from Kampala, your best option is the daily bus, which leaves from the central bus station in Kampala at 07.00 and arrives in Kigali in the late afternoon. It is also easy to get to Kigali from Kabale: plenty of pick-up trucks run from Kabale to the Katuna border post, from where there are regular shared taxis to Kigali – this journey takes half a day. A non-stop stream of minibus-taxis zips backwards and forwards between Kigali and Musanze, taking up to two hours. If you're looking for accommodation in Kigali, the central Hotel Gloria, close to the bus station, charges around US$15 for a clean self-contained double, while the nearby Belle Vie and New Modern Guesthouses both charge around US$10 for an acceptable room. More commodious options include the central Hotel Garni du Centre and Hotel Gorillas, where a self-contained double in the moderate category will cost around US$80–100.

Gorillas aside, there is plenty to see in Rwanda, a scenic and remarkably welcoming country slowly recovering from the tragic genocide of 1994. Musanze forms an excellent base from which to explore the curvaceous lakes Burera and Ruhondo, while Gisenyi, 60km west of Musanze, is a seductively faded resort town and tropical port on the shore of Lake Kivu. Further afield, the rolling green hills of Nyungwe – swathed in what is the largest extant forest in East Africa – ranks as one of the region's most accessible and underrated national parks. The L'Hoest's monkey is particularly common here, and troops of 400 Angola colobus can be tracked from the campsite, while a checklist of 275 bird species includes more Albertine Rift Endemics than are found in the whole of Uganda. For more detailed information, get hold of the third edition of the Bradt guide to Rwanda by Philip Briggs and Janice Booth, which was researched and published in 2006.

reasonable food served within 60 minutes but these ambitions remain unrealised. You can, however, watch DSTV at the bar while you wait. The food and service is no better at the Tourist Hotel's sister establishment, the budget **Skyblue Hotel** but it's cheaper and the roadside veranda is a better place to watch the world go by. There are two cheap eateries on the street north of Main Street. The Mgahinga

Straddling the borders of Uganda, Rwanda and the DRC, the Virungas are not a mountain range as such, but a chain of isolated freestanding volcanic cones strung along a fault line associated with the same geological process that formed the Rift Valley. Sometimes also referred to as the Birunga or Bufumbira Mountains, the chain is comprised of six inactive and two active volcanoes, all of which exceed 3,000m in altitude – the tallest being Karisimbi (4,507m), Mikeno (4,437m) and Muhavura (4,127m). Three of the eight mountains lie partially within Uganda: Muhavura and Gahinga (3,475m) straddle the Rwandan border, while Sabinyo (3,669m) stands at the junction of the three national borders.

The names of the individual mountains in the Virunga chain reflect local perceptions. Sabinyo translates as 'old man's teeth' in reference to the jagged rim of what is probably the most ancient and weathered of the eight volcanoes. The lofty Muhavura is 'the guide', and anecdotes collected by the first Europeans to visit the area suggest that its perfect cone, topped today by a small crater lake, still glowed at night as recently as the early 19th century. The stumpier Gahinga translates as 'small pile of stones', a name that becomes clear when you see local people tidying the rocks that clutter their fields into heaps named *gahingas*. Of the volcanoes that lie outside Uganda, Karisimbi – which occasionally sports a small cap of snow – is named for the colour of a cowrie shell, while Visoke simply means 'watering hole', in reference to the crater lake near its peak.

The vegetation zones of the Virungas correspond closely with those of other large East African mountains, albeit that much of the Afro-montane forest below the 2,500m contour has been sacrificed to cultivation. Between 2,500m and 3,500m, where an average annual rainfall of 2,000mm is typical, bamboo forest is interspersed with stands of tall *hagenia* woodland. At higher altitudes, the cover of Afro-alpine moorland, grassland and marsh is studded with giant lobelia and other outsized plants similar to those found on Kilimanjaro and the Rwenzori.

The most famous denizen of the Virungas is the mountain gorilla, which inhabits all six of the extinct or dormant volcanoes, but not – for obvious reasons – the more active ones. The Virungas also form the main stronghold for the endangered golden monkey, and support relic populations of elephant and buffalo along with typical highland forest species such as yellow-backed duiker and giant forest hog. The mountains' avifauna is comparatively poorly known, but some 150 species are recorded including about 20 Albertine Rift Endemics.

Still in their geological infancy, none of the present Virunga Mountains is more than two million years old and two of the cones remain highly active. However, eruptions of earlier Virunga volcanoes ten–12 million years ago marked the start of the tectonic

park rangers appreciate the good local food at the **community group restaurant** while travellers have recommended the nearby **New Moonlight Hotel** as serving excellent roast pork. You'll get best results if you can give a couple of hours' advance notice and go for the 'lean' pork option. Whatever you do, insist on the roasted rather than fried-with-cabbage option. Prices are negotiable but still firmly in the budget value range.

LISTINGS

Tourist information The Mgahinga National Park office opposite the Kisoro Tourist Hotel can provide information about the national park as well as other tourist attractions in the region. They can also put travellers in touch with reliable local guides and special-hire vehicles to get to Mgahinga.

processes that have formed the western Rift Valley. The most dramatic volcanic explosion of historical times was the 1977 eruption of the 3,465m Mount Nyiragongo in the DRC, about 20km north of the Lake Kivu port of Goma. During this eruption, a lava lake that had formed in the volcano's main crater back in 1894 drained in less than one hour, emitting streams of molten lava that flowed at a rate of up to 60km/h, killing an estimated 2,000 people and terminating only 500m from Goma Airport.

In 1994, a new lake of lava started to accumulate within the main crater of Nyiragongo, leading to another highly destructive eruption on 17 January 2002. Lava flowed down the southern and eastern flanks of the volcano into Goma itself, killing at least 50 people. Goma was evacuated, and an estimated 450,000 people crossed into the nearby Rwandan towns of Gisenyi and Musanze for temporary refuge. Three days later, when the first evacuees returned, it transpired that about a quarter of the town – including large parts of the commercial and residential centre – had been engulfed by the lava, leaving 12,000 families homeless. The lava lake in Nyiragongo's crater remains active, with a diameter of around 50m, and although there has been no subsequent eruption, red and white plumes reaching a height of up to 3km were regularly observed above the crater in late 2002.

Only 15km northwest of Nyiragongo stands the 3,058m Mount Nyamuragira, which also erupted in January 2002. Nyamuragira is probably the most active volcano on the African mainland, with 34 eruptions recorded since 1882, though only the 1912–13 incident resulted in any fatalities. Nyamuragira most recently blew its top on 26 July 2002, spewing lava high into the air, along with a large plume of ash and sulphur dioxide, and destroying large tracts of cultivated land and forest.

It is perhaps worth noting that these temperamental Congolese volcanoes pose no threat to visitors to Uganda. The three cones shared by Uganda are all dormant or extinct and while the plumes from the Congolese volcanoes might well be seen at night from around Kisoro, no active lava flow has touched Ugandan soil in recorded history. That might change one day: there is a tradition among the Bafumbira people of the Ugandan Virungas that the fiery sprits inhabiting the crater of Nyamuragira will eventually relocate to Muhavura, reducing both the mountain and its surrounds to ash.

Another Bafumbira custom has it that the crater lake atop Mount Muhavura is inhabited by a powerful snake spirit called Indyoka, which only needs to raise its head to bring rain to the surrounding countryside. It is said that Indyoka lives on a bed of gold and protects various other artefacts made of precious metal, and that it can extend itself as far as Lake Mutanda to a lakeshore sacrificial shrine at Mushungero. An indication of its presence at the lake and associated shrine is the inundation of the seasonal Gitundwe Swamp near Lake Mutanda.

Foreign exchange There is a Stanbic Bank in Kisoro which offers the bank's usual forex services.

Shopping There are no decent stores in Kisoro and you're best to stop in Kabale to stock up on commodities. The main market – busiest Mondays and Thursdays – is a short distance along the Kabale road opposite the California Inn.

EXCURSIONS The most popular destinations from Kisoro are Mgahinga National Park, Parc National des Virungas or in the Parc National des Volcans in Rwanda for hiking and gorilla tracking (covered elsewhere in this chapter). Note that gorilla tracking is not presently available in Mgahinga as the habituated gorillas had been in Rwanda for 18 months prior to the research of this edition. In July 2006, however, they were reported to have crossed the frontier back into Mgahinga, so hopefully they will now resume residence in Uganda. The area around Kisoro is also great walking country, and there are several worthwhile goals for day hikes even if you never set foot in any of the gorilla reserves. Local guides can be arranged through the national park office in town.

Echuya Forest Reserve Extending over 340km² of hilly terrain between Lake Bunyonyi and Kisoro, Echuya is one of the least-visited and most under-researched reserves in Uganda, yet it is still ranked among the top six sites in the country in terms of forest biodiversity. With an altitude span of 2,200m to 2,600m, the reserve protects a range of montane habitats including evergreen and bamboo forest, while the adjacent Muchuya Swamp is one of the most extensive perennial high-altitude wetlands in East Africa, harbouring the largest-known population of the globally endangered Grauer's swamp warbler. Little information is available about the reserve's non-avian fauna, but it is likely to be similar to the forest belt of nearby Mgahinga National Park and includes at least four small mammal species endemic to the Albertine Rift. Until recent times, Echuya was permanently inhabited by Batwa Pygmies. Several Pygmy communities living on the verge of the forest still derive their livelihood from bamboo and other resources extracted from within the reserve.

A surprisingly low bird checklist of 100 species suggests that scientific knowledge of Echuya is far from complete, but even so 12 Albertine Rift Endemics have been recorded, and it is the only locality outside of the national park system

GORILLA TRACKING IN THE PARC NATIONAL DES VIRUNGAS, DRC

In the early 1990s, Djomba Gorilla Reserve in the Parc National des Virungas, in what was then Zaïre, was the most popular place to track gorillas in East Africa, and indeed there were times when it was the only 'gorilla reserve' open to tourism. The reserve effectively closed to tourism in 1998, when four tourists were abducted after crossing into the DRC from Uganda and a persistent civil war ensured that tracking remained closed until 2005. But things change quickly in this part of Africa, and with strong indications that the civil war in the DRC is drawing to an end, gorilla tracking is once again possible in the Congolese Virunga. Information and permits are provided by the Kampala Backpackers' Hostel (see *Kampala* listings, page 147) and Nile River Explorers (see *Jinja and Bujugali Falls* listings, pages 407–8).

DRC permits, at face value, are the cheapest available at USS$300. In real terms they are more expensive than anywhere else (though this may no longer be the case after Uganda permits increase to US$500 in July 2007). Firstly, travellers with a single-entry visa intending to leave and return to Uganda (eg: to track gorillas in Uganda or DRC) must purchase another US$30 visa on re-entry. If however you intend to spend less than seven days in Uganda before leaving again, you can purchase a transit visa for only US$15. Secondly, it has been so arranged that the only people available to take you from the border to Djombe is a company called Jambo Safaris. They'll charge you a hefty US$100, irrespective of whether you are one person or five. Nobody else will take you for less and you are not allowed to take your own vehicle across or walk to Djombe. Welcome to DRC!

If you are in a group of three, transport and visas will cost you either US$393 (or US$363 if you have a multiple-entry visa for Uganda). A party of two will pay US$380 or US$410. It's all rather complicated. Some outlets such as Backpackers simply charge groups of three or more a flat US$340 to include the transport. You pay a deposit of US$15 and the balance is paid at the border. You can save a few dollars by

where a comparable selection of these sought-after specialities is resident. The most accessible part of Echuya Forest Reserve is the northern sector, transected by a 6km stretch of the Kibale road, starting about 20km out of Kisoro. With patience, a good selection of forest- and bamboo-associated species can be observed by walking along this stretch of road, as described in the box *Birding Echuya: a personal account* below.

Lakes Mutanda and Mutolere These pretty mountain-ringed lakes lie a short distance north of Kisoro. The easiest way to reach them is by driving or walking for about 6–8km out of Kisoro along the road heading directly north towards Nkuringo (Bwindi). The marshy southern tip of Mutanda, the larger of the town lakes, can also be reached cross-country, since it lies barely 3km from Kisoro as the crow flies. Local guides are available to direct travellers to Mutanda and to a nearby cave wherein a 10m python is regularly encountered. Lakeside accommodation is provided by the Nkuringo Safari Lodge and the Mutanda Ecotourism Centre (see *Where to stay*, pages 250–1).

Shozi Crater and Caves Shozi Crater, reaching an altitude of 2,000m, is a relic of the volcanic activity that shaped this mountainous corner of Uganda. Close by is a 400m-long cave, formed by a petrified lava flow, which houses a colony of thousands upon thousands of bats. The crater and cave can be reached by following the Kabale road out of Kisoro for about 5km, then taking a left turn towards Mutolere trading centre for another few hundred metres.

arranging everything at the border but I'd say it's worth the extra for the peace of mind provided by a firm booking (not to mention useful travel updates) before you make the long haul west.

If you're intent on seeing these magnificent animals, your first priority will be to obtain a permit to do so, and it's far easier to do so for DRC than in Uganda and Rwanda. You might want to know, however, that your permit fees in Uganda and Rwanda do directly support conservation, gorilla tracking in Bwindi supporting activities in loss-making parks such as Semliki and Mount Elgon. I'd be very surprised on the other hand if your US$300 or your visa fees for that matter are used for anything accountable.

The Congolese border is at Bunagana, about 15km from Kisoro. To get to Bunagana, take the Horizon bus from Kampala at 05.00 to Kisoro (Ush20,000) then the following morning take a special hire taxi to the border (Ush20,000). Your best budget bet in Kisoro is the new Golden Monkey Hotel where Sheba, the helpful owner will sort out your travel arrangements (m *0772 435148*).

The main base for gorilla tracking in the DRC is Djombe, about 8km from the Ugandan border and an hour or so from where the gorillas live. Eight daily permits are available for this location. I'm told that there are another 24 permits available for another site about 45km inside DRC and about 1.5 hours' drive. This is about as far as you'd be advised to go in DRC right now and I'd certainly want further information before heading there. It may be tempting to roam further afield across the western Rift Valley, perhaps cutting down to Lake Kivu or up to the Ishasha border post beside Queen Elizabeth National Park but, unless definitely advised to the contrary, I'd suggest that right now you might be pushing your luck. It's worth noting that DRC territory around Bunia beyond the Semliki Valley is definitely off-limits unless you're part of the UN Peace Keeping Force in the area.

Derek Schuurman

If a lack of gorilla-tracking permits (or time) dissuades any birdwatcher from visiting Bwindi National Park, no better alternative exists than the Echuya Forest Reserve near Kisoro, certainly when it comes to ticking a few Albertine Rift endemics. Emmy Gongo of the Uganda Bird Guides Club and I arrived at Echuya on 17 March 2003 at about 08.00. Our driver dropped us on the road where the forest begins and agreed to collect us about 2km further along the road at 11.30.

For the most part, the short stretch of evergreen montane forest we explored was packed with birdlife. Just after we started, the first Albertine Rift endemic (ARE) came into view – a male Rwenzori batis, which sat in full view singing its little head off. This was followed by corking views of cinnamon bracken warbler, while overhead a white-necked raven mercilessly harassed an African harrier-hawk, the two birds wheeling, dodging and diving dramatically between the trees. The site proved excellent for African hill babbler, which posed in a low shrub at the roadside. Metres away, a flock of black-headed waxbills settled in roadside herbage where Chubb's cisticolas were noisy and conspicuous.

Up in the trees, we found – among other things – least honeyguide, cinnamon-chested bee-eaters and the lovely white-tailed blue flycatcher hawking insects. We also absorbed a blizzard of sunbird sightings, including the stunning regal (ARE), blue-headed (ARE though not one of the 12 listed for the site), olive-bellied and variable sunbirds. White-browed crombec, chestnut-throated apalis and the red-faced woodland warbler (ARE) were not difficult to find. Small groups of black saw-wings had their burrows in a low roadside bank and a few metres behind that we leisurely watched a pair of strange weavers (ARE) building their nest in a thin vine. Greenbuls seen included Shelley's and mountain, and Emmy spotted a Doherty's bush-shrike flying low between shrubs.

All too soon, our time was up and we drove uphill to the impressive Bamboo zone, where we saw a second instance of a raptor being harassed – this time a tiny shikra was doing a surprisingly convincing job of mobbing a brown snake eagle. In the bamboo, we constantly heard evergreen forest warbler but did not have time to lure it out. This account lists just a small sample of what we saw in Echuya Forest that day – without a doubt we only scratched the surface and I don't doubt that visiting birders stopping by there would be in for a very rewarding time.

MGAHINGA GORILLA NATIONAL PARK

Mgahinga National Park protects the Ugandan part of the Virunga Mountains (see box, pages 254–5) and its three main peaks: Muhavura, Gahinga and Sabinyo. Established in 1930 as the Gorilla Game Sanctuary, the national park was gazetted in 1991, when more than 2,000 people were relocated from within its boundaries. Covering less than 34km^2, Mgahinga is the smallest national park in Uganda, but it forms part of a cross-border system of contiguous reserves in Rwanda and the DRC extending over some 430km^2 of the higher Virungas. Small it might be, but Mgahinga is also arguably the most scenic park in Uganda, offering panoramic views that stretch northward to Bwindi, and a southern skyline dominated by the steep volcanic cones of the Virungas, surely one of the most memorable and stirring sights in East Africa.

Mgahinga protects 76 mammal species, including the golden monkey (a localised and distinctive race of the blue monkey), black-and-white colobus, mountain gorilla, leopard, elephant, giant forest hog, bushpig, buffalo, bushbuck, black-fronted duiker and several varieties of rodents, bats and small predators.

Bafflingly, only 115 bird species have been recorded, possibly a reflection of the park's small size, but also suggesting that no serious study of its avifauna has ever been undertaken. However, the park is still of great interest to birdwatchers, as several of the species recorded are localised forest birds, and 12 are considered to be endemic to the Albert Rift region.

Mgahinga is best known to tourists for gorilla tracking. Oddly enough, no gorillas live permanently within the park, but a fair number move freely between Uganda and the neighbouring Parc National des Volcans in Rwanda, and one habituated troop frequently spends months at a stretch within Mgahinga. Unfortunately late on in 2004 the park's habituated group was subjected to attacks from a belligerent lone silverback and fled across the border into Rwanda. The silverback has remained on the Ugandan slopes where it frustrates any attempts by the habituated gorillas to return to Mgahinga. However, in July 2006 they were tracked by UWA rangers along the Uganda–Rwanda border in the watershed between mounts Sabinyo and Mgahinga. They are presently being monitored to see whether tracking for tourism can recommence. Check the Bradt website/email newsletter for updates (see page i for details). In the meantime, it's just as well that Mgahinga offers a far broader range of activities than any of the other 'mountain gorilla reserves' including caving, forest walks, and day hikes to the three volcanic peaks. Anybody who enjoys challenging day hikes or who has an interest in natural history could happily spend a week based at Mgahinga without ever going gorilla tracking.

The national park's office in Kisoro always has current information regarding Mgahinga, as well as sometimes stocking maps and pamphlets. The best source of background information is the 96-page booklet *Mgahinga Gorilla & Bwindi Impenetrable National Parks*, written by David Bygott and Jeannette Hanby, and published by UWA in 1998. The wider Rift Valley setting is described in *Uganda's Great Rift Valley* by Andrew Roberts. Payments, bookings and enquiries are handled in a new visitors' centre 100m beyond the entrance gate.

Non-residents pay a visitation fee of US$25/35/50 for one/two/three or more nights. East African residents pay discounted rates of US$15/20/25 on production of proof of residency. An entrance permit is valid for 24 hours from time of entrance. These fees are included in the prices for volcano climbing and caving but are not applicable to overnight stays at the community campsite at the park gate.

GETTING THERE AND AWAY Ntebeko Entrance Gate lies roughly 14km from Kisoro along a dirt road. Historically a shocker, this infamous route has recently been hugely improved and it should now take no more than 30 minutes from Kisoro. A 4x4 may still be necessary after heavy rain. To get to Mgahinga from the national park's office in Kisoro, follow the main road towards the DRC for about 100m, turn left at the first main junction, immediately before the Travellers Rest Inn, then turn right about 100m further. Follow the stone cairns up to Ntebeko.

If you don't have a vehicle, the national park's office in town will know whether any official vehicles are heading out to the entrance gate. You can also normally hire a park vehicle to take you there – this costs around Ush25,000, which is not too expensive for a group. The other option is to walk: it's quite a hilly road, but it shouldn't take you much longer than three hours to get there. You might be able to pick up a lift some or all of the way. If you do walk, fork right at Nturo trading centre roughly 1km out of Kisoro for a considerably shorter and prettier route. You can drive this route too but it's a tooth-rattling ride with plenty of rocks.

WHERE TO STAY It's perfectly possible to visit Mgahinga as a day trip from one of the lodges in Kisoro, but more atmospheric to stay at the upmarket and shoestring accommodation at the Ntebeko Entrance Gate.

Upmarket

🏠 **Mount Gahinga Rest Camp** ☏ 0414 346464/5; m 0752 741718; f 0414 341718; e sales@ volcanoessafaris.com; www.volcanoessafaris.com. This attractive little lodge, situated a few hundred metres from the entrance gate, consists of about half-a-dozen spacious s/c stone cottages with hot showers and large beds, and a private balcony looking towards Lake Mutanda beyond Kisoro. Also constructed from stone, the cosy restaurant/bar has a useful library of local-interest books and is warmed up by a log fire on the chilly highland evenings. *US$180 pp sharing a twin, US$240 sgl, all FB plus drinks.*

Shoestring and camping

⚊ **Mgahinga Community Campground** The community campsite just outside the entrance gate to Mgahinga has a truly spectacular setting, with Muhabura, Gahinga and Sabinyo peaks forming an arc to the south, and a grandstand view over Lake Mutanda and the rolling hills of Bwindi to the north. Very simple meals such as potatoes and mixed vegetables can be prepared with plenty of notice and cost Ush5,000. You'll eat far better at the nearby Mount Gahinga Rest Camp but expect to pay US$25 for a 3-course meal including drinks. *Dbl bandas US$11 per bed, camping US$1.60 per tent.*

ACTIVITIES

Gorilla tracking Roughly 45 gorillas spend part of the year in Mgahinga moving to and from the adjoining protected forests in Rwanda and DRC. Unfortunately, however, the park's habituated gorillas migrated across the volcanic saddle between Muhuvura and Mgahinga into Rwanda 18 months ago and, for reasons explained above, may well remain there. UWA has been negotiating with its cross-border counterparts in Rwanda and DRC to establish a mechanism whereby gorillas habituated in one country can continue to be tracked commercially in a neighbouring state. In this case, Uganda's gorillas would be tracked in Parc National des Volcans and the proceeds shared between UWA and Rwanda's ORTPN. In July 2006 however, the habituated group showed signs of returning to Mgahinga NP. It remains in the balance whether you will be able to track them in Uganda or Rwanda. Check the Bradt newsletter or enquire from UWA or tour agents or hostels in Kampala.

Mountain hikes Guided day hikes to each of the three volcanic peaks in Mgahinga cost US$40 per person, inclusive of the guide and visitation fee. A reasonable level of fitness and an early start is required for any of the mountain hikes, and good boots, raingear and warm clothes are recommended. The least-demanding mountain hike, the six- to seven-hour round trip from Ntebeko up Mount Gahinga, offers a good chance of seeing various forest birds in the bamboo zone, while duikers and bushbuck inhabit the marshy crater at the peak. The tougher ascent from Ntebeko to Sabinyo, which takes at least eight hours there and back, passes through montane forest and moorland, and culminates in three challenging climbs up rock faces using ladders.

The most challenging hike is to the peak of Muhabura, the highest peak. This starts at a base camp a few kilometres from the entrance gate (it is advisable to camp here the night before the hike) and the round trip will take at least nine hours. The open moorland that characterises Muhabura offers great views in all directions, as well as the opportunity to see Afro-Alpine endemics such as the beautiful scarlet-tufted malachite sunbird. A small crater lake at the top of Muhabura is encircled by giant lobelias. Hikers might feel altitude-related symptoms near the peak, due to the rapidity of the ascent.

Golden monkey visits The next-best thing to seeing the mountain gorilla is the chance to track the golden monkey *Cercopithecus kandti* (sometimes treated as a distinctive race of the more widespread blue monkey *C. mitis*), a little-known bamboo-associated taxa primate listed as 'endangered' by the World Conservation Union. Endemic to the Albertine Rift, the golden monkey is characterised by a bright orange-gold body, cheeks and tail, contrasting with its black limbs, crown and tail end. Until a few years ago, this pretty monkey was common in Rwanda's Gishwati Forest Reserve, most of which was chopped down by returned refugees in the aftermath of the 1994 genocide, and unconfirmed sources indicate that a small population might occur further south in the same country's Nyungwe National Park. More likely, however, that the Virunga Volcanoes harbour the only remaining viable breeding population of this localised monkey. Fortunately, the golden monkey is the numerically dominant primate within this restricted range – a 2003 survey estimated a population of 3,000–4,000 in Mgahinga National Park, but no figures are available for neighbouring parks in Rwanda and DRC. Golden monkey tracking can be undertaken at Mgahinga daily and costs US$20, excluding the visitation fee.

Nature walks Nature trails concentrating on the forest zone run out of Ntebeko at a charge of US$10 per person (irrespective of whether it is a full or half day's walk). Of particular interest to birders, the three- to four-hour Sabinyo Gorge Trail ascends through the heath around Ntebeko into a stand of bamboo forest before following a small stream through a lushly forested gorge. The bamboo forest is a good place to see the pretty golden monkey, as well as handsome francolin, Kivu ground thrush and regal sunbird. The evergreen forest harbours such localised birds as Rwenzori turaco, western green tinkerbird, olive woodpecker, African hill babbler, Archer's ground robin, Rwenzori batis, montane sooty boubou, Lagden's bush-shrike and strange weaver, several of which are Albertine Rift Endemics.

Another day trail leads to Rugezi Swamp, where, in addition to the usual forest animals and birds, you stand a fair chance of seeing elephants and, in the late afternoon, giant forest hog. A flat rate of US$30 is charged to visit Garama Cave, 4km from Ntebeko, which was occupied by humans during the late Iron Age and later used by the Batwa as a hiding place from neighbouring Bantu-speaking tribes. Exploration goes as deep as 300m, but the cave is rumoured to cut right through the mountain to Rwanda. No experience of caving is required, but you do need to bring a good torch and spare batteries (don't rely on these being available at the park headquarters). The round trip takes about three hours and the terrain is surprisingly flat.

BWINDI IMPENETRABLE NATIONAL PARK

The Bwindi Impenetrable Forest is regarded to be one of the most biologically diverse forests in Africa, largely due to its antiquity (it dates to before the Pleistocene Ice Age, making it over 25,000 years old) and an altitude range of between 1,160m and 2,607m above sea level. Bwindi is a true rainforest, spread over a series of steep ridges and valleys that form the eastern edge of the Albertine Rift Valley. The national park has an average annual rainfall of almost 1,500mm, and it is a vital catchment area, the source of five major rivers, which flow into Lake Albert. Until about 500 years ago, when agriculturists started planting crops in the Kisoro area, Bwindi was part of a much larger belt of forest stretching south to the slopes of the Virunga Mountains.

Tourism to Bwindi focuses on gorilla tracking at two locations, Buhoma and a recently established location at Nkuringo. Slightly more than half the world's mountain gorilla population is resident in Bwindi: an estimated 320 individuals living in 15 troops. Given the focus on gorillas, it may come as a surprise to learn that Bwindi harbours at least 120 mammal species, more than any national park except Queen Elizabeth. This list consists mainly of small mammals such as rodents and bats, but it does include 11 types of primate, including a healthy chimpanzee population and substantial numbers of L'Hoest's, red-tailed and blue monkey, as well as black-and-white colobus and olive baboon. Of the so-called big five, only elephants are present, though the herd of 30 animals in the southeast of the park – assigned to the forest race – is very seldom seen by tourists. Buffaloes and leopards were present until recent times, but they are thought to have been hunted to extinction. Six antelope species occur in the park: bushbuck and five types of forest duiker.

A total of 350 bird species have been recorded in Bwindi, a remarkably high figure when you consider that, unlike most other national park checklists, it includes very few water-associated birds. Of particular interest to birders are 23 species endemic to the Albertine Rift, and at least 14 species recorded nowhere else in Uganda, among them the African green broadbill, white-tailed blue flycatcher, brown-necked parrot, white-bellied robin chat and Frazer's eagle owl. In addition to its extensive bird checklist, Bwindi is also home to at least 200 butterfly species, including eight Albertine Rift Endemics, and dedicated butterfly watchers might hope to identify more than 50 varieties in one day.

Non-residents pay a visitation fee of US$25/35/50 for one/two/three or more nights. East African residents pay discounted rates of US$15/20/25 on production of proof of residency. An entrance permit is valid for 24 hours from time of entrance. These fees are included in the prices for gorilla tracking and are not applicable to stays at the Buhoma Homestead and Community Campground.

The UWA offices in Kampala, Kabale and Kisoro can give up-to-date information on gorilla tracking and other travel practicalities in Bwindi and Mgahinga. The best source of background information is the 96-page booklet *Mgahinga Gorilla & Bwindi Impenetrable National Parks*, written by David Bygott and Jeannette Hanby and published by UWA in 1998. A full checklist of the birds recorded in Bwindi can be bought for a nominal price at the park headquarters.

BWINDI IMPENETRABLE

The name Bwindi derives from the local phrase Mubwindi bwa Nyinamukari, which most probably originally referred to the Mubwindi Swamp in the southeast of the park rather than the forest itself. The story behind this name goes back to about a century ago, when, it is said, a family migrating northwards from the Kisoro area found themselves standing at the southern end of a seemingly impenetrable swamp. The parents asked the swamp spirits for guidance, and were told that only if they sacrificed their most beautiful daughter, Nyinamukari, would the rest of the family cross without mishap. After two days of deliberation, the family decided that they could not turn back south, and so they threw the girl into the water to drown, and went on their way safely to the other side. When news of the sacrifice spread, people began to avoid the swamp, calling it Mubwindi bwa Nyinamukari – 'Dark Place of Nyinamukari'.

The forest was proclaimed as the Impenetrable Forest Reserve in 1932, its official name until 1991 when it was gazetted as a national park and named Bwindi. Realising that this local name has less allure to tourists than the colonial name (though the two words are close in meaning), UWA expanded it to be the Bwindi Impenetrable National Park. Today, most people refer to the park as plain Bwindi, though the murderous swamp is still known by the more correct name of Mubwindi.

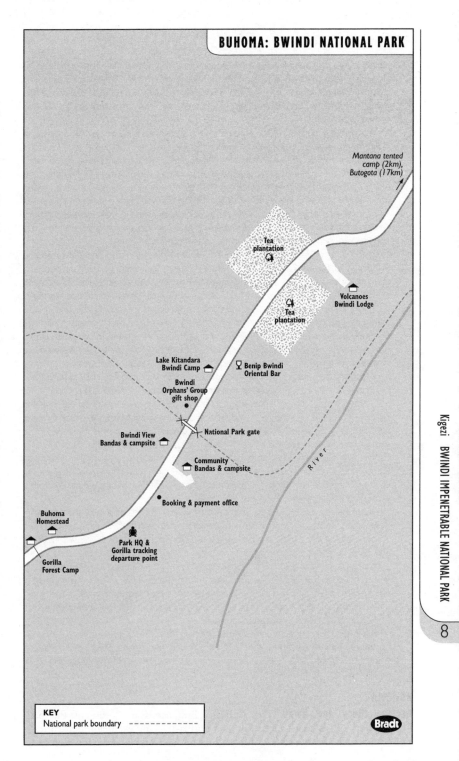

BUHOMA: BWINDI NATIONAL PARK

Mantana tented camp (2km), Butogota (17km)

Tea plantation

Tea plantation

Volcanoes Bwindi Lodge

Lake Kitandara Bwindi Camp

Benip Bwindi Oriental Bar

Bwindi Orphans' Group gift shop

National Park gate

Bwindi View Bandas & campsite

Community Bandas & campsite

River

Booking & payment office

Buhoma Homestead

Park HQ & Gorilla tracking departure point

Gorilla Forest Camp

KEY
National park boundary ----------

Bradt

Over the two decades following the European discovery of mountain gorillas, at least 50 individuals were captured or killed in the Virungas, prompting the Belgian government to create the Albert National Park in 1925. This protected what are now the Congolese and Rwandan portions of the Virunga Mountains, and was managed as a cohesive conservation unit.

The gorilla population of the Virungas is thought to have been reasonably stable in 1960, when a census undertaken by George Schaller indicated that some 450 individuals lived in the range. By 1971–73, however, the population had plummeted to an estimated 250. This decline was caused by several factors, including the post-colonial division of the Albert National Park into its Rwandan and Congolese components, the ongoing fighting between the Hutu and Tutsi of Rwanda, and a grisly tourist trade in poached gorilla heads and hands – the latter used by some sad individuals as ashtrays! Most devastating of all perhaps was the irreversible loss of almost half of the gorillas' habitat between 1957 and 1968 to local farmers and a European-funded agricultural scheme.

In 1979, Amy Vedder and Bill Webber initiated the first gorilla tourism project in Rwanda's Parc National des Volcans, integrating tourism, local education and anti-poaching measures with remarkable success. Initially, the project was aimed mainly at overland trucks, who paid a paltry – by today's standards – US$20 per person to track gorillas. Even so, gorilla tourism was raising up to ten million US dollars annually by the mid 1980s, making it Rwanda's third-highest earner of foreign revenue. The mountain gorilla had practically become the national emblem, and was officially regarded to be the country's most important renewable natural resource. To ordinary Rwandans, gorillas became a source of great national pride: living gorillas ultimately created far more work and money than poaching them had ever done. As a result, a census undertaken in 1989 indicated that the local mountain gorilla population had increased by almost 30% to 320 animals.

Despite the success of ecotourism, there are still several threats to the ongoing survival of mountain gorillas in the wild. For the Virunga population, the major threat is undoubtedly political. In 1991, the long-standing ethnic tension between Rwanda's Hutu and Tutsi populations erupted into a civil war that culminated in the genocide of 1994. In context, the fate of a few gorillas does seem a rather trivial concern, even if you take into account the important role that gorilla tourism is playing in rebuilding Rwanda's post-war economy, and the fact that the integrated conservation of their habitat will also protect a watershed that supplies 10% of the country with water.

Nevertheless, the Rwandan conflict had several repercussions in the Virungas. Researchers and park rangers were twice forced to evacuate the Parc National des Volcans, leaving the gorillas unguarded. Tourism to Rwanda practically ceased in 1991, and although gorilla tracking has been available since 1999, tourist arrivals have yet to approach the level of the 1980s. Remarkably, however, when researchers were finally able to return to the Parc National des Volcans in the late 1990s, only four gorillas could not be accounted for. Two of the missing gorillas were old females who had most probably died of natural causes. The other two might have been shot, but might just as easily have succumbed to disease.

But in this most unstable part of Africa little can be taken for granted. Just as Rwanda started to stabilise politically, the DRC descended into anarchy. For years, eastern Congolese officials, who lived far from the capital, received no formal salary and were

BUHOMA

Getting there and away The Buhoma Entrance Gate – site of the park headquarters, all its accommodation, and gorilla-tracking excursion departures – can be approached using several different routes, converging at the junction town

forced to devise their own ways of securing a living, leading to a level of corruption second to none in the region. At least 16 gorillas were killed in three separate incidents in the DRC between 1995 and 1998, since when the Congolese part of the Virungas has effectively been closed to tourists and researchers alike. Under the circumstances, it is remarkable to learn that the latest gorilla count – undertaken in 2003 – shows a continued increase to at least 380 individuals in the Virungas, representing a population growth of around 20% in 15 years, while the Bwindi population increased by around 7% between 1997 and the most recent census, which returned an estimate of around 320 individuals in 2002.

The Bwindi population is probably more immediately secure than are the gorillas in the Virungas. Bwindi is not divided by arbitrary political borders, which means that the entire population can be protected within one well-managed and carefully monitored national park. Nevertheless, the habituation of the Bwindi gorillas has increased their vulnerability to poachers, who, during 1995, killed a total of seven habituated mountain gorillas. These incidents were linked to one dealer's attempts to acquire an infant gorilla, so it would perhaps be an overreaction to view them as a trend. Nevertheless, the very fact that habituated gorillas were targeted does highlight an area of vulnerability linked directly to tourism and research.

Less critical perhaps, but something that directly affects readers, is that humans and gorillas are genetically close enough for there to be a real risk of a tourist passing a viral or bacterial infection to a habituated gorilla. To reduce this risk, there is a restriction on the number of people allowed to visit a troop on any given day, and visitors are asked to keep a few metres' distance between themselves and the animals. It is up to individual tourists to forego their gorilla-tracking permit if they are unwell – easier said than done when you've already spent a small fortune to get all the way to Uganda, but perhaps not if you imagine the consequences if even one individual were to be infected by a contagious disease to which gorillas have no acquired resistance.

Given the above, a reasonable response might be to query the wisdom of habituating gorillas in the first place. The problem facing conservationists is that gorillas cannot be conserved in a vacuum. For instance, roughly 2,000 farmers were evacuated from Mgahinga when it was gazetted as a national park in 1993, a situation that created some local resentment of gorillas. However, against this immediate deprivation can be balanced the long-term consideration that 10% of revenue raised by gorilla tourism in Uganda is handed to local communities, in addition to which community campsites outside the national parks can generate funds at a grassroots level. So long as gorilla tourism can generate revenue and create employment opportunities locally, there is a strong incentive for neighbouring communities to perceive the gorillas' survival to be in their long-term interest. Without tourism, why should they give a damn?

Less parochially, mountain gorillas form the cornerstone of Uganda's national tourist industry: the majority of people who come to Uganda to see gorillas will also spend money in other parts of the country, thereby generating foreign revenue and creating employment well beyond the immediate vicinities of the mountain gorilla reserves. Tourist revenue is probably integral to the survival of the mountain gorilla; the survival of the mountain gorilla is certainly integral to the growth of Uganda's tourist industry. This symbiotic situation motivates a far greater number of people to take an active interest in the fate of the gorillas than would be the case if gorilla tourism were to be curtailed.

of Butogota 17km before the park entrance. All of the approach routes involve some driving along dirt roads that may become slippery after rain, so an early start is recommended to be certain of reaching the park before dark. It's advisable to carry all the fuel you need; but, if you run short, there are two filling stations in

The largest living primates, gorillas are widespread residents of the equatorial African rainforest, with a global population of perhaps 100,000 concentrated mainly in the Congo Basin. Until 2001, all gorillas were assigned to the species *Gorilla gorilla*, split into three races: the western lowland gorilla *G. g. gorilla* of the western Congo Basin, the eastern lowland gorilla *G. g. graueri* in the eastern DRC, and the mountain gorilla *G. g. beringei*, which lives in highland forest on the eastern side of the Albertine Rift. The western race was formally described in 1847, but the eastern races were only described in the early 20th century – the mountain gorilla in 1903, a year after two individuals were shot on Mount Sabinyo by Oscar van Beringe, and the eastern lowland gorilla in 1914.

The conventional taxonomic classification of gorillas has been challenged by recent advances in DNA testing and fresh morphological studies suggesting that the western and eastern gorilla populations, whose ranges lie more than 1,000km apart, diverged some two million years ago. For this reason, they are now treated as discrete species *G. gorilla* (western) and *G. beringei* (eastern). One distinct western race – the Cross River gorilla *G. g. dielhi* of the Cameroon–Nigeria border region – fulfils the IUCN criteria for 'Critically Endangered', since it lives in five fragmented populations, only one of which is protected, with a combined total of fewer than 200 individuals. In 2000, the Cross River gorilla and mountain gorilla shared the dubious distinction of being placed on a shortlist of the world's 25 most endangered primate taxa.

The status of the western gorilla is relatively secure, since it is far more numerous in the wild than its eastern counterpart, and has a more extensive range spanning half-a-dozen countries. Recent estimates place the total population of western gorillas at around 80,000, but numbers are in rapid decline, largely due to hunting for bushmeat and the lethal ebola virus. The fate of the eastern gorilla – still split into a lowland and mountain race – is far less certain. In the mid 1990s, an estimated 17,000 eastern lowland gorillas remained in the wild, but is widely thought that the population has halved – or worse – since the outbreak of the ongoing civil war in the DRC. Rarer still, but more stable, is the mountain gorilla, which just 700 individuals confined to two ranges: the border-straddling Virunga Volcanoes and Bwindi National Park in Uganda.

The first study of mountain gorilla behaviour was undertaken in the 1950s by George Schaller, whose pioneering work formed the starting point for the more recent research initiated by Dian Fossey in the 1960s. The brutal – and still unsolved – murder of Fossey at her research centre in December 1985 is generally thought to have been the handiwork of one of the many poachers with whom she crossed swords in the Virungas. Fossey's acclaimed book *Gorillas in the Mist* remains perhaps the best starting point for anybody who wants to know more about mountain gorilla behaviour, while the synonymous movie, a posthumous account of Fossey's life, drew global attention to the plight of the mountain gorilla.

The mountain gorilla is distinguished from its lowland counterparts by several adaptations to its high-altitude home, most visibly a longer and more luxuriant coat. It is

Kihihi, roughly 15km north of Kanyantorogo on the road towards Ishasha. Travellers heading to Bwindi using public transport should refer to the box *Butogota and the Buhoma road* below.

From Kabale The 108km drive from Kabale to Buhoma follows dirt roads the whole way, and it typically takes about three hours, a bit longer after rain. Follow the Kisoro road out of Kabale for 18km, then turn right at the turn-off signposted for Buhoma. (Whatever else you do, don't confuse this junction with the turn-off

on average bulkier than other races, with the heaviest individual gorilla on record (of any race) being the 220kg dominant silverback of Rwanda's Sabinyo Group. Like other gorillas, it is a highly sociable creature, moving in defined troops of anything from five to 50 animals. A troop typically consists of a dominant silverback male (the male's back turns silver when he reaches sexual maturity at about 13 years old) and sometimes a subordinate silverback, as well as a harem of three or four mature females, and several young animals. Unusually for mammals, it is the male who forms the focal point of gorilla society; when a silverback dies, his troop normally disintegrates. A silverback will start to acquire his harem at about 15 years of age, most normally by attracting a young sexually mature female from another troop. He may continue to lead a troop well into his 40s.

A female gorilla reaches sexual maturity at the age of eight, after which she will often move between different troops several times. Once a female has successfully given birth, however, she normally stays loyal to the same silverback until he dies, and she will even help defend him against other males. (When a male takes over a troop, he generally kills all nursing infants to bring the mothers into oestrus more quickly, a strong motive for a female to help preserve the status quo.) A female gorilla has a gestation period similar to that of a human, and if she reaches old age she will typically have raised up to six offspring to sexual maturity. A female's status within a troop is based on the length of time she has been with a silverback: the alpha female is normally the longest-serving member of the harem.

The mountain gorilla is primarily vegetarian, with bamboo shoots being the favoured diet, though they are known to eat 58 different plant species in the Virungas. They may also eat insects, with ants being a particularly popular protein supplement. A gorilla troop will spend most of its waking hours on the ground, but it will generally move into the trees at night, when each member of the troop builds itself a temporary nest. Gorillas are surprisingly sedentary creatures, typically moving less than 1km in a day, which makes tracking them on a day-to-day basis relatively easy for experienced guides. A troop will generally only move a long distance after a stressful incident, for instance an aggressive encounter with another troop. Gorillas are peaceable animals with few natural enemies and they often live for up to 50 years in the wild, but their long-term survival is critically threatened by poaching, deforestation and exposure to human-borne diseases.

It was previously thought that the Virunga and Bwindi gorilla populations were racially identical, not an unreasonable assumption given that a corridor of mid-altitude forest linked the two mountain ranges until about 500 years ago. But recent DNA tests indicate the Bwindi and Virunga gorillas show sufficient genetic differences to suggest that they have formed mutually isolated breeding populations for many millennia, in which case the 'mountain gorilla' should possibly be split into two discrete races, one – the Bwindi gorilla – endemic to Uganda, the other unique to the Virunga Mountains. Neither race numbers more than 400 in the wild, neither has ever bred successfully in captivity, and both meet several of the criteria for an IUCN classification of 'Critically Endangered'.

to Ruhija about 5km further towards Kisoro – the Ruhija road may look quicker on paper but it's in very poor condition.) Shortly after turning onto the Buhoma road, you pass through a tollgate at Hamurwa Swamp, where a nominal fee must be paid. About 45km further on, Kanungu is a substantial town with a post office, a bank, a basic resthouse and a few fairly well-stocked shops, but no petrol pump. At Kanyantorogo, 15km past Kanungu, turn left at the fork signposted for Buhoma. After 12km, you reach Butogota, which is similar in size to Kanungu (several resthouses and shops) but doesn't appear under that name on any maps. From Butogota, it's 17km to Buhoma, with all forks signposted.

From Kabale, an erratic trickle of pick-up trucks heads directly to Butogota, an inexpensive but cramped option. If these aren't available, ask about pick-ups heading to Kihihi – these will normally take you to Butogota for an extra few thousand shillings. There is also at least one bus daily between Kabale and Kihihi, leaving in mid morning. This can drop you at Kanyantorogo, where you should be in plenty of time to connect with the bus coming from Mbarara. The only danger with getting off at Kanyantorogo is that there is no formal accommodation if you do get stuck. A final option is a special hire from Kabale direct to Buhoma, which costs around Ush120,000 per group, depending on your negotiating skills – the Highland Business Centre is a good place to arrange this.

From Kampala Coming directly from Kampala, the best route to Bwindi entails following the surfaced road towards Kabale as far as Ntungamo, roughly 60km past Mbarara. At Ntungamo, you need to turn right to zip up a newly surfaced road for 45km to Rukungiri. From here, you will need to follow dirt roads in a roughly westerly direction through Kambuga (see box *Ihimbo Hot Spring* below) to Kanungu, where you converge with the route from Kabale described above.

Two bus services – Silverline and Mai – cover the road from Kampala to Butogota, travelling in opposite directions on alternate days, which effectively means that there is one bus daily in either direction except on Sundays. Buses leave from the central bus station in Kampala at around 07.00, passing through Mbarara towards midday and – depending on the state of the road – arriving in Butogota in the afternoon or early evening.

From Kasese/Fort Portal Travellers coming from northern destinations such as Kasese, Fort Portal or Queen Elizabeth National Park can use two routes to Buhoma. The more interesting route, via Katunguru, Ishasha and Kihihi, takes three to five hours, and is discussed in some detail in *Chapter 9, Getting there and away* under *Ishasha*. The alternative route entails following the surfaced Mbarara road as far south as Ishaka, where a right turn on to the unsurfaced old main road to Kabale leads for 33km to Kagamba at the junction with the newly surfaced Ntungamo–Rukungiri road. From here, directions are as for the route from Kampala. Public transport along this route is limited – instead of trying to travel directly, I would recommend heading to Mbarara to pick up the bus from Kampala.

BUTOGOTA AND THE BUHOMA ROAD

While it's easy enough to reach Butogota using public transport, the final 17km stretch to Buhoma is more of a challenge without a private vehicle. Bearing in mind that public transport to Butogota often arrives in the late afternoon or even after dark, travellers with pre-booked gorilla permits who are dependent on public transport should aim to get there with a full day left to spare to reach Buhoma. Two basic but good local lodges are available in Butogota: the **Travellers Rest House** and **Pineapple Club and Lodge** both charge around US$4/6 for single/double rooms with nets and have a restaurant attached.

At least one pick-up truck daily normally covers the road from Butogota to Buhoma, but this cannot be relied upon completely. Hitching is not impossible – there's a fair amount of private traffic now that the park has caught on with fly-in tourists. Another possibility, definitely worth thinking about if there are a few of you, is to arrange a special hire, which should cost around Ush20,000 one way. Quite a few travellers walk: the terrain is fairly hilly, but the gradients are reasonably gentle and it shouldn't take more than five hours.

If you're driving through Kambuga on the way between Rukungiri and Bwindi, you might want to ask about the location of the hot spring known locally as Ihimbo. Discovered by a Bakiga settler in the 1950s, the boiling water that bubbled from the spring rapidly acquired national fame for its therapeutic powers. One legend tells of a flat-chested girl who bathed there and emerged with an enviably voluptuous bosom, another of a man who lost his leg in an accident and regained it after swimming in the hot water. At its peak of popularity, Ihimbo attracted up to 1,000 invalids annually from all around the county, but whether it still receives visitors today, I cannot say.

Where to stay and eat You'll see a big gap in the listings below between 'Upmarket' and 'Budget' since locations whose facilities would naturally be categorised as Moderate are elevated to Upmarket for reasons of price. Note that for the first four camps/lodges below, East African residents are entitled to discounted rates.

Upmarket
Gorilla Forest Camp 0414 340290; f 0414 230254; e gfcamp@africaonline.co.ug. Owned by Sanctuary Lodges, this fabulous tented camp is easily the plushest option at Bwindi, cut into a lush forest glade about 500m inside the park entrance at Buhoma. The secluded s/c walk-in twin tents are protected beneath a thatch roof extending over a private deck, while meals and drinks are served in an organically decorated open-sided common area. A good variety of birds and (more occasionally) monkeys regularly pass through the grounds. *US$364/560 sgl/dbl FB.*

Mantana Tented Camp f 0414 321552; m 0772 403067 or 401391; f 0414 320152; e mantana@africaonline.co.ug; www.kimbla-mantana.com. This classic tented camp adjoins a small patch of forest rustling with birdlife. The s/c tents all have solar lighting, an eco-friendly toilet and a private veranda. The present site is 4km from Buhoma but there are plans for a site closer to the park gate with more expansive valley/forest views. *US$175/270 sgl/dbl FB.*

Volcanoes Bwindi Lodge 0414 346464/5; m 0752; f 0414 341718; e sales@

volcanoessafaris.com; www.volcanoessafaris.com. This attractively low-key camp consists of several secluded s/c standing tents and cottages carved into individual clearings in the surrounding scrub. The restaurant and bar is on a wooden deck with a great view over the gallery forest on the park boundary. *US$335/500 sgl/dbl FB (inc drinks and a massage).*

Buhoma Homestead 0414 321479; m 0772 502155; f 0414 321479; e info@wildfrontiers.co.ug. Now managed by Entebbe-based G&C Tours, the once rather crumby old Buhoma Homestead is undergoing an overhaul. Plans include an elevated lounge-dining deck with panoramic views across the forested Buhoma Valley. *US$120/205 s/c cottages sgl/dbl and US$85/140 for non-s/c rooms sgl/dbl, all FB.*

Lake Kitandara Bwindi Camp 0312 277304 and 0414 220494; f 0414 255288; e kitanda@infocom.co.ug; http://www.lkttsafaris.co.ug and www.visituganda.com/ads/kitandara.htm. This new camp consists of a few basic s/c standing tents in a cramped plot situated immediately outside the park entrance. It's exceptionally poor value. *US$100/190 sgl/dbl FB. Camping US$5 pp.*

Budget and camping
Buhoma Community Rest Camp m 0772 384965/529081 (poor reception so send text message if no signal); e buhomacrc@yahoo.com; www.traveluganda.co.ug/buhoma-community. This attractive complex is set in wooded grounds immediately inside the park entrance gate on a slope facing a forest gallery. It's by far and away the most popular budget option in the locale. No

visitation fee is levied for staying here, unless you go on a walk into the park. Basic 3-course dinners can be ordered in advance for Ush10,000, and beers and sodas are also available. *6-berth dormitory US$8 pp, twin and dbl bandas US$10 pp, s/c twin rooms US$25, rooms using shared facilities US$10/19 sgl/dbl, camping US$3 pp.*

On the morning of 17 March 2000, a larger than normal congregation gathered in the church of Kanungu's Movement for the Restoration of the Ten Commandments of God (MRTCG). The assembled cultists had been promised that today, finally, after long years of waiting, the apocalypse of fire spoken of by the Virgin Mary would sweep the earth. The Blessed Virgin had also asserted, or so the congregation was told, that the only survivors of the terrible inferno would be the select few assembled within the church, which should be sealed to ensure that nobody wandered outside at the wrong moment.

While the congregation sang their praises, a person or persons unknown locked the church doors for the last time, boarded and nailed closed the windows, then doused the wooden building with 40 litres of sulphuric acid purchased illegally four days earlier by cult leader Dominic Kataribabo. A match was struck, and the building exploded in a fireball of such intensity that many of its occupants' skulls exploded. Later, the remains of 330 charred bodies would eventually be identified, but church records indicate that more than 500 people must have died in the blaze. The only certain survivor was a teenage boy who had slipped out to buy some food shortly before the building was boarded up.

Initial police investigations indicated that the cremated cultists had been participants in a mass suicide pact. But then six more bodies were found buried in the Nyabugoto compound, and over the next six weeks a further 450 corpses were unearthed in mass graves at four other cult-associated properties. The buried victims had clearly not been acquiescent suicides, but had instead been strangled, clubbed or poisoned to death by the cult leadership. The police duly changed their verdict to mass murder – the largest cult killing in world history.

Years later, the circumstances surrounding the MRTCG massacre remain shrouded in mystery, as does the origin of the doomsday cult itself. Its chief apostle was a 68-year-old retired schoolteacher and civil servant called Joseph Kibwetere, deeply religious despite having fathered several illegitimate children, and once diagnosed as manic depressive after he claimed to have died and been resurrected. Kibwetere reputedly founded the cult after he overheard a conversation in which Jesus and the Virgin Mary complained about the world's departure from the Ten Commandments, and then decided to set the apocalypse for the turn of the millennium.

Subsequent investigations suggest that the MRTCG's true leader was not Kibwetere but Credonia Mwerinde, a 48-year-old school dropout who passed through four unsuccessful marriages, and produced a similar number of offspring, before she ended up a bar-girl and prostitute in Kanungu's Independence Bar. While working there, she became the seventh wife of a local Mukiga man – polygamy is still widely practised in the area – but the relationship fell apart when she was unable to conceive. One day, probably in early 1989, Mwerinde visited the Nyabugoto Caves, formerly associated with the Nyabingi fertility cult (see pages 232–3) and more recently with visitations by the Virgin Mary, who duly appeared to say that the baby had been withheld so that Mwerinde could serve as Mary's medium. Over the months that followed, Mwerinde established a cult not dissimilar to that of Nyabingi, curing infertile and ill women as the oracle of the Blessed Virgin.

In mid 1989, Mwerinde met Kibwetere and his wife Teresa, and was invited to relocate her spiritual practice to their home in Ntungamo. A year later, the MRTCG was officially launched, and by 1991 some 200 followers were living at the house, and Mwerinde and Kibwetere had become lovers. In 1993, Teresa and her children bade

🏠 **Bwindi View Bandas and Campsite** Situated directly opposite the community campsite, this private set-up is considerably cheaper than the opposition, but the grounds are less attractive. Meals are available. Bookings can be made through the national park information office in Kabale. *4-bed dormitory US$6 pp or US$20 for full unit, 2-bed bandas US$6/8 sgl/dbl, camping US$2.50 pp.*

Kibwetere and his growing cult – the membership eventually reached 5,000 – a less than fond farewell when it relocated to a 5ha hillside plot near Kanungu. Here, the cult was joined by a disgraced priest called Dominic Kataribabo, who would effectively become third-in-command to Mwerinde and Kibwetere.

In 2002, a Uganda Human Rights Commission team report on the MRTCG indicated that its leaders had violated 'all human rights' even before the killing started. The rank and file were forbidden from talking, worked long hours of hard manual labour, given limited food, could not wear shoes, and were forced to sleep on the floor of the compound's unsanitary and overcrowded dormitories. Children were separated from their parents, sex was forbidden even between married couples, and contact with neighbouring communities was banned. Upon joining the cult, members were expected to sell all their property and other possessions, the proceeds from which were to be donated to the cult, whose increasingly wealthy leaders suffered no such deprivations in their large modern house.

The MRTCG was centred on the Virgin Mary's announcement, relayed via Mwerinde and Kibwetere, that the world would end at midnight on 31 December 1999, and that the only survivors would be those cult members who had shed all their money and possessions and were gathered at the Nyabugoto camp when the moment came. And inevitably, once that long-awaited moment did come, and then went, without event, the mood of the dispossessed and formerly compliant cultists changed. Some left and never returned. Those who took up the leaders' invitation to submit a written complaint ended up in the mass graves later discovered by the police. And about 500 followers were appeased by a statement to the effect that the Virgin had contacted the leaders to say that Armageddon had not been cancelled, only rescheduled. It would take place on 17 March.

Who actually started the blaze and whether they survived remain open questions. International arrest warrants have been issued against Mwerinde, Kibwetere, Kataribabo and other prominent cult leaders, and a handsome police reward is at stake for information leading to their detainment. Some say that all the main leaders died in the inferno, but of them Kataribabo alone has been identified among the bodies, and then only tentatively. Another hypothesis is Kibwetere had been diagnosed with AIDS in 1999 and died some time before 17 March, either of natural causes, or by the hand of his angry lover Mwerinde – some surviving cultists say he had not been seen since October. Contradicting this are reports of Mwerinde and Kataribabo having been observed together shortly after the massacre, headed in the direction of the nearest border – only 25km distant – and presumably across to the DRC. Kibwetere's car, though present in the compound on the morning of the fire, has not been sighted since. Clearly, somebody escaped.

The promised judicial inquiry into the cult killings never materialised owing to lack of funding. Several other doomsday cults as potentially deluded and/or murderous as the MRTCG still operate in Uganda, though the more prominent ones have been disbanded by the authorities. In January 2003, journalist Kalungi Kabuye visited the site of the massacre and wrote in the *New Vision*: 'There is nothing left but empty, rotting buildings and overgrown bush… no plaque commemorating their passage… Where was the church that was burnt down? Where are the mass graves?… Shouldn't there be something to warn coming generations of just how bad man can be?'

Listings
Internet A Ugandan NGO, Conservation Through Public Health (CTPH) provides an internet service costing Ush500 a minute. It might be 20 times cheaper in Kabale but probably worth it to share your post-gorilla tracking 'high' with

distant family and friends. CTPH is 4km back towards Butogota from the Bwindi gate; turn right at the Mantana Camp and continue for a few hundred metres.

Activities

Gorilla tracking Two gorilla groups, Mubare and Habinyanja, have been habituated for tourist visits in the vicinity of Buhoma. In mid 2003, however, the Habinyanja group spilt into two groups now known as Habinyanja A and Habinyanja B. Eight permits are now available for each of the three Buhoma groups to bring the daily total to 24.

Gorilla-tracking excursions leave from Buhoma at 08.00 and the round trip might take anything from three to ten hours, depending on the proximity of the gorillas and how easily they are located. The success rate is as good as 100% – one Kampala operator who has sent hundreds of clients to Bwindi annually reckons that they have failed to see gorillas only twice in the past six years.

A gorilla-tracking permit costs US$375 for foreign visitors and US$355 for residents, though this will increase to US$500 for foreigners and US$475 for residents as of July 2007. They can only be arranged through the UWA headquarters on Kiira Road in Kampala (↞ *0414 355000*) or through a tour agent or backpackers' hostel. These 32 permits are often booked up by tour operators months in advance. There is absolutely no point in heading to southwest Uganda with the express goal of seeing gorillas unless you are either in possession of a Bwindi permit or are prepared to nip across the border from Kisoro to track the DRC gorillas.

Guided day walks from Buhoma Bwindi is widely thought to support the greatest biodiversity of any East African forest, and the Buhoma area has more to offer than just gorilla tracking. Five different day-trails, ranging from 30 minutes to eight hours in duration, lead from Buhoma, offering the opportunity to enjoy the tranquillity of the forest and to see several different monkey species. For birders, roughly 190 bird species have been recorded in the Buhoma area, ten of which are either listed in the *Red Data Book* or else endemic to the Albertine Rift.

The Muyanga River Trail lies outside the national park and so no guide is required. It's only a half-hour walk, starting at the end of the Buhoma road, from where it follows the Bizenga River to its confluence with the Muyanga, before returning to the Buhoma road at the community campsite. Birding can be good in the early morning and late afternoon, with the shining blue kingfisher being a particular speciality.

Guided trails cost US$10 per person for a day's walk – well worth it, since most of the guides are very knowledgeable and good at finding animals that you'd probably miss. A tip is not mandatory but it is more or less customary, bearing in mind that the rangers are very poorly paid. For monkeys and general scenery, the best of the guided walks is probably the three-hour Waterfall Trail. This leads for 2km along an abandoned road before heading into what I consider one of the most beautiful areas of forest in Uganda and following the Munyaga River on the ascent to the 33m-high waterfall. Other trails are the Mazubijiro Loop Trail and Rushara Hill Trail, which both take about three hours and offer good views across to the Virunga Mountains. The eight-hour Ivo River Walk, which leads to the Ivo River on the southern boundary of the park, offers a good opportunity for seeing monkeys, duikers and a variety of birds.

Birdwatchers with a limited amount of time in Bwindi are strongly urged to stick to the main road that runs into the forest from the entrance gate. It is easier to see birds from the road than from a forest path, and on a good morning you could hope to see around 40–50 species over a slow 2km walk, a high proportion of them more easily seen here than in any other similarly accessible part of Uganda. Among the great many remarkable birds that are commonly seen along this road, some of the more readily identifiable include the great blue and black-billed turacos; dusky and barred long-tailed cuckoos; bar-tailed trogon; black bee-eater; grey-throated barbet; Petit's cuckoo-shrike; Elliot's woodpecker; red-tailed bulbul; mountain, icterine and yellow-whiskered greenbuls; white-bellied robin-chat; white-tailed ant-thrush; rusty-faced warbler; white-browed crombec; yellow-eyed black flycatcher; white-tailed blue flycatcher; white-tailed crested monarch; narrow-tailed starling; McKinnon's grey shrike; Luhder's and Doherty's bush-shrikes and black-headed waxbill. Indulgent as the above list may sound to non-birders, it is really no more than a taster! In addition to the outstanding birding, this road supports a dazzling array of colourful butterflies, and the lovely L'Hoest's monkey is often encountered.

Village walks A recent introduction is a three-hour stroll through Buhoma and its margins to see the customs and practices of the Bakiga and Batwa people. The tour takes in varied activities such as farming, brewing local beer, dispensing traditional medicines and concludes with dancing displays by members of the Batwa community. The walk costs Ush15,000 per person and is organised through the Buhoma Community Rest Camp (see *Where to stay*, page 269).

NKURINGO Uganda's newest gorilla-tracking location is the Nkuringo sector of Bwindi National Park. Covering the southwestern part of the forest, it's just 40km north of Kisoro, but feels far more remote and although densely settled by farming communities is extremely undeveloped on account of its location on a dead-end road ending at the nearby DRC border. Tourism facilities are limited to a basic campsite but an upmarket lodge is planned.

It's an extremely beautiful area with good potential for hiking. The approach along the Nteko Ridge provides grandstand views across the Kashasha river valley to the Bwindi Forest which cloaks its northern slopes. 'Nkuringo' means 'round stone' and refers to a knoll-like forested hill beside the river, dwarfed by loftier ridges above it. To the south and west, superb panoramas include the western Rift Valley and the entire length of the Virunga volcanic range.

One group of gorillas has been habituated at Nkuringo. This consists of 18 individuals: two silverbacks, three black-backed males, four adult females, one sub-adult female, five juveniles and three infants. The group ranges over a 10km section of the Kashasha river valley which forms the boundary of the national park. They are usually encountered in the forest but do also range along the public lands to eat crops on the southern slopes of the valley. The International Gorilla Conservation Programme has purchased a 10km long by 400m wide strip of public land along the river as a buffer zone. Land-use practices such as pasture and tea are planned for this area since these are not appealing to gorillas and will encourage them to remain in the park.

Getting there and away The trailhead for tracking in Nkuringo is in Ntungamo village on the Nteko Ridge which can be reached by vehicle from either Kabale or Kisoro.

From Kabale Ntungamo is a 3–3½-hour drive from Kabale. Fork right just beyond Muko, about 43km out of Kabale (and 3km past the Lake Bunyonyi overflow; see directions to Kisoro/Mgahinga, pages 248–50). At the top of the following hill, you need to turn right off the main road for a slow and windy drive of at least two hours, turning right again just after the small Kashasha valley town of Rubugeri

(12km before Nkuringo). This route is more direct but slower speeds mean that it won't be much quicker than passing via Kisoro.

From Kisoro To reach Kisoro, see directions for Kisoro/Mgahinga. From Kisoro, Ntungamo is a straightforward, if windy and bumpy drive that shouldn't take much more than an hour. The road out of town leaves the Main Street next to the storied petrol station almost opposite the SkyBlue Hotel. The route is clearly signposted and passes the scenic Lake Mutolere before climbing into the Bwindi hills. It also passes the turning to the lovely Lake Mutanda with its unforgettable Virunga backdrop. The Kisoro–Ntungamo road is usually in reasonable condition although the route in the hilly section is narrow and windy with steep drops. Heavy rain and steep terrain also mean that landslides can occasionally block the road and a 4x4 vehicle driven at a sensible speed is recommended in wet conditions.

There's no public transport to Ntungamo village from Kisoro and the infrequent vehicles from Kabale stop at Rubugeri Town, 12km away. However, the walk along the ridge-top road does offer marvellous views. Indeed, with time and energy you might consider finding a guide and walking along local paths from Kisoro or the Lake Mutanda campsites. Alternatively, the Golden Monkey Hotel can hire a Pajero (seats four) for USh100,000 return trip or a minibus (seating five–six people) for Ush80,000.

Where to stay At present most people stay in Kisoro (see *Kisoro* listings, pages 250–1) because the options at Nkuringo are limited and ambitiously priced, presumably because of the lack of competition. If you do have your own camping equipment or are happy to stay somewhere basic then the campground at Nkuringo is a lovely spot. Note that mobile phone reception along Nteko Ridge is limited and you are better to send a text message.

Nkuringo Campground m 0772 413766; www.traveluganda.co.ug/nkuringocampsite. This basic campsite offers *bandas* or standing tents. I haven't seen the facilities, which I'd imagine are pretty basic, but the site itself is lovely with views north across Bwindi with Buhoma village, Lake Edward and the Rwenzori visible beyond. There's no electricity or running water (the latter is in critically short supply along Nteko Ridge; if insufficient rainwater can be collected, it must be carried in jerrycans up the hill from the Kashasha river 600m below). Take your own food. *US$20 pp for bandas or standing tents; pitch your own tent for US$5.*

Hammerkop Guesthouse m 0782 995802. This reportedly very basic new lodge near the UWA office in Ntungamo is expensive, and charges may or may not be negotiable. *US$30 FB.*

Clouds Gorilla Lodge ☎ 0414 251182; e tusc@africaonline.co.ug; www.safariuganda.com. A lodge is planned at Nkuringo through a partnership between the Uganda Safari Company, African Wildlife Foundation and the local community. It will occupy a superb site on Nteko Ridge looking south towards the Virungas and the DRC Rift Valley floor. *Prices will be US$300/380 FB and will include a payment of US$30 per night to the community.*

Activities

Gorilla tracking The staging point for gorilla tracking is the small UWA office in Ntungamo trading centre on the Nteko Ridge above the park boundary. You need to check in at 08.00. Nkuringo is the most physically challenging of all gorilla-tracking locations. Unlike existing tracking sites at Buhoma and Mgahinga, there is no vehicle access from the Nteko Ridge to the park boundary which follows the Kashasha River. The closest road is the Rubugiri–Ntungamo–Nteko road on the ridge 600m above the river. Trackers face a steep one-hour descent simply in order to cross the river and enter the forest. After the arduous but rewarding business of gorilla tracking, you'll face a one–two-hour climb back up to the ridge. This is not a problem for the fit, but Nkuringo is definitely not for the unfit or faint-hearted. A number of routes have been improved by the addition of steps and gentler switchback turns. The gorillas range along the Kashasha Valley so you can walk or drive (if you have a vehicle) to the most convenient descent. It's hotter on the open hillside than in the forest so do take plenty of water with you. Porters can be hired to carry your bag to and from the forest if required for Ush10,000.

Note: There is a semblance of a road descending the steep hillside below Ntungamo; an astonishingly inept attempt at road contruction by Kisoro District that has created a precipitous and already dangerously gullied scar winding just two-thirds of the way down the hill. You'd be ill advised to risk a vehicle on it. You might get down but you may well fail to get back up.

At present, Nkuringo permits are obtained at the UWA headquarters in Kampala but this might change. An upmarket lodge is planned at Ntungamo as a partnership between African Wildlife Foundation, UWA and the local community and to enable this to succeed, it has been proposed that this lodge would have first option on all eight permits. This is a controversial issue to which there are, as usual, two sides. While this would generate a useful levy of US$30 per person per night for community development in an extremely poor area it would also effectively exclude tourists unwilling to pay US$300 per night for accommodation over and above the already high cost of a gorilla permit. Given the additional consideration of access, tracking at Nkuringo would be restricted to a limited clientele that is more than usually wealthy and healthy. The proposal has proved controversial with the wider tourism industry and also with Kisoro District administration which obviously wants tourists to have the option of staying in Kisoro hotels.

Hiking Nkuringo is a superbly scenic area with great potential for hiking outside the forest. Community walks will at some stage become available. I would suggest though, that this is not an area for haphazard exploration, though in all probability, the available options are pretty limited. The steep nature of Nteko Ridge means that the main alternatives for a pleasant stroll are either west along the ridge-top road towards DRC or east towards Rubugeri. Bear in mind that Ntungamo lies about 8km from the Congolese border and it is a sensitive area. Tourism development has been subject to all manner of evaluations to ensure visitor safety. It's most unlikely that you'd wander off into DRC, or indeed be allowed to. However I would recommend that if walking any distance in that direction (and it's a lovely road) you engage a local guide. Another option, and one for which a guide, and probably a porter, would *certainly* be required, is if you want to find your way back over the hills to Kisoro or Lake Mutanda.

Batwa Village A Batwa (Pygmy) community lives a few kilometres from Ntungamo and according to Phil Stein, a visit is one of the 'advertised' attractions. Phil's trip never materialised. 'UWA wouldn't let us go without an armed escort which they refused to provide. They gave a feeble excuse along the lines that these Batwa had never met white people before and would run away. They talked about them as if they were mountain gorillas and needed 'habituation' which they were in the process of doing.' Nkuringo could do with some additional 'attractions' but as mentioned elsewhere in this book, tourism involving the marginalised Batwa people is a controversial, not to say tricky, subject that requires sensitive handling if it is to work to the benefit of all concerned. It's clearly not got off on the right foot here and we'd be interested to hear how the situation progresses from future visitors.

RUHIJA Ruhija was the research centre and headquarters for the Impenetrable Forest Reserve before it was gazetted as a national park in 1991. It is one of the most beautiful places I've ever seen: from the resthouse, situated at 2,300m, the view stretches over forested ridge after forested ridge to the Virunga volcanoes on the Rwandan border. Few people visit Ruhija these days – few people ever did – and it's practically inaccessible without a private vehicle.

The roads around Ruhija offer good monkey viewing, with black-and-white colobus particularly common. Because it lies at a higher altitude than Buhoma, Ruhija has a tree composition more characteristic of Afro-montane forest than lowland forest, and it supports a significantly different avifauna, making it an essential stop for enthusiasts with the time and means to reach it. It is one of the few places where you stand a chance of seeing all four crimson-wings recorded in Uganda, and other specialities include a variety of apalis species, Lagden's bush-shrike, African green broadbill, and the handsome francolin. The only Ugandan record for the uncommon yellow-crested helmet-shrike is an unconfirmed sighting at Ruhija.

Based from Ruhija, it is possible to organise guided walks along the three-hour Mubwindi Swamp Trail, which lies off the Kabale–Ruhija road and passes through the only part of the park where elephants are resident. The Mubwindi Swamp Trail is one of most alluring bird walks in Uganda, with the possibility of some 20 bird species listed in the *Red Data Book* and/or endemic to the Albertine Rift, notably the extremely local African green broadbill and Grauer's rush warbler. The six-hour Bamboo Trail leads to Rwamunyoni Peak, at 2,607m the highest point in the park, and it is also notable for good birding.

To get to Ruhija from Kabale, follow the Kisoro road for roughly 25km, then turn right at the turn-off signposted for Ruhija. This road is not very well maintained and a high-clearance vehicle with 4x4 will be necessary. Sections crossing smooth bedrock beyond Ruhija can be worryingly slippery after heavy rain. An additional excitement can be forest elephants on the road. These, being more aggressive than their savanna cousins, have been known to menace and even rock vehicles. If you do encounter them, keep your distance and wait until they have moved some way off the road (so far as you can tell!).

Where to stay The **Institute of Tropical Forest Conservation** runs a small hostel with two four-bed rooms with basic ablutions outside the building. It's not cheap at US$15 per person but the price will be justifiable to keen birders. At 2,340m above sea level it can get chilly so take a warm jumper.

9

Kasese and Environs

The most populous centre in western Uganda after Mbarara – and ninth-largest in the country according to the 2002 census – Kasese is of little inherent interest to travellers, lacking even the urban cohesion and scattering of quaint colonial structures that redeem the likes of Kabale and Fort Portal from small-town tedium. Kasese is, however, sandwiched by two superb and strongly contrasting national parks, and although the town is seldom visited by package tours, it does form a useful base for exploring these parks for independent travellers.

Immediately west of Kasese, the Rwenzori foothills rise to a string of glacial peaks – topped by Africa's third-highest mountain – the upper slopes of which are protected within the Rwenzori Mountains National Park, one of the most popular hiking destinations in east Africa. Overshadowed by the Rwenzori, the Queen Elizabeth National Park immediately south of Kasese is, along with Murchison Falls, the oldest in the country, established in 1952 to protect a fabulous tract of moist savanna, interspersed with extensive patches of tropical rainforest, numerous small crater lakes and the more open waters of lakes Edward and George on the Rift Valley floor.

KALINZU FOREST RESERVE

Flanking the Kasese–Mbarara road southeast of Queen Elizabeth National Park, the 137km² Kalinzu Forest Reserve is essentially an eastern extension of the better-known Maramagambo Forest (within Queen Elizabeth National Park) and it supports a similar range of forest species. In addition to an alluring variety of forest birds, Kalinzu protects six diurnal primate species: chimpanzee, olive baboon, black-and-white colobus and red-tailed, blue and L'Hoest's monkey, as well as the rare pygmy antelope. Nocturnal primates such as potto and two varieties of galago can be sought on night walks, when you're also likely to hear the eerie shrieking of the tree hyrax. A recently developed ecotourism site within the reserve offers camping facilities and guided and unguided walks along a series of trails that follow the ridges and valleys of the Rift Valley Escarpment, offering views to the Rwenzori, Lake Edward and the Kazinga Channel. It forms an excellent alternative to Maramagambo for budget-conscious travellers, since entrance fees are low compared with national park fees and access is relatively straightforward on public transport. For further information, ring the National Forest Authority in Bushenyi (✆ 04854 42365) or call the NFA Kampala HQ (✆ 0414 230365). You may hear or read of another ecotourism facility in the nearby Kasyoha-Kitomi Forest Reserve but this has closed down.

GETTING THERE AND AWAY The booking office and campsite lies at Nkombe Forest Station about 20km north of Ishaka, practically adjacent to the main Mbarara–Kasese road. Any public transport heading along the main road can drop you there.

🏠 **WHERE TO STAY** Campers need to be self-sufficient, though water and firewood are available and basic supplies can be purchased at a nearby trading centre. Camping costs US$3 per person. Visitors not wishing to camp can stay at the inexpensive but adequate Homeland Hotel in Ishaka (↘ *04834 42226*) or at the Abbey Guesthouse or Kookaburra Camp near Rugazi on the Kichwamba Escarpment (see *QENP* listings, pages 290–2).

ACTIVITIES Four forest trails have been developed, all of which involve some clambering over hilly terrain, so ask the local guides for advice. All day trails cost US$10 for residents or US$20 for non-residents. Aside from Kibale Forest, this is the only reserve in Uganda where night walks are offered. There is a real chance of seeing chimpanzees – well habituated by Japanese researchers who have worked there since 1992 – on all day walks.

The most straightforward walk is the 2.5km River Trail, which loops along the Kajojo (Elephant) River and shouldn't take longer than one hour. Although elephants are now scarce, the trail passes some fine specimens of *Parinari excelsia* and a huge strangler figure. Monkeys are often observed, while chimpanzee nests might be seen in the treetops.

The 5km circular Palm Trail takes up to two hours, traversing relatively flat terrain studded with fascinating forest trees such as the flame tree, with its large, red, tulip-like flames, said to have aphrodisiac properties when eaten by women, and numerous raffia palms, used for making local mats.

The most demanding hike is the 11km Waterfall Trail, which takes four to five hours to cover, passing over some hilly and, in parts, rather soggy terrain. The highlight of the trail is the Kilyantama Waterfall – the name somewhat curiously translates as 'sheep eater' – but you can also expect to see a variety of monkeys, birds and interesting trees, including the type of fig regarded to make the finest barkcloth.

QUEEN ELIZABETH NATIONAL PARK

Uganda's most popular and accessible savanna reserve, the 1,978km² Queen Elizabeth National Park (QENP) is bounded to the west by the Ishasha River and Lake Edward along the Congolese border, to the north by Kasese and the Rwenzori foothills, to the east by Lake George, the Kyambura (pronounced and sometimes spelt 'Chambura') Gorge and Kalinzu Forest Reserve, and to the south by the Kigezi Wildlife Reserve. QENP is primarily associated with open savanna, studded in some areas with a dense cover of acacia and euphorbia trees, but it also embraces large areas of swamp around Lake George, the extensive Maramagambo Forest in the southeast, and the forested Kyambura Gorge along the border with the Kyambura Game Reserve. At least ten crater lakes lie within the park, including a highly accessible cluster immediately north of the main road to Mweya Lodge, as does the entire Ugandan shore of Lake Edward, the northern and western shores of Lake George, and the connecting Kazinga Channel.

A total of 95 mammal species have been recorded in QENP, the highest for any Ugandan national park. Ten primate species are present, including chimpanzee, vervet, blue, red-tailed, and L'Hoest's monkey, black-and-white colobus and olive baboon. Around 20 predators are found in the park, including side-striped jackal, spotted hyena, lion and leopard. The most common antelope species are Uganda kob, bushbuck, topi and Defassa waterbuck. The elusive semi-aquatic sitatunga antelope occurs in papyrus swamps around Lake George, while four duiker species are primarily confined to the Maramagambo Forest. Buffaloes are common and often reddish in colour due to interbreeding with the redder forest buffalo of the

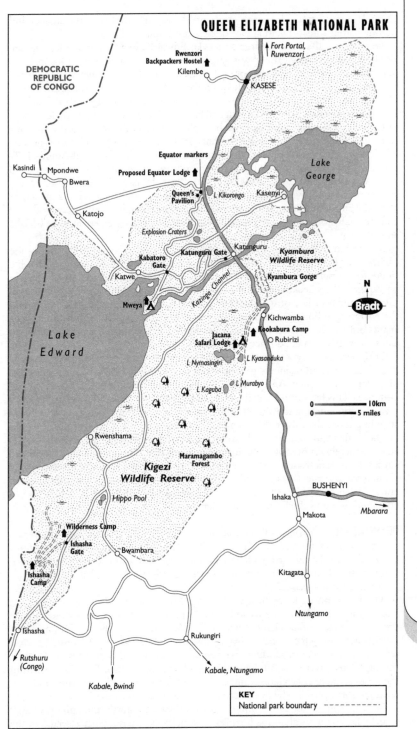

QUEEN ELIZABETH NATIONAL PARK

DEMOCRATIC
REPUBLIC
OF CONGO

↑ Fort Portal,
Ruwenzori

Rwenzori
Backpackers Hostel ↑
Kilembe

KASESE

Kasindi   Mpondwe
        Bwera

Katojo

Equator markers

Proposed Equator Lodge ↑

Queen's
Pavilion

L Kikorongo

Kasenyi

Lake
George

Explosion Craters

Katunguru Gate   Katunguru

Kabatoro
Gate

Katwe

Kyambura
Wildlife Reserve

Kyambura Gorge

Kazinga Channel

Mweya

Lake
Edward

Kichwamba

Kookabura Camp

Rubirizi

Jacana
Safari Lodge

L Nymasingiri   L Kyasanduka

L Murabyo

L Kaguba

N

Bradt

0   10km
0   5 miles

Rwenshama

Kigezi
Wildlife Reserve

Maramagambo
Forest

Hippo Pool

BUSHENYI

Ishaka

Mbarara

Makota

Wilderness Camp

Ishasha
Gate

Bwambara

Ishasha
Camp

Kitagata

Ishasha

Ntungamo

Rutshuru
(Congo)

Rukungiri

Kabale, Ntungamo

Kabale, Bwindi

KEY
National park boundary - - - - -

Kasese and Environs   QUEEN ELIZABETH NATIONAL PARK

9

Congolese rainforest. The park's elephants display affinities with the smaller and slightly hairier forest-dwelling race of elephant found in the DRC.

Protected as the Lake George and Lake Edward game reserves since the late 1920s, the present-day QENP was gazetted as the Kazinga National Park in 1952, to protect the varied landscapes of prolific wildlife of the Rift Valley floor between Lake Edward and the Rwenzori. It was renamed QENP in 1954 to commemorate a visit by the British monarch (it was also temporarily called Rwenzori National Park during the Amin era, and might still be shown under that name on older maps of Uganda, potentially confusing as the higher slopes of the Rwenzori Mountains were gazetted as the Rwenzori National Park in 1991). QENP's once-prolific wildlife declined greatly during the years of instability that followed Amin's 1971 coup, with the elephant population dropping from a high of 4,000 to perhaps 150 in 1980, and buffalo from 18,000 to 8,000. Over the past 15 years, however, the situation has improved greatly. The elephant population is today estimated at around 2,500, while lions, once rare and elusive, are thought to number at least 200 and are readily observed in the Kasenyi Plains and to a lesser extent around Ishasha and Mweya.

More than 610 bird species have now been recorded in QENP, possibly the highest total for any national park in Africa, if not the world, and a truly remarkable figure for a reserve that is relatively small by continental standards. In addition to 54 raptors, the checklist includes virtually every waterbird species resident in Uganda, and a variety of woodland and forest birds, the latter largely confined to the Maramagambo Forest. Birding anywhere in the park is good, but the Mweya stands out for the myriad waterbirds on the Kazinga Channel, while the riparian forest at Ishasha is a good place to see more unusual species.

Non-residents pay a visitation fee of US$25/35/50 for one/two/three or more nights. East African residents pay discounted rates of US$15/20/25 on production of proof of residency. An entrance permit is valid for 24 hours from time of entrance. This fee is valid for all sectors of the park, but you will need to show the receipt upon entering the various entrance gates to different sectors. The deal for spending more than three days is particularly attractive for QENP, since it would not be difficult to spend a week exploring its various sectors. No visitation fee is charged merely for driving along the public roads that run through the park, ie: the surfaced Mbarara–Kasese road, the dirt road to Katwe, and the dirt road between Katunguru and the Ishasha border post. Vehicles (less than two tonnes) pay an entrance fee of Ush20,000. Ugandan-registered 4x4 vehicles pay Ush30,000 to enter and foreign vehicles pay Ush74,000.

ORIENTATION A variety of natural and artificial barriers cut QENP into a patchwork of discrete sectors. The most important of these barriers is the Kazinga Channel and Lake Edward, which divides the park into its northern and southern components, linked only by an artificial bridge across the channel at Katunguru on the main Mbarara–Kasese road.

The main tourist focus in QENP is the Mweya Peninsula – site of the park headquarters as well as a luxury lodge, budget hostel and campsite – which lies on the northern bank of the channel at its confluence with Lake Edward. This northern tourist circuit is itself chopped in two by the surfaced Kasese road. Mweya, the small town of Katwe and surrounding crater lakes, and a network of game-viewing roads through dense riverine scrub lie to the west of the main road. Running east from the Kasese road to Lake George, the Kasenyi Plains, despite lacking accommodation facilities, form perhaps the prime game-viewing circuit in the park.

Little developed for tourism in comparison with the north, the bulk of QENP actually lies to the south of the Kazinga Channel, where it is further bisected by the

Mbarara road. The small area of the park to the east of this road is the site of the Kyambura Gorge, an important site for chimp tracking, while the fantastic Maramagambo Forest, immediately west of the Mbarara road, is the site of one small upmarket lodge and an underrated forest campsite. Further southwest – indeed, a good two-hour drive from the Katunguru Bridge along a back route to Bwindi National Park – the remote Ishasha Plains are crossed by a little-used road circuit best known for its population of tree-climbing lions.

The sectional nature of QENP makes it unrealistic to cover the park as one entity below. Instead, each sector is covered discretely under its own heading, with details of getting there and accommodation provided as though it were a destination in its own right. Also included below under separate headings is coverage of the Kyambura Game Reserve and Kalinzu Forest Reserve, both of which abut QENP and can be visited from the 20km stretch of the Mbarara road south of the Kazinga Channel.

FURTHER READING Queen Elizabeth National Park is described in *Uganda's Great Rift Valley* by Andrew Roberts. QENP is central to this publication which is an offshoot of the 2002 project that resulted in the Mweya Information Centre. The 184 page book should be available at the Information Centre and tourism sites throughout the park.

ISHASHA The remote Ishasha Plains in the southwest of QENP, though bypassed by most tour groups, ranks with the most alluring game-viewing areas in the country, as much for its untrammelled mood as its varied wildlife. Ishasha Camp, the only tourist base in the area, situated on the eastern bank of the Ishasha River facing the DRC, is also surprisingly accessible, assuming you have private transport and are in any case travelling between QENP and Bwindi National Park.

Ishasha is well known for its tree-climbing lion population, which currently consists of around 40 individuals split across three prides. Unusual elsewhere in Africa, the tree-climbing behaviour at Ishasha might be observed throughout the year but is most frequently encountered during the rainy seasons. The explanation for this localised behaviour is open to conjecture. Limited studies undertaken in Tanzania's Lake Manyara National Park, also noted for its tree-climbing lions, indicate that the custom of ascending trees is culturally ingrained rather than a response to any immediate external stimuli, though it may well have been initiated to escape the attention of biting flies during an epidemic of these irksome creatures. In Ishasha, the sycamore fig and to a lesser extent Albezia trees are favoured over other trees, and the lions are most likely to be seen in arboreal action in the heat of the day, descending back to the ground before dusk.

The Ishasha River, which can be explored on foot from the trio of campsites along its bank, supports a healthy hippo population, most easily observed from Campsite Two. The fringing riparian forest harbours good numbers of bushbuck and black-and-white colobus monkey, and an interesting variety of birds including black bee-eater, broad-billed roller and the localised Cassin's grey flycatcher. Away from the river, light acacia woodland and savanna support large herds of Uganda kob, topi and buffalo, while elephants are seasonally common.

Two main game circuits run out of Ishasha, the northern and southern loops, both of which are roughly 20km in length. The southern circuit is the more productive for lion sightings, since it passes through the main kob breeding grounds – as in Kasenyi, the predators often stick close to their prey, and their presence is often revealed by the antelope's alarm calls. The northern circuit, which passes through the Lake Edward Flats, is better for general game viewing and it also skirts an extensive swamp where birdwatchers should look out for black coucal, compact weaver, fan-tailed widow and other water-associated birds.

An 8km road extending north from this road loop leads to the marshy shore of Lake Edward, another good site for waterbirds, including various herons, storks and plovers. This area often harbours decent concentrations of elephant, buffalo, kob, topi and waterbuck, and it currently ranks as one of the most reliable spots in Uganda for shoebill (we had two good sightings in three visits in mid 2006). Road conditions around Lake Edward are erratic so do seek advice from the rangers before striking out alone, particularly after rain.

Ishasha Camp is quite wonderful at night – I can't remember ever being treated to such a diverse litany of animal calls. An incessantly high-pitched white noise, supplied by a myriad insects and frogs, is punctuated by the regular grunting of hippos, the eerie baying of spotted hyenas, the repetitive twittering of nightjars and the hysterical shrieking of disturbed plovers. Listen closely, and you'll probably pick out elephants trumpeting in the distance, and even the occasional throaty lion communication.

The Ishasha River Gorge, outside the park and upstream of the camp, is said to be outstandingly beautiful and rumoured to harbour a population of chimpanzees. At present the gorge can only be accessed by foot from the camp, but if a planned hydro-electric plant goes ahead, it may be quite easy to get there by vehicle. The Kigezi Game Reserve lies on the opposite side of the Katunguru–Ishasha road from Queen Elizabeth National Park. It protects similar species to the national park, with a major attraction being the hippo pool described below under *Getting there and away* below. The reserve is not at present developed for tourism, and plans to construct a low-key campsite and establish walking trails to the hippo pools and other interesting areas are evidently on hold.

Getting there and away

Ishasha Camp can be approached from one of two directions: Kabale and Bwindi National Park in the south or from Katunguru on the main Mbarara–Kasese road. It is thus easily visited *en route* between Bwindi and Mweya in the north of QENP, though road conditions are such that it would be difficult to explore the game-viewing tracks thoroughly without spending a night there.

From Kabale/Bwindi via Kihihi

Ishasha can be approached from Kabale or Bwindi National Park via Kihihi. Coming directly from Kabale, take the road towards Bwindi for roughly 75km (see *Chapter 8*, pages 226–7) but instead of turning left at Kanyantorogo for Bwindi, continue straight on to Kihihi. Coming from Bwindi, you must retrace the 30km to Kanyantorogo, then turn left towards Kihihi. The dirt road between Kanyantorogo and Ishasha is generally in good condition; you can get through in an hour or so in a private vehicle, though it might take longer after heavy rain.

The small town of Kihihi, 10–15km north of Kanyantorogo, appears on few maps, but it is nevertheless quite a jacked-up little place, with a filling station (the only reliable source of fuel if travelling between Kabale or Bwindi and Ishasha), a bank, at least one basic guesthouse and a few shops. At least one bus daily runs from Kabale to Kihihi, passing through Kanyantorogo in the mid afternoon, as does the occasional pick-up truck. From Kihihi, it's another 10–15km to the T-junction with the Ishasha–Katunguru road, an easy 20-minute drive in dry conditions. There is no regular public transport along this road, but a regular trickle of pick-up trucks connects Kihihi to Ishasha town on the Congolese border.

When you arrive at the T-junction, turn left in the unlikely event that you're heading towards the DRC border, and right if you're heading towards Ishasha Camp or Katunguru. From the junction, it's another 15km or so to the park entrance gate. With the Kigezi Game Reserve to your right and QENP to your left, game can be plentiful from the road, in particular topi and Uganda kob.

Travellers who've managed to pick up a vehicle heading to Ishasha Town have the option of disembarking at the junction and hitching to the gate from there. Plenty of trucks use this route, so you're practically certain to get a lift, provided that you arrive at the junction early in the day. On the other hand, if you don't get a lift, you'll be stuck in the middle of nowhere – not the most tempting scenario unless you have a tent, are self-sufficient in water and food, are prepared to risk the wrath of any conservation authority who finds you camping wild, and find the prospect of nocturnal visits from lions and elephants exciting rather than daunting. The conservative option would be to continue on to Ishasha town, where there are a few guesthouses should you be unable to secure transport back towards Katunguru via the Ishasha Entrance Gate.

From Kampala via Rukungiri If coming directly from Kampala, the best option is to turn off the main Mbarara–Kabale road at Ntungamo and follow the new 45km tarmac road to Rukungiri. Beyond Rukungiri, its 70km along murram roads to Ishasha via Kihihi. However a right turn about 4km out of Rukungiri (signposted to Rwenshama, a Lake Edward fishing village) provides a slightly shorter route, stepping down in several stages onto the Rift Valley floor before passing through the grasslands of the Kigezi Wildlife Reserve, and joining the Katunguru–Ishasha road about 15km from the sector gate.

From Kasese/Mbarara via Katunguru Ishasha Entrance Gate lies roughly 70km southwest of the Kasese–Mbarara road, and is reached via a dirt track that forks west roughly 3km south of Katunguru Bridge and continues to the Congolese border at Ishasha Town. Ishasha Entrance Gate lies about 20km before the border post, and is clearly signposted. Although the Katunguru–Ishasha road passes through QENP for most of its length, it is considered public – in other words no entrance fee is charged for driving along it although there's surprisingly little game to be seen. On the left side of the road coming from Katunguru, about 15km before Ishasha Entrance Gate, a small, hyacinth-covered seasonal pool used to harbour at least 20 hippos, as well as attracting kob and other antelope, and a host of water-associated birds, notably the attractive African jacana and small black crake. Unfortunately this pool dried up in 1997 and there is no telling when or indeed whether it will ever refill again.

A few years back, the Ishasha road was a mud bath strewn with pot-holes, and trucks passing this way were regularly bogged down for days after heavy rain. Today, the road is generally well maintained, and under normal conditions the drive between Katunguru and Ishasha Entrance Gate shouldn't take more than two hours. The road still tends to deteriorate quickly during the wet season, however, and it has also been subject to sporadic outbreaks of bandit attacks in recent years, so do ask local advice before using it. A 4x4 is recommended, though any robust saloon car should get through with ease except after heavy rain.

If you don't have private transport, the only way to get to Ishasha is to try to hitch a lift from the junction 3km south of Katunguru. A steady stream of trucks passes this way, so the chances of picking up a lift as far as the entrance gate are reasonably good. From the entrance gate, it's a further 8km to the camp. The ranger at the gate can radio through for a vehicle to fetch you, at a cost of around US$16. It may be permitted to walk to the camp, but with lion in the area this is not to be encouraged.

Where to stay

Upmarket

Ishasha Wilderness Camp (8 tents) 0414 321479; m 0772 502155; f 0414 321479; e info@wildfrontiers.co.ug; www.wildfrontiers.co.ug and www.wildfrontiers.com. Ishasha has long lacked for any decent accommodation, so the opening of this excellent new tented camp in 2005 was a most welcome development indeed. Operated by Wild Frontiers/G&C Tours, the camp lies in riverine forest beside the Ntungwe River near an elephant crossing point, and it attracts plenty of exciting birds and mammals, with elephant, hippo and various monkeys all being regular visitors. Eight comfortable, beautifully appointed and s/c tents are perfectly positioned minutes away from the prime Northern Circuit game track. *US$280/340 sgl/dbl, US$150/198 sgl/dbl for Ugandan residents.*

Budget

Ishasha Camp and Campsites This lovely, isolated retreat consists of 2 basic *bandas*, rather disappointingly situated on a piece of flat ground several hundred metres from the Ishasha River. Since the *bandas* collectively sleep only 4–5 people, it is advisable to book in advance through the UWA headquarters in Kampala, or to try to radio through an enquiry from the park headquarters at Mweya or Bwindi National Park. The chances of a vacancy are pretty good, even if you do pitch up without a booking. As a last resort, there's a basic hostel nearby. Three campsites are also available, and in direct contrast to the *bandas* each one is discreetly carved from the riparian forest along the river, and has a covered sitting area. Campsite One has a particularly intimate atmosphere, while Campsite Two offers the best game viewing – black-and-white colobus monkeys haunt the riverbank, a couple of dozen hippos live a short distance upstream, a pair of fish eagles is resident, and the trees are rustling with forest and woodland birds. Facilities are limited to pumped water, fit for washing but not for drinking, and basic but clean pit toilets. Visitors must bring all food with them, as well as cooking utensils. Firewood is available, and you can normally buy beers and sodas from the staff village near the camp. *Bandas US$8/14 sgl/dbl.*

MARAMAGAMBO FOREST AND KYAMBURA (CHAMBURA) GORGE The southeastern section of QENP is strikingly different in character from the southwest and the north, dominated by the extensive Maramagambo Forest, which possibly harbours a greater biodiversity and faunal affinity with central Africa than any east African forest bar Semliki and Budongo. Relatively undeveloped for tourism, Maramagambo is nevertheless very accessible, especially following the construction of a superb, exclusive lodge and lovely low-key campsite overlooking Nyamasingiri and Kyasanduka crater lakes. Several worthwhile guided walks can be undertaken, offering the opportunity to observe a selection of the rich forest avifauna, as well as elusive mammals such as chimpanzee, red-tailed and L'Hoest's monkey, potto, giant forest hog, yellow-backed duiker, pygmy antelope and giant elephant shrew.

The most popular tourist draw in this part of QENP, however, is the Kyambura Gorge, where a community of chimpanzees – unlike those in Maramagambo, fully habituated – can be tracked within the confines of a forested river gorge carved into the surrounding flat savanna. The gorge forms the border between QENP and the Kyambura Wildlife Reserve, a little-visited tract of savanna notable less for its wildlife viewing than the waterbirds – in particular flamingo – attracted to its lovely crater lakes.

Getting there and away All the sites described under this heading can be accessed from the surfaced Mbarara road running south from the Katunguru Bridge across the Kazinga Channel.

Fig Tree Camp on the rim of the Kyambura Gorge lies 2.5km east of the main road along a turn-off that is clearly signposted some 9km south of the bridge. Travellers without private transport can ask any bus or shared taxi to drop them at this junction. You're permitted to walk along the 2.5km track to Fig Tree Gorge unguided, though some risk of encountering elephant, buffalo or other potentially dangerous animals does exist. Alternatively, charter a taxi from Katunguru, or from the village of Kyambura about 4km further south.

The dirt turn-off to Maramagambo Forest lies 2.5km further south, on the west side of the Mbarara road, where it is clearly signposted for Jacana Safari Lodge. The visitors' centre and campsite lies 14km along this dirt road (in fair condition, though it can become erratically sticky after rain) and Jacana Safari Lodge is situated another 1km past the visitors' centre. There's no public transport along this road, and private vehicles aren't sufficiently regular for hitching to be a realistic proposition. Travellers without private transport will either have to walk, or must arrange a taxi or *boda-boda* from Kyambura trading centre, which flanks the Mbarara road less than 2km south of the turn-off to the forest. A taxi should cost around Ush25,000 one-way, and you'll probably want to arrange for it to collect you at an agreed time.

The turn-off to Kyambura Game Reserve runs east from Kyambura village, 13km south of the Katunguru Bridge, where it is clearly signposted. The reserve entrance lies 4km past the turn-off, and it's another 9km from there to Flamingo Lake. Although this road isn't in great condition, you'll have no problems in a 4x4, and it is traversed by a fairly steady trickle of shared taxis terminating at a small fishing village on the southern shore of Lake George.

Where to stay
Upmarket

Jacana Safari Lodge ☎ 0414 258273; f 0414 233992; e geolodges@africa.com; www.geolodgesafrica.com. Owned by Geolodges, who also run Nile Safari Camp in Murchison Falls and the new Mabira Forest Lodge, this fabulous wood-and-thatch construction straddles the steep wall of the jungle-fringed Lake Nyamasingiri, comprising 5 interlocking craters at the northern end of the Maramagambo Forest. Accommodation is in 8 luxurious, wooden, dbl stes with a private veranda overlooking the picturesque lake and piping-hot showers. The open-sided bar and restaurant are suspended over the lake, and overlook a great lakeshore swimming pool. There's plenty of faunal activity too – olive baboon, black-and-white colobus, red-tailed and more occasionally L'Hoest's monkey clatter through the canopy overhead, chimps are regularly heard calling across the lake, while common birds include the fish eagle, the localised African darter and a variety of robin-chats, greenbuls and sunbirds. Walking activities can be arranged through the visitors' centre, 1km distant, and boat trips are offered on the lake. The North Kasenyi Plains, the best game-viewing area in Central QENP, lie about an hour's drive away. In a nutshell, this is one of the most aesthetically satisfying and underrated wilderness retreats in east Africa – and reasonably priced, too. Extras include the 'Captain's Table', a motorised flat-bottomed raft with shade which can be hired for meals (US$20) or exploring Lake Nyamusingire (1hr costs US$30) while a village walk costs US$5 pp and a 1hr massage US$20. Day visitors are welcome to use the pool (US$10). *US$110/180 sgl/dbl FB.*

Camping

Maramagambo Campsite A rustic and attractive campsite cut into a forest glade close to Lake Kyasanduka. Facilities are limited to cold showers and firewood, but it's possible to eat at the lodge, only 1km away. The birdlife around the campsite is superb, and monkeys are all over the place. *US$6 pp to pitch a tent.*

Å Fig Tree Camp This campsite is perched on the western rim of the Kyambura Gorge, and also forms the trailhead for chimpanzee tracking in the forest.

The site isn't properly developed for tourism at this stage – nor is there any indication it will be in the foreseeable future – but there is a pit latrine, running water (but no shower) and a shaded eating *banda.* You should bring all the food you need with you. *US$6 pp.*

Activities

Chimp tracking (Kyambura Gorge) The Maramagambo Forest and abutting forest reserves collectively protect one of the largest chimpanzee populations in east Africa, but the only habituated community at the time of writing is resident in the gorge carved by the Kyambura River along the eastern boundary of QENP. Some 16km long and 100m deep, the gorge protects an isolated and contained cover of riparian forest, surrounded for the most part by more open savanna, which means that the resident chimpanzee community has a restricted territory and is normally quite easy to locate by sound. In addition to chimps, black-and-white colobus, vervet monkey and olive baboon are regularly observed in the gorge, while less visible residents include red-tailed monkey and giant forest hog. For birdwatchers, Kyambura is one of the best places in Uganda for black bee-eater and blue-bellied kingfisher, and a good range of other forest birds is present.

Guided chimp-tracking excursions depart at 08.00 and 13.00 daily from Fig Tree Camp, which lies on the rim of the gorge 2.5km east of the Mbarara road. A maximum of eight permits (two groups of four people) is issued for each morning or evening session at US$20/30 for residents/non-residents – no additional visitation fee is charged, assuming that you've already paid this elsewhere in QENP. The success rate currently stands at around 85%, probably the highest in Uganda after Kibale Forest, and once the chimps have been located it is often possible to get within 5m of them. Permit availability can be checked, and bookings made, by radio from the park office at Mweya or the visitors' centre at Maramagambo.

Maramagambo Forest walks The 1km stretch of road between the visitors' centre and Jacana Lodge passes through lush primary forest and can be walked unguided at no charge other than the standard visitation fees. Plenty of monkeys are likely to be seen – most commonly black-and-white colobus, red-tailed and vervet – and there's a slimmer chance of encountering the lovely L'Hoest's monkey, chimpanzee and even leopard. Birdwatchers could pace up and down this several times without exhausting the opportunities to identify a confusing assembly of forest greenbuls, sunbirds, woodpeckers and other more elusive species.

Three different guided walks can be undertaken from the visitors' centre at Maramagambo. A full day's walk costs US$10 per person. The most straightforward walk loops around the forested shore of Lake Kyasanduka, and shouldn't take much longer than an hour, depending on how interested you are in the prolific birdlife. A more popular walk, of roughly 90 minutes' duration, leads to a large cave where significant concentrations of bats are resident, as well as a rock python that's regularly observed by visitors. For dedicated birdwatchers, the most rewarding walk is likely to be the longer loop around the back of Lake Nyamasingiri, which typically takes half a day to complete, and offers the opportunity to seek out rarities such as scaly-breasted illadopsis, snowy-headed robin-chat and chestnut wattle-eye.

Kyambura Wildlife Reserve Based on our exploration, the densely wooded savanna that characterises this small wildlife reserve, which is divided from

QENP by the Kyambura Gorge, cannot be regarded as prime game-viewing territory, though you might see the occasional kob. Its main point of interest is a series of scenic crater lakes, of which two are readily accessed from the signposted dirt track that runs between Kyambura trading centre on the tarred Mbarara road and a small fishing village on Lake George. The road runs along the rim of the first of these lakes some 10km out of Kyambura village, offering the opportunity to alight from the car and scan its surface for waterbirds such as little grebe and various ducks. About 3km further, the road offers distant views over the aptly entitled **Flamingo Lake**, where impressive concentrations of thousands upon thousands of greater and lesser flamingo gather when conditions are conducive. The lake lies within a nestled crater, and although the roughly 1km track leading down from the outer crater rim to the inner wall is just about motorable, it would probably be a safer bet to head down on foot. Either way, to reach the lakeshore you'll need to walk along an ill-defined footpath through a field of tall grass. The road continues past this lake to skirt a third crater lake after another 10km or so, then 2km further it terminates at a marshy bay on the southern shore of Lake George. Assuming that you've paid the visitation fee for QENP, no additional fee is charged to enter the Kyambura Wildlife Reserve.

There is talk of developing Kyambura Wildlife Reserve as a launching site for boat trips to Mpanga Falls (see box, page 327).

MWEYA AND THE NORTHERN CIRCUIT

Flanked by Lake Edward to the northwest and the Kazinga Channel to the southwest, the Mweya Peninsula is a roughly 10km² wedge of hilly land connected to the mainland by a narrow natural isthmus little wider than the road that traverses it. The main tourist focus within QENP, Mweya is also the site of the park headquarters and staff quarters, creating an oddly village-like atmosphere subverted by the prolific and exceptionally habituated resident game. The peninsula also has a magnificent location, with spectacular views across the channel to the glacial peaks of the Rwenzori Mountains on the rare occasions when they're not blanketed in cloud. A good network of game-viewing roads runs between the peninsula and the main Kasese road north of the channel, and the game-viewing circuit on the Kasenyi Plains is only 45 minutes' drive away, while the launch trips on the Kazinga Channel below the lodge are for most visitors a highlight of QENP.

Although most tourists on the peninsula are resident at Mweya Safari Lodge, the combination of affordable accommodation and relatively easy access makes it a realistic goal for backpackers, especially as it has plenty of game that can be seen without moving outside the village. Herds of buffalo and elephant often amass on the channel shore facing the lodge, while Defassa waterbuck, hippo and warthog are certain to be seen from the roads on the peninsula – there is no restriction on walking within the village, but do be cautious of hippos in particular. Giant forest hogs sometimes emerge on to the airstrip towards dusk, a family of habituated banded mongooses lives in the lodge grounds, and lion and spotted hyena are heard – and seen – with a frequency that might unnerve solitary campers! Birdlife is prolific, too. Marabou storks regularly roost on a bare tree between the lodge and canteen, a hamerkop pair has built one of their vast nests in the wooded dip just before the campsite, while the exquisite red-throated sunbird, black-headed gonolek and a variety of weavers are among the more common residents of the lodge grounds. It's also well worth taking a bottle of beer down to the end of the peninsula airstrip to watch the sun set behind the DRC mountains – but ask which track to use, as driving down the airstrip itself is prohibited for obvious reasons.

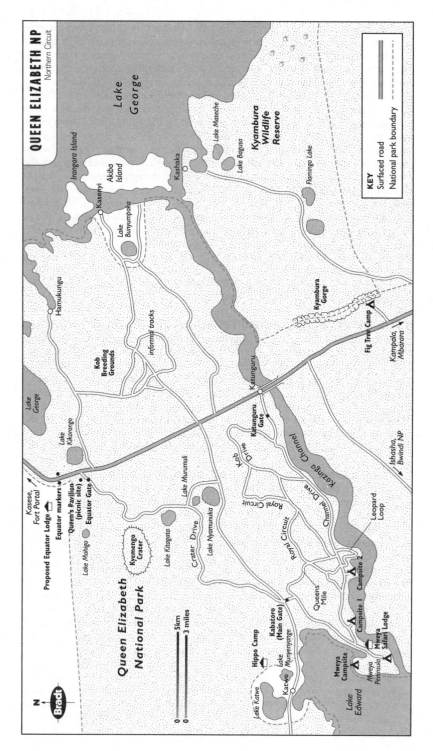

QUEEN ELIZABETH NP
Northern Circuit

KEY
Surfaced road
National park boundary

Lake George

Irangara Island

Akiba Island

Kaseryi

Lake Bunyumpaka

Hamukungu

Kashaka

Lake Maseche

Lake Baguso

Kyambura
Wildlife
Reserve

Flamingo Lake

Kob
Breeding
Grounds

informal tracks

Lake George

Lake
Kikorongo

Kyambura Gorge

Fig Tree Camp

Katunguru

Kampala,
Mbarara

Kasese,
Fort Portal

Equator markers

Proposed Equator Lodge

Queen's Pavilion
(picnic site)
Equator Gate

Lake Mohigo

Lake Murumuli

Katunguru Gate

Kyemengo Crater

Lake Kitagata

Crater Drive

Lake Nyamunuka

Kob Drive

Royal Circuit

Royal Circuit

Kazinga Channel

Ishasha,
Bwindi NP

Queen Elizabeth
National Park

Queens Mile

Channel Drive

Leopard
Loop

Campsite 2

Hippo Camp

Kabatoro
(Main Gate)

Campsite 1

Lake
Munyenyange

Mweya Safari Lodge

Mweya Campsite

Mweya Peninsula

Lake Katwe

Katwe

Lake Edward

N

Bradt

0   5km
0   3 miles

288

Getting there and away Mweya lies roughly 15km east of the surfaced Mbarara–Kasese road as the crow flies. There are two main approach routes. Coming from the direction of Mbarara, the most direct route is to turn right from the main road at the signpost for Katunguru Gate, which lies near Katunguru trading centre, a few hundred metres north of the bridge over the Kazinga Channel. From Katunguru Gate, follow Channel Drive for roughly 20km until you reach a T-junction, where you need to turn left to get to Mweya. Coming from the north, the quickest route is to turn left 35km south of Kasese, along the public road to Katwe, which is signposted for Mweya Safari Lodge. After about 15km, turn left into Kabatoro Main Gate, from where it's about 6km to Mweya.

Mweya Camp is easy to reach without your own transport, and there are several ways of going about it. The cheapest option is to ask around in Kasese for a pick-up truck heading for Katwe. These generally leave at around 11.00. Ask to be dropped off at the Kabatoro Entrance Gate, only 100m from the main road. It's customary for park and lodge staff to hitch along the 6km stretch of road between the gate and Mweya, and the rangers are generally helpful when it comes to finding lifts for backpackers too.

Alternatively, you can engage a 'special hire' taxi at Katunguru, which should cost around Ush20,000 one-way. Try Moses (m *0782 767495*). This is cheap enough if you're in a group – the park and lodge staff also often use taxis for this trip. It would also be possible to charter a taxi out of Kasese, which saves some hassle but is obviously costlier on account of the greater distance – expect to pay around Ush40,000–50,000 one-way. When you're ready to leave Mweya, it should be easy to hitch a lift to one of the entrance gates from the vehicle barrier gate at the road entrance to the peninsula.

Where to stay
Upmarket

🏠 **Mweya Safari Lodge** ✆ 031 260260/1; f 0414 253399; e mweyaparaa@africaonline.co.ug; www.mweyalodge.com. To contact the lodge directly: ✆ 0414 340054 or 04834 44266. One of the most beautifully situated lodges in Uganda, and following recent renovations now also one of the plushest, the 49-room Mweya Safari Lodge was aptly described by one recent visitor as a 'Sheraton in the Bush'! The dining areas and bar offer a grandstand view over the facing bank of the Kazinga Channel, which routinely attracts large herds of buffalo and elephant, with the Rwenzori Mountains providing an incomparable backdrop on a clear day. The lodge gardens are rustling with animal life, ranging from warthogs and banded mongoose to a variety of lizards and slender-billed weavers and marsh flycatchers that approach the veranda so closely you can practically touch them. The restaurant is excellent, with an extensive à la carte menu of Indian and Continental dishes in the Ush10,000–15,000 range, while the snack menu on the patio offers a good selection of filling meals for less than Ush10,000. At very busy times a buffet (Ush27,000) is served, presumably to discourage walk-in diners. The renovated s/c rooms are well appointed with large beds enclosed in walk-in mosquito netting, and a private veranda, some with sliding glass doors. Facilities and activities include daily game drives, a television lounge with DSTV, a good curio shop and a foreign-exchange facility. Credit-card payments attract a surcharge of 5%. US$99/190 sgl/dbl for residents of east Africa, US$223/275 sgl/dbl for non-residents, all FB.

🏠 **Hippo Hill Camp** ✆ 031 2277 304; f 00256 41 255288; e kitanda@infocom.co.ug; www.lkttsafaris.co.ug. This new camp, due to open in late 2006, overlooks Lake Munyenyange in the Katwe town enclave just outside the park. With a bit of landscaping to this rather exposed location the QENP management plan considered this a suitable location from which overland truck groups would shuttle into the park in smaller vehicles less damaging to game tracks. However, with rates of US$100/190 sgl/dbl for full board the developer, Lake Kitandara Tours, is clearly targeting a different market.

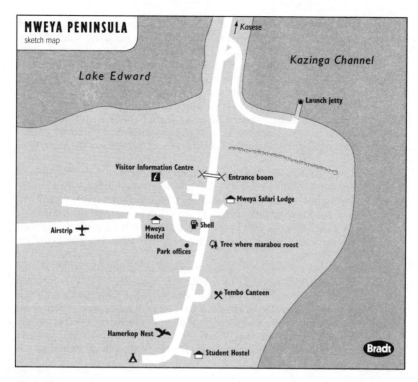

MWEYA PENINSULA
sketch map

↑ *Kasese*

Kazinga Channel

Lake Edward

● Launch jetty

Visitor Information Centre
ℹ ⤬—⤬ Entrance boom

⌂ Mweya Safari Lodge

Airstrip ✈

⌂ Mweya Hostel

⛽ Shell

● Park offices

⌬ Tree where marabou roost

✗ Tembo Canteen

Hamerkop Nest ✦

⛺

⌂ Student Hostel

Bradt

Moderate

⌂ **Equator Lodge** m 0782 728208;
e equatorlodge@yahoo.co.uk. As we go to press,
we receive reports of a new lodge under
construction on a hillside beyond the equator, just
outside the national park. Due to open in March
2007, Equator Lodge should enjoy a fine view across

Lakes Kikorongo and George. Attractively located for
arrivals from Fort Portal and Kibale forest, it is also
conveniently placed for the Kasenyi lion area and for
planned walking safaris around the Explosion craters
and Shoebill Swamp. *Cottages will cost in the region
of US$100/ double.*

Budget

⌂ **Mweya Hostel** ☏ 0414 373050 (Kampala Office)
m 0782 802650/ 0772 609969/ 0782 802650/
0782 381576; e rift_hostelmweyayahoo.co.uk.
Situated opposite the new Visitor Information Centre,
this recently privatised hostel is a convenient if
basic option. Twelve rooms with nets use shared
facilities while 2 guesthouses contain bedrooms
provided with nets and fans and a lounge, kitchen
(useful if you have your own provisions, stove and
utensils) and veranda. Due to the lack of alternative
options in this category at Mweya, the hostel is
frequently booked solid, so it's worth making a
reservation. *Rooms US$16/32 sgl/dbl B&B. Six bed/
four bed guesthouses costs US$97/65 B&B. Rates
pp are US$3 cheaper if b/fast is not required.*

⌂ **Student Camp** Technically this hostel is for
students only, and often it is full with them.

However UWA has permitted tourists to sleep there
but as 'a last resort'. The rooms are very basic and
I've heard reports of theft, so be careful. *US$6.*

⛺ **Kookaburra Camp** Kichwamba Escarpment;
m 0774 114477; e kookaburracamp@gmail.com;
www.kookaburracamp.com. Alternatively, contact
Kampala Backpackers' Hostel (see *Chapter 6*, page
147). Kampala's popular Backpackers' Hostel has
opened a new campsite on the Kichwamba
Escarpment above QENP in the Bunyaruguru explosion
crater field, just 10km from the Kazinga Channel.
Campers can pitch their own tents beside the lovely
Lake Ruijongo or use furnished tents. Hot showers
and flush toilets are provided. Rates below exclude
b/fast but affordable meals and snacks from the
Kampala Backpackers' menu are available from
Ush3,000–15,000. The site is perfectly located to

Connected by the 40km Kazinga Channel, lakes Edward (known locally as Ruisamba) and George lie on the Albertine Rift floor at an identical surface altitude of 913m above sea level, and both are regarded to be relics of a much larger lake that extended across the region during the most recent Ice Age. In other respects, however, these linked lakes could not be more different in character. Lake Edward, extending over almost 2,000km², is the smallest of a quartet of major freshwater bodies – starting with Lake Albert in the north and terminating with Lake Tanganyika in the south – that arcs through the base of the Albertine Rift floor along the border with the DRC and Uganda, Rwanda, Burundi and Tanzania. In common with the rest of these lakes, Lake Edward, roughly three-quarters of which falls in the DRC, is elongated in shape with a broadly north–south orientation following the contours of the Rift Valley, and it is relatively deep – up to 120m in parts. The 250km² Lake George, by contrast, is essentially an extension of Lake Edward fed by the Kazinga Channel: roughly circular in shape, it is nowhere more than 3.5m deep, and is bordered by extensive marshes, especially to the north.

Although geologically calm in recent millennia, the area around lakes Edward and George has been subject to massive volcanic upheaval over the past half-million years, as evidenced by a total of at least 35 crater lakes and numerous dry volcanic calderas clustered in the area 10km north and 20km south of the Kazinga Channel. The geological and archaeological records indicate that a particularly violent bout of volcanic activity occurred perhaps 7,000 years ago, temporarily denuding the area of practically its entire fauna and flora.

The most enduring casualty of this episode was the crocodile, which subsequently vanished from the archaeological record and was not known to occur around the lakes or channel until recent historical times. The lack of crocodiles was a subject of considerable debate during the colonial era. Some biologists attributed their absence to a physical or chemical factor, a theory that had little grounding in fact, since crocodiles are elsewhere tolerant of far more extreme water temperatures and levels of alkalinity and other chemical dilutes than are presented by either of the lakes in question. As a Cambridge scientific expedition to Uganda in 1931 noted: 'Lake Edward seems to be an ideal habitat for crocodiles; there are plenty of quiet beaches and swamps and an abundance of fish and other food.'

The other prevalent notion was that crocodiles had been unable to recolonise the lake on account of their inability to navigate a series of rapids and gorges on the Semliki River, the only major waterway connected to the lake that is inhabited by crocodiles. Implausible as this theory might sound, it would appear to be at least halfway correct. It was probably not the rapids or gorges per se that inhibited the crocodiles, but rather the obstacle they presented in tandem with the surrounding rainforest, a habitat that would be likely to impede their movement. Following widespread deforestation along the relevant stretch of the Semliki in the 1980s, crocodiles made an unexpected reappearance on Lake Edward towards the end of that decade. Today, large crocodiles are quite often seen during launch trips along the Kazinga Channel, and their numbers have proliferated in the reedy shallows of Lake George to the extent that they're regarded as a hazard by local fishermen.

explore the crater field and hike along the escarpment which provides stunning views over QENP's Maramagambo Forest towards Lake Edward and the Rwenzori Mountains. Day/overnight guided walks cost from Ush5,000–15,000 including a 25% community contribution. To get to Kookaburra from Mbarara, look for a signpost on the left about 1.5km beyond Rubirizi village after passing Rugazi hospital and a road cutting through volcanic rock. Approaching from QENP, you'll find the turning about 1.5km after a lay-by with a Rift Valley panorama and a shack selling local honey. The Horizon bus is recommended for travellers setting off from either Fort Portal or Kabale. *S/c chalets US$30 dbl, furnished tents US$15, pitch your own tent for US$4.50.*

Shoestring

🏠 **Excellent Lodge** Katwe. One of a few small basic lodges in Katwe, which borders the national park on the shore of Lake Edward and is readily accessible on public transport from Kasese, this has cleaner rooms than its flaking exterior might suggest, and is more affordable than anything at Mweya. Even if you don't formally enter QENP from Katwe, the road there is as reliable as any in the park for elephant, while the likes of warthog and waterbuck stroll around the outskirts of town, together with an abundance of waterbirds and hippos frequent the Lake Edward shoreline. *US$3/6 sgl/dbl.*

🏠 **Rwenzori Salaam Lodge** Katunguru. This very basic and inexpensive lodge lies in Katunguru village on the north side of the bridge across the Kazinga Channel, with its resident hippo and plentiful birds (including the localised papyrus gonolek in the reed beds). It's straightforward to arrange game drives into the park with local taxi drivers. I've had conflicting reports recently whether there is 'anywhere reasonable' to stay in Katunguru so perhaps it wouldn't be wise either to rely too much on finding somewhere to stay there – or if you do, to expect too much from it. *US$3.*

🏠 **Abbey Guesthouse** Rugazi; m 0772 367588. This small hotel on the Kichwamba Escarpment just north of Rugazi village has been recommended to us as being clean, reasonably priced and conveniently located for QENP. *US$14/19 sgl/dbl.*

⚑ **Mweya Campsite** This fabulously located rustic campsite on the north end of the peninsula has few facilities, and is rattling with wildlife – potentially dangerous after dark if you don't have a vehicle, as hippo pass through en masse nightly and lions are also frequent visitors. And beware the termites that 'chewed millions of holes in the groundsheet' of one reader's tent. If you intend cooking for yourself, bring your own food. Alternatively you could brave the hippos and wander up to the Tembo Canteen for a meal, but be careful after dark, and don't even think about it without a good torch. *US$6 pp.*

⚑ **Channel Campsites 1 and 2** If you have your own vehicle and are self-sufficient in food and water, you might prefer to camp at one of the secluded exclusive campsites which lie along Channel Drive about 5km from Mweya. Camping here is relatively expensive, but nocturnal encounters with large mammals are thrown in for free. Campsite #2 has a good reputation for leopard sightings, but do ask advice about security in advance. *US$12 pp.*

✗ Where to eat There must be few more attractive places to enjoy a meal than the patio of **Mweya Safari Lodge**, which serves excellent food – the snack menu in particular is pretty reasonably priced given the quality and location. Cheaper meals – around Ush4,000–5,000 – such as fish or chicken and chips or rice are served at the **Tembo Canteen**, which also has a good location overlooking the Channel and serves inexpensive beers and other drinks. Over the years I've eaten food (in the same price range) at the **Mweya Hostel** which ranges from dreadful to below average so I'm pleased to relay recent reports of some slight improvements.

Listings

Tourist information The national park's booking office near the entrance to Mweya Safari Lodge can provide information about game-drive routes as well as radio through to other national park accommodation, such as Kibale Forest or Ishasha, to check availability and current road conditions. It sells maps and postcards and you can make MTN calls for a small charge. Information and bookings are handled in the excellent new, purpose-built Mweya Visitor Information Centre. This well-planned facility contains clear and concise interpretive exhibits. The centrepiece is a topographic model which, complete with buttons and flashing lights to identify landscape features, clearly illustrates QENP's setting within the dramatic Albertine Rift Valley. Outside, a covered timber deck overlooks the dramatic panorama across Lake Edward towards the Semliki Valley and the Rwenzori. It's probable that services within the information centre will be expanded to include internet and refreshments.

Foreign exchange The only place to change money is the forex desk in the Mweya Safari Lodge. Fair rates are offered for cash. Travellers' cheques attract lousy rates and the service is limited to guests.

Fuel Diesel and petrol are available from the filling station at Mweya which charges the same prices as in Kasese.

Ranger/guides Although it is not mandatory to take a ranger/guide on private game drives, it is strongly recommended, at least until such time as you get to know your way around the park, and will greatly improve your odds of seeing lions and leopards. The fee for a guide is UshUS$20 per party.. Guided nature walks on the peninsula can also be arranged at US$10 per person. Guides can be booked through the visitor information centre.

Activities and game drives The activities and game-viewing circuits described below all lie on the north side of the Kazinga Channel. For those without private transport, organised game drives along Channel Drive to the Kasenyi Plains are offered by Mweya Safari Lodge. Guests are charged US$120 per vehicle and non-residents US$155. A cheaper option is to arrange with a Katunguru taxi driver to collect you for the three–four-hour early morning Kazinga–Kasenyi game drive. We were quoted US$60 in 2006. Maramagambo Forest and the Kyambura Gorge and Wildlife Reserve, although they lie to the south of the channel and are described under the separate heading *Maramagambo Forest and Kyambura (Chambura) Gorge*, pages 284–7, can easily be visited as a day trip out of Mweya. Chimp-tracking excursions in the Kyambura Gorge can be booked at the tourist office on the peninsula. The drive from Mweya to either Kyambura or Maramagambo shouldn't take significantly longer than one hour. A UWA ranger guide costs US$20 for a full day. Night game drives have recently been introduced, accompanied by a guide at a cost of US$25.

Kazinga Channel launch The most popular activity at Mweya is the launch trip to the mouth of the Kazinga Channel, which leaves daily at 09.00, 11.00, 15.00 and 17.00 and lasts for roughly two hours. Although not perhaps as spectacular as its equivalent in Murchison Falls, it's a great trip, with elephant, buffalo, waterbuck, Uganda kob and large hippo pods seen on a daily basis, and giant forest hog, leopard and lion also observed from time to time. Keep an eye open for the enormous water monitor lizard, which is common in the riverine scrub, as well as crocodiles, seen with increasing regularity since first colonising the area in the early 1990s. Waterbirds are plentiful, in particular water thickknee, yellow-billed stork and various plovers, while pink-backed pelicans and white-bellied cormorants often flock on a sandbank near the channel mouth. One smaller bird to look out for is the black-headed gonolek, a member of the shrike family with a dazzling red chest – and look closely, as the localised papyrus gonolek, similar in appearance but with a yellow crown, has also been recorded in the area.

The 15.00 departure is most likely to yield good elephant sightings, particularly on a hot day, when these thirsty creatures generally gravitate towards water from midday onwards, sometimes bathing in the channel. The 08.00 and 17.00 departures should be more rewarding photographically, as the light will be softer, though this might be countered by the increased probability of camera shake on a rocking boat in low light. The odds of seeing predators and other nocturnal

SALT PRODUCTION AT KATWE

The highly saline Lake Katwe, separated from the northern shore of Lake Edward by a narrow sliver of dry land, lies in the base of an extinct volcanic cone that last erupted between 6,000 and 10,000 years ago. In pre-colonial times, salt was regarded to be as valuable as any precious metal, and control of the lake regularly shifted between the rulers of the various kingdoms of western Uganda. When Speke travelled through Uganda in 1862, he recorded several local references to a legendarily wealthy salt lake near the base of the Mountains of the Moon, almost certainly Lake Katwe. For much of the 19th century, Katwe was part of the Toro kingdom, an offshoot of Bunyoro, but in the late 1870s it was recaptured by the Banyoro king, Kabalega, setting the scene for the first military confrontation between Bunyoro and a combined British–Toro expedition led by Captain Lugard.

Lugard arrived at Katwe in 1890 and recorded that: 'Everywhere were piles of salt, in heaps covered with grass, some beautifully white and clean. On our right was the Salt Lake, about three-quarters of a mile [1km] in diameter, at the bottom of a deep crater-like depression with banks some 200ft [70m] high. The water was of a claret red, with a white fringe of crystallised salt about its margin. A narrow neck, only some 40 yards [40m] across at the top, and perhaps 300 yards [300m] at its base, divided the Salt Lake from [Lake] Edward.' Lugard and his Toro entourage had little difficulty claiming the site – the resident Banyoro were not soldiers but miners and businessmen, and evidently they subscribed to the view that discretion forms the better part of valour – and built there a small fort of which little trace remains today before continuing northwards to Fort Portal.

Lake Katwe today is not the rich claret apparition encountered by Lugard and other early European visitors. Particularly in the harsh midday light, however, Lake Katwe still retains the vaguely foreboding atmosphere described by E J Wayland: 'stifling and malodorous… a fiend-made meeting place for the Devil and his friends.' Commercial salt extraction from the lake peaked in the late-colonial era, when the faded plant that dominates Katwe village pumped out up to 2,000 tons of salt annually. Extraction of the lake's characteristic pink-hued coarse salt remains the main source of local income – judging by the state of the village, not quite so lucrative an activity as it was in Katwe's heyday – and visitors can watch the miners at work.

creatures coming to drink are highest in the late afternoon. In practice, however, the departure time chosen by independent travellers is likely to depend on when other groups are doing the launch trip. The reason for this is that the fee of US$15 per person applies only when ten or more passengers are on board – smaller groups will have to make up the total of US$150 so that two people must pay US$75 each, for instance, or five people US$30 apiece. Enquiries and bookings can be made at the new visitor centre roughly opposite the hostel.

Channel Drive circuit A compact network of game-viewing tracks emanates from Channel Drive – the road running roughly parallel to the northern shore of the Kazinga Channel between Mweya and Katunguru. The vegetation along these roads is generally quite dense and scrubby, and notable for the cactus-like euphorbia trees that protrude above the tangled thickets. The most common large mammals here are warthog, bushbuck and waterbuck, while elephant often cross the tracks from midday onwards, heading to or from the water. Leopard Track and the short side road to Campsite #2 are the best places to look for the unusually habituated leopards that frequent the area, while lions – generally more skittish than on the Kasenyi Plains – are seen fairly regularly. This is one of the few places anywhere in Africa where the massive giant forest hog – larger, darker and hairier than the warthog – are regularly seen in daylight hours, especially during the dry season. Because it lies so close to Mweya and consists of several interconnecting tracks, this network can easily be explored over two hours from the lodge.

Katwe Crater Lakes Katwe is an odd urban enclave enclosed by the park boundaries on three sides: monumentally rundown but also, perversely, rather charming, with the aura of a recently resettled ghost town. It has a superb situation, on a grassy rise flanked to the south by Lake Edward and to the north by two saline crater lakes, both of which also lie outside the park boundaries, and have formed one of the most important sources of coarse salt in Uganda for centuries (see box *Salt production at Katwe*, above). Hippos and warthogs are common in the area, and elephants can sometimes be seen on the opposite shore. The birdlife can be spectacular: most notably the large flocks of flamingo that amass seasonally on the crater lakes, together with a wide selection of waders. For those who cannot afford a full-scale safari into QENP, Katwe is accessible by public transport – with a good chance of encountering elephant on the way – and budget accommodation is available.

In total, some seven crater lakes and a similar number of dry calderas stud the northern hills of QENP, including the impressive **Lake Nyamunuka**, its green waters often attended by herds of buffalo, visible from the Katwe road about 5km west of the junction with the surfaced Kasese road. With a solid 4x4 and at least two hours to spare, it's also worth exploring the rough, rocky and occasionally vertiginous Katwe Explosion Craters Track, which runs for 27km from opposite the Kabatoro Entrance Gate (6km from Mweya) and the Queen's Pavilion alongside the Kasese road. This track offers some splendid views over Lake Kyemengo as well as a number of other deep craters, each with its own micro-habitat – some lushly forested from rim to rim, others supporting a floor of practically treeless savanna. Although more notable for its scenic qualities than its game viewing, the hilly country traversed by this road is frequently haunted by large elephant herds in the dry season, and the thick woodland is the best place in QENP for acacia-associated birds.

Immediately west of Katwe, the Pelican Point sector of QENP was suggested as the location for the park's first lodge in the 1950s, but Mweya was selected owing to its more central location. Despite its proximity to Mweya, this sector has a remote, unspoiled flavour, and although wildlife volumes are relatively low, buffalo, kob, warthog, hippo and lion are all present. The main attractions are excellent views across Lake Edward and the opportunity to explore off-road. There are currently no facilities in the area, not even tracks, but the QENP management plan proposes that a basic campsite be cleared in the near future.

Kasenyi Plains and Lake George Stretching east from the Kasese road towards Lake George, the Kasenyi Plains probably support the largest concentrations of game anywhere in QENP, and a very different selection of species from those most frequently observed around Mweya. It's also perhaps the most reliable place in Uganda for lion sightings, assuming that you know where and how to locate them, and get there as soon after sunrise as possible. The drive from Mweya takes 45–60 minutes, so aim to head out at 06.30 when the gates open. The fastest route is to drive 6km from the peninsula to Kabatoro Gate, turning right on to the Katwe road (in the opposite direction to Katwe itself) until after about 15km you reach the junction with the Kasese road, where you need to turn left on to the blacktop then almost immediately afterwards right on to the dirt road to Kasenyi. An alternative route from Mweya entails following Channel Drive through Katunguru Gate, turning left on to the Kasese road, then after another 4.5km (not even 100m past the junction for Katwe to the left) turning right on to the Kasenyi road. Note that a second road to Kasenyi branches east from the Kasese road 3km north of Katunguru, but based on our experience it offers less reliable game viewing.

About 5km from the junction with the Kasese road, a series of unofficial but clear tracks run north and south from the Kasenyi road through an extensive area of short-grass savanna interspersed with solitary euphorbia trees and small clumps of thicket. This plain is one of the most important breeding grounds for Uganda kob – thousands congregate here at times – and it is also frequented by numerous buffalo and more skittish pairs of bushbuck. The two or three well-fed lion prides resident in the area are generally quite easy to find, at least for the first hour or two after sunrise, after which they tend to retreat into the shade of thicker bush. If you can't locate them directly by sight or sound, pay attention to the male kobs, whose high whistling alarm call is often a reliable indicator that a lion is lurking in a nearby thicket. The Kasenyi Plains also support an interesting selection of grassland birds, including grey-crowned crane, red-throated spurfowl and yellow-throated longclaw, while abandoned lion kills often attract flocks of squabbling vultures – most commonly white-backed and white-headed – and more occasionally spotted hyenas.

Follow the informal tracks that lead north from the Kasenyi road for about 10km and you'll eventually reach a proper dirt road where a left turn leads back to the main Kasese road, bypassing Kikorongo Crater Lake, and a right turn brings you to the fishing village of Hamukungu on Lake George. North of this road, between lakes Kikorongo and George, lies a tract of swamp. This is part of a larger wetland area which extends across the expansive but inaccessible northern sector of QENP and which constitutes Uganda's first Ramsar Wetland Site. It is possible to approach the southern tip of the Kikorongo swamp in a 4x4 vehicle, though only in the company of an official ranger/guide and access may be difficult during the rains. The main attraction here is one of the country's most substantial breeding populations of shoebill. Other swamp inhabitants include the elusive sitatunga antelope, various papyrus endemics such as white-winged warbler, papyrus gonolek and papyrus warbler, and during the northern winter large concentrations of migrant waders and waterfowl.

KASESE

Hot, dusty and rundown, Kasese is not the most prepossessing of Ugandan towns, and its poky atmosphere contrasts oddly with its attractive setting at the base of one of Africa's largest mountain ranges. As the terminus of the railway line from Kampala, Kasese was once a popular springboard for independent travel in western Uganda, but following the suspension of passenger-train services it has fallen off the travel map somewhat. It remains the obvious place to arrange Rwenzori hikes and could also be used as a base for visits to Queen Elizabeth National Park, but otherwise it offers little to travellers and has far less going for it than Fort Portal, only 75km to the north. Should you have a spare afternoon in Kasese, you could amuse yourself with a walk out to the Margherita Hotel, or hire a bicycle from the Saad Hotel and cycle the 11km to the (presently closed) Kilembe Copper Mine, passing *en route* a colony of thousands of fruit bats.

GETTING THERE AND AWAY There is plenty of road transport connecting Kasese to Mbarara, Kabale and Fort Portal – just go to the bus station and wait for the next

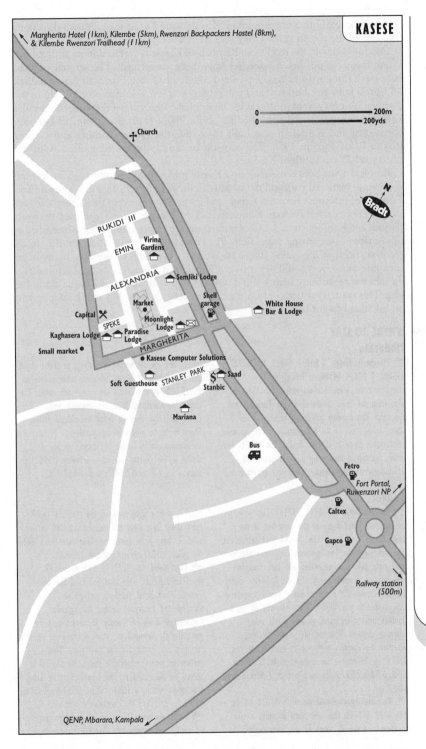

KASESE

Margherita Hotel (1km), Kilembe (5km), Rwenzori Backpackers Hostel (8km), & Kilembe Rwenzori Trailhead (11km)

Church

0 ———————— 200m
0 ———————— 200yds

RUKIDI III

EMIN

Virina Gardens

ALEXANDRIA

Semliki Lodge

Market

Shell garage

White House Bar & Lodge

Capital

SPEKE

Moonlight Lodge

Kaghasera Lodge

Paradise Lodge

Small market

MARGHERITA

Kasese Computer Solutions

Soft Guesthouse STANLEY PARK

Saad

Stanbic

Mariana

Bus

Petro

Fort Portal, Ruwenzori NP

Caltex

Gapco

Railway station (500m)

QENP, Mbarara, Kampala

vehicle to leave. Direct buses between Kampala and Kasese leave in both directions throughout the morning, and they take around six hours.

Driving yourself, the road from Kampala to Kasese is surfaced in its entirety and a few formerly pot-holed stretches have been resurfaced. The stretch of road between Katunguru and Kasese passes through the Queen Elizabeth National Park – Uganda kobs are abundant and you might even see an elephant or buffalo in the distance. You may want to stop at the Crater Lake Pavilion overlooking the circular Lake Kikorongo on the top of a hill about 200m from the mainroad between Katunguru and Kasese. It was built to receive the Queen Mother and George Rukidi III of Toro in 1958. The turn-off to the pavilion is signposted from the main road, 26km south of Kasese.

People driving between Kabale and Kasese might think about using a back route via Bwindi National Park and the Ishasha sector of Queen Elizabeth National Park. The part of this route between Kabale and Bwindi is covered in the *Getting there and away* section under Bwindi National Park in *Chapter 8*, and the part between Bwindi and Katunguru in the *Getting there and away* section under Ishasha earlier in this chapter (see map, pages 226–7). Provided that you stick to the roads recommended in this guide (there are several other roads in the area, many in an appalling state), you could get between Kabale and Kasese in six or seven hours – though the probability is that you'd want to stop at Bwindi and Ishasha along the way. This route is also an option for backpackers, though they will be dependent on hitching lifts for much of its length.

WHERE TO STAY
Moderate

Margherita Hotel ↘ 04834 44015; m 0772 695808; f 04834 44380; e info@hotel-margherita.com; www.hotel-margherita.com. Situated 3km from the town centre along the Kilembe road, this large and recently privatised hotel, with its commanding view of the Rwenzori, is easily the most comfortable place to stay in Kasese. The public areas retain the faintly depressing aura of outmoded institutionalism characteristic of former government hotels, and the restaurant is nothing to shout about, charging Ush8,000 for an adequate main course or Ush15,000 for a 3-course set menu with coffee. The rooms, renovated in 2002, are spacious and comfortable but they do seem ambitiously priced. There might be a lack of comparable accommodation in Kasese but there's plenty of choice in Fort Portal just an hour away. *US$50/60 standard sgl/dbl, US$70/80 sgl/dbl with TV/AC.*

Budget

Mariana Hotel m 0772 537331. This new multi-storey hotel is about the smartest in the town centre, and has a fair ground-floor restaurant, bar and nightclub. The spacious and clean s/c twins have nets, cold running water and balconies, but are perhaps a touch overpriced. Much better value are the similar dbl rooms. Even if you're travelling solo, better to pay slightly extra for one of these doubles than a cramped, gloomy single using common showers. However, it's worth checking whether the upstairs nightclub is open when you visit if you're hoping for a quiet night. *S/c twins US$16 B&B, US$10 dbl inc b/fast for 1 person only, US$8 sgl.*

Rwenzori International Hotel ↘ 04834 44148; m 0772 462783. This new hotel occupies a quiet location in a suburb south of the town centre. The hotel is clearly signposted off the Mbarara–QENP road about 2km from the roundabout. B&B in this solid, 2-storey hotel seems excellent value. *US$16/22 s/c sgl/dbl, US$11 sgl using shared showers.*

Saad Hotel m 0772 499552; e info@newsaadhotel.com; www.saadhotel.com. The once-popular Saad Hotel, reached through an unsignposted courtyard behind the Uganda Commercial Bank off Stanley Rd, seems to have gone slightly downhill in recent years. Even so, the standard s/c rooms are not bad value. The restaurant serves reasonable meals. No alcohol is served on the premises, but several bars lie along Stanley Rd within a 100m radius. *US$14 sgl/dbl inc b/fast for 1, US$19 for 'executive' rooms with AC.*

Virina Gardens This superficially attractive set-up consists of several s/c thatched bandas in a small but green garden on the back streets north of the market. Unfortunately, the rooms are rather dark and cramped with small beds are less than terrific value. The twin rooms (using shared showers) in the main building are better value at inc b/fast. *US$22 dbl B&B with cold water only for twin rooms.*

🏠 **White House Guesthouse** \ 04834 44706. Unquestionably the pick of the budget accommodation in Kasese, the new White House is a brightly painted dbl-storey building situated off Kilembe Rd, roughly opposite the Shell garage at the junction with Margherita St. The dbl rooms are small but clean. A decent bar and restaurant with DSTV are attached. *US$7 with common showers, US$10 dbl s/c with hot water.*

🏠 **Ataco Holiday Inn** Previously recommended as the pick of Stanley Road's shoestring lodges, this is no longer the case, not least because a price hike of over 50% has elevated it into the Budget listings. However tiled floors and bathrooms squeezed into (now cramped) rooms can't disguise the Ataco's shoestring origins. At *US$11/14 for s/c double/ twin rooms and US$6 for a single using shared showers* the 'New' Ataco is rotten value compared to the nearby White House Guesthouse.

Shoestring

🏠 **Soft Lodge** At the far (and presumably quieter) end of the line of cheapies on Stanley Rd, the Soft Lodge represents astonishing value for perfectly clean sgl/dbl rooms with nets using common showers. Admittedly the view hardly compares with that provided at Kasese's Margherita Hotel and AC and TV are lacking from the rooms but a couple can sleep soundly at the Soft Lodge in the knowledge that they've saved themselves a useful *US$77! US$3 single/dbl.*

✕ **WHERE TO EAT AND DRINK** If you're looking for a feast after climbing the Rwenzori, you'll be disappointed in Kasese. For what it's worth, the **White House Guesthouse**, **Saad Hotel** and **Mariana Hotel** offer about the best eating in town. If you fancy a walk out of town, there's nothing much wrong with the food at the **Margherita Hotel** (though it's not exactly memorable either) and the view from the balcony is great. For a cold beer, the open-air **Virina Gardens** is recommended, but there must be a dozen other bars on Stanley Road alone.

LISTINGS

Tourist information The Rwenzori Mountain Services (RMS) (m *0782 325431;* f *04834 44235;* e *rms@africaonline.co.ug or uwa@uwa.or.ug*), though a private company, has the sole concession to run Rwenzori hikes, and will be putting together the ground arrangements of your hike whichever company you book through. Hiking arrangements can also be made directly with the RMS, through their office beneath the Saad Hotel and they are also the best source of other travel information for Kasese.

Foreign exchange Stanbic Bank (next to the Saad Hotel) offers national bank rates for cash and American Express travellers' cheques (virtually the same for both). The only place in the area where travellers' cheques are accepted, albeit at a very poor rate, is Mweya Safari Lodge in Queen Elizabeth National Park.

Internet Kasese Computer Solutions provide internet and fax services on Margerita Road. A generator ensures constant service. However as a sign of the times, internet costs Ush50 per minute when mains electricity is available, and Ush100 per minute when the backup system is required.

Shopping Travellers who want to stock up for a Rwenzori hike are advised to buy all packaged and imported produce in Kampala or Mbarara. Otherwise a few supermarkets dotted around the central market in Kasese stock a limited range of dry foods such as spaghetti and soup.

This 996km² national park protects the upper slopes of the Rwenzori Mountains, which run for almost 120km along the Congolese border west of Kasese and Fort Portal. The Rwenzori Mountains are thought to have been the source of the legend of the Mountains of the Moon, the snow-capped range cited as the source of the Nile by the Roman geographer Ptolemy cAD150. The first Europeans to see these legendary mountains were Arthur Jephson and Thomas Parke, members of Stanley's cross-continental expedition to rescue the Emin Pasha, which passed through the area in 1889. The range was first comprehensively explored by Europeans in 1906, when an expedition led by Luigi da Savoia conquered all the major peaks.

The Rwenzori is the highest mountain range in Africa. Its loftiest peaks, Margherita (5,109m) and Alexandra (5,083m) on Mount Stanley, are exceeded in altitude elsewhere in Africa only by Kilimanjaro and Mount Kenya, both of which are extinct volcanoes standing in isolation above the surrounding plains. The Rwenzori Mountains are unique among east Africa's major peaks in that they are not volcanic in origin, but they do rise directly from the Rift Valley floor and their formation, like that of Kilimanjaro and Kenya, was linked to the geological upheaval that created the Rift. In addition to Mount Stanley, there are four other glacial peaks in the Rwenzori: Mount Speke (4,890m), Mount Emin (4,791m), Mount Gessi (4,715m) and Mount Luigi da Savoia (4,627m).

The Rwenzori is known primarily for its challenging hiking and climbing possibilities, but the range also supports a diversity of animals, including 70 mammal and 177 bird species, several of the latter being Albertine Rift Endemics. It is the only national park in Uganda where the Angola colobus has been recorded, though identification of this localised monkey will require careful examination as the similar and more widespread black-and-white colobus also occurs on the mountain.

Like other large east African mountains, the Rwenzori range can be divided into several altitude zones, each with its own distinct microclimate and flora and fauna. The forest zone, which starts at around 1,800m, has the most varied fauna. The only mammals you are likely to see in the forest are the aforementioned colobus and blue monkeys, though several other large mammals are present, including elephant, golden cat, servalline genet, chimpanzee, yellow-backed duiker and giant forest hog. At night, listen out for the distinctive and eerie call of the southern tree hyrax.

The forest zone is home to a diversity of birds, including Rwenzori turaco, barred long-tailed cuckoo, long-eared owl, handsome francolin, cinnamon-chested bee-eater, Archer's ground robin, white-starred forest robin, Rwenzori batis, montane sooty boubou, Lagden's bush shrike, slender-billed starling, blue-headed sunbird, golden-winged sunbird, strange weaver, and several varieties of barbet, greenbul, apalis, illadopsis, flycatcher and crimsonwing.

Above an altitude of roughly 2,500m, true forest gives way to dense bamboo forest stands. Higher still, spanning an altitude of roughly 3,000m to 4,500m, the open vegetation of the heather and Alpine zones is renowned for its otherworldly quality: forests of giant heather plants, and giant lobelias and groundsel up to 10m high. The striking *Lobelia wollanstonii* and *Senacio admiralis* are most common above 3,800m. Mammals are scarce above the forest zone, but there are a few birds worth looking out for: the lammergeyer (bearded vulture) and black eagle are occasionally seen soaring overhead, while the alpine and scarce swifts and scarlet-tufted malachite sunbird are practically restricted to high-altitude habitats in east Africa.

Do not attempt to climb the Rwenzori unless you are reasonably fit, nor if you have heart or lung problems (although asthma sufferers should be all right). Bear in mind, however, that very fit people are more prone to altitude sickness because they ascend too fast.

Above 3,000m you may not feel hungry, but you should try to eat. Carbohydrates and fruit are recommended, whereas rich or fatty foods are harder to digest. You should drink plenty of liquids, at least three litres of water daily, and will need enough water bottles to carry this. Dehydration is one of the most common reasons for failing to complete the climb. If you dress in layers, you can take off clothes before you sweat too much, thereby reducing water loss.

Few people climb above 3,500m without feeling at least minor symptoms of altitude sickness: headaches, nausea, fatigue, breathlessness, sleeplessness and swelling of the hands and feet. You can reduce these by allowing yourself time to acclimatise by taking an extra day over the ascent, eating and drinking properly, and trying not to push yourself. If you walk slowly and steadily, you will tire less quickly than if you try to rush each day's walk. Acetazolamide (Diamox) helps speed acclimatisation and many people find it useful; take 250mg twice a day for five days, starting two or three days before reaching 3,500m. However, the side effects from this drug may resemble altitude sickness and therefore it is advisable to try the medication for a couple of days about two weeks before the trip to see if it suits you.

Should symptoms become severe, and especially if they are clearly getting worse, then descend immediately. Even going down 500m is enough to start recovery. Sleeping high with significant symptoms is dangerous; if in doubt descend to sleep low.

Pulmonary and cerebral oedema are altitude-related problems that can be rapidly fatal if you do not descend. Symptoms of the former include shortness of breath when at rest, coughing up frothy spit or even blood, and undue breathlessness compared to accompanying friends. Symptoms of high-altitude cerebral oedema are headaches, poor co-ordination, staggering like a drunk, disorientation, poor judgement and even hallucinations. The danger is that the sufferer usually doesn't realise how sick he/she is and may argue against descending. The only treatment for altitude sickness is descent.

Hypothermia is a lowering of body temperature usually caused by a combination of cold and wet. Mild cases usually manifest themselves as uncontrollable shivering. Put on dry, warm clothes and get into a sleeping bag; this will normally raise your body temperature sufficiently. Severe hypothermia is potentially fatal: symptoms include disorientation, lethargy, mental confusion (including an inappropriate feeling of well-being and warmth!) and coma. In severe cases the rescue team should be summoned.

There is a good network of trails and huts on the mountains. The peaks are generally only tackled by experienced climbers. Most people stick to the Loop Trail (see box, page 303), which takes six to seven days and reaches an altitude of 4,372m. It is possible to do a shorter three-day hike through the forested foothills into the moorland zone, or to spend longer on the mountain in order to divert from the main loop to some of the peaks. It should be stressed that hiking in the Rwenzori requires above-average fitness and stamina, largely due to the muddy condition of the trails (in parts, you might literally have to walk through waist-high mud). Most people regard the Rwenzori Loop Trail to be a tougher hike than the ascents of either Mount Kilimanjaro or Mount Kenya.

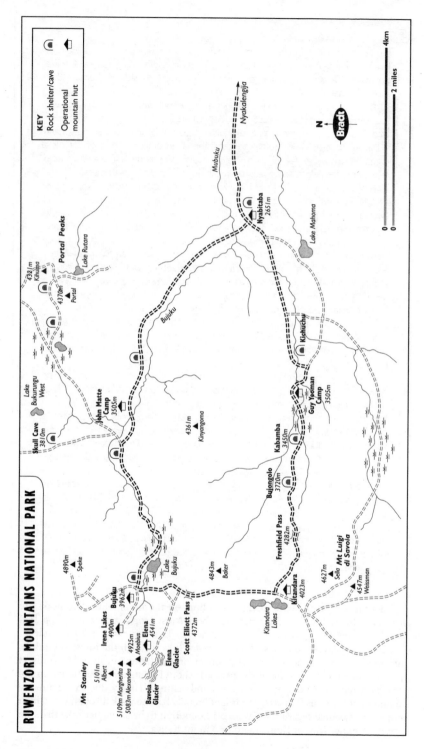

RUWENZORI MOUNTAINS NATIONAL PARK

KEY

◖ Rock shelter/cave

⌂ Operational mountain hut

Mt Stanley
5101m
Albert ▲
5109m Margherita ▲
5083m Alexandra ▲
4925m
Moebius ▲

Irene Lakes
4900m

Bujuku
3962m ⌂

Speke
4890m ▲

Elena
4541m ▲

Bavoia
Glacier

Elena
Glacier

Scott Elliott Pass
4372m

Lake
Bujuku

Skull Cave
3810m ◖

Lake
Bukurungu
West

◖

◖

**John Matte
Camp**
3505m ⌂

Bujuku

◖

Kinyangoma
4361m ▲

Portal Peaks
4370m ▲
Portal

Kihuma
4391m ◖

Lake
Rutara

◖

◖

Mubuku

Nyabitaba
2651m ◖

Lake Mahoma

Nyakalengija

Kichuchu ◖

**Guy Yeoman
Camp**
3505m ⌂

◖

Kabamba
3450m ▲

Bujongolo
3720m ▲

Freshfield Pass
4282m

Kitandara
4023m ▲

4843m
Baker ▲

Kitandara
Lakes

4627m ▲
Sella Mt Luigi
di Savoia

4547m ▲
Wessman

N

Bradt

0 _____ 2 miles
0 _____ 4km

302

This is traditionally the trail favoured by most tourists. However, the recent increase in hiking costs, combined with the tough walking conditions on the Rwenzori, mean that more and more travellers opt for a shorter hike that follows the loop trail for two days, descending back along the same route on the third day. The RMS can also organise day hikes into the forest zone, an option that will be of considerable interest to those with restricted time or funds, or for whom the forest birds and wildlife are more alluring prospects than spending days wandering about in the mud and rain. The RMS offers tailored advice on all routes and timings.

DAY ONE: NYAKALENGIJA (1,615m) TO NYABITABA HUT (2,651m) The trailhead is at Nyakalengija, 22km from Kasese off the Fort Portal road. The RMS can arrange transport from Kasese to its main office at Nyakalengija, where you will pay park fees and finalise arrangements. There is a campsite and safe parking near the office. From Nyakalengija it's a 10km, five-hour ascent to the Nyabitaba Hut, passing first through cultivation then through forest. There is a piped water supply at the hut.

DAY TWO: NYABITABA HUT TO JOHN MATTE HUT (3,505m) This is the longest and most strenuous day's walk; expect it to take a minimum of seven hours. From Nyabitaba Hut, the path descends through forest for a short time before it crosses the Bujuku River at the Kurt Schafer Bridge (built in 1989). Between the bridge and Nyamileju Hut, the path is good for the first couple of hours, but it becomes steeper and very rocky as you enter the moorland zone, where heather plants are prolific.

You will probably want to stop for lunch at Nyamileju, where there is a little-used and rather rundown hut, as well as a rock shelter. After leaving Nyamileju, the path passes a giant heather forest and follows the Bujuku River. John Matte Hut is about a two-hour walk from Nyamileju. The hut is in good condition and about 200m from the Bujuku River, where you can collect water.

DAY THREE: JOHN MATTE HUT TO BUJUKU HUT (3,962m) This takes up to five hours, depending on the condition of the two Bigo Bogs, which are often knee-deep in mud. On the way to the hut you will pass Lake Bujuku, which has a magnificent setting between mounts Stanley, Speke and Baker. There is water 20m from Bujuku Hut.

Bujuku Hut is the base for reaching Mount Speke, and you will need to spend an extra night there in order to do this. If you want to climb to the highest point in the range, Margherita Peak on Mount Stanley (5,109m), you must do this from Elena Hut (4,541m), which is about 2km off the Loop Trail and three to four hours' walk from either Bujuku or Kitandara huts.

DAY FOUR: BUJUKU HUT TO KITANDARA HUT (4,023m) From Bujuku Hut you will ascend to the highest point on the Loop Trail, Scott Elliot Pass (4,372m), before descending to the two Kitandara lakes. The hut is next to the second lake.

DAY FIVE: KITANDARA HUT TO GUY YEOMAN HUT (3,505m) This is a five-hour walk, starting with a steep ascent to Freshfield Pass (4,282m) then a descent to Bujongolo Cave (3,720m), the base used by the 1906 expedition. Further along the trail at Kabamba Cave (3,450m) there is an attractive waterfall and a rock shelter where you can stay overnight as an alternative to Guy Yeoman Hut.

DAY SIX/SEVEN: GUY YEOMAN HUT TO NYAKALENGIJA It's a five-hour descent from Guy Yeoman Hut to Nyabitaba Hut. You can either stay overnight at the hut or else continue to the trailhead at Nyakalengija, which will take a further three hours.

The guides and porters on the Rwenzori are almost exclusively Bakonjo, a group of Bantu-speaking agriculturists who inhabit the Rwenzori footslopes – some 500,000 in Uganda as compared with more than four million in the DRC – and are known for their stocky build and hardy nature. Unlike most other Bantu-speaking peoples in Uganda, the Bakonjo have no clear traditional origin. Some say that they migrated westward from Mount Elgon, not settling anywhere until they found a similar montane environment to cultivate. Other traditions claim that the Bakonjo descend from an ancient ancestor who emerged from one of the caves in the Rwenzori – oddly echoing the prevalent creation legend among the Bagisu of Elgon. They also have no paramount leader, but are divided into a number of small clans, each of which is associated with a particular spur on the Rwenzori foothills.

Traditionally, the Bakonjo seldom ventured on to the higher slopes of the Rwenzori, which is inhabited by a number of powerful deities and spirits that place a curse on any human who glimpses them, and will sometimes strike the observer dead. Paramount among these is Kitasamba – The God Who Never Climbs – said to live on the apex of the jagged peaks, in a snowy environment associated by the Bakonjo with semen and potency. Tradition has it that Kitasamba will only remain the source of Bakonjo procreative powers so long as he is untainted by the act itself – for which reason his spirit manifests itself only in male virgins, and adult men will abstain from intercourse for a period before ascending to the Rwenzori snowline.

Kitasamba has one wife, called Mbulanene – Heavy Rain – but a more important female spirit is his sister Nyabibuya, who safeguards female fertility and protects children. The third most important spirit of the mountains is Endioka, a dark serpentine inhabitant of rivers, capable of rendering men or women infertile, as well as indulging in other acts of black sorcery. The centrality of fertility and potency in their spiritual affairs notwithstanding, sex before marriage is frowned upon in traditional Bakonjo society, monogamy is customary, divorce rare, and pregnancy outside of wedlock was formerly punishable by execution.

Agriculture has always been the main food-producing activity of the Bakonjo, but hunting also plays an important role in their traditional society, partly as sport, but also for food. The spirit of hunting and shepherd of all wild animals is a one-eyed, one-legged, one-armed being called Kalisa, known for his addiction to pipe smoking, as well as his partiality to fresh meat. Before setting off on any hunting expedition, Bakonjo men traditionally leave an offering of *matoke* or chicken to Kalisa in a shrine consisting of a pair of small hut-like shelters (the largest about 1m high) made of bamboo and/or thatch, then place a small fence of bamboo stakes across their path to prevent evil spirits following. After a successful hunt, a further offering of meat off-cuts would be left for Kalisa at the site of the slaughter.

HIKING ARRANGEMENTS The Rwenzori National Park was forced to close to tourism in 1997 as a result of instability along the Congolese border, but it finally reopened in July 2002. There are now two routes up to the high Rwenzori which is explored by the Central Circuit that winds between the main peaks The established route is the ascent along the Mobuku and Bjuku valleys from Nyakalengija while an another route, long closed to tourists, route along the Nyamwamba valley above Kasese is currently being re-opened

The trail is operated and the mountain huts owned (and supposedly maintained) by the Rwenzori Mountain Service (RMS) which until recently was the sole concessionaire for hikes. RMS will make all arrangements whether you book directly through their offices in Kasese (see *Listings*, page 299 for details) or UWA Headquarters in Kampala. Alternatively, you can book through most local tour operators. Of these the Adrift Adventure Company provides the most comprehensive arrangements, rather than simply dropping you at the trailhead to

The advent of colonial rule robbed the Bakonjo of Uganda of much of their former independence, since their territory was placed under the indirect rule of the Toro monarchy, to which they were forced to pay hut taxes and other tributes. Widespread dissatisfaction with this state of affairs led to the Bakonjo Uprising of 1919, which endured for two years before its leader, Chief Tibamwenda, and his two leading spiritual advisers were captured by the authorities and executed. But the strong resentment against Toro that still existed amongst the Bakonjo and their Bwamba neighbours resurfaced 40 years later, during the build-up to independence.

In 1961, the Bakonjo and Bwamba, frustrated by Toro's unwillingness to grant them equal status within the kingdom, demanded that they be given their own federal district of Ruwenzururu (Land of the Snow), to be governed independently of Toro. This request was refused. In August 1962, two months before Uganda was to gain independence, the Bakonjo took up arms in the Ruwenzururu Rebellion, attacking several Toro officials and resulting in a number of riots and fatalities. In February 1963, the central government declared a local State of Emergency in affected parts of Toro, and the Bakonjo were invited to elect their own government agents to replace the local representatives of Toro. Instead, the Bakonjo and Bwamba unofficially but effectively ceded from Uganda, by establishing their own Ruwenzururu kingdom, ruled by King Mukirania, and placing border posts and immigration officers at all entry points.

In 1967, the researcher Kirstin Alnaes, who had made several previous study trips to the region, noted that: 'The difference... from 1960 was marked... Earlier... spirit possession rituals were performed surreptitiously. Now people sported houses and shrines for the spirits, and were more than willing to talk about it. It was as if the establishment of their own territory in the mountains had released a belief in themselves and their cultural identity [formerly] suppressed not only by government regulations and missionary influence, but also by their own fear of seeming "backward", "uncivilised", "monkeys" and the many other epithets the Batoro had showered upon them.'

The situation in Ruwenzururu deteriorated after 1967, as government troops made repeated forays into the breakaway montane kingdom to capture or kill the rebel ringleaders. Ironically, it was only under Amin, who came to power in 1971, that the right for self-determination among the Bakonjo and Bwamba was finally accorded official recognition, with the creation of Rwenzori and Semliki districts, which correspond to the modern districts of Kasese and Bundibugyo. Even so, clan elders must still today obtain a permit from the authorities before they may visit centuries-old sacrificial shrines to the various mountain spirits situated within the national park.

take your chances with RMS (see box *Ascending the Rwenzori peaks*, page 307) they supply an experienced expatriate expedition leader with technical mountaineering skills, first aid training and cooking skills (see *Rafting*, page 161 for contact details).

The cost of a seven-day, six-night hike along the Central Circuit loop trail, as described overleaf, is fixed at US$500 per person for non-residents and US$460 per person for east African residents. This fee is paid to Rwenzori Mountaineering Services (RMS).

RMS is a local community tourism group established to provide local Bazonzo people with the wherewithal to benefit from tourism on the mountain that has for centuries been central to their existence and cosmology. Local men are employed as guides and porters and profits are supposed to be invested in community projects. Unfortunately, although expected to be a model of its type, and for a while a favourite with donor organisations, the reality of RMS proved otherwise. The closure of the park due to the ADF war didn't help but then neither has an even longer history of creative accountancy and other duplicitous practices within the organisation which has seen the organisation shunned by its erstwhile sponsors. A lack of competition on the mountain has meant that RMS could charge whatever it likes (as evidenced by a 20% price hike for the Central Circuit in August 2006), whilst failing to resolve consistently poor standards of guiding, trails and hut facilities. It is therefore greatly to be hoped that the allocation of a concession (which will also be required by UWA to be strongly community oriented) to access the Central Circuit along the Nyamwamba Valley will lead to improved standards on the mountain and induce RMS to improve on its own services and consider more carefully its pricing structure. At the time of writing, UWA has yet to process applications and select an operator for the new Kilembe Trail. If present activity is anything to go by, the clever money might be on an organisation called Rwenzori Trekking Services (m *0774 114499;* e *rwenzoritrekking@gmail.com; www.rwenzoritrekking.com*) which has already established a base camp, the Rwenzori Backpackers Hostel, in Kilembe (see Where to Stay below). If RTS is successful in its application for montane activities, I'm assured that daily prices will be significantly cheaper than the RMS rates stated above. Access to the peaks on the Kilembe Trail will not be as quick as on the Nyakalenjija route, taking four days rather than three to reach the peaks. However from all accounts the scenery in this area appears to be magnificent, the new route ascending the Nyamwamba valley and descending the stunning Nyamugasani valley which contains a chain of eight glacial lakes. As a tourist trail this route is, incidentally, older than the established Nyakalenjija trail. The Nyamwamba valley was first ascended in 1895 by Professor Scott Elliot, 11 years before the Italian Duke of Abruzzi pioneered the more direct route along the Bujuku valley.

GETTING THERE AND AWAY The Nyakalenjija trailhead is 22km northwest of Kasese. The Rwenzori Mountains National Park (RMNP) is signposted off the tarmac Fort Portal highway about 7–8km out of Kasese by an electric substation between the road bridges over the Mubuku and Sebwe rivers. Transport can be arranged through the RMS or any private taxi driver for around Ush30,000–35,000 one-way per party. Secure parking is available at the RMS HQ.

WHERE TO STAY Many people overnight in Kasese immediately before and following their ascent (see *Listings*, pages 298–9). There are, however, two options at the Nyakalenjija trailhead.

⚑ Ruboni Campsite m 0752 503445; e ucota@ africaonline.co.ug; www.rwenzori.org.conservation. This good community-run site offers hillside cottages with a dbl bed, nets and good mountain views. Morning/afternoon walks through the Bakonzo communities cost US$6 pp. *US$17 cottage, camping US$3.*

⌂ RMS Guesthouse ☎ 04834 44936. This long-serving but unprepossessing facility close to the pretty Mubuku River is currently undergoing a renovation, after which charges for improved rooms will increase and meals will be provided. *Rooms presently US$8, camping around US$2.*

In addition to accommodation options in Kasese there is presently only a single facility in Kilembe itself:

Rwenzori Backpackers Hostel m 0774 199022; e rwenzoribackpackers@gmail.com; www.backpackers.co.ug/rwenzorihostel.html This new facility lies in the deep Nyamwamba river valley,11km out of Kasese at the far (west) end of the copper mining town of Kilembe. The hostel occupies restored miner's housing (the mine closed 20 years ago) at the end of the motorable

ASCENDING THE RWENZORI PEAKS

The RMS guides are generally adequately experienced to lead hikes around the Central Circuit below the snowline. Several have also recently undergone training by international mountain guides to acquire the skills necessary to lead parties on snow and ice at high altitude. However the extent to which this has improved their professional abilities remains to be seen. Certainly the consensus over several years of reader feedback has been that most if not all of their guides, are not competent, sometimes dangerously so, to ascend the glacial peaks. Unless you have experience in Alpine climbing conditions and carry your own map, compass and GPS, it's highly questionable whether you will be safe above the snowline. Here's an extract from one letter written after the park reopened in 2002:

The guides vary enormously in terms of quality and experience. We had two guides, one of whom spoke no English and was utterly useless from start to finish. He had no cold-weather equipment and became a serious liability on the summit day because he had only thin cotton trousers, a light anorak and no hat. He also wore gumboots, which cannot realistically take crampons, all the way to the summit. On the glacier stages we had to continually stop in cold and windy weather while he tried in vain to get his crampons to stay on.

Our second guide at least spoke English and had a basic idea of the plants and animals of the mountains. He was a nice guy and meant well. But his technical skills were extremely rusty and on the summit day he became alarmingly confused about how to rope up and how to set up a belay. His climbing calls were all wrong, he gave no instruction to the team, and on a particularly steep and exposed rock face below the summit he was essentially hauling us up with brute strength from a non-belayed position – until we as a team made clear our climbing knowledge and insisted on better protection.

On the Stanley Plateau we got lost in thick mist and the guides became stubborn and silent when we insisted that we stop and assess our situation. As a group we had carried a map, a compass and a GPS, so knew exactly where we were and which way we should proceed. Meanwhile the guides had no such aids and were going on memory alone. It was only our team's skill that averted a disaster. Even when we located cairns and flags that marked the summit route, the guides still maintained the pretence that we were not going the right way, apparently to protect their own pride. All in all quite frightening and unprofessional.

road into the mountains; it's a 3km walk to the park boundary and the start of the Kilembe Trail. Camping costs US$4.5; four-bed dormitories cost US$9 per person and double rooms cost US$18. Flushing toilets and hot showers are provided.

CLIMBING THE MOUNTAIN The cost of a seven-day, six-night hike along the Central Circuit loop trail, as described below, is fixed at US$500 per person for non-residents and US$460 per person for east African residents. This fee is paid to Rwenzori Mountaineering Services (RMS). The price includes hut fees, a guide and four porters per person. Note, however, that it is exclusive of park entrance, payable to the national park office. This is set at US$25/day bringing the cost of the standard circuit to US$675. The RMS can arrange hikes of shorter and longer durations as required. Prices for climbers wishing to scale a peak are based on the flat rate for the Central Circuit plus the necessary additional days. Example rates for foreign residents/east African residents are: Mt Stanley US$650/605; Mt Speke US$570/530; Mt Baker US$570/530; Mt Luigi di Savoia US$610/570; Mt Gessi

US$700/600 (plus park entrance). Packages for climbers wishing to scale more than one peak (there are four on Mt Stanley alone) can be arranged at a cost of US$91 for each additional day on the mountain. Shorter hikes can also be arranged. If intending to climb a peak it is essential to report to the RMS office on the day before your intended departure, so that equipment such as ice-axes, crampons and walking sticks can be sized, fitted and paid for, without misunderstandings and other delays on the day of departure.

Clothing and equipment Cold and wet conditions are normal on the mountain, and it is essential that you are properly prepared. You will need plenty of warm clothing for the nights. The driest months are from late December to early March and from late June to early September, but you should be prepared for rain at all times of year. The paths are incredibly muddy after rain (knee-deep in parts), particularly around the Bigo Bogs, Lake Bujuku, and on some parts of the trail between Kitandara and Guy Yeoman huts. It is advisable to wear gumboots and a waterproof jacket and trousers. Before you climb, waterproof your matches and seal your clothes in plastic (it's worth saving up plastic bags for this purpose).

Most of the hiking and climbing equipment you need can be hired from the RMS, for between US$3 and US$10 per article. Items for hire include *pangas*, cooking pots, ice-axes, gumboots, crampons, gaiters, sleeping bags and mats, climbing boots and climbing ropes. A reasonable range of dry foods is available in Kasese; the RMS can advise you on how much to bring. On the loop walk, you can normally cook on the porters' fire, but a portable stove would be an advantage and it is essential if you plan on scaling any peaks. If you can't get hold of waterproof clothing, I met someone who bought a length of clear plastic in Kasese and had trousers made up by a local tailor.

Food should be pre-packed and labelled for each day, which makes the life of the cook easier and saves you having to think too hard once in the mountains. Ideally, pack a separate packet for each day's evening meal and drinks, and one for the next day's breakfast, lunch and snacks. You may end up with lots of spare food as your appetite diminishes at altitude, but better to have extra in case you need an additional day or two due to bad weather. Variety is essential – if possible, don't repeat any meal two days in a row. Ensure that you have a wide variety of snacks for munching on the go, some sweet and some savoury; crunchy oat bars and pre-mixed trail mix are both good.

If you intend to climb one of the glacial peaks, you will need climbing rope, an ice-axe, crampons and climbing boots. Snow goggles, a compass and an altimeter will also be useful.

Health Altitude is not a major concern below the snowline. On the loop trail, you are likely to be affected by the altitude only around Scott Elliot and Freshfield passes; this will probably be no more than a headache. Only if you climb the peaks is there a serious risk of developing full-blown altitude sickness. The guides are trained to recognise altitude-related symptoms; they will force you to turn back immediately if they feel it is unsafe for you to continue.

Maps and guides A simple map of the Central Circuit sold at the RMS office is up to date and is adequate for ordinary hikers. If you plan to climb the peaks, it is advisable to buy the excellent 1:25,000 contoured map of the Central Rwenzori from the Dept of Lands and Surveys, PO Box 1, Entebbe. Alternatively, Andrew Wielochowski's *Rwenzori Map and Guide* also shows contours and has plenty of practical and background information on the reverse side. It may be available in Nairobi; otherwise order it electronically (**e** ewp@ewpnet.com; www.ewpnet.co.uk).

Serious climbers and walkers with wide interests are advised to get hold of the definitive and recently revised *Guide to the Rwenzori* (Henry Osmaston, 2006), available through bookshops or from West Col Productions, Goring, Reading RG8 9AA, UK, or in Uganda from Geolodges (☏ *0414 258273*). Andrew Roberts is presently preparing a historical/regional guide for the Rwenzori. Intended to complement Osmaston's book, this will provide plenty of wider information for travellers to absorb during those lazy afternoons at the mountain huts and on regional lodge verandas.

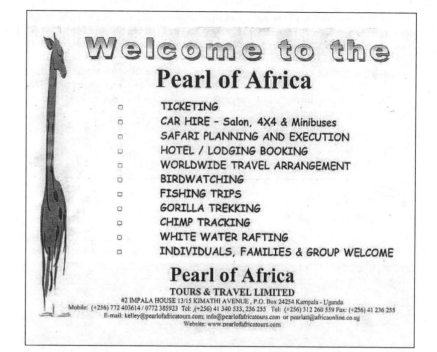

310

10

Fort Portal

Situated in the northern foothills of the Rwenzori Mountains, some 50km north of Kasese and 320km west of Kampala, Fort Portal is a likeable enough town, but of greatest interest to travellers for lying at the epicentre of a cluster of highly alluring and reasonably accessible national parks and other tourist attractions. Foremost among these is probably Kibale National Park, which – situated about 30km south of town – is not only the best place to track chimpanzees in Uganda, but also harbours its greatest primate diversity and a thrilling variety of forest birds. Other popular destinations around Fort Portal include a field of several-dozen crater lakes near Kibale Forest, and the forested National Park and more open Semliki Wildlife Reserve at the base of the northern Rwenzori foothills.

Marked by a remarkable amount of new tourist development in recent years, the Fort Portal area hosts perhaps the greatest density of successful community-based ecotourism projects anywhere in Africa, most of which are strongly geared towards backpackers. This is perhaps the most positive trend I've seen in many years of African travel, and a model for new tourist development elsewhere on the continent. Community ecotourist projects such as the Bigodi Wetland Sanctuary and Lake Nkuruba Nature Reserve deserve the support of travellers, not least because they provide a genuine foundation to the sometimes glib assertion that independent travel is of greater benefit than package tourism at a grassroots level.

FORT PORTAL

Fort Portal is perhaps the most attractive town in Uganda, situated amid lush rolling hillsides swathed in neat tea plantations and – clouds permitting – offering excellent views across to the glacial peaks of the Rwenzori Mountains to the west. The town centre has seen a great deal of renovation since the early 1990s, including plenty of new hotels and restaurants, and what with ongoing resurfacing of its internal roads, it is barely recognisable from the rundown 'Fort Pot-hole' of a few years back.

Fort Portal is named after a British fortress constructed between 1891 and 1893, on the site of the town's present-day golf club, with the aim of protecting the Toro kingdom (see box, pages 216–17) from guerrilla raids by King Kabalega of Bunyoro. Fort Gerry, as it was originally known, was named posthumously after the British Consul General of Zanzibar Sir Gerald Portal, who arrived in Buganda in late 1892 to formalise its protectorateship and died of malaria on Zanzibar a few months later. Norma Lorimer, who travelled to Fort Portal in 1913, referred to the settlement as 'Toro', adding that it then consisted of 'about six bungalows, the bank, the Boma, the huts for a few KARs [King's African Rifles], the Indian bazaar and the native settlement'. The 'splendid native market... at the bottom of the hill' mentioned by Lorimer is still in position today, opposite the Gardens Restaurant.

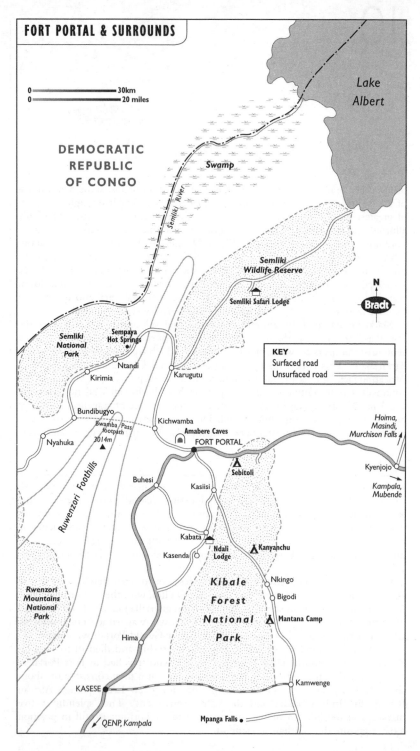

FORT PORTAL & SURROUNDS

0 ———————— 30km
0 ———————— 20 miles

DEMOCRATIC
REPUBLIC
OF CONGO

Swamp

Lake
Albert

Semliki River

Semliki
Wildlife Reserve

Semliki Safari Lodge

N
Bradt

Semliki
National
Park

Sempaya
Hot Springs

Ntandi

Kirimia

Karugutu

KEY
Surfaced road
Unsurfaced road

Bundibugyo

Bwamba Pass
footpath

Kichwamba

Nyahuka

3014m

Amabere Caves
FORT PORTAL

Hoima,
Masindi,
Murchison Falls

Ruwenzori Foothills

Buhesi

Kasiisi

Sebitoli

Kyenjojo

Kampala,
Mubende

Kabata

Kasenda

Ndali
Lodge

Kanyanchu

Rwenzori
Mountains
National
Park

Kibale
Forest
National
Park

Nkingo

Bigodi

Mantana Camp

Hima

KASESE

QENP, Kampala

Kamwenge

Mpanga Falls

312

Fort Portal boasts few urban landmarks of note. There is the faintly preposterous statue of a gun-wielding Sir Gerald Portal that stands sentinel on the roundabout opposite the Gapco garage, subverted by a howler of a plaque – Sir Gerald was neither a major nor an explorer, he never set foot within a 100km radius of the town, nor for that matter did he ever personally carry a firearm! Perched on a hill above Fort Portal is the large circular Toro Palace; built in the 1960s for Omukama Kasagama's son and successor, Rukidi III, this was destroyed and looted after the abolition of the old kingdoms under Obote and was only recently restored with Libyan money. Kasagama and Rukidi III are buried at the Karambi Tombs, 5km out of town on the Kasese road.

GETTING THERE AND AWAY The 300km-long road from Kampala to Fort Portal has recently been surfaced. This can be driven along at a comfortable 80–100km/h and the drive takes a little under four hours. The reliable Post Bus from Kampala leaves from the central post office on Kampala Road at 08.00 daily except Sundays, arriving in Fort Portal five to six hours later, but the return trip starts at a less convenient 05.30. Also recommended is the Kalita Coach between Kampala and Fort Portal, which leaves in either direction at 07.00, 08.30, 10.00, 12.00 and 14.00 daily and takes four to five hours. The fare is Ush14,000.

Fort Portal lies only 60km north of Kasese – less than an hour's drive – along a recently resurfaced and rather nippy road covered by regular buses and minibuses throughout the day. On the way you pass through Hima, famed throughout Uganda for its cement factory, but otherwise notable only for the Snow View Hotel, a name covering all eventualities since in clear weather it looks towards the Rwenzori snow peaks while in more frequently hazy conditions (I'll spell it out for you), there'S no View to speak of. Fort Portal Town can also be approached from Masindi in the northwest via Hoima, a full day's drive, or possibly two using public transport, along a route covered more fully in *Chapter 11*.

WHERE TO STAY

Upmarket A couple of upmarket locations are being developed in and around Fort Portal though at the time of writing neither is open:

Mountains of the Moon Hotel m 0712 200800; e byaruhanga@lawyer.co.ug. Fort Portal's oldest hotel, which stands 2km out of the town centre in the leafy suburb of Boma, is presently closed and undergoing a much-needed major renovation, and remains hidden behind a screen of corrugated tin. Its expected to reopen in 2007. Hopefully the upgrade will respectfully improve upon the original decaying colonial gem of a building with its beautiful clay-tiled veranda overlooking manicured grounds (teeming with birdlife) but it will certainly be a welcome development for hot bathing water to once more arrive through the taps rather than being delivered by staff in a plastic bucket. If this is indeed the case and that other aspects of the upgrade meet expectations, the hotel will be very

reasonably priced indeed with *rates of US$60/100 s/d B&B.*

Lake Kyaninga Resort m 0772 999750; e kyaningalodge@yahoo.com. A new lodge is under construction beside Lake Kyaninga a few kilometres north of Fort Portal along the Kijura road. Kyaninga is one of the loveliest of the many crater lakes in the Fort Portal area and the site enjoys a lovely Rwenzori backdrop. This log cabin lodge is scheduled to open in November 2007 but I'd phone for an update or ask around Fort Portal before you head up there. Lake Kyaninga is 8km from Fort Portal. 2km out of town along the Kampala road turn left up the Kijura road by the bridge and then left again after 2km at a signposted turning. Continue for 4km to the lodge.

Moderate

Rwenzori View Guesthouse ☎ 04834 22102; m 0772 722102; e ruwview@africaonline.co.ug.

Fort Portal's outstanding hostelry is this universally praised guesthouse on the outskirts of town, reached

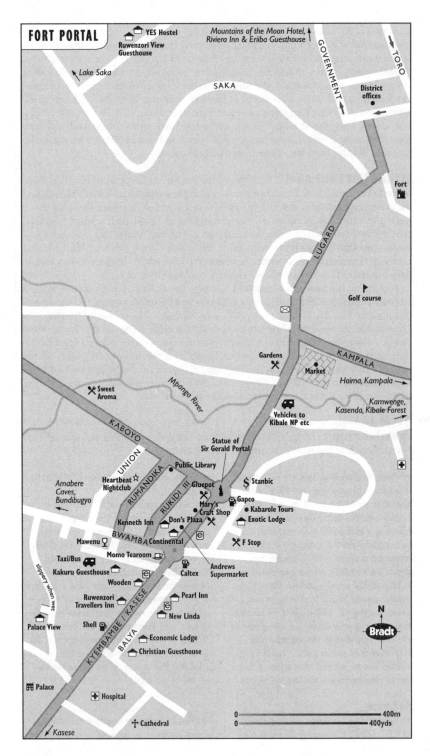

FORT PORTAL

YES Hostel
Ruwenzori View
Guesthouse

Mountains of the Moon Hotel,
Riviera Inn & Eriiba Guesthouse

SAKA

GOVERNMENT

TORO

Lake Saka

District
offices

Fort

LUGARD

Golf course

KAMPALA

Gardens

Market

Hoima, Kampala

Sweet
Aroma

Mpanga River

Kamwenge,
Kasenda, Kibale Forest

KABOYO

Vehicles to
Kibale NP etc

Statue of
Sir Gerald Portal

UNION

Public Library

RUMANDIKA

Stanbic

Amabere
Caves,
Bundibugyo

Heartbeat
Nightclub

RUKIDI III

Gluepot

Gapco

Mary's
Craft Shop

Kabarole Tours

Kenneth Inn

Don's Plaza

Exotic Lodge

BWAMBA

Continental

Mawenu

F Stop

Taxi/Bus

Momo Tearoom

Kakuru Guesthouse

Wooden

Caltex

Andrews
Supermarket

slippery when wet

KYEMBAMBE / KASESE

Ruwenzori
Travellers Inn

Pearl Inn

Palace View

Shell

New Linda

BALYA

Economic Lodge

Christian Guesthouse

Palace

N

Bradt

Hospital

Cathedral

0 ———————— 400m
0 ———————— 400yds

Kasese

314

by following the Saka road past the golf course for about 1km then turning right for another 200m or so. Owned and managed by a friendly Dutch–English couple, the guesthouse offers comfortable accommodation in airy s/c rooms with hot water, and including a great b/kfast. The wonderful home-cooked dinners are a refreshing change from bland hotel fare. The pretty flowering gardens face the glacial peaks of the Rwenzori. At the price, difficult to recommend too strongly! Advance booking is essential. Outside diners should phone for a reservation since as a rule non-residents are only served when the guesthouse is not full. The guesthouse has a selection of baskets and other local crafts for sale and is in the process of constructing a sauna. *US$24/32 sgl/dbl.*

🏠 **Eriiba Guesthouse** (2 rooms) m 0712 446304. Situated on Njara Road on the northern edge of Fort Portal beyond the Mountains of the Moon (fork right at the hotel gate) this new guesthouse is the family home of a charming retired Ugandan couple (so it's not really the place if you intend rolling in from Heartbeat disco in the small hours). Their smart home enjoys a lovely view across a forested valley and the golf course towards Fort Portal, the Omukama's palace and the Rwenzori. The 2 s/c dbl rooms are truly pristine and good value. Advance booking is suggested. *US$22/27 sgl/dbl inc b/fast.*

🏠 **Toro Resort** m 0772 888900. 3km from Fort Portal Town, signposted off to the south side of the Kampala road, the new Toro Resort stands in a lovely pastoral/wooded landscape with a Rwenzori backdrop. The s/c dbl rooms in the main building are nothing out of the ordinary; far more attractive are the round s/c cottages in the garden (same price). *US$27 inc b/fast.*

🏠 **Rujuna Guesthouse** 📞 04834 25077; e rujunaguesthouse@yahoo.com; www.traveluganda.co.ug/rujunaguesthouse. This new establishment enjoys a fabulous location 6km south of Fort Portal. The 2-storey house is set on a high grassy slope above the Kasese road looking towards the Rwenzori Mountains. The grounds include what must be western Uganda's only croquet lawn. Meals include 'full English, African traditional buffet and international cuisine'. Ndali Lodge redirects potential guests here when they are full, and it's a far more attractive option than anywhere in Kasese for travellers coming out of QENP. *US$30/40/80 sgl/dbl/family rooms, US$150 safari ste.*

🏠 **Riviera Inn** m 0772 681817. Situated about 1km past the Mountains of the Moon Hotel, the new Riviera Inn is housed in an attractive dbl-storey building in large green gardens. The s/c rooms with hot bath are more than adequate, though not quite in the same league as the 2 hotels listed above. A bar and basic restaurant are attached. *US$22/28 sgl/dbl.*

🏠 **Fort Motel** m 0772 731307/0712 220259; e reservations@fortmotel.com; www.fortmotel.com. This brand-new establishment opened too late for me to visit it but I passed its attractively restored and extended building which enjoys a pleasant location above the golf course. It's about 400m up the hill past the Post Office. *Rooms cost between US$40 and US$100.*

Budget

🏠 **Rwenzori Travellers Inn** 📞 04834 22075; m 0712 400570; e travellersinn2000@yahoo.com. Opened in September 2002, this smart 3-storey block on the Kasese road is easily the most comfortable place to stay in the town centre. It's also very good value. There's a good restaurant on the ground floor, serving simple but tasty main dishes for around Ush5,000–6,000. The lively new rooftop bar provides a panoramic view over the town centre. On the downside, this also gives little chance of an early night although I'm told by the Englishman who financed the hotel that the music should reduce to an acceptable level at 23.00. However his Ugandan wife owns it so you'll probably have to discuss the matter with her after the clock chimes eleven. *US$16/22 for a spotless s/c sgl/dbl or twin with netting/hot water. US$35–46 executive rooms.*

🏠 **Continental Hotel** m 0772 484842. Conveniently located on the main roundabout opposite the Caltex garage, the once-popular Continental Hotel has gone slightly downhill in recent years, though it remains one of the better compromises between cost and comfort in the town centre. *US$11 s/c dbl, US$5/6 sgl/dbl using common showers.*

🏠 **Palace View Hotel.** There's not much of a view but this new hotel is excellent value, and occupies a quiet and attractive suburban location on the hillside above the taxi park. From town, turn right off the Kasese road immediately before the palace hill and shortly afterwards, right again. *US$14 for a clean s/c room sleeping 1 or 2 people, inc b/fast.*

🏠 **Soka Hotel** m 0772 472320. 2km out of town down the Kasese Road, the Soka is good value and occupies a pleasant roadside location (well out of earshot of the Heartbeat disco). If that's not enough,

Fort Portal lies at the physical and political heart of Toro, the youngest of Uganda's traditional kingdoms, ruled – aptly – by the world's most youthful monarch, not quite four years old when he took the throne in 1995. Corresponding roughly with the present-day administrative districts of Kabarole and Kasese, Toro started life as a southern principality within the Bunyoro kingdom, from which it broke away to become an independent kingdom in the late 1820s under Prince Kaboyo, the son of the Bunyoro king, Nyakamaturu.

In the mid 1820s Nyakamaturu, reaching the end of his 50-year reign, was evidently regarded as a weak and unpopular ruler. As a result, Kaboyo, the king's favourite son and chosen heir to the throne, had become impatient to claim his inheritance. In part, Kaboyo's haste might have been linked to a perceived threat to his future status: Nyakamaturu had already survived at least one attempted overthrow by a less-favoured son, while the elders of Banyoro openly supported his younger brother Mugenyi as the next candidate for the throne. While on a tour of Toro c1825, Kaboyo came to realise the full extent of his father's unpopularity in this southern part of Bunyoro, and he was persuaded by local chiefs to lead a rebellion that left Toro a sovereign state.

Nyakamaturu's army had the better of the rebels in the one full-scale battle that occurred between them, but the ageing king was not prepared for his favourite son to be killed, and he eventually decided to tolerate the breakaway state. It has even been suggested that Kaboyo was invited to succeed the Banyoro throne after Nyakamaturu's death in the early 1930s, but declined, leaving the way clear for Mugenyi to be crowned King of Bunyoro. By all accounts, Kaboyo's 30-year reign over Toro was marked by a high level of internal stability, as well as a reasonably amicable relationship with Bunyoro.

The death of Kaboyo c1860 sparked a long period of instability in Toro. Kaboyo's son and nominated successor Dahiga proved to be an unpopular leader, and was soon persuaded to abdicate in favour of his brother Nyaika, who was in turn overthrown, with the assistance of the Baganda army, by another brother called Kato Rukidi. Nyaika was exiled to the present-day DRC, where he rebuilt his army to eventually recapture Toro, killing Kato Rukidi and reclaiming the throne as his own. Toro enjoyed a brief period of stability after this, but Nyaika was not a popular ruler, and the long years of civil strife had left his state considerably weakened and open to attack.

The start of Nyaika's second term on the Toro throne roughly coincided with the rise of Bunyoro's King Kabalega, who avowed to expand his diminished sphere of influence by reintegrating Toro into the ancient kingdom, along with various other smaller breakaway states. In 1876, Kabalega led an attack on Toro that left its king dead. The Banyoro troops withdrew, and a new Toro king was crowned, but he too was captured by Kabalega and tortured to death, as was his immediate and short-lived successor. The remaining Toro princes fled to Ankole, where they were granted exile, and for the next decade Banyoro rule was effectively restored to Toro.

And that might have been that, had it not been for a fortuitous meeting between the prominent Toro Prince Kasagama (also known as Kyebambe) and Captain Lugard in May 1891, at the small principality of Buddu in Buganda. Kasagama was eager for any assistance

---

additional facilities include DSTV in the bar/restaurant, a gym (Ush3,000), wood-fired sauna (Ush4,000), massage (Ush5,000) and secure parking. US$6 non-s/c sgl and US$14 s/c dbl.

⌂ **Wooden Hotel** m 0772 402770. The oldest-serving hotel in the town centre – also overlooking the roundabout and Caltex garage – was once the established favourite with budget travellers and may

become so again following a recent drop in price and rise in standards. The large, clean rooms are slightly rundown, but they all come with net and fan, and seem good value. However over the years, I've found the disco on the ground floor to be noisy, while the hotel is consistently staffed by anonymous flip-flop shod women who display an utter disinterest in the hotel and catering industry.

that might help him to restore the Toro throne, while Lugard quickly realised that the young prince might prove a useful ally in his plans to colonise Bunyoro – 'Inshallah, this may yet prove a trump card' he wrote of the meeting in his diary! Kasagama and his entourage joined Lugard on the march to Ankole, where they gathered together a small army of exiled Toro royalists. They then proceeded to march towards Toro, recapturing one of its southern outposts and most important commercial centres, the salt mine at Lake Katwe, then continuing north to the vicinity of Fort Portal, where a treaty was signed in which Kasagama signed away Toro sovereignty in exchange for British protection.

When Lugard left for Kampala in late 1891, leaving behind a young British officer named De Winton, the kingdom of Toro had to all intents and purposes been restored, albeit under a puppet leader. De Winton oversaw the construction of a string of small forts along the northwestern boundaries of Toro, designed to protect it from any further attacks by Kabalega, and manned by 6,000 Sudanese troops that had been abandoned by the Emin Pasha on his withdrawal from Equatoria a few years earlier. In early 1862, however, De Winton succumbed to one or other tropical disease, leaving Toro at the mercy of the Sudanese troops, who plundered from communities living close to the forts, and rapidly established themselves as a more powerful force than Kasagama and his supporters. The withdrawal of the Sudanese troops to Buganda in mid 1893 proved to be a mixed blessing: in the absence of any direct colonial presence in Toro, Kasagama briefly enjoyed his first real taste of royal autonomy, but this ended abruptly when Kabalega attacked his capital in November of the same year. Kasagama retreated to the upper Rwenzoris, where several of his loyal followers died of exposure, but was able to return to his capital in early 1864 following a successful British attack on Kabalega's capital at Mparo.

Toro functioned as a semi-autonomous kingdom throughout the British colonial era. Kasagama died in 1929, to be succeeded by King George Rukidi II, a well-educated former serviceman who is regarded as having done much to advance the infrastructure of his kingdom prior to his death in 1965. In February 1966, King Patrick Kaboyo Rukidi III ascended to the Toro throne, only eight months before the traditional monarchies of Uganda were abolished by Obote. The king lived in exile until the National Resistance Movement took power in 1986, after which he enjoyed a distinguished diplomatic career serving in Tanzania and Cuba.

In July 1993, the traditional monarchies were restored by Museveni, and two years later the Toro king returned to Fort Portal for a second coronation. He died a few days before this was scheduled to take place, to be succeeded by his son Prince Oyo Nyimba Kabamba Iguru Rukidi IV – only three years old when he came to power and currently a scholar in Kampala. The first years of the restored monarchy have been marked by controversy. The sudden death of the former king just before he would have been restored to power has attracted allegations of foul play from certain quarters. The three regents originally appointed to assist the young Oyo Nyimba included Toro prime minister, John Katuramu, who was arrested for his alleged involvement in the murder of another prince in 1999. Three new regents were appointed in August 2002.

Moreover it's incapable of providing a decent dinner, or any sort of breakfast before 9am. That said, there's no reason why you shouldn't save a few dollars sleeping here and go elsewhere to enjoy yourself. US$5/6 sgl/dbl using common showers, US$6/8 s/c sgl/dbl.

⌂ **Kenneth Inn** m 0772 992076. This new town-centre hotel on Rukidi III Road has comfortable s/c rooms with tiled floors and nets. A pleasant 1st-fl veranda/bar looks across the townscape towards the mountains but it's not an especially restful location; the loud bar closes at midnight, only to be replaced by thudding from the nightclub in the next street.. Note that the front door is locked at midnight and there is on-street parking only. US$14/19 sgl/dbl inc b/fast.

Shoestring

⌂ **Exotic Lodge** Centrally located alongside the Kabarole Tours office behind Don's Plaza, this friendly, excellent-value family-run lodge has been the pick of Fort Portal's cheapies for some years now. The clean rooms all have nets and although the common showers have cold running water only, the staff will boil up water on request for a hot bucket-shower. *US$3/4 sgl/dbl.*

⌂ **Youth Encouragement Services (YES)** e yesuganda@gmail.com. A Fort Portal NGO which supports orphans, YES provides cheap dormitory accommodation. The fee includes the use of a self-catering kitchen equipped with a gas stove and utensils. Located near the Rwenzori View Guesthouse, YES occupies an unprepossessing 2-storey building but one which faces a lovely pastoral setting with mountain views to the rear. *US$3 per night.*

⌂ **Pearl Guesthouse** The best of a row of mostly rather scruffy and similarly priced budget lodgings running along Balya Road parallel to the main Kasese road, the Pearl is a clean, family-run lodge. For what it's worth, the **New Linda Lodge** and **Christian Guesthouse** are about the best of the rest. *US$5 for an adequate sgl.*

✖ **WHERE TO EAT AND DRINK** Patience is not so much a virtue in Fort Portal's eateries as a survival tool. The restaurants mentioned below all serve perfectly decent food but the service, provided by woefully ill-trained staff, is slow even by the usual standards of upcountry Uganda. Order your meal with good humour and tolerance and take along a good long book or enthusiastic conversationalist.

The best place to eat in the town centre is probably the **Rwenzori Travellers Inn**, which eventually serves grills and stews for Ush4,000–5,000 indoors or on the pavement patio from which you can count cars while you wait. Also on the main road, **Don's Plaza** is a friendly restaurant and bar, where the emphasis is on drinking, though good snacks are also available. The **Glue Pot Bar** opposite is a similar set-up.

More alluring than anywhere in the town centre is the **Gardens Restaurant** opposite the Mpanga River Bridge and market. The spacious veranda is a pleasant place to watch Fort Portal go by accompanied by a cold beer and the extensive menu of Western and Indian dishes is reasonably priced at around Ush5,000 for a main course. The food was a bit disappointing last time we ate here, but it's been good on other occasions. The pork escalope is a good change from the ubiquitous fish or pepper steak. You can also make paper boats and race them down the adjacent stream while your order is being prepared; you'll have time for quite a few mini-regattas.

If dinner arrives slowly, breakfast can be even more of a challenge. Fort Portal wakes up slowly and there's unlikely to be much activity in your hotel kitchen before 08.00. If you're intent on an early start, head straight to the **Momo Tea Room** right on the main Caltex roundabout (which you'll be noting by now is rather a strategic location) which provides a cheap and fast breakfast menu. The Momo has no sign but you can't miss the building which is painted green and emblazoned 'Hima Cement'. Long before 09.00 (a more acceptable hour for breaking one's fast in Fort Portal), the place is packed with locals which is always a good sign.

Heartbeat disco, Uganda's best upcountry nightclub, is located on Rumandika Road. It's a fine place for an evening out but less so for a quiet night in. Heartbeat's resonant pulse can be heard and felt to varying extents throughout the town centre so it's worth selecting rooms that face away from Rumandika Road.

LISTINGS

Tourist information and activities Kabarole Tours (☏ 04834 22183; m 0772 661752; f 04834 22636; e ktours@infocom.co.ug; www.traveluganda.co.ug/kabaroletours; open Mon–Sat 08.00–18.00, Sun 10.00–16.00) is a commendable set-up of more than ten years' standing, whose positive attitude to budget travellers complements an active role in the development and support of most of the community ecotourism projects around Fort Portal. Their office on Moledina Street, behind Don's Plaza, is plastered with flyers and information sheets about local tourist attractions, and effectively functions as the local tourist information office. Although Kabarole Tours has recently expanded its services to include countrywide tours, it remains very active locally and can arrange a variety of very reasonably priced day- or overnight-driving excursions to the likes of Kibale Forest and nearby crater lakes, the Semliki Valley or Queen Elizabeth National Park. They have also set out a 35km bicycle tour taking in a variety of crater lakes, caves and waterfalls around Fort Portal (US$5 per person inclusive of sketch map and bicycle) and the Rwenzori mini-trek described later in the chapter.

Foreign exchange Stanbic Bank's Fort Portal branch provides it's usual range of forex (cash and travellers' cheques) and ATM services. You'll find long queues so it's worth bringing sufficient funds with you to enable you to change money at your convenience rather than from necessity.

Internet Three internet cafés close to the Caltex roundabout charge Ush50 a minute. The best service is said to be provided by the S S Mugasa stationery shop on Balya Road opposite the Rwenzori Travellers Inn. Others are in the Wooden Hotel building and Voice of Toro building.

Shopping **Andrews Supermarket** on the main road stocks a huge range of local and imported food and drinks, as well as fresh bread (salt as well as sweet). **Mary's Craft Shop** a couple of doors down is a good place to buy local handicrafts and other souvenirs.

EXCURSIONS Fort Portal is the normal springboard for visits to the Semliki Valley, Kibale Forest and Kabarole Crater Lakes, covered under separate headings later in this chapter. The following, more local sites of interest can be visited as day or overnight excursions out of Fort Portal.

Amabere Caves The Amabere Caves (alternatively known as the Nyakasura Caves) lie roughly 8km west of Fort Portal off the Bundibugyo road, in a hilly area dotted with crater lakes. The attractive and peaceful private campsite just above the caves is one of the little-known gems of the Fort Portal area – in the right frame of mind you could happily spend several days here, resting up and exploring the surrounding countryside. The cycling tour offered by Kabarole Tours goes past the caves.

The full name of the caves is Amabere ga Nyinamwiru – Breasts of Nyinamwiru – and refers to a live stalactite formation supposedly shaped like a pair of breasts (but actually more reminiscent of deformed cow udders, certainly in numerical terms). According to local tradition, Nyinamwiru was the daughter of a local king called Bukuku, so beautiful that no man could leave her alone, and constantly plagued by marital proposals from unsuitable suitors. Bukuku cut off Nyinamwiru's breasts in the hope it would reduce her charms, but even this wasn't enough to deter his lovely daughter's many admirers, so eventually he hid her away in the caves. Whilst there, Nyinamwiru was impregnated by the Batembuzi King Isaza to give birth to Ndahura, the future founder of the Bacwezi dynasty, and – lacking breasts herself – she fed the infant with the cloudy limestone 'milk' that drips from the breast-like stalactites. Legend has it that after Ndahura surrendered the Bacwezi throne to his son, he retired to his birthplace – his footprints can still reputedly be seen in the caves' vicinity.

The main cave, though small, is very pretty, supported as it is by several pillars formed where stalactites and stalagmites have met in the middle. Local tradition has it that anybody who touches these formations will get lost in the caves or be visited by misfortune – during the colonial era, or so the story goes, a European schoolteacher removed one of the stalactites, causing the surrounding area to be swept by destructive winds until he was persuaded to replace it. A powerful little waterfall lies next to the main cave – it's an exhilarating feeling to stand on the moss-covered rocks behind the waterfall, and to see a sheet of ice-cold water plunge down right in front of you, kicking spray back into your face. It's said to be OK to swim in the pool below the falls, though the water is very chilly. A couple of other caves, or more accurately overhangs, lie downstream of the waterfall. The riparian forest around the waterfall is rattling with birds, and it supports a few black-and-white colobus monkeys.

The attractive **Amabere Caves Campsite**, set in a private garden about 500m from the caves, consists of two separate sites. In theory, the one in the garden is for backpackers and the one in the field above the caves is for overland trucks, but both sites are more often than not deserted and backpackers can choose where they camp. The site above the caves is fringed by riverine forest, and it has much more atmosphere than the garden site. Camping costs US$3 per person. Tents are available for hire. Sodas and meals are available. A self-contained two-bedroom chalet and a lovely veranda with mountain views costs US$27.

To get to the Amabere Caves, follow the Bundibugyo road out of Fort Portal for 6km before turning right into the signposted turn-off. After a further 1.1km, turn right into a signposted dirt road. You'll soon pass a swimming pool to your right. Around 800m from the turning, turn right again to reach the campsite. No more than ten minutes' walk away from the campsite, Kigere Crater Lake is surrounded by dense stands of plantains and palms, and reportedly safe to swim in. You can walk around the crater rim to get a view of a smaller, less attractive lake. Another empty crater stands directly above the campsite. A visit to the caves costs US$3 and a tour of the lakes the same amount.

Lake Saka Lake Saka is the largest lake in the immediate vicinity of Fort Portal. Not strictly speaking a crater lake, but rather a flooded valley dammed by a crater, Saka is one of the few lakes to support fish large enough for commercial harvesting, and it is safe to swim in. The lake lies on church property, so there are no tourist facilities, and vague plans to build a campsite on the lakeshore have been shelved. The cycling tour offered by Kabarole Tours goes past Lake Saka. It's also possible to walk there from the Amabere Caves over a couple of hours, following a path running to the right of Lake Kigere, then behind it, and finally following a right fork that goes downhill to ford a river and leads to the Saka road near Kagote Prison. If you get lost, ask directions for Kagote.

Lake Saka can be approached directly from Fort Portal. From the town centre, follow Lugard Road towards the Mountains of the Moon Hotel for about 1km, then immediately after passing the golf course, turn left into Saka Road (signposted for the Rwenzori View Guesthouse). The lake is about 7km out of town. Walking through the church grounds isn't encouraged; better to leave the road at a col about 1km before the lake, then walk left up a steep hill to a crater rim from where you can follow the rims of two adjoining craters. If you don't have private transport, there's a fair chance of getting a lift some of the way, but be prepared to walk. A genuine crater lake called Kaitabarogo can be reached by following a 1km track that runs north from the Saka road opposite Kagote Prison.

Mugusu and Rwimi markets The colourful weekly markets at Mugusu and Rwimi, which lie along the Kasese road below the peaks of the Rwenzoris, are important social events locally, and well worth visiting if you're in town on the right day. The market at Mugusu, about 12km south of Fort Portal, takes place on Wednesdays, and is mostly concerned with secondhand clothing, attracting buyers from as far afield as Kampala. The market at Rwimi, about 45km south of Fort Portal, is a more conventional rural market, but very large and colourful, with a spectacular setting.

Rwenzori mini-hike Pioneered by Kabarole Tours and Abanya Rwenzori Mountaineering Association (m *0772 621397*), this hike crosses between Fort Portal and Bundibugyo via the northern tip of the Rwenzori Mountains National Park using the 'Bwamba Pass', at one time the only access route between the Semliki Valley and Fort Portal. Despite being relatively strenuous – six to eight hours if you are driven to the trailhead, and up to 12 hours if you walk there from Fort Portal – the walk has become increasingly popular with travellers who are reluctant to pay the high fees asked for longer Rwenzori hikes based out of Kasese.

An attractive option, particularly for those who are walking all the way from Fort Portal, is to break up the hike at the Mountains of the Moon Campsite, a community project situated in Kighomu trading centre. Kabarole Tours in Fort Portal have played an advisory role in developing this campsite, and they can supply independent hikers with current information about the trail, as well as sketch maps, guides and advice on where to pay national park entrance fees.

The trailhead lies at an altitude of about 1,650m in Kazingo trading centre, roughly 8km southwest of Kichwamba along a side road branching from the Bundibugyo road some 15km out of Fort Portal and 3km before Kichwamba. Kazingo is a good four- to five-hour walk from Fort Portal, though you can cut a significant chunk from the distance by catching Bundibugyo-bound public transport as far as the turn-off. From Kazingo, the steep 1hr 15min ascent to Kighomu (2,050m) follows a clear footpath through grassy and partly cultivated slopes.

The community campsite lies a short distance above Kighomu; it charges around US$2 per person to camp, and there are also a few inexpensive rooms. Bedding and meals are available by prior arrangement, either at the village or else through Kabarole Tours, and a limited selection of soft drinks is sometimes available. Several trails radiate from the campsite, so you could easily spend a few days walking in the surrounding area. There are rumoured to be chimpanzees present in a nearby forest, though they are not as yet habituated and the chances of seeing them are slim.

From Kighomu, there are two paths over the ridge. The east to west path is the easier, climbing to the forest edge (2,150m) then to the bamboo-covered ridge (2,450m) over about 1hr 15min. The east to west path climbs to an altitude of around 3,000m – local guides are available to show you the different routes. Either way, it's a bit of a slog up to the ridge, with some consolation for the leg-strain being that this is the best area for seeing the four monkey species present in the forest, including the Angola colobus.

From the ridge of the mountain, a muddy path leads through bamboo forest before descending steeply towards Bundibugyo. It takes one or two hours to get from the ridge to the base of the mountain, depending on how slippery the path is and on which route you used from Kighomu. Shortly after reaching the base the path widens into a motorable track, leading first across an area of rolling hills and then, as you approach Bundibugyo, crossing relatively flat terrain. The walk from the base of the mountain to Bundibugyo takes roughly three hours.

Kabarole Tours offers a one-night hiking package inclusive of transportation to Kazingo, accommodation at the Vanilla Hotel in Bundibugyo and a guide, for US$45 per person. This can be extended to spend an additional day visiting Semliki National Park and Sempaya Hot Springs for US$130 inclusive of park fees, accommodation and meals, minimum three people. A three-day, two-night hiking package ascending to roughly 2,800m, with one night camping high in the mountains, costs US$160 per person all inclusive.

KIBALE FOREST NATIONAL PARK

Kibale Forest National Park, together with the nearby Kasenda Crater Lakes, are close to being an independent traveller's dream, blessed with the tantalising combination of inexpensive accommodation, easy access, wonderful scenery and a remarkable variety of activities. The park is highly alluring to nature lovers of all budgets for its excellent chimpanzee tracking and birdwatching, not to mention the greatest variety and concentration of primates of any forest in East Africa. Gazetted in October 1993, the 766km² national park extends southwards from Fort Portal to form a contiguous block with the Queen Elizabeth National Park. Interspersed with patches of grassland and swamp, the dominant vegetation type is rainforest, spanning altitudes of 1,100–1,590m and with a floral composition transitional to typical eastern Afro-montane and western lowland forest.

At least 60 mammal species are present in Kibale Forest. It is particularly rich in primates, with 13 species recorded, the highest total for any Ugandan national park. The nine diurnal primates found at Kibale are vervet, red-tailed, L'Hoest's and blue monkeys, grey-cheeked mangabey, red colobus, black-and-white colobus, olive baboon, and chimpanzee. The Kibale Forest area is the last Ugandan stronghold of the red colobus, although small numbers still survive in Semliki National Park. Visitors who do both the forest and the swamp walks can typically expect to see around five or six primate species.

Kibale Forest offers superlative primate viewing, but it is not otherwise an easy place to see large mammals – this despite an impressive checklist which includes lion, leopard, elephant, buffalo, hippo, warthog, giant forest hog, bushpig, bushbuck, sitatunga, and Peter's, red and blue duikers. The elephants found in Kibale Forest are classified as belonging to the forest race, which is smaller and hairier than the more familiar savanna elephant. Elephants frequently move into the Kanyanchu area during the wet season, but they are not often seen by tourists.

Roughly 335 bird species have been recorded in Kibale Forest, including four species not recorded in any other national park: Nahan's francolin, Cassin's spinetail, blue-headed bee-eater and masked apalis. Otherwise, the checklist for Kibale includes a similar range of forest birds to Semliki National Park, with the exclusion of the 40-odd Semliki 'specials' and the inclusion of a greater variety of water and grassland species. A recent first sighting of a green-breasted pitta caused some excitement in Ugandan ornithological circles, while the truly optimistic might want to look out for Prigogine's ground thrush, a presumably endemic species or race collected once in the 1960s and yet to be seen again! The best birdwatching spot is the Bigodi Wetland Sanctuary, where a four-hour trail has been laid out, and experienced guides will be able to show you several localised species which you might otherwise overlook.

Non-resident visitors to Kanyanchu and Sebitoli pay a visitation fee of US$25/35/50 for one/two/three or more nights. East African residents pay discounted rates of US$15/20/25 on production of proof of residency. An entrance permit is valid for 24 hours from time of entrance. This is, more than any other park, a consideration when planning your itinerary, given the additional attractions just outside the park. It obviously doesn't make sense to pay for park entrance and check into park accommodation then, with the 24-hour clock ticking, head off for 'out-of-park' birdwatching in the Kihingami and

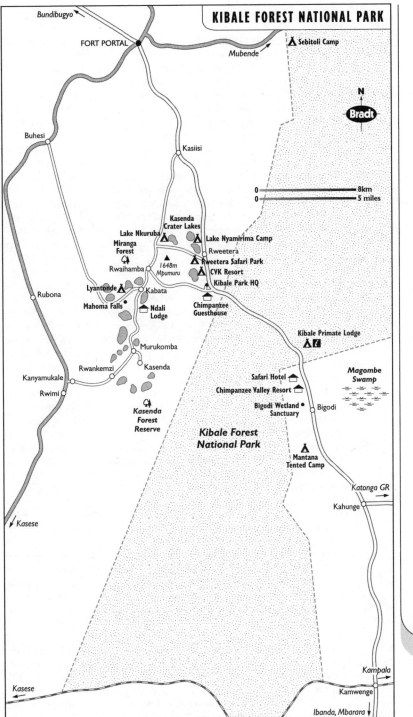

KIBALE FOREST NATIONAL PARK

Bundibugyo

FORT PORTAL

Mubende

Sebitoli Camp

N

Bradt

Buhesi

Kasiisi

0   8km
0   5 miles

Kasenda
Crater Lakes

Lake Nkuruba   Lake Nyamirima Camp

Miranga
Forest   Rweetera

Rwaihamba   1648m   Rweetera Safari Park
          Mpumuru   CVK Resort

Lyantonde   Kibale Park HQ
         Kabata

Rubona

Mahoma Falls   Chimpanzee
         Ndali   Guesthouse
         Lodge

        Murukomba   Kibale Primate Lodge

Rwankemzi   Kasenda

Kanyamukale   Magombe
                      Safari Hotel   Swamp
Rwimi   Chimpanzee Valley Resort

                 Bigodi Wetland   Bigodi
Kasenda   Sanctuary
Forest
Reserve   Kibale Forest
          National Park   Mantana
                           Tented Camp

                           Katonga GR

Kasese   Kahunge

                               Kampala

Kasese   Kamwenge

                           Ibanda, Mbarara

You'll hear them before you see them: from somewhere deep in the forest, an excited hooting, just one voice at first, then several, rising in volume and tempo and pitch to a frenzied unified crescendo, before stopping abruptly or fading away. Jane Goodall called it the 'pant-hoot' call, a kind of bonding ritual that allows any chimpanzees within earshot of each other to identify exactly who is around at any given moment, through the individual's unique vocal stylisation. To the human listener, this eruptive crescendo is one of the most spine chilling and exciting sounds of the rainforest, and a strong indicator that visual contact with man's closest genetic relative is imminent.

It is, in large part, our close evolutionary kinship with chimpanzees that makes these sociable black-coated apes of the forest so enduringly fascinating. Humans, chimpanzees and bonobos (also known as pygmy chimpanzees) share more than 98% of their genetic code, and the three species are far more closely related to each other than they are to any other living creature, even gorillas. Superficial differences notwithstanding, the similarities between humans and chimps are consistently striking, not only in the skeletal structure and skull, but also in the nervous system, the immune system, and in many behavioural aspects – bonobos, for instance, are the only animals other than humans to copulate in the missionary position.

Unlike most other primates, chimpanzees don't live in troops, but instead form extended communities of up to 100 individuals, which roam the forest in small, socially mobile subgroups that often revolve around a few close family members such as brothers or a mother and daughter. Male chimps normally spend their entire life within the community into which they were born, whereas females are likely to migrate into a neighbouring community at some point after reaching adolescence. A highly ranking male will occasionally attempt to monopolise a female in oestrus, but the more normal state of sexual affairs in chimp society is non-hierarchical promiscuity. A young female in oestrus will generally mate with any male that takes her fancy, while older females tend to form close bonds with a few specific males, sometimes allowing themselves to be monopolised by a favoured suitor for a period, but never pairing off exclusively in the long term.

Within each community, one alpha male is normally recognised – though coalitions between two males, often a dominant and a submissive sibling – have often been recorded. The role of the alpha male, not fully understood, is evidently quite benevolent – chairman of the board rather than crusty tyrant. This is probably influenced by the alpha male's relatively limited reproductive advantages over his potential rivals, most of whom he will have known for his entire life. Other males in the community are generally supportive rather than competitive towards the alpha male, except for when a rival consciously contests the alpha position, which is far from being an everyday occurrence. One male in Tanzania's Mahale Mountains maintained an alpha status within his community for more than 15 years between 1979 and 1995!

Prior to the 1960s, it was always assumed that chimps were strict vegetarians. This notion was rocked when Jane Goodall, during her pioneering chimpanzee study in Tanzania's Gombe Stream, witnessed them hunting down a red colobus monkey, something that has since been discovered to be common behaviour, particularly during the dry season when other food sources are depleted. Over subsequent years, an

Magombe swamps near Sebitoli and Kanyanchu respectively. The 24-hour deadline is also a factor when deciding whether to stay a second night in park accommodation or head to another location that is not subject to a US$25 surcharge on the bed rate. No park fee is charged for passing through the park on the Fort Portal–Kamwenge road, for staying at the guesthouses in and around Bigodi, or for visiting the Bigodi Wetland Sanctuary.

average of 20 kills has been recorded in Gombe annually, with red colobus being the prey on more than half of these occasions, though young bushbuck, young bushpig and even infant chimps have also been victimised and eaten. The normal modus operandi is for four or five adult chimps to slowly encircle a colobus troop, then for another chimp to act as a decoy, creating deliberate confusion in the hope that it will drive the monkeys into the trap, or cause a mother to drop her baby.

Although chimp communities appear by and large to be stable and peaceful entities, intensive warfare has been known to erupt within the habituated communities of Mahale and Gombe. In Mahale, one of the two communities originally habituated by researchers in 1967 had exterminated the other by 1982. A similar thing happened in Gombe Stream in the 1970s, when the Kasekela community, originally habituated by Goodall, divided into two discrete communities. The Kasekela and breakaway Kahama community coexisted alongside each other for some years. Then in 1974, Goodall returned to Gombe Stream after a break to discover that the Kasekela males were methodically persecuting their former community mates, isolating the Kahama males one by one, and tearing into them until they were dead or terminally wounded. By 1977, the Kahama community had vanished entirely.

Chimpanzees are essentially inhabitants of the western rainforest, but their range does extend into the extreme west of Tanzania, Rwanda and Uganda, which have a combined population of perhaps 7,000 individuals. These are concentrated in Tanzania's Mahale and Gombe national parks, Rwanda's Nyungwe Forest, and about 20 Ugandan national parks and other reserves, most notably Budongo, Kibale, Semliki, Maramagambo and Bwindi. Although East Africa's chimps represent less than 3% of the global population, much of what is known about wild chimpanzee society and behaviour stems from the region, in particular the ongoing research projects initiated in Gombe Stream and Mahale Mountain national parks back in the 1960s.

An interesting pattern that emerged from the parallel research projects in these two reserves, situated little more than 100km apart along the shore of Lake Tanganyika, is a variety of social and behavioural differences between their chimp populations. Of the plant species common to both national parks, for instance, as many as 40% of those utilised as a food source by chimps in the one reserve are not eaten by chimps in the other. In Gombe Stream, chimps appear to regard the palmnut as something of a delicacy, but while the same plants grow profusely in Mahale, the chimps there have yet to be recorded eating them. Likewise, the 'termite-fishing' behaviour first recorded by Jane Goodall at Gombe Stream in the 1960s has a parallel in Mahale, where the chimps are often seen 'fishing' for carpenter ants in the trees. But the Mahale chimps have never been recorded fishing for termites, while the Gombe chimps are not known to fish for carpenter ants. Mahale's chimps routinely groom each other with one hand while holding their other hands together above their heads – once again, behaviour that has never been noted at Gombe. More than any structural similarity, more even than any single quirk of chimpanzee behaviour, it's such striking cultural differences – the influence of nurture over nature if you like – that bring home our close genetic kinship with chimpanzees.

GETTING THERE AND AWAY Kibale Forest National Park is most normally approached from Fort Portal using the Kamwenge road. If you're driving from Fort Portal town centre, follow Lugard Road north for about 1km. Immediately before the bridge across the Mpanga River, turn right. You know you're on the right road when after about 500m you pass a hospital to your right (with signposts reading 'blood bank' and 'canteen' perched in intriguingly close proximity). About 12km out of Fort

Portal, you reach a major junction, where you need to fork left (the right fork, incidentally, leads to Lake Nkuruba and Ndali Lodge in the heart of the Kasenda Crater Lake Field). After another 8.5km you pass the signpost for the Lake Nyamirama Camp and then 2.5km later Crater Valley Resort and Chimpanzee Guesthouse, from where it's another 12km to Kanyanchu Campsite and a further 5km to Bigodi.

Public transport to Kanyanchu used to be restricted to two or three dangerously overcrowded pick-up trucks running daily between Kamwenge and Fort Portal. These have recently been supplemented by more regular minibus-taxis, which run back and forth between Bigodi and Fort Portal throughout the day and are far more comfortable and safer than the trucks. Tourists are routinely overcharged by taxi touts, so it's advisable to check what local passengers are paying. There is normally no transport on Sunday. It's likely that when the new Chimp Valley Resort near Kanyanchu gets going it will run a shuttle. Enquire at Andrew's Supermarket in Fort Portal.

A little-used alternative route to Kibale Forest runs north from Mbarara via Ibanda and Kamwenge. This route is covered as far north as Ibanda (see pages 221–3). North of Ibanda the road is unsurfaced but mostly in pretty good condition, and in a private vehicle the drive should take three hours. Using public transport, you'll probably have to change vehicles at Ibanda and Kamwenge and may well have to overnight at one or other town – both possess a few cheap guesthouses. You can easily pick up transport from Kamwenge on to Fort Portal via Kanyanchu. If you're heading this way, you might want to investigate the Mpanga Falls and nearby cycad field between Kamwenge and Ibanda (see box *Mpanga Falls*, opposite).

WHERE TO STAY All of the accommodation listed below lies along the Fort Portal–Kamwenge road within 10km of the tourist centre at Kanyanchu. With private transport, it is also possible to visit the park as a day trip out of Fort Portal or from any of the lodges around the Kabarole Crater Lakes. Assuming that you want to track chimps in the morning (excursions depart at 08.00), allow a good hour to get to Kanyanchu from Ndali Lodge or Fort Portal, and 30 minutes from the Chimpanzee Guesthouse.

Upmarket

🏠 **Mantana Tented Camp** (8 tents) ⅂/f 0414 321552; m 0772 525736/401391; f 0414 320152; e mantana@africaonline.co.ug; www.kimbla-mantana.com. Carved into a patch of secondary forest outside the national park, this excellent bush camp consists of 8 comfortable, s/c standing tents, each in its own private clearing,

with eco-friendly toilets, hot showers and solar electricity. The jungle atmosphere is reinforced by the presence of screeching monkeys, parrots and other forest fauna. To get to the camp, head south from Bigodi towards Kamwenge for 5km, then take the signposted 2km turn-off to the right. *US$175/270 sgl/dbl FB.*

Budget and camping

🏠 **Kibale Primate Lodge** (*5 bandas, tree houses, 8 luxury tents*) Great Lakes Safari ⅂ 0414 267153/0772426368; f 0414 267153; e gls@ utlonline.co.ug or info@safari-uganda.com; www.ugandalodges.com. The long standing park rest camp at Kanyanchu enjoys a superb site surrounded by forest and alive with mysterious rustles and birdcalls during the day and, after dark, washed over by an almost deafening choir of cicadas and

other insects. It has for years been a favourite with budget travellers but this will change following the site's recent allocation to a private concessionaire and the price increases (and rise in standards) that will result. Developments will include the renovation or replacement of five existing bandas and a 'tree house' overlooking the Kanyanchu river swamp, the addition of 2 additional 'tree houses', construction of an eight

Also known as Beaton Falls, this impressive waterfall is formed by the Mpanga River as it tumbles over the rim of the 1,200m Mount Karubaguma some 15km before emptying into Lake George. Estimated to be about 50m high, the waterfall is enclosed by a steep gorge and supports a lush cover of spray forest. A remarkable feature of the gorge's vegetation is the profusion of the cycad *Encephalartos whitelockii*, a species which, so far as I can ascertain, is endemic to this single location. Perhaps the closest thing among trees to living fossils, the cycads are relics of an ancient order of coniferous plants that flourished some 300 to 200 million years ago, with the aptly prehistoric appearance of an overgrown tree fern perched on top of a palm stem up to 10m tall. Many modern species are, like *Encephalartos whitelockii*, extremely localised, and classified as endangered, partly because of their very slow life cycle. The colony in Mpanga Gorge, however, has been described to me as possibly the largest anywhere in Africa.

Undeveloped for tourism and practically unvisited at the time of writing, the Mpanga Falls can be reached with reasonable ease as a day trip from Kibale Forest or as a diversion from the main road between Kamwenge and Ibanda. Mpanga Gorge lies in the remotest corner of QENP. UWA intends to establish a boat trip across Lake George from Kyambura Wildlife Reserve to the Mpanga estuary for the hike to the gorge. In the meantime, it can be reached from Kamwenge Town which can be approached either from Fort Portal (about 1.5 hours' drive on 70km of *murram*) or Mbarara via Ibanda (100km, including 60km of tarmac). The north side of the gorge is another 22km out of Kamwenge. From the roundabout in the middle of the town, head 3/4km south along the Mbarara road then turn right on the hilltop. Drive past the District HQ and take the left fork in each village. The falls are only visible from a rather oblique viewpoint, though I was told that it's possible to cross the river and scramble down to reach the foot of the waterfall on the south side. My ranger and I demurred, mindful that one slip and we'd be floating fast towards a 50m drop down a river swollen by recent rain. I'd strongly suggest a rope would be a good idea if you intend to try this. You should report to the QENP Dura sector office in Kebuko village (18km from the main road) to pay the park entrance fee and obtain a ranger guide (a) to guide you along the last 4km of the route which is unclear and (b) to take you into the national park. It may also be possible to reach the falls from the south via Rwengo trading centre (roughly 2km south of where the road crosses the river) and view the falls from the top of the ridge without entering the park. I'd imagine that it's quite a hike from the road though unless a motorable track exists to eat up a few kilometres.

If you're dependent on public transport, minibus-taxis do cover the Kamwenge–Ibanda road, albeit rather infrequently, but it should be possible to visit the falls as a day trip out of Kamwenge. Alternatively, the owner of Kabarole Tours in Fort Portal knows the waterfall well and can arrange day trips there in a private vehicle.

unit tented camp and a lodge building. Meals will no doubt improve on those currently boiled to order by members of the Bigodi Women's Association. *Rates until August 2007 will be bandas US$11/16 sgl/dbl; s/c banda US$32; treehouse US$21 sgl/dbl; and camping US$6pp. Thereafter new and improved facilities will cost US$60/80 sgl/dbl*

B&B for bandas, US$90/140 sgl/dbl FB for tree houses and US$130/240 FB for s/c tents. You'll still be able to pitch your own tent for around US$6. I'm informed that guests do not pay the UWA entrance fee for an overnight stay but only if they go for activities in the forest.

Shoestring

⌂ **Safari Hotel** m 0772 468113; e comm-tour@infocom.co.ug. This small family-run lodge lies about 3km past Kanyanchu, on the right side of the road to Bigodi. In 2003, I wrote that 'The somewhat basic accommodation might put off the squeamish' but happily it's been renovated following a change in management. The new owner was a Kanyanchu guide before being headhunted to work for Uganda Community Tourism Association and Uganda Heritage Trails. He's now home and using his considerable experience to rejuvenate tourism activities in and around his home village. There's a choice of rooms in the main building, thatched huts and tents. Local and international meals are available and cost Ush3,000–5,000 including fruit salad or pineapple pie. A clean pit toilet and warm basin showers. Bicycles can be hired to explore the area. *US$6 pp per night for rooms/huts/tents, US$3 to pitch your own tent.*

⌂ The new owner of Safari Hotel also offers visitors the chance to stay with his family in his home next to the Magombe Swamp visitors' centre. He can accommodate 3 people inside his house and other guests outside in tents. Billed as a cultural experience, visitors share meals with the family and can assist with food preparation, as well as planting or harvesting crops in the garden. Lunches (Ush7,000) are available. Food is served in a traditional setting eg: barefoot and sitting on mats on the floor and 'includes but is not limited to posho, potatoes, beans, peanuts, green bananas, rice, beef, mixed vegetables (carrots, egg plants, spinach, tomatoes, onions, cabbages, etc) cassava, yams, pumpkins, millet bread and fruits in season (jackfruit, avocado, bananas, papaya, pineapples and mangoes)'. Sounds filling! *US$14 per day FB to stay in the owner's house.*

⌂ **Chimp Valley Resort** m 0772 554602. This new facility is strategically located between Kanyanchu and Magombe Swamp. At the time of writing it's not yet open but by 2007 should be offering camping and rooms. 'CVR' occupies an attractive 30-acre site (already landscaped) bordered by natural forest in the valley below (contiguous with Magombe swamp) which should offer good birdwatching. Enquire at Andrew's Supermarket in Fort Portal for an update. *Rates expected to be US$6 for rooms, less than US$3 for camping.*

ACTIVITIES The most popular activity in the national park is the guided chimp-tracking excursion out of Kanyanchu. Almost as popular is the guided walking trail through the Bigodi Wetland Sanctuary, which is probably better for general monkey viewing and one of the finest birding trails in the country. There is also plenty of potential for unguided exploration in the area, both along the main road through the forest, and around Bigodi trading centre and Kanyanchu Camp. If time is limited, it's advisable to do the activity that most interests you in the morning – this is not only the best time to see chimpanzees, but also when birds are most active.

Guided forest walks A highlight of any visit to Kibale Forest will be the chimp-tracking excursions that leave from Kanyanchu at 08.00 and 14.00 daily at a cost of US$70 for non-residents and US$50 for East African residents *excluding* park entrance. Chimp sightings are not guaranteed on these walks, but the odds of encountering them have improved greatly in recent years, and stand at over 90% in 2006. The chimpanzee community whose territory centres on Kanyanchu has also become far more habituated over the past few years, with the result that visitors often get to within a few metres of them.

Whilst in the forest you can expect to see at least two or three other types of primate, most probably grey-cheeked mangabey and red-tailed monkey. You will hear plenty of birdsong, but it's very difficult to see any birds in the heart of the forest – you're better off looking for them in the rest camp and along the road. The guides are knowledgeable and will identify various medicinal plants, bird calls and animal spoor.

For dedicated chimp enthusiasts or aspiring researchers seeking field experience, a chimpanzee habituation experience which involves staying with the chimps all day with habituators and taking notes on their behaviour. One, two or three days for non-residents/East African residents respectively cost costs US$150/100; US$200/150 and US$300/200. This includes guide fees and park entrance but not accommodation.

Another novelty is the guided night walks with spotlights, which run from 19.30 to 22.00 daily and cost US$10 per person, and offer a good chance of sighting nocturnal primates such as the bushbaby and potto.

Bigodi Wetland Sanctuary This small sanctuary, which protects the Magombe Swamp, adjacent to Bigodi trading centre and immediately outside the national park boundary, is an admirable example of conservation and tourism having a direct benefit at grass-roots level. Run by the Kibale Association for Rural and Environmental Development (KAFRED), all money raised from the trail is used in community projects in Bigodi – it has so far funded the creation of a small local library as well as the construction of a new secondary school in the village. The guided 4.5km circular trail through the swamp is also one of the best guided bird trails in East Africa, as well as offering a realistic opportunity to see up to six different primate species in the space of a few hours.

The trail starts at the KAFRED office on the Fort Portal side of Bigodi. Here you must pay a fee of US$11 per person and will be allocated a guide. Serious birdwatchers should mention their special interest, since some guides are better at identifying birds than others – and if you don't have a field guide and binoculars, then make sure your guide does. Afternoon walks technically start at 15.00 and generally take around three hours, but dedicated birders will need longer and are advised to get going an hour earlier – there are enough guides for you to start whenever you like. For morning walks, it is worth getting to the office as early as you can, or possibly even arranging a dawn start a day in advance. The trail is very muddy in parts, and if you don't have good walking shoes, then you'd do well to hire a pair of gumboots from the KAFRED office – this costs less than US$1. For general monkey viewing, it doesn't matter greatly whether you go in the morning or afternoon, but birders should definitely aim to do the morning walk.

The sanctuary's main attraction to ornithologists is quality rather than quantity. You'd be very lucky to identify more than 40 species in one walk, but most of these will be forest-fringe and swamp specials, and a good number will be west African species at the eastern limit of their range. There are other places in Uganda where these birds can be seen, but not in the company of local guides who know the terrain intimately and can identify even the most troublesome greenbuls by sight or call. One of the birds most strongly associated with the swamp is the great blue turaco, which will be seen by most visitors. Another speciality is the papyrus gonolek, likely to be heard before it is seen, and most frequently encountered along the main road as it crosses the swamp or from the wooden walkway about halfway along the trail. Other regularly seen birds include grey-throated, yellow-billed, yellow-spotted and double-toothed barbets; speckled, yellow-rumped and yellow-throated tinker-barbets; yellowbill; brown-eared woodpecker; blue-throated roller; grey parrot; bronze sunbird; black-crowned waxbill; grey-headed Negro-finch; swamp flycatcher; red-capped and snowy-headed robin-chats; grosbeak and northern brown-throated weavers; and black-and-white casqued hornbill.

Butterflies are abundant in the swamp, and it is also home to sitatunga antelope, serval, a variety of mongoose and most of the primate species recorded in the forest. The red colobus is the most common monkey, often seen at close quarters, but you are also likely to observe red-tailed monkey, L'Hoest's monkey, black-and-white colobus and grey-cheeked mangabey. If you are extremely fortunate, you might even see chimpanzees, since they occasionally visit the swamp to forage for fruit.

Unguided walks Tourists are forbidden to walk along forest paths or in Magombe Swamp without a guide, but they are free to walk unguided elsewhere. Kanyanchu itself is worth a couple of hours' exploration. A colony of Viellot's black weaver nests in the camp, while flowering trees attract a variety of forest sunbirds. You can also expect to see or hear several types of robin and greenbul, often difficult to tell apart unless you get a good look at them (little greenbul and red-capped robin appear to be most common around the camp). A speciality of the camp is the localised red-chested paradise flycatcher, a stunning bird that's very easy to find once you know its call. Other interesting birds I've seen regularly at Kanyanchu are the great blue turaco, hairy-breasted barbet, black-necked weaver and black-and-white casqued hornbill. The short, self-guided grassland trail which circles the camp is good for monkeys.

It is permitted to walk unguided along the stretch of the main road between Fort Portal and Kamwenge as it runs through the forest. The most interesting section on this road is the first few kilometres running north towards Fort Portal from Kanyanchu, where you're almost certain to see a variety of monkeys, genuine forest birds such as Sabine's spinetail, blue-breasted kingfisher and Afep pigeon, as well as butterflies in their hundreds gathered around puddles and streams. The road south from Kanyanchu to Bigodi passes through a variety of habitats – forest patches, swamp and grassland – and is also productive for birds and monkeys.

Sebitoli and the Kihingami Wetlands

Sebitoli lies inside the northern part of Kibale National Park. It is little visited, which is a shame, since it is conveniently located just metres off the main Fort Portal–Kampala road and is far easier to reach than Kanyanchu. A new development, Sebitoli opened in 2002 to help ease tourist pressure on the Kanyanchu sector of the park. It offers similar activities and facilities to Kanyanchu, with the exception of chimpanzee tracking, and is far more accessible for day trippers from Fort Portal. Guided forest walks cost US$10 per person for a full day (excluding UWA entrance fee) and offer a good chance of seeing red and black-and-white colobus and blue and vervet monkey, as well as a varied selection of the (rapidly expanding) local checklist of 236 bird species – chimpanzees are present in the area but not habituated. Guided walking or cycling tours to the nearby Kihingami Wetlands outside the park offer excellent birdwatching and a visit to local tea estates, and leave daily at 07.30 and 15.00, and cost US$10 per person. Sebitoli is also the trailhead for a four-day, 66km hike through the national park to Kanyanchu, with accommodation with overnight stays in simple community-built *bandas* on the forest edge. To date however, just one group has completed the walk since it was established in 2003. It took rather longer than the expected four days while the accommodation tended towards the unacceptable side of 'simple'. If you're up for it, and I'd strongly suggest taking your own tent, it's actually very reasonably priced at US$30 per person per day including entrance fees and guide.

Getting there The Sebitoli Gate lies 100m off the Fort Portal–Kampala road, less than 1km west of the Mpanga Bridge and 15km from Fort Portal. It is simple to reach by either private vehicle or public transport.

Where to stay Sebitoli is convenient to reach from hotels in Fort Portal. Alternatively, the Sebitoli Camp provides three cottages containing two double rooms apiece, as well as a lovely campsite in a forest clearing. Accommodation is good value at US$11/16 single/double and camping costs US$6. Remember though, that you will have to pay the UWA entrance fee as well. Simple meals should be available for around Ush3,000 but it would be sensible to enquire. Plenty of monkeys and birds can be seen in the camp.

The part of western Uganda overshadowed by the Rwenzori is pockmarked with one of the world's densest concentrations of volcanic crater lakes. According to local legend, these lakes were created by Ndahura, the first Bacwezi king, when he retired to the area after abdicating in favour of his son Wamala. Less romantically, the craters are vivid relics of the immense volcanic and geological forces that have moulded the western Ugandan landscape, from the Albertine Rift to the Rwenzori and Virunga mountains. The lakes are conventionally divided into four main groups: the Fort Portal Cluster immediately northwest of the eponymous town, the Kasenda Cluster to the west of Kibale Forest National Park, Katwe Cluster in part of the Rift Valley protected within Queen Elizabeth National Park, and the Bunyaruguru Cluster straddling the Rift Valley Escarpment southeast of QENP.

The most accessible and extensive of these crater lake fields is the Ndali or Kasenda Cluster, which formed about 10,000 years ago and consists of about 60 permanent and seasonal freshwater lakes centred on Kasenda, Rweetera, Rwaihamba and Kabata trading centres, some 20–30km south of Fort Portal. The Kasenda lakes are all different in character and most are very beautiful, while the lush surrounding countryside, rattling with birds, monkeys and butterflies, provides limitless opportunities for casual exploration below the majestic backdrop of the glacial peaks of the Rwenzori. Despite this, the Kasenda area has only recently started to catch on with travellers, in large part as a result of the erection of a few excellent community campsites as well as the sumptuous Ndali Lodge. For any visitor looking to spend a few inexpensive days rambling and hiking in beautiful unspoilt surrounds, it is difficult to think of any part of Uganda as suitable as the Kasenda area.

GETTING THERE AND AWAY The Kasenda Crater Lakes are usually approached from Fort Portal, following the road to Kibale Forest National Park for 12km to Kasisi, where there is a major fork in the road. If you're heading to the more easterly lakes, then take the left fork at Kasisi, as you would for Kibale Forest National Park, and you'll pass Lake Nyamirima Campsite and then CVK Resort and Chimpanzee Guesthouse after 8.5km and 11km respectively. Any minibus-taxi or pick-up truck heading to Kamwenge or Bigodi can drop you at these places.

To reach the main cluster of lakes, you need to fork right at Kasisi for Kasenda trading centre, passing Lake Nkuruba, Rwaihamba and Kabata/Ndali Lodge after 8km, 10km and 13km respectively. At least three pick-up trucks to Rwaihamba and Kasenda leave Fort Portal daily, from the same stand as transport to Kibale Forest market. Generally one truck will leave in the early morning, one at around noon, and one at 15.00, though there is a lot more transport on market days (Mondays and Thursdays). Vehicles heading to Rwaihamba can drop you at Lake Nkuruba Nature Reserve, but stop 2km short of Kabata. *Boda-bodas* are available at Rwaihamba.

Using private transport, the crater lakes can also be approached from Rubona trading centre on the main Kasese–Fort Portal road, following a dirt road branching east through Rwakenzi and Murukomba to arrive in Kabata after 16km. During the rainy season, this road will probably be suitable for 4x4 vehicles only.

If you're driving in a 4x4 from Ndali Lodge or Lake Nkuruba to Kibale Forest for the morning chimp-tracking excursion, you can either go back through Kasisi or use one of two short-cuts between the Kasenda and Kamwenge roads: an 8.5km dirt and murram track between Rwaihamba and CVK via Isunga or a 5km dirt track between Lake Nkuruba and Rweetera. Both shortcuts may be impassable after rain, so seek local advice with regard to the best route.

Fort Portal NDALI-KASENDA CRATER LAKES

10

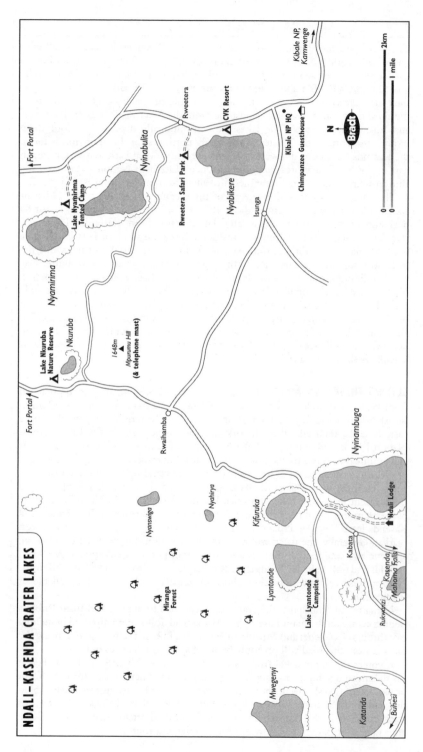

NDALI–KASENDA CRATER LAKES

Fort Portal

Nyamirima

Lake Nkuruba
Nature Reserve

Nkuruba

1648m
Mpuramu Hill
(& telephone mast)

Fort Portal

Rwaihamba

Nyamirima

Lake Nyamirima
Tented Camp

Nyinabulita

Rweetera

Rweetera Safari Park

CVK Resort

Nyabikere

Isunga

Kibale NP HQ

Chimpanzee Guesthouse

*Kibale NP,
Kamwenge*

Nyanswiga

Nyahirya

Miranga
Forest

Mwegenyi

Kifuruka

Lyantonde

Lake Lyantonde
Campsite

Kabata

Nyinambuga

Ndali Lodge

Rukwanzi

*Kasenda,
Mahoma Falls*

Buhesi

Katanda

Bradt

N

0   2km
0   1 mile

Kabarole Tours runs a scheduled day tour taking in at least four crater lakes and Mahoma Falls every Saturday and Sunday. This leaves Fort Portal at 08.00, returning at 17.00, and costs US$20 per person. Unscheduled shared tours to the crater lakes cost US$80.

WHERE TO STAY
Upmarket

Ndali Lodge (8 cottages) m 0772 221309/487673; e ndali@bushnet.net; www.ndali.co.uk. Situated about 1km from Kabata trading centre by road, the family-run Ndali Lodge is one of Uganda's most widely praised upmarket retreats. It has a stunning location on a magnificent dual viewpoint high on the rim of Lake Nyinambuga. While the veranda overlooks this lake, the rooms and lawns face additional crater lakes set in undulating farmland that extends towards the Rwenzori. In clear weather the snow peaks are visible, as are Lake George and the Rift Valley floor at Queen Elizabeth National Park. The airy and tastefully decorated lounge and dining area, set in

colourful flowering gardens, have something of an English country-house ambience, with a good library and superb candlelit home-cooked four-course dinners. The spacious s/c cottages have been recently refurbished, with piping hot baths and a private veranda. In addition to exploring Kibale Forest and the other crater lakes, visitors to Ndali are welcome to look around the active coffee farm on which it lies and to follow a lovely walking trail through the property. A steep trail leads down a jetty where you can take a boat out on Lake Nyinambuga. A swimming pool is imminent. From June 2007, cottages cost *US$210/285 sgl/dbl FB, with a discount offered to Uganda residents.*

Budget

Chimpanzee Forest Guesthouse m 0772 486415. This lovely new guesthouse lies on a hillside close to the Kibale road just beyond the Kibale National Park Headquarters. Set in a beautiful garden, it's essentially a low-budget equivalent of the Ndali Lodge, insomuch as it's a homely facility owned and run by the Ugandan descendants of a British tea planter named Switzer. When he built the main house for himself and his Mutoro wife in the 1950s, he included a bright and airy lounge to enjoy fabulous views beyond a lawny garden and across the tea plantation towards Kibale Forest. The style of its furniture suggests that it came with the house, while the room abounds with old black-and-white photographs and books. I gather the meals could be improved upon – Ush6000 (with meat) and Ush4000 (veg) – but it's early days yet; in such a genuinely lovely setting it's easy to be gracious! A range of guided walks are offered. *US$11/19/22 sgl/dbl/twin s/c rooms excluding b/fast (Ush2,000 extra for tea and omelettes). US$16 for a thatched banda (sleeps up to 3) and less than US$3 for camping.*

Rest Camp Lake Nyamirima m 0782 532533; e highland@imul.com. This lovely site high above the cliff-and-forest-lined Lake Nyamirima (previously occupied by an under-utilised community-run campground) has been taken over by the management of the Overland Camp at Lake Bunyonyi (near Kabale). Food is available. *US$13/19*

sgl/dbl for furnished tents and you can pitch your own tent for US$2.

CVK Resort m 0772 492274; e cvk.resortbeachlodge@infocom.co.ug; www.visituganda.com/cvk.htm. The long-standing Crater Valley Kibale Forest Resort – to give it its full name – has an idyllic position on the lushly vegetated rim of Lake Nyabikere, and it's conveniently located for chimp tracking in Kibale Forest since it lies alongside the Fort Portal–Kamwenge road just before the Kibale National Park HQ. The birdlife around the lake is excellent – more than 100 species recorded including African grey parrot, pygmy goose, fish eagle and an array of colourful sunbirds – and red-tailed monkey and black-and-white colobus are resident. Said somewhat improbably to be 400m deep, Nyabikere means 'lake of frogs' and you'll usually hear plenty of these croaking through the night. Close-by attractions include the Isunga Hot Springs and a small waterfall on the Nyabikere River. Location notwithstanding, CVK seems a bit tired and lacking in character these days and it's certainly overpriced compared with newer, fresher options nearby. Accommodation is in a terraced line of rather ordinary s/c dbl rooms and some tatty *bandas*. A variety of very basic meals is served, with prices starting at around Ush4,000, and cold beers and sodas are available. There's an MTN payphone and craft shop on-site. *US$27/32 twin/dbl, bandas US$8 pp (not s/c), camping US$4 pp.*

Shoestring and camping

⌂ **Lake Nkuruba Nature Reserve** m 0772 400101.
Protecting a stunning jungle-fringed crater lake
immediately east of the Kasenda road 2km before
Rwaihamba, this well-maintained community-run
reserve and rest camp (proceeds fund a local
primary school) is a perfect base from which to
explore the crater lakes on a budget – indeed, many
travellers end up spending a week or longer enjoying
its laidback atmosphere. There is accommodation in
basic 4-bed *bandas* above the crater rim, while
camping is permitted. Shared facilities are provided;
flush toilets are under construction. There is a
solitary dbl *banda* set on the edge of Lake Nkuruba
Good meals are available for around Ush6,000, using
fresh local produce grown in the reserve's private
vegetable garden, and self-catering is also permitted
(basic foodstuffs can be bought at nearby Rwaihamba
on the market days of Monday and Thursday). Beers
and sodas are sold on-site, boiled water is provided
to campers, and paraffin lamps can be hired for a
nominal fee. Other facilities include mountain-bike
hire and a short hiking trail. Guided walks to
Mahoma Falls, 'Top of the World', etc. are offered at
reasonable rates. Visitors (as opposed to guests) are
charged Ush5,000 (non-resident) and Ush3,000
(resident) to visit the site. *US$6 pp for bandas,
US$17 for Lake Nkuruba banda for 1 or 2 people,
camping US$2.70 pp (add US$1 for tent hire).*

▲ **Lake Lyantonde Campsite** m 0772 562513;
e lakelyantonde@yahoo.com. Situated about 1km
from Kabata and 5km south of the Lake Nkuruba
Nature Reserve, the more basic and less publicised
but equally attractive campsite on the rim of Lake
Lyantonde also functions as a community project
aimed at conserving the area's natural attractions.
There are basic *bandas* and camping (no tents
available for hire) and local meals and drinks are
available. Swimming is safe and guided walks to the
Mahoma Falls and other local attractions are offered
at Ush2,000–6,000 pp, as is a 2hr traditional dance
show for Ush20,000 per party. *US$6/8 sgl/dbl
bandas, camping US$2 pp.*

▲ **Rweetera Safari Park and Tourist Camping Centre**
A secluded campsite on Lake Nyabikere, close to the
CVK Resort. Meals, firewood and cooking facilities are
available. The staff organise guided walks into the
nearby forest and to several other sites of interest
in the area. A marshy dormant crater lies about
100m from the camping ground, and there is
another empty crater about 10mins' walk away. To
reach the site, follow a turn-off signposted for
Rweetera Fish Project, roughly 200m south of
Rweetera trading centre. *Camping US$3 pp.*

⌂ **Planet Rwigo Beach Resort** This curiously named
development is apparently to be found beside the
remote Lake Kasenda at the southern end of the
crater field. I gather, as one would expect, that
facilities are on the basic side but I'd be grateful to
hear more.

EXPLORING THE CRATER LAKES There are few organised activities in the area, and
many people will be quite content to spend their time idling in the blissful
surrounds of their lodge or campsite. For those who want to explore, part of the
joy of this area is that it's largely up to the individual traveller to take the initiative.
Kabarole Tours will be able to fill you in on new developments in the area, and can
give advice to walkers and hikers. Serious walkers would do well to get hold of the
1:50,000 maps of Kuhenge (map no 66/2) and Fort Portal (map no 56/4), which are
sold by the Department of Lands and Surveys in Entebbe.

Around CVK Resort If you're based at CVK Resort, you're rather isolated from the
main cluster of lakes. The trail encircling Lake Nyabikere is certainly worthwhile:
you should see monkeys as well as a variety of birds – among the more interesting
species found around the lake are Ross's and great blue turaco, pygmy goose, little
bittern and night heron. Two more crater lakes, Nyinabulita and Nyamirima, lie
next to each other roughly 2km north of the resort. They can be reached with ease
by following the road back towards Fort Portal for 2.5km then turning left on to
the motorable track signposted for the Lake Nyamirima Camp.

Hiking between lakes Nyabikere and Nkuruba A very attractive and easy walk,
wherever you are based, is along the motorable track which crosses between the
Kamwenge and Kasenda roads. The track leaves the Kamwenge road at Rweetera

trading centre, roughly 100m north of the derelict tea factory, and it emerges on the Kasenda road a few hundred metres south of Lake Nkuruba. The walk takes about two hours, and on the way you'll see lakes Nyamirima, Nyinabulita and Nyabikere. There are great views over the crater lake region from Mpurumu Hill to the south of the track.

Lake Nkuruba and surrounds Lake Nkuruba, though small, is very beautiful, enclosed by a steep forest-lined crater in which red-tailed monkey, red colobus and black-and-white colobus are resident, together with at least 100 species of bird (a regularly updated checklist is pinned up in the office). With a bit of luck, you will also make acquaintance with the solitary hippo that divides its time between Nkuruba and a couple of nearby lakes. The water here is considered free of bilharzia, so unless the itinerant hippo is in close attendance, there's no obstacle to swimming. That said, Ndali Lodge management claim (very honestly I must say) that there is bilharzia in their own lake. If one can catch it here then this rather overturns the accepted means of transmission and usual precautions ie: leaping into deep water off jetties rather than paddling in muddy shallows.

Based at Lake Nkuruba, you're well positioned to explore the main cluster of lakes, including those at Kabata (see below). Closer to Lake Nkuruba, the tiny Lake Nyahirya on the fringe of the Miranga Forest can be reached by walking south along the road to Kabata, passing through Rwaihamba trading centre after 2km, then about 1km further there's a sharp westward kink in the road. The lake lies 500m west of this kink – if you're uncertain, ask in Rwaihamba for directions. The Miranga Forest could also be worth exploring, and a second crater lake, Nyanswiga, lies 1km directly to the north of Nyahirya. Rwaihamba hosts a large, colourful market on Mondays and Thursdays.

Kabata This small junction village, which lies 5km south of Lake Nkuruba by road, is the site of Ndali Lodge and the Lake Lyantonde Campsite. Coming from Nkuruba, two more crater lakes are first glimpsed about 500m before Kabata. On the left side of the road, Lake Nyinambuga – named for its mildly saline water – is one of the largest lakes in the area, enclosed by steep cliffs on which stands Ndali Lodge. On the right side of the road, the smaller Lake Kifuruka is one of the prettiest lakes in the region, enclosed by riparian forest and covered in floating water lilies. A troop of black-and-white colobus is evidently resident in the area, and often seen from the road, as are Ross's and great blue turaco, African grey parrot, yellow-billed duck and pygmy goose.

Turn right into the Buhesi road at Kabata and after about 500m you'll see Lake Lyantonde to your right – a fairly small lake surrounded by a thickly vegetated crater, reminiscent in appearance of Lake Nkuruba. About 2km further towards Buhesi, the road skirts past lakes Katanda and Mwegenyi. Further along the Buhesi Road, the Kabata Cave is large enough to hold 20 people.

Mahoma Falls From Kabata, you can also visit the Mahoma Falls, where the Mahoma River surges with more than a little conviction over a series of large boulders into a forested valley. Below the waterfall, you can swim in the river – it flows at a velocity that should negate any fears about bilharzia, and the crisp water is a welcome treat after a sweaty walk. Guides are available for about Ush3,000 from the Lake Lyantonde Campsite. To reach the waterfall, follow the motorable track leading west from the centre of Kabata, passing through grasslands and cane fields for about 2km before climbing to Rusona, a small village church situated on a rise above a forested crater to the right and the northern extension of Lake Mwamba to the left. If you have a vehicle, park it at Rusona, from where it's about

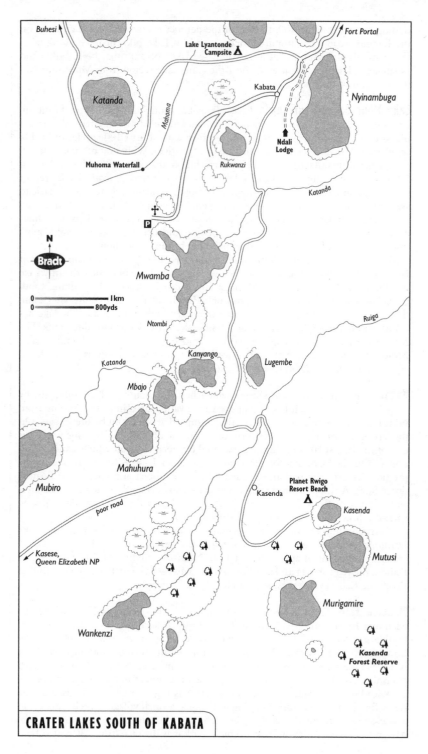

CRATER LAKES SOUTH OF KABATA

1km to the waterfall along a footpath that passes through cultivated fields and rural homesteads before the final steep descent to the river. About 2km from Rusona – you'll need a local guide to find it – a small but immeasurably deep crater called Mwitampungu (literally, the place that kills birds) is said locally to suck in any bird that flies directly over it.

Towards Kasenda Three further crater lakes can easily be seem from the 6km road running south from Kabata to Murukomba. About 1.5km past the main junction in Kabata, Lake Rukwanzi lies only 100m to the right of the road, but is invisible from it. Another 1.5km further, also on the right, Lake Mwamba is one of the largest lakes in the Kasenda region, with an irregular outline suggesting that it fills two or three different collapsed calderas. Finally, another 1.5km towards Murukomba, the stunning Lake Lugembe lies at the base of a very deep and sheer-sided steep crater, no more than 25m left of the road, but also invisible from it. Directly opposite Lugembe, the larger Lake Kanyango lies within 200m of the road, also hidden by a cliff.

Everybody has their saturation point, even when it comes to crater lakes, but a group of five lakes form an arc running about 2km south of Kasenda trading centre, which lies 2km south of Murukomba. Unless you have private transport, you'll have to base yourself in Kasenda to explore the lakes further south. There's no accommodation here, but you should be able to pitch a tent somewhere around the trading centre with permission. You could cover lakes Kasenda, Mutusi and Murigamire in a circular day walk of roughly 6km southeast of Kasenda trading centre. More ambitiously, you could continue west from Lake Murigamire to Lake Wankenzi and an adjoining forested crater, a circular walk of roughly 10–12km starting and ending at Kasenda.

THE SEMLIKI VALLEY

The magnificently scenic Semliki Valley lies at the base of the Albertine Rift to the west of Fort Portal, where it is hemmed in by the Rwenzori foothills to the south, Lake Albert to the north, and the Semliki River along the border with the DRC. The northern Rwenzori foothills divide the Semliki Valley into two geographically discrete and ecologically divergent sectors. Stretching northeast of the mountains through to the marshy southern shores of Lake Albert lies the moist woodland and savanna of the Semliki Wildlife Reserve. The northwestern footslopes, by contrast, give way to a tract of steamy lowland jungle protected within the Semliki National Park, whose affinities with the contiguous Congolese rainforest are reflected by the presence of dozens of bird species and other creatures found nowhere else in Uganda.

The largest town in the Semliki Valley is Bundibugyo, which lies 72km from Fort Portal along a breathtaking dirt road that hugs the steep contours of the Rwenzori for about 50km – offering spectacular views to Lake Albert and the Semliki River – before it descends the western footslopes to form the eastern boundary of Semliki National Park. At Karugutu trading centre, some 30km out of Fort Portal, a signposted right fork runs northeast from the Bundibugyo road to the Semliki Wildlife Reserve and Ntoroko, a fishing village on the shores of Lake Albert.

In the mid-to-late 1990s, the Semliki Valley was subjected to regular attacks by the Allied Democratic Front (ADF), a small but brutally sadistic band of DRC-based guerrillas whose precise identity and agenda are both open to conjecture. The Semliki Wildlife Reserve remained operational throughout this period of instability, but the national park – situated closer to the Congolese border – was

10

One of the first Europeans to enter the Semliki Valley was Dr Albert Cook, who visited it on foot in 1898, an experience he would later describe vividly in his memoir *Ugandan Memories*:

The ground descended abruptly at our feet, and we looked out over a vast plain. Beneath us the Semliki River twisted in and out across the plain like a large snake. Beyond to the west was the commencement of Stanley's Great Forest. It looked like a dark green carpet, stretching away until it was lost in the haze... After a short rest, we began to descend from the summit of the pass into the Semliki Valley. Down, down, down for seven thousand feet, we had to leap like goats from rock to rock, and it was with bleeding fingers that we reached the bottom, for there were plenty of thorns.

At the bottom ... was a village of the Bwamba, hill tribes who inhabit the western slopes of the Rwenzoris. The village was composed of little beehive shaped huts, each with its own porch. The people were splendid specimens ... stalking about with spears in their hands ... They file their front teeth to a point, and dress their hair very carefully, frizzing it into long curls like a poodle dog. They wear brass rings on their arms and legs [and] nothing but a wisp of cloth passed between the legs and secured by a girdle.

In the afternoon we went to the celebrated hot springs ... Emerging from the long grass we suddenly came on a belt of rich tropical foliage ... paved with slabs of rock. From these, great sheets of steam were rising ... all along the upper edge were springs of boiling water, bubbling furiously ... in front were clouds of steam. In some of the holes, we boiled plantains, in other potatoes, and in a third we stuck our kettle.

forced to close between 1997 and 1998. Security in the Semliki Valley has improved greatly since the late 1990s, and there is no substantial risk to travellers at the time of writing, but so long as the ADF remains active on the Congolese side of the border, it would probably be wise to ask about security before heading in this direction. Travelling along the Bundibugyo road after dark is not recommended.

FURTHER READING *Uganda's Great Rift Valley* by Andrew Roberts provides a chapter on Semliki National Park and a couple of pages on Toro-Semliki Wildlife Reserve.

SEMLIKI WILDLIFE RESERVE This 545km^2 sanctuary, Uganda's oldest wildlife reserve, was originally gazetted in 1932 as the Toro Game Reserve, and is still marked as such on many maps. It lies to the northeast of the Bundibugyo road, extending to Ntoroko on the southern shore of Lake Albert. The dominant vegetation type is open acacia-combretum woodland and grassy savanna, interspersed with patches of borassus palm forest, significant belts of riparian woodland along the main watercourses, as well as some extensive swamps towards Lake Albert. The reserve itself is topographically unremarkable, set at a relatively low altitude of around 600–700m above sea level, but on a clear day the setting is truly awesome, with the sheer Rift Valley Escarpment rising sharply from the eastern shore of Lake Albert, the 2,500m-high Congolese Blue Mountains on the western horizon, and the mighty glacial peaks of the Rwenzori visible to the north.

In its pre-Amin heyday, the vast geographic scale of Semliki Wildlife Reserve was complemented by some of East Africa's most prolific plains game. More than 10,000 Uganda kob were resident in the reserve, together with large herds of Jackson's hartebeest, Defassa waterbuck, elephant and buffalo. As for predators, the hunter Brian Herne wrote of Semliki: 'The area is famous for the number of massive maned lions that live there. I have never seen so many big lions in other parts of Africa... Leopard were numerous throughout... None of the cats in Semliki had to work very hard for their dinner; they could simply lie in the grass and throw out a paw, for some animal or another was always about.' Isolated from similar habitats by various mountain ranges, Semliki was also at one point mooted as the site of a bizarre scheme to introduce tigers to Uganda for commercial hunting purposes. Six pairs of tiger were imported to Entebbe to be released into the reserve, before the scheme was abandoned as potentially detrimental to the indigenous predators.

Semliki's wildlife was heavily poached during the civil war, and it only really started to recover from the slaughter following the opening of Semliki Safari Lodge in 1997. Uganda kob, the population of which plummeted to below 1,000 in the early 1990s, today number about 8,000, and are most commonly seen in areas of short grass, along with pairs of common reedbuck. Roughly 1,000 buffalo, up from about 50 in the early 1990s, are also resident, along with small numbers of elephant and waterbuck, but they are not seen on an everyday basis and tend to be rather skittish when approached by a vehicle. Primates are well represented, with black-and-white colobus, olive baboon and red-tailed and vervet monkey all regularly observed in gallery forest close to the lodge and along the Wasa and the Mugiri and their tributaries. Leopards are still common and quite often spotted on night drives, while lion – at one point poached to local extinction – are gradually recolonising the area, though they are more often heard than seen. A community of roughly 40 chimpanzees resident in the Mugiri River Forest is in the process of being habituated by volunteers from the University of Indiana, and guided forest walks offer a roughly 25% chance of chimp sightings as well as the possibility of encountering the localised forest race of elephant.

For the average tourist, Semliki is arguably more attractive for its vast scenery and wild, untrammelled atmosphere than for its game viewing, which doesn't really compare to Murchison Falls or Queen Elizabeth national parks. But it is highly alluring to birdwatchers, with 350–400 species recorded. Game drives on the open plains are likely to yield Abyssinian ground hornbill and a variety of raptors, while areas of rank vegetation are good for marsh tchagra and African crake. The Mugiri River Forest is regarded to be the best site in Uganda for the elusive leaflove, and also hosts a variety of other localised forest species. Night drives are good for owls, as well as the improbable pennant-winged and standard-winged nightjars.

Boat trips on Lake Albert, offered by the lodge or by private fishermen at Ntoroko, are particularly worthwhile. For birdwatchers, this is one of the most reliable sites in Uganda for shoebill, as well as a profusion of more common waterbirds and the dazzling red-throated bee-eater, which forms large breeding colonies on sandbanks near Ntoroko between December and March. Less ornithologically minded visitors are usually boated to the base of the unexpectedly impressive Nkusi Falls, which – like a smaller replica of Murchison Falls – explode through a cleft in the Rift Valley Escarpment before tumbling noisily into the lake.

Entrance fees of US$20/25/30 for non-residents and US$15/20/25 for residents are levied for visits of one/two/three days' duration.

Getting there and away

The turn-off to the Semliki Valley Wildlife Reserve is signposted 30km along the Bundibugyo road at the small trading centre of Karugutu, halfway between Kichwamba and Itojo. A 40km-long road connects Karugutu to Ntoroko on Lake Albert, running right through the heart of the reserve. Semliki Safari Lodge lies about 25km down this road, about two hours'

The community of roughly 70 Bambuti Pygmies based at Ntandi, about 5km past Sempaya along the Bundibugyo road, are more closely affiliated to the Basua Pygmies of the Congolese Basin than to the Batwa of Kigezi and Rwanda. I first visited them more than a decade ago, an occasion described in previous editions of this book as follows: 'One of the most depressing experiences I've had in Africa. Far from offering an insight into another lifestyle and culture, the Ntandi Pygmies are basically a bunch of shorter-than-average people who spend the day hanging around their banana-leaf huts, smoking dope, drinking and waiting for the next bunch of tourists to arrive. I've yet to meet anyone who left these people without feeling disturbed.' And many visitors who followed in my footsteps weren't merely disturbed, but also hassled, ripped off or stolen from, culminating in an incident in the mid 1990s in which an aid worker from Fort Portal was stabbed in the hand.

What I didn't realise then is that this aggression towards tourists was a manifestation of a deeper resentment against the sort of prejudice discussed in the box *Batwa Pygmies*, pages 244–5 – among their neighbours, the Bambuti are regarded to be dirty ne'er-do-wells, stigmatised by such unacceptable customs as eating snakes and monkeys, growing and smoking marijuana, and the women walking around topless. Until recently, tourist fees supposedly paid to the Ntandi community were regularly confiscated by non-Bambuti guides (something that still reportedly occurs at certain Batwa communities in Kigezi) and the Bambuti, like the Batwa, were forbidden to use their traditional hunting grounds after Semliki National Park was gazetted in 1991. So far as I can ascertain, relations between the Bambuti and visiting tourists remained tense until as recently as 2001.

So it's pleasing to report that when we returned to Ntandi in late 2002, our worst expectations were totally confounded. If our visit is representative, the small community now genuinely welcomes tourists, and it really couldn't be friendlier or more hassle-free once a fee has been agreed. The reason for this seems to boil down to increased political empowerment in the past couple of years. The self-styled 'king' of the Ugandan Bambuti,

drive from Fort Portal – take the first right turn (signposted) after crossing the Wasa River Bridge.

If you're using public transport, plenty of trucks and the occasional minibus run directly between Fort Portal and Ntoroko on most days. Alternatively, any vehicle heading to Bundibugyo can drop you at Karugutu, from where it's usually easy enough to catch a lift on one of the pick-up trucks that transport fish from Ntoroko. There's a good chance you'll see some game from the road. Once at Ntoroko, there is accommodation and camping, you can walk freely in the immediate vicinity of the village, and a boat trip on to the lake – where you should encounter hippos and shoebills – will probably work out at around US$20 with local fishermen. Note that overloaded passenger boats do ply erratically along the lakeshore from Ntoroko all the way north to Butiaba and Wanseko, but accidents are commonplace and often result in passengers drowning.

⌂ Where to stay
Upmarket
⌂ **Semliki Safari Lodge** ☎ 0414 251182; m 0772 489497; f 0414 344653; e tusc@ africaonline.co.ug; www.safariuganda.com. Built on the site of an older, eponymous hunting lodge that was gutted in the early 1980s, Semliki Safari Lodge is widely and justifiably regarded to be the most luxurious bush retreat in Uganda. Accommodation is in large thatched tents with 4-poster beds, Persian carpets, hand-carved furniture, eco-friendly log bathroom and a private veranda. The main lodge is

Geoffrey Nzito, talked enthusiastically about a local teacher who is voluntarily schooling the whole community in English – most of the elders are now at upper primary school level – which has allowed them to deal directly with tourists rather than through the medium of crooked guides. The Bambuti's relationship with the national park has also improved greatly following a recent concession allowing them limited rights to fish and hunt within its boundaries (the main restriction being against hunting larger mammals such as elephant, buffalo and chimps) and to barter the forest produce with other local communities. According to the king, they are also the only 60 people in Uganda who are legally permitted to grow and smoke marijuana – the latter they do constantly and with great enthusiasm, through bubble pipes, especially – and somewhat incredibly – before they go hunting.

It's not all roses for the Bambuti by any means. The men complain that while the Batwa women are regularly impregnated by outsiders, partially due to the belief that sleeping with one cures certain diseases, they themselves have little hope of finding a partner outside their own community due to their unacceptable customs. And this interbreeding means that the genetic stock of Uganda's most ancient inhabitants is rapidly being diluted – already, the average height of its teenagers far exceeds that of the adults. The community does, however, remain strongly committed to its hunter-gatherer ways – they recently built a village with 'proper' houses, which they quickly abandoned in favour of their own simple traditional huts. I do still feel, as I did ten years earlier, that the nature of tourist visits to the Bambuti veers uncomfortably close to reducing them to a freak show exhibit – look at the short people, shake their hand, snap a photograph, and off we go. It would, I think, be more edifying for all parties were the community to be encouraged to offer visitors guided walks into the national park and to show off their consummate knowledge and mastery of the rainforest and its fauna and flora. But even as things stand, our most recent visit to Ntandi was a highly instructive and positive experience, tempered only by the sad consciousness of the uncertain future faced by the Bambuti and their ancestral lifestyle.

built of stone, log and thatch using materials recycled from the original lodge, and decorated in a manner that emphasises its earthy, organic, open-air feel. Facilities include a large swimming-pool area overlooking a stretch of riverine forest inhabited by black-and-white colobus and vervet monkeys. The 3-course meals and full b/fasts are superb, with freshly baked bread and real Uganda coffee served every morning. A full range of guided activities is offered: game drives, night drives, birdwatching walks in the adjacent forest, chimp tracking in a patch of forest 6km away, boat trips on Lake Albert and day trips to the forested Semliki National Park. Accommodation is FB, with a discount of around 25% offered to East Africa residents pp sharing. Activities are extra, and range in price from US$10 pp for a forest walk, US$30 pp for a night drive, to US$220 for a party of up to 4 people for a full-day motorboat trip on Lake Albert. *US$220/330 sgl/dbl FB.*

Shoestring and camping There are least three small lodges in **Ntoroko**, all decidedly scruffy but charging no more than Ush5,000 for a single room. Far more attractive, the **UWA campsite** (US$6 pp) lies on a sandbank overlooking the lake about 500m from the village.

SEMLIKI NATIONAL PARK The 220km² Semliki National Park was gazetted in October 1993, prior to which it was more widely known as the Bwamba Forest, a name you'll come across regularly in old ornithological literature about Uganda. Situated within the Albertine Rift at an average altitude of around 700m, the national park is bounded to the northwest by the Semliki River, which runs along the Congolese border into Lake Albert, and to the east by the Fort Portal–Bundibugyo road. It protects a practically unspoilt tropical lowland forest, essentially an easterly extension of the vast Ituri Forest that stretches all the way from Uganda to the Congo River. Separated only by the Semliki River, the two forests form an ecological continuum, for which reason Semliki National Park harbours an exciting range of lowland forest species associated with the Congo Basin. At least 300 species of butterflies have been identified in the park, including 46 species of forest swallowtails (75% of the national total), together with 235 moth species.

Considering its small size, Semliki National Park protects an extraordinary faunal diversity. It is of particular interest to birdwatchers: 435 bird species have been recorded, including a high proportion of forest birds and roughly 45 species that occur nowhere else in Uganda (see box *Semliki's special birds*, opposite). For amateur ornithologists, Semliki is not only certain to throw up a clutch of 'lifers' – it also offers a faint but real possibility of a brand new East African record. Three of the seven 'recent records' depicted in Stevenson and Fanshawe's 2002 East African field guide were discovered in Semliki during the 1990s, namely Congo serpent-eagle, grey-throated rail and black-throated coucal.

Only 53 mammal species have been recorded in Semliki, though the patchy look of the existing checklist (it includes no nocturnal primates or small carnivores, and just one species of duiker) suggests that it is far from complete. Of the listed species, 11 occur nowhere else in Uganda, including the pygmy antelope, two types of flying squirrel and six types of bat. Semliki is the only East African stronghold for the peculiar water chevrotain, a superficially duiker-like relic of an ancient ungulate family that shares several structural features with pigs and is regarded to be ancestral to all modern-day antelopes, deers, cows and giraffes. Persistent rumours that Semliki harbours an isolated population of eastern lowland gorilla probably have no factual foundation, but the national park does support a healthy chimpanzee population, not as yet habituated to humans, as well as seven other diurnal primates: red-tailed, vervet, blue and De Brazza's monkeys, grey-cheeked mangabey, olive baboon and black-and-white colobus. Other large mammals recorded in the park include elephant, bushpig, buffalo, sitatunga and white-bellied duiker. Hippos and crocodiles are common along the Semliki River.

The most popular attraction in Semliki National Park is the cluster of hot springs at Sempaya, which can be reached via a short walking trail. Longer guided walks, taking the best part of a day, can also be arranged at Sempaya, as can overnight hikes deep into the forest. Roughly 5km from Sempaya, in the direction of Bundibugyo, the Pygmy village at Ntandi is also popular with travellers, and a far less disturbing experience than it was a few years back. Ntandi is also the site of the park headquarters, but any unspecified references to the park office in the following information can be taken as referring to the office at Sempaya.

Visits of one/two/three days' duration are charged at US$20/25/30 for non-resident tourists and US$15/20/25 for residents. Unless you are a keen bird- or primate-watcher, the main attraction of this national park is a visit to the hot springs, so, as this doesn't take much more than an hour, the entrance fee might be considered rather steep – especially as you'll have to pay an further US$10 each for a guide to accompany you down to the springs. To get your money's worth you'd need to be prepared to walk some of the additional trails. No park entrance fee is charged for driving or walking along the main road to Bundibugyo, which forms the southern boundary of the park.

Getting there and away The park office and campsite at Sempaya are clearly signposted on opposite sides of the Semliki road, roughly 52km (two to three hours' drive) from Fort Portal. For details of driving there, or getting there by public transport, see *Bundibugyo, Getting there and away*, page 345.

The main attraction of the road to the Semliki National Park is its scenery. Travelling by public transport you'll probably be too busy hanging on for dear life to take much notice of anything outside the vehicle, let alone sit back and enjoy the views. For this reason, many travellers organise private transport to Semliki National Park, visiting it as a day trip from Fort Portal. It's best to form a group and organise a *matatu* through Kabarole Tours (see *Chapter 14*, pages 318–19). You could try to fix a private deal with a driver at the bus station, but Kabarole Tours will be more reliable, and the last time I tried I couldn't find anybody who was prepared to undercut their price. They charge Ush130,000 for the vehicle plus fuel (an estimated Ush35,000 to the Hot Springs and back).

Where to stay Aside from the basic guesthouse and campsite listed below, there is no accommodation within the national park. It can realistically be visited as a day trip from Fort Portal or Semliki Safari Lodge in the Semliki Wildlife Reserve – allow about 90 minutes each way for the drive, longer after heavy rain – but this is likely to prove frustrating to serious birdwatchers, as they'll miss out on the peak avian activity of the early morning and late afternoon. Reasonable self-contained rooms are available in Bundibugyo, only 20km past Sempaya (see page 345).

Kirimia Guesthouse Basic local lodge in the village of Kirimia, which lies on the forested banks of the river of the same name, 100m from the start of the Kirimia Trail to the Semliki River, and about 10km from Sempaya in the direction of Bundibugyo. Basic food is usually available. *Rooms US$3.*

National Park Bandas and Campsite A new self-catering campsite with *bandas* has recently opened alongside the main Bundibugyo road about halfway between Sempaya and Ntandi. Water and a kitchen building are provided and staff will cook for you but you should take your own provisions. Do also take insect repellent to discourage the annoying midges around the hours of sunrise and sunset. Long-sleeved shirts buttoned at the cuff and long trousers tucked into socks are also advisable. *Rooms US$9 twin pp, camping US$6 pp.*

Sempaya Restcamp In 2005, a private developer was in the process of building cottages opposite the park gate at Sempaya but this seems to have stalled. Updates on further progress would be appreciated.

ACTIVITIES All guided walks listed below cost US$10 per person for a full-day walk. The guides at Semliki are exceptionally knowledgeable and enthusiastic about birds – some can even call up responsive species such as ant-thrushes and robin.

Sempaya Hot Springs and eastern boundary A short guided trail leads from the roadside tourist office to the Sempaya Hot Springs. Ringed by forest and palm trees and veiled in a cloud of steam, these springs are a primeval, evocative sight and well worth the diversion. The largest spring is a geyser which spouts up to 2m high from an opening in a low salt sculpture. The emerging water has a temperature of more than 100°C, so the geyser shouldn't be approached too closely. The trail to the springs leads through a patch of rainforest where red-tailed monkey, grey-cheeked mangabey and black-and-white colobus are common. Among the more interesting birds regularly seen along this trail are eight forest hornbills, blue-breasted kingfisher, red-rumped and yellow-throated tinkerbird, Frasier's ant-thrush and honeyguide greenbul. Another spring, more of a broad steaming pool than a geyser, lies on the far side of the swampy clearing reached by a boardwalk. Rather than retracing your steps to Sempaya, you might ask whether UWA has finally re-opened an old trail that creates an attractive loop passing through forest and a lovely tract of swamp/grassland.

Once you've seen the springs, you can ask to be taken to **Mungiro Waterfall**, which lies on the north side of the main road in the North Rwenzori Forest Reserve. This is an excellent site for white-crested hornbill, red-billed dwarf hornbill and the massive black-casqued wattled hornbill. A more ambitious option is the walk along the eastern margin of the park along the Red Monkey Trail to the Semliki River, which takes at least three hours in either direction and offers exposure to a far greater variety of localised birds than the trail to the springs. The trail can be undertaken as a day trip, or, if you carry your own tent and food, as an overnight trip camping on the bank of the river. In addition to birds, you can expect to see a variety of monkeys, hippos and crocodiles on the river, and possibly even buffalo and elephant.

The 5km stretch of road between Sempaya and Ntandi is fringed by forest, and because it lies outside the national park, you can walk there for free, without a guide (though you'll miss out on quite a bit without the local expertise). As is so often the case, you've a better chance of seeing a good variety of birds from the road than you have in the depths of the forest, and also of getting clear views of monkeys. The patch of fig and palm forest about halfway between Sempaya and Ntandi is worth scanning carefully for the likes of swamp greenbul and various forest hornbills.

Kirumia River Trail Highly recommended to dedicated birdwatchers is the 15km foot trail that runs north from the village of Kirimia on the main Bundibugyo road to the banks of the Semliki River, crossing the Kirimia River twice, as well as passing a succession of forest-fringed oxbow lakes. This hike offers visitors the best opportunity to see a good selection of Semliki 'specials', but realistically it can only be undertaken as a two- to four-night self-sufficient camping expedition. Among the 20–30 bird species associated with the oxbow lakes and their environs, but unlikely to be seen in the vicinity of the main road or elsewhere in Uganda, are spot-breasted ibis, Nkulengu rail, black-throated coucal, yellow-throated cuckoo, lyre-tailed honeyguide, grey ground thrush, blue-billed malimbe, Maxwell's black weaver and Grant's bluebill, while Hartlaub's duck and white-throated blue swallow are resident on the Semliki River. The hike works out at around US$20 per person per day inclusive of guide, camping and visitation fees.

The first 4km of this hike, as far as the first crossing of the Kirumia River, can be undertaken as a guided day hike from the main road. This section of the trail passes through secondary forest in which African piculet, red-sided broadbill and lemon-bellied crombec are resident, while the riverine forest harbours the likes of long-tailed hawk and black-faced rufous warbler.

The exceptionally detailed site description of Semliki National Park contained in Jonathon Rossouw and Marco Sacchi's *Where to Watch Birds in Uganda* will prove invaluable to any birdwatcher wanting to maximise the possibility of locating rare species confined to particular stretches of the trail.

BUNDIBUGYO This pretty, rather remote little town lies at the northwestern base of the Rwenzori Mountains, about 15km past Ntandi in the Semliki National Park. The town itself is nothing special, but it does offer wonderful views across to the mountains and the forested floor of the Albertine Rift Valley, and there is plenty of walking potential in the immediate vicinity. The Rwenzori mini-hike offered by Kabarole Tours terminates in Bundibugyo, and the town is a relatively comfortable base from which motorised travellers can explore the Semliki National Park.

Getting there and away Bundibugyo probably lies little more than 20km west of Fort Portal as the crow flies, but the daunting obstacle provided by the Rwenzori means that the driving distance is closer to 75km. The road from Fort Portal to Bundibugyo is rather erratic in quality, and conditions can vary greatly depending on how recently it was graded or when it last rained. There are several blind corners along the way, which local drivers tend to rush around with rash impunity, hooting loudly and hoping for the best. An average driving speed of around 30km/h is probably realistic, ideally in a 4x4 or a pick-up truck with good clearance, so expect the trip to take the best part of three hours.

There is no formal public transport along this road, but a few pick-up trucks serve as informal (and generally very crowded) shared taxis between Bundibugyo and Fort Portal. These generally leave Bundibugyo before 08.30 and they start the return trip from Fort Portal at around 13.00 – but there is no fixed schedule, so you are advised to ask for departure times at the bus station in Fort Portal. Vehicles heading to Bundibugyo can drop you at Karagutu (the turn-off to Semliki Valley Wildlife Reserve) or at the Semliki National Park offices at Sempaya or Ntandi.

⌂ Where to stay

⌂ **Hotel Vanilla** The newest and by far the best lodging in Bundibugyo offers accommodation in 7 clean, s/c rooms as well as cheaper rooms using common showers. Decent food and DSTV are available. *US$7/12 sgl/dbl.*

⌂ **Picfare Guesthouse** Similar in standard to the above, but a little more rundown, this offers clean

accommodation using common showers. There is electricity, a television lounge and bar, and the staff speak English. *US$5 dbl.*

⌂ **Semliki Guest House** The best of the rest, this has acceptable rooms as well as communal showers with running water, and sit-down toilets. *US$3/6 sgl/dbl.*

NYAHUKA This small, little-visited trading centre lies roughly 40 minutes' drive from Bundibugyo towards the Congolese border. The views of the Rwenzori peaks are even better here than they are from Bundibugyo, and the Saturday market is well worth a visit. From Nyahuka, it's possible to hike to two beautiful Rwenzori waterfalls, Nyahuka Falls and Ngite Falls. Both are rigorous three-hour hikes, best undertaken with a local guide (the guides are good and the fee will be minimal). Clean rooms and meals are available at a local resthouse calling itself the **Holiday Inn**.

KYEGEGWA There's nothing remarkable about this small town on the Fort Portal road 42km west of Mubende, other than the junction of the northern approach to Katonga Wildlife Reserve (see *Chapter* 7, pages 222–4). However it is well worth stopping for a break or perhaps even overnight to experience the truly eclectic Gilman Valley Resort.

Where to stay, eat and drink

Gilman Valley Resort m 0712 846510. Fronted by an unremarkable bar/restaurant on the main road, the appeal of Gilman Valley lies in the so-called 'Magic Valley' that lies behind. Three means of descent are possible into this partially cleared area of swamp forest: a cable runway, a canopy walkway of Indiana Jones rickettyness and a concrete amphitheatre. Oh, and some steps too. Footpaths run between a number of elevated timber structures which provide good vantage points to scan for birdlife or, more usually I suspect, drink beer. Accommodation is provided in the 'Rock House', a pink 2-storey structure of some

individuality constructed on a rock kopje. All rooms are s/c: those on the ground fl stand on natural rock; the inconvenience of a 30° slope has been countered by suspending the beds on chains from the concrete ceiling. Rooms on the 1st fl are more conventional. Additional accommodation in the valley is provided by mud *bandas* which are probably best avoided; there is also a choice of adequate rooms behind the roadside bar. Local and international food costs Ush3,000–5,000. *US$14 sgl and dbl, US$16 twin, rooms by the roadside bar US$5–7 non s/c, US$8 s/c.*

MUBENDE

Mubende is one of Uganda's prettier small towns, set roughly halfway along the main Fort Portal–Kampala road amidst lush, rolling countryside studded with sites associated with the legendary Bacwezi rulers, whose centralised medieval polities

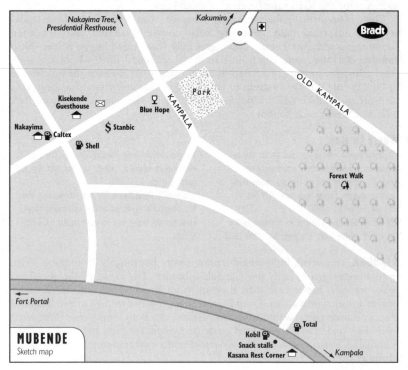

MUBENDE
Sketch map

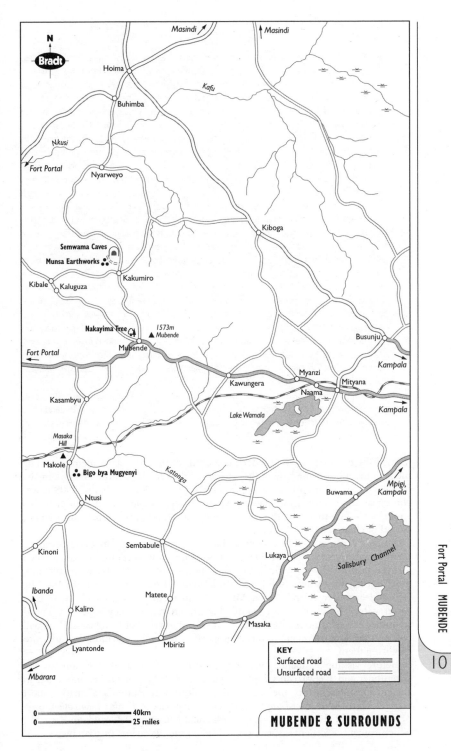

Fort Portal **MUBENDE**

10

KEY
Surfaced road
Unsurfaced road

MUBENDE & SURROUNDS

0 ———— 40km
0 ———— 25 miles

Oral tradition has it that the sacred status of Mubende Hill dates to pre-Bacwezi times, when it was settled by a sorceress called Kamwenge, who hailed from the vicinity of present-day Mbarara. The sorceress's two sons established themselves as important local rulers, and their capital on Mubende Hill – or Kisozi as it was known at that time – rapidly became one of the largest settlements in the region. The site was later usurped by the Bacwezi ruler Ndahura, who resided there for several years before abdicating in favour of his son Wamala to retire to his birthplace near Fort Portal, probably in the late 15th century. The specifics of these oral traditions are open to some debate, but their broad sweep is corroborated by archaeological excavations that suggest an important settlement existed on the crest of Mubende Hill at around the time when Ndahura would have lived.

The most prominent feature on Mubende Hill today is the Nakayima Tree, which according to oral tradition harbours the spirit of Ndahura, deified by both the Banyoro and Baganda as the god of smallpox. The tree is named after a hereditary line of sorceresses, which according to some sources claimed direct descent from Ndahura's wife Nakayima, but might also have been founded by a priestess from Ankole who adopted her name. Traditionally, the *nakayima* was not only the caretaker of the tree, but she was also regularly possessed by the spirit of Ndahura, on which occasions her extremities became covered in smallpox marks for several days. Her supernatural powers are said to have included the ability to cure and prevent smallpox and other fatal diseases, and to help infertile women bear children. The nakayima was probably the most important single spiritual figure in pre-colonial Buganda and Bunyoro, receiving regular tributes from the kings of both of these polities, and also overseeing ritual ceremonies that involved the sacrifice of cows, sheep and more occasionally teenage boys and girls.

If oral tradition is to be believed, the nakayima lineage was for a full four centuries an acknowledged spiritual figurehead to both the rulers and the peasantry of Buganda and Bunyoro. Yet its end was remarkably abrupt. The first intimation of its demise came in

formed the precursor of the modern kingdoms of the interlacustrine region. The modern town lies at the base of the 1,573m Mubende Hill, whose breezy climate, fertile soil and clear springs so impressed the early colonials that in 1908 it was chosen as the site of a hill station, where weary Entebbe-based administrators could, according to a contemporary issue of the *Mengo Notes*, 'repair thither for a period of change and invigoration'.

Mubende has not sparked comparable enthusiasm among modern travellers, but for anybody wishing to avoid Uganda's obvious tourist centres, the small town forms a useful base from which to visit a number of low-key Bacwezi cult sites, most notably the wonderfully gnarled Nakayima Tree on the crest of Mubende Hill and extensive earthworks at Munsa 40km further north. While these sites could scarcely be described as recognised tourist attractions, they do serve as a vivid reminder that African history did not start with the arrival of Europeans. Both will reward interested travellers in direct proportion to the imagination they put into exploring them.

Before visiting Mubende, you might want to look at the section on the Batembuzi and Bacwezi in *Chapter 1*, pages 7–8. If you're further interested in ancient Ugandan history, then get hold of Kihhumuro Apuuli's fascinating short book *A Thousand Years of Bunyoro-Kitara* (see *Appendix 3, Further Information*, page 476). You could also pay a visit to the National Museum of Uganda in Kampala, which contains excellent displays on Ntusi and the Nakayima matriarchy.

1888, when the religious conflict that rocked Buganda forced the incumbent nakayima, Nyanjara, to flee from Mubende. When she returned a year later, all but one of the seven huts traditionally inhabited by the nakayima had been razed, while the graves of her predecessors had been defaced, and her sacred drums had vanished. This attack had no immediate impact on the nakayima's influence in Bunyoro, then relatively unexposed to exotic religions – indeed, King Kabalega made a special visit to Mubende to pay Nyanjara tribute in 1899. But as foreign missionaries persuaded the Baganda élite to turn away from traditional beliefs, so the Nakayima's spiritual importance in Buganda diminished.

In 1902, the political autonomy that had characterised the once-feared and revered spiritual community led by the nakayima was curtailed when Mubende Hill was placed under the indirect colonial rule of a Muganda Saza chief appointed by the British administration at Kakumiro. Nyanjara retired to Bugogo, where she died in 1907, the first nakayima not to be interred in the traditional cemetery near the sacred tree, though eventually she was buried in isolation at the base of Mubende Hill. Her fantastic regalia, confiscated by the authorities, now forms one of the most impressive displays in the National Museum in Kampala – together with two large and ancient pots, probably used in Bacwezi-related religious rituals, unearthed during excavations at the base of the Nakayima Tree.

No credible successor to the Nakayima title ever emerged. In 1926, one Muhima sorceress briefly took up residence on Mubende Hill, while ten years later a young Ankole girl dressed in full regalia reputedly spent several nights screeching at the base of the Nakayima Tree before presumably vanishing back whence she had come. All the same, the Nakayima Tree remains to this day an important pilgrimage site for Bacwezi cultists, whose offerings can be seen scattered around its base. In 1996, I met an informal caretaker who claimed to be the grandson of Nyanjara and to have lived below the tree since 1965. I was inclined to believe this at the time, but it could as easily have been invented for my benefit – the only other people I've met who visited the tree said they were shown around by a woman who claimed to be nothing less than the nakayima reincarnate.

GETTING THERE AND AWAY Mubende lies about 1km off the main Kampala–Fort Portal road, and is roughly 160km from either of these towns. The road east of Mubende to Kampala is surfaced and in excellent condition – it can comfortably be covered in under two hours. The road west to Fort Portal is in less impressive shape, unsurfaced for most of its length and severely pot-holed in parts – even in private transport, it's a four-hour drive. Any minibus or bus connecting Kampala and Fort Portal – including the excellent Post Bus – will be able to drop you at Mubende. There are also direct minibuses between Kampala and Mubende, leaving Kampala from the new taxi park.

WHERE TO STAY

Presidential Resthouse Situated on Mubende Hill, a few hundred metres from the Nakayima Tree, the colonial sanatorium built in 1908 now serves as a presidential resthouse on the one or two occasions annually when Museveni opts to repair thither for a period of change and invigoration. Assuming that your visit doesn't coincide with a presidential thither – furthermore that you can find the caretaker, and that the caretaker can find the key – it should be possible to make an informal arrangement to sleep over. On the off-chance of finding a room, it's probably not worth manually heaving your luggage up a hill whose name derives from a local word meaning 'to break your back', but if you're motorised, this would be a lovely place to stay – electricity, kitchen, hot water and great views! *US$3.*

Nakayima Hotel The best rooms in the town centre are to be found in this clean, comfortable family-run hotel. *US$11 s/c dbl, US$8 sgl and dbl with shared facilities. Camping US$3 per tent.*

🏠 **Homeland Lodge** On the opposite side of the Caltex garage to the Nakayima Hotel, the accommodation here is pretty much as you'd expect for the price. *US$4/6 sgl/dbl.*

🍴 **WHERE TO EAT** The **Nakayima Hotel** and **Kisekende Lodge** both serve reasonable chicken and chips and other standard Ugandan fare. There's not much to choose between the two in terms of quality, but the Kisekende is considerably cheaper. The **Kasana Rest Corner** at the Fort Portal minibus stage as you come into Mubende has been recommended. **Margaret's Bar**, opposite the council office, does good chips, meat and chicken, and it has a Scrabble set. A popular place for a drink, right next to the Kisekende Lodge, is **Fred's Bar**, run by a Freddie Mercury lookalike who reportedly never smiles.

EXCURSIONS FROM MUBENDE

Mubende Forest Walk Only 500m from the town centre, an informal 8km walk passes through patches of indigenous forest and riverine woodland. The best place to start the walk is at the main crossroads next to the park. From here, walk out along the new Kampala road until you reach the patch of forest about 100m past the community centre, where a footpath to the left leads downhill to a river and then uphill again.

After roughly 500m, the footpath emerges on the old Kampala road, where you should turn right. There are normally plenty of butterflies and birds along this road, and you also stand a good chance of seeing black-and-white colobus monkeys. Along the way, to the left of the road, you should see local brick-makers going about their business.

Roughly 4km along the old Kampala road, you should take a side road leading to the right. This road soon becomes a footpath which itself diverges into several branching paths leading between homesteads. Provided that you keep asking for directions towards Mubende, there's no real danger of getting lost. You should, after walking for 2–3km, emerge on to the new Kampala road about 300m from the community centre.

Mubende Hill The Nakayima Tree on the summit of Mubende Hill, roughly 4km from the town centre, is the most accessible and compelling of the Bacwezi-related sites in the Mubende area (see box *The Nakayima of Mubende Hill*, on pages 348–9). It can be reached along a dirt road leading uphill from the main crossroads next to the park in central Mubende. The road is fairly steep and possibly too rough for anything but a 4x4 vehicle. If you're walking, you should make it up in an hour, depending on how often you stop to enjoy the prolific birdlife and views south to Masaka Hill. Once at the summit, it's worth continuing another 1km or so past the Nakayima Tree to the large artificial lake that supplies water to Mubende Town.

It is not difficult to see why this particular tree has become a spiritual focus of such note. It is a compelling piece of natural engineering, towering above its park-like surrounds like an oversized surrealist sculpture – almost 40m high, many centuries old, and supported by fin-shaped buttressed roots that fan out from the base to create several cavernous hollows. Contrary to expectations – given that the last of the sorceresses associated with the site died almost 100 years ago – it remains an active shrine, visited by cultists from all around Buganda and Bunyoro. In some of the hollows, especially the one where the Nakayima is said to have addressed her followers, a scattering of coins and cowrie shells has been left by worshippers hoping for the Nakayima's blessing. Nakayima cultists occasionally spend a night by the tree, where they roast a goat or pig as a sacrifice to the priestess.

Munsa Earthworks The Munsa Earthworks, which lie about 40km north of Mubende, consist of a maze of deep trenches (now silted up) surrounding Bikekete

Hill, a prominent granite outcrop riddled with tunnels and caves. The Munsa Earthworks are the second largest in Uganda, superseded in area only by their less-accessible counterpart at Bigo near Ntusi. Their name is derived from the Runyoro expression Mu-ensa, meaning 'place of trenches'. The site is associated by local oral traditions with a Bacwezi prince called Kateboha, a name that probably derives from a Runyoro term meaning 'one who locks himself in', suggesting it was applied posthumously to a local chief or more likely a dynasty of local rulers.

The oral tradition linking Munsa to the Bacwezi is vindicated by archaeological evidence suggesting that the earthworks and occupation of Bikekete Hill date back to the 14th century. Archaeologists also concur with the traditional convention that the ruler of Munsa lived within Bikekete Hill, in a cave large enough to seat 50 people. It is probable that the surrounding earthworks, which are up to 7m wide and 3m deep and were excavated in a V shape making them difficult to cross, were fortifications to protect the rocky royal stronghold. The orientation of the trenches implies that its excavators originated from further north and were mostly concerned with possible attacks from unknown lands further south.

The most recent archaeological studies on Bikekete Hill, which took place in late 1995, have done a great deal to further our understanding of the site. Among the more significant discoveries were an intact clay furnace used for smelting iron, glass beads, suggesting some sort of trade link with the coastal Swahili, and what was presumably a royal burial ground. One of the skeletons at Bikekete was discovered beneath a second, inverted skeleton. This, almost certainly, would have been a royal burial – it was the rather grisly custom that a king should be buried below one of his servants, the latter buried alive in order that he could look after his master.

Long-standing talk of developing Munsa for tourism, by erecting a site museum to house local artefacts currently stored in the National Museum in Kampala and building a basic guesthouse in the adjacent church property, has yet to translate into action. All the same, the earthworks are easy enough to visit, and the local priest – also the official caretaker of the site – generally welcomes the few curious travellers who do pitch up. With a torch and a local guide, it is possible to enter the cave that was once inhabited by Kateboha, reached by crawling through a tight tunnel. From the hilltop, the shape of the silted-up earthworks is clearly visible once you are shown what to look for. About 150m south of the base of the hill, two deep, narrow holes in a slab of flat granite were probably created artificially along existing cracks in the rock – according to local tradition, these holes were used as receptacles from where Kateboha drank beer offerings from his subjects at the start of the harvest season.

The springboard for visits to Munsa is Kakumiro trading centre, which lies 35km from Mubende along a fair dirt road flanked by some impressive forest patches and papyrus swamp. The drive should take no more than one hour, whether in a private vehicle or in one of the minibus-taxis that ply between Mubende and Kakumiro every hour or so. The earthworks lie 6km out of Kakumiro: follow the Hoima road for about 2km out of town, then turn left into the road signposted for Munsa Primary School. The inconspicuous track to the earthworks runs to the left about 3.5km along this road, practically opposite the primary school and perhaps 50m before a distinctive church. Roughly 700m down this track, and only 100m before the earthworks, lies the home of the local priest and official caretaker, who should be consulted by all visitors. There is no public transport beyond Kakumiro, but the earthworks can be reached by *boda-boda*. Munsa makes a feasible goal for a day trip out of Mubende, even if you're dependent on public transport. There is no accommodation in the Kakumiro area, but it should be possible to camp in the priest's garden for a small fee.

Semwama Hill This flat-topped granite outcrop, which lies immediately to the right of the road between Kakumiro and Munsa, contains a network of shelters and caves that is traditionally held sacred by the local people and also provided them with refuge against invaders. The most accessible cave consists of two main chambers, known locally as *ebidongobo* or waiting rooms, which are sometimes used as an overnight shelter for cattle. Within the chambers lies an ancient Bacwezi shrine where offerings of leaves, seeds and straw can still be seen, left behind to protect visitors against demonic spirits. The cave is said to have been where Kateboha of Munsa once held council with his elders and advisors, sitting above them on the flat slab of stone in the main chamber. From this opening you can scramble up a succession of rock chimneys, assisted in one or two places by rough ladders, then a near-vertical rock face to the top of the hill. You'll need a local guide to locate the entrance to a network of tunnels that runs right through the hill, and which can be traversed over about six hours with a torch and rope – and ideally some experience of caving.

Semwama Hill lies 3.5km from Kakumiro, on the right side of the road towards the Munsa Primary School precisely 1km after the junction with the Hoima road. The overgrown but motorable 200m track to the caves lies immediately after you pass a house distinguished by a balcony supported by four columns.

NTUSI AND BIGO

Ntusi trading centre lies about 80km south of Mubende and 100km northwest of Masaka. Though little more than a village today, Ntusi lies on the site of what was probably the most ancient large settlement in Uganda. Ntusi was occupied for at least 300 years in the first half of the last millennium; and it is thought to have peaked in importance in the 12th and 13th centuries, at which time it was probably the largest settlement in the East African interior and the capital of an empire that stretched as far north as Lake Albert.

The identity of Ntusi's ancient inhabitants is something of a mystery. They almost certainly pre-dated the Bacwezi, making it more than probable that they were the source of the Batembuzi legends that permeate local oral histories. Ntusi is thought to have had a mixed economy; evidence of iron-smelting and ivory and woodcarving has been found, as have large amounts of pottery. One of the most unusual objects discovered at Ntusi is a small fired-clay cylinder, covered in knobs and thought to have been used for ritual divination.

Within 20km of Ntusi lie two Bacwezi-related archaeological sites: Masaka Hill and the Bigo bya Mugyenyi earthworks.

GETTING THERE AND AWAY Ntusi can be approached from any of three directions: from Mubende to the north, from Masaka to the southeast, or from Lyantonde to the south.

Coming from Mubende, follow the Fort Portal road out of town for roughly 20km, then take the left turn towards Kasambyu. After about 15km, you'll reach Kasambyu trading centre, from where it's another 40–50km to Ntusi. The drive should take three to four hours in a private vehicle.

There is no direct public transport between Mubende and Ntusi, and travellers heading this way face the distinct possibility of getting stuck overnight at Kasambyu, which has no formal accommodation. At least three minibus-taxis run daily in either direction between Mubende and Kasambyu, and at least one runs between Kasambyu and Ntusi every day, as does an early morning bus heading on to Masaka. In the opposite direction, there should be at least one minibus-taxi heading from Ntusi to Kasambyu in the morning, and the bus from Masaka passes through Ntusi in the late afternoon, reaching Kasambyu at around 20.00.

Goodness knows what will happen when you try to visit Bigo. When I drove there a few years back, it proved to be one of those excursions that yields little in the way of hard travel information – any visit will be an individual experience, and the best I can do is describe what happened to me.

I made it to Ntusi easily enough, where I picked up an English-speaking guide who didn't actually know which road led to Bigo, for which reason he arranged a second, more inherently useful guide at the hydrometeorological station. The second guide directed us along the 17km road until we reached a group of rural homesteads, where it was established that neither of my existing guides knew how to proceed to the earthworks. A further three guides were appended to the party, one of them so drunk that he twice fell over on the 30-minute walk to our goal, lending a *Carry On Livingstone* feel to what was already descending into a farcical exercise.

We passed the outer earthworks: silted up and covered in thicket-like scrub, it would have taken a trained eye to recognise them for anything more remarkable than a non-perennial or underground watercourse. Within the ancient royal compound, uninhabited due to a combination of fear and respect for ancestral spirits, I felt a distinctly haunted atmosphere, though admittedly one that I've often sensed while walking through less exalted tracts of abandoned African bush. Our goal, it transpired, was the large euphorbia tree that is said to hold Mugyenyi's spirit: a pilgrimage site whose sandy base is littered with coins and cowrie shells. The guides knelt at the base of the tree, and suggested that I join them to pray for good luck. I asked them to whom I should pray; they said to whomsoever I wanted, a refreshingly non-sectarian attitude.

After walking back to the group of homesteads, and trying to explain that the fee they asked would be fair enough for one guide but was a little steep multiplied by five, I drove back to Ntusi with my initial two guides. On the way we got bogged down for half an hour in a muddy stream, when I discovered that the true purpose of having duplicate guides was so that they could push the vehicle in opposite directions and thus neutralise each other's efforts. Eventually, in a rare moment of co-ordinated shoving, we broke free of the mud and made it to Ntusi as the sun was setting.

There is, as I say, not a great deal to see at Bigo – certainly I found it to be less impressive and accessible than the Munsa Earthworks – and one could argue that this obscure site doesn't really belong in a travel guide. But getting there is bound to be an adventure, and an instructive one at that – surely what travelling in Africa is all about?

The 100km road between Masaka and Ntusi is reportedly in poor condition, though perfectly navigable in a sturdy 4x4. The daily bus between Masaka and Kasambyu via Ntusi leaves Masaka at around 14.00 and reaches Ntusi at about 17.00. In the opposite direction it passes through Ntusi at around 09.00. The alternative to using the bus to Ntusi is to catch a shared taxi from Nyondo, 2km from Masaka on the Kampala road.

The 60km road between Lyantonde (on the main Masaka–Mbarara road) and Ntusi is in remarkably good condition. It's the only road to Ntusi which can be navigated by practically any vehicle – in fact, provided that you keep an eye open for the one or two large pot-holes along the way, you can cruise it comfortably at around 40km/h. So far as I'm aware, there's no public transport along this road, but I saw enough private traffic to suggest that hitching would be feasible; though it would be advisable to get an early start, by spending the night before you travel at one of the many basic lodges in Lyantonde.

WHERE TO STAY Good question! There is no formal accommodation in Ntusi. If you have a tent, you should be allowed to camp in the grounds of the district headquarters in the small town centre; otherwise you will have to take your chance and ask around for a private room.

EXCURSIONS FROM NTUSI

Ntusi Mounds The most notable features of Ntusi are two immense mounds, known locally as the male and female mound. Excavations have shown them to be a massive pile of bones, pottery shards and other waste material: they are huge refuse heaps, deposited over a 300-year period during the first half of the second millennium AD. Their importance has always been recognised by more recent inhabitants; the name Ntusi means mound. There are several scraped depressions around the village, the largest of which, the 20m-deep Bwogero depression, lies 150m from the male mound. Bwogero was probably a part of an extensive irrigation system, traces of which still exist today. The mounds at Ntusi are within 1km of the district headquarters, so they can be visited on foot over a couple of hours.

Bigo bya Mugyenyi Of the several earthworks excavated by the Bacwezi, Bigo bya Mugyenyi is by far the largest and the most archaeologically important. Lying at the confluence of the Katonga and Kakinga rivers, Bigo bya Mugyenyi literally translates to mean 'Fort of the Stranger', and while it is said locally that Mugyenyi was the name of the Bacwezi prince responsible for excavating the earthworks, it could as easily be that this name was applied posthumously to a ruler whose name has been forgotten. Oral traditions suggest that the earthworks were originally created to protect the eastern extreme of the core Bacwezi Empire, but that towards the end of Wamala's reign, when the Bacwezi status quo was threatened by the arrival of Luo upstarts from Sudan, the king himself moved to Bigo and made it his capital.

Bigo bya Mugyenyi consists of two concentric sets of earthworks: an outer ditch system almost 10km long and an inner royal enclosure built on a small hill and used to protect Mugyenyi's cattle. Many of the earthworks are 5m deep and excavated from solid rock. Although Bigo was contemporaneous with the Shirazi cities of the Kenyan and Tanzanian coast, no evidence has ever been found at the site to indicate trade links between the two. The earthworks are still treated with respect by the local people, and are believed to have supernatural powers.

For all its historical and archaeological importance, there isn't an awful lot to see at Bigo, and the hassle involved in getting there will probably put off all but the most determined or obsessive. The edge of the site is 17km along a road which leaves Ntusi from alongside the hydrometeorological station opposite the district headquarters. The road is actually a barely motorable and in parts barely discernible track – don't even think about attempting it without a 4x4 and a reliable guide (the district headquarters will help you out with the latter). Without your own transport, the best way to get to Bigo would be to try to hire a bicycle (it's too far from Ntusi to be a realistic day walk), though, again, you would definitely need a guide to find your way. See box *Visiting Bigo,* on page 353.

Masaka Hill This hill, surrounded by two concentric ramparts, is on the north bank of the Katonga River 18km upstream from Bigo. It is thought to have been the site of the last capital of the Bachwezi leader, Wamala; as a consequence it has been a place of Bachwezi cult worship and pilgrimage for centuries. It is said that when Wamala abandoned the hill he gave his royal drum to a local clan for safekeeping. This drum became an important symbol of the Ankole kingdom and remained so until 1888, when the Ankole capital was looted and the drum disappeared (some sources claim it was taken to Mubende Hill). On top of Masaka Hill is a circular grove of ancient fig trees which are thought to have some ritual significance.

MITYANA

Possibly the most interesting thing about this compact and relatively prosperous-looking town, situated on the Mubende road about 70km from Kampala, is its name, which somewhat obtusely derives from a Luganda phrase Miti-eyana meaning 'the trees creak'. We visited Mityana to take a look at Lake Wamala, which, as it transpired, is quite pretty but hardly worth making a special effort for. A more convincing reason to stop off in Mityana is that there is plenty of cheap accommodation; if you are heading to or coming from Fort Portal, staying in Mityana would save you the hassle and expense of an overnight stay in Kampala.

If you want to take a look at Lake Wamala – which, according to local legend, was formed by water leaked from the water-skin of the Bacwezi leader for which it is named – jump on to any vehicle heading towards Fort Portal and ask to be dropped at the village of Naama, 8km from Mityana. From there it's a 20-minute walk to the lakeshore along footpaths which weave between mud huts, coffee trees and patches of indigenous bush. You should have no difficulty finding somebody to direct you. There is a large island on the lake and it might be possible to talk someone into rowing you across; there are plenty of dugout canoes on the lake's shore.

Another little-known point of interest near Mityana is the deep and narrow Tanda Pits, which, legend has it, were excavated by the creator's son Kayikuzi (literally, 'Digger of Holes') in his failed attempt to capture his brother Walumbe during the momentous battle described in the boxed text *In the Beginning...* in *Chapter 1*, page 6. Kiganda tradition has it that the sinister pits at Tanda are still sometimes used as a refuge by the malevolent spirit Walumbe, and are thus associated with ill fortune and death.

GETTING THERE AND AWAY Regular minibuses to Mityana leave Kampala from the new taxi park, and they take about an hour. If you are heading to Fort Portal from Mityana, you may have to wait a while for a vehicle coming from Kampala with a spare seat, but I doubt you would have too much trouble finding something.

WHERE TO STAY

Enro Hotel m 0772 442007. Situated on the north side of the main road on the way in from Kampala this smart 2-storey hotel is the first choice for expatriates visiting the tea plantations beyond the town. They consider the rooms clean and pleasant and their only gripe is the occasional disco in the hotel grounds. *US$20/27 sgl/dbl inc b/fast.*

New Highway Hotel Situated opposite the Shell garage on the Kampala side of town, this unexpectedly smart hotel is good value, and it has a pleasant outdoor restaurant where main courses cost around US$2. *US$8/11/13 sgl/twin/dbl.*

Kolping Society Hotel Run by the Mityana Women's Project, this church-affiliated hostel has clean, comfortable rooms, with a good restaurant attached. *US$5 ordinary dbl, US$12 s/c dbl.*

Wamala View Inn Spotless, spacious rooms with views over the town, at slightly cheaper rates than the Kolping Society.

11

Murchison Falls and the Northwest

Flanking the Victoria Nile some 300km northwest of Kampala, Murchison Falls National Park is the largest protected area in Uganda, and one of the most exciting. The waterfall for which the park is named is the most electrifying sight of its type in East Africa, while daily launch trips from Paraa offer the opportunity to see a profusion of hippos, crocodiles and waterbirds, including the elusive and bizarre shoebill. Terrestrial wildlife, too, is recovering from the heavy poaching of the 1980s, and a wide variety of mammals – including elephant and lion – are now routinely sighted along the road circuit north of the Nile.

The other major established attraction in the Murchison region is the Budongo Forest, effectively a southern extension of the national park, protected within the Budongo and Kanyiyo Pabidi forest reserves. The Budongo Forest harbours one of the most varied forest faunas in East Africa, and is a premier site for birdwatchers, as well as one of the best – and most affordable – places to track chimpanzees in East Africa. There are two tourist sites in Budongo Forest, both of which offer camping, basic accommodation, and chimp tracking and other forest walks. Organised tours and travellers with private transport will normally visit the Kanyiyo Pabidi tourist site in the northern section of Budongo along the more direct route between Masindi and Murchison Falls. Busingiro Tourist Site, situated within the Budongo Forest Reserve about 20km west of Masindi, is more accessible for travellers using public transport, and it is also cheaper, since no national park entrance fees must be paid.

The largest town in this part of Uganda is Masindi, about three hours in a private vehicle from Kampala along a (mostly) surfaced road, or a day's drive from Fort Portal along a wild 250km dirt road through Hoima. From Masindi, there are two different routes up to Murchison Falls. The shorter (85km) route runs directly north from Masindi to Paraa, cutting through the Kanyiyo Pabidi Forest Reserve and bypassing Sambiya Lodge. The longer (135km) and more scenic route runs west from Masindi through Budongo Forest Reserve and the Butiaba Escarpment, then north along the Lake Albert littoral, veering east at Bulisa, then bypassing Nile Safari Camp, before it enters the national park to connect with the direct route south of Paraa.

A couple of worthwhile new attractions have opened in this area in recent years. The more contrived and better publicised of the two, situated along the Kampala–Masindi road, is the Ziwa Rhino Sanctuary, which protects four reintroduced black rhino and provides an interesting diversion along the otherwise unremarkable journey north towards Murchison Falls. By contrast, the newly opened and little-known Kabwoya Wildlife Reserve make for an appealing overnight detour off the long 350km drive between Fort Portal and Murchison Falls. Situated on the shores of Lake Albert west of Hoima, Kabwoya was created in 2002 from the remnants of a denuded Controlled Hunting Area, and is enjoying a new lease of life under the committed conservation management of a private concessionaire.

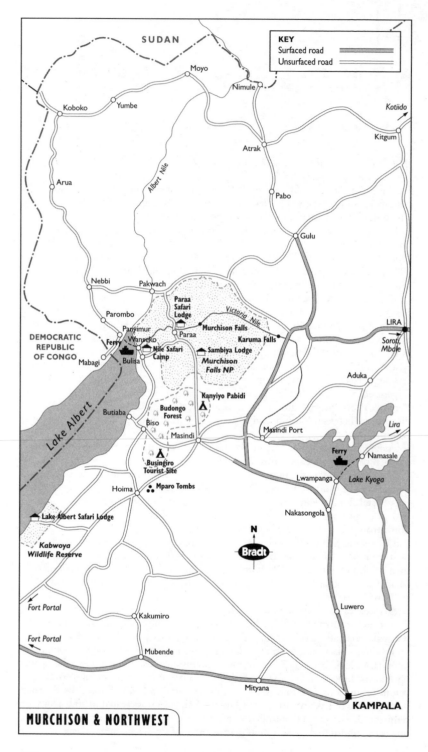

KEY
Surfaced road
Unsurfaced road

SUDAN

Moyo
Nimule
Koboko
Yumbe
Kotiido
Kitgum
Atrak
Arua
Pabo
Gulu
Nebbi
Pakwach
**Paraa
Safari
Lodge**
Victoria Nile
LIRA
Parombo
*Soroti,
Mbale*
Panyimur
Murchison Falls
Wanseko
Paraa
Karuma Falls
Ferry
**Nile Safari
Camp**
Sambiya Lodge
DEMOCRATIC
REPUBLIC
OF CONGO
Bulisa
*Murchison
Falls NP*
Mabagi
Aduka
Kanyiyo Pabidi
Lira
Butiaba
**Budongo
Forest**
Biso
Masindi Port
Masindi
Ferry
Namasale
**Busingiro
Tourist Site**
Lwampanga
Lake Kyoga
Hoima
Mparo Tombs
Nakasongola
Lake Albert Safari Lodge
*Kabwoya
Wildlife Reserve*
N

Bradt

Luwero

Fort Portal
Kakumiro

Fort Portal
Mubende

Mityana
KAMPALA

Albert Nile
Lake Albert

MURCHISON & NORTHWEST

358

HOIMA

The rather out-of-the-way town of Hoima sees little traveller traffic and is of interest primarily as a staging post between Fort Portal and Masindi. The pretty, almost park-like surrounds notwithstanding, the compact town centre feels unusually rundown and neglected, as if it has been bypassed by the restoration and development that has characterised Uganda over the past decade. Still, Hoima is a pleasant enough place, and the local historical sites arguably add up to a good reason to hang around for a day. Mparo, 4km from the town centre, was the 19th-century capital of Omukama Kabalega, and the reigning Omukama Solomon Iguru Gafabusa has his main residence in Hoima Town.

GETTING THERE AND AWAY Hoima stands at a minor route junction. It is the main town between Fort Portal and Masindi, and there is also a road connecting it to Kampala in the east and to Lake Albert in the west. All approach roads to Hoima are unsurfaced and prone to deteriorate after heavy rain, in which case the driving times mentioned below will be rather optimistic. The Kampala road is sealed for the first 40km out of from the capital and roadworks are underway to tarmac it up to Hoima – perhaps within the lifespan of this edition. Regular minibus-taxis run between Hoima and Masindi throughout the morning and early afternoon, and the trip takes around three hours. A few minibuses run daily between Kampala and Hoima, also taking around three hours. The Post Bus from Kampala runs to Hoima via Masindi and costs Ush10,000. Probably the only reason why you would head straight from Kampala to Hoima is to continue to Kabwoya Wildlife Reserve (see pages 364–5) and it would be difficult and uncomfortable (but by no means impossible) to attempt this by public transport. If you are heading from Fort Portal to Murchison Falls or the Budongo Forest, you could bypass Masindi by using one of the pick-up trucks that leave Hoima for Wanseko daily at around 10.00. There is limited transport between Fort Portal and Hoima: your best option is to take the bus that leaves in either direction on alternate days at around 08.00, taking about six hours.

WHERE TO STAY
Budget
Crown Hotel m 0772 970150/0712 206093. Top of the range for Hoima, this smart new hotel lies just outside the town centre beyond the post office off Kizungu Mandela Road. The s/c rooms are good value and there's a large swimming pool (Ush5,000) to while away those long Hoima afternoons albeit with perhaps the most uncomfortable veranda chairs in the country. US$16/19/24 sgl/dbl/trpl B&B.

Kolping Society Guesthouse 0465 40167; f 0465 40313; e hoikolping@yahoo.com. About 500m out of town along the Butiaba road, this clean, church-run guesthouse lies in attractive grounds. Acceptable food is available. US$14/19 s/c sgl/dbl.

Africa Village Guest Farm m 0772 412876. This peaceful and welcoming lodge lies in a large plot just outside the town centre. There's plenty of birdlife around and an unexpected camel. Accommodation is in comfortable s/c cottages. Good food is available – many locals come just for the restaurant. US$16 dbl B&B.

Riviera Hotel 0464 523310. This sprawling but rather characterless establishment on the Kampala road is reasonably priced. US$6 sgl (sharing common showers), US$16 s/c dbl.

Shoestring
Nsamo Hotel Cheerful and conveniently located close to the taxi park, the long-serving Nsamo Hotel is also good value. The food is the best in the town centre, which isn't saying a lot. US$4 sgl room using common showers, US$7/8 s/c sgl/dbl with nets.

Classic Inn Situated on the southern edge of the town centre just off the Fort Portal road, this small lodge has bright, clean rooms. US$3/4 sgl/dbl.

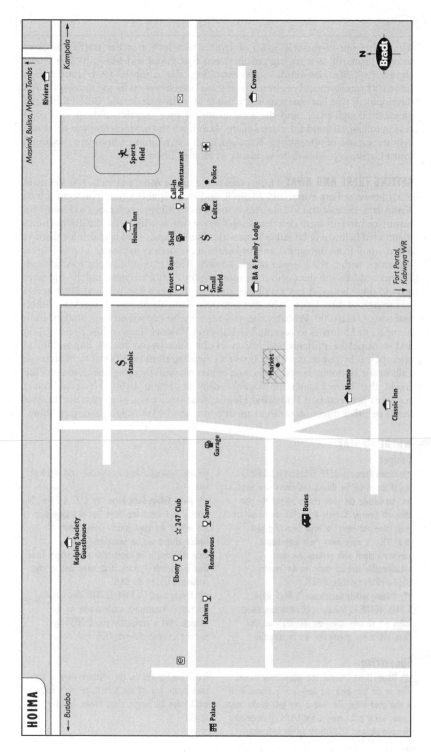

HOIMA

Traditionally, within what is today Uganda, the birth of twins was seen as an event of great significance, though some cultures regarded it as a great blessing while others perceived it be an omen of ill. Speke, while stuck in Bunyoro in 1862, compared some of the customs he had come across on his travels:

A Munyoro woman, who bore twins that died, now keeps two small pots in her house, as effigies of the children, into which she milks herself every evening, and will continue to do so for five months, fulfilling the time appointed by nature for suckling children, lest the spirits of the dead should persecute her. The twins were not buried, as ordinary people are buried, under ground, but placed in an earthenware pot, such as the Banyoro use for holding pombe [beer]. They were taken to the jungle and placed by a tree, with the pot turned mouth downwards. Manua, one of my men, who is a twin, said, in Nguru, one of the sister provinces to Unyanyembe, twins are ordered to be killed and thrown into water the moment they are born, lest droughts and famines or floods should oppress the land. Should any one attempt to conceal twins, the whole family would be murdered by the chief; but, though a great traveller, this is the only instance of such brutality Manua had ever witnessed in any country.

In the province of Unyanyembe, if a twin or twins die, they are thrown into water for the same reason as in Nguru; but as their numbers increase the size of the family, their birth is hailed with delight. Still there is a source of fear there in connection with twins, as I have seen myself; for when one dies, the mother ties a little gourd to her neck as a proxy, and puts into it a trifle of everything which she gives the living child, lest the jealousy of the dead spirit should torment her. Further, on the death of the child, she smears herself with butter and ashes, and runs frantically about, tearing her hair and bewailing piteously; whilst the men of the place use towards her the foulest language, apparently as if in abuse of her person, but in reality to frighten away the demons who have robbed her nest.

WHERE TO EAT All of the hotels listed under the budget category serve food, though the inferior but still acceptable restaurant at the **Nsamo Hotel** is more central. Plenty of restaurants and bars serving cheap local fare and cold beers are scattered around the town centre. The **Rendezvous bar/club** does a decent lunchtime buffet for Ush5,000 while the little garden outside the **Call-In pub** on the corner beside the sports ground and Caltex is perhaps the leafiest spot in the town for a cold drink.

LISTINGS

Internet Internet facilities are available at Kolping House (not the guesthouse) behind the Classic Inn at Ush3,000 per hour.

Foreign exchange Forex services are provided by the Stanbic Bank.

Nightclubs The **Rendezvous** and **247 Club** in the middle of town both provide the opportunity to stay up late. If one doesn't take your fancy, the other is just a few metres away.

WHAT TO SEE

Mparo Tombs Situated about 4km out of Hoima along the Masindi road, Mparo was chosen as the capital of Omukama (King) Kabarega of Bunyoro in 1872, after Sir Samuel Baker forced his retreat out of Masindi. It was from Mparo that he led

11

On 9 September 1862, Speke and Grant became the first Europeans to set foot in the capital of the kingdom of Bunyoro, Mruli, near present-day Masindi Port. Grant described the site as 'bare and dreary'. Speke dismissed the royal palace as 'a dumpy, large hut, surrounded by a host of smaller ones... nothing could be more filthy', adding that 'it was well, perhaps, that we were never expected to go there, for without stilts and respirators it would have been impracticable'. Nor were Speke and Grant much taken with Kamurasi, the King of Bunyoro, who – understandably troubled by 'absurd stories which he had heard from the Baganda' about the cannibalistic, mountain-eating, river-drying powers of the white man – left his European visitors waiting for nine days before finally granting them an audience. When finally they met, Speke wrote: 'Kamurasi was enshrouded in his mbugu dress, for all the world like a pope in state – calm and actionless. One bracelet of fine-twisted brass wire adorned his left wrist, and his hair, half an inch long, was worked up into small peppercorn-like knobs by rubbing the hand circularly over the crown of the head... Kamurasi asked [Speke's translator] Bombay, "Who governs England?" "A woman." "Has she any children?" "Yes," said Bombay, with ready impudence; "these are two of them" (pointing to Grant and myself). That settled, Kamurasi wished to know if we had any speckled cows, or cows of any peculiar colour, and would we like to change four large cows for four small ones, as he coveted some of ours.'

Speke was clearly frustrated by the mixed reception accorded to him by Kamurasi, not to mention the king's endless demands for gifts, but he also regarded him to be a more benevolent ruler than the despotic Mutesa of Buganda. 'Kamurasi conducts all business himself,' Speke wrote, 'awarding punishments and seeing them carried out. The most severe instrument of chastisement is a knob-stick, sharpened at the back... for breaking a man's neck before he is thrown into the lake. But this severity is seldom resorted to, Kamurasi being of a mild disposition compared with Mutesa, whom he invariably alludes to when ordering men to be flogged, telling them that were they in Buganda, their heads would suffer instead of their backs.'

The king's attitude towards his family, Speke explained, was somewhat dictatorial: 'Kamurasi's sisters are not allowed to wed; they live and die virgins in his palace. Their only occupation in life consisted of drinking milk, of which each one consumes the produce daily of from ten to twenty cows, and hence they become so inordinately fat that they cannot walk. Should they wish to see a relative, or go outside the hut for any purpose, it requires eight men to lift any of them on a litter. The brothers, too, are not allowed to go out of his reach. This confinement of the palace family is considered a state necessity, as a preventive to civil wars, in the same way as the destruction of the Baganda princes, after a certain season, is thought necessary for the preservation of peace there.'

The only other Europeans to visit Bunyoro during Kamurasi's rule were Samuel and Florence Baker, who arrived at Mruli on 10 February 1864, remarking that it was a 'delightful change to find ourselves in comparative civilisation'. Baker waxed lyrical about 'the decency of the clothing' in the 'thickly populated and much cultivated' kingdom. 'The blacksmiths,' he noted 'were exceedingly clever and used iron hammers instead of stones... they made a fine quality of jet black earthenware, producing excellent tobacco pipes, extremely pretty bowls, and also bottles. The huts are very large... made entirely of reeds and straw, and very lofty... like huge inverted baskets, beehive shaped.'

his raids into the neighbouring kingdoms of Toro and Buganda before the British drove him into hiding in 1891. After he died in exile in 1923, his body was returned to Hoima and interred at Mparo. This burial of Kabarega was in most respects traditional, but certain customs were deemed obsolete. The most grisly of these involved digging a 10m-deep hole, the floor of which would be covered in

Kamurasi, once again, made a poor impression, badgering his guests with interminable demands for gifts, culminating in the suggestion that Baker leave his wife behind at Mruli as a royal consort. But after the Bakers left Mruli for Lake Albert, they received a message from Kamurasi requesting another meeting, at which it transpired that the 'king' they had met at Mruli was an impostor, installed by Kamurasi for reasons that remain unclear. The real Kamurasi impressed Baker as 'a remarkably fine man, tall and well-proportioned … beautifully clean', but still perturbed by the earlier deceit in Mruli, he also observed in Kamurasi a 'peculiarly sinister expression'. When the king started with the customarily outrageous requests for gifts, Baker 'rose to depart, telling him I had heard that Kamurasi was a great king, but that he was a mere beggar, and was doubtless [another] impostor'.

In April 1872, the recently knighted Sir Samuel Baker returned to Bunyoro as governor of Egypt's Equatoria Province, accompanied by a detachment of Egyptian troops, and charged with stopping the Arab slave trade out of the region. Kamurasi had died three years earlier, to be succeeded by his son Kabarega. Baker was impressed by the physical attributes of the new king, describing him as 'excessively neat [and] very well clad, in a beautifully made bark-cloth striped with black… about twenty years of age… five feet ten inches in height, and of extremely light complexion'. Kabarega welcomed Baker's attempt to suppress the slave trade, but he also resented his kingdom being placed under Egyptian sovereignty, and relations between the two men – whose fort and capital lay within a few hundred metres of each other at Masindi – swiftly deteriorated. On 8 June 1872, Kabarega led a surprise attack on Baker's fort, expecting that resistance would be minimal, since he had craftily arranged for poisoned beer to be supplied to the Egyptian troops on the previous day. But Baker repulsed the attack, and having done so burned Kabalega's capital to the ground. Kabarega retreated southward to Mparo (close to modern-day Hoima), where he established a new capital. A decade earlier, Baker had written of Bunyoro that 'the deceit of this country was incredible'. The apparently unprovoked attack on Masindi only confirmed his earlier judgement.

Britain's colonial policy towards Bunyoro was to a great extent moulded by the antipathy expressed by Sir Samuel Baker, who left Equatoria in 1873, towards its 'cowardly, treacherous, beggarly drunkard' of a ruler. Yet a very different impression is given in the writings of the first European to built a lasting relationship with Kabarega: Emin Pasha, who visited Mparo in 1877 to negotiate the peace between Equatoria and Bunyoro, and then served as Governor of Equatoria between 1878 and 1889. 'I have often visited Kabarega,' he wrote, 'and cannot say that I have ever heard him utter an improper word or make an indecent gesture, or that he was ever rude… Kabarega is cheerful, laughs readily and much, talks a great deal, and does not appear to be bound by ceremony, the exact opposite to Mutesa, the conceited ruler of Buganda. I certainly cannot charge Kabarega with begging; on the contrary he sent me daily, in the most hospitable manner, stores… which although they were intended to last one day, could easily have been made to last us a fortnight. I received a detailed account of all the events that happened during Baker's visit, a curiously different account from that given [by Baker]. I had to listen to a long account of the doings of the Danaglas [Egyptian soldiers]… the sum and substance of all being that [Kabarega] had been continually provoked and attacked by them, although he, as occupant on the throne, was entitled to rule over them.'

barkcloth on the morning of the burial. One of the late king's wives – usually the eldest or the favourite – would be seated in the hole, holding in her lap a parcel containing the dead man's jawbone. Onlookers were then seized randomly from the crowd, their limbs were amputated, and then they were thrown into the hole one by one until it was filled.

The tomb is protected within a large domed construction made mostly from natural materials, and not dissimilar in appearance to the more famous Kasubi Tombs in Kampala, though considerably smaller. The grave itself is surrounded by many of Kabarega's personal effects, including some spears and crowns said to be handed down from the Bacwezi dynasty. It is covered with a type of white spotted brown cowhide called *entimba*, held in place by nine traditional hoes. Kabarega's son and successor Omukama Tito Winyi is also buried at Mparo. A plaque outside the main enclosure at Mparo marks the spot where Kabarega granted an audience to the Emin Pasha in 1877.

Coming in a private vehicle, the tombs are clearly visible along the main road towards Masindi. The best way to get there otherwise is on a *boda-boda*, which can be hired opposite the bus station.

Hoima Palace The throne room of Bunyoro-Kitara in the present palace at Hoima also opens to visitors but by prior arrangement. In addition to the traditional nine-legged throne/stool swathed in leopardskins and barkcloth, an array of spears, royal headdresses and musical instruments are on display. Contact the Omukama's Private Secretary (and respected local historian) Yolamu Nsamba (m *0772 471251;* e *nsambay@yahoo.com*).

Katasiha Fort Katasiha, situated only 2km from Hoima along the Butiaba road, was the largest of the forts built by General Colville after Kabarega abandoned his capital at Mparo in late 1893. All that remains of the fort today is the 8m dry moat (now filled in) that surrounded it, and a nearby small cave that was used as a hiding place by Kabarega and later as an arsenal by the British. Still, it's a fair goal for a short walk or bicycle ride out of the town centre.

KABWOYA WILDLIFE RESERVE

Text taken from Uganda's Great Rift Valley *by Andrew Roberts*

Uganda's newest protected area, the 87km² Kabwoya Wildlife Reserve, occupies an isolated but superbly scenic lake plain sandwiched between Lake Albert and the Rift's Bunyoro escarpment. It is presently completely unknown to tourists although this situation will quickly change with the opening of an excellent new safari lodge by the lake. In a previous incarnation – the 227km² Kaiso-Tonya Controlled Hunting Area – Kabwoya's grasslands were famous during the 1960s for large and varied herds of game, and represented an important part of a migration route along the Rift between Semliki and Murchison Falls. This wildlife spectacle has since been lost; most animals were wiped out by poachers and the remainder dispersed when the lake plain was invaded by cattle herders. In a belated effort to protect remnant game, Kabwoya Wildlife Reserve was created in 2002 from the southern section of the Kaiso-Tonya Controlled Hunting Area when this category of protected area was deemed obsolete and discontinued. The northern part of Kaiso-Tonya was afforded the new (and some would say equally meaningless) title of 'Community Wildlife Area', Uganda's lowest category of protected area.

Uganda Wildlife Authority has leased Kabwoya and Kaiso-Tonya to a private tourism/conservation operator who works in partnership with UWA staff and Hoima District. It has been uphill all the way for the new management team. In 2002, Land Rovers had to be winched over the escarpment to reach a reserve full of cattle but obviously not game. A further issue concerning conservationists is oil prospecting in the reserve for it seems probable that significant reserves do lie underneath it. There is a silver lining, for the no-expense-spared prospecting operation has constructed an excellent access road down the escarpment to the reserve, making Lake Albert considerably easier to reach than it was for Samuel and Florence Baker when they struggled down to its shore in 1864.

Conservation progress has been impressive in Kabwoya. With the backing of local politicians and Bunyoro royalty, cattle have been relocated from the wildlife reserve to the adjacent Community Wildlife Area and game is increasing quickly in response. Buffalo now graze the airstrip near Lake Albert Safari Lodge and hippos have taken up residence in the lake below it. Uganda kob, warthog, duiker and bushbuck are now common in Kabwoya's *Combretum* savanna and even an occasional lion is seen. Hartebeest are to be reintroduced from the nearby Bugungu Wildlife Reserve near Butiaba. Primates include black-and-white colobus monkey and chimpanzee, which inhabit riparian forests along the Hoywa and Wambabya rivers and tributaries, as well as the baboon troops that clamber over the lake cliff near the lodge. A full bird list has yet to be compiled but with habitats including savanna, riverine forest and lakeshore, birders are unlikely to be disappointed.

As a game-viewing destination, Kabwoya has a long way to go, being presently in a similar situation to that of neighbouring Semliki Wildlife Reserve ten years ago, before the lodge owners kick-started conservation activities there. The reserve does have two other, significant areas of appeal. Firstly, it is a prime location to appreciate the Albertine Rift Valley and its wide-ranging history. Secondly it allows an attractive detour and overnight stop from the interminable 350km section of the tour itinerary between Fort Portal and Paraa (Murchison Falls).

Getting there Kabwoya Wildlife Reserve lies 70km southwest of Hoima and 215km north of Fort Portal. From Hoima, follow the Fort Portal road south for 26km and turn right off the main road at Kiziranfumbi. After 26km, take a left fork then after another 9km turn right at Kaseta. The reserve boundary on the Rift Valley Escarpment is 8km further on. The safari lodge and lakeshore lie another 14km across the plain. Approaching from Fort Portal, follow the tarmac Kampala road east for 50km to the northbound (*murram*) Hoima road at Kyenjojo. It's 121km to Kiziranfumbi where you turn left and follow the directions above. Travellers bound for Murchison Falls from Kabwoya can bypass Hoima by turning left in the village 9km beyond Kaseta. Around 18km further on (after crossing the Wambabya River), turn right at Busereka to reach the Hoima–Butiaba road (27km). Turn left here to reach Murchison Falls (Bugungu Gate) via Biso and the viewpoints on the Rift Valley Escarpment above Butiaba.

Where to stay

🏠 **Lake Albert Safari Lodge** m 0772 221003; e info@lakealbertlodge.com or reservations@lakealbertlodge.com; www.lakealbertlodge.com. This excellent new lodge has been developed by the reserve concessionaire at a stunning location on top of the 60m lakeshore cliffs. It's a perfect place to watch the sun set over the Blue Mountains of DRC across 40km of water and even to get up in the middle of the night to experience the *son et lumière* that accompanies the frequent storms on the lake. Accommodation is provided in attractive canvas-sided and immaculately thatched s/c cottages facing the lake and a tented camp nearby. A small swimming pool is a welcome feature since it gets hot in the trough of the Albertine Rift Valley. *US$80 pp fb for cliftop bandas. US$60 pp for standing tents. Pitch your own tent for US$15 pp (US$45 fb).*

Activities Entrance to the reserve costs US$10 for foreign visitors and US$5 for residents. There's no entrance gate at present and fees are settled at the lodge where activities are organised. Game drives are of course available. However since this presently compares poorly to the experience in Murchison Falls or Queen Elizabeth National Park, a range of additional activities are offered. These include

11

walking safaris, birdwatching, fossil hunting and visits to some lovely waterfalls dropping over the Rift Escarpment.

MASINDI

The gateway to Murchison Falls and Budongo Forest, Masindi is a sleepy small town (population estimate 15,000), slumped in an aura of subdued commercial activity that reflects its location along a road that today leads to nowhere of great economic consequence. In the colonial era, by contrast, Masindi was a thriving hub of international trade, situated at the pivot of three key transportation routes: from Butiaba across Lake Albert to the northern DRC, north along the Nile to southern Sudan, and across Lake Kyoga to the Busoga Railway which connects to the main Uganda–Mombasa line. Commerce declined after 1962, when the rising level of Lake Albert enforced the closure of Butiaba Port, and it was further undermined by the havoc wrought on the national economy and transport infrastructure under Idi Amin. Masindi's capacity for economic recovery during the Museveni era has been restricted by several factors: the effective closure of the Sudanese and Congolese borders, the ongoing unrest in the northwest of Uganda, and the decreased significance of Lake Kyoga following the collapse of the Busoga railway link.

Masindi's compact town centre isn't much to look at: a tight grid of erratically surfaced roads, dusty or muddy depending on how recently it last rained, emanate from a central market, lined with the faded colonial-era shopfronts that characterise so many small Ugandan towns. Rather more appealing is the green, leafy stretch of suburbia that runs north from the town centre past the golf course. In 1924, Etta Close was charmed by Masindi and its 'European officials [who] live in trim little bungalows with little gardens full of European flowers placed in a circle around a golf course and two lawn tennis courts, the one and only hotel being not far off.' The European officials are gone, but this description otherwise feels surprisingly apposite today, right down to the recently renovated Masindi Hotel, built in 1923 and once host to the writer and hunting enthusiast Ernest Hemingway.

A group of Masindi-based VSO volunteers has just produced an informative brochure that identifies a trail around the town taking in interesting buildings and landmarks and providing a little of the history of the town. Visit or contact the Court View Hotel for a copy (see *Where to stay*, below).

GETTING THERE AND AWAY Masindi lies 215km north of Kampala and is reached by following the surfaced Lira–Gulu road, which is in good condition for much of its length, though a few stretches are quite heavily pot-holed. Roughly 170km north of Kampala, a 45km dirt road to Masindi – not signposted but easily identified by a couple of billboards – branches left from the Gulu road. This dirt road is in fair condition, though some stretches might be slippery after rain, and it passes through a few seasonal marshes that often hold significant concentrations of waterbirds. The drive shouldn't take much longer than three hours in a private vehicle. The Post Bus to Masindi (Ush8,000) leaves Kampala at 08.00 daily except for Sundays, and sets off in the opposite direction at 07.00. Other buses and minibuses between Kampala and Masindi run regularly throughout the day, charging Ush7,000, and taking about four hours in either direction. Travellers with private transport might well want to stop at the Ziwa Rhino Sanctuary *en route* (see page 370). The junction of the two roads to Murchison Falls lies about 1km north of the town centre, opposite the Shell garage (the last opportunity to fill up at normal fuel prices) and between the police station and the Masindi Hotel. A right

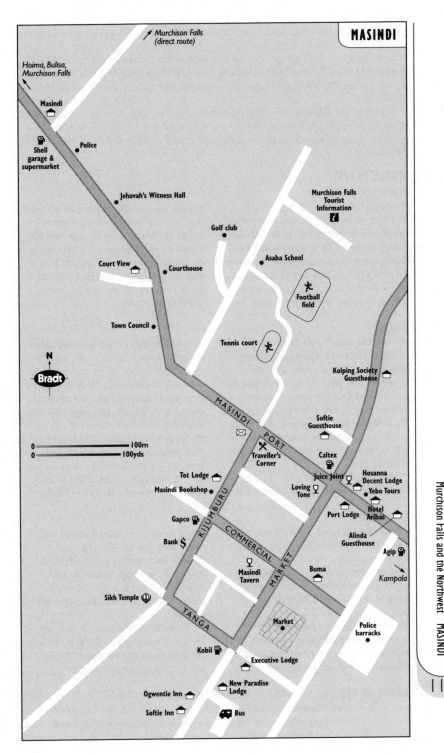

MASINDI

Murchison Falls
(direct route)

Hoima, Bulisa,
Murchison Falls

Masindi

Shell
garage &
supermarket

Police

Jehovah's Witness Hall

Golf club

Murchison Falls
Tourist
Information

Court View

Courthouse

Asaba School

Football
field

Town Council

Tennis court

N

Bradt

Kolping Society
Guesthouse

MASINDI PORT

Softie
Guesthouse

0   100m
0   100yds

Caltex

Juice Joint

Hosanna
Decent Lodge

Traveller's
Corner

Tot Lodge

Masindi Bookshop

Loving
Tone

Yebo Tours

Port Lodge

Hotel
Aribas

KIJUMBURU

Gapco

Alinda
Guesthouse

Agip

Bank $

COMMERCIAL

Kampala

Masindi
Tavern

Buma

Sikh Temple

MARKET

TANGA

Market

Police
barracks

Kobil

Executive Lodge

New Paradise
Lodge

Ogwentie Inn

Softie Inn

Bus

Murchison Falls and the Northwest   MASINDI

11

367

turn at this junction (signposted for Paraa via Kichumbanyobo) takes you along the direct 85km route to Paraa via Kanyiyo Pabidi and Sambiya Lodge. Continue straight past the Shell garage for the 135km route to Paraa via Busingiro, Butiaba, Bulisa and Nile Safari Camp. There is no public transport to Paraa along either route, but on the latter, one bus daily connects Kampala to Wanseko via Masindi and Bulisa.

Heading for Hoima in a private vehicle, follow the Busingiro road out of Masindi past the Shell garage for about 3km until you reach a fork in the road, where you must branch to the left. Regular minibuses run between Masindi and Hoima.

WHERE TO STAY
Moderate

Masindi Hotel 0465 20023; m 0712 447676; e masindihotel@gmail.com. This rambling colonial-era hotel (built in 1923 by the East Africa Railways Commission) lies in attractive wooded grounds roughly 1km northwest of the town centre. The hotel became decidedly rundown and cobwebbed prior to being privatised in 2000, since when a series of restorations have restored its period character. The refurbished s/c rooms are airy and clean, with tiled floors, hot water and internet facilities. The Hemingway Bar has large-screen DSTV, a swimming pool is planned and a buffet meal in the Kabarega Restaurant costs Ush15,000. A lot of effort has gone into this hotel but it might still be slightly pushing its luck with its asking prices. *US$47/65 sgl/dbl B&B.*

Budget

Court View Hotel 0465 20461; m 0772 693458; e courtview@utlonline.co.ug. Situated opposite the municipal courtroom about halfway between the town centre and the Masindi Hotel, the recently opened Court View offers accommodation in small but clean s/c *bandas* with nets and hot water. The *bandas* are somewhat tightly clustered, but the grounds are pretty, and the restaurant serves decent grills, curries and salads at around Ush5,000–6,000. *US$16/22 sgl/dbl.*

Alinda Guesthouse m 0772 550710/520382. This friendly dbl-storey guesthouse, built around a large courtyard with chairs and tables, is comfortably the best budget option in the town centre, with clean s/c rooms with fan, net and hot water and similar rooms using common showers. The restaurant serves dishes such as chicken and chips, beef stew or spaghetti in the Ush2,000–4,000 range. *US$11/13 s/c sgl/dbl, US$11/12 non s/c rooms.*

Kolping House Guesthouse 0465 20458. Set in green grounds less than 500m from the town centre, this is a clean and reliable church-run hostel, with a fair restaurant attached. *US$11 for a twin using common showers, US$13/14 s/c twin/dbl.*

Shoestring

Buma Hotel Clean and centrally located, very close to the bus station. *US$8/9 for a s/c sgl/dbl with cold water only.*

Hotel Aribas This quiet hotel is nothing special, but it's a notch better than most of the dumps around the bus station. *US$5/6 sgl/dbl using common showers.*

Executive Lodge (aka Kyateketera Hotel) Optimistically named and one of a few scruffy guesthouses dotted around the bus station, with adequate rooms with nets and most noteworthy perhaps for the notice reading 'Prostitutes not allowed accept your own wife'. *US$5.*

Softie Guesthouse Once popular with budget travellers, this increasingly rundown but still acceptable lodge (not to be confused with the inferior Softie Inn) offers clean rooms with nets. *US$4 pp.*

Hosanna Decent Lodge Adequately clean and seemingly as decent as it pertains to be, this lodge nevertheless feels rather overpriced. *US$5/6 for a basic sgl/dbl using common showers.*

WHERE TO EAT
The out-of-town **Masindi Hotel** serves buffet meals (Ush15,000) while the **Court View** offers the usual grills and stews for around Ush6,000 plus some tasty Indian and Chinese items and home-grown salads enlivened with tuna, egg, etc. These items, together with apparently swift service, make a refreshing change

In 1970, some 300 black rhinos roamed wild in Uganda, divided between Murchison Falls and Kidepo national parks, while a population of roughly 120 white rhinos was resident in Ajai Wildlife Reserve, some later relocated to the more secure Murchison Falls. Within little more than a decade, both species had been poached to local extinction: Uganda's last white rhino was shot in Murchison Falls in 1982, and no black rhino has been observed in either Murchison or Kidepo since 1983. The main cause of this sudden decline was poaching – rhino horns, used as dagger handles in the Middle East and as an aphrodisiac in parts of Asia, fetch up to US$ one million on the black market – exacerbated by the general atmosphere of lawlessness that prevailed during and after the 1979 war in which Idi Amin was ousted.

Founded in 1998, the Rhino Fund Uganda is an NGO dedicated to reintroducing both species of rhino to their former Ugandan haunts. The first step in this process took place in December 2001, when a pair of two-and-a-half-year old white rhinos, bought from the Solio Ranch in Kenya, landed at Entebbe to a festive reception. The rhinos – named Kabira and Sherino – currently reside in a holding pen in the Uganda Wildlife Education Centre in Entebbe. The focus of the reintroduction programme has now shifted to the 7,000ha Ziwa Ranch in Nakasongola District, about 120km north of Kampala, where they will be the first residents of a fenced 80km² sanctuary that will eventually contain about 30 black and 20 white rhinos. Four white rhinos were introduced in 2005 and more will be added as funds become available. Once the populations have reproduced and stabilised, the intention is to release the rhinos back into Murchison Falls and Kidepo.

Unlike Entebbe, Ziwa, which is located within the Kafu River basin, lies within the historical range of the black rhino which was restricted to northern Uganda and, unlike Entebbe, the ranch contains represents natural rhino habitat of *Combretum* savanna similar to that in Murchison Falls National Park. The ranch is necessarily sealed off within a 2m-high electric fence and as further security, the animals and the perimeter are monitored 24 hours by 40 rangers.

Uganda's recently imported white rhinos are of the southern race *Ceratotherium s. simum* rather than the indigenous northern race *C. s. cottoni*. Ziwa's first four southern whites were introduced in 2005. Unfortunately, the chances of reintroducing the indigenous northern white rhino of northern Uganda, the DRC, Sudan, Chad and the Central African Republic are now practically zero. Before the recent wars in DRC, the wild population was reduced to just 30 animals in Garamba National Park in northeastern DRC. Two censuses of the park, carried out in 2006 with possible relocation of the last wild northern white rhinos in mind, spotted only four animals. All is not *quite* lost however, for nine more animals are held in zoos in San Diego and the Czech Republic. Some conservationists have suggested that the two rhinos in the Czech zoo, which were taken from Uganda during the Amin era, should be returned – but the zoo argues, not unreasonably, that they are probably safer kept exactly where they are now.

to the upcountry norm. The **Alinda Guesthouse** can be recommended to those on a tighter budget or seeking a more central location. Otherwise, the usual scattering of cheap local eateries and bars aside, there is only one genuinely alluring restaurant in Masindi.

✕ **Travellers Corner Restaurant** The best restaurant in the centre of Masindi, this is housed in a colonial-era building with a wide balcony from where you can watch the town go by over a cold drink. It serves good pizzas, roast chicken, steak, burgers and pasta dishes. *Meals around Ush6,000.*

LISTINGS

Tourist information Current rates and other practical information relating to Murchison Falls National Park and associated conservation areas (Budongo Forest, Bugungu Wildlife Reserve) is available at the **Murchison Falls Conservation Area tourist office** (☎ *0465 20428*), which lies on the outskirts of town, off the road towards Masindi Hotel. The office also usually stocks the useful booklet on Murchison Falls National Park.

Vehicle hire **Yebo Tours** (☎ *0465 20029;* **m** *0772 637493;* **f** *0465 20411;* **e** *yebotours@hotmail.com or yebotours2002@yahoo.com*). The Masindi-based Yebo Tours can provide vehicle hire to Murchison Falls and other local attractions at a very reasonable daily rate of US$70 per day for a 4x4 and US$80 for a minibus (inclusive of driver and unlimited kilometres, but exclusive of fuel). Yebo can also arrange all-inclusive camping tours to Murchison Falls. The office is a few doors down from the Alinda Guesthouse.

Shopping One of the better central supermarkets lies out along the Kampala road, about 100m past the Agip garage. It stocks frozen meat, imported tinned foods and biscuits, and packet soups. It's a good place to stock up if you're heading off to camp for a day or two – though expensive by comparison with similar places in Kampala. There's also a small supermarket attached to the Shell garage opposite the Masindi Hotel. Local handicrafts are sold at a stall attached to the Court View Hotel.

Foreign exchange Forex services are provided by the Stanbic Bank.

EXCURSIONS The most popular destinations for excursions out of Masindi are Budongo Forest and Murchison Falls, both covered later in the chapter. An excellent diversion *en route* to Masindi is the Ziwa Rhino Sanctuary, which lies about two hours' drive out of Kampala.

Ziwa Rhino Sanctuary (**m** *0772 713410;* **e** *info@rhinofund.org; www.rhinofund.org*) Ziwa Rhino Sanctuary is a 7,000ha ranch about 120km (two hours' drive) out of Kampala on the Masindi–Gulu road. It presently contains four rhinos (more to arrive soon) and a range of smaller game species. The rhinos can be tracked on foot in the company of a ranger at a cost of US$15 (plus entrance fees below). They are habitually found in wetland areas so be appropriately shod for the conditions.

Entrance to Ziwa costs US$20 for non-residents (children 5–12yrs US$10). East African residents pay US$10 (children US$5). Ugandan citizens pay Ush5,000 (children Ush2,000). Day trips from Kampala can be organised. Costs – including transport, lunch and ranger guide for rhino tracking – are US$65 for non-residents, US$55 for East African residents and US$50 for Ugandan citizens.

Accommodation is presently limited to camping though a wider range of facilities is planned. Camping costs US$15 and US$10 for children. Bring your own provisions though lunches are available for pre-booked groups (minimum 5 people) at Ush7,500.

Masindi Port Masindi Port, which lies 40km east of the town of Masindi, fringes the marshy area where the Victoria Nile exits Lake Kyoga. The port peaked in importance during the colonial era, but no commercial boats sail from it today. The surrounding marshes are of potential interest to birdwatchers, and there are quite a few hippos around. You'd be unlikely to have any problems organising a dugout to explore Lake Kyoga, and the Nile River is navigable to the top of Karuma Falls,

70km downstream, though exploring the latter would be highly inadvisable in the present political climate in the northwest.

Little if any formal public transport runs to Masindi Port, though on most days a pick-up truck or two heads out from Masindi Town to the port. An erratic but free ferry service crosses the Nile between Masindi Port and Maiyunge on the opposite bank, taking about ten minutes. When it's not running, you can hire a dugout to take you across for a few hundred shillings. From Maiyunge, a road heads north to Lira, an area that is unsafe for travel at the time of writing. There is no accommodation in Masindi Port, but a basic lodge exists in Maiyunge.

Boomu Women's Group (m *0772 448950, due to poor reception, it's best to SMS, and messages are checked every half hour;* e *ucota@africaonline.co.ug; www.boomuwomensgroup.org*). Shortly before going to print, we received an email from Lan-Any Pham, a volunteer working with this women's group (and member of the Uganda Community Tourism Association) located outside the main park entrance gate to Murchison Falls National Park, 35 minutes' ride from Masindi by *boda-boda* or special hire. The group has set up a small tourism project in a cosy location with trees and flowers, and it aims to offer visitors a participatory experience in community tourism in rural Uganda. It contains four *bandas* with mosquito nets at Ush10,000 per person B&B twin or Ush15,000 per person B&B double, as well as camping (Ush3,000), showers, toilets, a scenic community walk (Ush6,000), a unique 'process of cooking tour' (Ush8,000) and basic meals and drinks. An all-inclusive package including both tours, one night's *banda* accommodation, dinner and breakfast costs Ush20,000. Also scheduled to open soon is a short (30 minutes each way) guided walk for a picnic lunch on Kyabatwa Hill, which lies in Murchinson Falls Conservation Area and offers a 360° view of the surrounding area.

The menu will be expanded in the future as the group is planning a project farm, hen house and small fish pond. All proceeds from the community walk and a percentage of accommodation turnover goes towards a fund for community projects, the first of which will be a nursery. There is also a basketry group that can demonstrate its craft and show visitors how to make their own basket. A shop sells a variety of crafts.

BUDONGO FOREST

The 790km² Budongo Forest Reserve is one of the most extensive and ecologically diverse in East Africa, with some 465 plant species recorded, most impressively perhaps a dense concentration of buttressed giant mahoganies reaching up to 60m tall. Budongo's population of 800 chimpanzees, the largest anywhere in Uganda, has been the subject of scientific research for several decades. Other common primates include red-tailed monkey, blue monkey, black-and-white colobus, potto and various forest galago species. More than 250 butterfly species have been recorded.

Budongo Forest is of great ornithological significance, with some 366 bird species recorded, including 60 west or central African birds known from fewer than five locations in East Africa. The yellow-footed flycatcher, often associated with ironwood trees, is known from nowhere else in Uganda, while the Ituri batis, lemon-bellied crombec, white-thighed hornbill, black-eared ground thrush and chestnut-capped flycatcher are known from only one other East African forest. The Royal Mile, the stretch of road connecting Nyabyeya Forestry College to the main research station, is regarded by some as the single best birdwatching site in Uganda. The main road past Busingiro also offers superb birdwatching.

Fourteen years ago, Budongo was totally undeveloped for tourism and the only habituated chimpanzees in the forest were those being studied by researchers. In 1992, the Budongo Forest Ecotourism Project was founded with the aim of conserving Budongo and the nearby Kanyiyo Pabidi Forest through the development of tourist projects that are of direct benefit to local communities. Two tourist sites were created using foreign funding. The Busingiro Tourist Site is situated within the Budongo Forest proper, and reached by following the Bulisa route towards Murchison Falls. The other site lies within the Kanyiyo Pabidi Forest (and, because it is reached by following the direct route from Masindi to Murchison Falls, coverage is included separately later in this chapter).

The National Forest Authority has recently transferred the management of both its Budongo tourism sites to the Jane Goodall Institute (JGI), a leading chimpanzee conservation organisation. Notwithstanding the excellent of the tracking experience at both locations, JGI has decided (reasonably enough) that having two under-utilised, poorly managed, and inadequately financed chimp tourism sites in one forest was excessive. As a result, chimp tracking has been discontinued at Busingiro where, although general forest walks will remain available, JGI will concentrate on educational activities. Chimp tourism will focus on the Kanyiyo Pabidi site which will benefit from concentrated investment in accommodation and services. Profits made from these sites will assist with the protection of Budongo Forest and to encourage through education and community benefits, closer collaboration between local communities and NFA.

GETTING THERE AND AWAY The Busingiro Tourist Site lies right alongside the Bulisa road, 43km west of Masindi, and is clearly signposted. The 2km turn-off to Nyabyeya Forestry College is about 10km closer to Masindi, and also signposted. The drive from Masindi should take about an hour in a private vehicle. Using public transport, any minibus-taxi or bus heading from Masindi to Butiaba or Wanseko can drop you at the camp, though you'll probably have to pay the full Ush3,000 fare to Butiaba. A 4x4 with driver can be hired in Masindi through Yebo Tours (see *Listings*, page 370).

For details of continuing from Busingiro to Murchison Falls via Lake Albert, see the heading *Masindi to Murchison via Lake Albert*, page 375.

WHERE TO STAY

Busingiro Tourist Site 🔌 0414 252711. Cut into a tall forest glade, this stunningly attractive and admirably rustic camp is alive with birdlife and monkeys, while the nocturnal chorus of insects is regularly interrupted by the alarming shrieks of tree hyraxes. *Camping costs US$5.*

Nyabyeya Forestry College 🔌 039301258/ 039301114; m 0772358755/0772496051; e nfc@infocom.co.ug. The small resthouse at the Nyabyeya Forestry College is about 10km from Busingiro. Its main advantage over Busingiro is that it is positioned close to the Royal Mile. Water and firewood are available at the resthouse, but you must bring your own food. *Around US$6 for a bed.*

ACTIVITIES Though no longer used for chimp tracking, Busingiro's complex and extensive trail system remains open for forest walks. Some routes are of note, variously, for trees, birds or butterflies so it is worth discussing any special interests and preferences with the guides, who will tailor your walks accordingly. A three-hour forest walk will cost US$10 until June 2007 when it will increase to US$15. Birdwatching will cost US$10/15 (half/full day) for a half day with a specialised guide. This will rise to US$15/20 in 2007. Although you may walk unaccompanied along the main road, visitors may enter the forest on either side only when accompanied by a guide.

The best place to do a guided bird walk is along the **Royal Mile**, which runs between Nyabyeya Forestry College and the research station. Unfortunately, the Royal Mile lies about 14km from Busingiro, so it's not really a viable option for a day trip unless you have private transport or stay at the forestry college. Generally regarded as being one of Uganda's best forest-birding sites, the Royal Mile supports a wide variety of localised species, with the sought-after African dwarf, blue-breasted and chocolate-backed kingfishers all very common. A long list of other local specials includes Cassin's hawk eagle, Nahan's francolin, white-thighed hornbill, yellow-billed barbet, lemon-billed crombec, black-capped apalis, forest flycatcher, yellow-footed flycatcher and Jameson's wattle-eye. Various monkeys are also likely to be seen, along with giant forest squirrels and the bizarre chequered elephant-shrew. Equally bizarre in this remote patch of forest is a large church built by Polish refugees who were settled in the area during World War II. Many of the footpaths in this part of the forest are a legacy of the same refugees.

The alternative to visiting the Royal Mile is to walk along **the main road past Busingiro**. Though not on a par with the Royal Mile, the birding here is still excellent and it is generally easier to locate birds than it is in the forest proper. Among the species to look for on the road and around the campsite are brown-crowned eremomela, Ituri batis, chestnut-capped flycatcher, Cassin's and Sabine's spinetails, and grey and yellow longbills. The chocolate-backed kingfisher, common in the area, is most easily located by call. A small pool by the side of the road about 1km back towards Masindi is a reliable place to see the shining blue kingfisher and black-necked weaver. In addition to birds, you should also see at least three types of primate on this stretch of road. There's nothing to prevent you from walking along the road alone, but it's worth taking a guide – they are very knowledgeable, particularly with regard to bird calls, and they all carry binoculars and a field guide. With a vehicle and spotlight, the road could be worth exploring by night – on our last visit we were shown a colony of gigantic hammerhead bats along the road between Busingiro to the aforementioned pool, and the nocturnal potto and tree pangolin are also resident.

KANYIYO PABIDI FOREST

The 268km² Kanyiyo Pabidi Forest, the second largest of the four forest blocks within the Budongo Forest Reserve, is essentially an eastern extension of the main Budongo Forest, to which it is linked by a forested corridor crossing the Paraa road. Kanyiyo Pabidi harbours a similar though not identical fauna and flora to Budongo, and because it has never been logged it contains a far higher proportion of large buttressed mahogany and ironwood trees. A similar range of forest primates to Budongo is present, notably black-and-white colobus and blue monkey, while large troops of olive baboon are a regular sight along the main road. Owing to the proximity to Murchison Falls, herds of elephant and buffalo regularly visit Kanyiyo Pabidi, while the occasional wandering lion supplements the resident leopard population.

The Kanyiyo Pabidi Tourist Site was established along similar lines and by the same organisation as Busingiro, but it is more convenient for people driving through to Murchison Falls, since it lies alongside the main Masindi–Paraa road.

Kanyiyo Pabidi protects a similar range of birds to Busingiro, though the denser vegetation of the pristine forest can make birding more difficult. The best place to look for birds is around the campsite, especially the gallery forest between the staff quarters and the main road, and a 600m nature trail offers good views into the canopy. Among the species we saw on a recent visit were the common shrike-flycatcher, chestnut wattle-eye, Narina trogon, little greenbul, chestnut-winged

11

You'd scarcely credit it today, but back in the colonial era, the port of Butiaba – situated on the lakeshore 8km west of the Masindi–Bulisa road – was a commercial centre of some significance. In the 1920s, the colonial government earmarked the existing administrative station – contemporaneously described by Etta Close as 'a few native huts, an Indian store, and three little European houses by the edge of the water' – for a major harbour development. A regular steamer service was established out of Butiaba, effectively extending the existing import–export route between Masindi and Mombasa further west, to the Congolese port of Mahagi and to Nimule on the Sudanese border.

Butiaba's stock rose further in 1931, when it was selected as a landing site for the first seaplane flights between Cairo and East Africa. Over the subsequent decade, it also became something of a tourist focus, after a freshly dredged channel through the Victoria Nile estuary allowed boats from Butiaba to divert to a landing point a short distance downstream of Murchison Falls. During the production of the classic Bogart/Hepburn movie *The African Queen*, a boat called the *Murchison* was chartered by director John Huston to carry supplies and run errands between Butiaba and the nearby filming location.

Butiaba's celebrity connections don't end with Bogart and Hepburn. The American writer Ernest Hemingway and his fourth wife Mary Welsh arrived there on 23 January 1954, somewhat the worse for wear after a bruising 24-hour trip to Murchison Falls. The day before, their chartered Cessna had dipped to avoid hitting a flock of birds, in the process clipping a wing on an abandoned telegraph wire, and forcing a crash landing in which Hemingway dislocated his right shoulder and Mary cracked several ribs. The injured passengers and their pilot spent the night huddled on the riverbank below Murchison Falls, to be rescued the next morning by a boat headed to Butiaba.

At Butiaba, Hemingway chartered a De Haviland to fly him and his wife back to Entebbe the next morning. On take-off, however, the plane lifted, bumped back down,

starling, grey apalis, dwarf and pygmy kingfishers, and a great many forest sunbirds and hornbills. A local speciality is Puvel's illapopsis, which, although it was recorded here for the first time only recently, and is known from no other locality in East Africa, is very common. The extremely localised and magnificently garish green-breasted pitta has also been recorded here.

GETTING THERE AND AWAY Kanyiyo Pabidi Tourist Site lies alongside the main Paraa road, 29km from Masindi, and it is clearly signposted. In a private vehicle, it would be easy enough to stop here for a walk *en route* between Masindi and Paraa. The site also lies about an hour's drive from Sambiya Lodge, and is often visited as a day trip from there. There is no public transport along this road, so travellers without a vehicle are better off heading to Busingiro in the Budongo Forest.

WHERE TO STAY

🏠 **Kanyiyo Pabidi Tourist Site** ✆ 0414 252711. This is a very similar set-up to Busingiro in the Budongo Forest. Happily, you can expect facilities and services to improve drastically (though prices will inevitably rise) by the end of 2007. At present, facilities include a cooking shelter, clean borehole water, hot showers and accommodation in adequate but rather musty *bandas* costing about US$11 per person. Camping costs US$5 per person. Beers and sodas are normally available, but you will need to bring your own food. Guided walks cost US$20 for foreign visitors and US$10 for residents. JGI plans accommodation in log cabins with tentative prices of US$16 for a self-contained twin, US$32 for a 4-bed family unit and US$11 per bed in a bunkhouse.

crashed, and burst into flames. Mary and the pilot escaped through a window. Hemingway, too bulky to fit through the window and unable to use his dislocated arm, battered open the buckled door with his head, to emerge with bleeding skull and a rash of blistering burns. The battered couple were driven to Masindi to receive medical attention and spent a few days recuperating at the Masindi Hotel. On 25 January 1954, the *Daily News* broke the news of the accident under the headline 'Hemingway Feared Dead in Nile Air Crash'. A spate of premature obituaries followed before it was discovered that the writer had survived, if only just.

Hemingway had, in addition to the dislocated arm and several first-degree burns, limped out of the burning plane with a collapsed intestine, a ruptured liver and kidney, two crushed vertebrae, temporary loss of vision in one eye, impaired hearing, and a fractured skull. In October of that year, he was awarded the Nobel Prize for Literature, but was too battered to attend the ceremony. Nor did he have the energy to work the 200,000 words he wrote on safari into publishable shape – an edited version finally appeared in 1999 under the name *True At First Light*. It is widely asserted, too, that the injuries Hemingway sustained at Butiaba sparked the gradual decline in his mental well-being that led ultimately to his suicide in 1961.

In 1962, coincidentally the same year that Uganda gained independence, unusually heavy rains caused the level of Lake Albert to rise by several metres overnight, sinking all of the ships in Butiaba harbour and leaving much of the town submerged. The port was officially abandoned in 1963, never to be redeveloped. Today it is little more than an overgrown fishing village. The airstrip where Hemingway so nearly died in 1954 still flies a windsock, but it sees little aerial activity other than ducks and herons flapping overhead. The only other remaining evidence of Butiaba's former significance is a ruined cotton factory on the outskirts of town, and the wreck of the stalwart lake steamer SS *Coryndon* (named after Sir Robert Coryndon, Governor of Uganda 1918–22), which sank during the floods of 1962.

ACTIVITIES Note that activities much be booked through JGI's agent and that visitors turning up will pay a US$5 surcharge on all activities.

The three-hour chimp walk will cost US$17 until June 2007 when it will increase to US$30. Another option is chimp habituation where you can go out with the field researchers and habituators and experience a full day (minimum six hours, starting at 07.00) in the life of chimpanzees. This costs US$50 until June 2007 and thereafter US$80. A maximum of two people is allowed. A birding walk costs US$10/15 (resident/non resident) for a half/full-day's walk until June 2007 then US$15/20. Other walks are available. The four-hour loop taking in the Pabidi Hill viewpoint costs US$15, rising to US$20. The easy 45-minute Mahogany Trail (US$5) visits what is apparently the oldest (300 years old) mahogany tree found in East Africa. It's certainly the largest I've seen standing in Uganda.

MASINDI TO MURCHISON VIA LAKE ALBERT

Although most organised tours favour the direct route between Masindi and Paraa, the longer alternative route via Lake Albert is among the most scenic roads in Uganda, with quite a number of possible diversions along the way. Foremost among these – and covered under a separate heading above – is the Busingiro Tourist Site in Budongo Forest, well worth visiting even if you have no intention of going on to the national park.

11

GETTING AROUND The 135km road between Masindi and Murchison Falls via Lake Albert is unsurfaced in its entirety. It is generally in fair condition, and the drive shouldn't require more than three hours, though certain stretches might need to be taken carefully after a serious downpour. The road initially runs northward out of Masindi for about 1km before passing a Shell garage at the signposted junction for the direct route to Paraa. A kilometre further on it bears west in a small tatty suburb and a couple of kilometres further on you'll need to turn right on to the Bulisa road (the main road continues towards Hoima and Kabwoya Wildlife Reserve). The next major landmark, 43km out of Masindi, is Busingiro Tourist Site in Budongo Forest (see pages 371–3), while another 10km past Busingiro a secondary road to Hoima branches to the south at Biso.

Beyond Biso, the road snakes down the Butiaba Escarpment to the Rift Valley floor – baboons are usually present in this area, and the view across Lake Albert to the Blue Mountains of the DRC is stunning. At the base of the escarpment a left turn leads west to the lakeshore port of Butiaba (see box, pages 374–5) while the main road continues north, running roughly parallel to the Lake Albert shore through the Bugungu Wildlife Reserve for 40km, to the small trading centre of Bulisa. From Bulisa, the road continues north for 6km to terminate at the lakeshore port of Wanseko. Those heading for Murchison Falls, however, must turn right at Bulisa (clearly signposted), from where it's another 20km to Bugungu Entrance Gate (passing the turn-off to Nile Safari Camp along the way). About 5km after entering the national park, the road from Bulisa connects with the main Masindi Road roughly 7km south of Paraa.

Public transport along this route has improved greatly in recent years, with the breakdown-prone bus that once ran thrice weekly between Kampala and Wanseko having been rendered obsolete by minibus-taxis, which leave Masindi for Wanseko and/or Butiaba throughout the day. All transport between Masindi and Butiaba or Wanseko will pass the Busingiro Tourist Site in Budongo Forest, but transport to Butiaba will not pass through the Bugungu Wildlife Reserve to Bulisa. In addition, there is a less regular direct minibus service to Wanseko, Bulisa and Butiaba from Hoima, possibly the better option if you're heading to Murchison Falls from Fort Portal rather than from Kampala. Vehicles leave Wanseko for Hoima at around 05.30 and start the return trip from Hoima at around 10.00.

It should be stressed that no public transport runs east from Bulisa towards Murchison Falls. It used to be possible to hire a bicycle at Bulisa cheaply and cycle the roughly 33km to Paraa, but I've not heard of anybody doing this for a long time. The alternative will be to hitch to Paraa – by no means impossible, though bear in mind that most people drive to Murchison Falls along the more direct route.

BUGUNGU WILDLIFE RESERVE This small reserve protects an area of savanna and seasonal swamp lying at the base of the Rift Valley Escarpment to the west of Murchison Falls National Park. It supports many of the same species as the neighbouring national park, with an estimated 1,200 head of oribi and 600 Uganda kob as well as substantial populations of leopard, buffalo, warthog, hippo, reedbuck, sitatunga, waterbuck, bushbuck, dik-dik, black-and-white colobus and baboon. Roughly 240 bird species have been recorded, including Abyssinian ground hornbill, shoebill and saddle-billed stork. There are no tourism facilities at present (a basic campsite seems to have closed down).

BULISA The only likely reason why you'd stop over at this wretched junction town might be to hire a bike to cycle to Murchison Falls – an option that's faded in popularity over recent years. Still, any transport continuing to Wanseko will drop you at Bulisa, and inexpensive beds are available at the rundown **Bulisa Corner Guesthouse**.

WANSEKO Situated 6km north of Bulisa, where the Nile Estuary opens into Lake Albert, Wanseko is a hot, dusty fishing village whose Wild West feel is compensated for by some impressive views across the lake to the Congolese Blue Mountains, and the estimable virtue of not being Bulisa. Definitely worth a look are the reed-beds near the estuary, only a few minutes' walk from town, and home to the odd hippo or crocodile as well as a profusion of birds, notably crowned crane and, with a bit of luck, shoebill. The only place to stay is the reasonably clean and comfortable and thoroughly inexpensive **Wanseko Lodge**. Fishing boats act as a ferry service between Wanseko and Panyimur on the northern shore of Lake Albert – for details of this trip, see pages 395–8.

MURCHISON FALLS NATIONAL PARK

Uganda's largest protected area, the 3,840km² Murchison Falls National Park lies at the core of the greater Murchison Falls Conservation Area, which also embraces the Bugungu and Karuma wildlife reserves and the Budongo Forest. Gazetted in its modern form in 1952, the national park previously formed part of the Bunyoro Game Reserve, which was proclaimed in 1910 following the evacuation of the local human population during a sleeping-sickness epidemic. During the Amin era, Murchison Falls was officially re-christened Kabarega Falls, after the former King of Bunyoro, a name that still appears on some maps of Uganda, even though it fell into official and vernacular disuse soon after Amin departed the country. But, whatever one elects to call it, Murchison Falls – the wide, languid Nile being transformed into an explosive froth of thunderous white water as it funnels through a narrow cleft in the Rift Valley Escarpment – is easily the most impressive sight of its type in East Africa.

Spanning altitudes of 619m to 1,292m, Murchison Falls National Park is low lying by Ugandan standards, and of those parts of the country that are regularly visited by tourists, it is the only one that regularly becomes stiflingly hot. The average annual rainfall of 1,085mm, though significantly lower than in the forests of the southwest, compares favourably to most other East African savanna ecosystems. The Victoria Nile, flowing in a westerly direction between Lake Kyoga and Lake Albert, divides the park into two roughly equal parts. North of the river, the vegetation broadly consists of tall, green grassland interspersed with isolated stands of borassus palms, acacia trees and riverine woodland. South of the river, the park is characterised by denser woodland, giving way in the southeast to closed canopy forest around Rabongo Hill, the highest peak in the park.

In the 1960s, Murchison Falls – with its spectacular waterfall, prolific game and clutch of outstanding lodges – was universally regarded to be one of East Africa's most compelling national parks. It was particularly renowned for its prolific elephant population: herds of 500 or greater were a common sight, and the total count of 14,500 was probably the densest on the continent. According to the 1969 census, the park also supported around 26,500 buffalo, 14,000 hippo, 16,000 Jackson's hartebeest, 30,000 Uganda kob and 11,000 warthog, as well as substantial populations of Rothschild's giraffe and both black and white rhinoceros, the latter introduced from the west Nile in the early 1960s. Ironically, in hindsight, the main conservation issue associated with Murchison Falls in the 1960s was overpopulation, particularly of elephant, and associated environmental destruction – indeed the authorities opted to cull some 3,500 elephants and 4,000 hippos during the last years of the decade.

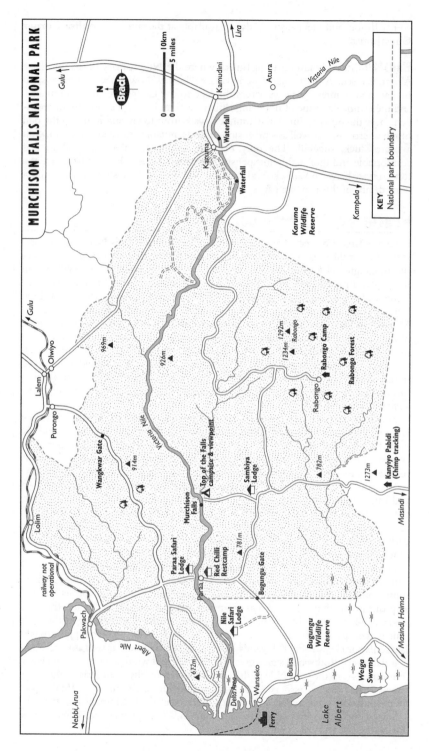

MURCHISON FALLS NATIONAL PARK

N

Bradt

0   10km
0   5 miles

Gulu

Lira

KEY
National park boundary

Kampala

Karuma Wildlife Reserve

Atura

Victoria Nile

Waterfall

Kamudini

Karuma

Waterfall

Gulu

Olwiyo

Lalem

Purongo

Lolim

969m

926m

Victoria Nile

914m

Wangkwar Gate

Murchison Falls

Top of the Falls campsite & viewpoint

Sambiya Lodge

1234m
1292m
Rabongo

Rabongo Camp

Rabongo Forest

Rabongo

782m

1273m

Kanyiyo Pabidi (Chimp tracking)

Masindi

railway not operational

Nebbi, Arua

Pakwach

Albert Nile

672m

Delta area

Wanseko

Bulisa

Masindi, Hoima

Paraa Safari Lodge

Red Chilli Restcamp

Paraa

781m

Bugungu Gate

Nile Safari Lodge

Bugungu Wildlife Reserve

Weiga Swamp

Lake Albert

Ferry

378

Murchison Falls remained a popular tourist draw in the early days of the Amin regime, but the gates closed in September 1972, when foreign visitors were banned from Uganda. Within a couple of years, conservation activities within the national park had practically ceased, making its wildlife easy prey for commercial and subsistence poachers. In 1980, a year after Amin was ousted, aerial surveys indicated that the number of elephants and hippos had been reduced to around 1,400 and 1,200 respectively, while buffalo and other large-mammal populations stood at half of what they had a decade earlier. During the turbulent 1980s, the slaughter continued unabated, as a succession of military factions occupied the park and treated it as a moving larder. By 1990, fewer than 250 elephant and 1,000 buffalo survived, the hartebeest and kob herds had plummeted to around 3,000 and 6,000 respectively, rhinos and African hunting dogs had been hunted to local extinction, and the dwindling populations of giraffe and lion threatened to go the same way. Meanwhile, the combination of declining tourist arrivals and ongoing guerrilla activity had rendered all three of the park's lodges inoperative.

This downward trend was reversed in the early 1990s, and although wildlife populations have yet to re-approach their pre-Amin highs, nobody who has visited the park regularly over the past decade will be in doubt as to the steady and significant growth in animal numbers. A recent aerial census indicated that the elephant population has risen to roughly 1,100, with herds of several hundred occasionally observed north of the Nile. In 2002, the buffalo population, based on partial counts, was estimated at 8,200, an increase of 50% from 1999. The numbers of kob, hartebeest and giraffe have doubled or perhaps even trebled in recent years. Particularly pleasing has been a sudden explosion in the lion population: scarce and skittish into the late 1990s, lions are now readily located on the plains north of the Nile, and it has been credibly estimated that the park supports a healthy population of 150–200 lions across some 15–20 prides. Previously unrecorded in Murchison Falls, a solitary cheetah was observed by rangers in the northern sector on several occasions in 2002.

In total, 76 mammal species have been recorded in Murchison Falls. Aside from those species already mentioned, bushbuck, Defassa waterbuck, Bohor reedbuck, oribi, warthog and side-striped jackal are frequently observed on game drives, as are vervet monkey and olive baboon. Also present on the plains, but less frequently observed, are leopard, spotted hyena and the localised patas monkey. The Rabongo Forest harbours black-and-white colobus, chimpanzees and other forest primates. The bird checklist of 460 confirmed and 19 unconfirmed species is headed in desirability by the shoebill, most common along the stretch of river between Nile Safari Camp and the estuary into Lake Albert. Many other water-associated birds are prolific along the river, while raptors make a strong showing on the checklist with 53 species recorded.

Paraa, situated alongside the Nile a few kilometres downriver of Murchison Falls, is the focal point of tourist activities in the national park. All access roads leading into the park converge at Paraa, where a regular motor ferry provides the only means of crossing between the northern and southern banks of the Nile within the park. The popular launch trip to the base of the falls departs from Paraa, as does the main game-viewing circuit north of the river. Paraa is also the site of Paraa Safari Lodge, on the north bank of the river, while the budget Red Chilli Rest Camp faces it on the south bank. The other two lodges servicing the park, Sambiya Lodge and Nile Safari Camp, both lie about one hour's drive from Paraa, the former along the direct road to Masindi, and the latter off the road to Bulisa. It's worth noting here that the Chobe and Pakuba safari lodges, still present on several maps of Uganda, both fell into disuse in the pre-Museveni era and are unlikely to be renovated in the foreseeable future.

Murchison Falls borders the volatile northwest of Uganda, and both the national park and the roads approaching it have been subject to sporadic security problems throughout the past 15 years. The original Paraa Lodge was burned down by bandits in 1988, after which the part of the national park north of the Nile was declared unsafe for travel and the present Paraa Camp was built on the south bank. In 1996, the park closed briefly when clashes between Joseph Kony's Lord's Resistance Army and the military spread into its boundaries, but for several years after this, no incident of armed banditry was reported within the park or along its southern approach roads.

In March 2001, however, a detachment of Lord's Resistance Army rebels opened fire on a field study group of Kampala-based catering students as they were driving on the Pakuba road a few kilometres north of Paraa. Nine students were killed instantly, together with catering institute director Jimmy Ssekasi, and a national park ranger, and another student died of gunshot wounds a few days later. The incident attracted almost no international media attention – unlike the massacre at Bwindi in 1999, no foreign nationals were involved – and it has had surprisingly little effect on tourism to the area. In the aftermath, UWA suspended all game drives to the north of the Nile while security was restored. The north of the park has subsequently reopened: game drives continue as normal, and visitation levels over 2002 were not dramatically down on what they had been two years earlier. In October 2002, we spent a week in the park, including five days north of the river, and over several discussions with rangers and hotel managers, we were assured that the UPDF has responded to the incident, as it did to the Bwindi massacre, by completely tightening up the security.

This appeared not to be the case in November 2005 when Steve Willis, the owner of the Red Chilli backpacker camps, was shot by rebels in northern Murchison. Steve was returning to Paraa after helping to rescue a rafting group following an accident on the river above Murchison Falls. The event shocked Kampala's tight-knit expatriate society and brought messages of condolence from across the world from Steve's travelling and backpacking guests. It is important though, for the purposes of this book, that a couple of points be made. Firstly, the incident took place to the east of the Paraa–Pakwach road in an area long off-limits to tourists due to perceived or actual insecurity. Secondly, UWA, knowing that the area was potentially unsafe, dispatched the rescue party with an armed escort of 30 rangers and soldiers. It was tragically unfortunate that after the successful rescue, Steve sped back to Paraa in front of the escort, ironically because he was late for a security meeting with the US embassy. One might infer from this incident that UWA and its military partners are well aware where the trouble spots are and that consequently no escort is required in the Buligi area because there is no risk.

Not everyone would agree. The US State Department still advises its citizens to stay away from the park, as do several other international embassies in Kampala, where it is widely held that Murchison Falls is totally unsafe for travel.

Realistically, for so long as northwestern Uganda remains politically volatile, there also exists some risk – however slight – of another attack in Murchison Falls. Then again, in the current global political climate, it could be argued that this much, to a greater or lesser extent, is true of practically anywhere in the world. Is Murchison Falls more or less safe than, say, New York, or Johannesburg, or Mombasa? Who knows? As things stand, I personally would have few qualms about spending time in Murchison Falls. But that is a personal decision, not one that I can – or should be prepared to – make for readers. We can only hope that ongoing peace talks between the government and the rebels of northern Uganda will made the need for such a text box redundant by the time we print the sixth edition of this book.

Non-residents pay a visitation fee of US$25/35/50 for one/two/three or more nights. East African residents pay discounted rates of US$15/20/25 on production of proof of residency. An entrance permit is valid for 24 hours from time of entrance. In addition, the standard vehicle entrance fees are applied.

FURTHER READING Shaun Mann's 36-page *Guide to Murchison Falls National Park and the Surrounding Game Reserves* (1995, revised in 2004) is an exemplary booklet with good ecological and historical coverage of the national park. It also includes a pull-out checklist of birds and mammals, and colour maps and photographs. The booklet costs Ush10,000 and can normally be purchased at the UWA office in Kampala or the national park office in Masindi, and sometimes even in the national park itself. Andrew Robert's '*Uganda's Great Rift Valley*' includes additional information relating to the waterfall, its early visitors and its rift valley setting.

GETTING THERE AND AWAY

Self-drive All travellers heading to Murchison Falls from Kampala must first drive to Masindi, which usually takes about three hours (see *Masindi*, pages 366–71). From Masindi, there is a choice of two different routes to Paraa. The direct route is 85km long and can be covered in two to three hours, depending on road conditions. The more scenic 135km route via Lake Albert (see *Masindi to Murchison Falls via Lake Albert*, pages 375–7) can take up to five hours. Both routes are generally in fair condition, but sections become muddy after heavy rain. If you are heading to Paraa or Sambiya Lodge, the direct route is definitely the best choice from a practical point of view. Heading to Nile Safari Camp, it doesn't make a great deal of difference which route you take, though if you have no intention of entering the park on the day that you drive up, you will avoid paying park fees for that day by using the Bulisa Route. Do note that no fuel is available along either route, so fill up at Masindi. Petrol and diesel are available from the garage at Paraa Safari Lodge, albeit about 20% more expensive than elsewhere in the country.

Murchison Falls can also be approached from the north, along the Karuma–Pakwach road which branches off the Kampala–Gulu road just north of Karuma Bridge. The park is entered at Tangi Gate just before Pakwach. This route has been considered unsafe for security reasons for several years, and it was particularly bad a couple of years back, when the Karuma Bridge was a regular site of murderous bandit attacks. Local sources suggest the situation is significantly improved in late 2006, but still you are strongly advised to make enquiries with UWA or similar before you think about heading up this way.

Incidentally, the managers of the Red Chilli Camp at Paraa who have seen people arrive on moped and even bicycle *boda-bodas* from Masindi 85km away suggest that this is *not* a sensible thing to do on account of buffalo and other potentially stroppy animals on the road. They advise that a special hire from Masindi costs about Ush100,000.

Tours Organised tours to Murchison Falls can be organised from any tour agent in Kampala (see *Chapter 3, Tour operators*, page 72). In addition, Red Chilli Hideway and Kampala Backpackers' hostels both run budget excursions for backpackers. A typical Backpackers' trip includes return transport, park entrance, overnight camping in Budongo Forest, chimpanzee tracking, game drive, launch trip on the Nile and visit to the Top of the falls viewpoint. Charges range from US$200 per person for a group of six to US$260 per person for three people. The notice boards at both hostels may advertise other options or carry notices from travellers seeking to form a group for a trip.

All visitors who stay at Paraa Safari Lodge or do a game drive north of the Nile will need to make use of the motor ferry at Paraa, which takes about five minutes to cross the river. The ferry usually runs between 07.00 and 19.00, and is scheduled to leave once an hour on the hour, in either direction, except at 13.00 when it stops for a two-hour lunch break, but do note that shortly before going to print it was reported that the ferry was only sailing every second hour starting at 08:00. Clearly, it is physically impossible for any boat to simultaneously cross a river in opposite directions, but in practice the crossing generally does take place within ten minutes either side of the scheduled departure. Anybody who plans on taking the last ferry of the day, scheduled for 19.00, or who urgently needs to cross at a specific time, should thus be ready and waiting at the jetty about ten minutes ahead of schedule.

A daily fee of Ush20,000 per vehicle and Ush2,000 per passenger or pedestrian is charged to use the ferry, good for as many scheduled crossings that are made on that day. No fee is charged for taking motorbikes or bicycles on the ferry. Unscheduled crossings can be arranged, but at a cost of Ush100,000.

Public transport The most straightforward way for travellers without private transport to reach Murchison Falls is to take a special hire from Masindi (Ush100,000). Note that the minibus service offered by Red Chilli Rest Camp (see *Where to stay*, page 383) is no longer operating. Another possibility is to ask about lifts at the national park's office in Masindi – a national-park vehicle usually heads up from Masindi to Paraa a few times a week, most often leaving at around 14.00, and the driver will normally give travellers a lift, space permitting. More of a long shot, but by no means impossible, would be to try to hitch to Paraa from the junction opposite the Shell garage in Masindi – though do make sure that the vehicle will be going as far as Paraa to drop you at the Rest Camp. The management there, incidentally, have welcomed guests arriving on *boda-bodas* and even on the back of a pedal bike from Masindi, but suggest that, for your own safety, you employ transport that provides greater protection from buffalo.

The closest that any public transport comes to Murchison Falls is Bulisa (see *Masindi to Murchison Falls via Lake Albert*, pages 375–7), where the Bulisa Corner Guesthouse rents out bicycles at around Ush5,000 per day. If you want to cycle to the park, the road from Bulisa to Paraa is reasonably flat most of the way, but very sandy in parts, and you'll do well to get through in less than two hours. The condition of the bicycles is variable, and you should be very sure that both of your brakes are working before you attempt the steep descent about 2km past the entrance gate – if in doubt, I suggest you walk this stretch. Don't expect to be provided with a pump, and bear in mind that although there is a village a few kilometres before the entrance gate where somebody can repair tyres, you could be in for a long walk if you have a puncture. To avoid the risk of arriving at the park after dark, it's probably best not to leave Bulisa after about 14.00.

WHERE TO STAY
Upmarket

Paraa Safari Lodge \ 0312 260260/1; f 0312 260262; e mweyaparaa@africaonline.co.ug; www.paraalodge.com. Situated on the north bank of the Nile opposite the launch jetty, Paraa Safari Lodge was reconstructed in 1997 over the shell of the original lodge built in 1959 and gutted by bandits during the civil war. Architecturally, Paraa falls firmly into the 'hotel in the bush' category of lodges – a double-storey monolith that in most respects wouldn't look out of place on a beach or in a city – but the extensive use of natural materials and African interior décor give it a definite organic feel. The large and luxuriously decorated rooms all have a private balcony facing the river, walk-in mosquito netting and a spacious bath or shower. There are 2 disabled rooms, as well as a ste in the cottage that was slept in by the Queen Mother when she visited Uganda in 1959. The 3-course meals cost Ush20,000 and have a strong international flavour, plus a daily choice for vegetarians, and there's also a good, inexpensive snack menu for casual passers-by. The grounds are dominated by a curvaceous swimming pool and offer a clear, if rather distant and less than awe-inspiring view over the Nile (visit the ruined Pakuba Lodge in the Buligi area for a lesson in exactly how to locate a lodge). Logistically, this is the most conveniently located of the upmarket lodges for game drives in the north and the launch trip to the base of Murchison Falls. *US$114/181sgl/dbl FB.*

⌂ **Nile Safari Lodge** ☎ 0414 258273/0312 260758; f 0414 233992; e info@geolodgesafrica.com; www.geolodgesafrica.com. Run by Geolodges (formerly Inns of Uganda) Nile Safari Lodge is situated a short distance west of the park boundary on the southern bank of the Nile. This is a superb luxury tented lodge, not quite so upmarket as Paraa, but smaller and more personalised with a compelling 'bush' character and riverbank location. The camp consists of several standing tents and wooden cottages on stilted wood frames. Each has an en-suite toilet and shower and a private veranda overlooking the Nile. The communal deck and restaurant are made almost exclusively of natural materials, and the whole camp blends unobtrusively into the surrounding bush. The camp itself is overrun with colourful agama lizards and rustling with birdlife, while hippos, crocodiles and a variety of waterbirds can be seen on the river, and the facing northern bank and midchannel island is regularly visited by waterbuck and elephants. Nile Safari Lodge is particularly recommended to birders. The inexpensive afternoon boat trips to the island opposite offer a better than even chance of encountering a resident pair of shoebills. The 1km guided walk (US$5 pp) through the adjacent riverine forest is likely to yield 30–40 bird species in the space of an hour, and is perhaps the best place in East Africa for sightings of the localised white-crested turaco, red-headed lovebird and red-winged grey warbler. A village walk is offered for the same price. The food and service are excellent, and the swimming pool boasts a serene view over the Nile. The camp lies 11km from the Paraa–Bulisa road, and the turn-off is clearly signposted about 5km from the park entrance gate in the direction of Bulisa. No entrance fees are levied for staying here, and you needn't pass through the park at all if you approach the camp from Bulisa. If you are doing the launch trip, it is possible to arrange a boat transfer from Nile Safari Lodge to the jetty at Paraa (US$25 one-way/US$35 return). There is also now a road linking the lodge to Paraa via the park staff village at Mubako. This is considerably shorter than returning to the main road and entering through Bugungu Gate. *US$110/180 sgl/dbl FB. Pitching your own tent at a campsite with toilet/shower block on an attractive riverside plateau 5–10mins' walk from the main camp costs US$10 pp.*

Moderate

⌂ **Sambiya Lodge** ☎ 0414 233596; ☏/f 0414 344855; e afritour@africaonline.co.ug; www.afritourstravel.com. Situated 500m from the main road between Masindi and Paraa, near the turn-off to the top of the falls, Sambiya Lodge enjoys a pleasant but unspectacular woodland location in the small Sambiya River Valley. The main lodge offers accommodation in 20 s/c cottages with solar-powered hot showers and a fan, but more basic *bandas* and a campsite are also available. Sambiya is conveniently located for chimp tracking and birding at Kanyiyo Pabidi in the Budongo Forest, and is only a 20min drive from the Top of the Falls, but it is almost an hour from Paraa. Facilities and services include a swimming pool and guided walks through the bird-rich riverine forest. The rather mundane location notwithstanding, cottages are very reasonably priced. Special offers are sometimes available. *Cottages US$70/120 sgl/dbl B&B, bandas US$46/80 sgl/dbl FB, US$17 pp B&B, or US$12 pp without food. There is also a campsite where you can pitch a tent for US$6.*

Budget and camping

⌂ **Red Chilli Rest Camp** m 0772 709150; e chilli@infocom.co.ug; www.redchillihideaway.com. Managed by Kampala's popular Red Chilli Hideaway, the former Paraa Rest Camp is situated on the south side of the Nile, in a patch of bush frequented by warthog, bushbuck and a wide variety of birds. The accommodation is in s/c and brick *bandas* provided with electricity, fans and mosquito

IN SEARCH OF KING WHALE-HEAD

Perhaps the most eagerly sought of all African birds, the shoebill is also one of the few that is likely to make an impression on those travellers who regard pursuing rare birds to be about as diverting as hanging about in windswept railway stations scribbling down train numbers. Three factors combine to give the shoebill its bizarre and somewhat prehistoric appearance. The first is its enormous proportions: an adult might stand more than 150cm (5ft) tall and typically weighs around 6kg. The second is its unique uniform slaty-grey colouration. Last but emphatically not least is its clog-shaped, hook-tipped bill – at 20cm long, and almost as wide, the largest among all living bird species. The bill is fixed in a permanent Cheshire-cat smirk that contrives to look at once sinister and somewhat inane, and when agitated the bird loudly claps together its upper and lower bill, rather like outsized castanets.

The first known allusions to the shoebill came from early European explorers to the Sudan, who wrote of a camel-sized flying creature known by the local Arabs as Abu Markub – Father of the Shoe. These reports were dismissed as pure fancy by Western biologists until 1851, when Gould came across a bizarre specimen amongst an avian collection shot on the Upper White Nile. Describing it as 'the most extraordinary bird I have seen', Gould placed his discovery in a monotypic family and named it Balaeniceps Rex – King Whale-Head! Gould believed the strange bird to be most closely allied to pelicans, but it also shares some anatomic and behavioural characters with herons, and until recently it was widely held to be an evolutionary offshoot of the stork family. Recent DNA studies support Gould's original theory, however, and the shoebill is now placed in a monotypic subfamily of Pelecanidae.

The life cycle of the shoebill is no less remarkable than its appearance. One of the few birds with an age span of up to 50 years, it is generally monogamous, with pairs coming together during the breeding season (April to June) to construct a grassy nest up to 3m wide on a mound of floating vegetation or a small island. Two eggs are laid, and the parents rotate incubation duties, in hot weather filling their bills with water to spray over the eggs to keep them cool. The chicks hatch after about a month, and will need to be fed by the parents for at least another two months until their beaks are fully developed. Usually only one nestling survives, probably as a result of sibling rivalry.

The shoebill is a true swamp specialist, but it avoids dense stands of papyrus and tall grass, which obstruct its take-off, preferring instead to forage from patches of low floating vegetation or along the edge of channels. It consumes up to half its weight in food daily, preying on whatever moderately sized aquatic creature might come its way, ranging from toads to baby crocodiles, though lungfish are especially favoured. Its method of hunting is exceptionally sedentary: the bird might stand semi-frozen for several hours before it lunges down with remarkable speed and power, heavy wings stretched backward, to

nets. The bar has a fridge, and the restaurant serves decent meals in the Ush5,000–6,000 range. Though river views from the site itself are rather distant, Red Chilli enjoys a strategic location close to the Paraa Jetty. The launch is just 10mins' walk down the hill for backpackers while motorised tourists are ideally placed for the early-morning ferry across the Nile to access the Buligi game tracks. An 8-seat 4x4 open-top minibus for game viewing can be hired for US$175 for up to 5 people or less or US$30 pp for larger groups. The drive to the Top of the Falls costs US$80 for up to 5 people and US$15 pp for larger groups. *Bandas with shared facilities US$16,*

s/c bandas US$24/33/49 twin/trpl/family (5 beds). Camping US$6.

⚡ Rabongo Camp Bookings through UWA (see pages 158–9). Set in the remote southeast of the park, this camp lies roughly 40km from the main road between Masindi and Paraa, along a rough track signposted between Kanyiyo Pabidi and Sambiya Lodge. It lies within the Rabongo Forest, which consists of eight relic patches of a formerly more extensive forest that suffered heavily as a result of elephant overpopulation in the 1960s and 1970s. It is home to a variety of primates, including black-and-white colobus and chimpanzees, and roughly 150

grab an item of prey in its large, inescapable bill. Although it is generally a solitary hunter, the shoebill has occasionally been observed hunting co-operatively in small flocks, which splash about flapping their wings to drive a school of fish into a confined area.

Although the shoebill is an elusive bird, this – as with the sitatunga antelope – is less a function of its inherent scarcity than of the inaccessibility of its swampy haunts. Nevertheless, *BirdLife International* has recently classified it as near-globally threatened, and it is classed as CITES Appendix 2, which means that trade in shoebills, or their capture for any harmful activity, is forbidden by international law. Estimates of the global population vary wildly. In the 1970s, only 1,500 shoebills were thought to exist in the wild, but this estimate has subsequently been revised to 10,000–15,000 individuals concentrated in five countries – Sudan, Uganda, Tanzania, DRC and Zambia. Small breeding populations might also survive in Rwanda and Ethiopia, and vagrants have been recorded in Malawi and Kenya.

The most important shoebill stronghold is the Sudd floodplain on the Sudanese Nile, where 6,400 individuals were counted during an aerial survey undertaken over 1979–82, followed by the inaccessible Moyowosi–Kigosi Swamp in western Tanzania, whose population was thought to amount to a few hundred prior to a 1990 survey that estimated the population to be greater than 2,000. Ironically, although Uganda is the easiest place to see the shoebill in the wild, the national population probably amounts to fewer than 1,000 birds, of which perhaps half are concentrated in the Kyoga–Bisina–Opeta complex of wetlands. For tourists, however, the most reliable locations for shoebill sightings are Murchison Falls National Park, Semliki Wildlife Reserve and the Mabamba Swamp near Entebbe – none of which is thought to hold more than a dozen pairs. Visitors to Uganda who fail to locate a shoebill in the wild might take consolation from the Wildlife Orphanage in Entebbe, where a few orphaned individuals are kept in a large aviary.

The major threat to the survival of the shoebill is habitat destruction. The construction of several dams along the lower Nile means that the water levels of the Sudd are open to artificial manipulation. Elsewhere, swamp clearance and rice farming pose a localised threat to suitable wetland habitats. Lake Opeta, an important shoebill stronghold in eastern Uganda, has been earmarked as a source of irrigation for a new agricultural scheme. A lesser concern is that shoebills are hunted for food or illegal trade in parts of Uganda. In the Lake Kyoga region, local fishermen often kill shoebill for cultural reasons – they believe that seeing a shoebill before a fishing expedition is a bad omen. As is so often the case, tourism can play a major role in preserving the shoebill and its habitat, particularly in areas such as the Mabamba Swamp, where the local community has already seen financial benefits from ornithological visits.

forest birds have been recorded in the area. The stretch of the Wairingo River that runs through the camp lies in a good place to see the shining blue kingfisher and African finfoot. Firewood is available for cooking, but you must bring all food with you. *Camping by the river US$6 pp.*

⋏ Top of Murchison Falls Visitors with a private 4x4 vehicle might prefer to pitch a tent at this secluded and little-used campsite about an hour from Paraa by car a couple of hundred metres upstream from the waterfall. The site has a beautiful location above a natural pool that's safe for swimming, and there's great birding — look out for the localised bat hawk towards dusk. *Camping US$6 pp.*

⋏ Nile Safari Camp Contact details above. Attached to this superb lodge is a lovely shaded campsite in a clearing in the riverine forest overlooking the Nile. Camping fees include access to the lodge's bar, restaurant and swimming pool. Self-catering is permitted, too. Because the site lies outside the national park, no visitation fees are paid simply for being there. *Camping US$10 pp.*

⋏ Sambiya Lodge A small campsite where self-catering is permitted, or you can eat and drink in the lodge restaurant. *US$6 per tent.*

Murchison Falls is first alluded to in the writings of Speke, who upon visiting Karuma Falls to the east in 1862 was told that a few other waterfalls lay downriver, mostly 'of minor importance' but 'one within ear-sound... said to be very grand'. Speke does not record the name by which this waterfall was known locally, but his guide did inform him that a few years earlier 'at the Grand Falls... the king had the heads of one hundred men, prisoners taken in war against Rionga, cut off and thrown into the river'. Two years later, partially to fulfil a promise they had made to Speke, Samuel and Florence Baker became the first Europeans to explore the stretch of river between Lake Albert and Karuma Falls. As they were paddling about 30km east of the estuary, Samuel Baker wrote:

We could distinctly hear the roar of water [and] upon rounding the corner a magnificent site burst upon us. On either side of the river were beautifully wooded cliffs rising abruptly to a height of about 300 feet [100m]; rocks were jutting out from the intensely green foliage; and rushing through a gap that cleft exactly before us, the river, contracted from a grand stream, was pent up in a passage of scarcely 50 yards [50m] in width; roaring furiously through the rock-bound pass, it plunged in one leap of about 120 feet [40m] perpendicular into a large abyss below. The fall of water was snow white, which had a superb effect as it contrasted with the dark cliffs that walled the water, while the graceful palms of the tropics and wild plantains perfected the beauty of the view. This was the greatest waterfall of the Nile, and in honour of the distinguished president of the Royal Geographic Society, I named it the Murchison Falls, the most important object through the entire course of the river.

Sean Mann, in his erudite booklet to the national park, reckons that the above description more closely fits the more northerly of the two waterfalls described under the heading Top of Murchison Falls (see page 387), as does the sketch made by Baker at the time. If that is the case, then, ironically, it was that second waterfall which Baker saw and named after the president of the Royal Geographic Society in 1864 – and the Bakers presumably had no inkling of the existence of the cataract today known as Murchison Falls.

ACTIVITIES

Nile launch trip Deservedly popular, the superb launch trip from Paraa to the base of the Murchison Falls leaves twice daily, generally at 08.00 and 14.00, though the departure time is sometimes changed by request (or at whim!). The return trip takes three hours, so keen photographers are advised to ask about leaving slightly earlier in the morning and later in the afternoon to capture the best light. In addition to taking you close to the base of the waterfall, the launch trip follows a stretch of the Nile with a compelling African atmosphere, fringed by borassus palms, acacia woodland and stands of mahogany. Game viewing is excellent – hippos in their hundreds, some of the largest crocodiles left in Africa, small herds of buffalo, waterbuck and kob, and as often as not giraffe, bushbuck and black-and-white colobus. Elephant are frequently observed playing in the water, often within a few metres of the launch, and fortunate visitors might even see a lion or leopard.

The birdlife on the papyrus-lined banks is stunning, with the top prize being the shoebill, seen here less often than it is on the trip to the delta, but nevertheless a distinct possibility in the dry season. More certain to be seen are African fish eagle, Goliath heron, saddle-billed stork, African jacana, pied and malachite kingfishers, African skimmer, piacpiac, rock pratincole, black-headed gonolek, black-winged red bishop, yellow-mantled widowbird, yellow-backed weaver and at the right time of year a variety of migrant waders. The dazzlingly colourful red-throated bee-eater nests in sand banks between Paraa and the falls, and is more likely to be seen here than anywhere in East Africa. The guides who run these trips are very knowledgeable about the local birds, and they normally carry a field guide.

The launch trip costs US$15 (Ush28,000) per person. A minimum charge of Ush300,000 is required for a trip which therefore requires 11 people. Smaller numbers can share the cost of a voyage, if for example eight people are prepared to pay Ush37,500 each. These days, it's increasingly unusual for the afternoon trip to attract fewer than eight passengers, but check in advance with the booking office at Paraa to find out how many people are boarding on any given day.

Top of Murchison Falls As viewed from the launch trip, Murchison Falls is impressive indeed, but the combination of distance and the rumbling boat engine do much to mute its full impact. For sheer sensory overload it is recommended that you visit the picnic site at the top of the falls, reached along a roughly 15km road (graded in 2002 but sometimes tricky after rain) that branches north from the main Masindi–Paraa road a few hundred metres from Sambiya Lodge. From the picnic site, a short footpath leads downhill to a fenced viewpoint right above the waterfall's head. Here only can one truly appreciate the staggering power with which the Nile crashes through the narrow gap in the escarpment, not to mention the deafening roar and voluminous spray associated with the phenomenon.

From the main viewpoint, a longer footpath, perhaps 20 minutes' walking time, leads to a saddle offering a face-on view not only of Murchison Falls, but also of a comparably voluminous waterfall a few hundred metres to its north. Some sources state that this second waterfall was created when the Nile flooded in 1962, a theory that is refuted by old aerial photographs, as indeed it might be by Sir Samuel Baker's original sketch and description of the waterfall (see box *The Bakers at Murchison Falls*, page 386). Whatever the case, the face-on view of the two cataracts – separated by a lushly forested hillock – is truly inspiring, but surpassed perhaps by following another footpath leading downhill from this saddle to the base of the short gorge below the main waterfall. If you want to check out all the viewpoints, allow at least two hours – ideally in the afternoon, when the sun is better positioned for photography.

There's not much wildlife to be seen around the falls – a relief perhaps if you opt to walk the footpaths unaccompanied by one of the rangers from the picnic site – though you might encounter a troop of baboons or black-and-white colobus. The so-called 'bat cliff' immediately south of the main waterfall (visible from the viewpoint on the saddle) is worth scanning with binoculars for raptors and swallows. Wait around until dusk and you should also see some impressive flocks of bats emerging from the caves in this cliff, as well as a few bat hawks soaring around in search of a quick dinner. After dusk, the drive from the top of the falls back to the main road is particularly good for nocturnal birds. The spotted eagle owl is likely to be encountered on the road throughout the year, as – in season – are Africa's three most spectacular and distinctive species of nightjar: long-tailed (March–August), pennant-winged (March–September) and standard-winged (September–April).

Delta boat trip The launch to the base of the falls is the highlight of most trips to Murchison Falls, but the boat trip downriver from Paraa towards the Lake Albert Delta is favoured by birdwatchers, since it offers perhaps *the* best opportunity to see shoebills anywhere in Africa, particularly during the rainy season. The two occasions on which I've done this trip yielded a total of eight sightings, but not everybody is so fortunate – one of the guides told me that he once took a visitor along this stretch of river on three successive days without luck. Without the shoebill as a motivating factor, the trip towards the delta is not as worthwhile as the one to the base of the falls, since there is less wildlife to be seen and the general birding more-or-less duplicates what you would see from the launch. The boat trip to the delta costs Ush150,000 per party for up to six hours. You would be fortunate to find other people who are willing to share the expense.

Note that one of the places where shoebills are most regularly encountered *en route* to the delta is the island opposite Nile Safari Camp – one pair has been resident there for at least five years. Nile Safari Camp offers short boat trips to this island for Ush60,000 per party.

Nile River Company (m *0772 221003;* e *nileriverco@infocom.co.ug*). This new company offers boat cruises from the Paraa Jetty through the Nile delta to the Albert Nile to cruise the shores of the park's prime game-viewing Buligi area. Importantly, the *Madi Gras* launch (the Madi are a tribe of northern Uganda) has an overhead sunshade and a 'loo with a view'. One or two day trips are offered. The latter includes an overnight bush camp in the Buligi area where guests can sleep in mossie-netted compartments on the boat or in tents on the shore. This is to my knowledge the first time in 20 years when camping in this beautiful wilderness area has been permitted. It's a tremendous experience; the shoreline *vibrates* with nocturnal sounds including lion, hyena and hippo. Day trips cost US$25 per person and US$60 for the overnight and require a minimum of four persons and a maximum of eight. The boat can be chartered for a daily cost of US$350. The overnight price includes dinner, breakfast and drinking water but excludes your beer and camping fees. Park entrance is applicable to day and overnight voyages.

Game drives The bulk of Murchison Falls' wildlife is concentrated to the north of the Nile, and the best area for game drives is the circuit of tracks that run west from the ferry jetty at Paraa to the Lake Albert Delta (see box *Game viewing on the Delta Circuit*, pages 390–1). The only other road north of the river, connecting Paraa to the Wankwar Gate, is closed at the time of writing for security reasons, but should it reopen during the lifespan of this edition, a recommended stop is at Nyamsika Gorge. Lions and buffaloes often come to the gorge to drink, while the cliffs host seasonal colonies of several types of bee-eater, and the shallows are one of the few places in East Africa where the dashing Egyptian plover is frequently recorded.

The combination of dense vegetation and low concentrations of wildlife mean that game viewing is generally poor south of the river though there is a lovely open area along the Sambiya–Karuma road beyond the Rabongo turning where Uganda kob, Jackson's hartebeest, waterbuck, baboon and oribi may be encountered as – more occasionally – are elephant and lion. This road was reopened in 1998 and I've driven along it to the Gulu road, though the eastern section is monotonously bushy and it took about 2.5 hours from Sambiya. I gather however that it has since become overgrown due to disuse.

It is permitted to drive in the main tourism areas of the park without an armed ranger, but there are several advantages in hiring one. They will generally know where the wildlife is concentrated at any given time, and are also more adept at spotting well-camouflaged animals such as lion and leopard. Most of them are also very knowledgeable about animal behaviour. There is less risk of getting lost or heading into potentially insecure areas when in the company of a ranger. The services of a ranger cost US$20. Visitors with an ornithological bent should specify this in advance, since some of the rangers are extraordinarily knowledgeable about the local birdlife, others somewhat less so.

Travellers without their own transport can arrange game drives through Red Chilli Rest Camp (see *Where to stay*, page 383–4) or – more expensively – through Paraa Safari Lodge.

On the north side of the river, you should ask advice before driving off to the east of the Paraa–Pakwach road at the Pakaba–Karuma crossroads. It may be considered safe to visit the Nyamsika Cliffs just a few kilometres away but not at present to continue further east towards either Chobe (near Karuma Falls) or Wankwar Gate to exit onto the Karuma–Pakwach highway.

Forest walks **Rabongo Forest**, in the far southeast of the park, is reached via a signposted and tsetse-infested road that branches from the main Paraa–Masindi road a few kilometres south of Sambiya Lodge. General forest walks at Rabongo are of interest mostly to birdwatchers, though black-and-white colobus and red-tailed monkeys are also likely to be seen, and the number and variety of butterflies is impressive. Guided nature walks cost US$10 per person. Frankly, unless you are staying at Rabongo Camp, there is better forest birding and a greater chance of seeing chimps at the more accessible Kanyiyo Pabidi (see pages 373–5) on the Paraa–Masindi road.

Fishing If you have your own tackle, there is good fishing from the banks of the Nile, with large Nile perch and tiger fish offering the main challenge. The largest confirmed perch taken from the bank of the Nile on rod and line weighed 73kg, and was caught by C D Mardach in 1959. However, a fish recorded as 106kg was caught in 2001. Local fishermen have netted specimens weighing up to 160kg.

A LOOP THROUGH THE NORTHWEST

Culturally and economically, the far northwest of Uganda has always been somewhat dislocated from the rest of the country, a situation exacerbated in recent years by the campaign of terror against local villagers undertaken by Joseph Kony and the Lord's Resistance Army (LRA – see also box, pages 396–7). At the time of writing, there is strong reason to hope that a negotiated settlement will put an end to the civil war that has gripped the region for the past two decades. The section that follows is included in the hope that peace will prevail, but the situation remains somewhat volatile, and it is impossible to predict whether the region will become safe for travel during the lifespan of this edition.

Even at the best of times, the northwest will hold little appeal for those who expect their entertainment to come packaged and sealed. Aside from a couple of brief ferry crossings, the crumbling remains of Baker's Fort at Patiko and the Emin Pasha's long-vanished camp at Wadelai, the loop described in this section has few genuine points of interest, and there is certainly nothing to match the manifold attractions found further south. In West Nile, alert map-readers may pick out Rhino Camp east of Arua. At one time, this was the last refuge for the rare northern race of white rhinoceros. Since 1994, however, it has been home to about 10% of the estimated 200,000 Sudanese refugees who live in refugee settlements established by the Ugandan government in the northwest. Of the towns, only Pakwach, perched on the west bank of the Albert Nile, has any great inherent appeal. What most struck the few people who visited this area in happier times was the friendliness of the people and the low cost of travel: the far northwest genuinely lies off any beaten tourist track, and it is arguably worth exploring for that reason alone.

A loop of sorts runs through the northwest. Starting in Masindi or Kampala, you can get to Lira directly by road or, a more interesting option, by using the daily ferry across Lake Kyoga. From Lira, there are regular buses and trains through to Gulu and Pakwach. North of Pakwach, the main road leads further north through Nebbi to Arua, something of a dead end in travel terms. From Nebbi and Pakwach, a couple of side roads head south to Panyimur on Lake Albert. Panyimur is linked

11

by ferry to Wanseko, from where you can detour to Murchison Falls National Park or bus directly through to Masindi or Kampala. Note that the train service that once connected Kampala to Pakwach via Tororo, Lira and Gulu ceased operating in early 1998 and is unlikely to resume in the foreseeable future.

KAMPALA TO LIRA VIA LAKE KYOGA Although it's perfectly possible to catch the Post Bus or any other bus or minibus going directly to Lira from either Masindi or Kampala, a more interesting option (though considerably less straightforward and one that might take several days) is to go to Lira via the ferry which crosses Lake Kyoga between Shengebe and Namasale.

The first place you need to get to is Nakasongola trading centre, roughly midway along the main road between Kampala and Masindi. Any minibus running between these towns will be able to drop you there. Nakasongola lies in a swampy area dotted with a few hills, which are worth climbing for the views across the surrounding scrub and cultivated plains. There are two basic lodges in Nakasongola: the one on the Kampala side of town is probably the better, with an obliging owner and acceptable rooms for US$1.50 per person including breakfast.

There isn't a great deal of transport from Nakasongola to Shengebe, but you can generally rely on there being a few minibuses in the early morning and another at

---

GAME VIEWING ON THE DELTA CIRCUIT

Situated about an hour's drive from the Paraa ferry jetty, the perhaps 20km² of grassland fringing the delta formed by the Victoria Nile as it flows into Lake Albert is the focus of most game drives north of the river. And, whatever might be said about game viewing elsewhere in Murchison Falls National Park, few could fail to be impressed by the concentrations of wildlife found around the delta.

The delta circuit is reached by following the rutted Pakwach road northwest from the jetty for 7km, and then turning left at the junction for the airstrip. About 3km past this junction, the road passes through a patch of whistling thorns, a type of acacia whose marble-sized round pods – aerated by insects – whistle softly when a wind comes up. About 3km further, the disused Buligi Track branches off to the left, then about 3km further the road passes the fenced airstrip. The above roads pass through a scenic area of rolling grassland studded with tall borassus palms, where game concentrations are unpredictable, but generally highest in the rainy season.

About 2km past the airstrip, the road forks twice in the space of a kilometre, giving one the option of following three different tracks, all of which lead west towards the delta. For those with limited time, the central 10km Queen's Track is not only the shortest route, but also the smoothest, and generally the most productive for game viewing. The 12km Albert Nile Track to its north is in relatively poor condition, passing through patches of dense acacia woodland that will be as attractive to birdwatchers as they are, unfortunately, to tsetse flies. The 25km Victoria Nile Track to the south is far longer and game concentrations are generally low, except as it approaches the delta.

The three tracks converge on a grassy peninsula, flanked by the delta to the south and the Albert Nile to the north, and crossed by a network of interconnecting tracks that run through several kob breeding grounds. Large concentrations of Uganda kob are a certainty, as are family parties of Defassa waterbuck and the rather doleful-looking Jackson's hartebeest, as well as small groups of the dainty oribi. A striking feature of the area is its giraffe herds, which often number 50 or more, something I've seen nowhere else in Africa on a regular basis. Substantial buffalo herds are also common around the delta, usually containing a few individuals whose colouration indicates some genetic input from the smaller, redder forest buffalo of west Africa. About 3km south of the main kob

---

around 16.00. Best to get the earliest minibus possible: the ferry might go at any time from 08.00, and there's no formal accommodation at Shengebe. It's difficult to imagine that the ferry wouldn't wait for the early-morning minibuses, but if you do miss the ferry or you want to spend a while in Shengebe, the police station 2km down the road at Lwampanga will probably let you sleep on the floor or pitch a tent in the compound. The ferry may leave Shengebe at any time between 08.00 and 10.00. It takes one hour and costs US$1.

The ferry terminates at Namasale on the northern shore of Lake Kyoga. On arrival, you may have to register with the police – they don't see too many travellers here and they're more likely to express concern for your safety than to give you any hassle. Formalities completed, it's about 2km from the jetty to the trading centre, which you'll almost certainly have to walk. Once you're in the trading centre, you'll see a large tree, probably with several people sitting underneath it – this is where pick-up trucks heading to Lira wait for passengers. Unfortunately, most of the transport to Lira leaves in the early morning. You might be lucky, but it will probably be less frustrating to resign yourself to spending a night in Namasale than to wait around, probably in vain – there's a good little lodge near the tree where you can get a room for US$2.50/4 single/double. With an early start the next morning, you should have no difficulty finding transport to Lira.

breeding grounds, the Victoria Nile Track runs adjacent to the delta for a few hundred metres – plenty of hippos around, and elephants are present practically from late morning until late afternoon.

The limitless supply of kob has attracted several prides of lion to the delta area. One of the best places to look for these languid predators is along an anonymous 2.5km track (marked 'lion track' on the map) connecting the Albert Nile and Queen's tracks. At least one pride maintains an almost permanent presence in this area, often lying out in the open in the early morning and late afternoon, but generally retreating deep into the thicket during the heat of the day. The most reliable way to locate the lions is by observing the behaviour of the male kobs that always stand sentry on the edge of a herd. If one or two kobs persistently emit their characteristic high wheezing alarm whistle, they are almost certainly conscious that lions are around, so follow their gaze towards the nearest thicket. Conversely, should you hang around a kob herd for a few minutes and not hear any alarm calls, you can be reasonably sure that no lions are to be found in the immediate vicinity. The 'lion track', incidentally, is also a good place to look for the endearingly puppyish side-striped jackal and troops of the localised and rather skittish patas monkey.

The delta area offers some great birdwatching. Noteworthy ground birds include the preposterous eye-fluttering Abyssinian ground hornbill, the majestic grey crowned crane and saddle-billed stork, the localised Denham's bustard, the handsome black-headed and spur-winged lapwings, and the Senegal thickknee. The tall acacia stands that line the Albert Nile Track immediately north of the junction with Queen's Track harbour a host of good woodland birds, including the rare black-billed barbet and delightfully colourful swallow-tailed, northern Carmine, blue-breasted and red-throated bee-eaters. Herds of grazers – in particular buffalo – are often attended by flocks of insectivorous cattle egret, piacpiac and red-billed and yellow-billed oxpeckers. An abundance of aquatic habitats – not only the rivers and lake, but also numerous small pools – attracts a wide variety of waterfowl, waders, herons and egrets, while the mighty African fish eagle and both species of marsh harrier are often seen soaring above the water. We've seen shoebill in flight at the part of the delta fringed by the Victoria Nile Track (referred to above), while the hippo pool about 1km further along the track evidently hosts a resident osprey.

11

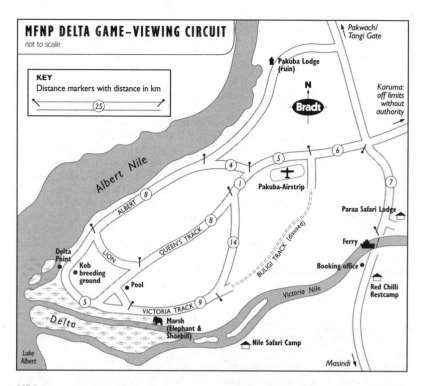

MFNP DELTA GAME-VIEWING CIRCUIT
not to scale

Pakwach/
Tangi Gate

KEY
Distance markers with distance in km

25

Pakuba Lodge
(ruin)

N

Bradt

Karuma:
off limits
without
authority

Albert Nile

5

6

4

1

Pakuba-Airstrip

7

ALBERT

8

Paraa Safari Lodge

8

QUEEN'S TRACK

BULIGI TRACK (disused)

Ferry

14

LION

Delta
Point

Kob
breeding
ground

Pool

Booking office

Red Chilli
Restcamp

5

Victoria Nile

VICTORIA TRACK

9

Delta

Marsh
(Elephant &
Shoebill)

Nile Safari Camp

Lake
Albert

Masindi

LIRA The gateway to the northwest, Lira used to be a very pleasant, spacious town, though this may no longer be the case following an influx of rural refugees that has seen its population more than treble over the past decade, from fewer than 30,000 in 1991 to almost 90,000 in 2002. There's not a great deal to do in Lira – if you're restless, it's worth walking out to the park and parade ground, where large numbers of fruit bats congregate in a tree. The **Lira Hotel** (⟍ 0473 20086), formerly owned by the government but now in private hands, has acceptable rooms for around US$20. Cheaper accommodation is available at the **Tourist Motel** (⟍ 0414 257426), and there are also several local guesthouses along the main road.

In addition to the route across Lake Kyoga, Lira can be approached from Soroti (see *Chapter 13*, page 458). Lira lies 128km from Soroti along a well-maintained all-weather *murram* road. Several minibuses cover this route every day.

GULU Gulu is today the second-largest town in northern Uganda, with a population of 113,000; large because, for the same reason as Lira, its population has more than trebled in the past decade. Even before the present civil war, it was one of the few towns in Uganda to still bear obvious scars of damage done during the previous civil war that led to the installation of Museveni in 1986. The only potential tourist attraction in the area is what remains of Baker's Fort at Patiko, which lies about 25km north of Gulu. You can hire a bicycle-taxi to Patiko, though there isn't much left to see, and the caretaker used to be officious to the point of absurdity.

Several minibuses go from Lira to Gulu every morning. You're unlikely to want to stay in Gulu but, as minibuses on to Pakwach leave in the early morning, you may have to. The former government hotel, the **Acholi Inn** (*central reservations;* ⟍ 0471 22560; e *acholiug@ios.com*), has rooms for around US$20, and there are several good local lodgings such as the Roma (15$) and Rainbow Guesthouses (10$ - internet facilities in the same street) and a fair **Church of Uganda Hostel**. Gulu can also be reached directly from Kampala – a Post Bus leaves at 08.00 daily except Sundays and minibuses take about six hours. You could also try the new **Hotel Pearl Afrique** (m *0772 435032*), which is listed in Kampala's *The Eye* magazine under Gulu.

PAKWACH There is little more to Pakwach than a main street, but it's the most attractive urban centre in the area, perched on the west bank of the Albert Nile. As you enter Pakwach, you cross the Nile on what is the only bridge connecting Nebbi and Arua districts to the rest of Uganda. The military are understandably sensitive about this vital communication link: walking on the bridge is forbidden, as is photographing it. You can, however, walk down to the Nile from several points in Pakwach – the main street runs parallel to the river. Nobody with a sense of African history could fail to be conscious of the fact that the Emin Pasha's camp at Wadelai once stood on the west bank of the Nile, roughly 30km north of Pakwach. Sadly, Wadelai is difficult to reach without private transport, and about the only trace of Emin Pasha's former occupation of the site is the inevitable plaque.

Several minibuses run between Gulu and Pakwach in the morning. There's no formal public transport later in the day, and hitching is slow. There are a few guesthouses in Pakwach. **Dreamers Lodge** on the main road has small double rooms for US$4 and larger ones for US$5. The **Executive Lodge**, signposted from the main road, also has reasonably priced rooms. A recent recommendation is the **Accord Hotel**, which has rooms for US$5. The best food is at the **Family Hotel**.

ARUA This relatively large town lies near the Congolese border about 130km northwest of Pakwach. It is famous for being the hometown of Idi Amin, whose overt favouritism towards the people of Arua and West Nile meant that the area suffered a degree of isolation and rejection after his fall in 1979. Despite being so isolated from the rest of Uganda, it's a bustling little place, with a lively market and a sizeable aid-worker and missionary presence. From Pakwach, you can get to Arua by pick-up or truck, or wait for the daily buses between Kampala and Arua to pass through.

Arua offers few attractions, though the hill above the Nebbi roundabout is worth climbing for the views east towards the Nile and west into DRC, while the West Nile Golf Course is a pleasant setting for a stroll – wait for the newly built swimming pool to be finished and the place will be perfect. There's a good little craft shop in the town centre near the bus stop offering handmade sandals and vibrantly patterned waxed cotton from DRC. It's also worth noting that the Aruans are among the friendliest people one could hope to meet. There's no better way to 'sightsee' than to engage a *boda-boda* cyclist to pedal you about Arua's excellent tarmac streets and have him proudly point out the town's 'major' landmarks, which include the hospital, police station, several mosques, and a market rated to be one of the biggest in Uganda, with a wide selection of vitenge (sarongs) from the Congo for sale.

You'll find several cheap hotels in the town centre of which the best (being the regular choice of the Eagle Air pilots) are the **Hotel Pacific** (adequate US$11/14 single/doubles, s/c with nets and breakfast) in the town centre and the quieter **Pacific Annex** (same rates) just out of town on the Moyo road. Several more attractive options lie down a pretty lane with the unlikely name of Weatherhead Park Road on the edge of town (turn off at the Nebbi roundabout). The long-established **White Rhino Inn** (↖ *0414 235915*), is half torn down and unlikely to stand again, but the newer **Heritage Gardens** (m *0772 451689*), **Heritage Bamboo Guesthouse** and **Mvara View Inn** offer comfortable rooms further down the same road for around US$20 single/double. Heritage Gardens enjoys an attractive garden setting and serves excellent roast meat, while the nearby Heritage

The present-day civil war in the Acholi districts of Kitgum and Gulu has deep roots. They stretch to the beginning of the colonial era, when the culturally divergent northern territories were arbitrarily annexed to the Uganda Protectorate and effectively placed under joint British–Baganda rule. And they reach back through 60 years of colonial underdevelopment: education in the northwest and associated prospects of employment were deliberately stifled by the British, in order that the region might remain a ready source of military recruits and manual labourers. The roots of the present-day conflict are also embedded in the complex Jok system of spiritual belief, possession and sorcery that informs Acholi culture past and present. And they cannot easily be disentangled from the teachings of the early Christian missionaries who appropriated traditional Acholi spiritual concepts and icons into their biblical translations, in order that they might better hawk their exotic religious product to the locals.

As good a place to start as any, however, is June 1985 when Alice Auma, or Alice Lakwena as she had recently started calling herself, was introduced to General Tito Okello at the Acholi Inn in Gulu. Auma was then a 29-year-old Acholi woman whose largely undistinguished life – divorced, childless, eking out a living as a fish-seller in Pakwach – had been transformed three months earlier when she was possessed by the spirit of an Italian soldier called Lakwena. Okello, by contrast, was the chief of the Defence Force (UPDF): slowly coming to the realisation that his troops would be unable to hold out indefinitely against the rebel National Resistance Army (NRA), and frustrated at President Obote's refusal to negotiate with NRA leader Yoweri Museveni, Lakwena was made aware of Okello's plans to oust Obote, and offered her services as his spiritual advisor, to be passed over in favour of a established peer. Whether the general and the medium ever met again goes unrecorded, but both would play a leading role in national events over the next two years.

On 27 June 1985, the Obote regime was toppled by Okello and his Acholi supporters within the military. In the aftermath of this coup, the NRA captured Fort Portal, to eventually assume control over western Uganda as close to the capital as Masaka. Okello, who had no great personal ambition to power, formed a broad-based Military Council (MC) that included representatives of all political factions except the NRA. Museveni was invited to the party, and in December 1985, following protracted negotiations in Nairobi, a peace accord was signed leaving Okello as chairman of the MC and installing Museveni as vice-chairman. On 25 January 1986, less than two months after the accord had been signed, the NRA marched into Kampala to topple Okello.

Museveni's given reason for breaking the peace accord was the ineffectiveness of Okello's MC and in particular its inability to curb atrocities against civilians being perpetrated by its defence force. To the Acholi, the coup against Uganda's first Acholi head of state was betrayal pure and simple. And whatever the rights and wrongs of the matter, Museveni's coup undeniably did represent a loss of power and prestige to the Acholi. It also prompted thousands of Acholi soldiers to flee north for fear of reprisal, while the subsequent NRA occupation of Acholi territory was allegedly accompanied by a spate of unprovoked civilian killings. Put simply, in 1986, when most Ugandans perceived or willed Museveni to be a national saviour, the Acholi viewed him as a liar and an oppressor – indeed, a full ten years later, Museveni would poll a mere 20% of the Acholi vote in the 1996 presidential election, as compared to 75% countrywide.

Court offers a (kind of) gym and sauna. **Oasis Inn** on the same road offers the best food in town, amongst others excellent roast meat. In the main street in Arua there is an Indian restaurant which serves good Indian food at low prices. Internet facilities to be found in the main street shortly after Stanbic bank.

After being rebuffed by Okello, Alice Lakwena continued using her powers as a medium and healer to tend wounded Acholi soldiers. On 6 August 1986, however, the spirit Lakwena ordered his medium to abandon her healing to form the Holy Spirit Mobile Forces (HSMF) and lead a war against the forces of evil in Uganda. Alice assembled an initial force of 150 Acholi men, all of whom had served in the UPDF prior to the NRA coup, and made them undertake an elaborate purification ritual, laced with elements of both Christian and traditional Acholi ritual, as laid out to her by the spirit Lakwena. The newly inducted soldiers were also issued with a list of 20 commandments – the Holy Spirit Safety Precautions – ranging from the predictable 'Thou shalt not commit adultery' to the decidedly left-field 'Thou shalt have two testicles, neither more nor less'.

A compelling book could be – and indeed has been – written about the outwardly contradictory aims and beliefs of the HSMF (see *Appendix 3, Further Information*, page 476). One central aim of the movement was the elimination of witchcraft (allegations of which were rife in the early days of the HIV pandemic) in favour of Christian values. Yet it could be argued that the movement's obsession with sorcery itself stood in contravention of biblical teachings, as certainly did some of its more obtuse beliefs, for instance that smearing a soldier's body with *shea* butter would make him immune to bullets. And even if Alice herself was sincere in her beliefs, it is difficult to say whether her mostly ex-UPDF followers – at least 3,000 at the movement's peak – were motivated primarily by spiritual considerations or simply by the prospect of exacting revenge on the hated NRA.

Whatever their motives, this improbable army came closer to ousting Museveni than anybody has since or before. Led by the spirit Lakwena and his earthly vessel Alice, the HSMF marched through Kitgum, Lira, Soroti, Kumi, Mbale and Tororo, inflicting significant defeats on the NRA and replacing the dead and wounded with new recruits along the way. Defeat came finally in November 1987, on the outskirts of Jinja, where the HSMF enjoyed little public support and its movements were relayed to the government forces by local villagers. After the defeat, the spirit of Lakwena abandoned Alice in favour of her father Severino, who resuscitated the HSMF with some success, at least until March 1988, when 450 of his followers were killed in an attack on Kitgum. Six months later, Severino was captured and beaten up by the UPDA (a rival anti-NRA army) and informed by a leading officer – an HSMF deserter – that there would be no more talk of spirits.

Following the defeat at Jinja, Alice fled into exile in Kenya, where she currently resides, though her expressed wish to return to Uganda was cleared in January 2003 when Museveni announced that she would be covered by an act pardoning combatants who surrender voluntarily. Alice's father escaped from the UPDA in May 1989, was arrested by the NRA six months later, and released in 1992. The spirit of Lakwena eventually abandoned Severino, and father and daughter have both renounced violence in favour of prayer and fasting. The UPDA officer who so violently exhorted Severino against spiritual talk back in 1988 has subsequently stated that he is possessed by Lakwena, a claim publicly refuted by Severino, who describes his former tormentor as a 'devil'. And that former UPDA officer, whether spirit medium or devil, has exerted a murderously destabilising influence over the whole of northern Uganda for almost two full decades. His name is Joseph Kony, and the chilling story of his subsequent career continues overleaf.

PAKWACH TO WANSEKO VIA PANYIMUR From Pakwach, you can cut back towards Masindi by taking a ferry across Lake Albert between Panyimur and Wanseko. There are two ways of getting from Pakwach to Panyimur. The more direct road is 31km and follows the course of the Albert Nile. The longer route is to go from

Since Museveni assumed power in January 1986, the civil war between rebel factions and government forces in Kitgum and Gulu districts has occasionally abated but never ceased. After the HSMF (see box *The rise and fall of Alice Lakwena*, pages 394–5) ran out of steam in November 1987, the most important rebel force in the region was the UPDA, consisting mostly of ex-soldiers who'd served under Obote and Okello. The first six months of 1988 saw significant progress towards peace in the northwest, with the surrender of 20,000 rebels under an amnesty offered by Museveni. And in May, following months of negotiation, a peace accord was signed with the UPDA leadership. But some factions in the UPDA were dubious – Museveni had, after all, reneged on a similar accord with Okello in 1985 – and these dissenters decided to throw in their lot with the newly established Ugandan People's Democratic Christian Army (later the Lord's Resistance Army, or LRA) and its charismatic leader Joseph Kony.

Kony's sketchy biography varies with the teller. At various times, he has claimed to be related to Alice Lakwena, and to be possessed by the spirit Lakwena (among many others), and almost certainly he served briefly with the HSMF. Some time in 1987, when Kony first became possessed by a spirit, he was instructed to start a new movement to 'liberate humans from disease and suffering'. Initially, Kony's doctrines were based primarily on the Christian HSMF's 20 'safety precautions', but many Muslim rituals were incorporated into the LRA in the 1990s. And Kony's ferment of possessive spirits often guided him along paths less ascetic than those cut by Lakwena – the precaution 'Thou shalt not fornicate', for instance, would eventually be discarded in favour of something along the lines of 'Thou shalt abduct, rape and sexually enslave schoolgirls at whim'.

The LRA's political objective has eluded most observers; certainly, any pretence to provide meaningful resistance to the government long ago evaporated. As early as 1988, Kony seemed to be more concerned with attacking rival liberation movements than he did government targets. And since 1989, when Kony launched several unprovoked assaults on villages he perceived to be disloyal, the LRA has essentially been at war with the people it is ostensibly trying to liberate: the rural Acholi. In 1991, a government campaign called Operation North significantly reduced rebel activity, but violence flared up again in 1993, prompting an amnesty and peace talks that fell apart when Kony asked for a full six months to demobilise his troops. The next three years saw suffering like never before in the form of mass abduction of children and the callous massacres of innocent villagers.

Perhaps the single most important reason why the Ugandan government failed to disband the LRA was the support Kony has received from the National Islamic Front (NIF) government of Sudan. For years, the NIF struggled to suppress the rebel Sudanese People's Liberation Army (SPLA), whose stronghold was southern Sudan along the border with Uganda. The SPLA was supported by the Ugandan government, for which reason the NIF regarded the LRA as an ally. Furthermore, it has been alleged that a large proportion of the children abducted by the LRA are handed over to NIF forces in southern Sudan as cannon fodder against the SPLA. Between 1993 and early 2002, Kony and the LRA were based in Sudan, able to flee across the border whenever things heated up in Uganda. And any attempted Ugandan incursion into Sudan to capture Kony would have been treated as a military invasion by the Sudanese government.

In March 2002, Sudan signed a protocol allowing the UPDF to pursue LRA rebels into southern Sudan, and Museveni arrived in Gulu to launch Operation Iron Fist, promising that by the end of the year his forces would have captured or killed Kony. Several UPDF victories over LRA units followed, but the latter part of 2002 also witnessed some of the LRA's most vicious civilian attacks yet. On 24 July, Kony's rebels killed 48 people in a village near Kitgum – the adults hacked apart with machetes and knives, the young children beaten against a tree until their skulls smashed open – before abducting an estimated 100 teenagers. On 24 October, the *New Vision* printed a chilling picture of a singularly callous attack: the LRA executed 28 villagers, chopped off their heads and limbs, boiled them in a pot, and had been about to force the surviving villagers to eat the human stew when the government army arrived on the scene.

Operation Iron Fist did greatly reduce the LRA's military resources, but despite Museveni's promises, Kony was still on the loose in mid 2006.

The LRA became more vulnerable following the signing of the Sudanese Comprehensive Peace Agreement between the Sudanese government and the SPLA (formerly Kony's prime backer) in January 2005. Later that year, the outside world finally took a firm stance on the LRA notice when the International Criminal Court (ICC) in The Hague issued warrants against Kony and his deputies for crimes against humanity. In July 2006, the Uganda government and representatives of the LRA joined in peace talks in Juba mediated by the government of southern Sudan, with all involved parties having good reasons to push for peace. Aside from wanting to put an end to the suffering in the north, the Ugandan government has no wish to be embarrassed by a high profile atrocity in November 2007 when it hosts visitors from around the world for the Commonwealth Heads of Government Meeting. Kony's erstwhile allies in Sudan have good reason to push the war towards discreet closure rather than risk being implicated by the ICC for their role in perpetuating events. The insurgents themselves, wearied by 20 years of war, seem moved to seek a settlement rather than risk being hunted down to join Saddam Hussein in the international dock.

Progress has been made and an agreement signed but it is not yet a done deal. As I write (Sept 2006), an estimated 3000 rebels have massed at identified centres in southern Sudan to be demobbed and returned to the Acholi tribal society from which most of them were abducted and forcibly conscripted into the rebel ranks. A lot have already started moving back to their original communities. Reintegration will involve forgiveness through a traditional cleansing ritual. The same process will apply to Kony and his deputy Vincent Otti but both men have yet to appear in person, demanding that the ICC charges first be dropped. Museveni has offered an amnesty to end the terror, in spite of which the ICC still insists that the culprits must be brought to justice. Having come so far, it is probably unlikely that Kony and his child soldiers will melt back into the bush and the terror will resume, but the story is unfolding day by day.

By the time you read this book, the result of the Juba talks will be apparent, one way or the other. Even in the event of a happy outcome, it will take time and effort for northern Uganda to shed the legacy of 20 years of civil war. The civilian death toll in Gulu and Kitgum districts alone has exceeded 10,000 over the two decades. A similar number of schoolchildren have been abducted, thousands more people have been maimed or disabled, and roughly half of the rural inhabitants – some 400,000 souls – have sought refuge in towns or protected camps offering limited food, facilities and sanitation. More than 50 schools have been destroyed, while the lamentable medical facilities are highlighted by a 30% mortality rate among children under the age of five. The average annual per capita household income (US$30) is just 10% of the national average, while the number of cattle has been reduced to only 2% of what it was in 1986, as compared to an increase of 100% countrywide. Whenever the outcome, northern Uganda has already endured some thirty-five years of instability, twenty more than the country as a whole suffered during the excesses of Amin and Obote. It will take years to recover.

Pakwach to Nebbi, 50km along the Arua road, and from there to cut south to Panyimur via Parombo, a distance of 60km. There is reportedly not a lot of transport along the shorter route, though it would obviously be worth asking around in Pakwach to see if anything is going that way.

The route you're most likely to follow is via Nebbi and Parombo. You'll have no problem getting transport to Nebbi from Arua or Pakwach. If you do get stuck in Nebbi there's at least one proper hotel in town, as well as several local lodgings. Nebbi is slightly larger than Pakwach, and of some regional importance because of its proximity to the Mahagi border crossing into the DRC. On Wednesdays, there's a busy little market in **Nebbi**. Quite a few people from Wanseko come to Nebbi on market day, and correspondingly it's also the day when the volume of traffic between Nebbi and Panyimur is the greatest. There is some transport on other days, though generally you'll have to change vehicles at Parombo – an early start is advisable. The road between Nebbi and Panyimur is very scenic with great views down the Rift Valley Escarpment to Lake Albert.

The ferry itself is basically a fishing boat, often very crowded and reputedly dangerous in bad weather. I'm aware of two storm-related incidents in recent years in which boats crossing this way have overturned, resulting in dozens of fatalities, so you're strongly advised to stay put if there's a high wind or any warning signs of an oncoming storm. Oil exploration workers at Kaiso-Tonya tell me that a few dozen people drown on the lake each month. Anyway, the crossing between Panyimur and Wanseko costs US$2 and it takes about one hour. The boat normally crosses twice in each direction before noon. On Wednesdays, it also crosses at about 18.30, crowded with returnees from the market – personally I would be reluctant to make use of an overcrowded fishing boat at night, and would feel much safer sleeping over in Panyimur and waiting until the next morning. There are basic rooms and fish-based meals available at the Lake View Lodge near Panyimur Jetty.

There is a lodge at Wanseko, and several vehicles leave there in the early morning for Masindi and Kampala, on the way passing through Bulisa (from where you can cycle into Murchison Falls National Park) and the Budongo Forest. Wanseko and other places of interest along the Masindi road are covered in this chapter (see pages 375–7).

12

Jinja

Uganda's second-largest town (assuming that one treats the satellite settlement of Njeru on the opposite bank of the Nile as a suburb), Jinja lies about 80km east of Kampala, overlooking the point where the Nile flows out of Lake Victoria. And it is the mighty river rather than the moderately interesting town that attracts visitors to Jinja. The thrilling series of grade-five rapids below Bujagali Falls, rafted by three different companies, has emerged in recent years as perhaps the single most popular tourist activity in Uganda, surpassing even the mountain gorillas of the southwest. There is, too, a certain poignancy attached to standing on the slopes from where Speke first identified that geographical Holy Grail which, less than a decade earlier, had lured an obsessed (and hopelessly misdirected) Livingstone to a feverish death near Lake Bangweulu in Zambia. No less impressive is the knowledge that the water flowing past these green slopes will eventually drain into the Mediterranean, following a 6,500km journey through the desert wastes of Sudan and Egypt.

JINJA

Jinja has an attractively lush location on the northern shore of Lake Victoria above the Ripon Falls, identified by Speke in 1862 as the Source of the Nile, but submerged following the construction of the Owen Falls Dam in the 1950s. Jinja was formerly the industrial heartland of Uganda, and its present population stands at 86,500, while that of Njeru exceeds 50,000, making it a substantial settlement by local standards. Still, it's no metropolis – first-time visitors wandering around the compact, low-rise town centre might reasonably reflect on what they can expect of the country's fourth-largest town!

Jinja suffered badly during the Amin years and subsequent period of economic and political turmoil, but a more recent economic upswing (see box *Jinja in History*, pages 402–3) has been mirrored by its emergence as a major travel focus. The town centre admittedly boasts little of genuine historical note, though some fine colonial-era Asian architecture – epitomised by the restored 1919 Madvhani House on Main Street – complemented by a spread of thickly vegetated residential suburbs carved from the surrounding jungle, does give Jinja a compelling sense of place.

GETTING THERE AND AWAY Jinja lies along the surfaced Nairobi–Kampala road, 82km east of Kampala and 131km west of Tororo. Depending to some extent on the traffic leaving Kampala, the drive shouldn't take much longer than an hour in a private vehicle. On the outskirts of Jinja, the road from Kampala crosses the Owen Falls Dam, shortly after which there is a roundabout where a right turn leads to the town centre and a left turn to Bujagali Falls.

Using public transport, regular minibus-taxis to Jinja leave Kampala from the old taxi park throughout the day. Tickets cost Ush5,000 and the trips take about 90

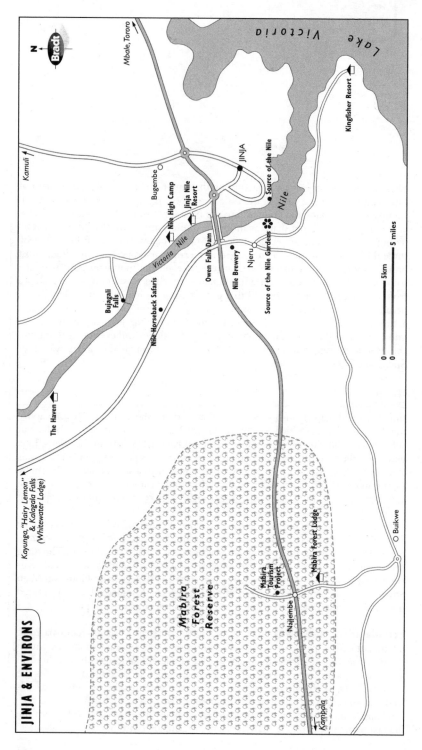

JINJA & ENVIRONS

N

Bradt

Mbale, Tororo

Kamuli

Lake Victoria

Bugembe

JINJA

Source of the Nile

Kingfisher Resort

Nile High Camp

Jinja Nile Resort

Victoria Nile

Nile

Owen Falls Dam

Bujagali Falls

Nile Horseback Safaris

The Haven

Kayunga, "Hairy Lemon" & Kalagala Falls (Whitewater Lodge)

Nile Brewery

Njeru

Source of the Nile Gardens

0 5km

0 5 miles

Mabira Forest Reserve

Mabira Tourism Project

Najjembe

Mabira Forest Lodge

Buikwe

Kampala

minutes. There is also plenty of public transport from Jinja to Tororo and to Mbale via Iganga. It's worth noting that all four rafting companies offer a free transfer from Kampala as part of their rafting package.

Many regular commuters between Kampala and Jinja (among them Adrift rafters and Nile Breweries executives) now prefer a northerly route via Gayaza and Kayunga to the increasingly busy main Jinja highway. The alternative is 30km longer but the road allows a quiet, safe and enjoyable drive while the journey takes the same time. To get to Gayaza, head north out of Kampala through either Wandegere junction or Mulago hospital roundabout. These roads meet after 1km at a roundabout where you bear right (turn left and you'll head to northern Uganda). The first 10km or so to Gayaza is pretty hectic but beyond this small town (fork right at the petrol station) it's a quiet road all the way to Jinja (the road emerges onto the Kampala – Jinja highway opposite Nile Breweries at Owen's Falls dam. Snack sellers at Nakifuma (almost halfway) sell good roasted meat and are less hassle than their counterparts on the main highway.

WHERE TO STAY
Upmarket

Gately on Nile Kisinja Rd; ✆ 0434 122400; m 0772 469638; e gately@utlonline.co.ug; www.gately-on-nile.com. Homely, characterful and refreshingly non-institutionalised, this popular Australian-managed retreat is situated a short walk south of the town centre. It consists of 2 lovingly restored and lavishly decorated colonial homesteads set in an expansive tropical garden overlooking the lakeshore. It's not cheap, but it has a good restaurant – worth visiting even if you're staying elsewhere in town – which serves continental and Mexican dishes in the Ush10,000 range. Facilities include office and email services, DSTV, local travel advice and bookings, and massage and reflexology. The number of rooms is limited, so it's advisable to make reservations well in advance. *US$68/92 s/c sgl/dbl B&B, rooms in an outlying cottage US$75/105 sgl/dbl.*

Kingfisher Safaris Resort m 0772 510197/632063; e mail@kingfishersafaris.com;

www.kingfishersafaris.com. Another relatively new out-of-town lodge, the Kingfisher Resort has a pretty, peaceful location near the Source of the Nile on the opposite side of the river to central Jinja. The compact, green grounds, separated from the water by a strip of cultivation, are centred on a trio of connected swimming pools. Clean, airy s/c accommodation is offered in whitewashed stone *bandas*. Unfortunately, the *bandas* are clustered rather close together and close to the pool, creating a somewhat crowded atmosphere when the resort is busy. To get there from Jinja, follow the Kampala road across the Owen Falls Dam, then take the next left turn (immediately before Nile Breweries) and follow the signposts for another 5.5km. *US$50/60 sgl/dbl B&B or US$60/80 sgl/dbl FB (a discount of around 25% is offered to residents and a more substantial discount to missionaries).*

Moderate

Palm Tree Guesthouse Kisinja Rd; m 0772 500400/563636; e palmtreejinja@yahoo.com. Situated a few gates up from Gately on Nile, this new lodge is another restored colonial homestead in a large garden (with swimming pool) near the Nile. A range of brightly decorated dbl rooms is offered. An attractive terrace restaurant serves good, reasonably priced food with a Mexican touch. Palm Tree is closely involved with an orphanage down the road (www.amanibabycottage.org); the kids love visitors coming to play with them; no strings are attached. *Dbl rooms US$38–75 B&B depending on whether they are s/c and/or have a balcony.*

Sunset Hotel International Kiira Rd; ✆ 0434

120115; m 0712 120155 or 0772 120155; f 0434 120741; e sunset@utlonline.co.ug; www.crosswinds.net/~sunsethotel. This long-serving establishment has a superb location on a ridge facing west towards the Owen Falls Dam, the shore of which is reliably dotted with various herons, cormorants, storks and fish eagles. The patio cafeteria serves substantial snacks as well as reasonable Chinese food. Compared to other options nearby, the rather ordinary rooms are not great value. *US$46 standard dbl B&B, US$54 upwards for a dbl ste.*

Hotel Paradise on the Nile ✆ 0434 121912. Just round the corner from the Sunset Hotel, this new hotel seems much better value for comfortable s/c

A somewhat elegiac tone informs the first written description of the site of modern-day Jinja, less to do perhaps with the its inherent scenic qualities than with Speke's conviction that he was staring at the long sought-after headwaters of the Nile:

> The 'stones', as the Waganda call the falls, was by far the most interesting sight I had seen in Africa… It attracted one to it for hours – the roar of the waters, the thousands of passenger-fish leaping at the falls with all their might; the Wasoga and Waganda fishermen coming out in boats and taking post on all the rocks with rod and hook, hippopotami and crocodiles lying sleepily on the water, the ferry at work above the falls, and cattle driven down to drink at the margin of the lake – made, in all, with the pretty nature of the country – small hills, grassy-topped, with trees in the folds, and gardens on the lower slopes – as interesting a picture as one could wish to see… I felt as if I only wanted a wife and family, garden and yacht, rifle and rod, to make me happy here for life, so charming was the place.

Speke named the falls after the Marquess of Ripon, a former president of the Royal Geographic Society, while a second set of rapids about 1km downriver subsequently became known as Owen Falls, after Major Roddy Owen, a member of Sir Gerald Portal's 1893 expedition to Uganda. But the local name for the site has survived, too, since Jinja is a corruption of Ejjinja (Stones), which is not only the original Luganda name for the Ripon Falls, but also that of a village and associated sacrificial stone that stood close by.

An informal European settlement was founded at Jinja in 1900, when the rocky waterfall was selected as the most suitable place for the telegraph line to Kampala to cross the Nile. At this time, the administrative centre for Busoga was at Iganga, regarded by Governor Sir Harry Johnston to be 'not a very healthy place, and, so to speak, "nowhere"'. In 1901, however, Johnston relocated the headquarters to Jinja, with its 'aggregation of European settlers' at the head of a potentially important riverine transport route north along the Nile and Lake Kyoga.

Jinja's rapid emergence as a pivotal commercial centre and international transport hub was encouraged by the completion of the railway line from Mombasa to the lake port of Kisumu, and the introduction of a connecting ferry service. The local economy was further boosted by the successful introduction of cotton as a cash crop for export, and by the construction of a railway line north to Namasagali in 1912. Even so, Sir Frederick Treves, writing in 1913, dismissed Jinja as 'a little tin town… a rough settlement of some size [but] purely utilitarian and without the least ambition to be beautiful'. Jinja's importance as a port undoubtedly diminished after the late 1920s, when the railway line was extended to Kampala, but by this time the town was firmly established as an administrative and retail centre servicing the local cotton industry.

Instrumental in Jinja's post-World War II emergence as Uganda's major industrial and manufacturing centre was the construction of a dam and an associated hydro-electric plant at Owen Falls. As early as 1904, the Uganda Company had mooted erecting 'an electric generating station to be worked by waterpower from the Ripon Falls'. Winston Churchill, who visited the falls three years later, supported this notion enthusiastically: 'So much power running to waste, such a coign of vantage unoccupied, such a lever to

rooms with DSTV. The name implies proximity to the river rather than a broad vista across the Nile Valley, though the river can be glimpsed from some 2nd-floor rooms. A gym and swimming pool is under construction. *US$24/32 sgl/dbl B&B.*

🏠 **Hotel Triangle Annex** ✆ 0434 122098/9; **m** 0772 490340; **e** hoteltriangle@source.co.ug. In

stark contrast, the Triangle Annex provides a fabulous river panorama, though how this concrete monstrosity was permitted to blight the fabled headwaters of the Nile is a mystery. Aesthetic niceties apart, the hotel enjoys a superb shoreline location between the sailing club and golf course with comfortable and affordable rooms with carpet,

control the natural forces of Africa ungripped, cannot but vex and stimulate imagination. And what fun to make the immemorial Nile begin its journey by driving through a turbine!'

Only in 1946, however, did the colonial administration look seriously at damming the lower Nile, initially as part of a proposed Equatorial Nile Project that involved Egypt, Sudan, Uganda and other indirectly affected nations. The broad idea behind this scheme was that Egypt would fund the construction of a large dam at the outlet of each of the two largest lakes along the Nile's course: Victoria and Albert. The advantage to Uganda was that the dams could be harnessed as a reliable source of hydro-electric power, not only for domestic use, but also to sell to neighbouring Kenya. At the same time, the dams would transform the lakes into vast semi-artificial reservoirs from where the flow of the Nile downriver to Sudan and Egypt could be regulated to prevent the sporadic flooding and droughts that had long been associated with annual fluctuations in the river's water level.

Protracted and often acrimonious negotiations between the various governments over the next two years eventually broke down as both Uganda and to a lesser extent Kenya objected to the significant loss of land that would result from the construction of the proposed dams. In 1949, Egypt reluctantly signed a treaty allowing Uganda to build a hydro-electric plant at Owen Falls, provided that it did not significantly disrupt the natural flow of the river and that an Egyptian engineer would regulate the water flow through the dam. The Owen Falls Dam cost seven million pounds sterling to construct, and was formally opened in 1954.

Jinja's proximity to this reliable source of cheap electricity proved attractive to industry, and several textile and other manufacturing plants, including the country's major cigarette factory and brewery, were established. For two decades, the local economy boomed. The modern town centre – one of the few in East Africa to display clear indications of considered urban planning – essentially dates to the early 1950s, when the population increased from 8,500 to more than 20,000 in the space of three years. A settler community of 800 Europeans and 5,000 Asians is reflected today in the ornate Indian façades of the town centre, as well as the sprawling double-storey mansions that languish in the suburbs. Other relics of this period are the impressive town hall and administrative buildings at the southern end of the town centre.

Jinja's fortunes slumped again following the expulsion of Asians from Uganda in 1973. Most of the town's leading industries had been under Asian management, and the cohorts of Amin who were installed in their place generally lacked any appropriate business experience or managerial skill, resulting in a total breakdown in the local economy. As recently as the early 1990s, the town centre's boarded-up shops and deeply pot-holed roads epitomised a more general aura of lethargy and economic torpor. Today, however, while Jinja remains somewhat sleepy by comparison with Kampala, it no longer feels unhealthily so. Many of the industries have returned, and the freshly painted shopfronts that line the neatly tarred roads of the town centre seem emblematic of a broader sense of urban rejuvenation, as are the once-rundown suburban mansions that have been restored as private houses or hotels.

hot water, fan, DSTV, telephone and private lake-facing balcony. The restaurant serves unexciting but reasonably priced meals. *US$28/33 s/c sgl/dbl.*

🏠 **Crested Crane Hotel** Hannington Sq; ☎ 0434 121954. This suburban government hotel (which doubles as a tourism training college) has undergone a major facelift. The s/c rooms have hot water, nets,

fan and DSTV, and are good value. *US$27/32 sgl/dbl B&B.*

🏠 **Two Friends** Jackson Crescent. This expatriate-run facility provides comfortable rooms in an annex next to the restaurant of the same name. It's located in Jackson Crescent behind the Crested Crane. *US$21/43 sgl/dbl B&B.*

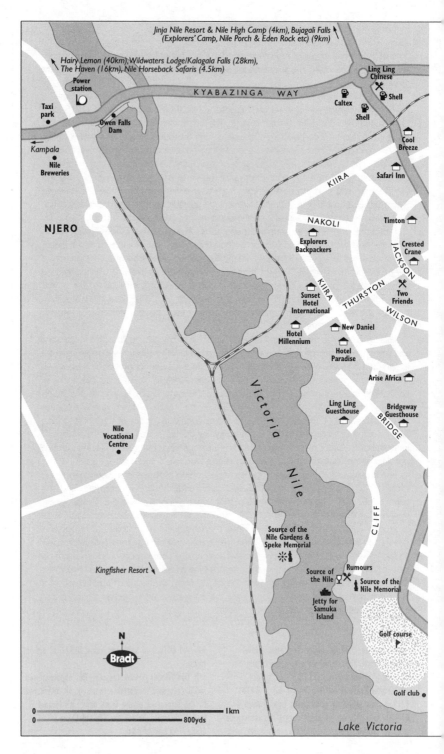

Jinja Nile Resort & Nile High Camp (4km), Bujagali Falls
(Explorers' Camp, Nile Porch & Eden Rock etc) (9km)

Hairy Lemon (40km), Wildwaters Lodge/Kalagala Falls (28km),
The Haven (16km), Nile Horseback Safaris (4.5km)

Power
station

Taxi
park

KYABAZINGA WAY

Ling Ling
Chinese

Shell

Caltex

Shell

Cool
Breeze

Kampala

Owen Falls
Dam

Nile
Breweries

KIIRA

Safari Inn

NJERO

NAKOLI

Timton

Explorers
Backpackers

Crested
Crane

JACKSON

KIIRA

THURSTON

Two
Friends

WILSON

Sunset
Hotel
International

Hotel
Millennium

New Daniel

Hotel
Paradise

Arise Africa

Nile
Vocational
Centre

Ling Ling
Guesthouse

Bridgeway
Guesthouse

BRIDGE

Victoria

Nile

CLIFF

Source of the
Nile Gardens &
Speke Memorial

Rumours

Kingfisher Resort

Source of
the Nile

Source of the
Nile Memorial

Jetty for
Samuka
Island

Golf course

N

Bradt

Golf club

0   1km
0   800yds

Lake Victoria

404

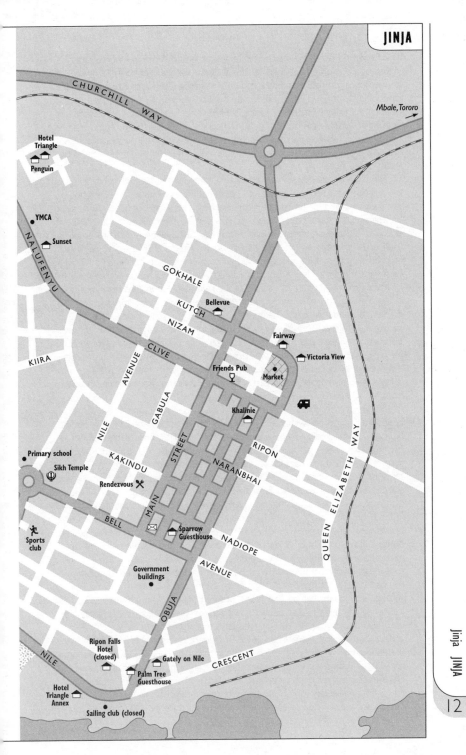

The Reverend James Hannington first set foot in East Africa in June 1882 as the leader of a reinforcement party for the Victoria Nyanza Mission in Kampala, but he was forced to return to England before reaching Uganda due to a debilitating case of dysentery. In June 1884, he was consecrated in London as the first Bishop of Eastern Equatorial Africa. In November of the same year, he left England to assume his post, inspired by Joseph Thomson, who months earlier had become the first European to travel to Lake Victoria through Maasailand, rather than the longer but less perilous route pioneered by Speke around the south of the lake.

Thomson advised future travellers against attempting to reach Buganda through the territory occupied by the militant Maasai, but Bishop Hannington – attracted by its directness and better climatic conditions – paid him no heed. And, as it transpired, Hannington and his party of 200 porters negotiated the route without encountering any significant resistance from the Kikuyu or Maasai, to arrive at Mumias (in present-day western Kenya) on 8 October 1885. A few days later, accompanied by a reduced party of 50 porters, Hannington continued the march westward, obtaining his first view of Lake Victoria on 14 October.

Hannington had been fully aware of the risks involved in crossing Maasailand, but he had no way of knowing about the momentous change in mood that had marked Buganda since the death of King Mutesa a year earlier. Mutesa was succeeded by his son Mwanga, who became increasingly hostile towards outsiders in general and the Anglican Church in particular during the first year of his reign. Worse still, Mwanga was deeply affected by a vision that foretold the destruction of Buganda at the hands of strangers who entered the kingdom through the 'back door' – the east – as opposed to the more normal approach from the southwest.

On 21 October 1885, Hannington and his party entered the fort of Luba, an important Basoga chief with strong loyalties to the King of Buganda. Hours later, the bishop was attacked and imprisoned, and Luba sent a party of messengers to Mwanga to seek instructions. The messengers returned on 28 October accompanied by three Baganda soldiers. The next morning, Hannington wrote in his diary: 'I can hear no news. A hyena howled near me last night, smelling a sick man, but I hope it is not to have me yet.' On the afternoon of 29 October, Hannington was informed that he would be escorted to Buganda immediately. Instead, he was led to a nearby execution rock, stripped of his clothes and possessions, and speared to death. That night, Luba's soldiers massacred the bishop's entire party of 50 porters, with the exception of three men who managed to escape and one boy who was spared on account of his youth.

It is said locally that the murder of Bishop Hannington displeased the spirits and resulted in a long famine in Busoga. King Mwanga, not entirely plausibly, would subsequently claim that he had never ordered Hannington's death; instead, his instructions to release the bishop had been misinterpreted or disregarded by overzealous underlings. In 1890, the bishop's skull – identifiable by his gold fillings – and some of his clothes were brought to Sir Frederick Jackson in Mumias by the one member of Hannington's party who had been spared by Luba's soldiers. The mortal remains of Bishop Hannington were interred at Namirembe Cathedral on 31 December 1892 in a lavish ceremony attended by Mwanga. On 29 October 1939, the 54th anniversary of his death, a bronze memorial dedicated to Bishop Hannington was erected on a boulder near the small port of Buluba (Place of Luba), some 60km east of Jinja.

🛏 **Samuka Island Retreat** m 0772 401508; e island@source.co.ug; www.traveluganda.co.ug/samukaisland. The newly opened Samuka Island is billed as a bird sanctuary (with over 50 species of resident and migratory birds recorded; it is also one of two breeding sites in Uganda for long-tailed cormorants and little

egrets) and a botanical garden (with 100 plus plant species). A boat transfer from Rumours Café within the Source of the Nile site costs Ush8,000 pp (minimum 5 people). Buffet suppers costs Ush10,000. *A range of s/c cottages cost US$25–40/30–45 sgl/dbl B&B, US$8 camping.*

Budget The last few years have seen the establishment of several good budget hotels in suburban Jinja, most of them similar in standard, consisting of converted colonial houses in pretty gardens. These hotels cater primarily to local business travellers, and are popular conference venues, which means – although most of them are very quiet most of the time – one or two are likely to be fully occupied on any given night.

🛏 **Explorers Backpackers** ☎ 0434 120236; m 0772 422373; f 0434 121322; e rafting@starcom.co.ug; www.raftafrica.com. This well-run backpacker lodge, situated around the corner from the Sunset Hotel, is the base for the rafting company Nile River Explorers (NRE). Explorers used to be the most popular budget option in the Jinja area, and it remains probably the first choice within the town limits – though these days most travellers prefer to stay at Bujagali Falls. Travellers who go rafting with NRE are given one free night's accommodation. There's a lively bar with a free pool table and DSTV, and good, inexpensive meals can be ordered. The management can also book gorilla permits for Uganda and Rwanda. Rafters unlucky enough to break a nail during their river adventure need not panic; NRE considerately bring a Kampala beautician out to their hostel every Wednesday. After she's patched you up she'll give you a facial and a massage too. *Dormitory accommodation US$5 pp, 2 dbl rooms US$20, camping US$3 pp.*

🛏 **Hotel Triangle** ☎ 0434 121613; m 0772 758081; e hoteltriangle@source.co.ug. Once little more than a glorified guesthouse, this is now a rather smart multi-storey business hotel, somewhat bland, but the s/c rooms with hot baths are good value. The garden restaurant is good and reasonably priced. *US$19/24 sgl/dbl.*

🛏 **Arise Africa Guest House** Wilson Rd. This spacious, old-fashioned, clean, friendly, Christian guesthouse on a quiet suburban road (behind Two Friends) has been praised by readers as superb value. *US$19 for B & (a plentiful) B.*

🛏 **Bellevue Hotel** ☎ 0434 120328; m 0712 889900; e bellevuehotel@yahoo.com. This long-standing favourite is only a short walk away from the taxi park, making it perhaps the most convenient, if sometimes noisy option in this range.

It has undergone a recent facelift under new Indian management and now seems very good value. *US$6 for a clean sgl using common showers or US$8/14 for a s/c sgl/dbl.*

🛏 **Safari Inn (previously Annesworth Hotel)** ☎ 0434 122955. Situated more or less opposite Cool Breeze, this long-serving hotel stands in pretty green grounds. Newly renovated and tastefully furnished dbl rooms upstairs seem a bargain. A choice of more basic rooms are also excellent value given the quiet suburban setting. *US$27 upstairs rooms, US$8/13 sgl/dbl B&B.*

🛏 **New Daniel Hotel** ☎ 0434 121633; m 0772 666137. The New Daniel, 100m or so from the Sunset Hotel International has been awaiting a facelift for years. Still it's reasonable value for a room with hot bath or shower. There's a pleasant garden restaurant and a sitting room with DSTV. *US$14/20 s/c sgl/dbl.*

🛏 **Cool Breeze Hotel** Nalufenya Rd; m 0712 897766. One of the smarter hotels in this range, Cool Breeze lies in large gardens close to the main Kampala roundabout. There's DSTV in the bar, but the restaurant looks less than inspiring. Check whether an evening function is planned before you check in; Cool Breeze has quite a reputation locally for keeping its neighbours awake. *US$17/21–33 sgl/dbl, depending on whether they are s/c and/or have a balcony.*

🛏 **Hotel Ling Ling** m 0772 489616. Affiliated to the eponymous restaurant, this Chinese-owned guesthouse is housed in a modern white double-storey building off Cliff Road, near to the Source of the Nile. The clean dbl rooms lack character, but they're reasonable value. *US$17–33 depending on size.*

🛏 **Timton Hotel** Jackson Crescent; ☎ 0434 121233. Situated close to the Crested Crane Hotel, this long-serving suburban budget hotel has lovely grounds and an attractive outside bar/dining area. The promised renovation programme needs to get a

move on to warrant the asking price. *US$19/30 sgl/dbl.*

Shoestring

⌂ **Victoria View Inn** \ 0434 122319. The multi-storey Victoria View Inn is a perennial budget favourite, with a central location practically alongside the taxi park – 1 or 2 rooms even offer the vaunted view over the town centre to the lake. It's good value, too, for a slightly rundown but spacious and reasonably clean s/c dbl or twin. *US$6.*

⌂ **Fairway Guesthouse** Situated a couple of doors up from the Victoria View, and similar in standard. *US$5/6 for an acceptable sgl/dbl.*

⌂ **Khalinie Hotel** m 0772 456904. The standard

of accommodation varies wildly. The upstairs rooms are OK, even including a distant lake view over unfinished concrete rooftops, while the downstairs rooms are pretty grotty. *US$6/8 sgl/dbl for all rooms.*

⌂ **Sparrow Guesthouse** m 0772 553586. Not quite the unmitigated dump it was a few years ago, the centrally located Sparrow Guesthouse is still no better than adequate. *US$5/6 sgl/dbl using common showers.*

⌂ **Arc Nile Hotel** The flaking exterior reflects the state of the rooms, which are decidedly basic, rundown and poor value. *US$8/11 sgl/dbl.*

⚑ Camping There are several camping options in and around Jinja, all charging around US$2–3 per person. Most popular within the town centre is **Explorers Backpackers**, a good place to meet other travellers, but the **Timton Hotel** can also be recommended. You can also camp at the **Source of the Nile Gardens**, but the absence of showers and inconvenient location (unless you have private transport) count against it. Camping is also possible at the nearby **Mabira Forest** and **Bujagali Falls** (covered later in this chapter).

✗ WHERE TO EAT AND DRINK The hotels listed under the upmarket and moderate headings all have decent restaurants serving Western-style food. Worth singling out is **Gately on Nile**, which lies within easy walking distance of the town centre and serves excellent (mostly continental) food in the Ush8,000–10,000 range. Nearby, the **Palm Tree Guesthouse** offers good Mexican food including tacos made from home-ground cornflour with delicious dips. The bar at **Explorers Backpackers** is often a good place to meet travellers and volunteers, particularly when major sports events are screened on DSTV. Numerous small bars and local eateries, not listed individually below, are scattered along Main Street and around the market area. If you've got transport, you might drive the 9km out to Bujugali Falls to try the steaks at the excellent **Black Lantern** (main courses Ush10,000–15,000).

✗ **Ling Ling Chinese Restaurant** The location, on the roundabout at the Kampala bypass, is neither particularly convenient nor inspiring, but the food – predominantly Chinese dishes – is of a good standard and the large portions are good value. *Around Ush8,000 for a main course.*

✗ **Ozzie's Café** This great little Australian-run restaurant, situated directly opposite the Source Café has become a 'home from home' for scores of local volunteers and gap-year students over the years. It serves toasted sandwiches, steaks, burgers and vegetarian dishes. *Meals in the Ush3,000–5,000 range. She closes at around 18.00 except on Fri and Sat, when Ozzie's stays open until around 21.00.*

✗ **Barazza's** This new restaurant on the corner of Main St and Ripon Rd serves good pizzas from its own wood oven. A lively bar-pool room is attached.

✗ **Source Café** Set in a restored 1920s' warehouse on Main St, this excellent café – a kind of 'African Starbucks' – serves freshly brewed coffee, including cappuccino and mochas, and juices, plus a variety of cakes and light meals. It's a pleasant place to hang out, with an attached internet café (Ush75 per min) and several tables on the pavement. Source Café is a non-profit initiative helping schools in the area. *Meals up to Ush5,000. Open Mon–Sat 09.00–18.00.*

✗ **Rendezvous Bar and Restaurant** More a drinking hole than an eatery, this relatively smart bar does serve decent, affordable meals such as fish and chips.

✗ **Meera Restaurant** Not much to look at from the outside, Meera – situated on the ground floor of the Khalinie Hotel – serves good, authentic and inexpensive Indian food.

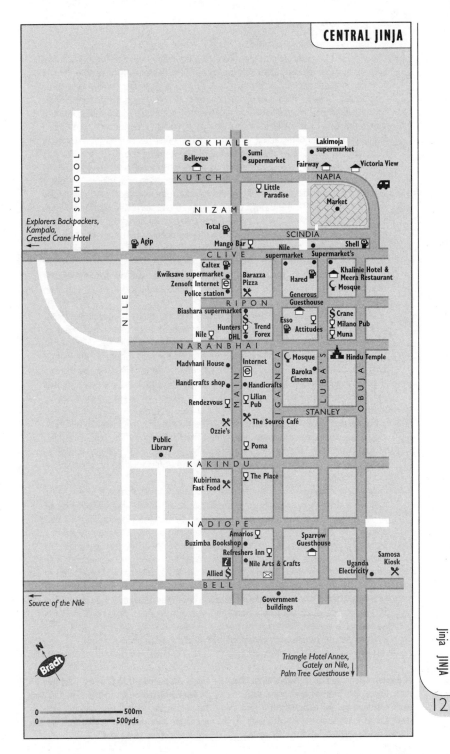

CENTRAL JINJA

GOKHALE

Bellevue

Sumi supermarket

Lakimoja supermarket

Fairway

Victoria View

KUTCH

NAPIA

Little Paradise

Market

NIZAM

Explorers Backpackers, Kampala, Crested Crane Hotel

Total

SCINDIA

Agip

Mango Bar

Nile supermarket

Shell

CLIVE

Supermarket's

Caltex

Kwiksave supermarket

Zensoft Internet

Police station

Barazza Pizza

Hared

Khalinie Hotel & Meera Restaurant

Mosque

RIPON

Generous Guesthouse

Biashara supermarket

Crane

Milano Pub

Hunters

Trend Forex

Esso

Attitudes

Nile

DHL

Muna

NARANBHAI

Madvhani House

Internet

Mosque

Hindu Temple

Handicrafts shop

Handicrafts

Baroka Cinema

Rendezvous

Lilian Pub

STANLEY

Ozzie's

The Source Café

Poma

Public Library

KAKINDU

Kubirima Fast Food

The Place

NADIOPE

Amarios

Sparrow Guesthouse

Buzimba Bookshop

Samosa Kiosk

Refreshers Inn

Nile Arts & Crafts

Uganda Electricity

Allied

BELL

Government buildings

Source of the Nile

N

Bradt

Triangle Hotel Annex, Gately on Nile, Palm Tree Guesthouse

0   500m
0   500yds

SCHOOL

NILE

MAIN

IGANGA

LUBAS

OBUJA

The Victoria Nile, running past Jinja, forms the boundary between the kingdoms of Buganda and Busoga, the latter being the home of the Basoga, Uganda's second most populous linguistic group. The Basoga speak a Bantu language very similar to Luganda – particularly close to the dialect of the Ssese Islands – but they claim a different origin from the Baganda, and traditionally adhere to a far less centralised political structure. It is also the case that many traditional Basoga customs – for instance, the largely abandoned practice of extracting six teeth from the lower jaw of a boy as an initiation to adulthood – are clearly influenced by the Nilotic-speaking Luo.

Basoga has been subject to numerous migrations and a great deal of cultural intermingling over the past few centuries, for which reason its traditions are more diverse and contradictory than those of Uganda's other kingdoms. It is generally agreed, however, that the Basoga originate from the eastern side of Mount Elgon. A popular tradition has it that Busoga was founded by a hunter called Makuma, who crossed the western slopes of the mountain accompanied by his wives, dogs and other followers about 600 years ago to settle in the vicinity of present-day Iganga. Makuma had eight sons, each of whom was appointed ruler of a specific area of Busoga. Makuma was buried at Iganga, where it is said his tomb magically transformed into a rock that is known today as Buswikara and forms the site of an important ancestral shrine.

Uniquely, Busoga's modern status as a kingdom is not rooted in any pre-colonial political or social structure, but is instead a result of 20th-century developments. Pre-colonial Busoga was divided into about 70 autonomous principalities ruled by hereditary chiefs who originally paid tribute to the king of Bunyoro, but had mostly transferred allegiance to the King of Buganda by the end of the 19th century. This traditional system of decentralised government was undermined in 1900 when Britain divided Busoga into 14 larger principalities for administrative and tax purposes. It was shattered entirely six years later, when Busoga was amalgamated into one cohesive political entity, modelled on Buganda, and administered by a Muganda 'president' Semei Kakunguru. The office occupied by Kakunguru was abandoned after his retirement in 1913, but the traditional leaders of Basoga put pressure on the British authorities for it to be reinstated – and awarded to a prominent Musoga.

In 1919, Britain created the title of *kyabazinga*, transforming Busoga into a centralised monarchy that enjoyed a similar status within the Uganda Protectorate to the ancient kingdoms of Bunyoro or Buganda. Ezekieri Wako Zibondo was crowned as the first kyabazinga, to be succeeded by Sir Wilberforce Nadiope Kadhumbula, whose active rule was terminated when Obote abolished the traditional kingdoms of Uganda in 1967. In 1996, when the kingdoms were reinstalled, Henry Wako Muloki – the son of the first kyabazinga – was instated to the throne. Today, the kyabazinga is regarded as the overall leader of Basoga, but he is supported by a parliament of 11 semi-autonomous hereditary Saza chiefs. Five of these chiefs claim accession from Makuma, the founder of Busoga, and the kyabazinga is picked from one of these élite families using a system of rotating accession, to be succeeded only upon death, abdication or serious illness.

✗ **Rumours Café** Situated at the Source of the Nile, about 10mins' walk from the town centre, this stilted waterfront bar and restaurant has a good stereo and DSTV, and serves sophisticated meals. It also has a well-equipped little barge for booze cruises. *Meals in the Ush5,000–10,000 range.*

✗ **Two Friends** Jackson Crescent. Formerly Club Oasis, this outdoor bar, set in a large suburban garden is one of the more chilled-out drinking holes in town, and it also serves good pizzas.

LISTINGS

Tourist information The most useful sources of current travel information for Jinja and environs are **Gately on Nile** and **Nile River Explorers** (see *Where to stay, Explorers Backpackers*, page 407) as well as the backpacker lodges at Bujagali Falls.

4x4 rental Several readers have recommended the four well-maintained Land Rovers rented out by **Walter Egger** (\f *0434 121314;* m *0772 221113;* e *wemtec@source.co.ug*) for use around Jinja or for longer safaris countrywide. Two of the vehicles are 109 soft-tops and the other two 110 hardtops. All run on petrol and can seat up to six with luggage. A driver is provided.

Foreign exchange Jinja is not as well equipped with forex bureaux as Kampala, but there are several banks that can exchange major foreign currencies at reasonable rates. **Trend Forex** on Main Street has competitive rates for US dollars cash (about 1% lower than the best rates in Kampala at the time of writing). It will also exchange travellers' cheques at about 5% lower than the best rates offered in Kampala, though proof of purchase and identity must be provided. Foreign exchange is also possible at **Nile**, **Stanbic** and **Standard Chartered** banks. The ATM at the last accepts Visa cards.

Internet There are several internet cafés along Main Street, most of which charge Ush50 per minute. The excellent **Source Café** is the most attractive setting for catching up on your emails but also more expensive at Ush75 per minute.

Shopping For fresh produce, the **central market** near the taxi park has a lively but non-intimidating atmosphere. Among the better supermarkets are the **Kwiksave** next to the Caltex garage on Main Street, the **Biashara Supermarket** diagonally opposite, and **Sumi Supermarket** further north along the same road. A number of good craft shops lie along Main Street between Ozzie's and the Rendezvous Bar.

Jinja Golf Club This lovely course, overlooking the Nile and at one time famous for games being interrupted by a stray hippo, is open to non-members at Ush10,000 per round, and golf clubs are available. A fee of Ush5,000 is charged to visitors who want to use the 10 x 25m swimming pool or squash or tennis courts.

WHAT TO SEE

Source of the Nile (*Admission Ush2,000 pp plus Ush1,200/2,000 for a car/minibus*) The Ripon Falls, the natural landmark associated with the Source of the Nile, was submerged in the early 1950s following the construction of the Owen Falls Dam a short distance upriver. But the site remains worth visiting, and there is a park and a plaque situated on both banks of the Nile as it exits Lake Victoria.

The **eastern bank** is the more accessible from central Jinja, and can be reached by *boda-boda* or a 30-minute walk. From the post office on Main Street, follow Bell Street west to the roundabout with Nile Crescent, cross the roundabout and continue for 200m along Bridge Street, then turn left into Cliff Road and follow it to its end. The best time to visit is early or late in the day, when it is not crowded by school trips. The timber-stilted **Rumours Café** and **Source of the Nile Bar** lie within the park, and on Sunday afternoons, from 16.00 until 18.00, the Nile Beat Artists – probably the best group in Busoga – perform here (they can also give interested travellers information about local music in nearby villages). Shaded fishing boats with outboard engines await to take you for a cruise on the lake. Some haggling will be necessary but within a

The first European to see Lake Victoria was John Hanning Speke, who marched from Tabora to the site of present-day Mwanza in 1858 following his joint 'discovery' of Lake Tanganyika with Richard Burton the previous year. Speke named the lake for Queen Victoria, but prior to that Arab slave traders called it Ukerewe (still the name of its largest island). It is unclear what name was in local use, since the only one used by Speke is Nyanza, which simply means 'lake'.

A major goal of the Burton–Speke expedition had been to solve the great geographical enigma of the age, the source of the White Nile. Speke, based on his brief glimpse of the southeast corner of Lake Victoria, somewhat whimsically proclaimed his 'discovery' to be the answer to that riddle. Burton, with a comparable lack of compelling evidence, was convinced that the great river flowed out of Lake Tanganyika. The dispute between the former travelling companions erupted bitterly on their return to Britain, where Burton – the more persuasive writer and respected traveller – gained the backing of the scientific establishment.

Over 1862–63, Speke and Captain James Grant returned to Lake Victoria, hoping to prove Speke's theory correct. They looped inland around the western shore of the lake, arriving at the court of King Mutesa of Buganda, then continued east to the site of present-day Jinja, where a substantial river flowed out of the lake after tumbling over a cataract that Speke named Ripon Falls. From here, the two explorers headed north, sporadically crossing paths with the river until they reached Lake Albert, then following the Nile to Khartoum and Cairo.

Speke's declaration that 'The Nile is settled' met with mixed support back home. Burton and other sceptics pointed out that Speke had bypassed the entire western shore of his purported great lake, had visited only a couple of points on the northern shore, and had not attempted to explore the east. Nor, for that matter, had he followed the course of the Nile in its entirety. Speke, claimed his detractors, had seen several different lakes and different stretches of river, connected only in Speke's deluded mind. The sceptics had a point, but Speke had nevertheless gathered sufficient geographical evidence to render his claim highly plausible. His notion of one great lake, far from being mere whimsy, was backed by anecdotal information gathered from local sources along the way.

Matters were scheduled to reach a head on 16 September 1864, when an eagerly awaited debate between Burton and Speke – in the words of the former, 'what silly tongues called the "Nile Duel"' – was due to take place at the Royal Geographic Society (RGS). And reach a head they did, but in circumstances more tragic than anybody could have anticipated. On the afternoon of the debate, Speke went out shooting with a cousin, only to stumble while crossing a wall, in the process discharging a barrel of his shotgun into his heart. The subsequent inquest recorded a verdict of accidental death, but it has often been suggested – purely on the basis of the curious timing – that Speke deliberately took his life rather than face up to Burton in public. Burton, who had seen Speke less than three hours earlier, was by all accounts deeply troubled by Speke's death, and years later he was quoted as stating 'the uncharitable [say] that I shot him' – an accusation that seems to have been aired only in Burton's imagination.

Speke was dead, but the 'Nile debate' would keep kicking for several years. In 1864, Sir Samuel and Lady Baker became the first Europeans to reach Lake Albert and nearby

couple of minutes' discussion they'll agree to around Ush20,000 for a small group (less than five) or Ush5,000 per person for more.

The original plaque on the east bank commemorated Speke's discovery of the source of the Nile, but this was removed some years back on the basis that local people knew the place long before any European arrived there. Frankly, this

Murchison Falls in present-day Uganda. The Bakers, much to the delight of the anti-Speke lobby, were convinced that this newly named lake was a source of the Nile, though they openly admitted it might not be the only one. Following the Bakers' announcement, Burton put forward a revised theory, namely that the most remote source of the Nile was the Rusizi River, which he believed flowed out of the northern head of Lake Tanganyika and emptied into Lake Albert.

In 1865, the RGS followed up on Burton's theory by sending Dr David Livingstone to Lake Tanganyika. Livingstone, however, was of the opinion that the Nile's source lay further south than Burton supposed, and so he struck out towards the lake along a previously unexplored route. Leaving from Mikindani in the far south of present-day Tanzania, Livingstone followed the Rovuma River inland, continuing westward to the southern tip of Lake Tanganyika. From there, he ranged southward into present-day Zambia, where he came across a new candidate for the source of the Nile, the swampy Lake Bangweulu and its major outlet the Lualaba River. It was only after his famous meeting with Henry Stanley at Ujiji, in November 1871, that Livingstone (in the company of Stanley) visited the north of Lake Tanganyika and Burton's cherished Rusizi River, which, it transpired, flowed into the lake. Burton, nevertheless, still regarded Lake Tanganyika to be the most likely source of the Nile, while Livingstone was convinced that the answer lay with the Lualaba River. In August 1872, Livingstone headed back to the Lake Bangweulu region, where he fell ill and died six months later, the great question still unanswered.

In August 1874, ten years after Speke's death, Stanley embarked on a three-year expedition every bit as remarkable and arduous as those undertaken by his predecessors, yet one whose significance is often overlooked. Partly, this is because Stanley cuts such an unsympathetic figure, the grim caricature of the murderous pre-colonial White Man blasting and blustering his way through territories where Burton, Speke and Livingstone had relied largely on diplomacy. It is also the case, however, that Stanley set out with no intention of seeking headline-making fresh discoveries. Instead, he determined to test methodically the theories advocated by Speke, Burton and Livingstone about the Nile's source. First, Stanley sailed around the circumference of Lake Victoria, establishing that it was indeed as vast as Speke had claimed. Stanley's next step was to circumnavigate Lake Tanganyika, which, contrary to Burton's long-held theories, clearly boasted no outlet sufficiently large to be the source of the Nile. Finally, and most remarkably, Stanley took a boat along Livingstone's Lualaba River to its confluence with an even larger river, which he followed for months with no idea as to where he might end up.

When, exactly 999 days after he left Zanzibar, Stanley emerged at the Congo mouth, the shortlist of plausible theories relating to the source of the Nile had been reduced to one. Clearly, the Nile did flow out of Lake Victoria at Ripon Falls, before entering and exiting Lake Albert at its northern tip to start its long course through the sands of the Sahara. Stanley's achievement in putting to rest decades of speculation about how the main rivers and lakes of East Africa linked together is estimable indeed. He was nevertheless generous enough to concede that: 'Speke now has the full glory of having discovered the largest inland sea on the continent of Africa, also its principal affluent as well as its outlet. I must also give him credit for having understood the geography of the countries we travelled through far better than any of us who so persistently opposed his hypothesis.'

particular concession to political correctness strikes me as somewhat delusional. Of course, Speke did not really 'discover' Lake Victoria or the Ripon Falls: people had been living there for millennia before any European arrived. But Speke was the first person to make the connection between the effluent from Lake Victoria and a sacred river that flows into the Mediterranean 6,500km further north.

Ironically, the new plaque stating that 'this spot marks the place from where the Nile starts its long journey to the Mediterranean' is itself somewhat contentious. The Ripon Falls is *a* source of the Nile, but its semi-official status as *the* Source of the Nile is arbitrary and sentimental – posthumous recognition of Speke's momentous but contemporarily controversial discovery – rather than being based on any geographical logic. The most remote headwater of the Nile is in fact the most distant spring of the Kagera River and the location of this is another cause for debate. German explorer Oscar Baumann placed it in Burundi's Kabera Forest in 1892 and his countryman, Richard Kandt located a spring in Rwanda's Nyungwe Forest in 1903. However in March 2006, modern GPS equipment led an expedition mounted by Jinja rafter Cam McLeay up the Nile from Alexandria to a 'new' source in Rwanda, 15km from the location identified by Kandt in 1903. Cam claims the length of the river to be 6,718km – 107km longer than previously thought. This might be the most distant headwater but there are still other alternative sources to consider. The Victoria Nile is the only river to flow into Lake Albert, from which the true Nile emerges. This lake is also fed by the Semliki which receives streams from the river's highest and certainly most fabulous source on the Rwenzori Mountains. Nyungwe, Rwenzori or the effluent of Lake Albert – any of these would be a more logical candidate than Jinja for the spot where the Nile starts its journey to the Mediterranean. At the Jinja source an additional plaque with a sculpted bust close to the river commemorates Mahatma Gandhi, part of whose ashes were scattered into the river here following his death in 1948.

The **Source of the Nile Gardens** on the western bank can be reached by canoe from the east bank, or by following the Kampala road across Owen Falls Dam, then taking the next left turn (before Nile Breweries) and following it for about 5km. It is from this side of the river that Speke originally viewed the Ripon Falls, an event commemorated by an inscribed pillar which was erected in 1954 (and has thus far survived any attempt to replace it with something more politically correct). Long-standing plans to develop further facilities remain dormant and though you can enter the site (a caretaker will materialise to ask you for a small sum) the Nile Gardens seem all but closed down.

Nile Breweries Tours (☏ *033 210009; tours are available during normal office hours (08.30–17.00) on all weekdays except Mon*) Nile Breweries in Njeru hosts brewery tours with pleasure and free of charge. These can be arranged by contacting the brewery and asking to speak to the tour co-ordinator Herbert Ngobi. The brewery is usually able to oblige at very short notice but prior arrangements are appreciated: they occasionally have large groups booked and may have to turn away anybody who arrives unannounced. After the tour, you can visit a small gift shop selling a limited selection of branded clothing and other items such as watches, key rings, pens, coasters, etc. For more technically oriented people it is better to contact the Technical Director at the same telephone number, so that a tour guide with more in-depth knowledge of the brewing process, the business and its objectives can be provided.

Jinja Sailing Club The sailing club has, for many years, been a pleasant lakeshore garden and restaurant rather than a centre for waterborne activity. In any case, it has been closed for a year or more awaiting renovation. Hopefully it will soon reopen as a pleasant and peaceful place to enjoy a drink or meal whilst pondering the ambiguities of the 'Crocodiles Do Not Swim Here' sign. You can walk to the sailing club by heading directly south from the town centre past the town hall, but a more scenic route along Nile Crescent leads past the very attractive golf course, an avenue of palm trees laden with fruit bats, and some fine old colonial houses

THE SPIRIT OF BUJAGALI

Based on information supplied by Speke Camp

The waterfall at Bujagali, held sacred by the local community, is named after a powerful river spirit that has manifested itself in more than 30 successive human reincarnations over the centuries. Anyone who claims to be the new reincarnation of the spirit is required to prove it by sitting on a magical piece of barkcloth and drifting across the rapids. Only if he succeeds in this risky venture will local villagers accept him as their new spiritual leader.

The last uncontested Bujagali died without nominating an heir in the 1970s, and the identity of his successor has been the subject of a heated dispute. Most villagers believe the spirit resides in a local called Ja-Ja, who is said to have crossed the rapids on the magical piece of barkcloth while evading military arrest during the Amin era. Ja-Ja's rival for the title is an outsider called Jackson, who dreamed that he was the reincarnation of Bujagali more than 20 years ago. Jackson arrived at the village to stake his claim and, assisted by a companion, he ran off with the magic barkcloth in order to float over the rapids. Before he could attempt the crossing, however, the villagers caught him and killed his companion. Jackson was banished from the village to live out his days on what is now known as Jackson's Island, opposite Speke Camp.

(many of these have been beautifully renovated though sadly no attempt has been made to restore and reopen the historic Ripon Falls Hotel).

BUJAGALI FALLS AND THE NILE

Only 12 years ago, tourism activity on the Nile north of Jinja was limited to a peaceful and rather obscure picnic site at Bujagali Falls – a series of impressive rapids about 10km downriver of the Source of the Nile – visited by a handful of travellers annually. Goodness, how this has changed! Today, the eastern bank of the Nile between Jinja and Bujagali has developed into East Africa's premier adventure tourism centre, serviced by four bustling backpacker facilities, and an upmarket tented camp and hotel. This is because the 50km stretch of the Nile north of Jinja is now a legendary white-water rafting and kayaking route, widely regarded to be as exhilarating as the more famous Zambezi Gorge below Victoria Falls. Additional activities include bungee jumping, an aerial runway and quad biking (more details below). Although most visitors to Bujagali are primarily there to undergo their trial by white water, it's a relaxed and scenic place to spend a few days, with the wide Nile fringed by lush riparian woodland rattling with birds and the odd monkey. Tourism facilities are also appearing along the equally scenic western bank of the river; these are rather laidback set ups that complement rather than compete with the high-adrenalin activities centred on Bujagali.

GETTING THERE AND AWAY There are two tourism hubs on the east bank of the river north of Jinja. The first of these, the Nile High Camp/Jinja Nile Resort hotel complex is about 4km along a fair dirt road leading off from the main roundabout on the Kampala–Kenya road which bypasses Jinja 2km north of the town centre. The second and larger centre is at Bujagali Falls, 9km from Jinja along the same road. Both sites are signposted off the roundabout, but the first landmark to look for here is the very obvious Chinese restaurant on the opposite side of the road. Occasional minibus-taxis run between Jinja and a junction about 500m from the waterfall. A *boda-boda* from Jinja direct to the falls costs Ush2,500. In practice, most visitors will not be dependent on public transport, since the rafting companies

Andy Roberts

Bujagali Falls is something of a phenomenon, not only because of its role as the adrenaline capital of East Africa but because of numerous initiatives through which the backpacker-driven tourism industry along the Nile corridor is actually giving back something back to the locality that supports it. This is as it should be. For while the Nile rafting industry and spin-offs generate an estimated US$1m annually, local schoolkids sit on hard benches catching jiggers in their feet through the earth floors of mud-and-thatch classrooms. Or rather they were. Thanks to Hannah Bayne, an English overland truck driver, conditions for many kids have recently improved in various ways. Dilapidated classrooms have been replaced by new brick structures with concrete floors, rainwater collection tanks fitted and safe latrines built. These date from 2000 when Hannah returned to Africa with the intention of doing something for some of the communities through which she had travelled over the years. Gravitating back, quite understandably, to the lovely Bujagali Falls her chance began when the Bwenda village community provided her with a plot of land, hoping that she would be able to provide them with a pre-school facility. And with the assistance of likeminded travellers willing to provide labour and financial assistance, Hannah was indeed able to. Today 120 AIDS orphans and other deserving infants attend a brightly painted brick-built school at Bwenda with a grassy compound and adventure playground. A school for another 120 kids followed at nearby Kyabirwa. These initial activities have been formalised as 'Soft Power Education', an English-registered charity and a name that few visitors to Buji will miss these days, Soft Power gained momentum in 2002 when Hannah married Bingo Small, co-director of Nile River Explorers, since when local schoolkids have benefited immensely from logistical backup, marketing and a ceaseless flow of donations and volunteers from NRE's Explorers Camp. NRE's bosses would be the first to wince at any suggestion that Mrs Bingo has transformed them into little saints but it's encouraging for our planet to see these leathery South African commercialists look engagingly proud of what the Soft Power–NRE union has achieved.

either operate regular shuttles from their bases in Jinja or provide transport from Kampala, including pick-ups from the main hotels.

WHERE TO STAY
Upmarket

Jinja Nile Resort 0434 122190/1/2 or 0414 233593; f 0434 122581; e nileresort@source.co.ug; www.madahotels.com. Opened in June 2000, the sumptuous Jinja Nile Resort – part of a Kenyan hotel chain – borders a stretch of the Nile studded with forested islands and babbling rapids, about 1km downriver of the Owen Falls Dam along the road towards Bujagali Falls. The atmosphere of bland internationalism may not be to everybody's taste, but taken on its own terms the resort is difficult to fault – especially the fabulous swimming pool and outdoor bar area. The plush, spacious mini-stes all have 2 beds (1 dbl, 1 sgl), a small sitting area with DSTV, and fan, netting and private balcony. Substantial lunches and dinners cost US$10, and facilities include a gym,

massage parlour, business centre, and squash and tennis courts. The resort caters mainly to business travellers and conferences during the week. The Nile High Camp, at the rear of the hotel, provides cheaper accommodation. *Stes US$80/100 sgl/dbl B&B (an extra US$20 for rooms facing the river), discounted weekend packages for 2 US$81 1 night, US$146 2 nights.*

The Nile Porch m 0782 321541 or 0772 990815; e relax@nileporch.com or rafting@starcom.co.ug; www.nileporch.com. Superbly located above a high forested river cliff, the Nile Porch is a new semi-permanent tented camp overlooking the swirling Nile as it approaches Bujagali Falls. The tents are spacious yet marvellously cosy, romantic even, with

Soft Power Education (*UK Contact: Soft Power Education, 55 Guildhall St. Bury St Edmunds, Suffolk IP33 1QF;* m *0772 903344;* e *info@softpowereducation.com; www.softpowereducation.com*) is now co-ordinated by two full-time volunteers funded by an unusually generous tourist and is presently halfway through a five-year plan intent on refurbishing all 20 schools in Budondo Sub County. Developmental cynics will be pleased to note that rather than relieving the local education authority of its responsibility for developing infrastructure, it liases with the authorities in order to work where funding is apparently not available. In 2005, Soft Power Education raised over £100,000 through the support of visiting overland passengers, independent long-term volunteers, groups of university students, standing orders, one-off donations (of up to £5,000) and fundraising by ex-volunteers in their home countries. It is presently completing an Education Centre in which Ugandan teachers will instruct daily groups of visiting schoolchildren in topics either poorly represented in the local curriculum or lacking in materials such as drama, arts and crafts, and computer use.

Local support from the tourism industry is not limited to Soft Power Education. An independent sister project, Soft Power Health provides improved health care to villagers at affordable prices. Upriver in Jinja, Ozzie's Café and Palm Tree Guesthouse both provide considerable support to orphans and orphanages. Back at Bujagali, All Terrain Adventures makes payments to the local parishes through which their ATVs (All Terrain Vehicles) pass. NRE is helping to train interested local people in kayaking, a process that has, for the most talented, led to opportunities exceeding their wildest dreams. The best among them have become professional river guides and some have acquitted themselves extremely well in international competitions in Switzerland and Australia. In 2003, a team of Ugandan villagers, Paulo Babi, Juma Kalakwani and Geoffrey Kabirya reached the quarter-finals of the World Championships in Australia while Babi was placed 8th in the 2004 European Championships in Switzerland. The stakes are even greater for 20-year-old Prossie Mirembe of Bujagali village, Uganda's first and only female trainee kayaker. For this pre-O Level school leaver, the Nile River offers the chance to escape the lifetime of digging local fields that will be the inevitable lot for most of her village girlfriends.

inner, walk-in mosquito netting and verandas facing the river. It's worth waking early to watch the day break over the misty valley. Ablutions provided along the outside of the bedroom tent are quite private but enjoy fresh air and river views. Meals are provided in the adjacent Black Lantern Restaurant (see *Where to eat,* page 421). The room rates (including a filling breakfast) are excellent value compared to other 'Upmarket' offerings along the Nile (see *Jinja* section, page 401). 2-bedroom cottages for families (sensibly set safely back from the river cliff) are also good value. *US$54/84 sgl/dbl, cottages US$120.*

Whitewater Lodge (20 cottages) ✆ 0414 252 720 or 0772 237 438; e raft@adrift.ug. This brand new lodge (opening in November 2007) enjoys a magnificent site on an private island in the Nile between two thunderous rapids at Kalagala Falls, 28km north of Bujagali. The thatched cottages look across the raging mid-river rapid into another, heavily forested, island. A pervading theme is the roar of the white water which, despite the volume, is (appropriately enough) 'white noise' that soothes rather than otherwise. The lodge is ideally placed for river rafting, being located directly at the end of the standard one-day excursion from Bujagali Falls. Gentle river cruises (searching for birds and otters) are available on the more placid section of river north of Kalagala Falls. The lodge is reached from the west bank, three kilometres east of Kangulumira town on the quiet tarmac Kayunga road that loops around Mabira forest. If driving yourself from Kampala, use the Gayaza route described in *Getting there and away* for Jinja above (the same applies to the Hairy Lemon and The Haven below. Alternatively, turn onto the Kayunga road at Mukono and follow it for 74km to Kangulumira, turning right when you meet a T-junction at Mukalagi. From Jinja, the Kangulumira turning is 26km up the Kayunga road from Nile Breweries. *FB accommodation costs US$130/200.*

The proposed construction of a 30m-high hydro-electric dam at Itanda, upriver of Bujagali Falls, has been the subject of ongoing controversy since it was announced in 1994. Contracted to the AES Corporation (the biggest independent power producer in the world) with considerable financial backing from the World Bank, the project is expected to cost US$550 million, the most substantial foreign investment ever made in East Africa.

AES and the Ugandan government have promoted the Bujagali Dam project as an important step in developing the infrastructure of a country in which only 3% of the population has access to electricity and many businesses lose the equivalent of 90 working days annually through power cuts. But, while it is true that the 250MW Bujagali station would practically double Uganda's electricity production, many claim that the above statistics are not primarily a function of an inadequate supply, but rather indicative of an inefficient and limited distribution network.

The project has also riled environmentalists. The International Rivers Network has noted that the dam would submerge a significant tract of productive agricultural land resulting in 'further watershed degradation and deforestation and a loss in soil productivity'. Countering this argument, it has been claimed that access to electricity would reduce many rural Ugandans' dependence on wood and charcoal for cooking, and thus have strong environmental benefits. According to Martin Musumba of the Save Bujagali Campaign, however: 'The real issue… is not electricity but poverty. Currently the majority of Ugandans have no money for electricity [and so] production of more electricity will not reduce use of fuel-wood and charcoal until deliberate programmes are evolved to reduce poverty and the cost of power.'

In any event, it is widely held that alternative sources of energy such as solar, wind or geothermal power could probably provide all the electricity Uganda requires at a far lower financial and environmental cost than another dam.

Another criticism of the proposed dam is that, by submerging Bujagali Falls and most of the other rapids used by the commercial rafters, it will destroy Uganda's fastest-growing and arguably most lucrative single tourist attraction. But while it is true that capsizing the rafting industry would result in a significant loss in tourist revenue, the reality is that the dam would inconvenience but not damage it – the activity will probably relocate downstream to a series of rapids below the dam.

The Bujagali project met with strong initial resistance from local residents, since hundreds of people's homes will be submerged, and thousands more will be affected by the destruction of communal land and sacred burial sites. AES has, however, largely neutered local opposition with money: it has agreed to compensate an estimated 400 affected landowners with cash, new dwellings or a comparable tract of land elsewhere.

In an environmental report submitted to the World Bank, AES states that 'it has been established that the dwelling places of a number of spirits will require relocation either before construction commences or before the reservoir area is inundated'. And so AES has undertaken to fund a ceremony at each of these sacred sites to relocate its resident spirit to a new home, and two mass ceremonies to appease the spirit of Bujagali. Over to John Kaggwa, an authority on local religion employed by AES to handle the logistics of this bizarre operation: 'Traditionally, community spirits are not supposed to be

Budget

Ă **Explorers Campsite** ⎰ 0434 120236; m 0772 422373; campsite bar, m 0782 320552; f 0434 121322; e rafting@starcom.co.ug;

www.raftafrica.com. Superbly located on a high rise overlooking Bujagali Falls, this neatly terraced campsite is a popular base for rafting, particularly

transferred. What we're doing is appeasing the spirits ... saying to them "Your home is going to be tampered with. Please allow us to continue."'

It remains to be seen when – or indeed whether – the spirits will ever need to be appeased on account of Bujagali Dam. In December 2001, the World Bank formally approved credits and guarantees to the value of US$225 million relating to the project, and the official ground-breaking ceremony took place in January 2002. But only weeks later, it emerged that a confidential report to the World Bank had categorised the project as 'high risk' on the basis that 'its electricity might become unaffordable for the average Ugandan.

The same report stated that the project violated World Bank working policies on five other counts including environmental assessment, involuntary resettlement, evaluation of investment operations, and disclosure of information, echoing many long-standing concerns of the anti-Bujagali lobby. As a result, some 120 NGOs from 34 countries, including Uganda, petitioned the World Bank in May 2002, suggesting that it withdraw its support for a project that had been approved 'on the basis of a distorted economic analysis' and 'manipulated data'.

Ever since its inception, the Bujagali project has been dogged by rumours of corruption and characterised by a disturbing lack of transparency. Incredibly, AES was awarded its original US$550 million contract without having to go through the standard process of competitive bidding. The Power Purchase Agreement, which defines Uganda's financial obligations to AES for the first 30 years after the dam is completed, was not made public until recently, despite years of lobbying for disclosure by various NGOs. In July 2002, however, the rumours were lent considerable substance following allegations that the Associate Director of the World Bank, Richard Kaijuka, had received a bank deposit of US$10,000 from a Norwegian subcontractor back in 1999 when he served as Uganda's Minister of Energy. Kaijuka claims that the deposit represented a legitimate payment, but nevertheless he has been removed from his post at the World Bank and recalled to Uganda, where an investigation is underway at the time of writing. The World Bank has also suspended all funding related to the dam until the results of this investigation are released.

In November 2002, the mysterious Power Purchase Agreement (PPA) between AES and the Ugandan government was finally made public, by order of the Uganda High Court. An independent report commissioned by the International Rivers Network (IRN) immediately after the PPA was released stated that the agreement fell short of international standards and would result in Uganda facing up to US$40 million in excessive payments annually should the project go ahead. Peter Bosshard of the IRN stated that the Bujagali project is 'fundamentally flawed [and] represents a serious burden for a highly indebted poor country like Uganda', furthermore that 'the World Bank has misled the public and provided bad advice to the Ugandan government'. Frank Muramuzi of Uganda's National Association of Professional Environmentalists (NAPE) responded by stating that 'Bujagali Dam is not in the best interest of the Ugandan people and should be cancelled'.

The project did indeed stall for three years. However, in November 2005 the government of Uganda signed an agreement with Bujagali Energy Limited, a American–Kenyan consortium. At the time of writing, the earlier concerns were being addressed through an updated Environmental Impact Statement and other reports. Construction of the dam, which is now expected to cost just US$500 million, is forecast to begin in early 2007.

with overland trucks. Good meals are served and there is a lively bar. Like its namesake in Jinja, Explorers is operated by NRE, and a free night's accommodation is offered to anybody who rafts with them. *Dormitory beds US$5 pp, dbl rooms in small bandas US$20/25 dbl/trpl, camping US$3 pp.*
🏠 **Speke Camp** 🕾 0414 220906; m 0752 584171; e bujagali@afsat.com; www.bujagali.co.ug. This

sprawling camp, situated right alongside the waterfall, is also the base for Equator Rafting. The open-sided restaurant/bar, which overlooks the waterfall, has a great atmosphere and serves decent, inexpensive meals. In addition to water-based activities, village walks and drumming lessons are offered. Unfortunately the site's crumbling *bandas* are in a shocking condition and are due for imminent demolition, pending construction of improved cottages and a hotel on the hilltop above. Even at US$15 for dbl occupancy they are eminently avoidable. Pitching a tent on the grassy riverside campsite or staying in a dorm are better options. Guests rafting with Equator get a night's free accommodation in the dorm or (lucky you!) US$5 off a *banda*. Visitors to the waterfall pay US$1.60 (foreign tourists) or US$1 (Ugandans and foreign residents) plus US$1 for a vehicle. Entrance fees are deducted from accommodation costs for overnight guests. *Dormitory beds US$5 pp, camping US$2 pp.*

🏠 **Eden Rock Bandas** Eden Rock centres on a large and spacious thatched restaurant/lounge building set in an expansive lawn. Accommodation is provided in a dormitory or in a row of s/c dbl bandas. The latter are clean if somewhat cramped and squeezed together, and they lack a view of the river. On the plus side, Eden Rock does not target overlanders and is significantly quieter than the two adjacent resorts. It's also the best option for families, since it lies some distance from hazards such as steep river slopes or the river itself. As this edition goes to print, big changes are planned for Eden Rock under new European management, including a complete upgrade of the toilet and shower buildings, and the construction of the larger bandas with bedroom, en-suite shower and toilet, and a small living room. *Dormitory beds US$6; bandas US$18/25 sgl/dbl B&B.*

🏠 **Nile High Camp** m 0772BUNGEE/286433; www.surfthesource.com. The activity centre for the rafting company Adrift, the camp is actually located several kilometres before Bujagali, behind the upmarket Jinja Nile Resort Hotel, 3km along the Bujagali rd from Jinja's Shell/Ling Ling roundabout. The site boasts an excellent timber bar-restaurant deck and wooden cottages, all perched on poles above the lofty river cliff and enjoying stunning views across the Nile valley. All facilities share a communal (hot) shower and toilet block artfully, indeed tastefully constructed using natural slates and cobblestones. Good food is prepared on site by chefs seconded from the adjacent hotel. English breakfast costs Ush5000 and dinner from Ush4000-15000. *Cottages and furnished tents US$40 for sgl and dbl*

occupancy, a bed in the timber dormitory, US$5 and camping, US$2.

🏠 **The Hairy Lemon** m 0772 828338 or 0752 893086; e lemononthenile@yahoo.com; www.hairylemonuganda.com. This great little camp, accessed from the west bank of the river, stands on a small private island in the Nile in Kayunga District, some 40km northwest of Jinja. There is an abundance of birdlife on the island, and red-tailed monkeys and a family of otters are resident. The atmosphere is very relaxed, but fishing equipment is available for hire (it's reportedly one of the top fishing spots on the river) and for those who like a little more action, the so-called Nile Special rapid (reportedly one of the best play-holes for kayakers in the world) is about a 15min paddle away. Kayakers must provide all their own equipment, but the owners can provide transport for kayakers with all their gear from Jinja to the island. Adjoining the island is a safe swimming area with a white-sand bottom and no bilharzia. The camp has a bar/restaurant, solar power, gas freezers and a gas oven. Meat eaters are well catered for but vegetarian food is a speciality... and not just meat meals minus the meat. Accommodation costs vary, depending on whether you pitch your own tent or stay in a *banda* or a standing tent, and is inclusive of 3 meals, tea or coffee at any time, bar snacks and boat transfers to and from the island. Note that advance booking is essential for overnight guests and that day visitors are not catered for. To reach the island, catch a minibus-taxi from Njeru taxi park (opposite Nile Breweries on the outskirts of Jinja) to Nazigo. Then take a *boda-boda* from Nazigo to the Hairy Lemon, bang on the yellow tyre rim on the riverbank, and they will come and collect you in the boat. From Kampala take a *matatu* from Nakawa taxi park (at the end of Port Bell Rd) to Kayunga, then take one *boda-boda* from Kayunga to Nazigo and another motorbike from Nazigo to the Hairy Lemon. *US$10-30 per night.*

🏠 **The Haven** m 0782 905959 or 0712 110055; e info@thehaven-uganda.com; www.thehaven-uganda.com. This brand-new camp occupies a stunning location on the west bank of the Nile. The site is divided by a small peninsula which separates two very different Niles, the river being broad and placid on the southern side whilst immediately to the north it rages down the Grade Five 'Overtime' rapid (passing rafters present a pleasant if brief diversion for guests lounging outside the lodge). Accommodation is provided by small, furnished tents and 2 spacious thatched rondavels, all of which use communal facilities in a palatial ablution block. This Anglo-German venture has been carefully constructed using natural materials and earthy tones, is powered by solar panels and the larger buildings innovatively designed to maximize rainwater harvesting. You'll only need to drop a hint to get the full design history from the enthusiastic manager. Wildlife abounds along the shore including fish eagles and other birds, red-tailed monkey, otters and monitor lizards. To get there from Kampala, turn north off the Kampala–Jinja highway opposite Nile Breweries, just before the Owen Falls Dam. Head north for 15km along the tarmac Kayunga road before turning right at a signposted junction onto a 3km dirt track. Guests and diners should be sure to book in advance. It's attractively priced at US$33 pp for the cottages, US$24 for the tents provided or US$19 to pitch your own, all FB.

✕ WHERE TO EAT Diners really are spoilt for choice these days along the Jinja Nile. Decent hotel food is dispensed at the **Jinja Nile Resort/Nile High Camp**, meals at the latter being served on a superbly positioned covered deck above the river and costing Ush4,000–15,000. 5km north, the **Black Lantern Restaurant** at NRE's **Nile Porch** probably serves the best riverside steaks along the 4,700km Nile. Main courses in the attractive and atmospheric thatched building cost Ush10,000–15,000 and a filling English breakfast is Ush11,000. Note that last orders for evening meals are taken at 21.15. Sunday events such as pig roasts cost around Ush12,000. On the west bank of the Nile at **The Haven**, a German chef combines presentation with imagination to dish up three-course suppers. Non-residents are welcome to book for Sunday lunch/barbecues at Ush10,000. Still further downriver, **Hairy Lemon Island** remains the best bet for good veggie food. At Bujagali Falls, all of the budget camps serve reasonable meals at affordable prices. Budget food is served at a couple of canteens opposite the entrance to Explorers Camp. Most notable is the Green Light which serves meals ranging from simple rice and beans (Ush700) to daily specials such as spicy fish and roast potatoes (Ush3,500). All Terrain Adventures next door are known for decent breakfasts and excellent juices and milkshakes on an attractive raised deck.

RAFTING AND OTHER ACTIVITIES Rafting trips on the Nile are offered by four companies: **Adrift**, **Equator Rafting**, **Nile River Explorers (NRE)** and **Nalubale Rafting**. Contact details for NRE, Equator and Adrift are listed on pages 418–20 under the entries for Explorers Campsite, Speke Camp and Nile High Camp respectively. Nalubale has an office at the Blue Mango complex in Kampala (**m** 0782 638938/9).

The first three also operate their own backpacker resorts in the vicinity of Bujagali. All four offer similar one-day itineraries starting at Bujagali Falls and finishing at Itanda about 20km downriver. This route includes nine major rapids, four of which are classed as Grade Five, namely Total Gunga, Big Brother, Overtime and Itanda. While on the river, you'll get to see a lot of different birds, and you can swim in the calm stretches of water between the rapids. The long-established Adrift and NRE charge US$95 for a full-day excursion, as does Nalubale, the youngest company on the river. The deal includes rafting equipment, return transportation from Kampala or Jinja, buffet lunch, and beers and sodas. These operators all have solid reputations, and the stiff competition ensures that they offer an ever-growing list of inducements such as free accommodation, a post-rafting barbecue, discounts for a second trip, and optional extras such as DVDs of the day's action, so it's worth checking out the different packages before you make a booking. Equator Rafting, based out of Speke Camp, charges just US$65 for a similar excursion, but it attracts fewer punters than its costlier rivals and feedback is less consistent. When making a choice between the four companies, you might also ask a few searching questions concerning guide experience, first-aid training, certificates, etc. Rafting excursions can be booked

12

Based partially on text kindly supplied by Laura Sserunjogi, of the Source of the Nile Gardens in Jinja

The Nile is the world's longest river, flowing for 6,650km (4,130 miles) from its most remote headwater to the delta formed as it enters the Mediterranean in Egypt. Its vast drainage basin occupies more than 10% of the African mainland and includes portions of nine countries: Tanzania, Burundi, Rwanda, the DRC, Kenya, Uganda, Ethiopia, Sudan and Egypt. While passing through southern Sudan, the Nile also feeds the 5.5 million hectare Sudd or Bar-el-Jebel, the world's most expansive wetland system.

A feature of the Nile Basin is a marked decrease in precipitation as it runs further northward. In the East African lakes region and Ethiopian Highlands, mean annual rainfall figures are typically in excess of 1,000mm. Rainfall in south and central Sudan varies from 250–500mm annually, except in the Sudd (900mm), while in the deserts north of Khartoum the annual rainfall is little more than 100mm, dropping to 25mm in the south of Egypt, then increasing to around 200mm closer to the Mediterranean.

The Nile has served as the lifeblood of Egyptian agriculture for millennia, carrying not only water, but also silt, from the fertile tropics into the sandy expanses of the Sahara. Indeed, it is widely believed that the very first agricultural societies arose on the floodplain of the Egyptian Nile, and so, certainly, did the earliest and most enduring of all human civilisations. The antiquity of the name Nile, which simply means 'river valley', is reflected in the ancient Greek (Nelios), Semetic (Nahal) and Latin (Nilus).

Over the past 50 years, several hydro-electric dams have been built along the Nile, notably the Aswan Dam in Egypt and the Owen Falls Dam in Uganda. The Aswan Dam doesn't merely provide hydro-electric power, it also supplies water for various irrigation schemes, and protects crops downriver from destruction by heavy flooding. Built in 1963, the dam wall rises 110m above the river and is almost 4km long, producing up to 2,100MW and forming the 450km-long Lake Nasser. The construction of the Aswan Dam enforced the resettlement of 90,000 Nubians, whilst the Temple of Abu Simbel, built 3,200 years ago for the Pharaoh Ramesses II, had to be relocated 65m higher.

The waterway plays a major role in transportation, especially in parts of the Sudan between May and November, when transportation of goods and people is not possible by road due to the floods. Like other rivers and lakes, the Nile provides a variety of fish as food. And its importance for conservation is difficult to overstate. The Sudd alone supports more than half the global populations of Nile lechwe and shoebill (more than 6,000), together with astonishing numbers of other water-associated birds – aerial surveys undertaken between 1979 and 1982 counted an estimated 1.7 million glossy

directly with the rafting company, or through the Kampala Backpackers' and Red Chilli hostels, or any tour operator.

Two-day rafting trips are available through the same companies at around US$150 per person all-inclusive. The first day covers the same ground as the day excursion, with an extra rapid called Novocain tagged on at the end. On the second morning, four more rapids are traversed: Hair of the Dog, Kula Shaker, Nile Special and Malalu. After lunch the going is smoother, though the day culminates with one last rapid called Weleba.

In addition to rafting, kayaking is also offered from NRE's Speke Camp. Contact NRE (m *0772 880332;* e *jamie@kayakthenile.com; www.kayakthenile.com*). Instructors are trained to the UK's BCU standard and options vary from a three-hour lesson costing US$60 to ten-day courses at US$1,200, the latter including airport shuttle and full-board accommodation. Sunset cruises in open kayaks are

ibis, 370,000 marabou stork, 350,000 open-billed stork, 175,000 cattle egret and 150,000 spur-winged goose.

The Nile has two major sources, often referred to as the White and Blue Nile, which flow respectively from Lake Victoria near Jinja and from Lake Tana in Ethiopia. The stretch of the White Nile that flows through southern Uganda is today known as the Victoria Nile (it was formerly called Kiira locally). From Jinja, it runs northward through the swampy Lake Kyoga, before veering west to descend into the Rift Valley over Murchison Falls and empty into Lake Albert. The Albert Nile flows from the northern tip of Lake Albert to enter the Sudan at Nimule, passing through the Sudd before it merges with the Blue Nile at the Sudanese capital of Khartoum, more than 3,000km from Lake Victoria.

The discovery of the source of the Blue Nile on Lake Tana is often accredited to the 18th-century Scots explorer James Bruce. In fact, its approximate (if not exact) location was almost certainly known to the ancients. The Old Testament mentions that the Ghion (Nile) 'compasseth the whole land of Ethiopia', evidently in reference to the arcing course followed by the river along the approximate southern boundary of Ethiopia's ancient Axumite Empire. There are, too, strong similarities in the design of the papyrus *tankwa* used on Lake Tana to this day and the papyrus boats depicted in ancient Egyptian paintings. Furthermore, the main river feeding Lake Tana rises at a spring known locally as Abay Minch (literally 'Nile Fountain'), a site held sacred by Ethiopian Christians, whose links with the Egyptian Coptic Church date to the 4th century AD. Bruce's claim is further undermined by the Portuguese stone bridge, built c1620, which crosses the Nile a few hundred metres downstream of the Blue Nile Falls and only 30km from the Lake Tana outlet.

By contrast, the source of the White Nile was for centuries one of the world's great unsolved mysteries. The Roman Emperor Nero once sent an expedition south from Khartoum to search for it, but it was forced to turn back at the edge of the Sudd. In 1862, Speke correctly identified Ripon Falls as the source of the Nile, a theory that would be confirmed by Stanley in 1875. Only as recently as 1937, however, did the German explorer Burkhart Waldecker locate what has since been recognised as the most remote of the Nile's headwaters, the source of the Kagera River, a hillside spring known as Kasumo (Gusher) and situated some 4° south of the Equator in Burundi. In 2006, however, the Uganda-based rafting expedition Ascend the Nile located what it claims to be an even more remote headwater of the Kagera in Rwanda's Nyungwe National Park, a source that will add almost 100km to the documented length of the world's longest river if formally accepted by geographers.

offered in Jinja at US$30. Other activities include river-boarding excursions at US$65 for a full day. NRE also operate sunset cruises for large groups such as overland trucks, while Adrift runs 5km float trips suitable for families. The latest step in Bujagali's development as East Africa's answer to the more southerly adventure-activity capital of Victoria Falls is a 44m bungee jump located at Adrift's Nile High Camp between Jinja and Bujagali. Jumpers leap from a 12m cantilevered steel structure on top of a 32m cliff above the Nile and pay US$55 for the pleasure. If one jump isn't enough a second will cost another US$20 and the third is free. If rafting with Adrift or NRE, a jump costs US$40. For contact details, see the entry for Nile High Camp above. A 'flight' across the Nile from NRE's Speke Camp on their imminent 700m aerial runway will cost around U$30. I assume this includes a boat ride back but you might want to check! If it's any reassurance, it's been designed to Australian Standards

When Speke prepared for his first audience with King Mutesa of Baganda, he put on his finest clothes, but admitted that he 'cut a poor figure in comparison with the dressy Baganda [who] wore neat bark cloaks resembling the best yellow corduroy cloth, crimp and well set, as if stiffened with starch'. .

The stiff, neat barkcloth cloak or *mbugu*, as described by Speke, was the conventional form of attire throughout Baganda for at least 100 years prior to the coronation of Mutesa. Exactly how and when the craft arose is unknown. One legend has it that Kintu, the founder of Baganda, imported the craft with him from the heavens, which would imply that it was introduced to the kingdom, possibly from Bunyoro. Another story is that the Bacwezi leader Wamala discovered barkcloth by accident on a hunting expedition, when he hammered a piece of bark to break it up, and instead found that it expanded laterally to form a durable material.

Whatever its origin, barkcloth has been worn in Baganda for several centuries, though oral tradition has it that the cloth was originally worn only by the king and members of his court, while commoners draped themselves more skimpily in animal skins. In the late 18th century, however, King Semakokiro decreed that all his subjects should grow and wear barkcloth – men draped it over their shoulders, women tied it around their waist – or they would be fined or sentenced to death. At around the same time, barkcloth exported from Baganda grew in popularity in most neighbouring kingdoms, where it was generally reserved for the use of royalty and nobles.

Ironically, the historical association between barkcloth cloaks and social prestige was reversed in Baganda towards the end of the 19th century, when barkcloth remained the customary attire of the peasantry, but the king permitted his more favoured subjects to wear cotton fabrics imported by Arab traders. During the early decades of colonial rule, the trend away from barkcloth spread through all social strata. W E Hoyle, who arrived in Kampala in 1903, noted that barkcloth clothing was then 'so very common'. By 1930, when Hoyle departed from Uganda, it had been 'discarded in favour of "amerikani" (cotton sheeting); and later *kanzus* (of finer cotton material known as "bafta"), with a jacket of the cheaper imported cloth and a white round cap the ideal "Sunday best"'. Hoyle also noted that while 'women kept to barkcloth much longer than men… by the 1920s many were attired in the finest cotton materials and silks'. In the early 1930s, Lucy Mair recorded that 'European [cloths] are popular and barkcloth is made for sale by not more than three or four men in each village'. By the time of independence, barkcloth had practically disappeared from everyday use.

Barkcloth – Olubugo in Luganda – can be made from the inner bark lining of at least 20 tree species. The best-quality cloth derives from certain species in the genus *Ficus*, which were extensively cultivated in pre-colonial Baganda and regarded as the most

AS3533.1-1997 which governs the design and construction of amusement rides Down Under. Also based at Bujagali is All Terrain Adventures (m *0772 377185*), which runs **quad-biking** trips between some stunning Nile viewpoints using local footpaths and tracks. Prices range from US$30 per person for two hours up to US$90 per person for a full day. Overnight trips down the Nile valley to explore the route of Winston Churchill's 1911 Busoga Railway can also be arranged.

As an alternative to noisy quad biking on the east bank you might try **horseriding** on the west back. **Nile Horseback Safaris** (\ *0774 101196;* e *info@nilehorsebacksafaris.com; www.nilehorsebacksafaris.com*), 4km up the Kayunga road (see directions to The Haven above), cater for all ages and abilities. It costs US$20 per hour with a minimum of two hours.

valuable of trees after the plantain. Different species of tree yielded different textures and colours, from yellow to sandy brown to dark red-brown. The finest quality rusty brown cloth, called Kimote, is generally worn on special occasions only. A specific type of tree that yielded a white cloth was reserved for the use of the king, who generally wore it only at his coronation ceremony.

The common barkcloth tree can be propagated simply by cutting a branch from a grown one and planting it in the ground – after about five years the new tree will be large enough to be used for making barkcloth. The bark will be stripped from any one given tree only once a year, when it is in full leaf. After the bark has been removed, the trunk is wrapped in green banana leaves for several days, then plastered with wet cow dung and dry banana leaves, to help it heal. If a tree is looked after this way, it might survive 30 years of annual use.

The bark is removed from the tree in one long strip. A circular incision is made near the ground, another one below the lowest branches, then a long line is cut from base to top, before finally a knife is worked underneath the bark to ease it carefully away from the trunk. The peeled bark is left out overnight before the hard outer layer is scraped off, then it is soaked. It is then folded into two halves and laid out on a log to be beaten with a wooden mallet on alternating sides to become thinner. When it has spread sufficiently, the cloth is folded in four and the beating continues. The cloth is then unfolded before being left to dry in the sun.

There are several local variations in the preparation process, but the finest cloth reputedly results when the freshly stripped bark, instead of being soaked, is steamed for about an hour above a pot of boiling water, then beaten for an hour or so daily over the course of a week. The steaming and extended process of beating is said to improve the texture of the cloth and to enrich the natural red-brown or yellow colour of the bark.

Although it is used mostly for clothing, barkcloth can also serve as a blanket or a shroud, and is rare but valued as bookbinding. At one time, barkcloth strips patterned with the natural black Muzukizi dye became a popular house decoration in Kampala. Sadly, however, barkcloth production appears to be a dying craft, and today it would be remarkable indeed to see anybody wandering around Kampala wrapped in a traditional bark cloak. It is still customary to wear it in the presence of the king, and at funerals, when barkcloth is also often wrapped around the body of the deceased.

One place where you can be certain of seeing some impressive strips of red barkcloth is at the Kasubi Tombs in Kampala. If you're interested in looking for barkcloth at source, the forests around Sango Bay in Buddu County, south of Masaka, are traditionally regarded to produce the highest-quality material in Baganda. The Ugandan artist Mugalula Mukiibi is dedicated to reviving the dying craft through his work, and a number of his abstracts painted on traditional barkcloth can be viewed online (*www.mugalulaarts.com*).

MABIRA FOREST RESERVE

Extending over more than 300km², the Mabira Forest Reserve, which straddles the Kampala–Jinja road about 20km west of Jinja, is primarily composed of moist semi-deciduous forest, in which more than 200 tree species have been identified. The forest is interspersed with patches of open grassland, while several of the valleys support extensive papyrus swamps. In the colonial era, Mabira was heavily exploited for timber and rubber (half a million wild rubber trees, *Funtuma elastica*, grow there), while its proximity to Kampala and Jinja led to an estimated 1,500 tons of charcoal being extracted annually in the 1960s. During the civil war of the early 1980s, roughly 25% of the forest was cleared or degraded by subsistence farmers, who were evicted in 1988. Since then, much of the

THE NAKALANGA OF MABIRA

'Mabira' is a Luganda word literally meaning Large Forests, and the first European survey of the area referred to it as Mabira Nakalanga: the Large Forests of Nakalanga, the latter being the name of the mischievous spirit said to inhabit it. According to folklore, Nakalanga is associated with one specific stream that runs through Mabira, the source of which was until recent times the site of an important sacrificial shrine consisting of several huts.

Several early colonial writers reported that Mabira harboured a Pygmy tribe called the Banakalanga (people of Nakalanga) and assumed that it was related to the Batwa Pygmies of the Congolese border area. Local Luganda legend, however, doesn't regard the Banakalanga as a tribe, but rather as sports of nature. The belief is that the forest spirit punishes families that have fallen out of favour by cursing one of its children to be a puny and often mildly deformed dwarf.

In the 1950s, Raper and Ladkin of the Uganda Medical Service investigated the Nakalanga and determined that they did indeed appear to be born randomly to physiologically normal parents with other healthy offspring. They concluded that the Banakalanga were affected by a form of infantilism linked to a pituitary defect, one that generally first showed itself when the afflicted person was about three years of age. The disease, Raper and Ladkin believed, was pathological rather than genetic in origin, but its precise cause was indeterminate, as was its apparent restriction to one small area around Mabira Forest. Subsequent studies confirmed that Nakalanga dwarfism is a complication of a pituitary malfunction caused by onchocerciasis (a disease spread by the Simulium black fly) and note that the condition also occurs in Kabarole District of western Uganda.

Interestingly, the first written references to the Banakalanga interchangeably calls them the Bateemba (people of the nets), evidently in reference to a hunting method used by pygmoid peoples elsewhere in Africa. Furthermore, Raper and Ladkin record that a local Saza chief in the early 20th century had stated that a race of true Pygmies did once live in the forest, but some time before Europeans arrived in the area. It seems probable, then, that both Nakalanga and the medical condition attributed to the spirit's mischief-making derive their name from that of a pygmoid tribe which once inhabited Mabira Forest.

degraded forest has recovered through the replanting of indigenous trees, and illegal felling has practically ceased.

Mabira is by far the largest remaining stand of indigenous forest in central Uganda, not only of immense ecological value, but also – situated so close to the country's two largest cities – offering great potential for recreation and tourist development. Certainly, the combination of accessibility, affordable accommodation, good monkey viewing and lovely walking trails makes it a highly recommended stopover for any traveller with an interest in natural history. Large mammals are relatively scarce today, though a small population of elephants was present as recently as the 1950s. The red-tailed monkey is regularly seen in the vicinity of the camp, however, and grey-cheeked mangabey and blue duiker are quite common. Leopards are reputedly present but unlikely to be seen. More than 200 species of butterfly have been identified from Mabira.

Mabira ranks as one of the most important ornithological sites in Uganda, with more than 300 (mostly forest-associated) species recorded, including several rarities. The excellent network of forest trails that emanates from the visitors' centre can be explored unaccompanied, but you'll benefit greatly from taking a guide, whose knowledge of bird calls will assist in locating more elusive forest species. Conspicuous larger birds include the stunning great blue turaco and more familiar African grey parrot, while three forest hornbill species and a variety of colourful sunbirds are often seen around the camp. Mabira is one of only two places in East Africa where the pretty tit hylia has been recorded, and this rare bird is seen here with surprising regularity. It is also one of the few places in Uganda where the localised forest wood-hoopoe, African pitta, purple-throated cuckoo-shrike, leaflove, Weyn's weaver and Nahan's francolin are regular. Note, however, that the forest's reputation as a good place to see the rare blue swallow is based on one vagrant sighting many years ago. One of the best individual birding sites at Mabira is a forest-fringed pond that can be reached by following the Jinja road east for 5km past the Najjembe then turning left on to a small dirt road for a few hundred metres.

The National Forest Authority is in the process of revising its tariffs upwards. By 2007, entrance to Mabira Forest is likely to be US$15 for foreign visitors and US$10 for East African residents. A guided walk will then cost another US$10. Contact the NFA in Kampala (✆ 0414 230365) for more details. Keen birders can phone Mabira's highly rated bird guide of 12 years' experience, Ibrahim Senfuma (m 0712 920515) to see whether he's on duty. Ibra's also happy to take leave to accompany birders on countrywide tours.

GETTING THERE AND AWAY Mabira Forest Reserve lies about 55km from Kampala along the surfaced road to Jinja. The drive from either Kampala or Jinja should take less than an hour in a private vehicle, and the 500m turn-off to the visitors centre is clearly signposted.

Using public transport, any minibus-taxi heading between Jinja and Kampala will drop you at Najjembe village from which it's a 5–10-minute walk to the visitors' centre and rest camp. When you're ready to leave the forest, just walk out to the road and wave your arms at any passing vehicle – although public transport heading past the forest is likely to be full, there's a strong likelihood of hitching a free lift.

WHERE TO STAY AND EAT
Upmarket

⌂ **Mabira Forest Lodge** ✆ 0414 258273; e geolodgesafrica.com or iou@africaonline.co.ug; www.geolodges. This brand-new lodge consists of several beautifully furnished timber cottages scattered across the side of the forested Gangu Hill, each set into a small clearing with excellent views into forest beyond. Hornbills, turacos and red-tailed monkeys abound. An elevated restaurant building and swimming pool enjoy similar views. Discounts are available for Ugandan residents. The lodge lies 2km south of Najjembe village; the turning from the main highway is directly opposite the track leading to the long-standing NFA tourism project. *Prices are likely to be in the range of US$110/180 sgl/dbl FB.*

Budget

⌂ **Mabira Forest Tourism Project** ✆ (National Forest Authority HQ) 0414 230365. In 1995, a community project was established at Mabira under the supervision of the Forest Department and with the assistance of a VSO volunteer. The main result of this was the construction of a beautiful rest camp consisting of 2 dbl *bandas* and 1 4-bed family unit, all with private balcony, garden and washing area (a bucket of hot water is provided on request). Unfortunately the volume of road haulage traffic has increased hugely since the camp was established and noise from trucks on the main road is audible day and night. This is perhaps the reason why the facilities are looking slightly tired these days as the NFA considers alternative locations. Your best bet is to pitch your own tent in the lovely but strangely under utilised campground. As with national parks, these fees are in addition to the reserve entrance fee. There is no need to bring food with you to Mabira. The staff will prepare reasonable meals for around Ush3,000 by advance order, and warm beers and sodas are available at the camp. Far better, however, to head back along the 500m track to Najjembe market on the main Kampala–Jinja road which is renowned by motorists for its cheap and succulent grilled

chicken. You can also buy a selection of fruits and vegetables there, as well as refrigerated beers and sodas. *Dbl bandas US$6 sgl/dbl, family banda US$10. Camping US$2.*

Shoestring

⌂ **Da Little Havana** m 0712 536133; e flandersrazaka@yahoo.com. Located in Najjembe village, this new Dutch-Ugandan lodge offers a small bar/restaurant with pool table with shoestring accommodation and camping behind. It's cheap but frankly the grubby rooms and ablutions are no

bargain, the campsite is overgrown and the bar seems to be the daytime hangout for local loiterers. It's all something of a diversion to the expected forest experience. *US$8 sgl and dbl with shared facilities, dorm bed US$4. Camping US$3.*

13

Eastern Uganda

The far east of Uganda is, with a handful of exceptions, rather poorly developed for tourism, and its attractions are relatively few and far between. The bulk of travellers who pass through the area are heading directly to Uganda from Kenya, and most will simply whizz from the border straight through to Jinja or Kampala. This, normally, is where I would make a comment along the lines that those who do explore this little-visited part of the country will be well rewarded for their efforts. They will, of course – but when western Uganda offers one of the most compact and rewarding travel circuits anywhere in Africa, few visitors with serious time restrictions are likely to stray in the direction of the Kenyan border.

What little tourist development that exists in eastern Uganda centres on Mount Elgon National Park and the town of Mbale at its western base. Mbale itself is among the more substantial and attractive towns in Uganda, without really offering any great incentive for visitors to linger. By contrast, Mount Elgon, a 4,321m extinct volcano straddling the Kenyan border, offers some superb hiking possibilities, and – although prices have crept up in recent years – it remains by far the most affordable of East Africa's Afro-alpine hiking destinations. For the more sedentary, the lovely Sipi Falls, which tumble down the footslopes of Elgon outside the national park, is a popular and very inexpensive place to while away a few days.

Other lesser-known landmarks of the region include the impressive Tororo Rock, a clutch of accessible rock-art sites, the remote lakes Bisina and Opeta, and the minimally developed but potentially fantastic Pian Upe Wildlife Reserve. Further north, nudging the Sudanese border, the remote Kidepo Valley National Park is one of Uganda's most alluring savanna reserves, but seldom visited on account of the poor access roads and recurrent incidents of banditry along them. Accessible – at a cost – by charter flight, Kidepo is seeing an upturn in tourist interest following the construction of an upmarket lodge in 2006.

BUSIA

Busia – the most normal crossing point between Kenya and Uganda – is the quintessential border town: scruffy, amorphous, and bustling with hustlers and con-artists. Busia lies well away from any major domestic road route, and you're likely to pass through it only if you're crossing to or from Kenya. Travelling by international coach or bus, as most people do, you'll not likely hang around a moment longer than border formalities or a dithering bus driver dictates. Even those travelling by minibus-taxi can expect to move on quickly from Busia, since there's plenty of transport eastwards to Jinja or westwards to Kisumu, the nearest sizeable town in Kenya. But, should you arrive late in the day and be inspired to spend the night, there are a couple of indifferent lodges to choose from. Assuming that you arrive during banking hours, a new Stanbic Bank provides a sedate alternative to changing hard currency with the assemblage of dodgy touts who loiter about the border post.

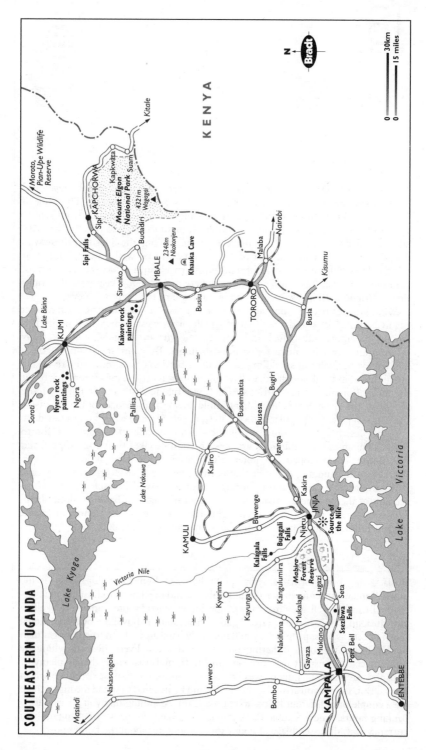

SOUTHEASTERN UGANDA

KENYA

30km
15 miles

Masindi
Nakasongola
Lake Kyoga
Sorati
Lake Bisina
KUMI
Nyero rock paintings
Ngora
Lake Nakuwa
Pallisa
Kakoro rock paintings
Sironko
Budadiri
Sipi Falls
Sipi KAPCHORWA
Morato, Pian–Upe Wildlife Reserve
Mount Elgon National Park
Kapkwata Suam
432m Wagagai
2348m Nkokonjeru
Khauka Cave
MBALE
Busiu
Kitale
TORORO
Malaba
Nairobi
Busia
Kisumu
Busembatia
Bugiri
Busesa
Iganga
Kaliro
Victoria Nile
Kamuli
Buwenge
Kakira
JINJA
Njeru
Source of the Nile
Bujagali Falls
Kalagala Falls
Kangulumira
Kyerima
Kayunga
Mabira Forest Reserve
Lugazi
Seta
Nakifuma
Mukalagi
Ssezibwa Falls
Gayaza
Mukono
Port Bell
Luwero
Bombo
KAMPALA
ENTEBBE
Lake Victoria

This medium to large town (population estimate 45,000) is situated a few minutes' drive from the Malaba border post with Kenya, just off the road to Jinja and Kampala. These days, few travellers pass through Tororo unless they make a specific effort. This is because the Busia rather than Malaba border crossing is normally used by traffic between Nairobi and Kampala, while public transport between Kampala and Mbale now uses the more direct Turini road from Iganga.

Supporting roughly 1,000 Asian and European settlers, well located for cross-border trade and the site of Uganda's main cement factory, Tororo ranked among the ten most populous and prosperous towns in Uganda in the 1950s. Today, the exaggeratedly wide pavements, lined with a straggle of flowering trees and colonial-era façades, pay testament to Tororo's former prosperity, as does a pair of impressive Hindu temples (one of which long ceased functioning), but one's overall impression is of a sleepy backwater that long ago saw its heyday. Altogether more diverting than the town centre is Tororo Rock, a steep volcanic plug that protrudes several hundred metres above the southern skyline. Visible from miles around, this distinctive isolated outcrop takes about an hour to climb – guides can be found at the Rock Classic Hotel in town – and offers panoramic views towards Mount Elgon and, reputedly, to Lake Victoria in very clear weather.

GETTING THERE AND AWAY Tororo lies along a good surfaced road connecting Mbale (40km to the north) to Jinja (130km to the east). Regular minibus-taxis connect Tororo to both of the above towns, charging Ush3,000 and Ush5,000 respectively. Note that all the public transport running directly between Kampala/Jinja and Mbale now bypasses Tororo in favour of a new, shorter surfaced road from Iganga. Regular minibus-taxis between Tororo and the Malaba border post cost a few hundred shillings.

WHERE TO STAY
Moderate
Rock Classic Hotel \/f 04544 45069; m 0772 468535; e rockclassichotel@yahoo.com. Totally renovated and refurbished, this former government hotel, set in wooded grounds near the golf course, is unrecognisable from its rundown state of a few years ago. The large, comfortable rooms with DSTV, hot bath and fan are very good value. Facilities include a gym, swimming pool and sauna, and a restaurant serving Continental dishes in the Ush6,000–7,000 range. The hotel lies about 3km out of town along the road to the Malaba border. On foot, the simplest route is to follow Malakasi Road out of town past the golf course, but there are also several short cuts behind Tororo Rock. *US$30/35 standard sgl/dbl, US$33/41 executive rooms.*

Budget
Crystal Hotel Bazaar Rd; \ 04544 45180; m 077 555174. This multi-storey building has for several years been the standout hotel in the town centre. It offers reasonably well-maintained s/c rooms with fan, hot water and a private balcony facing Tororo Rock. The ground-floor restaurant is pretty good, too. *US$11/14 sgl/dbl.*
Granite Apartments Hotel \ 04544 44479. This new out-of-town hotel offers rooms with a fan, net and television. It's pretty good value, but not madly convenient unless you have your own transport, being situated along a clearly signposted side road about 1.5km from the town centre along the Malaba road. *US$14 for a clean s/c dbl.*
CTS Country Inn m 0772 330295. Situated right next door to Granite Apartments, this new hotel doesn't seem quite as good – no nets or television in the rooms – and is costlier. *US$20 s/c dbl.*

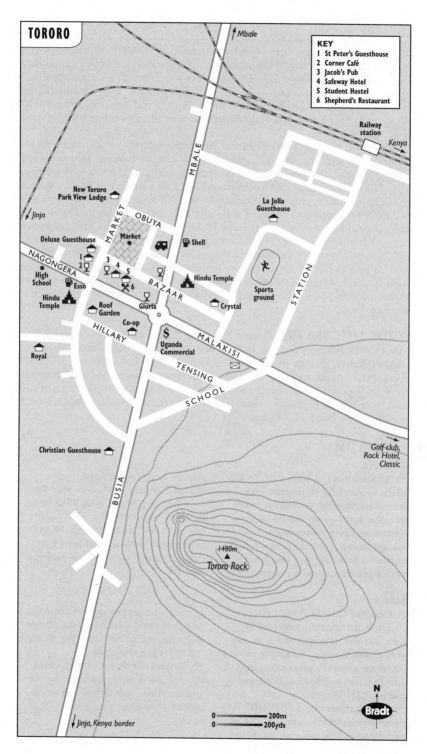

TORORO

KEY
1 St Peter's Guesthouse
2 Corner Café
3 Jacob's Pub
4 Safeway Hotel
5 Student Hostel
6 Shepherd's Restaurant

↑ Mbale

Railway station

Kenya →

New Tororo
Park View Lodge

↓ Jinja

La Jolla
Guesthouse

Deluxe Guesthouse

MARKET

OBUYA

Market

Shell

NAGONGERA

1
2

3

4 5

High
School

Esso

6

BAZAAR

Hindu Temple

Sports
ground

STATION

Hindu
Temple

Roof
Garden

Gloria

Co-op

Crystal

HILLARY

$

Uganda
Commercial

MALAKISI

Royal

TENSING

SCHOOL

Golf club,
Rock Hotel,
Classic

Christian Guesthouse

BUSIA

1480m
▲
Tororo Rock

N

Bradt

0 — 200m
0 — 200yds

↓ Jinja, Kenya border

Shoestring

⌂ **Deluxe Guesthouse** ↘ 04544 44986. Easily the pick of several cheapies dotted around the town centre, the Deluxe Guesthouse lies only a few mins' walk from the taxi park, and offers rooms with a private 1st-floor balcony, but no net or fan. Cheaper but scruffier singles using common showers are available downstairs. *US$8 for a clean s/c dbl.*

⌂ **La Jolla Guesthouse** m 0772 314133. This small, quiet, family-run guesthouse, situated behind the stadium offers very reasonable and clean s/c rooms with carpet, fan, net and double bed. *US$6 s/c rooms, similar rooms using common showers US$5.*

⌂ **Co-op Hotel** This long-serving crash pad has smartened up considerably in recent years, but not to the extent that most people would be prepared to pay what they're asking for a basic dbl room using common showers. *US$6.*

⌂ **New Silent Night Lodge** Neither new, nor particularly likely to offer silent slumber, this somewhat basic lodge is mitigated solely by having the cheapest rooms in town. *US$3 for a grubby single.*

⌂ **New Tororo Park View Guesthouse** More aptly named than the above – the catch being that the park in question is the taxi park – this lodge is conveniently located but nothing special. *US$4/6 for a dingy sgl/dbl.*

✗ **WHERE TO EAT AND DRINK** The best place for a meal is undoubtedly the **Rock Classic Hotel**, which also boasts serene grounds and a clean swimming pool, but it's not too convenient for those staying in the town centre. The food at the **Crystal Hotel** is pretty good and great value at around Ush3,000 for a generous plate of roast chicken or steak. Otherwise, several small inexpensive restaurants serving standard Ugandan fare are dotted around the town centre, **Shepherds Restaurant** on Nagongera Road being perhaps the pick. The best drinking hole in town is **Jacob's Pub**, which has a relaxed courtyard at the back and serves snacks such as grilled chicken and chips.

MBALE

Mbale was, until the recent (and possibly temporary) population boom in Gulu and Lira, the third-largest town in Uganda, with a population estimated at 75,000. Nestled at an altitude of around 1,200m in the Mount Elgon foothills, it has considerably more going for it than either Tororo or Busia. Dominating the eastern skyline of Mbale is Nkokonjeru, a 2,348m spur of the Mount Elgon massif whose rocky face is run down by several waterfalls. On a clear day, the volcanic peaks of the 4,321m Mount Elgon are also visible from the town centre. The area around Mbale is particularly worth visiting between August and December of even-numbered years, which is when the renowned – and conspicuous – Bagisu circumcision ceremonies take place.

Relatively few travellers pass through Mbale, and those who do are generally *en route* to Mount Elgon or the Sipi Falls. There is no overwhelming reason to stopover in town for longer than is required to change public transport, but if you do, you'll find the range of tourist facilities is among the best in Uganda. That Mbale was less scarred by the events of 1971–86 than most other Ugandan towns is reflected in the healthily bustling atmosphere of the modern town centre, and several well-preserved examples of colonial-era Asian and European architecture. The leafy suburbs around the Mount Elgon Hotel make for a pleasant afternoon stroll.

GETTING THERE AND AWAY Mbale lies about 235km from Kampala along a (mostly) good surfaced road through Jinja and Iganga. In theory, the drive should take less than three hours in a private vehicle, but increased congestion on the outskirts of Kampala, plus slow trailers and tankers on the Jinja road, and perennial roadworks around Iganga mean that trip will take rather longer. Turn left about 3km east of Iganga to avoid Tororo and follow the zippy and almost traffic-free Turini road (100km) straight to Mbale. There is plenty of public transport from Kampala to

In 1900, the narrow belt of no-man's-land that divided the cultivated footslopes of Nkokonjeru and its Bagisu inhabitants from the pastoralist people of the Kyoga Basin made a less than favourable impression on visitors. C J Phillips described the area as 'a long wilderness of scrub', William Grant deemed it 'a dreary waste', while one early Muganda visitor called it 'a small and fearsome place, swarming with wild animals'. Back then, certainly, it would have taken a bold soul to suggest this area would become the site of the third-largest town in Uganda! But then Mbale is possibly unique among comparably sized East African towns in that it isn't rooted in a pre-colonial settlement, nor is it truly a colonial creation, but was founded by the controversial Muganda administrator and soldier Semei Kakunguru.

Between 1889 and 1901, Kakunguru had single-handedly – or rather with the assistance of a private army of 5,000 Baganda soldiers – subjugated and administered the region of eastern Uganda known as Bukedi (a disparaging Luganda term meaning 'Land of Naked People') as an agent of the British Crown. By 1901, however, Kakunguru was perceived by his colonial paymasters to have developed into a tyrannical force – the self-appointed 'King of Bukedi' – that they could neither stem nor control. In the words of A L Hitching, Kakunguru had indeed 'first reduced [Bukedi] to order, cut the roads, and began to direct the local chiefs', but it was 'rather after the method of making desolation and calling it peace'. And bad enough that Kakunguru and his army evidently regarded Bukedi 'as a sort of El Dorado', raiding the local cattle and crops at whim. Worse still, the authorities at Entebbe had every reason to believe that their employee was less than scrupulous when it came to declaring and returning the tax he had collected in his official capacity for the Crown.

The Entebbe administration decided that this untenable situation could be resolved only by retiring the self-styled King of Bukedi from the colonial service. But how to achieve this when any hint of force might prompt Kakunguru's army to stage a rebellion the authorities would find difficult to contain? A series of tense communications resulted in a mutually agreeable compromise. Kakunguru would resign his post and hand over his fort at Budoka (30km west of present-day Mbale). In exchange, he would be given 20 square miles of land at a site of his own choosing. Kakunguru selected the plains below Nkokonjeru, which, although practically unoccupied, were run through by several perennial streams and lay close to a reliable supply of the favoured Baganda diet of *matoke*.

Kakunguru and his Baganda followers relocated to Mbale in March 1902, and immediately set about building a new township, one that by several accounts bore strong similarities to the Buganda royal enclosure on Kampala's Mengo Hill. The first European visitors to trickle through Mbale in early 1903 were astonished at the transformation wrought by Kakunguru in one brief year. Bishop Tucker reported that 'on what was little better than a wilderness... we found ourselves surrounded by gardens, well cultivated and well kept; houses, too, had sprung up on every hand, most of them well built'. An equally gushing William Grant described Mbale as 'flourishing with gardens, teeming with life' and added that 'good wide roads have been cut, rivers have been bridged and embankments made through marshy ground, all at [Kakunguru's] expense and for public use'. A map of Mbale dating to 1904 indicates that the central market was situated

Mbale. The Post Bus, which leaves Kampala from the main post office on Kampala Road at 08.00 daily except Sundays, costs Ush9,000 and takes about six hours. Regular minibus-taxis charge Ush10,000. They are a lot quicker, but are driven with less care. Regular buses and minibus-taxis connect Mbale to Jinja and Tororo, as well as on to Kumi, Soroti and Moroto in the north. Most local places of interest can be reached by minibus-taxi (details given under individual sites later in this chapter).

roughly where the clocktower stands today. Running southwest from the market, a wide road lined with shops and houses approximated the equivalent stretch of present-day Kumi Road. This road continued southwest for about 300m to Kakunguru's fortified compound, which consisted of a large rectangular stone building and seven smaller huts protected within a tall reed fence.

This rapid growth of Mbale was not solely due to its founder's estimable ambition and drive. One contemporary visitor, the missionary J J Willis, described the town's location as 'a natural centre' for trade, elaborating that 'An excellent road connects Mbale with Jinja to the southwest. A caravan route, very far from excellent, connects it with Mumias to the south. Caravans [from Karamoja] pass through Mbale laden with ivory. And to the northwest a caravan route passes through Serere and Bululu to the Nile Province.' Mbale usurped nearby Mumias as the most important regional trading centre; indeed its market soon became the largest anywhere in the protectorate after Kampala and Entebbe. The permanent population of the nascent metropolis – estimated by Willis to stand at around 3,000 – comprised not only Kakunguru's Buganda followers, but also a substantial number of Greek, Arab, Indian and Swahili traders.

In hindsight, it might be said that when Kakunguru handed over Budoka Fort to Britain, he did not so much abandon his 'El Dorado' as relocate it (and expand it) at his personal estate of Mbale. That much was recognised by the new commissioner, James Sadler, when he made a tour of Bukedi in January 1904. Sadler characterised the established administrative centre at Budoka as consisting of 'two wattle and daub houses and some dilapidated police lines' on a 'bad' site that was 'neither liked by Europeans nor natives'. Mbale, by contrast, impressed him as 'the natural trade centre of the district [and] centre of a Baganda civilisation [of] flourishing plantations [and] substantially built grass-roofed houses'. Sadler decided that Mbale should forthwith replace Budoka as the administrative centre of Bukedi, and attempted to reign in Kakunguru by reappointing him to the regional administration. (In 1906, the authorities realised that they would gain full control over Bukedi only in the physical absence of Kakunguru, which they achieved not by retiring him, but by tantalising him away to Jinja to serve as the official head of state of Busoga, a position he held until 1913.)

Mbale's rise to prominence had its setbacks. In 1909, Cook described it as a 'thriving little place entered along a broad well-kept road, nearly a mile in length, bordered by thousands of *emsambya* trees and numerous native houses... crowded with the once-turbulent Bagisu engaged in the peaceful activity of bartering their native produce'. A year later, the colonial administration – for a variety of opaque reasons – banned the ivory trade from Karamoja, causing foreign traders to desert Mbale and the district commissioner to bemoan that 'a legacy of debts is about all that remains of what used to be a profitable and flourishing business'. A few years later, tentative plans to relocate the regional administration to Bugondo, a newly developed ferry port on Lake Kyoga and the site of two large ginneries, were shelved following the outbreak of World War I. As it transpired, Bugondo's brief heyday would be curtailed by a post-war drought that left it high and dry, while the strategic location chosen by Kakunguru took on fresh significance with the rise of the motor vehicle as the natural hub of the road network east of Lake Kyoga.

WHERE TO STAY
Moderate

Mbale Resort Hotel \ 04544 33920/34485; f 04544 33922; e sales@mbaleresort.com; www.mbaleresort.com. The modern Mbale Resort Hotel lies in beautiful grounds with a superb swimming pool plus a gym and sauna. Even if you don't stay here it's a popular place to relax and (for a small fee) use the facilities. The attractive bar/restaurant and poolside bar are both provided

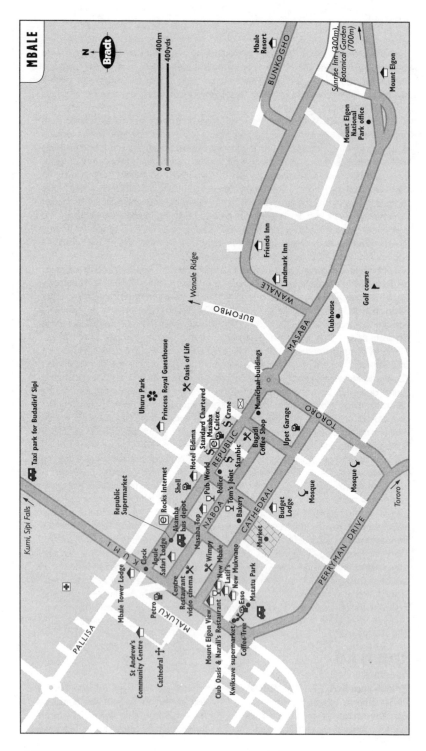

MBALE

N

Bract

0 ____ 400m
0 ____ 400yds

Kumi, Sipi Falls

PALLISA

St Andrew's
Community Centre

Cathedral ✝

MALUKU

Mbale Tower Lodge

Petro ⛽

Clock
Apule
Safari Lodge

Centre
Restaurant
video cinema

Mount Elgon View
Club Oasis & Narali's Restaurant
Kwiksave supermarket

Coffee-Tree
Esso

KUMI

Republic
Supermarket

Rockis Internet

Akamba
bus depot

Masaba top

Wimpy
New Mbale
Latif's
New Mukwano

Matatu Park

NABOA

Pub World
Police ●
Tom's Joint

Bakery

CATHEDRAL

Budget
Lodge

Market

Hotel Eldima

Standard Chartered
Masaba
Caltex

REPUBLIC

Stanbic

Bugdi
Coffee Shop

Municipal-buildings

Crane

Upet Garage

Mosque

TORORO

Mosque ☾

PERRYMAN DRIVE

Tororo

Uhuru Park

Princess Royal Guesthouse

✗ Oasis of Life

← Wandle Ridge

BUFOMBO

MASABA

Clubhouse ●

Golf course ⛳

WANDLE

Friends Inn

Landmark Inn

BUNKOGHO

Mbale
Resort

Sunrise Inn (300m),
Botanical Garden
(700m) →

Mount Elgon

Mount Elgon
National
Park office ●

Taxi park for Budadiri/ Sipi

436

with DSTV and are good places to watch English and international football fixtures. Unfortunately the rooms are rather cramped and the fittings increasingly shabby. The food is definitely nothing to write home about either, though you'll find plenty of time to catch up with your correspondence while you wait for your meal. Still, as a place to chill out at, the resort is not bad value, especially given the range of excellent alternative eateries in Mbale Town. The hotel is situated about 2km from the town centre and can be reached by following Republic Rd east *US$27/44 sgl/dbl inc b/fast.*

🏠 **Mount Elgon Hotel** ↘ 04544 33454. This stalwart former government hotel, situated about 2km from the town centre along Masaba Rd, has recently undergone an Italian-driven refurbishment. It is a very peaceful place, with lovely grounds enjoying superb views of the Wanale cliffs, and a bar with pool table. The Italian architect has included a crazy golf course, a feature which (free to residents and Ush2,000 to visitors) is as fun as it is unexpected. The s/c rooms are extremely large with new wooden floors, DSTV and hot baths. Prices have risen accordingly but are still acceptable; the hotel is often

Budget

🏠 **Botanical Gardens** ↘ 04544 33185. This Church-oriented guesthouse occupies a storeyed residential building set in a pleasant, palm-shaded garden. Its quiet, suburban location at the eastern end of town (follow the road past either the Sunrise or Mbale Resort hotels) is appealing, as are the rates. *US$14/16 for clean but basic s/c sgl/dbl rooms.*

🏠 **Landmark Inn** (3 rooms) ↘ 04544 33880; 📱 0782 751016. This converted colonial homestead – complete with red-tiled roof and pillared veranda – is set in attractive green gardens a short distance west of the town centre and is unbeatable value. The Indian chef provides the ground floor restaurant with arguably the best food in Mbale. If higher recommendation is required, this is where the Indian ambassador stays and eats out east. Recommended – though room space is limited, so it's advisable to ring in advance if you're on foot. *US$17 s/c dbl.*

Shoestring

🏠 **Royal Princess Guesthouse** 📱 0712 710056. Look no further! Rooms are an absolute bargain in this smart little lodge on Aryada Street, The slightly strange frontage is curiously suggestive of a cocktail bar but there's absolutely nothing odd about the clean s/c rooms inside. Located just down the hill behind the dismal Eldima Hotel, the new Royal

booked up. The hotel restaurant serves some average meals, reaching a culinary peak with small but tasty pizzas for around Ush6,000. The service however has not improved since the old Uganda Hotels days, with 'Spot the Manager' being a popular pastime for longer term guests. *US$27/32 B&B for a standard sgl/dbl, superior rooms US$46/51 sgl/dbl, basic s/c rooms in a guesthouse annex just across the road are great value at US$16/19 sgl/dbl inc b/fast.*

🏠 **Sunrise Inn** ↘ 04544 33090. A perennially popular establishment situated about 200m past the Mount Elgon Hotel, offering clean s/c rooms with DSTV, fan and hot water. A pleasant open-sided restaurant serves decent grills, pasta and Chinese dishes in the Ush5,000–6,000 range. *US$24/30 sgl/dbl.*

🏠 **Hotel Eldima** ↘ 04544 35225. The s/c rooms in this central multi-storey block are no better than those at several of the budget hotels listed below, and they aren't close in standard to anything else in the moderate price category. Prices have dropped drastically in this threadbare establishment since 2003 but it's still poor value. *US$12/17 sgl/dbl.*

🏠 **Mount Elgon View Hotel** 📱 0772 445562. The long-serving Mount Elgon View is the best hotel in the town centre, and very conveniently located for access to the taxi park, restaurants, bars and internet. Offers clean and spacious s/c dbls with netting, fan and a table and chair and similar-quality rooms using clean common showers. Bus horns will wake you before dawn but it's worth it to be able to wander onto the rooftop balcony to enjoy the sunrise over Mbale's townscape and the cliffs of Mt Elgon. The Mt Elgon Annex (just across Kumi Rd) offers large, s/c dbl rooms; secure parking is an advantage. *US$14 s/c dbl, US$6/8 sgl/dbl rooms with common showers.*

🏠 **Masaba Top Hotel** ↘ 04544 35378; 📱 0772 497842. This centrally located hotel is nothing special, but fair value at the price, offering s/c rooms with hot water. *US$9/11 sgl/dbl.*

Princess is already a favourite with volunteers in the area. Enjoying a quiet site 5mins' walk from Republic St, it is also temptingly close to the excellent Oasis of Life Restaurant. Vehicles can squeeze into the small forecourt to park. No food is served at present but a restaurant is being constructed. *US$8/11 sgl/dbl.*

THE ABAYUDAYA OF MBALE

Situated on the outskirts of Mbale, Nabugoye Hill is the site of the Moses Synagogue, spiritual home to a small, isolated community of Ugandan Jews known as Abayudaya. The Abayudaya are not officially accepted as Jews, nor will they be until they undergo an official conversion recognised by a court of rabbis. Nevertheless, they are devout in their observance of Jewish customs and rituals, recognising the same holidays as other Jews, holding their Sabbath services on Friday evening and Saturday morning, and keeping kosher according to Talmudic law. They do not participate in local Basigu circumcision rituals, but instead circumcise males eight days after birth. And those who marry outside the community are no longer considered Abayudaya unless their spouses agree to convert.

Abayudaya is simply the Luganda word for Jews, coined in the late 19th century when missionaries attempted to dissociate their exotic religion from British colonialism by explaining to locals that the Bible was written not by Europeans but by Jews – the People of Judea or Ba-Judea. This ploy backfired somewhat when the first Luganda translation of the Bible appeared and literate Muganda started to question why, for instance, their local tradition of polygamy was condemned by the missionaries when many of the Abayudaya in the Old Testament unashamedly possessed more than one wife.

The most prominent of these religious dissidents was Malaki Musajakawa, whose Africanist Christian sect called the Malakites managed to attract up to 100,000 Ugandans away from more conventional denominations during its short-lived heyday. The Malakite doctrine was based on a fairly random selection of Old Testament verses: it was vehemently against the consumption of pork and the use of any medicine whatsoever, and – of course – it came out in strong support of polygamy. Not surprisingly, the British colonists were less than enamoured with this development: tensions between the authorities and the sect came to a head in 1926, when the plague swept through Uganda and the Malakites launched a violent protest against the use of inoculations to combat the disease. In the aftermath, Malaki Musajakawa was imprisoned and exiled to northern Uganda, where he died after a protracted hunger strike, and the sect gradually disintegrated.

The main proponent of the spread of Malakitism in eastern Uganda was Semei Kakungulu, who – embittered with the colonial authorities after his retirement from the 'presidency' of Busoga in 1913 – heartily embraced the anti-establishmentarianism of the breakaway faith. Kakungulu withdrew from politics to focus his attention on spiritual matters, dedicating his life to reading the Bible and other Christian tracts. And, somewhat inevitably, he soon started to develop his own variations on the established Malakite doctrines, leading to a dispute that would eventually split the Mbale Malakites into two opposing factions. The key issue was male circumcision, which Kakungulu and his followers believed to be in line with Old Testament teachings, but which most other Malakites regarded as sacrilege. The true reason behind the widespread Malakite objection to circumcision was rooted in Kiganda tradition, which forbade bodily mutilation of any sort. But this was rationalised away by claiming that circumcision was the way of the Abayudaya, people who don't believe in Jesus Christ.

The present-day Abayudaya community was founded in 1920, when Kakungulu, fed up with the quarrelling, announced to the Malakites that 'because of your insults ... I have separated completely from you and stay with those who want to be circumcised: and we will be known as the Jews'. Kakungulu – at the age of 50 – was circumcised along with

---

🏠 **St Andrew's Community Centre** 📞 04544 33650. Attached to the eponymous cathedral on the west of the town centre, this Church-run hostel remains one of the best deals in Mbale. *Dormitory accommodation US$2 pp, while clean though rather cell-like private*

rooms with netting and a writing desk cost US$4/6 sgl/dbl. There are also smarter s/c rooms for US$12.
🏠 **Salem Brotherhood** 📞/f 04544 33368. The deservedly popular hostel run by the Salem Brotherhood lies in a rustic setting about 10km

his first-born son. He circumcised all his subsequently born sons eight days after their birth, and gave all his children Old Testament names. In 1922, he published an idiosyncratic Luganda religious text steeped in the Jewish religion, demanding complete faith in the Old Testament and all its commandments from himself and his followers.

In reality, Kakungulu's version of Judaism was a confused hotchpotch of Jewish and Christian customs. Neither he nor any of his followers had actually ever met a genuine Jew, and they knew little of real Jewish customs. As a result, the Abayudaya referred to their temple not as a synagogue but as a 'Jewish Church', and they placed as much emphasis on the Christian baptism of children as on the severing of their foreskins! That would change after 1926, however, when Kakungulu spent six months under the instruction of one Yusufu, the Jewish settler who effected the community's final conversion to Judaism. Under Yusufu's guidance, Kakungulu deleted all the Christian prayers from his book, and he instructed his followers to cease baptising their children, to observe the Saturday Sabbath, and to eat meat only if it had been slaughtered within the community according to Jewish custom. Ever the iconoclast, however, Kakungulu did remain vehement when it came to at least one pivotal Malakite doctrine that has no place in modern Judaism: the rejection of medicine. On 24 November 1928, Semei Kakungulu died of pneumonia, refusing to the last to touch the medication that might have saved his life.

By this time, a kibbutz-like community of 2,000 Jewish converts lived on Kakungulu's estate at Nabugoye Hill, also known as Galiraya, a Luganda rendition of Galilee. After their founder's death, the Abayudaya had little contact with their neighbours and eschewed materialistic values: it is said that they could be recognised in a crowd by their 'backward' attire of animal hides and barkcloth. The Abayudaya suffered mild persecution during these early years, especially from neighbouring Christian communities who regarded Jews to be Christ killers. But essentially the community thrived until 1971, when Idi Amin banned Judaism, closed 32 synagogues and ordered the Abayudaya to convert to Christianity or Islam. During the Amin years, some 3,000 Abayudaya abandoned their faith rather than risk being beaten or tortured by the military. And some of the more stubborn among them – one group, for instance, who were beaten to death by Amin's thugs for collecting remnants of a synagogue roof that had blown away in a storm – did not survive. Today, the national community of Abayudaya amounts to roughly 500 individuals, most of them living around Nabugoye Hill, the site of Kakungulu's original 'Jewish Church' and his engraved tomb. A smaller community and synagogue exist at nearby Namanyoyi, and two others lie further afield in the town of Pallisa and in a village called Namatumba.

Under Kakungulu, the Abayudaya developed a distinct style of spiritual music, setting the text of recognised Jewish prayers to African melodies and rhythms. Several of these songs, sung in Hebrew or Luganda over a simple guitar backing, are collected on a CD called *Shalom Everybody Everywhere*, available online (www.ubalt.edu/kulanu). The community generally welcomes visitors with a genuine interest in its faith. There is no charge for spending time with them, but a donation should be left behind. To get to the synagogue catch a minibus-taxi from central Mbale to Makadui, from where it's a short walk to the Semei Kakungulu High School on Nabugoye Hill. For more information contact the Abayudaya Community (*PO Box 225, Mbale, Uganda;* e *steno@swiftuganda.com – mark emails for the attention of the Abayudaya; www.kulanu.org*).

from Mbale along the Soroti road, 10mins' walk from the turn-off at Nakaroke. Good meals are available. All proceeds go towards the support of orphans. *US$10 for a private dbl, a dormitory bed US$4, camping US$2 pp.*

🏠 **Apule Safari Lodge** A clean, central cheapie, the Apule Safari Lodge offers spacious s/c dbls and smaller sgls using common showers. *US$5/8 sgl/dbl.*
🏠 **Mbale Tower Lodge** and **Sayona Lodge** Two eminently avoidable town-centre cheapies. *US$4/6.*

WHERE TO EAT AND DRINK

✗ **Mount Elgon Hotel** and **Sunrise Inn** (see hotel listings) both serve good Western dishes in the Ush5,000–7,000 range. The **Mbale Resort** is probably the best place to hang out with a drink, but its food is questionable.

✗ **Landmark Inn** (see hotel listings) Arguably the best place to eat in Mbale, both for the food and for the lush garden setting, the Landmark Inn serves top-notch Indian cuisine. *Around Ush5,000–6,000 for a main course inc rice, chips or naan bread.*

✗ **Narali's Café** Centrally located (below the Mount Elgon View Hotel), this excellent Indian restaurant serves a wide selection of meat and vegetarian dishes. The chicken tikka is particularly recommended. A selection of non-Indian dishes is available too. The smart bar is a good place to hang out at any time, and particularly popular when major sporting fixtures are shown on DSTV. *Meals Ush4,000–6,000 range.*

✗ **Oasis of Life** Aryada St; m 0782 430116. Just behind the Main St/Republic Rd, the Oasis of Life is another unexpected jewel, 100m beyond the excellent Royal Princess Guesthouse. Built and run by a British lay preacher, landscape designer, chef, and collector of model buses (check the display under the reception counter!), Oasis of Life offers a superb 'British-European' menu which provides the best non-

Indian food in Mbale. If the main dining room itself is slightly bland, the brick-paved courtyard outside is a lovely setting. *Open Mon and Tue 16.00–22.00, otherwise 10.00–22.00. Main courses Ush9,000–14,000.*

✗ **East Nile Restaurant** Around the corner from Narali's, this established local eatery serves reasonable and very inexpensive local dishes with a slight Indian touch.

✗ **Coffee Tree Bar and Restaurant** The menu here is rather limited and none too exciting – meat, rice and not much else – but it's a good place for a drink, and (with several DSTV screens) it tends to be packed on Sat/Sun afternoons during the English football season.

✗ **Club Oasis** ✆ 0772 552150. Mbale's nightclub is Club Oasis, situated next to Narali's Café. There's a disco on most nights and live music on occasion – a list of pending events is posted up at the entrance or you can ring the number listed above for details.

✗ **Resort Valley** This centrally located outdoor bar has a lively atmosphere and serves the usual chilled beer and substantial snacks.

✗ **Tom's Joint** Naboa Rd. Mainly a drinking hole, this cosy bar usually serves grilled chicken or meat in the evening.

LISTINGS

Tourist information The Mount Elgon National Park tourist information office (✆ 04544 33170; f 04544 33332; e *uwaface@imul.com*) lies about 15 minutes' walk from the town centre, on Masaba Rd just before the Mount Elgon Hotel. The helpful staff can arrange all aspects of hikes on Mount Elgon, including equipment hire, and will also do their best to provide current information about other sites associated with the mountain, such as Sipi Falls, and the Pian Upe Wildlife Reserve. A useful information board is posted with flyers from various hotels and restaurants within the Elgon region.

Foreign exchange Stanbic and Standard Chartered banks on the eastern end of Republic Rd, and Crane Bank just off it, will change foreign currency at their Kampala rates. Stanbic will also change American Express travellers' cheques.

Internet Masaba Internet Café near the Caltex on Republic Rd charges about Ush50 per min.

Shopping The best place to buy imported and specialised foodstuffs is the **Serve Supermarket**, around the corner from the Mount Elgon View Hotel. The central **market**, a short distance downhill from the taxi park, is usually overflowing with fresh produce from the surrounding agricultural lands.

WHAT TO SEE The main tourist attractions in the Mbale area are Mount Elgon National Park and the Sipi Falls, both covered later in this chapter. The

following two sites also make for interesting and straightforward day excursions out of Mbale:

Nkokonjeru Also known as Wanale Ridge, Nkokonjeru is the tall rocky spur of Elgon that dominates the eastern skyline of Mbale. A not-to-be-missed activity for visitors to Mbale is to drive up to the MTN masts at the southern end of the cliffs. The recently improved 20km road explores superb mountain scenery while the lofty panorama across Mbale from the masts is almost like looking at a map. The ridge is also accessible from Mbale using a steep footpath (find a guide in Mbale or at the UWA office) or on one of the few daily minibus-taxis. The national park offers two guided walking trails of 3km and 6km in length through the regenerating forest in the national park behind the main cliff face. An interesting geological feature along the trail is **Khauka Cave**, which contains logs of petrified wood. The cost of US$30pp including park entrance is rather off-putting, since walking along the road or public lands is equally attractive. No accommodation is available at present. Further details are available from the Mount Elgon tourist office in Mbale.

Kakoro Rock Paintings The Kakoro Rock Paintings (see box *Rock Art of Teso*, page 455) are situated on a small granite outcrop near Kabwangasi, which lies along a 10km dirt road that branches west from the Kumi road at Nakaroke, 10km from Mbale near the Salem Brotherhood Hostel. Any minibus-taxi running along the Kumi road can drop you at Nakaroke, where you can find a *boda-boda* to take you to the rock-art site. The actual paintings, which consist of two red panels of concentric circles and one separate white panel, are very faded and not as impressive as their counterparts at Nyero near Kumi. More unusual is the ancient rock gong that lies close to the paintings, not the only one of its type in Uganda, but certainly the most accessible. Very few tourists head out to Kakoro and the hill is rather overgrown, so wear long trousers and decent walking shoes. You may need to ask permission from the nearest *shamba* before climbing the hill – not a problem!

MOUNT ELGON NATIONAL PARK

Straddling the Kenyan border east of Mbale, Mount Elgon is the eighth-highest mountain in Africa, and it rises from the broadest base of any freestanding mountain in the world. Like most other major East African massifs, Elgon is the relic of an extinct volcano, whose formation was associated with the tectonic activity that created the Rift Valley several million years ago. This volcano probably first erupted at least 20 million years ago and it is thought to have remained active for another 14 million years, when it would have stood far higher than Kilimanjaro does today. Elgon's tallest peaks form a jagged circle around the more-or-less-intact caldera, which has a diameter of about 8km (making it one of the largest in the world) and is dotted with small crater lakes and hot springs created by Pleistocene glacial activity. The tallest peak, set on the Uganda side of the border, is **Wagagai** (4,321m), which lies on the southwest caldera rim. Other major peaks are **Kiongo** (4,303m) in the south, **Mubiyi** (4,210m) in the north, and **Jackson's Summit** (4,165m) in the east. Elgon is an important watershed, the main source of fresh water to more than two million people in Uganda alone.

Stanley obtained a distant view of Elgon in 1875, but the first European to reach the mountain's lower slopes was Joseph Thomson, who approached it from the direction of Maasailand in 1883. Thomson called the mountain Elgon, an Anglicisation of El Kony, the name given to both the massif and its inhabitants by

13

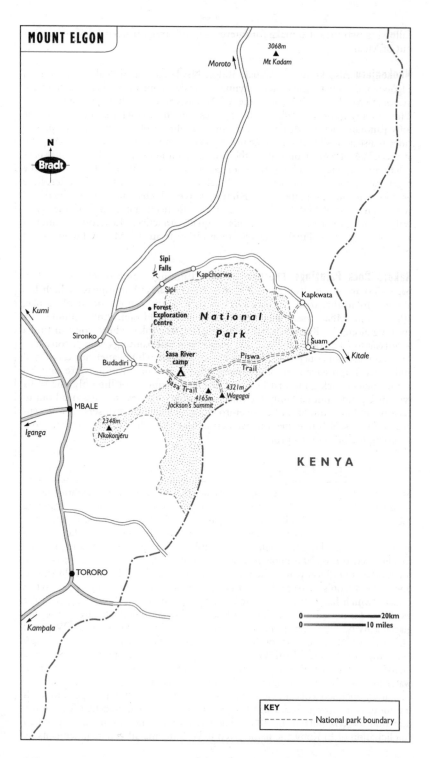

MOUNT ELGON

3068m
▲
Mt Kadam

Moroto ↗

N
Bradt

Sipi
Falls
Kapchorwa
Sipi
Kapkwata
Kumi ↗
● Forest
Exploration
Centre
National
Park
Sironko
Suam
Budadiri
Sasa River
camp
Å
Piswa
Trail
Kitale ↗
Sasa Trail
4321m
▲ Wagagai
4165m
▲
Jackson's Summit
MBALE
Iganga ↗
2348m
▲
Nkokonjeru
K E N Y A

● TORORO

Kampala ↗

0 ━━━━━ 20km
0 ━━━━━ 10 miles

KEY
– – – – – – National park boundary

442

Elgon lies below the snowline, but it can be very cold at night or in windy weather. You must be sure to bring enough warm clothing. It is not high enough for altitude sickness to be a major cause of concern, but you may experience headaches and other altitude-related symptoms near the peaks. Water on the mountain should be purified or boiled before drinking. The ascent of the escarpment via a tricky path known as the Wall of Death on the Sasa Route is not recommended if you are afraid of heights. It is mandatory for trekkers visiting the hot springs area between Mude and Hunters Caves to be escorted by an armed ranger.

the Maasai, who frequently visited the area on cattle raids. The local Bagisu call the mountain Masaba, the name of their founding ancestor, who is said to have emerged from a cave on the slopes several centuries ago. Masaba's spirit is believed to be personified by Jackson's Summit, which appears to be the tallest peak from many vantage points, while Wagagai is named after and associated with Masaba's wife. In February 1890, Jackson and Gedge ascended Elgon from a base camp at modern-day Kapchorwa, crossing the caldera and climbing one of the peaks (long assumed to have been Jackson's Summit, but more probably the taller Kiongo Peak). The Kenyan portion of Mount Elgon has been a national park for several decades. The Ugandan part of the mountain above the 2,000m contour was gazetted as a 1,145km² national park only in October 1993.

Elgon's vegetation zones are similar to those of other large East African mountains. Below the 3,000m contour, the mountain supports a contiguous belt of evergreen forest extending over roughly 750km² within Uganda. This forest belt can be divided into two broad strata: tall Afro-montane forest below 2,500m, and low-canopy montane forest and bamboo between 2,500m and 3,000m. The slopes below the 2,000m contour, which lie outside the national park, also supported significant forest cover a century ago, but much of this forest has been cleared for cultivation. Above 3,000m lies the heather belt, giving way at around 3,500m to otherworldly Afro-alpine vegetation studded with stands of giant lobelia and groundsel including the endemic *Senecio barbatipes* and *Senecio elgonensis*.

Hikers on Elgon are unlikely to encounter many large mammals aside from blue monkey and black-and-white colobus. But a small number of elephants are resident on the mountain, as is a population of the localised and striking De Brazza's monkey, as well as leopard, bushpig, buffalo, sitatunga and common duiker. The official checklist of 24 mammal species will surely expand when an intensive survey is done, especially as an increasing number of animals are crossing back to Uganda from Kenya.

The bird checklist of 305 species, of which more than 20% are unconfirmed, further indicates that more studies are required before knowledge of the park's fauna can be considered anywhere near complete. The mountain supports a rich variety of forest birds, as well as several which are endemic to East Africa's montane moorlands. Twelve of the species listed for Elgon occur in no other Ugandan national park, in many instances because Elgon lies at the most westerly extent of its range. Of particular interest are Jackson's francolin (recorded only once), moorland francolin (elsewhere common only in Ethiopia's Bale Mountains), moustached green tinkerbird, red-throated wryneck, black-collared apalis, Hunter's cisticola, Alpine chat, marsh widowbird and Weyn's weaver. The endangered bearded vulture or lammergeyer is regularly observed soaring at higher altitudes.

Despite its enormous hiking potential, Mount Elgon has never really caught on with hikers. In large part, this has been due to intermittent security problems, particularly on the Kenyan slopes, but it's probably also the case that Elgon lacks the popular mystique of Kilimanjaro, Mount Kenya or the Rwenzori. The ascent of Elgon is, however, far less financially draining than that of any other major massif in East Africa, while offering similar exposure to the weird and wonderful world of the Afro-alpine zone. In past decades, Elgon was most often climbed from Kenya, but this has changed with the creation of better facilities and guides in Uganda. Logistically, the trailheads of the Ugandan national park are far easier to reach on public transport than their Kenyan counterparts. It is also worth noting that Wagagai, the tallest peak, stands on the Ugandan side of the border. Note that it is now possible to traverse the mountain, ascending the Ugandan side and descending through the contiguous national park in Kenya. Ask at the Mbale UWA office for further details.

For less-serious hikers, Mount Elgon also offers plenty of alluring prospects. The lovely waterfall at Sipi, accessible from Mbale in less than an hour on a newly surfaced road, is entrenched as the most popular destination in this part of Uganda, and serviced by a range of accommodation to suit all budgets. The nearby Mount Elgon Exploration Centre at Kapkwai is a great base for day hikes on the footslopes of the Elgon massif. And more adventurous travellers might want to explore the seldom-used but scenic road leading past Sipi to Suam on the Kenyan border. These options are covered under the separate heading *Around Mount Elgon* on page 445.

GETTING THERE AND AWAY The national park can be explored only on foot, but most of the trailheads can be reached on public transport. The most established route up Elgon is the Sasa Route, the trailhead for which is at Budadiri on the western slopes. Two more recently established trails to the peaks lead from the northern footslopes: the Piswa Route (trailhead at Kapkwata) and the Sipi Route (trailhead at Kapkwai). For details of access to the trailheads, see the heading *Around Mount Elgon* overleaf. Transport from Mbale to any of the trailheads can also be arranged through the national park information office in Mbale.

WHERE TO STAY Accommodation exists at all three trailheads; see *Around Mount Elgon* overleaf for details. Once on the trail, however, camping is the only option. Hikers must either bring their own tent and sleeping bag, or else hire equipment from the national park office in Mbale. Porters will cut grass to make you a 'mattress' to put under your sleeping bag; this is useful for comfort and also warmth at higher altitudes.

HIKING Elgon is not a difficult mountain to climb. Aspirant hikers need to be reasonably fit, but no specialised equipment or skill are required to reach the peaks, and the mountain is not so high that there's a serious risk of the altitude-related illnesses that regularly afflict hikers on the upper slopes of mounts Kilimanjaro or Kenya. Elgon can be climbed at any time of year, though the dry seasons (June to August and December to March) are best, in particular November/December when the highland flowers are in bloom.

All hikes must be arranged directly through the national park staff. This can be done at the Mount Elgon tourist office in Mbale, which lies about 100m from the Mount Elgon Hotel, or the equivalent office at the trailheads of Budadiri, Kapkwata or Kapkwai. It doesn't really matter where you make arrangements, but it probably makes sense to drop into the central office in Mbale to talk through route options before you decide on a trailhead. Porters (carrying a maximum of 18kg each) must also be arranged through the national park offices. Most hikers cater for themselves, but this can be talked through with the park staff.

Several hiking routes are available. Traditionally, the most popular route has been a four-day round trip from Budadiri to Wagagai following the Sasa Route in both directions. Other possibilities include a five-day round hike from Budadiri, taking in Wagagai and the hot springs, and a six-day hike between Budadiri and Kapkwata via Wagagai and the hot springs. These days, however, it's probably best to ascend via the newer Piswa or Sipi routes, which start at much higher altitudes than Budadiri, making for a more gradual and far less strenuous ascent, then to return down using the Sasa Route. The experienced national park staff can give more detailed advice on the various options.

The first three days of all hikes out of Budadiri follow the same route. On the first day, the Sasa Trail involves a stiff six- to eight-hour walk from Budadiri (1,250m) via the village of Bumasifwa to Sasa River Camp (2,900m). This is followed on the second day by a four- to five-hour walk to Mude Caves (3,500m). Many people use the spare afternoon at Mude Caves to ascend Jackson's Summit (4,165m), which is a round trip of around five hours. On the third day, you will ascend from Mude Caves to Wagagai (4,321m) and back, an eight- to nine-hour trip. Hikers doing the four-day route will descend from Mude Caves back to Budadiri on the fourth day. Hikers doing the full trek to Kapkwata will on the fourth day walk from Mude Caves to Hunters Cave Camp (3,870m) via the hot springs, a trek of at least ten hours. On the fifth day, they will descend to Piswa Camp, a five-hour trek, and on the sixth day to Kapkwata, a further four hours. It is possible to combine the last two days into one, thereby cutting the duration of the trek to five days. As already noted, hikers who want to do the full route should consider starting at Kapkwata or Kapkwai rather than Budadiri.

Hiking prices are very reasonable when compared with other large mountains in East Africa. The daily hiking fee of US$30 per person per day includes the park entrance fee and the services of a guide. Camping costs US$6 extra for each night you spend on the mountain. Porters cost Ush8,000 per day. In 2006, the total cost of an Elgon hike using one porter per hiker and inclusive of food should work out at around US$45 per person per day – less than half the price of a hike up Kilimanjaro or the Rwenzoris.

Note A new hut is planned for Mude Cave campsite on the Sasa Route and will accommodate 16 people on wooden bunks. Trekkers will then be able to climb the mountain to the peak without carrying tents, ie: by trekking from Budadiri to Mude Cave on the first day, staying overnight at the new hut, and climbing to the peak and back to Mude Cave on the second day, then back to Budadiri on the third day.

AROUND MOUNT ELGON

The sites discussed below, starting in a clockwise direction from Budadiri, all lie on the footslopes of Mount Elgon, and in most cases they stand as worthwhile travel destinations in their own right, as well as being trailheads for hiking routes into the national park. Traditionally, the most popular destination in the Elgon area is Sipi Falls, which is not only readily accessible on public transport, but also offers a good range of accommodation for all budgets and several day-walking possibilities outside the national park. The Mount Elgon Exploration Centre at Kapkwai is, however, a more worthwhile goal for those with a strong interest in natural history, but also more costly as park visitation fees must be paid.

BUDADIRI Budadiri, a small trading centre situated a few kilometres outside the western park boundary, is the established starting point for hikes on Mount Elgon.

The western slopes of Mount Elgon are home to the Bagisu, a Bantu-speaking group with few cultural or historical links to the linguistically affiliated kingdoms of western Uganda. The origin of the Bagisu is uncertain: their oral traditions assert simply that the founding ancestor Masaba emerged from a cave in the synonymous mountain perhaps 500 years ago. Masaba – also the local name for the mountain – is said to still inhabit Elgon's upper slopes, where he holds meetings with lesser deities at a place where stones have been laid out to form chairs and tables. Bagisu society recognises no central leadership: each autonomous clan is presided over by its own non-hereditary chief, appointed by a committee of elders. Traditionally, the judicial powers of the chief were in many respects subservient to those of sorcerers and witch-finders, who used to exert a steel grip on the social affairs and perceptions of the Bagisu.

The Bagisu, together with their Sabiny neighbours, are the only Ugandans to practise male circumcision (unlike the Sabiny, however, the Bagisu do not circumcise females – see box, pages 450–1). The origin of this custom is obscure, and several contradictory traditions have been recorded. One somewhat improbable legend has it that the first Bagisu man to be circumcised had a reputation for seducing the wives of his neighbours, and was taken before the committee of elders, who decreed that he should be semi-castrated as both punishment and deterrent. This plan backfired when, having recovered, the offender went back to his seductive ways, and – it was whispered – had become an even more proficient lover due to the operation. After that, his rivals decided that they too would have to be circumcised in order to compete for sexual favours! Nice story, but all things considered it's more likely that the custom arose through contact with a neighbouring people who had an existing tradition of circumcision, for instance the Kalenjin of western Kenya.

Whatever its origin, the circumcision ceremony or *imbalu*, held on even-numbered years, is the pivotal occasion in Bagisu society, an individual rite of passage to manhood that involves the entire local community. Unusually among those African societies that practise circumcision, the year in which an individual will undergo the ritual is dictated not by strict convention nor by the council of elders, but by his own personal choice – any age between 16 and 26 is considered acceptable. Those who elect to be circumcised in any given year announce their intention in May or June, and spend the next few months preparing for the main ceremony. The most visible facet of the preparations involves the initiate, adorned in plantain fronds or animal skins and ash-plastered face, and accompanied by a band of cheering friends, parading and dancing through the streets to visit all his close relatives and seek their approval.

The climactic ceremony, according to certain historical sources, is traditionally held in August by the Bagisu and in December by the Sabiny, but these days it appears that both groups hold ceremonies during both of these months, though mainly in December. It normally takes place in the morning, well before 10.00, and involves all the initiates from a given clan – anything from one to several-dozen young men – being marched by a

Although non-hikers seldom visit Budadiri, one interesting local attraction is the **Numagabwe Cave**, which lies about 3km away and is decorated with ancient rock paintings. Either of the hotels in Budadiri can organise a day trip to the caves, as well as longer caving expeditions for those with the necessary equipment.

Getting there and away Budadiri lies about 35km from Mbale by road. The best route entails following the surfaced road towards Sipi and Kapchorwa out of town for 24km to Sironko, then after another 2–3km turning into the signposted dirt road to the right. Several minibus-taxis and pick-ups run daily to Budadiri from

whistling, cheering crowd to the circumcision ground. The initiates have their faces plastered in ash, and they are stripped below the waist on the way to the circumcision ground, where they must line up in front of a crowd of family and friends of both sexes and all ages. Elsewhere in Africa, the circumcisions are normally performed indoors, with only a handful of associates in attendance. This was previously the case with the Bagisu, as only the initiates and the circumcisor were allowed into the special initiation enclosure. Today, however, the circumcision is a public event that anybody – including tourists – may attend.

The operation lasts for about one minute. The initiate holds both his arms rigid in front of him, clasping a stick in his hands, and staring forward expressionlessly. The circumcisor then makes three bold cuts around the foreskin to remove it from the penis. When the operation is complete, a whistle is blown and the initiate raises his hands triumphantly in the air, then starts dancing, proudly displaying his bloodied member to an ululating crowd. Any initiate who cries out during the painful procedure is branded a coward (as is any Bagisu man who is circumcised by a doctor under local anaesthetic). Once the crowd is satisfied of his bravery, the initiate is led away to a quiet place by a few friends, and seated on a stool and wrapped in cloth while he waits for the bleeding to cease. He is then taken to his father's house, where he will be hand fed by his relatives for three days. Finally, the initiate's hands are ritually washed, after which he is permitted to eat with his own hands, and his rite to manhood is completed.

While it is wholly acceptable for a Bagisu man to delay circumcision into his late 20s, he will not be considered a true man until he has undergone the rite, and will be forbidden from marrying or attending important clan meetings. A man who refuses to be circumcised past the accepted age parameters will be hunted down by his peers, and cut by force. It is not unknown for octogenarian men to be denounced as uncircumcised by a younger wife, and dragged off by a mob for a forced operation. And in one famous incident a few years ago, a Bagisu man who had lived overseas for decades, and had thus far escaped the knife, was abducted by his peers when he arrived at Entebbe International Airport, and taken away to be circumcised. When I first visited Mbale in 1992, a local councillor made the front page of the national papers when, accused by his drinking pals of being uncircumcised, he dropped his trousers in a bar. When later he was accused of having faked a circumcised appearance using an elastic band, he responded by exposing himself at a public gathering, where doubters could ascertain his adulthood for themselves.

Travellers who visit Mbale, Sipi or Kapchorwa during the circumcision season are welcome to attend any local ceremonies that take place – they occur on practically a daily basis during December and to a lesser extent August, of all even-numbered years. The easiest way to find out about upcoming ceremonies is to ask local hotel staff. A small fee will usually be asked – particularly if you're thinking of taking pictures – but the Bagisu and Sabiny seem genuinely keen to have outsiders attend their most important ceremony. There is no taboo on women being present. Male visitors can expect a few (joking?) invitations to join the initiates as they line up to be cut!

Mbale, leaving from a stand along the Kumi road about 300m north of the clocktower, and taking roughly 45 minutes in either direction.

Where to stay

Rose's Last Chance (7 rooms) This shoestring guesthouse in Budadiri has been recommended warmly by several travellers. It's probably fair to say that the attraction lies in its homely atmosphere and friendly host rather than the standard of the accommodation.

Warm water is available for bathing, and good, reasonably priced meals can be prepared by advance order. The guesthouse can be contacted by radio through the national park office in Mbale. *The 7 sgl, dbl and trpl rooms cost US$4 pp, camping US$3 pp.*

13

SIPI FALLS The Sipi River rises on the upper slopes of Mount Elgon before cascading down the foothills over 7km to form a series of four pretty waterfalls culminating in a 99m drop at an altitude of 1,775m outside the small trading centre of Sipi, 60km from Mbale by road. Overlooking the main waterfall is a choice of resorts and campsites that cater to all budgets and make an agreeable base for gentle day walks in the surrounding hills, with their spectacular views over the Kyoga Basin and glimpses of the nearby Elgon peaks.

The most popular walking trail, only 20 minutes in each direction, leads from behind the post office in Sipi trading centre to the base of the main waterfall, where a small entrance fee is levied. If you choose, you can continue along this trail for another 20–30 minutes to reach a cluster of caves on the cliff above the river. The largest of these caves extends for about 125m into the rock face, and contains rich mineral salt deposits that have clearly been worked extensively at some time in the past, as well as traces of petrified wood. Walking back to the reading centre from the caves along the main road, you'll pass the top of the main waterfall, as well as an important local shrine set within a small forest-fringed cavern.

More ambitiously, it is possible to undertake a day hike from the main waterfall to the three smaller falls that lie upstream, one of which has a tempting swimming pool at its base. The second set of falls can easily be visited independently, since it's visible from the Suam road about 1km out of Sipi trading centre. It would be difficult to find the other waterfalls without a local guide. Unfortunately, Sipi trading centre is developing into one of these travel hotspots – the only one in Uganda – where it's difficult for a visitor to walk more than five paces without a local youngster latching on and asking to guide them. This is becoming a little bit of an issue. It's perhaps too soon to sound alarm bells after one incidence of camera theft and a couple of suggestions of 'add more money or find your own way back' but you'll enjoy peace of mind and save haggling if you sort a guide through your lodge rather than off the roadside. The guiding fees include a contribution to local landowners for access to each of the falls; so while it's quite safe to find your way around alone, it's probably simplest to pay your guide up front and let him take care of these issues.

A local company called **Rob's Rolling Rock** (m *0772 800702*) arranges abseiling trips down the face of the main waterfall.

Getting there and away Sipi trading centre lies about 60km from Mbale on the Kapchorwa–Suam road. From Mbale, follow the Kumi road out of town for 5km, then turn right on to the Moroto road. The turning to Kapchorwa lies 33km further on; the tarmac also turns right here, rather than heading to Moroto! The waterfall is clearly signposted just after you pass through Sipi trading centre. Formerly notoriously bad (the villagers immediately below Sipi did good business putting up bogged travellers), the road to Sipi has recently been surfaced in its entirety, and it is currently one of the best roads anywhere in Uganda.

Without private transport, the best way to get to Sipi is with one of the minibus-taxis or overcrowded trucks that head to Kapchorwa from Mbale at least once per hour. Transport heading in this direction leaves Mbale from the small taxi park on the Kumi road about 300m past the clocktower. Expect the trip to take between 60 and 90 minutes and cost about Ush5,000, depending on how often the driver stops to pick up and let out passengers.

⌂ Where to stay
Upmarket
⌂ **Sipi Falls Resort** ☎ 0414 346464/5; m 0752 741718; f 0414 341718; e sales@ volcanoessafaris.com; www.volcanoessafaris.com. Until recently a quaint, low-key resthouse built as a

governor's residence in the 1950s, the Sipi Falls Resort is now run by Volcanoes Tours. Set in attractive green grounds overlooking the main waterfall, the resort consists of several comfortable bamboo-and-thatch *bandas* with netting and en-suite hot shower and toilet. Day visitors are welcome (entrance fee Ush1000) to visit for meals and drinks. *US$90/130 sgl/dbl HB, US$96/144 sgl/dbl FB, discounted by roughly 25% for Uganda residents.*

Moderate

🏠 **Lacam Lodge** m 0752 292554; www.lacamlodge.co.uk. A welcome addition to Sipi's listings, this new lodge introduces some middle ground between the Sipi Falls Resort and the cheap and cheerful offerings at Moses's Campsite and the Crow's Nest. Lacam occupies a lovely site immediately beside the main Sipi Falls – so close that the waterfall is heard rather than seen, the exception being a single viewpoint looking, rather hypnotically, into tumbling strands of water. In the other direction, the view looks down the Sipi Valley to vast plains extending to Lakes Bisina and Kyoga. Three comfortable, spacious and attractively furnished timber guest cottages are provided with roofs thatched in the local style. These are s/c with hot showers and compost toilets. FB accommodation only is provided. The food is reportedly excellent. *Cottages with sgl and dbl bed and cater for sgl/dbl/trpl occupancy at US$47/71/90, a dormitory bed costs US$19 and you can pitch your own tent for US$13.*

Budget and shoestring

🏠 **The Crow's Nest** m 0752 286225 or 0772 687924/515389; e thecrownets@yahoo.com – note 'nets', not 'nest'!; www.sipifalls.isrepresenting.com. Built with the assistance of 2 former Peace Corps volunteers, the Crow's Nest has a wonderful situation on a small hill about 500m before Sipi trading centre, offering a grandstand view to all 4 waterfalls along the Sipi River as well as to the peaks of Mount Elgon. Accommodation is in cosy log cabins. Camping is permitted, and tents and sleeping bags are available for hire. Overland trucks are welcome, but the site is large enough to accommodate independent travellers without becoming crowded. The restaurant has a great view, and serves a selection of stir-fry, spaghetti and local dishes for around Ush3,500–5,000. There's no charge for exploring the small nature trail that encircles the camp, while guided walks to the various waterfalls as well as the Mount Elgon Exploration Centre at Kapkwai are offered for Ush4,000–9,500 pp. *Log cabins US$15 for a private dbl, dormitory bed US$6 pp, camping US$3 pp.*

🏠 **Moses's Campsite** Looking across the valley to the main Sipi waterfall, this is a family-run clifftop campsite with half-a-dozen *bandas* that might euphemistically be described as 'traditional.' That said, almost everybody who stays here agrees that the distinct lack of frills is offset by the friendly and helpful attitude of Moses and family. Simple meals cost Ush4,000, and lukewarm drinks are available, or you could pop up the road to Sipi Resort for better meals and cooler liquid refreshment. *US$5 pp to camp or sleep in the bandas.*

BULAGO An attractive excursion in the Sipi area is a visit to the scenic village of Bulago. Approaching from Mbale, turn off the new, tarmac Sipi road onto the *old* Sipi road at Kaserem about halfway up the mountainside. The turning is signposted to Kamu, an important local market centre. After 2–3km turn left up the mountain. The road winds beneath some superb cliffs and passes through a small but pretty rock gorge before reaching Bulago. The village stands on a clifftop above a lovely waterfall dropping into a pretty, grassy meadow. A rocky plateau beyond the village overlooks the Simu Valley to Butandiga Ridge and a path climbs to the cliffs bordering the national park, over which a couple of streams fall. There is no official accommodation in Bulago at present (we were kindly allowed to sleep in the clinic and departed with feet full of jiggers). Also bear in mind that the road to Bulago is steep and deteriorates quickly after rain so be aware of the weather and retreat if necessary.

KAPKWAI (MOUNT ELGON FOREST EXPLORATION CENTRE) The Forest Exploration Centre at Kapkwai, situated at an altitude of around 2,050m immediately within the national park boundary, was originally designed as an educational facility for

The Sabiny people of Kapchorwa District are the only ethnic group in Uganda to practise female genital mutilation (FGM) – often and somewhat euphemistically referred to as female circumcision. Traditionally, Sabiny girls are expected to succumb to the knife shortly after reaching puberty, but before they marry, in the belief that having the clitoris removed reduces the temptation to indulge in promiscuity. Should a female Sabiny refuse to be cut, she will forever be accorded the social status of a girl – forbidden from marrying, or from speaking publicly to circumcised women, or from undertaking women's tasks such as milking cows, collecting dung to plaster walls and drawing grain from the communal granary.

FGM is traditionally performed during the December of every even-numbered year. Several girls generally participate in one communal ceremony, and the festivities endure for several days before and after the actual operation, which takes only a few minutes to perform. One by one, the girls are instructed to lie down with their arms held aloft and their legs spread open. Cold water is poured on the vagina, and the clitoris is pulled and extended to its fullest possible length before it is sliced off, together with part of the labia minora. Should a girl cry out during the procedure, she will be branded a coward and bring shame and misfortune to her family. When all the participants have endured the operation, they are herded to a collective enclosure. Here, according to J P Barber, who witnessed a ceremony in the 1950s: 'they bend and kneel, they moan and whistle, in an attempt to lessen their extreme agony. Their faces... are drawn and contracted. They are too conscious of pain to notice or care about anything or anybody.'

No anaesthetic or disinfectant is used, and the operation is often performed on several girls in short succession using a non-sterilised knife or razor, or even a scrap of sharp metal or glass. Short-term complications that frequently follow on from the procedure include haemorrhaging, urinary retention and temporary lameness. In the years that follow, mutilated women often experience extreme pain during sexual intercourse, and bear an increased risk of complications related to childbirth. For some, circumcision will prove fatal. A small proportion of girls will die immediately or shortly after the operation due to uncontrolled bleeding, shock or infection. Others face a lingering death sentence: the HIV virus is occasionally transmitted during mass operations, and mutilated women are often prone to vaginal tearing during intercourse, which makes them especially vulnerable to sexually transmitted diseases.

Public debate around the subject of FGM is traditionally taboo. The first local woman to come out strongly against the custom was Jane Kuka, head of a local teacher-training college in the 1970s. Herself defiantly uncircumcised, Kuka educated her students about the dangers of FGM, hoping they would act as ambassadors to the wider community. In 1986, encouraged by Museveni's strong commitment to women's rights, and assisted by the local representative of the WHO, Kuka launched a more open campaign, one that met strong opposition from community leaders who felt that outsiders were criticising and interfering with their culture. In response to this provocation, a district by-law was passed in 1988 requiring all Sabiny women to undergo FGM – any woman who did not submit to the knife voluntarily would do so by force. Kuka visited the cabinet minister for women in Kampala, and together they flew a helicopter to Kapchorwa to rescue as many

schoolchildren living around Mbale. Over the past few years, it has also been developed for tourism with the opening of a network of day trails, a hiking trail to the Elgon peaks, and a comfortable rest camp consisting of four log cottages, a similar number of standing tents, and a good canteen. Only 1–1.5 hours from Sipi village on foot, Kapkwai is an excellent destination for travellers who don't want to do an extended hike on Mount Elgon.

victims as they could. At the minister's insistence, the by-law was revoked shortly after it came into being, but still too late for the hundreds of women that had been seized, bound and forcibly circumcised by the district authorities.

Kuka's major breakthrough came in 1992, with the formation of the Sabiny Elders Association, which aimed to protect the Sabiny culture by preserving songs, dances and other positive customs, but also wanted to eliminate more harmful traditions, notably FGM. At the same time, Kuka consolidated her network of local women's groups to launch the UN-funded REACH programme, which adopted a culturally sensitive strategy, endorsing most Sabiny traditional values but highlighting the health risks associated with FGM. In 1996, coinciding with the start of the initiation season, the two organisations staged the first Sabiny Culture Day, which highlighted the positive aspects of local traditions while doubling as a substitute for the traditional female initiation ceremony. In place of a rusty knife, female initiates were given a symbolic gift, and counselled on subjects such as HIV prevention, family planning and economic empowerment. The number of girls who underwent FGM in 1996 was 36% lower than it had been in 1994.

In 1996, Kuka swept to a landslide victory in local elections for a parliamentary representative, to be appointed minister of state for gender and cultural affairs, giving her a more prominent forum for her campaign. Her new appointment also ensured that she had the ear of President Museveni, who made a personal appearance at the 1998 Culture Day to deliver a speech about the dangers of FGM. The efforts of Kuka and Museveni were undermined that year by those of a short-lived organisation called the Promote Sabiny Culture Project, which outspokenly advocated FGM and offered a payment of US$100 and gifts of cloth and animals to families who agreed to cut their daughters. In reaction, an American non-profit anti-circumcision organisation called the Godparents started offering cattle, goats and money for scholarships to parents of girls who pledged not to undergo FGM.

Many Sabiny traditionalists regard female circumcision as integral to their cultural identity: the rite of passage that transforms a girl into a woman. In more remote parts of the district, uncircumcised women still experience social discrimination, and their families stand to gain materially from the substantial gifts they customarily receive from friends and relatives on the day of initiation. One strongly reactionary element is the female elders who are paid to perform the operations – finance aside, these women are not eager to relinquish their elevated status as community advisors and custodians of tradition and magic. But FGM is now illegal in Uganda, and while clandestine ceremonies are still held in certain remote areas, the number of women who undergo it today is a mere fraction of those who would have been cut a decade ago.

The remarkable progress made towards eradicating FGM locally within the space of one generation can be attributed partially to the Sabiny being culturally anomalous in Uganda – the rest of the population has never subscribed to the practice. It is sobering to realise that, according to WHO estimates, some 100 million women across 26 countries elsewhere in Africa have suffered some form of genital mutilation, and there are several countries in which more than 90% of females have undergone the procedure.

Three connecting, circular day trails run through the exploration centre. The 7km, four-hour Mountain Bamboo Loop leads past a cave before climbing to the main viewpoint (from where, on a clear day, the peaks of Mount Elgon can be seen), and then follows a ridge northwards through montane forest to a large bamboo forest. The popular 5km, three-hour Chebonet Falls Loop passes the eponymous waterfalls as well as involving a climb up a rock chimney and passing through areas of montane and bamboo forest leading to the main viewpoint. The 3km, two-hour Ridge View Loop involves a relatively easy ascent of the ridge, where it connects with the other trails at the main viewpoint.

In addition to passing through areas of regenerating forest, fields of colourful wild flowers and extensive stands of bamboo, the day trails offer a good chance of sighting black-and-white colobus and blue monkey. The centre is highly rewarding to birders, with a high proportion of the 305 species recorded in the national park present. The lovely cinnamon-chested bee-eater, Doherty's bush-shrike and golden-winged sunbird head a long list of highland species resident in the riverine scrub close to the rest camp. Among the more conspicuous birds of true forest – the Mountain Bamboo Loop is probably the most productive trail – are black-and-white casqued hornbill, Hartlaub's turaco, bar-tailed trogon, grey-throated barbet, montane oriole, mountain greenbul and black-collared apalis.

Note that the national park visitation fees of US$20/25/30 for non-resident tourists and US$15/20/25 for residents are applied for visits of one/two/three days' duration to the forest exploration centre. Guided walks cost US$10pp. It is not permitted to walk without a guide except in the immediate vicinity of the rest camp.

Getting there and away The exploration centre lies roughly 12km from Sipi by road. To drive there, follow the surfaced Kapchorwa road out of Sipi for 6km, where a prominent signpost to the right indicates the 6km dirt road to the entrance gate and rest camp. Except after heavy rain, the road should be passable in any vehicle. For those without private transport, there are two options. Most straightforward is to catch any vehicle running between Mbale and Kapchorwa via Sipi and ask to be dropped at the junction to Kapkwai, from where the 6km walk to the rest camp shouldn't take longer than 90 minutes. Alternatively, the guides at the Crow's Nest in Sipi can lead you along a more direct 90-minute walking trail for Ush9,000 per person. It should also be possible to arrange a special hire out of Sipi or Mbale.

Where to stay and eat

Kapkwai Cottages and Rest Camp ⤬ 04544 33170; f 04544 33332; e uwaface@imul.com. The rest camp at Kapkwai is a real gem, sprawling attractively across the slopes near the source of the Sipi River. 3 immaculate s/c log cabins with twin beds, hot water, solar lighting and private balconies are provided. A few s/c standing tents are also available, and camping is permitted. The attractive Bamboo Grove Canteen serves simple but decent meals at around Ush3,000 as well as beers and sodas. Cottages US$11 pp twin, US$28 sgl and dbl for a solitary 'executive banda' (containing a dbl bed). Camping in s/c tents US$11/17 sgl/dbl, with own tent US$6 pp.

KAPCHORWA Administrative headquarters of the synonymous district, Kapchorwa lies at the heartland of Uganda's main Arabica coffee-production area, and the major development within the town is a vast and recently rehabilitated coffee-processing plant. Kapchorwa is an odd little place: a vast but unfocused semi-urban sprawl of only 5,000 inhabitants that somehow manages to straddles the Suam road for perhaps 2km. An attractive and breezy montane setting go some way to compensating for the town's rather scruffy appearance, but one could argue – convincingly – that the best thing about Kapchorwa is the scintillating ascent road from Sipi, which offers some wonderful views to Lake Kyoga and the isolated Mount Kadam. If you're up to some exploration, the surrounding slopes must also offer plenty of good walking, with one possible goal being a little-known series of caves on a cliff outside of town.

Getting there and away Kapchorwa lies 14km past Sipi along the road to Suam (the road is surfaced as only far as the town but no further). Regular minibus-taxis run between Mbale and Kapchorwa, leaving Mbale from the taxi park about 300m north of the clocktower on Kumi Road, and stopping at Sipi on request.

Where to stay and eat
Budget
Tim's Guesthouse m 0772 659652. This reasonably smart guesthouse, which lies about 200m from the main road through Kapchorwa, isn't great value, but is easily the most comfortable accommodation in town. *US$11 small dbl using common showers, US$14 for a s/c dbl.*

Greenfields Resort ↘ 04544 51184; m 0772 418254. About 50m from the main road as you enter Kapchorwa from the Sipi side, this small resort offers two types of accommodation. The comfortable s/c wooden *bandas* with cold water only are excellent value. Bizarrely, the rooms in the main building cost twice as much, with the solitary

advantage of having running hot water, and the distinct disadvantage of being very ugly and scruffy. *US$6 for s/c bandas.*

Noah's Ark Guesthouse ↘ 04544 51100; m 0772 646364. This rambling lodge next door to (and under the same management) as Tim's Guesthouse has s/c rooms, and rooms using common showers. The rooms look somewhat timeworn and there is no running hot water (a bucket will be supplied on request), but all things considered it's reasonable value. The large restaurant and bar serves a limited menu of local dishes and cold beer. *US$11/14 s/c sgl/dbl, US$6/8 non-s/c sgl/dbl, all B&B.*

Shoestring
Paradise Lodge Situated alongside the main taxi park, this basic lodge offers less than heavenly sgl

rooms using common showers. It serves acceptable local food, as well as chilled beers and sodas. *US$4.*

KAPKWATA The small trading centre of Kapkwata, which lies about 30km from Kapchorwa along the *murram* road to the Kenyan border crossing at Suam, is of interest mainly as the trailhead for the Piswa Trail up Mount Elgon. In addition to being a trailhead, Kapkwata offers travellers heading to Suam a good excuse to break up the journey in the form of an obscure forestry resthouse, situated in the middle of a plantation at the rangers' post roughly 500m past the trading centre. The resthouse has three rooms – one single, one double and one six-bed dormitory – and accommodation costs US$6 per person. No park entrance fees are charged, because the resthouse lies in a forestry reserve outside the national park boundary, and camping is permitted. The resthouse staff can cook meals to order, or you can eat in one of the small restaurants in the trading centre. Free tea is served in the morning. Facilities include a solar-powered hot shower. There are several good day walks from the resthouse to local viewpoints.

SUAM Suam lies at an altitude of 2,070m on the Kenyan border, and it is only likely to be passed through by travellers crossing between Kitale and Mbale north of Mount Elgon. A few trucks run between Kapchorwa and Suam daily, taking roughly four hours when the road is dry and a great deal longer in wet conditions. This is likely to be a pretty hairy trip, so it would be worth trying to secure a seat in the front. There are a couple of basic lodgings in Suam, or you can continue directly across the border – which is connected to Kitale by a reasonable surfaced road and regular minibuses.

PIAN UPE WILDLIFE RESERVE

Extending over an area of 2,788km² to the north of Mount Elgon, the little-known Pian Upe Wildlife Reserve, recently brought under the management of the greater Mount Elgon Conservation Area, is the second-largest protected area in Uganda after Murchison Falls. It lies in semi-arid country, which usually receives some rain in April and more substantial showers from June to early September, but there are years when the rains fail completely. The predominant cover of mixed acacia-commiphora savanna is essentially the Ugandan extension of an eastern savanna belt encompassing much of northern Kenya and the Amboseli–Tsavo–Mkomazi complex of reserves on the border between Kenya and Tanzania. Providing dramatic contrast to the dry, scrubby plains of Pian Upe is Mount Kadam, an isolated range of spectacularly tortured turrets and bleak volcanic plugs that rises to an altitude of 3,084m on the reserve's eastern boundary.

Pian Upe is home to the two pastoralist tribes for which it is named: the Pian being part of a subgroup of the Karimojong, and the Upe a Kalenjin-speaking people more widely referred to as the Pakot within Kenya. These two tribes have a history of armed conflict, most of it related to cattle rustling. At times, the Pian and Upe have teamed up together to take on neighbouring tribes in Kenya or Uganda, at other times they have directed their violence at each other. This insecurity is the main reason why the reserve has seen little development for tourism to date.

No reliable wildlife population estimates exist for Pian Upe, and poaching has undoubtedly taken a heavy toll since the 1970s. But anecdotal information suggests that Pian Upe still harbours a wide variety of large mammals, furthermore that populations have stabilised or even increased in recent years. Leopard, cheetah and spotted hyena are all seen quite regularly by ranger patrols, and a small population of lion is present. Among the ungulate species are Burchell's zebra, buffalo, eland, hartebeest, greater kudu, topi, oribi, dik-dik and Uganda's last population of roan antelope. In addition to the widespread vervet monkey and olive baboon, the far more localised patas monkey is quite common on the savanna. Wildlife concentrations are highest in the vicinity of the Loporokocho Swamps, which lie near the eastern border and are inhabited by Upe pastoralists who (unlike the Pian) have no tradition of killing wild animals for food. Pian Upe is of some ornithological interest, since the dry plains harbour several dry-country species with a restricted distribution in Uganda, for instance ostrich, yellow-necked spurfowl, Hartlaub's bustard, Jackson's hornbill and white-headed buffalo weaver.

Though sporadic cattle-raiding continues, from a practical point of view the main restriction on exploring Pian Upe is the limited internal road network. Other than the main road between Mbale and Moroto, this is restricted to a recently reopened track leading towards Loporokocho Swamp. Given the limited options available, an additional disincentive is perhaps Pian Upe's new (and arguably premature) UWA classification as a Category B protected area for which fees of US$20/25/30 for non-resident tourists and US$15/20/25 for residents are levied for visits of one/two/three days' duration. No fee is charged for using the public road through the reserve. The reserve's headquarters at Morujore can provide basic *banda* accommodation (US$8 – take your own supplies) and arrange guided game walks (accompanied by an armed ranger) and informal visits to one of the Pian/Karimojong villages within the reserve. Current information regarding facilities (and the security situation) can be obtained from the Mount Elgon tourist office in Mbale.

GETTING THERE AND AWAY The headquarters at Morujore are situated right alongside the direct Mbale–Moroto road, roughly 90km from Mbale and 11km north of the reserve's southern boundary. For the first 30km (as far as the junction to Sipi) this road is surfaced and in a good state of repair, while the remainder is reasonably well-maintained *murram*, so the drive shouldn't take longer than two hours. You'll know you've entered the reserve when, shortly after passing through the trading centre of Chepsikunya, the road crosses a bridge over the forest-fringed

Kerim River. A few buses daily run directly between Mbale and Moroto, passing within a few metres of the park headquarters.

🏠 **WHERE TO STAY AND EAT** Four *bandas* have recently opened at the reserve headquarters. They cost US$6/8/11 single/double/triple. A canteen serves a limited selection of drinks and may in future provide meals, but for the time being you're advised to bring all the food you require from Mbale.

KUMI AND SURROUNDS

Kumi, founded in 1904 by Semei Kakunguru as an administrative substation of Mbale, is named after the jackal-berry tree *Diospyros mespiliformis* (known locally as *ekum*) that proliferates in the vicinity. Kumi is today the headquarters of Kumi District, a full 35% of which comprises wetland habitats associated with Lake Kyoga and its drainage basin, while the remainder is covered in dry savanna studded with spectacular volcanic outcrops. A rather sleepy and nondescript small town (population 12,000), Kumi is of interest to travellers primarily as the springboard for visits to the nearby Nyero Rock Paintings and Lake Bisina.

GETTING THERE AND AWAY Kumi straddles the surfaced Mbale–Soroti road roughly 55km north of Mbale and 45km south of Soroti. The drive from either of these towns should take less than an hour in a private vehicle. Plenty of minibus-taxis run along this road, stopping at Kumi.

🏠 **WHERE TO STAY**
Budget
🏠 **Green Top Hotel** (36 rooms) ☎ 0772 542340. This unexpectedly large hotel stands right alongside the Soroti road about 100m from the taxi park. It's a clean and comfortable set-up, a touch overpriced perhaps by standards elsewhere in eastern Uganda, but far and away the smartest option on offer in Kumi. A decent restaurant and bar with DSTV is attached. US$14 s/c sgls with ³/₄ bed, netting and a tiled floor, US$8/14 sgl/dbl for similar rooms using common showers.

🏠 **New Kumi Hotel** A smart new hotel, with a swimming pool planned, provides s/c dbl rooms including b/fast. US$21.

Shoestring
🏠 **Home Again Guesthouse** Comfortably the most attractive of several cheapies dotted around the town centre. A clean restaurant and bar is attached. US$6 for s/c sgl with ³/₄ bed.

WHAT TO SEE
Nyero Rock Paintings (*Admission of Ush5,000 is charged to non-residents and Ush3,000 to residents*) The finest of several rock-art sites scattered around this part of Uganda (see box *Rock Art of Teso*, page 441), Nyero is also perhaps the most accessible. Set on a prominent granite outcrop called Moru Ikara near Nyero trading centre, the site consists of three discrete panels, all of which lie within a few hundred metres of each other. The most impressive is Panel Two, which covers a 6m-high rock face reached via a narrow cleft between two immense boulders. At least 40 sets of red concentric circles are partially or wholly visible on the face, as is one 'acacia pod' figure. At the top right are the (very faded) remains of a painting of three zebras. The most striking naturalistic figures on the panel are two large canoes, of which one is about 1.5m long and evidently carrying people. Panel One is somewhat less elaborate: six sets of white concentric circles, as well as few 'acacia pod' figures. Panel Three consists of just one white set of concentric circles on the roof of a low rock shelter.

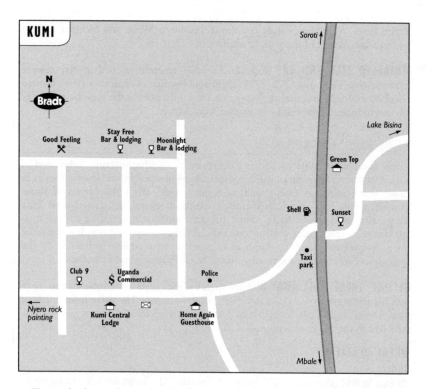

KUMI

N

Bradt

Soroti

Lake Bisina

Good Feeling

Stay Free
Bar & lodging

Moonlight
Bar & lodging

Green Top

Shell

Sunset

Taxi
park

Club 9

Uganda
Commercial

Police

Nyero rock
painting

Kumi Central
Lodge

Home Again
Guesthouse

Mbale

To reach the rock-art site, head out to the tiny trading centre at Nyero – somewhat incongruously the site of a large new private university – 8km from Kumi along the Ngora road. Continue for another kilometre past Nyero towards Ngora, and you'll see the 100m side road to the rock-art site clearly signposted on the right side of the Ngora road. Any public transport heading between Kumi and Ngora can drop you at the site; expect to pay Ush2,000. Nyero can easily be visited as a day trip from Mbale, Kumi or Soroti. If you like, however, it's permitted to pitch a tent at the clearing below the site – you'll have to negotiate a fee with the caretaker – though you'll need to bring all the food you need. There's a toilet at the site but no washing facilities.

At Ngora, 9km west of Nyero, another rock-art site can be found on Tank Rock. The solitary panel on this hill includes several red concentric circles, but unfortunately it was damaged in the 1960s. If you're interested, ask the caretaker at Nyero for directions.

Lake Bisina Formerly known as Lake Salisbury, Bisina is a long, narrow and shallow freshwater body extending over roughly 190km² along an eastern arm of the Kyoga drainage system. It's an attractive lake, fringed by extensive swamps and towered over by the normally obscured peaks of Elgon to the south and jagged outline of Mount Kadam to the east, but tourist development along the shores is non-existent. Lake Bisina is primarily of interest to birders, as the swamps support a number of localised species, including the legendary shoebill and localised papyrus gonolek, white-winged warbler, pygmy goose and lesser jacana. More significantly, it is also one of a handful of localities known to harbour Fox's weaver, a swamp fringe-associated bird endemic to this one small part of eastern Uganda.

A dozen discrete panels of prehistoric rock art are known from five different localities in Kumi and Soroti districts, namely Nyero, Kakoro, Obwin Rock, Ngora and Lolui Island (Lake Kyoga). The paintings are in most cases monochromatic – typically either red or white – and the predominant figures are sets of four or five concentric circles, and strange compartmentalised sausage-shaped figures reminiscent of acacia pods. It would be misleading to compare the impact of these geometric rock paintings, many of which are very faded, with their more naturalistic and better-preserved counterparts in central Tanzania or southern Africa. Nevertheless, a visit to one of the more accessible sites, in particular Nyero, is recommended to anybody with a passing interest in archaeology or human prehistory.

The limited palate drawn on by the artists of Kumi and Soroti was sourced from whatever natural materials were available to them. Red pigments were created by scraping the surface of a ferruginous rock, while white paint was derived from a combination of clay, dung and sap, and black from oxidised organic matter such as charcoal and burned fat. The raw ingredients would be ground finely then mixed into a thick liquid such as albumin to form an adhesive paste that was applied to the rock surface using a rudimentary brush of animal hair. Unless one assumes that the artists had one eye focused on posterity, it is reasonable to assume that the surviving paintings constitute a minute proportion of their work, much of which would have been painted on to exposed rocks or more ephemeral surfaces such as animal hide.

The age of the rock art is a matter for conjecture, as is the identity of the artists. The Iteso people who have inhabited the region for the last 300 years reckon that the art has always been there. Iteso tradition does relate that the region's rock shelters were formerly occupied by a short, light-skinned race of people, and excavations at Nyero have unearthed several microlithic tools of a type not used by the Iteso. Most likely, then, that the artists were hunter-gatherers with ethnic and cultural affiliations to the so-called bushmen who were responsible for much of the rock art in southern Africa. The paintings must be at least 300 years old, and are possibly much older.

As for the intent of the artists, the field is wide open. The circle is a universal theme in prehistoric art; its use could be mythological, symbolic (for instance, a representation of the cycle of the seasons) or more literal (the sun or moon). A possible clue to interpreting the rock art of eastern Uganda comes from a style of house painting practised in northeast DRC in association with rainmaking ceremonies. Here, concentric circles represent the sun, while wavy lines symbolise the moon's feet, which – it is said – follow the rain (a reference to the link between the new moon and stormy weather). Could a similar purpose reasonably be attributed to the rock art of eastern Uganda? Quite possibly, since Nyero is known to have been the site of Iteso rainmaking ceremonies in historic times. But it is a considerable part of these ancient paintings' mystique that they pose more questions than there are answers forthcoming – the simple truth is that we'll never know!

There are two access routes to Lake Bisina. The first is the 15km dirt road that runs northeast out of Kumi to a disused ferry landing on the southern shore. A more useful route entails following the surfaced Soroti road northwest out of Kumi for 22km to the village of Kipiri, where a side road to the right leads to the western tip of Bisina after about 2km. Once at the lakeshore, you'll need to hire a local dugout – expect to pay around Ush1,000 per hour – to the reedy northwestern shore, where up to 50 pairs of Fox's weaver have been recorded breeding.

Soroti, with a population of 42,000, is the headquarters of a district of the same name which, like Kumi to the south, is mainly populated by Iteso people. Few travellers pass through Soroti unless perhaps they are heading further north to Moroto or Kidepo or east towards Lira – routes that have been plagued by regular incidents of banditry in recent years – and the town itself offers little in the way of mandatory sightseeing. The most prominent local attraction is **Soroti Rock**, a striking granite formation that towers above the shady town centre, offering good views across to Lake Kyoga from the pinnacle. The steep footpath from the town centre to the peak is best attempted in the early morning, before the heat of the day sets in – look out for vervet monkeys on the way up.

A few other places of interest lie within easy striking distance of Soroti. About 7km south of town along the Mbale road stands a tall granite outcrop known as **Obwin Rock**, which means 'place of hyenas' in Ateso. You'd be fortunate to see any hyenas at Obwin today, but the formation is riddled with small caves and shelters, one of which is the site of an ancient red rock painting. There's just one pattern on the panel, a set of six concentric circles, but – unusually – the outer circle is decorated with eight rectangles, while what might be a pair of legs dangles from the circle's base. Another possibility is to catch a minibus-taxi to **Serere**, 30km southwest of Soroti near Lake Kyoga, and arrange to take a dugout canoe on to the lake with one of the local fishermen.

About 50km east of Soroti as the crow flies, **Lake Opeta** forms the centrepiece of a 550km² complex of swamps and other wetlands that may soon gain recognition as a Ramsar Wetland Site. The lake and swamps protect one of the most prolific shoebill populations in Africa, as well as the marsh-dwelling sitatunga antelope, breeding colonies of the endemic Fox's weaver, and several other localised species including rufous-bellied heron and papyrus gonolek. Lake Opeta cannot be reached on public transport. To get there in a private vehicle, follow the Moroto road out of Soroti for 55km, turning right a few hundred metres past the village of Katakwi. From here, it's another 50km or so to the lakeshore village of Peta, passing *en route* through the villages of Toroma and Magoro. A trip to Lake Opeta could be combined with a diversion to the northern shore of Lake Bisina, which lies about 10km south of Toroma.

GETTING THERE AND AWAY Soroti lies 100km northwest of Mbale along a good surfaced road, passing through Kumi and the marshy fringes of Lake Bisina on the way. There is plenty of public transport heading up to Soroti from Mbale – a few buses daily as well as the occasional minibus – and the trip shouldn't take longer than two hours. Direct buses from Kampala cost Ush12,000.

Several buses and minibuses daily leave Soroti for Lira to the west. Transport north to Moroto is less regular, but at least one bus does the run daily, leaving Soroti at around noon and taking five hours. Neither route is recommended at present due to regular incidents of banditry.

⌂ WHERE TO STAY

⌂ **Soroti Hotel** ☎ 0414 561269. This recently renovated hotel is set in pleasant grounds about 1km out of town along Serere Rd. To get there, follow the fading signposts from the Shell garage opposite Independence Circle. US$27 *for comfortable s/c dbls.*

The **Golden Ark** (US$21) and the **Garden Guesthouse** (US$13) have been recommended for decent self contained rooms, and the **Savanna Hotel** and **Company Inn** at US$4/6 for single/double rooms with shared showers.

This remote national park lies in the far northeast of Uganda, isolated from the rest of the country by the sparsely populated, arid badlands of Karamoja region. Seldom visited by tourists due to the expense and difficulty of getting there, Kidepo is nevertheless one of the most alluring destinations in the country, boasting a strong wilderness atmosphere, rugged mountain scenery and exceptional game viewing and birdwatching.

The park covers an area of 1,442km², and it has an altitude range of between 914m and 2,750m above sea level. The highest point in the park is Mount Morungole (2,750m) on the southeastern border. The slightly higher Mount Lutoke (2,797m), which lies just within the Sudanese border, is visible from several points in the park. The mountainous terrain is broken by the Narus Valley in the southwest and the Kidepo Valley in the northeast. The dominant habitat is open or lightly wooded savanna, interspersed with patches of montane forest, riparian woodland, thick miombo woodland, borassus palms and rocky koppies. Kidepo protects one of the most exciting faunas of any Ugandan national park although its total of 86 mammal species has been reduced to 77 after a rash of local extinctions in recent years.. The bird checklist of 463 confirmed and 26 unconfirmed species is second only to Queen Elizabeth National Park, and more than 60 of the birds listed have been recorded in no other Ugandan national park. That said, the variety of butterflies and other smaller creatures is far less than in the forested national parks of western Uganda.

Five primate species have been recorded in Kidepo, including the localised patas monkey. Predators are particularly well represented, with 20 species resident. Of these, the black-backed jackal, bat-eared fox, aardwolf, cheetah and caracal are found in no other Ugandan national park. Other predators recorded in Kidepo are the side-striped jackal, spotted hyena, leopard, lion, and a variety of mustelids, genets, mongooses and small cats. Twelve antelope species occur in Kidepo of which the greater kudu, lesser kudu, Guenther's dik-dik and mountain reedbuck occur nowhere else in Uganda. Other antelope species found in Kidepo are Jackson's hartebeest, eland, bushbuck, common duiker, klipspringer, oribi, Defassa waterbuck, and bohor reedbuck. Kidepo also supports populations of elephant, Burchell's zebra, warthog, bushpig and buffalo. The black rhinoceros recently became extinct in Kidepo, but giraffes have been saved from local extinction by the translocation of several animals from Kenya. Kidepo's long bird checklist is made even more impressive by the relatively small size of the park and the fact that as many as 100 of the birds listed are either dry-country species which within Uganda are practically confined to Kidepo, or else northern or eastern species which have been noted elsewhere only in the north of Murchison Falls National Park or in the Mount Elgon area. Raptors are particularly well represented: 56 species in total, of which the most commonly observed are the dark chanting goshawk, pygmy falcon, tawny eagle, bateleur, secretary bird and several types of vulture. Other birds which must be regarded as Kidepo specials, at least within Uganda, include the ostrich, kori bustard, fox and white-eyed kestrels, white-bellied go-away bird, carmine, little green and red-throated bee-eaters, Abyssinian roller, Abyssinian scimitarbill, d'Arnauds, red-and-yellow and black-breasted barbets, red-billed, yellow-billed and Jackson's hornbills, Karamoja apalis, rufous chatterer, northern brownbul, golden pipit, chestnut weaver, red-billed and white-headed buffalo weavers, and purple grenadier – to name only a few of the more colourful and/or visible species.

AROUND THE PARK Kidepo Valley National Park is ringed by mountains, but its area is dominated by the broad valleys of the Kidepo River to the north, and the

13

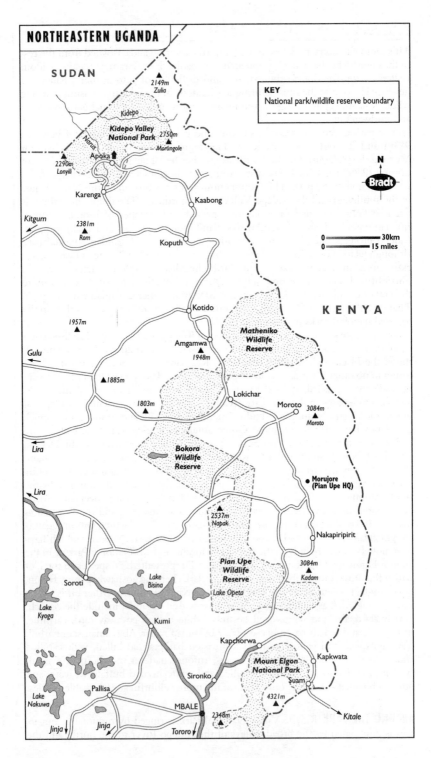

SUDAN

▲ 2149m
Zulia

Kidepo

*Kidepo Valley
National Park* ▲ 2750m
Morungole

Narus

▲ 2290m
Lonyili

Apoka

Karenga

Kaabong

Kitgum

▲ 2381m
Rom

Koputh

▲ 1957m

Kotido

K E N Y A

Gulu

Amgamwa
▲ 1948m

*Matheniko
Wildlife
Reserve*

▲ 1885m

▲ 1803m

Lokichar

Moroto
▲ 3084m
Moroto

Lira

*Bokora
Wildlife
Reserve*

Lira

● Morujore
(Pian Upe HQ)

▲ 2537m
Napak

Nakapiripirit

Soroti

Lake
Bisina

*Pian Upe
Wildlife
Reserve*

▲ 3084m
Kadam

Lake
Kyoga

Kumi

Lake Opeta

Kapchorwa

Kapkwata

Lake
Nakuwa

Pallisa

Sironko

*Mount Elgon
National Park*

Suam

MBALE

▲ 4321m

Jinja

Jinja

Tororo

▲ 2348m

Kitale

KEY
National park/wildlife reserve boundary
- - - - - - - - - - - - - - - - - - -

N

Bradt

0 ━━━━━━ 30km
0 ━━━━━━ 15 miles

Narus River in the south. Apoka, the site of the park's headquarters, lodge and hostel overlooks the Narus Valley which is the prime game-viewing area. The park enjoys just one wet season each year and during the long, hot dry season game migrates south from the semi-arid Kidepo Valley to find what moisture it can in swamps and remnant pools along the seasonal channel of the Narus. The Narus Valley is explored by three game loops, the Kakine, Katurum and Nagusokopire circuits. Game is scarce in the Kidepo Valley, a result of poaching by Sudanese visitors and dry conditions. Worth a visit is the Kidepo River itself which is beautiful in its unorthodox fashion. Lined by lovely borassus palm forest, it is for 95% of the year completely dry and its 50m-wide course is a swathe of white sand. Hot springs are found at Kanatarok on the Sudanese border though these are a low-key event which don't compare with those in Semliki National Park in western Uganda.

En route to the Kidepo Valley, the Kanatarok road passes through a rather incongruous 10km² enclosure contained within a 2m-high electrified fence. This was created in 2001 as a secure location for the introduction of locally extinct or endangered species, including giraffe, eland, Grant's gazelle and roan antelope. The intention is to import breeding pairs of each species and, as their numbers increase, release animals into the wild. A number of eland were brought up from Lake Mburo National Park in 2003. Unfortunately less than rigorous firebreak maintenance enabled fire to sweep through the compound in 2005, whereupon the eland crashed through the fence and dispersed. The empty compound presently awaits new residents.

THE KARAMOJA

The northeast is home to Uganda's most singular ethnic group, the Karamojong, nomadic pastoralists whose love of cattle has an obsessive quality rivalling that of the Maasai of Tanzania and Kenya. The Karamojong of northeastern Uganda are divided into six groups, each with its own dialect of the Nilotic Karamoja language. Two of these groups, the Napore and Nyangia, have largely forsaken their traditional ways for an agriculture-based lifestyle, while a third, the Tueso, are hunter-gatherers who have moved from the dry plains into the mountains.

The Karamojong are apparently something of an embarrassment to more Westernised Ugandans. When I discussed Moroto with people in Tororo and Mbale, I was repeatedly warned that people there are backward and run around half-naked (one hotel owner in Tororo looked at me as if I were half-crazed and asked 'Do you like to look at naked people?' – I refrained from giving him the qualified response his question deserved). Aside from the ugly ethnicity exposed by such accusations, they are also rather unfair: you won't see too many flashers in Moroto itself, though it is true that in rural areas most Karamojong people still dress in skimpy traditional attire. So what?

A more realistic cause for concern than being exposed to the occasional bare breast is the spasmodic outbursts of armed fighting to which this Kenyan border area is prone. Most of this violence is ethnic rather than directly political in nature, and it most often takes the form of cross-border cattle rustling. The ethnic problems in this region are not to be belittled: the target of most cross-border raids may be cattle, but human fatalities are commonplace. The park itself is quite safe. Under normal circumstances, the danger to tourists along the approach roads is probably not great, provided that they can resist the temptation to bring along a few cows, but as we go to print violence has flared up again and you should certainly make advance enquiries before heading up this way.

13

THE DRIVE TO KIDEPO

If you're thinking of driving to Kidepo, you will need a reliable 4x4, and whether you drive or use public transport, you are strongly advised to check out the current security situation and road conditions with the UWA headquarters or another reliable source in Kampala. The most frequently used route is via Mbale and Moroto, the latter the regional capital of the northeast. Two other routes can be used to reach Kidepo, one passing through Gulu and the other through Lira. The national park headquarters will be able to advise you should one of these be recommended over the standard Moroto route.

Few people appear to use the 224km road connecting Mbale directly to Moroto – though whether its unpopularity is because of poor road maintenance or because there's a greater risk of banditry closer to the Kenyan border, I cannot say. The more commonly used route, via Soroti, is about 50km longer, and should take six to seven hours to drive. On public transport, it takes two hours to get from Mbale to Soroti by bus or minibus. If you get to Soroti before noon, you can pick up a bus from there to Moroto the same day and be in Moroto before nightfall. Once in Moroto, the former government Moroto Hotel (PO Box 54, Moroto) has recently reopened. Rooms are reputedly rather basic for a hotel that charges around US$30 for an en-suite double, and running water cannot be guaranteed. There are several cheaper lodgings in town.

The distance between Moroto and Kidepo is roughly 250km, and the drive will take the best part of a day. Hitching from Moroto is recommended only to adventurous travellers with plenty of time on their hands – unless you are extraordinarily lucky, you can expect the trip to take a minimum of two days in each direction, and you could easily be stuck in the park for a week. In the park itself, there's little food available, so you will need to carry sufficient provisions.

The first goal for hitchers is Kotido, a village lying roughly 95km north of Moroto. There's no organised transport to Kotido but, if you ask around at the bus station in Moroto, there will be something heading up most days. The optimistically named Paradise Lodge in Kotido has basic singles for US$1.50. The next goal is Kaabong, another 95km north of Kotido. You shouldn't have too much difficulty finding a lift up here, and once you arrive you can stay at the mission for US$10 per person per night. Beyond Kaabong, transport is very unpredictable, and your best chance is with one of the park vehicles that do this run once or twice a week. What you don't want to do is take a lift part of the way, for instance to Karenga about 20km before the park entrance gate, as there's nowhere to stay between Kaabong and the national park.

Another option, increasingly used by the lodge and UWA vehicles, is to travel around the western side of Lake Kyoga via the historically insecure areas of Gulu and Kitgum. You'd certainly need to take some informed advice before attempting this, not least because the route to the park is not signposted and it's easy to take a wrong turning in wild country

For security reasons, it was not possible to check or update the information in this box during the course of researching the fifth edition of this guide. I would be glad to hear from anybody who does head up this way for inclusion in the update newsletter. However, as stated on the previous page, a recent upsurge in trouble in Karamoja in late 2006 means that you should not consider travelling in this area without official clearance.

GETTING THERE AND AWAY The small proportion of tourists who visit Kidepo generally do a fly-in safari from Kampala, which can be arranged through most local tour operators. If arranging your own transport, a four–five-seater charter from **Kampala Aeroclub** (m *0772 712553*) costs US$550 return per person for a group of four (assuming that each person and their luggage weighs less than 100kg). A party of five, light in both body and baggage, would pay US$450 each. This price allows for one night's stopover cost for the plane and pilot. For longer stays, the scheduled flight provided by **Eagle Air** (✆ *0414 232185*) is cheaper. Planes fly from Entebbe to Kidepo on Friday and collect on Monday. Passengers each pay US$460 (four people), US$360 (six) and US$275 (ten). It is theoretically possible to drive or even hitch up to the park, but the going is relatively tough, and at present it cannot be recommended due to the risk of banditry (see box *The Drive to Kidepo* above). However, once there, travellers without private transport can easily organise guided walks, which offer a high chance of seeing more common species such as elephant, buffalo, zebra, waterbuck and hartebeest. UWA can also provide game drives on a park truck at a cost of US$1.60 per kilometre.

WHERE TO STAY
Upmarket
⌂ **Apoka Lodge** ✆ 0414 251182; m 0772 489497; f 0414 344653; e tusc@africaonline.co.ug; www.safariuganda.com. The brand-new 20-bed Apoka Lodge occupies a superb location overlooking the rolling plains of the Narus Valley towards the Napore-Nyungea mountains. The seasonal Narus River and wetlands attract game year round, notably elephant, buffalo, waterbuck and zebra. The main lodge building occupies a large timber deck beneath a thatched roof set into the side of a kopje. Part of this outcrop has been used to create a magnificent swimming pool with a natural rock floor and typically panoramic Kidepo views. Accommodation is provided in spacious s/c cottages inside which walls of stretched canvas and vast mesh windows combine to create a light and airy interior with a near 180° outlook over the plains. Hot water is supplied to each cottage from its own solar heater. These provide ample water to supply a high-pressure bathroom shower and a romantically sized bathtub just outside, set into the rock. *FB accommodation (inc drinks, game drives and walking safaris) US$360/620 sgl/dbl. East African residents pay US$225/390.*

Budget
⌂ **Apoka Rest Camp** Only 500m from the lodge, this UWA camp consists of several s/c dbl *bandas* with solar-powered lighting and hot showers. Shared flush toilets and hot showers are provided. Bottled water, sodas and beers are usually available, but food must be brought with you. Don't expect to rely on the nearby lodge for meals (as you might at Mweya Lodge in Queen Elizabeth National Park). Apoka Lodge flies what it needs up from Kampala for its pre-paid guests so is unable to cater for outside guests. The Rest Camp is great value and bookings can be made through the UWA headquarters in Kampala. *US$11/16 sgl/dbl.*

Camping
Ⅹ **Kakine Campsite** UWA provides 2 campsites in the Narus Valley a few kilometres from Apoka, these are provided with basic shower/latrine blocks and shelters. You may need to fill water jerrycans at Apoka before heading out to a campsite. *US$6 pp.*

464

Appendix I

LANGUAGE

Although 33 local languages are spoken in Uganda, the official language is English, spoken widely by most urban Ugandans, and certainly by anybody with more than a moderate education level and/or who works in the tourist industry. The standard of English spoken, and the proportion of the population who are familiar with it, has tangibly increased over the past decade, particularly amongst younger people. It is not uncommon to come across Ugandans from different parts of the country using English to communicate, and most English-speaking visitors to the country will have no problem getting around.

Of the indigenous languages, the most widely spoken is Luganda, which to some extent serves as a *lingua franca* for the uneducated. So, too, does Swahili (more correctly KiSwahili), a Bantu language that is no more indigenous to Uganda than is English. Swahili developed on the East African coast about 1,000 years ago and has since adopted several words from Arabic, Portuguese, Indian, German and English. It spread into the East African interior along the 19th-century slave caravan routes and is today now the uncontested *lingua franca* in Tanzania and Kenya, as well as being spoken widely in parts of Uganda, Malawi, Rwanda, Burundi, DRC, Zambia and Mozambique.

There is a certain stigma attached to the use of Swahili in Uganda, particularly among the educated. This is perhaps rooted partially in the perception that it is a peasant language, but most of all because it gathered negative associations during the Amin and Obote eras, when it was the language of the military. Basically, it would not be the done thing to try out Swahili as a first choice of language in Uganda. Nevertheless, and contrary to what people might tell you, my experience is that in rural areas where English is not understood, Swahili generally will be. On the whole, it strikes me as more pragmatic to fall back on this widely spoken regional tongue in such circumstances, than it would be to attempt to learn a smattering of each of the dozen or more languages that are indigenous to the various parts of Uganda that might be passed through in the course of a standard trip.

Numerous Swahili–English dictionaries have been published, as have various phrasebooks and grammars. The most useful dictionary is DV Perrot's *Concise Swahili and English Dictionary* (Hodder and Stoughton, 1965) as it has two sections – one translating each way – as well as a basic grammar. Peter Wilson's *Simplified Swahili* (Longman) is regarded as the best book for teaching yourself Swahili. Of the phrasebooks, Lonely Planet's is probably the best. If you want a Swahili book, buy it before you arrive in Uganda, as it will be difficult once there.

For short-stay visitors, all these books have practical limitations. Wading through a phrasebook to find the expression you want can take ages, while trying to piece together a sentence from a dictionary is virtually impossible. What follows is no substitute for a proper dictionary or phrasebook; it is not really an introduction to Swahili, but more an introduction to communicating with Swahili speakers.

SWAHILI

Pronunciation Vowel sounds are pronounced as follows:

a   like the a in *father*
e   like the e in *wet*
i   like the ee in *free*, but less drawn-out
o   somewhere between the o in *no* and the word *awe*
u   similar to the oo in *food*

The double vowel in words like *choo* or *saa* is pronounced like the single vowel, but drawn out. Consonants are in general pronounced as they are in English. *L* and *r* are often interchangeable, so that *Kalema* is just as often spelt or pronounced *Karema*. The same is true of *b* and *v*.

You will be better understood if you speak slowly and thus avoid the common English-speaking habit of clipping vowel sounds – listen to how Swahili-speakers pronounce their vowels. In most Swahili words there is a slight emphasis on the second-last syllable.

Basic grammar Swahili is a simple language insofar as most words are built from a root word using prefixes. To go into all of the prefixes here would probably confuse people new to Swahili – and it would certainly stretch my knowledge of the language. They are covered in depth in most Swahili grammars and dictionaries. The following are some of the most important:

Pronouns

ni	I/me		*wa*	they/them
u	you		*a*	he or she
tu	us			

Tenses

na	present		*li*	past
ta	future		*ku*	infinitive

Tenses (negative)

si	present		*siku*	past
sita	future		*haku*	negative infinitive

From a root word such as *taka* (want) you might build the following phrases:

Unataka soda	You want a soda
Tutataka soda	We will want a soda
Alitaka soda	He/she wanted a soda

In practice, *ni* and *tu* are often dropped from simple statements. It would be more normal to say *nataka soda* than *ninataka soda*.

In many situations there is no interrogative mode in Swahili; the difference between a question and a statement lies in the intonation.

Vocabulary

Greetings There are several common greetings in Swahili. Although allowances are made for tourists, it is rude to start talking to someone without first using one or other formal greeting.

The first greeting you will hear is *Jambo*. This is reserved for tourists, and a perfectly adequate greeting, but it is never used between Africans (the more correct *Hujambo*, to which the reply is *Sijambo*, is used in some areas).

The most widely used greeting is *Habari?*, which more-or-less means *What news?* The polite reply is *Mzuri* (good). *Habari* is rarely used on its own; you might well be asked *Habari ya safari?*, *Habari ako?* or *Habari gani?* (very loosely, *How is your journey?*, *How are you?* and *How are things?* respectively). *Mzuri* is the polite reply to any such enquiry.

It is respectful to address an old man as *Mzee*. *Bwana*, which means *Mister*, might be used as a polite form of address to a male who is equal or senior to you in age or rank, but who is not a *Mzee*. Older women can be addressed as *Mama*.

The following phrases will come in handy for small talk:

Where have you just come from?	*(U)natoka wapi?*
I have come from Kampala	*(Ni)natoka Kampala*
Where are you going?	*(U)nakwenda wapi?*
We are going to Mbale	*(Tu)nakwende Mbale*
What is your name?	*Jina lako nani?*
My name is Philip	*Jina langu ni Philip*
Do you speak English?	*Unasema KiEngereze?*
I speak a little Swahili	*Ninasema KiSwahili kidigo*
Sleep peacefully	*Lala salama*
Bye for now	*Kwaheri sasa*
Have a safe journey	*Safari njema*
Come again (welcome again)	*Karibu tena*
I don't understand	*Sielewi*
Say that again	*Sema tena*

Counting

1	*moja*	40	*arobaini*
2	*mbili*	50	*hamsini*
3	*tatu*	60	*sitini*
4	*nne*	70	*sabani*
5	*tano*	80	*themanini*
6	*sita*	90	*tisini*
7	*saba*	100	*mia (moja)*
8	*nane*	150	*mia moja hamsini*
9	*tisa*	155	*mia moja hamsini na tano*
10	*kumi*	200	*mia mbili*
11	*kumi na moja*	1,000	*elfu* or, more commonly
20	*ishirini*		in Uganda, *mia kumi*
30	*thelathini*		

Swahili time Most Ugandans use Western time, but you may come across Swahili time at some point. The Swahili clock starts at the equivalent of 06.00, so that *saa moja asubuhi* (hour one in the morning) is 07.00, *saa mbili jioni* (hour two in the evening) is 16.00, etc. To ask the time in Swahili, say *Saa ngape?*

Day-to-day queries The following covers such activities as shopping, finding a room, etc. It's worth remembering that most Swahili words for modern objects, or things for which there would not have been a pre-colonial word, are often similar to the English. Examples are *resiti* (receipt), *gari* (car), *polisi* (police), *posta* (post office) and – my favourite – *stesheni masta* (station master). In desperation, it's always worth trying the English word with an *ee* sound on the end.

Shopping The normal way of asking for something is *Iko?*, which roughly means *Is there?*, so if you want a cold drink you would ask *Iko soda baridi?*. The response will normally be *Iko* or

Kuna (there is) or *Hamna* or *Hakuna* (there isn't). Once you've established the shop has what you want, you might ask *Nataka koka mbili* (I want two Cokes). To check the price, ask *Shillingi ngape?* If your Swahili is limited, it is often simpler to ask for a brand name: *Omo* (washing powder) or *Blue Band* (margarine), for instance.

Accommodation The Swahili for guesthouse is *nyumba ya wageni*. In my experience *gesti* or *lodgings* works as well, if not better. If you are looking for something a bit more upmarket, bear in mind *hoteli* means restaurant. We found self-contained (*self-contendi*) to be a good keyword in communicating this need. To find out whether there is a vacant room, ask *Iko chumba?*

Getting around The following expressions are useful for getting around:

Where is there a guesthouse?	*Iko wapi gesti?*
Is there a bus to Moshi?	*Iko basi kwenda Moshi?*
When does the bus depart?	*Basi ondoka saa ngapi?*
When will the vehicle arrive?	*Gari tafika saa ngapi?*
How far is it?	*Bale gani?*
I want to pay now	*Ninataka kulipa sasa*

Foodstuffs

avocado	*parachichi*	onions	*vitungu*
bananas	*ndizi*	orange(s)	*(ma)chungwa*
(cooked)	*matoke/batoke*	pawpaw	*papai*
beef	*(nyama ya) ngombe*	pineapple	*nanasi*
bread (loaf)	*mkate*	potatoes	*viazi*
bread (slice)	*tosti*	rice	
coconuts	*nazi*	(cooked plain)	*wali*
coffee	*kahawa*	rice (cooked	
chicken	*kuku*	with spices)	*pilau*
egg(s)	*(ma)yai*	rice	
fish	*samaki*	(uncooked)	*mchele*
food	*chakula*	salt	*chumvi*
fruit(s)	*(ma)tunda*	sauce	*mchuzi/supu*
goat	*(nyama ya) mbuzi*	sugar	*sukari*
maize porridge	*ugali*	tea	*chai (ya*
mango(es)	*(ma)embe*	(black/milky)	*rangi/maziwa)*
meat	*nyama*	vegetables	*mboga*
milk	*maziwa*	water	*maji*

Days of the week

Monday	*Jumatatu*	Friday	*Ijumaa*
Tuesday	*Jumanne*	Saturday	*Jumamosi*
Wednesday	*Jumatano*	Sunday	*Jumapili*
Thursday	*Alhamisi*		

Other useful words and phrases

afternoon	*alasiri*	no	*hapana*
again	*tena*	no problem	*hakuna matata*
and	*na*	now	*sasa*
Ask (I am asking for...)	*Omba (ninaomba...)*	OK or fine	*sawa*
		only	*tu*
big	*kubwa*	passenger	*abiria*
boat	*meli*	pay	*kulipa*

brother	*kaka*	person (people)	*mtu (watu)*
bus	*basi*	please	*tafadhali*
car (or any vehicle)	*gari*	road/street	*barabara/mtaa*
child (children)	*mtoto (watoto)*	shop	*duka*
cold	*baridi*	sister	*dada*
come here	*njoo*	sleep	*kulala*
excuse me	*samahani*	slowly	*polepole*
European	*smzungu (wazungu)*	small	*kidogo*
evening	*jioni*	soon	*bado kidogo*
far away	*mbali sana*	sorry	*polepole*
friend	*rafiki*	station	*stesheni*
good	*mzuri*	stop	*simama*
(very good)	*(mzuri sana)*	straight or direct	*moja kwa moja*
goodbye	*kwaheri*	thank you	
here	*hapa*	(very much)	*asante (sana)*
hot	*moto*	there is	*iko/kuna*
later	*bado*	there is not	*hamna/hakuna*
like	*penda*	thief (thieves)	*mwizi (wawizi)*
(I would like...)	*(ninapenda...)*	time	*saa*
many	*sana*	today	*leo*
me	*mimi*	toilet	*choo*
money	*pesa/shillingi*	tomorrow	*kesho*
more	*ingine/tena*	want	*taka*
morning	*asubuhi*	(I want...)	*(ninataka...)*
nearby	*karibumbali*	where	*(iko) wapi*
	kidogo	yes	*ndiyo*
night	*usiku*	yesterday	*jana*
		you	*wewe*

Useful conjunctions include *ya* (of) and *kwa* (to or by). Many expressions are created using these; for instance *stesheni ya basi* is a bus station and *barabara kwa Mbale* is the road to Mbale.

LUGANDA Luganda is the first language of Buganda and most widely spoken of the languages indigenous to Uganda. Pronunciation is very similar to Swahili. Some words and phrases follow. A detailed phrasebook and dictionary can be viewed online at www.buganda.com.

Greetings

Hello (informal)	*Ki kati*
How are you?	*Oli otya?*
I am OK	*Gyendi*
Have a nice day	*Siba bulungi*
Goodnight	*Sula bulungi*
Farewell	*Weraba*
See you later	*Tunalabagana*
Please	*Mwattu*
Thank you (very much)	*Webale (Nyo)*
Excuse me	*Owange*
Sorry	*Nsonyiwa*
Sir	*Ssebo*
Come here	*Jangu wano*
Madam	*Nnyabo*
Mr	*Mwami*
Mrs	*Mukyala*

Useful phrases

Where are you from?	*Ova mukitundu ki?*
I am from England	*Nva mu England*
Where have you come from?	*Ovude wa?*
I have come from Kampala	*Nvude Kampala*
Where are you going?	*Ogenda wa?*
I am going to Mbale	*Ngenda Mbale*
How can I get to Mbale?	*Ngenda ntya okutuka e Mbale?*
Does this bus go to Kampala?	*Eno baasi egenda e Kampala?*
Which bus goes to Kampala?	*Baasi ki egenda e Kampala?*
What time does the bus leave?	*Baasi egenda sawa meka?*
Where can I buy a bus ticket?	*Tikiti ya baasi nyinza kugigula wa?*
What time does the bus arrive?	*Baasi etuka ku sawa meka?*
Where is the road to Kampala?	*Olugudo lwe Kampala luliwa?*
Where is this taxi going?	*Eno taxi eraga wa?*
Where is it?	*Kiriwa?*
How far is it?	*Kiri wala wa?*
Is it far?	*Kiri wala?*
Is it near?	*Kiri kumpi?*
How much does it cost?	*Sente meka?*
Do you speak English?	*Oyogera oluzungu?*
Do you have any…?	*Olinayo ko…?*
I would like…	*Njagalayo….*
I want a room	*Njagala kisenge*
There is	*Waliwo*
There is not	*Tewali*
What is this called?	*Kino kiyitibwa kitya?*
What is your name?	*Amanya go gw'ani?*
My name is Philip	*Nze Philip*

Words

big	*kinene*	OK	*ye*
come (here)	*jangu (wano)*	please	*bambi*
good	*kirungi*	possible	*kisoboka*
here	*wano*	slow down	*genda mpola*
hurry up	*yanguwa*	small	*katono*
later	*edda*	today	*lero*
many	*bingi*	toilet	*toileti*
me	*nze*	tomorrow	*enkya*
morning	*kumakya*	water	*mazi*
no	*neda*	yes	*ye*
not possible	*tekisoboka*	yesterday	*jjo*
now	*kati*	you	*gwe*

Foodstuffs

avocado	*kedo*	melon	*wuju*
banana (green)	*matooke*	onion	*katungulu*
banana (sweet)	*menvu*	orange	*mucungwa*
beans	*bijanjalo*	pawpaw	*paapaali*
beef	*nte*	peanuts	*binyebwa*
cabbage	*mboga*	pepper	*kaamulali*
carrot	*kalati*	pineapple	*naanansi*
cassava	*muwogo*	pork	*mbizi*

chicken	*nkoko*	potato	*lumonde*
corn	*kasooli*	rice	*muceere*
fish	*kyenyanja*	salt	*munnyo*
garlic	*katungulu Ccumu*	sugar	*sukali*
goat meat	*mbuzi*	sugar cane	*kikajo*
lamb/mutton	*ndiga*	sweet potato	*lumonde*
mango	*muyembe*	tomato	*nyanya*
meat	*nyama*		

AFRICAN ENGLISH Although a high proportion of Ugandans do speak English as a second language, not all get the opportunity to use it regularly, and as a result they will not be as fluent as they could be. Furthermore, as is often the case in Africa and elsewhere, an individual's pronunciation of a second language often tends to retain the vocal inflections of their first language, or it falls somewhere between that and a more standard pronunciation. It is also the case that many people tend to structure sentences in a second language similar to how they would in their home tongue. As a result, most Ugandans, to a greater or lesser extent, speak English with Bantu inflections and grammar.

The above considerations aside, I would venture that African English – like American or Australian English – is over-due recognition as a distinct linguistic entity, possessed of a unique rhythm and pronunciation, as well as an idiomatic quality quite distinct from any form of English spoken elsewhere. And learning to communicate in this idiom is perhaps the most important linguistic skill that the visitor to Uganda (or any other Anglophone country in Africa) can acquire. If this sounds patronising, so be it. There are regional accents in the UK and US that I find far more difficult to follow than the English spoken in Africa, simply because I am more familiar with the latter. And precisely the same adjustment might be required were, for instance, an Australian to travel in the American south, a Geordie to wash up in my home town of Johannesburg, or vice versa.

The following points should prove useful when you speak English to Africans:

- Greet simply, using phrases likely to be understood locally: the ubiquitous sing-song 'How-are-you! – I am fine', or if that draws a blank try the pidgin Swahili *Jambo!* It is important always to greet a stranger before you plough ahead and ask directions or any other question. Firstly, it is rude to do otherwise; secondly, most Westerners feel uncomfortable asking a stranger a straight question. If you have already greeted the person, you'll feel less need to preface a question with phrases like 'I'm terribly sorry' or 'Would you mind telling me' which will confuse someone who speaks limited English.
- Speak slowly and clearly. There is no need, as some travellers do, to take this too far, as if you are talking to a three year old. Speak naturally, but try not to rush or clip phrases.
- Phrase questions simply, with an ear towards Bantu inflections. 'This bus goes to Mbale?' might be more easily understood than 'Could you tell me whether this bus is going to Mbale?' and 'You have a room?' is better than 'Is there a vacant room?'. If you are not understood, don't keep repeating the same question more loudly. Try a different and ideally simpler phrasing, giving consideration to whether any specific word(s) – in the last case, most likely 'vacant' – might particularly obstruct easy understanding.
- Listen to how people talk to you, and learn from it. Vowel sounds are often pronounced as in the local language (see Swahili pronunciation above), so that 'bin', for instance, might sound more like 'been'. Many words, too, will be pronounced with the customary Bantu stress on the second-last syllable.
- African languages generally contain few words with compound consonant sounds or ending in consonants. This can result in the clipping of soft consonant sounds such as 'r' (important as eem-POT-ant) or the insertion of a random vowel sound between running consonants (so that pen-pal becomes pen-I-pal and sounds almost indistinguishable from pineapple). It is commonplace, as well, to append a random

vowel to the end of a word, in the process shifting the stress to what would ordinarily be the last syllable e.g. pen-i-PAL-i.

- The 'l' and 'r' sounds are sometimes used interchangeably, less often in Uganda perhaps than in Tanzania or Malawi, but it does happen – Rubaga Hill in Kampala, for instance, is sometimes spelt Lubaga. This transference can cause considerable confusion, in particular when your guide points out a lilac-breasted roller! The same is to a lesser extent true of 'b' and 'v' (Virunga versus Birunga), 'k' and 'ch' (the Rwandan capital, spelt Kigali, is more often pronounced 'Chigari') and, very occasionally, 'f' and 'p'.

- Some English words are in wide use. Other similar words are not. Some examples: a request for a 'lodging' or 'guesthouse', is more likely to be understood than one for 'accommodation', as is a request for a 'taxi' (or better 'special hire') over a 'taxi-cab' or 'cab', or for 'the balance' rather than 'change'.

- Avoid the use of dialect-specific expressions, slang and jargon! Few Africans will be familiar with terms such as 'feeling crook', 'pear-shaped' or 'user-friendly'.

- Avoid meaningless interjections. If somebody is struggling to follow you, appending a word such as 'mate' to every other phrase is only likely to further confuse them.

- We've all embarrassed ourselves at some point by mutilating the pronunciation of a word we've read but not heard. Likewise, guides working in national parks and other reserves often come up with innovative pronunciations for bird and mammal names they come across in field guides, and any word with an idiosyncratic spelling (eg: yacht, lamb, knot).

- Make sure the person you are talking to understands you. Try to avoid asking questions that can be answered with a yes or no. People may well agree with you simply to be polite or to avoid embarrassment.

- Keep calm. No-one is at their best when they arrive at a crowded bus station after an all-day bus ride. It is easy to be short tempered when someone cannot understand you. Be patient and polite; it's you who doesn't speak the language.

- It can be useful to know that the Ugandan phrase for urinating is 'short call'. Useful, because often you will be caught short somewhere with no toilet, and if you ask for a toilet will simply be told there is none. By contrast, if you tell somebody you need a 'short call', you'll be pointed to wherever locals take theirs!

- Last but not least, do gauge the extent to which the above rules might apply to any given individual. It would be patently ridiculous to address a university lecturer or an experienced tour guide in broken English, equally inappropriate to babble away without making any allowances when talking to a villager who clearly has a limited English vocabulary. Generally, I start off talking normally to anybody I meet, and only start to refine my usage as and when it becomes clear it will aid communication.

Appendix 2

GLOSSARY

acacia woodland	any woodland dominated by thorn trees of the acacia family
Albertine Rift	western Rift Valley between Lake Albert and northern Lake Tanganyika
Amin, Idi	dictatorial President of Uganda 1971–79
Ankole	extant medieval kingdom centred on modern-day Mbarara
askari	security guard
Bacwezi	legendary medieval kingdom, centred on present-day Mubende
Baker, Lady Florence	wife and travel companion to Sir Samuel
Baker, Sir Samuel	first European to Lake Albert, Murchison Falls 1864, Governor of Equatoria 1872–73
balance	change (for a payment)
banda	any detached accommodation such as a hut or chalet
barkcloth	traditional material made from bark of fig tree
Batembuzi	legendary medieval kingdom, possibly centred on present-day Ntusi
Bell, Sir Henry Hesketh	Commissioner to Uganda 1905–09 after whom Port Bell (and thus Bell Beer) is named
boda-boda	bicycle or motorcycle taxi
boma	colonial administrative office
Buganda	extant kingdom for which Uganda is named, centred on modern-day Kampala
Bunyoro	extant kingdom centred on modern-day Hoima
Bwana	Mister (polite Swahili terms of address, sometimes used in Uganda)
chai	tea
Colville, Colonel	led attack on Mparo that drove Kabalega into hiding, 1894
cowrie	small white shell used as currency in pre-colonial times
Daudi Chwa, Kabaka	crowned King of Buganda at age one in 1897, ruled until death in 1939
DSTV	South African multi-channel satellite television service
duka	stall or kiosk
endemic	unique to a specific area
exotic	not indigenous, for instance pine plantations
forest	wooded area with closed canopy
forex bureau	bureau de change
fundi	expert (especially mechanic)
Grant, Captain James	accompanied Speke on journey to Source of the Nile, 1862
guesthouse	cheap local hotel
Hannington, Bishop James	Missionary killed on Mwanga's instructions *en route* to Buganda in 1885

hoteli	local restaurant
indigenous	occurring in a place naturally
Interlacustrine Region	area between Lake Victoria and Albertine Rift Lakes: Rwanda, Burundi, south Uganda, northwest Tanzania
Isuza	legendary Batembuzi ruler
Kabaka	King of Buganda
Kabalega, Omakuma	King of Bunyoro from 1870, exiled to Seychelles by British 1897, died there 1923
Kaggwa, Sir Apollo	Katikiro of Buganda 1889–1926, and copious chronicler of Kiganda folklore and history
Kakunguru, Semei	Muganda leader who conquered east Uganda for the British in the 1890s, founded Kumi and Mbale
Kamurasi, Omakuma	powerful Bunyoro King, ruled c1852–69, met by Speke and Baker
Katikiro	'Prime minister' of Buganda
Kiganda	relating to the culture or religions of Buganda
Kiira	Luganda name for Victoria Nile
Kintu	legendary founder of Buganda
Kony, Joseph	leader of LRA
koppie	small, often rocky hill (from Afrikaans meaning 'little head')
Kyebambe III, Omakuma	King of Bunyoro c1786–1835
LRA	Lord's Resistance Army
Lubaale (plural Balubaale)	important Kiganda spirit
Luganda	language of Buganda
Lugard, Captain Frederick	Representative of the Imperial British East Africa Company who signed a provisional treaty with Mwanga in 1890
mandazi	fried doughnut-like pastry
matatu	see *minibus-taxi*
matoke	staple made from cooking plantains (bananas)
mbugo	barkcloth (traditional dress of Buganda)
minibus-taxi	minibus used as shared taxi typically carrying ten–13 passengers
mishkaki	meat (usually beef) kebab
mobile	mobile satellite phone
MTN	main satellite phone provider in Uganda
Muganda (plural Baganda)	citizen of Buganda kingdom
Museveni, Yoweri	President of Uganda 1986–present
Mutesa I, Kabaka	King of Buganda 1857–84, hosted Speke 1862
Mutesa II, Edward Kabaka	King of Buganda 1939–66, President of Uganda 1962–66, died in exile 1969
muzungu	white person
Mwanga, Kabaka	King of Buganda 1884–93, exiled to Seychelles 1897, died there 1903
Namasole	'Queen mother' or more accurately mother of the Kabaka of Buganda
Ndahura	legendary founder of Bacwezi dynasty, son of Isuza
netting	mosquito net
NRM	National Resistance Movement (governing part of Uganda)
Nyerere, Julius	President of Tanzania who initiated war that ousted Amin in 1979
Obote, Milton	dictatorial President of Uganda, 1962–71 and 1981–85
Okello, Tito	military President of Uganda, July 1985–January 1986
Omakuma	King of Bunyoro/Toro

Omugabe	King of Ankole
Owen, Roderick	companion of Portal in 1893 for whom Owen Falls at Source of the Nile is named
panga	local equivalent of a machete
Pasha, Emin	Governor of Equatoria 1878 until 'rescued' by Stanley 1889
pesa	money
pombe	local beer
Portal, Sir Gerald	Governor of Zanzibar, visited Uganda 1893, Fort Portal named in his honour
QENP	Queen Elizabeth National Park (often called QE or QENP)
riparian/riverine woodland	strip of forest or lush woodland following a watercourse, often rich in fig trees
Ruhanga	legendary king of underworld and founder of Batembuzi dynasty
Runyoro	language of Bunyoro
safari	Swahili word for journey, now widely used to refer to game-viewing trip
savanna	grassland with some trees
Saza chief	ruler of a County (Saza) of Buganda, answerable to the kabaka
self-contained (s/c) en suite	room with private toilet and shower attached
shamba	small subsistence farm
short call	urinate
soda	fizzy drink such as Fanta or Coca-Cola
special hire	taxi
Speke, John Hanning	first European to visit Buganda, Bunyoro and Source of the Nile, 1862
Ssemogorere, Paul	one-time prime minister under Museveni, stood in 1996 presidential election.
Stanley, Henry Morton	explorer to Uganda in 1875–76 and 1889, discovering Rwenzoris on latter trip
surfaced (road)	road sealed with asphalt or similar
tented camp	rustic but generally upmarket small camp offering canvassed accommodation
Thomson, Joseph	in 1883, became the first European to enter present-day Uganda from the east
Toro	extant 19th-century kingdom centred on modern-day Fort Portal
tot packet	sachet of whisky or *waragi*
track	motorable minor road or path
trading centre	small town or village where local villagers would go to shop
ugali	staple porridge made from maize (corn) meal
UPDF	Uganda Peoples Defence Force
UWA	Uganda Wildlife Authority
Wamala	legendary Bacwezi ruler, son of Ndahura
Waragi	local brand of gin
wazungu	plural of Mazungu
woodland	wooded area lacking closed canopy

Appendix 3

FURTHER INFORMATION

BOOKS
History and background

Apuuli, K *A Thousand Years of Bunyoro-Kitara* Fountain, 1994. Inexpensive and compact locally published book that ranks close to being essential reading on pre-colonial events, despite being riddled with internal contradictions.

Behrend, Heike *Alice Lakwena & The Holy Spirits* James Currey, 1999. The bizarre and disturbing story of the emergence of the spirit medium in northern Uganda in 1986 which laid the foundation for the present-day Lord's Resistance Army and its brutal leader Joseph Kony. By no means easy reading, but worth the effort!

Bierman, J *Dark Safari* Albert Knopf, 1990. As the name suggests, a no-holds-barred biography of Henry Morton Stanley, who twice travelled through what would later become Uganda in the late 19th century. Its repugnant central figure might have been designed to give Victorian explorers a bad name – mercenary, avaricious, callous, unsympathetic to local customs, and utterly fascinating.

Blixen, Karen *Out of Africa* Penguin, 1937. Though based in Kenya, this famous autobiography offers fascinating glimpses into the colonial era, and just about everybody who sets foot in East Africa ends up reading it.

Carruthers, John *Mrs Carruthers is Black*, 2004. An autobiographical account by a Scottish insurance chairman of his marriage to a Ugandan during the days when mixed unions were more of an eyebrow raiser than they are today. The book covers some lively years prior to the family's flight from Uganda during the Amin regime and their return to live in Kampala some 20 years later. It's an entertaining read liberally seasoned with salacious tales in which names have been changed to protect the guilty. Available from Aristoc bookshop in Kampala.

Hall, Richard *Empires of the Monsoon: A History of the Indian Ocean and its Invaders* Harper Collins, 1996. Highly focused and reasonably concise book conveying a strong international perspective on the last 1,000 years of east and southern African to the general reader, with a good storytelling touch. Highly recommended, though centred on Kenya and Tanzania more than Uganda.

Herne, Brian *African Safaris* Winchester Press, 1979. Chatty, anecdotal and sometimes revealing accounts of hunting and other safaris in Uganda before the Amin coup.

Hibbert, C *Africa Explored: Europeans in the Dark Continent* Penguin, 1982. Useful overview of the careers of most major Victorian explorers. Readable and entertaining, the recommended starting point on this fascinating period.

Karugire, S *A Political History of Uganda* Heinemann, 1980. The most concise introduction to Ugandan history on the market, highly readable, with a useful chapter covering pre-colonial events and razor-sharp commentary on the colonial period.

Leggett, Ian *Uganda: An Oxfam Country Profile* Oxfam, 2001. Solid, up-to-date and not overwhelmingly academic overview of Uganda today, with special reference to social and economic issues such as HIV/AIDS.

Maxon, Robert *East Africa: An Introductory History* Heinemann, 1989. Probably the most reliable short one-volume general history covering East Africa, a useful if somewhat dry reference work.

Miller Charles *The Lunatic Express* 1971: reprinted Penguin Classics 2001. Eminently readable account of the Uganda Railway, most notably a history of the events in Uganda that brought about the project.

Moorehead, Alan *The White Nile* Hamilton, 1960. Classic example of the history-as-adventure-yarn genre, detailing the race to discover the Source of the Nile and its leading characters. A more recently published illustrated edition has plenty of good paintings and photos, too.

Mugaju, J B *Uganda's Decade of Reforms* Fountain, 1996. Rather superficial and partisan book about Uganda under Museveni, who contributes a moving introduction.

Museveni, Yoweri *Sowing the Mustard Seed* Macmillan, 1997. The acclaimed autobiography of Uganda's charismatic president, mostly devoted to his wilderness years fighting the Amin and Obote regimes, but with good coverage of post-1986 reconstruction. Inevitable bias notwithstanding, a frank, entertaining and insightful read.

Mutibwa, Phares *Uganda Since Independence* Fountain, 1992. Subtitled 'a story of unfulfilled hopes', no better overview exists on post-colonial Ugandan politics prior to the 1990s.

Nzita, Richard *Peoples and Cultures of Uganda* Fountain, 1993, third edition 1997. Useful introduction to the various ethnic groupings of Uganda, and the monochrome photos make for an interesting browse.

Oliver, R, and Fage, J D *A Short History of Africa* Penguin, 1988, sixth edition. Standard introduction to African history, though too compact to be satisfying on any specific region or period.

Osmaston Henry, *Guide to the Rwenzori: Mountains of the Moon* The Rwenzori Trust, 2006. This beautifully compact pocket-sized book represents the eagerly awaited revision of the long-out-of-print 1971 Osmaston and Pasteur *Rwenzori guide*, published to coincide with the 2006 celebrations of the mountain's first ascent by the Italian Duke of Abruzzi. It contains pretty much everything the aspiring Rwenzori visitor needs to know. It is also a fitting memorial to Henry Osmaston (84), the long-time sage of the Rwenzori, who died only a week after completing the exhausting task of overhauling his work of 35 years ago. It's distributed in the UK by West Col Productions (✆ *01491 681284*) and in Uganda by Geolodges (✆ *0414 258273*).

Packenham, Thomas *The Scramble for Africa* Weidenfeld and Nicolson, 1991. Gripping and erudite 600-page account of the decade that turned Africa on its head – a 'must read', aptly described by one reviewer as '*Heart of Darkness* with the lights switched on'.

Reader, John *Africa: A Biography of the Continent* Penguin, 1997. Bulky, and working the broadest canvas, this excellent introduction to Africa past and present has met with universal praise as perhaps the most readable and accurate book to capture the sweep of African history for the general reader.

Reid, Richard *Political Power in Pre-colonial Buganda* James Currey, 2002. Accessible and clearly written introduction to the kingdom that lies at the heart of Uganda.

Roberts, Andrew *Uganda's Great Rift Valley* New Vision, 2006. A concise but wide-ranging exploration of the Albertine Rift Valley including geology, human history and chapters on Queen Elizabeth and Semliki national parks. This volume is to be complemented by a guide/history of the Rwenzori in 2007.

Seftel, Adam *The Rise and Fall of Idi Amin* Bailey's African Photo Archives, 1993. This is a compelling as-it-happened document of Ugandan politics from 1955 to 1986 focusing mainly on events between the joyous coup that brought Amin to power in 1971 and the Tanzanian invasion that forced him into exile eight years later. Essentially a series of articles reprinted from the archives of the seminal *Drum Magazine*, the book peaks with a chapter entitled *The Truth About Amin* brilliantly capturing the uneasy realisation circa late 1972 that Uganda's new president was anything but the grinning saviour he had seemed initially. Superb and in some cases deeply moving (even gruesome) monochrome photographs, and chuckle-inducing reprints of original covers on which pouting dolly birds do their utmost to undermine the more serious content of 'Africa's Leading Magazine' – a wonderful period package!

Speke, John *Journal of the Discovery of the Source of the Nile*, 1863, reprinted Dover Press, 1996. The mirror image of the murderous Stanley, John Hanning Speke comes across as the most courteous and respectful of travellers, of his time for sure, and occasionally rather petty, yet with a wonderful ability to capture without judgement the flavour of local cultures he encountered, nowhere more so than in the series of chapters about the Buganda court under Mutesa contained in this unique document. An enjoyable, instructive and occasionally mind-boggling read!

Sutton, John *A Thousand Years of East Africa* BIEA, 1990. Notable in this context primarily for an excellent chapter on the Bigo and other earthworks in southwest Uganda.

Twaddle, Michael *Kakungulu and the Creation of Uganda* James Currey, 1993. Excellent and readable biography of the enigmatic and controversial Semei Kakunguru, a Muganda who started his career as a British expansionist and ended it as the founder of a bizarre Judaic sect that still thrives in the Mbale area to this day. Essential stuff!

Nature and wildlife If you have difficulty finding African natural history books at your local bookshop and you're not flying directly to South Africa (where you can pick them up easily) get hold of the Natural History Book Service (*2 Wills Rd, Totnes, Devon TQ9 SXN;* ✆ *01803 865913*), or Russel Friedman Books in South Africa; (✆ *011 702 2300/1;* ✆ *011 702 1403*).

Mammals

Dorst, J and Dandelot, P *Field Guide to the Larger Mammals of Africa* Collins, 1983. Once the standard mammal field guide to Africa, this has been rendered close to obsolete by several newer and better books listed here.

Erickson Wilson, Sandra *Bird and Mammal Checklists for Ten National Parks in Uganda* European Commission, 1995. Increasingly difficult-to-locate 88-page booklet containing a complete checklist of all mammals and birds known in Uganda, and in which national parks, if any, each species has been recorded.

Estes, Richard *The Safari Companion* Green Books UK, Chelsea Green USA, Russell Friedman Books South Africa, 1992. Not a field guide in the conventional sense so much as a guide to mammalian behaviour, this superb book is very well organised and highly informative, but rather bulky perhaps for casual safari-goers.

Fossey, Dian *Gorillas in the Mist* Hodder and Stoughton, 1983. Twenty years after its original publication, this seminal work remains the best introduction to gorilla behaviour in print. Read it!

Goodall, Jane *In the Shadow of Man* Collins, 1971. Classic on chimp behaviour based on Goodall's acclaimed research in Tanzania's Gombe Stream National Park.

Haltennorth, T *Field Guide to the Mammals of Africa (including Madagascar)* Collins, 1980. See comments for Dorst and Dandelot.

Kingdon, Jonathan *Field Guide to African Mammals* Academic Press, 1997. The definitive field guide of its type, with immense detail on all large mammals, as well as a gold mine of information about the evolutionary relationships of modern species, and good coverage of bats, rodents and other small mammals. Excellent illustrations, too. Arguably too pricey and heavy for casual safari-goers, but an essential – and in my case much-thumbed – reference for anybody with a strong interest in Africa's mammals.

Schaller, George *The Year Of the Gorilla* Chicago University Press, 1963. Subsequently overshadowed, at least in popular perception, by *Gorillas in the Mist*, this formative behavioural study of gorillas in the Virungas did much to dispel their violent image on publication in 1963, and it remains a genuine classic (with the somewhat parochial advantage over later gorilla books in that most of the action takes place in Uganda rather than Rwanda).

Stuart, Chris and Tilde *Field Guide to the Larger Mammals of Africa* Struik Publishers, 1997. Solid and well-organised field guide covering large mammals only, better suited than Kingdon's to space- and/or price-conscious travellers who are nevertheless serious about putting a name to any large mammals they encounter.

Stuart, Chris and Tilde *Southern, Eastern and Central African Mammals: A Photographic Guide* Struik Publishers, 1993. Commendably lightweight and inexpensive pocket book that manages to squeeze in detailed accounts and pictures of 152 mammal species – ideal for backpackers!

Stuart, Chris and Tilde *Africa's Vanishing Wildlife* Southern Book Publishers, 1996. Outstanding coffee-table book covering rare African species, highly recommended for reading in advance of a trip or as a souvenir.

Weber, Bill and Veder, Amy *In The Kingdom of Gorillas* Aurum Press, 2002. Written by the Americans who initiated gorilla tourism in Rwanda, this excellent new book includes detailed information about all aspects of the mountain gorillas of the Virungas. There's also good coverage of the monkeys of Nyungwe Forest, and an admirably unsentimental account of working alongside the notoriously strong-willed Dian Fossey. In 2003, *BBC Wildlife* listed it – along with the Goodall, Fossey and Schaller titles mentioned above – as one of 40 classic wildlife books of the past 40 years.

Birds

Russouw, Jonathan and Sacchi, Marco *Where to Watch Birds in Uganda* Uganda Tourist Board, 1998. No birdwatcher should think about travelling in Uganda without this compact, sensibly priced and engagingly written book, which can be bought from the UTB tourist information office in Kampala if nowhere else. It contains detailed descriptions and advice for all key birding sites in Uganda, with special reference to local rarities and specials, as well as an up-to-date national checklist referencing all the bird species recorded at each of 15 locations in Uganda. The ideal companion to a good field guide.

Stevenson, Terry and Fanshawe, John *Field Guide to the Birds of East Africa* T & A D Poyser, 2002. The best bird field guide, with useful field descriptions and accurate plates and distribution maps covering every species recorded in Uganda as well as Kenya, Tanzania, Rwanda and Burundi. No other book will suffice for serious birdwatchers, but it is much bulkier and pricier than Van Perlo's competing title.

Van Perlo, Ber *Illustrated Checklist to the Birds of Eastern Africa* Collins, 1995. Useful, relatively inexpensive and admirably compact identification manual describing and illustrating all 1,488 bird species recorded in Eritrea, Ethiopia, Kenya, Uganda and Tanzania. Unfortunately, however, the distribution maps and colour plates are often misleading, and the descriptions too terse, to allow for identification of more difficult genera.

Williams, John *Field Guide to the Birds of East Africa* Collins, 1971. Pioneering but obsolete field guide lacking plates for half the species found in Uganda and omitting a few hundred from the text. Still referred to in many travel guides and brochures, a sure sign that whoever compiled the information is desperately out of touch when it comes to East African birdwatching.

Zimmerman, Turner, Pearson, Willet and Pratt *Birds of Kenya and Northern Tanzania* Russell Friedman Books, 1996. A contender for the best single-volume field guide available to any African country or region, but lacking coverage for the 150 or so Ugandan species not recorded in Kenya. The exemplary text is, however, far more thorough than its counterpart in any field guide covering Uganda, and the plates are brilliant. Highly recommended to any serious birder as a supplement to Stevenson and Fanshawe.

Butterflies

Carter, Nanny and Tindimubona, Laura *Butterflies of Uganda* Uganda Society, 2002. Very useful albeit non-comprehensive field guide illustrating and describing roughly 200 of the more common butterfly species in Uganda.

Health Self-prescribing has its hazards so if you are going anywhere very remote consider taking a health book. For adults there is *Bugs, Bites & Bowels* by Dr Jane Wilson-Howarth, published by Cadogan 2006; if travelling with the family look at *Your Child: A Travel Health Guide* by Dr Jane Wilson-Howarth and Dr Matthew Ellis, published by Bradt Travel Guides (2005).

Coffee-table books

Guadalupi, Gianni *Discovery of the Source of the Nile* Stewart, Tabori and Chang, 1997. This hefty volume contains superb and lavish illustrated spreads of maps and coloured engravings from the age of exploration. The text (translated from the Italian) is notable primarily for the inclusion of explorers usually omitted from the standard Anglophonic accounts of the search for the Nile's origins.

Joynson-Hicks, Paul *Uganda: The Pearl of Africa* Quiller Press, 1994. The best general coffee-table book to Uganda, not perhaps quite up to the standard of the same photographer's subsequent Tanzania title, but the overall standard of photography is high and complemented by lively anecdotal text reflecting a clear passion for the country.

Michel, Kiguli, Pluth and Didek *Eye of the Storm: A Photographer's Journey Across Uganda* Camerapix, 2002. Sumptuous new book, which boldly contrasts evocative scenic and wildlife photography with more gritty urban and rural images reflecting the realities of day-to-day life in Uganda.

Pluth, David *Uganda Rwenzori: A Range of Images* Little Wolf, 1996. Absorbing photographic and verbal portrait of the legendary Mountains of the Moon, with contemporary photographs supplemented by old monochromes taken by the first Italian expedition to conquer it almost 100 years ago. An excellent post-trek souvenir.

MAPS The 1:800,000 map of Uganda recently published by International Travel Maps (ITMB) of Vancouver is the smallest-scale map available for the whole country, and more accurate than most, with one major error being a displacement of latitudinal lines causing the Equator, for instance, to be marked as 1°N etc. Also recommended, and easier to locate within Uganda, is Nelles's 1:700,000 map of Uganda, which we used on this latest trip and found to be mostly very accurate. The 1:1,350,000 *Uganda Traveller's Map* published by Macmillan is inferior to both, and contains several errors, most obviously the displacement of the Sempaya Hot Springs and Ntandi Pygmies in the Semliki Valley, but it does have good maps of Kampala and Queen Elizabeth and Murchison Falls national parks on the back. Most of the other maps I've come across lazily regurgitate antiquated sources from the 1960/70s – any map that depicts Grand Lodge on the site of the defunct Pakuba Lodge in Murchison Falls, or shows a mysterious Kenyege Lodge on the road connecting Masindi to Butiaba via Budongo Forest, should be regarded as highly suspect!

TRAVEL MAGAZINES For readers with a broad interest in Africa, an excellent magazine dedicated to tourism throughout Africa is *Travel Africa*, which can be visited online at www.travelafricamag.com. Recommended for their broad-ranging editorial content and the coffee-table-standard photography and reproduction, the award-winning magazines *Africa Geographic* (formerly *Africa Environment and Wildlife*) and *Africa Birds and Birding* can be checked out at the website www.africa-geographic.co.za. Another South African magazine devoted to African travel is *Getaway*, though this tends to devote the bulk of its coverage to southern Africa.

FICTION Surprisingly few novels have been written by Ugandans or about Uganda. Two notable exceptions are *The Abyssinian Chronicles* (Picador) by Moses Isegawa and *The Invisible Weevil* (FemRite, 1999) by Mary Karooro Okorot, a Ugandan MP. Both describe developments in Uganda since independence, as witnessed by local protagonists. As well as being a good read, the latter book provides an insight into the many problems (notably Ugandan men) that Ugandan women must endure. FemRite is an organisation that encourages Ugandan female writers. Its catalogue also includes a good anthology, *Gifts of*

Harvest. All these titles are available in Kampala's excellent Aristoc bookshop. More widely available is the Whitbread Prize-winning novel, *The Last King of Scotland* by Giles Foden (Faber & Faber, 1998), a fictional account of a young Scots doctor working in the service of Idi Amin. Also recommended is Paul Theroux's *Fong and the Indians*, set in post-colonial, pre-Amin Kampala, originally published in 1968 and reprinted in the three-book Penguin compedium *On The Edge of the Rift Valley* in 1996. Set in the Belgian Congo rather than Uganda, but still one if the most astonishing and insightful novels I've read about Africa in some time is Barbara Kingsolver's *The Poisonwood Bible* (HarperCollins, 2000).

UGANDA ONLINE The internet is an increasingly valuable tool when it comes to researching most aspects of a trip to Uganda or elsewhere in Africa, though it is advisable to be somewhat circumspect when it comes to heeding advice on personal websites. Do also be aware that the internet, even at this relatively youthful stage of its existence, is clogged up with sites constructed but never maintained and thus prone to be rather out of date. Websites for individual hotels, lodges, tour operators and other institutions are included alongside the relevant entries elsewhere in this guide. What follows is a list of more generic websites that might prove useful to travellers planning a trip in Uganda.

Uganda-specific sites

www.aboutuganda.com General information about Uganda, flights, safaris, etc.

www.visituganda.com Official website of Tourism Uganda (previously Uganda Tourist Board). Thorough and regularly updated, very well organised, with good links to numerous related sites and most upmarket hotels and lodges.

www.traveluganda.com Private site covering similar ground to Tourism Uganda, and well worth checking out for current news and information.

www.uwa.or.ug Official website of the Uganda Wildlife Authority, worth checking for the latest on gorilla-tracking permits and other fees and facilities in the national parks and wildlife reserves.

www.immigration.go.ug Current information about visa requirements and costs, and other immigration-related details.

www.backpackers.co.ug Budget-travel advice compiled and updated by the staff of Kampala Backpackers.

www.newafrica.com/profiles/uganda/htm Good Uganda section in site covering all Africa, but beware of out-of-date information.

www.newvision.co.ug News, travel features, etc posted by the country's most established English-language newspaper; also has thorough archives dating back several years and good search facilities.

www.monitor.co.ug Similar to above, though generally takes a more independent stance than the government-backed *New Vision*, but has inferior archiving and search facilities.

www.nationaudio.com/News/EastAfrican/Current Site of Kenya's East African weekly newspaper, most thorough news coverage for Uganda is compiled outside the country.

www.buganda.com Detailed historical and cultural essays about the Buganda kingdom past and present.

General sites

www.fco.gov.uk/travel British Foreign & Commonwealth Office site, containing up-to-date, generally rather conservative information on trouble spots and places to avoid.

travel.state.gov/uganda.html US State Department equivalent to above.

www.auswaertiges-amt.de/5_laende/index3.htm#fgypten German equivalent to above.

www.odci.gov.cia/publications/factbook/country.html Another site focusing on security and safety matters, based on CIA files; judgements once again tend to be on the conservative side.

www.brookes.ac.uk/worldwise/directory.html General practical information about visas, costs, transport, etc.

www.uk.multimap.com/world/places.cgi Free online maps of countries and major towns.

www.usatoday.com/weather/forecast/wglode.htm Weather forecasts and archives covering many remote parts of Africa; try also www.worldclimate.com or weather.yahoo.com/regional/Africa/Uganda.html

www.travelafricamag.com Site for the quarterly magazine *Travel Africa* – good news section, travel archives and subscriptions.

www.africa-geographic.com Site for the South Africa publications *Africa Geographic* and *Africa Birds & Birding* – useful news and archives, subscriptions, special offers and tours.

http://philipbriggs.wordpress.com A blog by Philip Briggs that provides an interactive update service for Bradt readers and other travellers, volunteers and service providers in Uganda.

Art

www.theartroom-sf.com Fine Arts Centre for East Africa, San Francisco.
www.kibuuka.com Website for artist David Kibuuka.
www.sekanwagi.com Website for artist Dan Sekanwagi.
www.nnyanziart.com Website for artist Nuwa Nnyanzi.
www.cwdl.com/Iwasakak Website for artist Patrick Iwasampijja.
www.y-art.net Canadian representative for Ugandan artists.

484

Index

Page numbers in bold indicate major entries; those in italic indicate maps or charts.

INDEX TO BOXED TEXT